CONTENTS

INTRODUCTION

The HNC and HND qualifications in Business are very demanding. The suggested content, set out by Edexcel in guidelines for each unit, includes topics which are normally covered at degree level. Students therefore need books which get straight to the core of these topics, and which build upon the student's existing knowledge and experience. BPP's series of Course Books have been designed to meet that need.

Unit 21: *Human Resource Management*, Unit 22: *Managing Human Resource Issues*, Unit 23: *Human Resource Development* and Unit 24: *Employee Relations* covers the Edexcel guidelines and suggested content in full, and includes the following features.

- The Edexcel guidelines

- A study guide explaining the key features of the book and how to get the most from your studies

- An index

Each chapter contains:

- An introduction and study objectives

- Summary diagrams and signposts, to guide you through the chapter

- Numerous activities, topics for discussion, definitions and examples

- A chapter roundup, a quick quiz, answers to activities and an assignment

BPP Publishing are the leading providers of targeted texts for professional qualifications. Our customers need to study effectively. They cannot afford to waste time. They expect clear, concise and highly-focused study material. This series of Course Books for HNC and HND Business has been designed and produced to fulfil those needs.

BPP Publishing
February 2001

Titles in this series:

Core Unit 1	Marketing
Core Unit 2	Managing Financial Resources
Core Unit 3	Organisations and Behaviour
Core Unit 4	Organisations, Competition and Environment
Core Unit 5	Quantitative Techniques for Business
Core Unit 6	Legal and Regulatory Framework
Core Unit 7	Management Information Systems
Core Unit 8	Business Strategy
Option Units 9-12	Business & Finance
Option Units 13-16	Business & Management
Option Units 17-20	Business & Marketing
Option Units 21-24	Business & Personnel

For more information, or to place an order, please call 020 8740 2211, or fill in the order form at the back of this book.

If you would like to send in your comments on this book, please turn to the review form on the last page.

HNC HND BUSINESS

Optional Units 21 to 24:

Business and Personnel

Course Book

BPP
PUBLISHING

3230097331

EDEXCEL HNC & HND BUSINESS

First edition February 2001
ISBN 0 7517 7043 4

British Library Cataloguing-in Publication Data
A catalogue record for this book is available from the British Library

Printed in Great Britain by Arrowsmith
Winterstoke Road
Bristol BS3 2NT

Published by
BPP Publishing Limited
Aldine House, Aldine Place
London W12 8AW

www.bpp.com

EDEXCEL GUIDELINES FOR UNIT 21: HUMAN RESOURCE MANAGEMENT

Description of the Unit

This unit provides an introduction to the concepts and practices of Human Resource Management within the United Kingdom. The aim of the unit is to provide an understanding of the personnel function of management through the consideration of systems and frameworks, which create and sustain the employment relationship within the organisation.

Summary of outcomes

To achieve this unit a student must

1   Examine the traditional view of **personnel management and the new approach of human resource management**

2   Evaluate the **procedures and practices for obtaining suitable employees**

3   Establish the effectiveness of **principles and procedures for monitoring and rewarding the employee**

4   Examine voluntary and involuntary forms of **employee exit from the organisation**

Content

1   **Personnel management and the new approach of human resource management**

   The nature and development of personnel management: historical context in the United Kingdom, the welfare tradition, the industrial relations tradition, the control of labour tradition, the professional tradition

   The roles and tasks of the personnel function: Tyson and Fell (clerk of works, Contracts manager, Architect), personnel as a specialist function, personnel policies, strategies and operating plans, personnel activities

   The shift in approach which has led to the term human resource management: political, economic, social context of change, human resource management within the organisation structure

2   **Procedures and practices used for obtaining suitable employees**

   Human resource planning: definition, purpose, processes and limiting factors

   The systematic approach to recruitment: recruitment policy, recruitment procedure, job analysis, job description, personnel specification, recruitment methods and media, evaluation

   The systematic approach to selection: the selection procedure, the design of application form, selection methods, references, the offer of employment, evaluation of process

3   **Principles and procedures for monitoring and rewarding the employee**

   Performance appraisal: definition, purpose of appraisal, appraisal procedures and techniques, the appraisal interview, follow up

Reward management: job evaluation purpose and methods, factors determining pay, payment systems, incentive schemes, legal framework on pay and benefits

Discipline and grievance procedures: definition, model disciplinary procedure, disciplinary interviews. ACAS code of practice, grievance procedures, grievance interviews

Human resource management information systems: personnel records and statistics, the use of statistics in HRM, computers in HRM, confidentiality, legal requirements, eg Data Protection Act (1984 and 1998)

4   **Employee exit from the organisation**

An introduction to the legal framework on employment protection: dismissal – wrongful, unfair and justified, role of Industrial Tribunals

Termination of employment; retirement, resignation, termination of contract, exit interviews

Dealing with the human aspects of termination employment: procedure for dismissal, counselling, training, notice of dismissal

Redundancy: definition, outline procedures for handling redundancy, selection for redundancy, out placement, redeployment, 'red circling', retraining

Outcomes and assessment criteria

Outcomes	Assessment criteria To achieve each outcome a student must demonstrate the ability to:
1 Examine the traditional view of **personnel management and the new approach of human resource management**	• discuss the historical development of human resource management • identify the role and purpose of human resource management • distinguish between 'personnel management' and 'human resource management' and discuss their historical development
2 Evaluate the **procedures and practices used for obtaining suitable employees**	• analyse the objectives and the process of human resource planning • evaluate the systematic approach to recruitment for a given organisation • investigate the selection procedures used for two different organisations

Outcomes	Assessment criteria To achieve each outcome a student must demonstrate the ability to:
3 Establish the effectiveness of **principles and procedures for monitoring and rewarding the employee**	• evaluate the application of appraisal procedures • carry out a job evaluation for a given organisation • evaluate the effectiveness of disciplinary and grievance procedures used by two organisations • explain the need for effective management of personnel records
4 Examine voluntary and involuntary forms of **employee exit from the organisation** and the termination of the employment relationship	• evaluate employee exit procedures used by two different organisations • discuss the need for effective management of employee dismissal • evaluate the selection criteria used for redundancy • propose alternative approaches for dealing with redundancy

Guidance

Generating evidence

Evidence of outcomes may be in the form of assignments, investigations of specific business organisations or case studies.

The following are suggestions, as a guide to possible methods of evidence collection:

- students could utilise their own experience and commercial contacts as a basis for collection and analysis of human resource management policies and practices

- a group role play assignment which simulates a panel selection interview

- case study(ies) which evaluate the effectiveness of the disciplinary procedure

- an individual role play of an employee appraisal interview

Links

The unit is part of the HN personnel pathway and forms a direct link with other personnel units in the programme: 'Organisations and Behaviour' (Unit 3), 'Managing Human Resources Issues' (Unit 22), 'Human Resource Development' (Unit 23) and 'Employee Relations' (Unit 24).

Links are also to be found with 'Legal and Regulatory Framework' (Unit 6), which covers employment protection legislation.

The unit covers some of the underpinning knowledge and understanding for the following units of the NVQ in Personnel at level 4:

- Area B – Resourcing
- Area D – Reward
- Area E – Relations with Employees
- Area F – Professionalism
- Area G – Management

This unit offers opportunities for demonstrating Common Skills in Communicating and Working with and Relating to Others.

Resources

Journals are a valuable source of information, eg *People Management* (bi-monthly) and the *Human Resource Management Journal*.

Companies such as Video Arts and Melrose produce a variety of videos which may be useful in covering human resource management topics.

World Wide Web user sites can be useful in providing information and case studies (eg http://www.bized.co.ac.uk. which provides business case studies appropriate for educational purposes).

Other sources of information can be provided by external organisation eg Advisory, Conciliation and Arbitration Service (ACAS) and the Institute of Personnel and Development (IPD).

Delivery

The unit can be delivered in a variety of ways. Case studies, role plays and student-centred learning can be utilised to enhance the delivery and student learning within the unit.

Investigations of human resource management policies and practices within organisations and talks from human resource management practitioners can both develop understanding and provide support for the knowledge base established within the unit.

Suggested reading

There is a wide range of textbooks which cover the areas contained in the unit. Examples are:

Bolton T – *Human Resource Management – An Introduction* (Blackwell, 1994)

Business Basics – *Human Resource Management* (BPP Publishing, 2000)

Cole G A – *Personnel Management* – 4th Ed. (Letts Education, 1997)

Dransfield et al – *Human Resource Management for Higher Awards* (Heinemann, 1996)

Foot M and Hook C – *Introducing Human Resource Management* (Longman, 1996)

Graham H T and Bennett R – *Human Resource Management* (Pitman, 1995)

Martin M and Jackson T – *Personnel Practice* (IPD, 1997)

Tyson S and York A – *Human Resource Management* (Longman, 1997)

Weightman J – *Managing Human Resources* (IPD, 1993)

EDEXCEL GUIDELINES FOR UNIT 22: MANAGING HUMAN RESOURCES ISSUES

Description of unit

The aim of this unit is to build upon the knowledge and understanding developed in the human resource management units.

A broader and wider perspective is undertaken in relation to the management of the employment relationship. Human resource management strategies and issues are considered. A comparative approach is also undertaken in relation to human resource practices in other countries.

Summary of outcomes

To achieve this unit a student must:

1   Examine the **differing perspectives of human resource management**
2   Examine ways of developing **flexibility within the workplace**
3   Examine the need for **equal opportunities within the workplace**
4   Discuss the need for **welfare provision** within organisations
5   Investigate **human resource practices** in the United Kingdom and overseas.

Content

1   **Differing perspectives of human resource management**

The different perspectives of human resource management (HRM): 'soft' and 'hard' human resource management, 'loose' and 'tight' human resource management (Guest)

Storey's definitions between HRM and IR and personnel practices: HRM – treating employees as an asset rather than a cost, emphasis on training and development, HRM – as a strategic form of management (devolution of function to line managers, employee empowerment)

2   **Flexibility within the workplace**

Flexible working methods: the core and periphery workforce model, employment of part-time and temporary staff, teleworking, homeworking, job sharing

Functional flexibility: multiskilling, job enrichment, job enlargement, flexible working groups, training needs, changing role of supervisor

Temporal flexibility: overtime, flexi-time, annual hours contracts, zero hours contracts, shift patterns

Labour market: labour market demographics, employment statistics, local, regional and national labour markets

3   **Equal opportunities within the workplace**

Discrimination in employment: forms of discrimination, eg gender, ethnicity, religion, disability, age, sexual orientation, education

The legislative framework: direct and indirect discrimination, legislation

Equal opportunities in employment: codes of practice, implementing policy, training requirements, equal opportunities practices and initiatives in the workplace, monitoring

Equal opportunity initiatives: Opportunity 2000, positive action approaches eg recruitment and selection policies, managing the diverse workforce

4   **Welfare provision**

The traditional welfare function: occupational health practices and policies, the management of ill health at work, bereavement, costs and absenteeism, accidents at work (statistics)

Health and safety legislation: welfare benefits and services, the role of the Health and Safety Commission, European Community Directives

New models of welfare: ergonomics, passive smoking, sick building syndrome, alcohol and drug abuse, stress management, private health care, employee assistance programmes, HIV and AIDS, workplace counselling, recognition of religious practices

5   **Human resource practices**

Human resource practices: recruitment, selection, welfare provision, training, reward

Human resource management in the United Kingdom: consider different human resource practices in the United Kingdom, eg case study examples of recruitment and selection

Human resource management in the European Union: comparison of human resource policies and practices across different European countries, European Commission directives, European Social Charter/Chapter, harmonisation, European Employment treaty – Aeria for Jobs

International comparisons in human resource management practices: comparison of human resource policies and practices in the United Kingdom, USA and Far East

Note. Since Unit 22 –especially section 5: *Human Resource Practices* – builds on topics already covered in Unit 21, this course book will cover selected aspects and case studies relevant to Unit 22 **in the chapters listed under Unit 21**. So, for example, Human Resource Practices in Recruitment and Selection, and comparisons of such practices in different countries, are included in Part A of the course book, in the chapters on Recruitment and Selection. Coverage will be cross-referenced to the guidelines in the 'Signpost' sections of each chapter. (see the *Study Guide* on page (xxiv)of this book).

Outcomes and assessment criteria

To achieve each outcome a student must demonstrate the ability to:

Outcomes	Assessment criteria
	To achieve each outcome a student must demonstrate the ability to:
1 Examine the **differing perspectives of human resource management**	• explain Guest's model of hard-soft, loose-tight dimensions of HRM • discuss the differences between Storey's definitions of HRM and Personnel and IR practices • examine HRM from a strategic perspective and its implications for the role of the line manager and employees.
2 Examine ways of developing **flexibility within the workplace**	• describe the types of flexibility which may be developed by an organisation and give examples of how they can be implemented • discuss the advantages and disadvantages of flexible working practices from both the employee and the employer perspective.
3 Examine the need for **equal opportunities within the workplace**	• describe the forms of discrimination that take place • discuss the implications of equal opportunities for human resource management • discuss how the legislative framework relating to discrim-ination in the workplace can be applied by an organisation • describe the role of the Equal Opportunities Commission and Commission for Racial Equality.
4 Discuss the need for **welfare provision** within organisations	• discuss the traditional welfare function and the models of welfare within organisations • examine implications of policy and practices of a welfare provision within an organisation • prepare a programme to introduce new welfare provision within a given organisation.

Outcomes	Assessment criteria
	To achieve each outcome a student must demonstrate the ability to:
5 Investigate **human resource practices** in the United Kingdom and overseas	• compare the implementation of a given human resource practice in the United Kingdom with that of one other country
	• discuss how the UK organisations have modified employ-ment practice in response to EU employment legislation
	• explain the impact of increasing European social and employment legislation and the response of organisations within the United Kingdom.

Guidance

Generating evidence

Evidence of outcome may be in the form of assignments, investigations of specific organisations or case studies. Students may also provide evidence of understanding and analysis, through the presentation of a seminar paper following an investigation into one particular area of human resource management or human resource practices within a business organisation.

Links

This unit is part of the HN personnel pathway and forms a direct link with the other personnel units in the programme: 'Organisations and Behaviour' (Unit 3), 'Human Resource Management' (Unit 21), 'Human Resource Development' (Unit 23) and 'Employee Relations' (Unit 24).

Links may also be found with: 'Organisations, Competition and Environment' (Unit 4), 'Legal and Regulatory Framework' (Unit 6), 'International Business Strategy' (Unit 8) and 'Quality Management' (Unit 22).

The unit covers some of the underpinning knowledge and understanding of the following units of the NVQ in Personnel at level 4:

• Area C – Development
• Area E – Relations with Employees
• Area G – Management

This unit offers opportunities for demonstrating Common Skills in Managing and Developing Self, Communicating, Managing Tasks and Solving Problems and Applying Design and Creativity.

Resources

Companies such as Video Arts and Melrose produce a variety of videos which may be useful in covering human resource management topics.

World Wide Web user sites can be useful in providing information and case studies (eg http://www.bized.co.ac.uk. which provides business case studies appropriate for educational purposes).

Information can also be obtained from external agencies eg:

- Equal Opportunities Commission
- Commission for Racial Equality
- Health and Safety Executive
- Institute of Personnel and Development
- Manpower Services Commission

Delivery

Students should be exposed to a variety of case studies to gain coverage of the different aspects of human resource issues and management.

The unit is intended to be 'topical' with students discussing current business organisation practice. This could involve:

- Student investigation into business organisation(s)

- A forum in which student discussion and debate can take place

- Students researching a 'live' topic through the collection of information from journal articles and newspaper references

- External speakers, eg from the Equal Opportunities Commission.

Suggested reading

There is a wide range of textbooks available covering the areas contained within this unit. Examples are:

Armstrong M – *A Handbook of Personnel Management in Practice* – 6th Ed. (Kogan Page London)

Beardwell I and Holden L – *HRM A Contemporary Perspective* (Pitman, 1996)

Bratton J and Gold J – *Human Resource Management* (Macmillan, 1994)

Johns T and Taylor S – *Employees Resourcing* (IPD, 1998)

Marchington and Wilkinson A – *Core Personnel and Development* (IPD, 1996)

Torrington D and Hall L – *Personnel Management: HRM in Action* – 3rd Ed. (Prentice Hall, 1995)

Journals

Employment Gazette

Human Resource Management Journal

International Human Resource Management Journal

People Management

Personnel Review

EDEXCEL GUIDELINES FOR UNIT 23: HUMAN RESOURCE DEVELOPMENT

Description of unit

This unit will develop students' understanding of the nature and role of training and employee development and consider the United Kingdom training scene and systems in operation. It look at different learning styles and how this relates to the delivery of effective training and development, within organisations.

Summary of outcomes

To achieve this unit a student must:

1   Examine **learning theory**
2   Examine the **systematic approach to training**
3   Evaluate the range of different **training methods**
4   Evaluate the range of **government-led training initiatives**

Content

1   **Learning theory**

Learning styles: Honey and Mumford (1982), learning styles, Activists, Reflectors, Theorists, Pragmatists, Kolb's (1979) Learning Style Inventory

Theories of learning: learning theory, learning cycle, learning curve, transfer of learning

2   **Systematic approach to training**

Training: the role of training within the organisation, attitudes to training, benefits of training, training policy

The systematic approach: identification of training needs, determining training objectives, training provision, evaluation of training, feedback and assessment

Modern approaches towards the learning organisation: developing a learning culture, employee development programmes, competency-based training, training for quality, British standards for quality systems, Investors in People

3   **Training methods**

On-the-job training: advantages and disadvantages of 'sitting Next to Nellie', training, action learning, assignments, projects, shadowing

Off-the–job training: college courses, assessment centres, training consultants, Open Learning, computer-based training

In-house training: training room instruction, coaching

Management training and development: management training in Britain, the Management Charter Initiative, development methods, the role of management succession and promotion planning, the value of management development, continuing professional development

4   **Government-led training initiatives**

General and vocational training schemes: training and development in the UK, Training and Enterprise Councils, The Qualifications Curriculum Authority and the National Training Framework

Recent initiatives: the Modern Apprenticeship scheme, University for Industry, National Training Organisations, the National Traineeship

Outcomes and assessment criteria

To achieve each outcome a student must demonstrate the ability to:

Outcomes	Assessment criteria
	To achieve each outcome a student must demonstrate the ability to:
1 Examine **learning theory**	• distinguish between different types of learning styles • explain the types of learning cycle and learning curve.
2 Examine the **systematic approach to training**	• explain how training contributes to the achievement of business objectives • explain the systematic approach to training • evaluate an organisation's approach to training
3 Evaluate the range of different **training methods**	• review a range of different training methods • discuss the effectiveness of 'on-the-job' training and 'off-the-job' training • devise 'on-the-job' and 'off-the-job' training programmes to meet the needs of a given organisation • explain the purpose of management development and evaluate its effectiveness for a given organisation
4 Evaluate the range of **government-led training initiatives**	• discuss the range of contemporary training initiatives introduced by the UK government • examine the role of the Training and Enterprise Councils • investigate a vocational training scheme

Guidance

Generating evidence

Evidence of outcomes may be in the form of written reports, presentations or role play skills training sessions.

Evidence could include:

- a case study approach which investigates employee training or employee development within an organisation

- an investigative report to examine the approach to training within an organisation

- a role play scenario which involves the student(s) in different training methods

- group based research and a group presentation which considers one of the government-led training initiatives introduced in recent years

Links

This unit is part of the HN personnel pathway and forms a direct link with the other personnel units in the programme: 'Organisations and Behaviour' (Unit 3), 'Human Resource Management' (Unit 21), 'Human Resource Issues' (Unit 22) and 'Employee Relations' (Unit 24).

The unit covers some of the underpinning knowledge and understanding of the following units of the NVQ in Personnel at level 4:

- Area C – Development
- Area F – Professionalism

This unit offers opportunities for demonstrating Common Skills in Working with and Relating to Others, Communicating, Managing Tasks and Solving Problems and Applying Design and Creativity.

Resources

Companies such as Video Arts and Melrose produce a variety of videos which may be useful for some topic areas. Specialised Human Resource Development journals are also a valuable resource.

World Wide Web user sites can be useful in providing information and case studies (eg http://www.bized.co.ac.uk. which provides business case studies appropriate for educational purposes).

Information can also be obtained from external agencies eg:

- Training and Enterprise Council
- Manpower Services Commission
- Department for Education
- Career Service
- Employment Occupational Standards Council (EOSC)
- Training and Development Lead Body
- MCI First line management standards

Delivery

Students' critical understanding of training and development can be developed through the use of directed reading, lectures, group work, videos and case studies. Skills can be developed through role plays and practical tasks. The students' experiences of this area should be utilised where appropriate.

Suggested reading

There are a wide variety of textbooks available covering the areas contained within this unit. Examples are:

Brookes J – *Training and Development Competence* (A Practical Guide, 1995)

Frances and Roland Bee – *Training Needs Analysis and Evaluation* (IPD London, 1994)

Hackett P – *Introduction to Training, Training Essentials Series* (IPD London, 1997)

Harrison R – *Employee Development* (IPD London, 1997)

Kenney J and Reid M – *Training Interventions* – 3rd Ed. (IPD London, 1997)

Reid M and Barrington H – *Training Interventions* (IPD London, 1997)

Thompson R and Mabey C – *Developing Human Resources* (Institute of Management, Butterworth-Heinemann, 1994)

Journals

Journal of European Industrial
People Management
Training Officer
Training and Development Journal

EDEXCEL GUIDELINES FOR UNIT 24: HUMAN RESOURCE MANAGEMENT

Description of unit

The main aim of this unit is to provide a general introduction to industrial relations and develop a knowledge and understanding of the changes which have taken place over the years with respect to employee participation and employee relations in the UK. The unit considers the nature of industrial conflict and the resolution of collective disputes. The processes of collective bargaining and negotiation are also explored.

Summary of outcomes

To achieve this unit a student must:

1 Explain the **unitary and pluralistic frames of reference** against a changing background

2 Examine the nature of **industrial conflict and the resolution of collective disputes**

3 Explore the processes of **collective bargaining and negotiation**

4 Analyse the concept of **employee participation**

5 Investigate the **shift from industrial relations to employee relations**

Content

1 **Unitary and pluralistic frames of reference**

The role of the trade union: types of trade union, the Trade Union Congress employer associations, trade union representatives

The history and development of trade unions: the rise of trade unionism, trade unions and the law, union growth and decline, the changing political and economic context and its relevance to industrial relations

The main actors in industrial relations: workers and their organisations, managers and their organisations, government agencies concerned with the workplace and work community

2 **Industrial conflict and the resolution of collective disputes**

The nature of industrial conflict: ideological framework, conflict and co-operation

Different types of dispute: collective disputes, strike action, strike statistics, ballots, no-strike agreements

Resolving conflict: dispute procedures, arbitration, the role of the Advisory, Conciliation and Arbitration Service (ACAS)

3 **Collective bargaining and negotiation**

The nature and scope of collective bargaining: role of shop stewards, union officials, employer associations and management

The collective bargaining process: institutional agreements for collective bargaining, local workplace bargaining, single-table bargaining

Negotiation processes: negotiation strategy, preparation for negotiation, conducting the case-settlement, disclosure of information

4 **Employee participation**

Consultation and employee participation: different forms of employee consultation and participation, joint consultation committees, upward-downward forms

Industrial democracy and employee participation: European Works Councils (European Objectives), the social dimensions of the European Union and supervisory boards, National differences

5 **Shift from industrial relations to employee relations**

Employee involvement techniques: sharing information, consultation, financial participation, commitment to quality, developing the individual, beyond the workplace

Empowerment: devolution of responsibility/authority to line managers/ employees, the role of human resource management, approach to employee relations

Outcomes and assessment criteria

To achieve each outcome a student must demonstrate the ability to:

Outcomes	Assessment criteria
	To achieve each outcome a student must demonstrate the ability to:
1 Explain the **unitary and pluralistic frames of reference** against a changing background	• explain the unitary and pluralistic frames of reference • assess the development of trade unions and nature of industrial relations • investigate the role of a trade union and its contribution to effective industrial relations
2 Examine the nature of **industrial conflict and the resolution of collective disputes**	• explain the ideological framework of industrial relations • discuss the different types of collective dispute • explain dispute procedures and the resolution of conflict • assess the effectiveness of dispute procedures in resolving conflict in a given situation
3 Explore the processes of **collective bargaining and negotiation**	• discuss the nature and scope of collective bargaining • describe the processes of negotiation • prepare and apply negotiation strategy for a given situation

Outcomes	Assessment criteria
	To achieve each outcome a student must demonstrate the ability to:
4 Analyse the concept of **employee participation**	• assess the effectiveness of arrangements made by two organisations to involve their employees in decision-making
	• analyse the influence of the EU on democracy in the UK
5 Investigate the **shift from industrial relations to employee relations**	• distinguish between industrial relations and employee relations
	• assess the effectiveness of employee involvement techniques
	• discuss the impact of human resource management on employee relations

Guidance

Generating evidence

Evidence of outcomes may be assessed as follows:

- Use of presentations as a context for conveying understanding of employee relations

- Use of role plays for exploring the processes of collective bargaining and negotiation

- Case studies to asses students' understanding of the nature of industrial conflict and the resolution of collective disputes

Links

This unit is part of the HN personnel pathway, and forms a direct link with other personnel units in the programme: 'Organisations and Behaviour' (Unit 3), 'Human Resource Management' (Unit 21), 'Managing Human Resource Issues' (Unit 22) and 'Human Resource Development' (Unit 23).

Links may also be found with 'Organisations, Competition and Environment' (Unit 4), 'Legal and Regulatory Framework' (Unit 6), 'Management Information Systems' (Unit 7) and 'Quality Management' (Unit 26).

This unit covers some of the underpinning knowledge and understanding of the following units of the NVQ in Personnel at level 4:

- Area E – Relations with Employees

This unit offers opportunities for demonstrating Common Skills in Working with and Relating to Others and Communicating.

Resources

Companies such as Video Arts and Melrose produce a variety of videos which may be useful in covering employee relations topics.

World Wide Web user sites can be useful in providing information and case studies (eg http://www.bized.co.ac.uk. which provides business case studies appropriate for educational purposes).

Information can also be obtained from external agencies eg: Advisory, Conciliation and Arbitration Service (ACAS).

Delivery

Students' understanding of employee relations can be developed through the use of a variety of training and learning methods including lectures, discussions, seminars, videos, role plays and case studies.

Suggested reading

There is a wide range of textbooks available covering the areas contained within this unit. Examples are:

Farnham D and Pimlott J – *Understanding Industrial Relations* – 5th Ed. (Cassell, 1995)

Gennard J and Judge G C – *Employee Relations* – 4th Ed. (Pitman, 1997)

Green G D – *Industrial Relations* – 4th Ed. (Pitman, 1994)

Salamon M – *Industrial Relations* – 3rd Ed. (Prentice Hall, 1995)

The texts suggested for 'Human Resource Management' (Unit 21) and 'Managing Human Resources Issues' (Unit 22) would also support this unit.

Journals

British Journal of Industrial Relations
Employment Gazette
Industrial Relations Journal
Industrial Relations Review and Report
People Management
Personnel Review

STUDY GUIDE

This text gives full coverage of the Edexcel guidelines. This text also includes features designed specifically to make learning effective and efficient.

(a)   Each chapter begins with a summary diagram which maps out the areas covered by the chapter. You can use the diagrams during revision as a basis for your notes.

(b)   After the main summary diagram there is an introduction, which sets the chapter in context. This is followed by learning objectives, which show you what you will learn as you work through the chapter.

(c)   Throughout the text, there are special aids to learning. These are indicated by symbols in the margin.

Signposts guide you through the text, showing how each section connects with the next.

Definitions give the meanings of key terms. The *glossary* at the end of the text summarises these.

Activities help you to test how much you have learnt. An indication of the time you should take on each is given. Answers are given at the end of each chapter.

Topics for discussion are for use in seminars. They give you a chance to share your views with your fellow students. They allow you to highlight holes in your knowledge and to see how others understand concepts. If you have time, try "teaching" someone the concepts you have learnt in a session. This helps you to remember key points and answering their questions will consolidate your knowledge.

Examples relate what you have learnt to the outside world. Try to think up your own examples as you work through the text.

Chapter roundups present the key information from the chapter in a concise format. Useful for revision.

BPP
PUBLISHING

(d)   The wide **margin** on each page is for your notes. You will get the best out of this book if you interact with it. Write down your thoughts and ideas. Record examples, question theories, add references to other pages in the text and rephrase key points in your own words.

(e)   At the end of each chapter, there is a **chapter roundup**, a **quick quiz** with answers and an **assignment**. Use these to revise and consolidate your knowledge. The chapter roundup summarises the chapter. The quick quiz tests what you have learnt (the answers often refer you back to the chapter so you can look over subjects again). The assignment (with a time guide) allows you to put your knowledge into practice. Answer guidelines for the assignments are at the end of the text.

(f)   At the end of the text, there is a glossary of key terms and an index.

PART A

UNIT 21: HUMAN RESOURCE MANAGEMENT

Chapter 1 :
THE DEVELOPMENT OF HRM

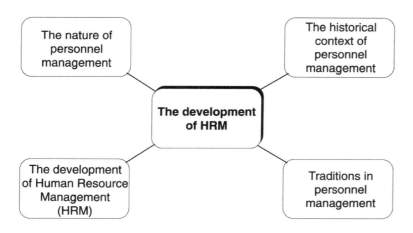

Introduction

It can be argued that people are an organisation's most important resource: after all, organisations are made up of people, and the way the organisation uses money, technology, information and other resources depends on human decisions. So it is generally recognised that the success of any business is greatly influenced by the calibre and attitude of the people who work for it.

It is therefore also commonly recognised that *someone* in every organisation will need to be responsible for the many matters that arise in connection with the recruitment, selection, training, motivation, payment and movement of staff through the organisation, as well as compliance with the various laws relating to employment. (We will discuss how those responsibilities may be structured in an organisation in Chapter 2).

However, as the pace of social and technological change has quickened, there has been a growing recognition that thought must be given to managing the vital human resource at an earlier stage and at a higher level of organisational planning than has previously been the case. This has encouraged a longer term, more proactive and strategic approach to people management, known as 'Human Resource Management' or HRM. In this chapter, we trace the development of this approach, while in Chapter 11, we explore its implications further, as an introduction to the various HR issues covered in Unit 22.

Your objectives

In this chapter you will learn about the following:

    (a)   The historical development of human resource management.

    (b)   The role and purpose of human resource management.

    (c)   The difference between 'personnel management' and 'human resource management' and their historical development.

NOTES

1 THE NATURE OF PERSONNEL MANAGEMENT

1.1 Personnel management

The main professional body for personnel managers is the Chartered Institute of Personnel and Development (CIPD), formerly known as the Institute of Personnel Management (IPM). The CIPD has defined the function of personnel management as follows.

Definition

'**Personnel management** is that part of management concerned with people at work and with their relationships within an enterprise...'

The CIPD statement continues: '(Personnel management's) aim is to bring together, and develop into an effective organisation, the men and women who make up an enterprise, having regard for the well-being of the individual and of working groups, to enable them to make their best contribution to its success.

'In particular, personnel management is concerned with the development and application of policies governing:

- Human resources planning, recruitment, selection, placement and termination

- Education and training; career development

- Terms of employment, methods and standards of remuneration

- Working conditions and employee services

- Formal and informal communication and consultation both through the representatives of employers and employees and at all levels throughout the enterprise

- Negotiation and application of agreements on wages and working conditions; procedures for the avoidance and settlement of disputes

'Personnel management must also be concerned with the human and social implication of change in internal organisation and methods of working, and of economic and social changes in the community.'

This statement highlights a number of useful ideas about personnel management.

(a) It is basically concerned with people and relationships. Thus it is founded on attempts to examine, describe, explain and as far as possible to predict and control human behaviour. (We will encounter some of these attempts – in the form of theories of learning, motivation and so on – in later chapters.) It also involves, perhaps more clearly than the management of other organisational resources, a moral or ethical dimension: the employment relationship has 'human and social implications', raising issues of human dignity and freedom, humane treatment, social responsibility, fairness and so on.

(b) It embraces not only 'soft' values to do with people and relationships – such as well-being – but also 'hard' values to do with the success of the enterprise: efficiency, effectiveness, contribution. These 'soft' and 'hard' perspectives,

BPP PUBLISHING

and HRM's role in seeking a 'fit' between them, are discussed in Part B of this Course Book.

(c)   It is a 'part of management'. Organisation of the personnel function may require a specialist department or departments under the control of a personnel manager (or director, where the function is represented on the Board), but it has been suggested that a separate personnel function need not exist at all: *all* line managers need to achieve results through the efforts of other people, and must therefore manage the employment relationship. (The issue of responsibility for personnel management is discussed in Chapter 2.)

FOR DISCUSSION

(a)   'How can you expect a corporation to have a conscience, when it has no soul to be damned and no body to be kicked?' (Baron Thurlow, George III's Chancellor)

(b)   'The only people who work this hard are people who want to. The only people who want to, are people with enough freedom to do the things they want to do.' (Comment on the Internet software company, Netscape.)

What do the above statements (quoted by Charles Handy, *The Hungry Spirit*) have to say about the concept of personnel management?

1.2   The personnel function

The traditional view of personnel management is essentially task-, activity- or technique-based, as reflected in the CIPD statement quoted above. Although, as we will see, this view has been changing, it is a useful introduction to what many personnel managers actually do. Dr Dale Yoder of the Graduate School of Business, Stanford University, defines the personnel management function as follows.

(a)   Setting general and specific management policy for employment relationships, and establishing and maintaining a suitable organisation for leadership and co-operation

(b)   Collective bargaining: negotiating working terms and conditions with employee representatives

(c)   Staffing and organisation: finding, getting and holding prescribed types and numbers of workers

(d)   Aiding the self-development of employees at all levels, providing opportunities for personal development and growth as well as requisite skills and experience

(e)   Developing and maintaining employee motivation

(f)   Reviewing and auditing manpower in the organisation

(g)   Industrial relations research, carrying out studies designed to explain employment behaviour and thereby improve manpower management

NOTES

Activity 1						(30 minutes)

The following headings represent the main components of a personnel manager's job. Think of typical duties which may be placed under these headings.

Organisation	Employee resourcing	Employee development	Reward	Employee relations	Health & Safety	Administration
1 Job design	1 Recruitment	1 Training	1 Pay systems	1 Trade unions	1 Complying with law	1 Record keeping
2	2	2	2	2	2	2
3	3	3	3	3	3	3

Graham and Bennett (*Human Resources Management*) suggest an alternative way of looking at personnel management by classifying its activities into three dimensions of management:

(a) **Utilisation** of people at work – recruitment, selection, transfer, promotion, separation, appraisal, training and development

(b) **Motivation** of people at work – job design, remuneration, fringe benefits, consultation, participation, negotiation and justice

(c) **Protection** of people at work – working conditions, welfare services, safety, implementation of appropriate legislation

If this seems too employee-centred a classification, it must be added that the overall *objective* of these dimensions of management is maintained or enhanced business performance.

We have immediately noted that there are some contentious issues inherent in the concept of personnel management. This has long been the case. There have been many different perspectives on organisation and management, which have developed in response to changes in the social, political and industrial contexts of work. Much of the ambiguity surrounding the personnel management function today arises from the baggage of its history. We will now briefly trace that development.

2 THE HISTORICAL CONTEXT OF PERSONNEL MANAGEMENT IN THE UK

2.1 The 'welfare worker'

It is generally agreed that the personnel function can be traced back to the benevolent attempts by some employers in the latter half of the nineteenth century to improve the working conditions and circumstances of workers, who had been hard hit by the first wave of industrialisation and urbanisation. Victorian entrepreneurs like Rowntree, Cadbury and Lever initiated programmes providing such facilities as company housing, basic health care, canteens and education for workers' families, managed on behalf of the employer by '**industrial welfare workers**'. There was a dual motivation for these measures.

(a) They reflected a wider programme of social reform and philanthropy, led by political and religious movements. Groups such as the Quakers, who in the USA were leaders in the abolition of slavery, strove to integrate successful business performance with the social, moral and spiritual betterment of their workers. This may seem unduly paternalistic to us today, but at the time brought much needed improvements in the quality of working life and the legal protection of workers.

(b)   Improved health and education, and the appreciation of their beneficiaries, secured an on-going pool of suitable labour for the employer. Cadbury considered welfare and efficiency as 'two sides of the same coin' at his model factory at Bournville.

Both motivations were highlighted when the British government attempted to recruit troops for the Crimean and Boer wars: so many volunteers were prevented from enlisting by medical deficiencies that there was an outcry about the health of the nation's labour force.

2.2   The science of productivity

Meanwhile, in the boom following the industrial revolution, businesses were growing larger and more complex, and it was recognised that a science or system of management was required.

Frederick W Taylor (1865–1915) was the first to argue that management should be based on 'well-recognised, clearly defined and fixed principles, instead of depending on more or less hazy ideas'. He pioneered the **scientific management** movement, which suggested that systematic investigation could indicate 'proper' methods, standards and timings for each operation in an organisation's activities. The responsibility of management was to select, train and help workers to perform their jobs 'properly': that is, to perform a single task or 'motion' in the most efficient way possible, eliminating all unnecessary physical movements. The responsibility of workers was simply to accept the new methods and perform accordingly, in return for increased pay.

Acute labour shortages during and following both World Wars created an urgent need to increase productivity, and Western governments encouraged the systematic study of the employment relationship and the human aspects of industrial work, which underpinned the personnel management function.

Henri Fayol (1841 – 1925) was a French industrialist who put forward and popularised the concept of universal, rational principles according to which organisations could be structured and managed: this came to be known as '**classical organisation theory**'. Among its principles were division of work (specialisation), the matching of authority and responsibility, the scalar chain of command or organisational hierarchy, unity of command ('one man, one boss'), unity of direction or purpose, discipline, equity, the subordination of individual interests to that of the organisation, and 'esprit de corps': these remain the foundations of bureaucratic management today.

Activity 2   **(10 minutes)**

Borderline Computers uses project teams to carry out research, deal with customer needs and to introduce new systems. Identify which of Fayol's principles would clash with this method of working.

2.3   The emergence of industrial relations

Meanwhile, the workers themselves were also becoming organised, and the legalisation of trade unions in 1871 raised the need for systematic frameworks for negotiation, conflict resolution and the management of relations between labour and management.

The increasingly active role taken by labour organisations was reflected in political recognition. The Labour Party was formed in 1900 (as the Labour Representation Committee, renamed in 1906), largely out of, and funded by, the trades-union movement of the 19th century. In 1911, the National Insurance Scheme established the first welfare provisions for workers in the event of unemployment or sickness. In 1916, the first Ministry for Labour was established to address wider workforce issues and consider wider representations.

Government policy during the Second World War was explicitly: '(i) to see that the maximum use was made of each citizen, (ii) to see that working and living conditions were as satisfactory as possible, (iii) to see that individual rights were reasonably safeguarded and the democratic spirit preserved. The growth of personnel management was the direct result of the translation of this national policy by each industry...' (Moxon, 1951).

Governmental influence on workforce and industrial relations continued, alongside general social reforms in education and healthcare, until the mid-1970s, when the idea that governments could and should maintain full employment finally gave way before the spectre of inflation and the rise of free market economics. The UK government declined to interfere in negotiated relationships between employers and employees, except in the area of trade union reform. (Many European governments, in contrast, continued to collaborate in strategic policy-making for the development of the national skill-base and workforce relations.) Nevertheless, the latter half of the 20th century saw a period of intense legislation in all areas of employment: health and safety, employment protection, equal opportunities and so on.

2.4   The emergence of industrial psychology

In the 1930s and 1940s, various academic theories of management were put forward and integrated with the emerging social and behavioural sciences. Scientific management was heavily criticised for dehumanising workers and treating them like mere cogs in the machine of production: it was realised that, by robbing the worker of any sense of contribution to the total product or task, the organisation was losing out on an important source of energy and creativity. Elton Mayo (1880–1949) wrote: 'We have thought that first-class technical training was sufficient in a modern and mechanical age. As a consequence we are technically competent as no other age in history has been, and we combine this with utter social incompetence.'

The 'human relations' approach emphasised a focus on people rather than on mechanics or economics: since both individuals and organisations share a desire for efficiency, it is possible to fulfil both individual and organisational objectives through human relations, motivation and teamwork. Mayo's famous studies at the Hawthorne plant of the Western Electric Company in the USA suggested that consultation, explanation, the encouragement of team-working and involvement of workers by management could raise commitment, self-management and productivity.

These ideas were followed up by various social psychologists, including Maslow, Herzberg and McGregor, who shifted attention to the 'higher' psychological needs of human beings for growth, challenge, responsibility and self-fulfilment. These were the new keys to the motivation of workers and the notion of 'job satisfaction' - since lasting satisfaction, according to Herzberg, was available only from factors in the job itself, not from 'maintenance' factors like pay and conditions. This phase was known as the Neo-human relations school. Most of its theorists attempted to offer guidelines to enable practising managers to satisfy and motivate employees and so, theoretically, to obtain the benefits of improved productivity.

FOR DISCUSSION

Peter Drucker warned that human relations thinking could manipulate workers just as effectively as bureaucratic rules, dictatorial management or scientific management techniques. It could be used as 'a mere tool for justifying management's actions, a device to 'sell' whatever management is doing. It is no accident that there is so much talk in Human Relations about 'giving workers a sense of responsibility' and so little about their responsibility, so much emphasis on their 'feeling of importance' and so little on making them and their work important.'

Do you think managers only pay lip service to 'enlightened' human relations – or personnel management – approaches? If so, why?

2.5 The growth of complexity

All the developments discussed above added to the perceived complexity of the relationship between employer and employee. And those are only the developments in employment! Add to them the accelerating pace of change in technology and communications, consumer power and sophistication, social and geographical mobility, culture and ideology – and so on – and you have a very post modern context for the employment relationship.

New models and metaphors of organisation and management emerged to reflect this changing world. Intensifying business competition and the introduction of new production technologies necessitated and facilitated change in classical structures and principles of organisation: 'chunking' (breaking structures into smaller units); 'horizontal' structures based on team-working and information-sharing rather than hierarchy, multi-skilling in place of job and occupational demarcation zones; concepts like 'chaos' and 'culture'.

The **systems** approach to management (developed at the Tavistock Institute of Human Relations in the 1950s) was one of the first to acknowledge complexity, by viewing the organisation as an open system.

Definition

An **open system** is an entity which consists of interdependent parts and which interacts with its environment.

Trist and Bamforth developed the model of the organisation as an open socio-technical system, consisting of at least three sub-systems:

(a) A **structure** (division of labour, authority relationships, communication channels)

(b) A **technological** *system* (the work to be done and the techniques and tools used to do it)

(c) A **social system** (the people within the organisation, the ways they think and interact with each other)

The task of management – and particularly personnel management - is to find a 'best fit' between the needs of the social and technical sub-systems.

NOTES

Activity 3 (15 minutes)

Below are a number of statements. Indicate whether they apply to the systems approach. Mark alongside T for True or F for False.

(a) The organisation is static.

(b) People, technology, organisation structure and environment are equally important in the systems approach.

(c) All sub-systems are in complete agreement.

(d) It is important that all employees are happy in their work.

(e) The organisation is aware of change affecting business.

(f) There is interdependence between all aspects of the organisation.

A **contingency** approach likewise developed as a reaction to the idea that there are 'universal principles' for designing organisations, motivating people and so on. Essentially, it all depends on the total picture of the internal factors and external environment of each organisation.

From these perspectives, personnel management began to be seen as increasingly involved with the full range of general business management and strategy. At the same time, however, the complexity of legislation and regulation, along with behavioural and managerial theory, had led to the development of specialisms within the personnel function (as we shall consider in Chapter 2): personnel management had become recognised as a discipline in its own right, which was broadly applicable – as an IPM statement declared – 'not only to industry and commerce but to all fields of employment'. Policy-setting and advice in areas such as labour planning, recruitment and selection, training and development, industrial relations, reward administration, employee appraisal and health and welfare came under the functional authority of personnel officers.

The need for a specialised body of knowledge – drawing on law, economics, administrative management and the social sciences (sociology, psychology and so on) – led to the establishment of a scheme of education and qualification and the professionalisation of the work of the personnel manager.

This more or less brings us to the picture we have of personnel management today. We will look briefly at how its historical development has created something of a 'rag-bag' of traditions, and a frustration that will, in Section 4, lead us towards a new perspective. The following classification of the four traditions from which personnel management has developed was suggested by Tyson and Fell.

3 TRADITIONS IN PERSONNEL MANAGEMENT

3.1 The welfare tradition

Building on the philosophy behind the 'industrial welfare worker', the welfare tradition suggested that much of the work and responsibility of the personnel officer was directed to the benefit of the employees, rather than to the strategic concerns of the enterprise and its management. Personnel management was in a sense the 'soft' or person-centred part or side of management. In specialised areas, such as occupational health, employee assistance schemes, workplace counselling services and so on, elements of this tradition may persist with some force. However it must be remembered that the personnel officer is not in any formal sense the representative of the workforce, and is paid to be part of the organisation's management team, as both representative and adviser.

3.2 The industrial relations tradition

A response to the legalisation and growing power of trade unions, through to the 1960s and '70s, the industrial relations tradition suggested that much of the work and responsibility of the personnel officer was to mediate and even arbitrate between the sides in industrial disputes, and to facilitate collective bargaining, negotiation and compliance with industrial relations law and regulation. The middle ground was an uneasy one to occupy: the 'diplomatic' role posed a dilemma of dual allegiance – particularly where there was lack of trust in the relationship between the personnel function and other (line) members of the management team. This arose particularly where close working relationships developed between personnel officers and trade union officials, despite potential (and actual) industrial disputes. Elements of this tradition may persist in the perception of the personnel officer and other parties to negotiation, conflict resolution, discipline and grievance procedures and so on.

3.3 The control of labour tradition

A response to the increasing pace of organisational growth and change, the control of labour tradition suggests that much of the work and responsibility of the personnel officer is to support management by standardising, monitoring and controlling the range and complexity of workplace activity: job allocation and performance, time-keeping and absenteeism, sick leave and holidays, pay and benefits, communication methods and media, training and promotion, rules and regulations and compliance checklists, preparation of workforce-related reports and returns, and so on. This is an essentially bureaucratic tradition and is still evident in many personnel departments. It has been supported by the ambiguity of personnel's role and authority in the management team: the application of rules, regulations, procedures and forms is one of the key methods of exercising influence over the activities of others, without direct positional or 'line' authority over them.

Activity 4   **(15 minutes)**

Whose side is the personnel manager on? Give three examples of the conflict which might exist between his or her position as a member of the management team and his or her special relationship with the workforce, and discuss what you feel are the issues involved. Where would *you* stand on these issues?

3.4 The professional tradition

The Institute of Personnel Management (now the Chartered Institute of Personnel and Development) has made determined efforts to establish personnel management as a profession, through a programme of learning and examinations leading to qualification; opportunities for professional communication and networking; and requirements for continuing professional development.

Employers in the UK value the CIPD qualification, but it must be noted (as Bolton points out) that 'many successful personnel managers are not specifically qualified, and lack of qualification has rarely been seen as a barrier to practice'. A wide body of detailed knowledge and skills is required, as mentioned above, in order for a personnel manager to be able to apply behavioural sciences to organisational systems and policies, ensure compliance with employment law, administer appropriate control systems and formulate strategic human resource plans in the light of wider economic and social factors. However, it may be argued that wider functional, general or change management experience may also be desirable, along with strategic awareness of the business enterprise (perhaps internationally), proactive planning and problem-solving skills, interpersonal competence and a range of other knowledge and skills would be an asset.

EXAMPLE

Team players with energy and vision

Resource manager

You will have overall management for the movement of resources within projects, be an active member in negotiations with departmental heads and project managers, have close links with other offices in order to utilise international resources, be responsible for defining yearly recruitment targets and identify detailed skill sets within each competence.

You must have 2+ years of resource or project-management experience. New media knowledge is desirable as well as knowledge of other European languages.

Training adviser

You will co-ordinate all aspects of the training cycle from identifying training needs to drawing up and implementing plans, sourcing external providers in order to develop enthusiastic and passionate employees. Working alongside department heads, HR and recruitment. You will be driving the development strategy together with the company.

You must be CIPD-qualified (full or part) with at least two years experience in a training environment.

HR officer

You will be an integral part of this dynamic company by providing the day-to-day HR function, defining resource requirements, tracking employees, ensuring appraisal objectives are met, assisting with the induction process.

You need to be CIPD-part qualified, have good time management skills, computer literacy and excellent communication skills.

People Management, 28 September 2000

Activity 5 (20 minutes)

Analyse the recruitment advertisement shown in the example above, in terms of the four 'traditions of personnel management' just discussed. What elements of each tradition can be seen, if any? What key words stand out as foreign to these traditions, and what do they suggest about the organisation, its environment and the role of personnel management within it?

3.5 Flaws in the traditional views

In 1968, Crichton (*Personnel Management in Context*) complained that personnel management was often a matter of 'collecting together such odd jobs from management as they are prepared to give up'.

Other writers have shared this view, notably Peter Drucker, who – while recognising the importance of human resources in the organisation – saw the personnel function of the time as 'a collection of incidental techniques without much internal cohesion'. According to Drucker, the personnel manager saw the role as 'partly a file clerk's job, partly a housekeeping job, partly a social worker's job and partly "fire-fighting" to head off union trouble or to settle it.' (*The Practice of Management,* 1955)

Activity 6   **(10 minutes)**

For each of Drucker's categories, cited above, give three examples of commonly perceived personnel management tasks. (Note that 'housekeeping' does not refer to maintenance of organisational premises, but maintenance tasks in general.)

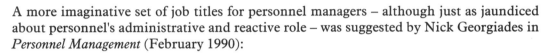

A more imaginative set of job titles for personnel managers – although just as jaundiced about personnel's administrative and reactive role – was suggested by Nick Georgiades in *Personnel Management* (February 1990):

(a)   'The administrative handmaiden' – writing job descriptions, visiting the sick and so on

(b)   'The policeman' – ensuring that both management and staff obey the rules, and keeping a watchful eye on absenteeism, sickness and punctuality

(c)   'The toilet flusher' – administering downsizing policies (cutting staff numbers)

(d)   'The sanitary engineer' – ensuring that there is an awareness of the unsanitary psychological conditions under which many people work

Figure 1.1 shows a simple diagram illustrating the personnel function and its place in the organisation, according to these traditional views.

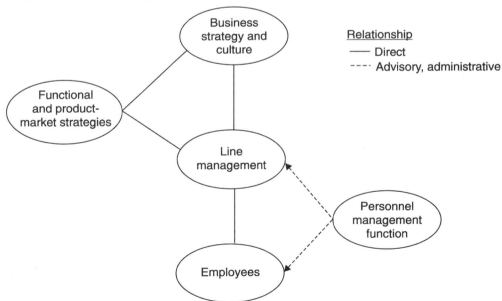

Figure 1.1 Personnel function and its relationships

In this model, note that personnel management is not directly involved in the strategic planning of the business.

The status and contribution of the personnel function is still often limited by its image as a 'fire-fighting' and 'housekeeping' function with an essentially reactive – even defensive – role. The personnel manager is judged according to his or her effectiveness in avoiding or settling industrial disputes, preventing accidents and ill-health (and their associated costs) and so on.

FOR DISCUSSION

'People may be regarded as a vital resource – at least plenty of lip service is paid to this concept by company chairmen in their annual statements – but many managers find it difficult to appreciate where the personnel department fits in, except in the simplest terms as a procurement and fire-fighting function.' (Armstrong, *A Handbook of Personnel Management Practice*)

Role-play a discussion between the company chairperson and the personnel manager about the role of the personnel function in the organisation.

This is a vicious circle. As long as personnel policy and practice are divorced from the strategy of the business and fail to be proactive and constructive, personnel will be perceived by line management as having little to do with the 'real' world of business management, or the 'bottom line' (profitability). Personnel specialists therefore command scant respect as business managers, and their activities continue to be limited to areas of little strategic impact.

'The real requirement is proactive and constructive rather than defensive and reactive. To discharge their true role, personnel managers must anticipate the needs of the organisation in the short and the long term. They must develop the policies to produce solutions to anticipated problems resulting from the external and internal environment, whilst influencing and creating the attitudes amongst employees needed for the enterprise's survival and success.' (Livy, *Corporate Personnel Management*)

Clearly, then, the concept of personnel management is of limited usefulness in the kind of complex, fast-changing we see today. A new concept has been developed to embrace and transcend traditional personnel management.

4 THE DEVELOPMENT OF HUMAN RESOURCE MANAGEMENT (HRM)

4.1 Context for a shift in perspective

Andrew Mayo (*People Management*, 22 January 1998) quotes Tom Watson, former president of IBM, as saying: 'All the value of this company is in its people. If you burnt down all of our plants and we just kept our people and information files, we would soon be as strong as ever. Take away our people and we might never recover.'

This represents a conceptual shift away from regarding employees as a cost to be managed and controlled, and towards regarding them as an asset to be nurtured and developed. According to Mayo, regarding employees as a key to adding value throws down a challenge to the human resource function. 'Forever fretting over whether "serious" business people see the function as adding value, HR now has no excuse for failing to make a major contribution.'

BPP
PUBLISHING

A former IBM President, Barry Curnow, likewise wrote (*Personnel Management*, October 1989): 'We've moved through periods when money has been in short supply and when technology has been in short supply. Now it's the people who are in short supply. So personnel directors are better placed than ever before to make a real difference – a bottom line difference. The scarce resource, which is the people resource, is the one that makes the impact at the margin, that makes one firm competitive over another.'

It seems that research is beginning to bear this out. Research findings reported in *People Management* ('*Profitable personnel*', 8 January 1998) showed that:

> 'the acquisition and development of skills (via selection, induction, training and appraisal) and job design are significant predictors of changes in both profitability and productivity. More broadly, the study concludes that – compared with, say, research and development, quality, technology and strategy – far the most powerful indicators of future business performance are the HR practices.'

At the same time, the increasing complexity of organisational models – such as the socio-technical system (see 2.5 above) – suggested that the personnel function was centrally concerned with issues of broader relevance to the business and its objectives: management of change and changing organisational forms, quality issues, meeting the long-term challenges of falling birthrates and skill shortages, empowering workers, facilitating team-working and flexible working methods, creating attractive 'employer brands' in the labour marketplace, managing diversity in the workforce, and creating and adapting organisational culture.

Increasing business competition was likewise demanding that personnel management justify itself in terms of contribution to the organisation's goals for growth, competitive gain and the improvement of 'bottom line' performance. Kramar, McGraw and Shuler also note that the payroll costs of many organisations today are of such magnitude (30-80% of total expenses) that 'senior managers must be concerned with human resources'.

In the social environment, advances in education, technological skills and general affluence have raised employee expectations of the quality of working life and awareness of their rights within the employment relationship: younger workers in particular appear to be more cynical and resistant to authority in the post-modern era. Meanwhile, the need to compete in innovative, technology- and quality-sensitive markets has put a premium on these highly skilled and knowledgeable employees, altering the balance of power in the employment relationship. Coercive and controlling psychological contracts of employment are no longer the norm (other than in very stable markets and/or areas of high unemployment): employees expect to have access to influence, responsibility and information related to their work. There has been a shift from compliance to commitment as the core of the psychological contract.

Definition

> A **psychological contract** is the set of values that determines what an organisation expects of its employees, and what they expect of it, in the employment relationship.

Politically, the UK government of the 1980s encouraged a shift away from trade union power and collective bargaining, instead emphasising entrepreneurialism, individualism and a 'unitary' perspective (discussed in detail in Part D of this Course Book) which assumed that management and employees shared a common interest in the success of the enterprise. It seemed possible that industrial conflict and collective negotiation could be pre-empted – and ultimately replaced by the proactive communication of shared goals, worker involvement, information-sharing and opportunities for personal and team

NOTES

development. This was supported by anti-union legislation and encouraged by the restructuring of the economy: the decline of old industries with entrenched industrial relations ideologies and the emergence of new technology- and knowledge-based industries and the service sector. In the USA, similar perceptions had been driven by the low productivity of the American worker and the declining rate of innovation in American industries compared to Japan, which was severely challenging the US economy by the early '80s.

The 1980s also saw major debate on management education, training and development (for example, in the influential report '*The Making of British Managers*' by Constable and McCormick, 1987), deficiencies in which were held partly responsible for the poor performance of British management. This made human relations issues of immediate strategic importance. Meanwhile, the popularity of the American anecdotal literature focusing on 'excellence' (for example, *In Search of Excellence* by Peters and Waterman) associated the success of high-performing companies with enlightened, customer-focused motivation styles, adding 'empowerment', 'culture' and 'commitment' to boardroom – and indeed popular – vocabulary.

4.2 Human resource management (HRM)

Definition

> **Human resource management** may (initially) be defined as 'a strategic and coherent approach to the management of an organisation's most valued assets: the people working there who individually and collectively contribute to the achievement of its objectives for sustainable competitive advantage' (Armstrong)

The term Human Resource Management (HRM) gained recognition in the USA in the late 1970s as a label for the way certain blue-chip companies such as IBM, Xerox and Hewlett Packard were managing their people. In order to give themselves a competitive edge over their rivals, these companies managed their people according to what David Guest defined (1989) as the four underlying principles of HRM, the combination of which (he asserts) create more effective organisations.

(a) **Strategic integration** – 'the ability of organisations to integrate HRM issues into their strategic plans, to ensure that the various aspects of HRM cohere and for line managers to incorporate an HRM perspective into their decision making'.

(b) **High commitment** – people must be managed in a way that ensures both their genuine 'behavioural' commitment to pursuing the goals of the organisation and their 'attitudinal' commitment, reflected in strong identification with the enterprise.

(c) **Flexibility** – HRM policies must be structured to allow maximum flexibility for the organisation, so it can respond to ever-changing business needs: for example, by encouraging functional versatility in employees and by creating 'an adaptable organisational structure with the capacity to manage innovation'.

(d) **High quality** – the notion of quality must run through everything the organisation does, 'including the management of employees and investment in high-quality employees, which in turn will bear directly on the quality of the goods and services provided'.

HRM is conceptually different from personnel management in that it is explicitly a strategy to use the human resources of an enterprise in order to gain competitive advantage. It integrates the various elements of personnel management into a whole strategic system: the various HR policies and plans of the organisation should 'fit' with each other and, crucially, with its overall business strategy.

Beer and Spector (1985) outline the 'new assumptions' which underpin policies identified with the 'HRM transformation' as follows.

New assumptions (HRM)	Old assumptions (personnel management)
• Proactive, system-wide interventions, with emphasis on fit, linking HRM with strategic planning and cultural change	• Reactive, piecemeal interventions in response to specific problems
• People are social capital, capable of development	• People are a variable cost
• Coincidence of interest between stakeholders can be developed	• Self interest dominates, conflict between stakeholders
• Seeks power equalisation for trust and collaboration	• Seeks power advantages for bargaining and confrontation
• Open channels of communication to build trust, commitment	• Control of information flow to enhance efficiency, power
• Goal orientation	• Relationship orientation
• Participation and informed choice	• Control from the top

Definition

> **Stakeholders** are all those individuals, groups and institutions who have a legitimate interest or 'stake' in the organisation's activities and performance. Examples include the shareholders, customers, suppliers, managers and employees of the organisation.

The emergence of HRM has sparked a lively debate among academics and practitioners about its relevance, whether it is a fair and ethical way to manage people and whether it makes any difference to organisational performance. Some commentators have noted a wholesale change in the use of terminology, with little difference in practice. However, where more than lip-service is paid to the concept, the following features might be noted.

(a) HRM implies a shift of emphasis in personnel management from the peripheral 'staff' role of the past to mainstream business management. Michael Armstrong has suggested that 'twenty years ago people in equivalent positions would have been more likely to talk about [personnel activities] as if these were techniques or areas of knowledge which had intrinsic value and did not need to be considered in terms of fit with business strategies or impact on business results'. The HR function is assumed to be centrally concerned with **issues of broader relevance to the business and its objectives,** such as change management, flexibility and the development of organisation culture.

> **Activity 7**   **(10 minutes)**
>
> List five 'changes' in an organisation or its environment that would have an impact on its employees or potential labour source.

(b) In the belief that human assets are the key to business success, personnel management can and should be integrated with the **strategic planning** of the enterprise, that is, with management at the broadest and highest level. The objectives of the HR function can and should be directly related to achieving the organisation's goals for growth, competitive gain and the improvement of 'bottom line' performance.

(c) Responsibility for HRM will also percolate **throughout the organisation**. *All* business planning should recognise that the ultimate source of 'value' is people and should appreciate the human resource implications and potential constraints associated with any long-term strategies evolved.

(d) The fit of people with organisation strategy will be reflected in **all areas and systems of HRM**.

(e) Personnel managers can and should be business people, even **entrepreneurs**. One definition of entrepreneurship is the 'shifting of economic resources out of the area of lower and into an area of higher productivity and greater yield' (JB Say) and this is essentially what HRM requires, in terms of finding, obtaining, retaining and developing the human resources of the business.

(f) The orientation of HRM will be towards **commitment and involvement** of employees, not mere compliance with organisational directives.

(g) Employee relations will reflect the conviction that there need be **no inherent conflict of interest** between management and employees (although this is a contentious assumption).

(h) The HR function will be a leader and communicator of organisational **culture and values**.

Definition

> The **culture** of an organisation is 'the way we do things round here': the collective self-image and style of the organisation, its shared values and beliefs, norms and symbols.

EXAMPLE: MAZDA

'The easiest way to get a compliant workforce is to recruit one. At the Mazda plant in Flat Rock, Michigan, for example, applicants underwent a five-stage series of tests before formally being offered a job... The process of weeding out "druggies, rowdies and unionists" is typical of Japanese firms elsewhere, and invariably results in a "green" workforce to match the site of the plant... As the Personnel Director of Kamatsu in north-east England made clear: "We haven't necessarily taken on the most skilled people, but the ones who have the right attitude to team working and flexibility".' (*Reassessing HRM*, ed. Blyton and Turnbull)

This integrated strategic viewpoint can be illustrated as in Figure 1.2 below. Compare this model with that shown in Figure 1.1.

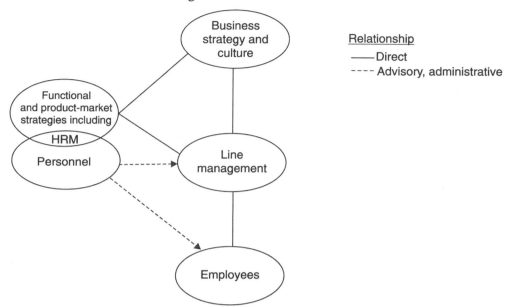

Figure 1.2 Strategic view of HRM

We will look in more detail at the perspectives, aims, ambiguities and implications of the HRM approach in Part B of this Course Book, covering Unit 22. Here, we will merely raise the question of how far the 'fashionable' terminology of HRM can be said to reflect a genuine shift in perspective and practice: is it just a glamorous new label?

4.3 HRM – more than a label?

The term 'HRM' has had a wide range of values, prescriptions and expectations put upon it: there is no universal definition or model of what it means in theory or in practice. The roots of HRM still leave doubt as to whether it emerged from academic description or practitioner developments, and whether it is a model of an 'ideal' employment relationship or a benchmark example of how that relationship actually is in certain leading-edge organisations. Beardwell and Holden note that 'HRM continues to provide agendas and prescriptions for debate amongst both practitioners and analysts that are contentious, compelling and have no set orthodoxy.' Does HRM exist? Are particular HRM policies effective in offering any kind of competitive advantage to organisations which use them? Are HRM policies merely a more subtle, psychologically-based form of manipulation than authoritarian or bureaucratic control?

One point of view is that 'HRM' is a term which practitioners have seized upon and applied to themselves, in the interests of their individual and professional status and self-esteem - whether or not they are in fact doing anything more than traditional personnel management. To some extent, widespread use of the term is unhelpful. It is rather a case of the Emperor's New Clothes: no personnel professional wants to admit that the term carries little meaning for him or her.

Another point of view, however, is that by continually focusing debate on the nature of the employment relationship and its role in business performance, HRM – whatever terminology is used – has fundamentally altered the orientation and practice of management and the expectation and experience of working life.

Activity 8 (30 minutes)

In June 1993, *Personnel Management (The magazine for human resource professionals)* published an article entitled 'The mystery of the missing human resource manager'. This reported a survey whose results suggested, amongst other things, that:

(a) Only 17% of establishments in the UK employing more than 25 people have a personnel specialist

(b) Only 44 out of 2,061 respondents used the 'HRM' title

(c) There was, however, some evidence to support the possibility that HRM is found at head offices, 'a strategic phenomenon at the strategic apex of the organisation'

The article continues:

'Perhaps predictably, the title does not necessarily reflect practice. IBM, for example, has retained the personnel title despite being frequently held up in the past as an exemplar of human resource management. Even in the US, where it has been estimated that over half of the top 50 corporations now use the human resource title, IBM has kept the personnel label. One explanation is that it only makes sense to change it if it provides some competitive advantage. Maybe establishments in the UK have taken that message on board. Certainly, we can refute the 'old wine in new bottles' argument that some of us promulgated. There may be some good wine around – some good human resource policy and practice – but it is still marketed in the old bottles.

Do you think the name of the function matters? Why?

Chapter roundup

- The personnel function takes different forms in different organisations. Traditionally, it has been regarded as a primarily administrative, reactive, problem-handling function, concerned with hiring and firing, employee welfare and industrial relations

- Personnel management developed from the appointment of industrial welfare workers by some Victorian employers, with the aim of improving the living and working conditions of employees. Even at this early stage, the motivation for this service was acknowledged to be both philanthropic and business-centred.

- Labour shortages associated with the World Wars fostered both a science of productivity and an increase in the power of organised labour. Management theory began with scientific management and was supposedly universalised by classical principles: each developed a portrait of the employment relationship. With the human relations school, the importance of socio-psychological or human factors to organisational effectiveness was more fully recognised.

- Growing complexity and accelerating change led to the development of less prescriptive models of management, including the systems and contingency approaches, which began to integrate human relations more directly with strategic business issues. At the same time, personnel management came to require bureaucratic controls and a specialised body of knowledge.

Chapter roundup (cont.)

- Four traditions therefore colour perceptions of personnel management: the welfare tradition, the industrial relations tradition, the control of labour tradition and the professional tradition.

- Human Resource Management (HRM) is a concept which seeks to recognise employees as an asset to be nurtured, rather than a cost to be controlled, and which views the sourcing, deploying and developing of these human resources as a key integrated element of business strategy.

- HRM developed out of influences such as: the increased complexity of business processes and their dependence on employee flexibility and commitment; the need for competitive advantage; the increased power and expectations of highly-skilled knowledge workers; and the identification of human relations policy as the key to management effectiveness and business 'excellence'.

- HRM terminology is often used interchangeably with more traditional personnel management ideas, but the proactive, integrated and strategic approach is distinctively 'HRM'.

Quick quiz

1 Outline the main areas of expertise which developed in the emergence of personnel management.

2 According to Drucker, the personnel manager's role is 'partly a file clerk's job, partly a housekeeping job, partly a social worker's job and partly 'fire-fighting'. Explain what is meant by each of these.

3 Why might it be considered important for personnel management to be linked to corporate strategy?

4 List four underlying principles of HRM.

5 List four influences in the business environment, which contributed to the shift from personnel management to HRM.

6 List the five main theoretical approaches to management and organisation.

7 What was the distinctive contribution of the neo-human relations approach to management?

8 Suggest four influences that the management of war had on personnel management.

9 In what contexts might (a) the welfare tradition and (b) the industrial relations tradition of personnel management still persist?

10 List Beer and Spector's 'new assumptions' underpinning HRM policy.

Answers to quick quiz

1 Welfare, recruitment, training, reward systems, human resource planning and employment legislation. (see paragraph 2)

2 Administration and record-keeping; maintaining order in staffing issues and related bureaucracy; counselling and welfare; industrial relations, conflict resolution. (para 3.5)

3   So that it can make (and demonstrate) a contribution to the 'bottom line' or added value.   (para 3.5)

4   Strategic integration, commitment, flexibility, quality.   (para 4.2)

5   Increased complexity of business processes and their dependence on employee flexibility and commitment; the need for competitive advantage; the increased power and expectations of highly-skilled knowledgeable workers; and the identification of human relations policy as the key to management effectiveness and business 'excellence'.
                                                                         (para 4.2)

6   Scientific management, classical organisation, human relations, systems and contingency.   (para 2.2 and 2.3)

7   A focus on motivation via job satisfaction, based on human beings' 'higher order' needs for challenge, responsibility and self-development.
                                                                         (para 2.4)

8   The Crimea and the Boer War highlighted poor health and encouraged government intervention to secure the workforce. Skill shortages during and after the World Wars encouraged a focus on productivity management. Skill shortages during and after the World Wars empowered trade unions. Wartime policy modelled an emphasis on utilisation of resources, improvement of conditions and security of rights.
                                                                         (para 2.1)

9   (a) In employee counselling, welfare services, health and safety. (b) In grievance procedures, industrial dispute resolution and (where it still exists) collective bargaining.   (para 3)

10   Proactive, system-wide interventions, with emphasis on fit, linking HRM with strategic planning and cultural change; people are social capital, capable of development; coincidence of interest between stakeholders can be developed; seeks power equalisation for trust and collaboration; open channels of communication to build trust, commitment; goal orientation; participation and informed choice.   (para 4.2)

Answers to activities

1   Personnel managers' additional duties with the given components may include:

     Organisation: job analysis and design, organisation design

     Resourcing: HR planning, selection, termination

     Development: appraisal, career management, succession planning

     Reward: market surveys, benefits, incentive schemes

     Relations: involvement, communication

     Health and safety: welfare, stress management, occupational health schemes

     Administration: management information, statistical analysis and returns, data protection

2   Borderline Computers' methods would conflict with Fayol's principles of specialisation, the scalar chain of command and unit of command. Sticking to those principles would prevent rapid decision-making and communication and reduce the efficiency of the team's performance.

3   Systems approach methods, applied to the given statements, are as follows. (a) F, (b) T, (c) F, (d) F, (e) T, (f) T.

4   Examples of conflicts of interest might include the following.

   (a)   The need for downsizing or delayering for organisational efficiency. The workforce may well see this as a betrayal, yet it is part of resource management to know when to liquidate assets: organisational survival may even depend on increased efficiency/flexibility or cost reduction.

   (b)   The negotiation of reward packages. As a member of management, you may wish to minimise increases in the cost of labour, or rationalise them in some way (eg through job evaluation). The workforce perceives pay rises as a 'right' or as an indication of the value the organisation puts on its services, and may be disappointed.

   (c)   Disciplinary procedures. The interests of management may best be served by 'clamping down on absenteeism, poor time-keeping and so on in order to keep general discipline and efficiency – but the workforce, and particular individuals, will often feel that rules are unfair or unfairly applied.

Broadly, these are issues of the way power is used in organisations. The personnel function can go a long way to minimising the potential hurt and conflict caused by applying and communicating the decisions of management fairly and sensitively.

5   Welfare tradition: very little sign of such an orientation in the job descriptions – except perhaps in the HR Officer's responsibility for 'assisting with the induction process', although even this seems more likely to be performance-oriented rather than for the psychological comfort of the recruits.

Industrial relations tradition: very little of this, either, in the traditional sense. The word 'negotiations' crops up (Resource Manger), but more in the sense of collaborative responsibility for project resourcing. The phrase 'enthusiastic and passionate employees' (Training Advisor) suggests a unitary perspective on the employment relationship: no inherent conflict anticipated. The stressing of 'individuality' (Footnotes) likewise suggests an absence of collectivism.

Control of labour tradition: targets, competence frameworks, plans, co-ordination, the 'tracking' (monitoring) of employees against appraisal objectives, the requirement for computer literacy: this suggests the presence of administrative control systems in the organisation. However, these elements are tempered with more 'dynamic' elements (such as the word 'fun' in the footnotes!)

Professional tradition: the Training Advisor and HR officer are required to have CIPD qualifications, and the Training Advisor additionally requires specific specialist experience. However, other skills and experience are also mentioned: project management, new media, European languages, communication and time management skills and so on.

Non-traditional concepts: the key word seems to be integration. 'In negotiation with departmental heads and project managers... links with other offices... overall management...' (Resource Manager). 'Driving the development strategy together with the company' (Training Adviser). 'Integral part' (HR officer). This language fits with Icon's field and self-image or culture as expressed in the footnotes: 'only the best... individuality... creativity... fun... focussing on strategic solutions... integrated business solutions... as client needs evolve...'

6   Your examples may be different, but here are some suggestions.

(a)   Keeping and updating personnel records (eg on employee training, pay, disciplinary actions etc); retrieving information on employees and the workforce as a whole for managers (eg when appraisal or pay negotiations are imminent); ensuring that the organisation has up-to-date information on relevant employment legislation.

(b)   Gathering and disseminating statistics on the workforce in 'returns' to government departments and agencies; hiring and firing on request; co-ordinating training programmes; administering pay and benefits.

(c)   Employee counselling; handling disciplinary action; co-ordinating welfare programmes.

(d)   Conflict resolution meetings with employee representatives; grievance handling; pay negotiations.

7   Again, there is a wide variety to choose from, but suggestions include:

(a)   Relocation of the organisation's premises

(b)   Restructuring of departments or levels of management

(c)   The introduction of new technology in the workplace

(d)   The introduction of new work methods such as teamworking or shifts

(e)   The entry into the market of a competitor offering higher rates of pay

(f)   The harmonisation of educational/professional qualifications within the European Union

8   It clearly matters to some of the people who perform the function, for their own sense of self-esteem and the status of their profession. An important consideration is whether the employees – the humans whom the function manages – view the idea of themselves as 'resources' positively or negatively and whether practice justifies the more 'enlightened' sounding title, or is indeed viewed cynically as the same 'old wine' in a fancy 'new bottle'. Adoption of the title may be a sign of conflict and power struggles within the organisation or it may enhance the organisation's reputation or 'brand' as an employer in the labour market.

Assignment 1

Class One Insurance Services

Background

Class One Insurance Services is a small but growing business specialising in household and commercial insurance. It has developed over the years by acquisition and merger but now wishes to consolidate its current base. Around 200 employees work in three divisions and at headquarters. The headquarters is based in East London, sharing premises with the Motor Insurance division. The Home Insurance division is based in Borehamwood, Hertfordshire while the Personal Insurance division runs from offices in Basildon, Essex.

Staffing

The company is staffed as follows:

Headquarters: Managing director, other directors, office manager, personnel officer and 50 administrative and clerical staff.

Motor insurance: Divisional director plus 30 specialist and administrative staff, 35 telephone enquiry and sales clerks, 25 sales representatives.

Home insurance: Divisional manager plus 20 specialist and administrative staff, 15 telephone sales clerks, 12 sales representatives, office manager.

Personal insurance: Divisional manager plus 5 administrative staff, 12 telephone enquiry and sales clerks, 10 sales representatives.

Business and personnel factors

The state of business and personnel factors in each of the firm's main units are as follows:

Head office: In order to achieve greater integration, the directors have increased headquarters' role in developing financial and administrative procedures for the whole organisation. A full-time personnel officer has just been appointed. Administrative and clerical staff are mostly local people and staff turnover is very low. Salaries are reasonable without being generous.

Motor insurance: This division is maintaining its market position but at an increasing cost to the company. Salaries are modest, but generous commission payments can be earned by sales staff. Staff turnover is high among this group. Administrative staff are paid at competitive rates and staff turnover here is low. Although morale appears high, there is a feeling of the division being in a state of flux, with people leaving and joining on a weekly basis.

Home insurance: Business is just being maintained in the face of fierce competition from the main building societies. Wages are high in comparison to other sections of the company. The workforce is stable and the employees are generally older than in other divisions. Most employees are members of MSF trade union

Cont…

NOTES

Assignment 1 *cont…*

Personal insurance: Business is expanding and the division has increased its market share in the Essex region. Salaries are lower than in other divisions, but staff turnover is also lower (except on the sales side). All staff are members of MSF.

Your task

You are the newly appointed personnel offer at headquarters, with a responsibility for staff in all divisions. Your task is to identify the problems which are likely to face you over the first six months in the job. Then take a longer term view, say over the next 1-2 years, and identify which aspects of personnel management should receive your special attention.

BPP
PUBLISHING

Chapter 2 :
THE PERSONNEL FUNCTION IN THE ORGANISATION

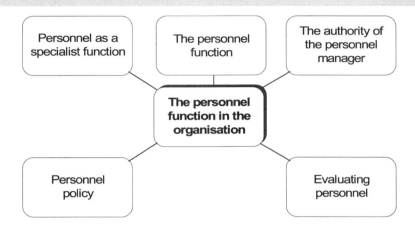

Introduction

In this chapter we look at how responsibility for human resource management tasks can be structured in an organisation, and at the relationship between personnel and other managers.

We noted in Chapter 1 that personnel management may be carried out as a separate function or department in the organisation, but is also the responsibility of managers and supervisors within their own departments and teams. We also suggested that, despite the claims of HRM to a key strategic role in a business's ability to add value, some personnel departments remain 'administrative handmaidens' to operational managers. So what kind of authority, if any, does the personnel function really have? We will attempt to answer the question in this chapter.

Your objectives

In this chapter you will learn about the following:

    (a)   The role and purpose of human resource management

    (b)   The implications of HRM for the role of the line manager and employees

    (c)   How responsibilities for personnel can be shared and structured within the management team

NOTES

1 THE PERSONNEL FUNCTION

1.1 HRM functions, activities, aims and objectives

As we suggested in Chapter 1, HRM – as opposed to personnel management – is seen as a broadly-distributed organisational competence rather than a 'function' in the sense of a department of functional specialists. The HR function may be thought of as the integration of people management systems throughout the organisation, rather than a particular set of roles and activities.

In this chapter, we will be looking primarily at the role and authority of the personnel function or department within the organisation structure. Before we do that, however, it is worth summarising the wider HRM perspective in its organisational context. The diagram on the next page, loosely based on the work of Shuler et al (1995), may be read from the bottom up (following the classical hierarchy of planning), or from the top down (from a functional perspective).

1.2 Ambiguities in the role of personnel

As we have seen in Chapter 1, personnel managers may operate in different areas and at different levels: from crisis handling and routine administration on the one hand, to policy-making and innovation on the other.

Charles Handy (*Understanding Organisations*) suggested that the effectiveness of the traditional personnel department is reduced by ambiguity about the role of the department or conflict between different roles of the department. He noted that personnel managers are expected to act in a variety of roles.

(a) As **line managers** – with direct authority over their own departments, as well as over certain specialist functions such as negotiating and implementing settlements with trade unions or enforcing safety procedures

(b) As **advisers** to line managers – for example, in welfare situations or in helping with behavioural or motivational problems in line departments

(c) As **service providers** to line managers – for example, in developing and implementing recruitment and training schemes, administering employee records and providing management information

(d) As '**auditors**' – for example, in monitoring and evaluating appraisal or training systems, or carrying out management audits

(e) As **co-ordinators and planners** – for example in human resource forecasting and planning

NOTES

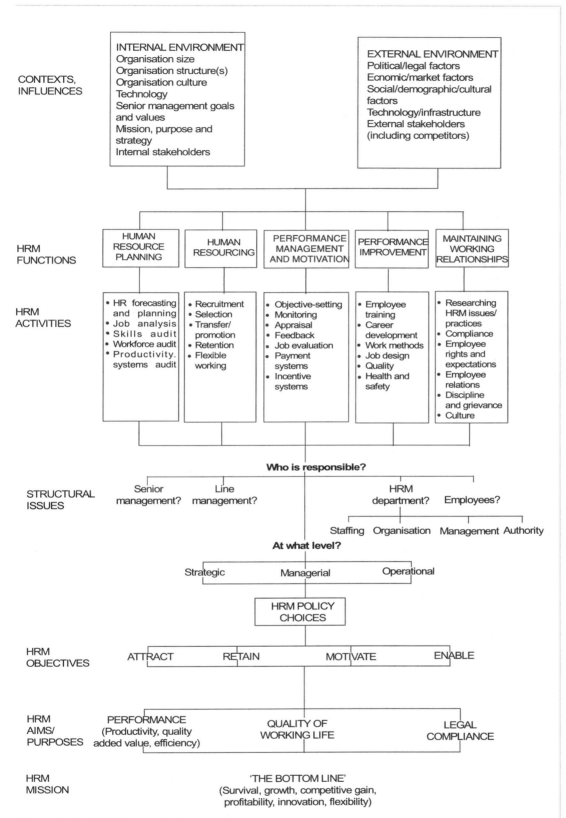

CONTEXTS, INFLUENCES

INTERNAL ENVIRONMENT
Organisation size
Organisation structure(s)
Organisation culture
Technology
Senior management goals and values
Mission, purpose and strategy
Internal stakeholders

EXTERNAL ENVIRONMENT
Political/legal factors
Ecnomic/market factors
Social/demographic/cultural factors
Technology/infrastructure
External stakeholders (including competitors)

HRM FUNCTIONS

HUMAN RESOURCE PLANNING | HUMAN RESOURCING | PERFORMANCE MANAGEMENT AND MOTIVATION | PERFORMANCE IMPROVEMENT | MAINTAINING WORKING RELATIONSHIPS

HRM ACTIVITIES

- HR forecasting and planning
- Job analysis
- Skills audit
- Workforce audit
- Productivity. systems audit

- Recruitment
- Selection
- Transfer/ promotion
- Retention
- Flexible working

- Objective-setting
- Monitoring
- Appraisal
- Feedback
- Job evaluation
- Payment systems
- Incentive systems

- Employee training
- Career development
- Work methods
- Job design
- Quality
- Health and safety

- Researching HRM issues/ practices
- Compliance
- Employee rights and expectations
- Employee relations
- Discipline and grievance
- Culture

STRUCTURAL ISSUES

Who is responsible?

Senior management? | Line management? | HRM department? | Employees?

Staffing | Organisation | Management | Authority

At what level?

Strategic | Managerial | Operational

HRM POLICY CHOICES

HRM OBJECTIVES

ATTRACT | RETAIN | MOTIVATE | ENABLE

HRM AIMS/ PURPOSES

PERFORMANCE (Productivity, quality added value, efficiency) | QUALITY OF WORKING LIFE | LEGAL COMPLIANCE

HRM MISSION

'THE BOTTOM LINE'
(Survival, growth, competitive gain, profitability, innovation, flexibility)

Figure 2.1: HRM in context

Handy suggested that this ambiguity leads to inefficiency and a loss of authority for the personnel function, which attempts to bolster its influence by expansion and by proliferation of rules and procedures as a form of influence and control over line management. In other words, the personnel department may develop a bureaucratic culture – regardless of the culture of the organisation. One solution put forward by Handy was to split the personnel function, within the organisation structure, into separate 'executive', 'advisory', 'service', 'auditing' and 'planning and co-ordinating' functions.

A more flexible alternative, put forward by Karen Legge, is a **matrix structure**.

Definition

> **Matrix organisation** is a structure, typically shown as a grid, which provides for the formalisation of management control between different areas of authority, while at the same time maintaining functional departmentalisation. It is typically used in project, product or brand management, where project/product/brand managers have authority over members of functional departments insofar as their activity is relevant to the project/product/brand, while in other matters, authority rests with the functional department managers.

In Legge's proposal, the key **functions** of personnel (such as human resource planning, selection, training and welfare) are on one axis of the grid, with key **process activities** (such as policy-making, innovation, the establishing of routines and crisis handling) on the other. Key personnel roles can then be allocated in a more rational manner.

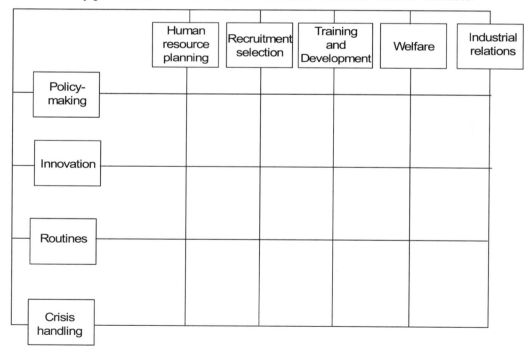

Figure 2.2: An HR matrix

A further ambiguity may exist for the personnel function in determining whose interest to serve: who is its 'customer' or 'client'. We noted that the welfare tradition of personnel management assumed an orientation towards the employee; the control of labour tradition, towards the employer; the industrial relations tradition, towards an intermediary position between the two; and the professional tradition, towards the profession itself. According to the CIPD's Code of Professional Practice in Personnel Management, these orientations are not mutually exclusive: the personnel manager has three principal areas of responsibility.

(a)   'A personnel manager's primary responsibility is to his **employer**.'

(b)   He will 'resolve the conflict which must sometimes exist between his position as a member of the **management team** and his special relationship with the **workforce** in general and with individual **employees**.'

(c)   He will 'use his best endeavours to enhance the standing... of his **profession**' in dealing with other bodies.

There are further ambiguities in the role of personnel management in the organisation structure, arising from line, staff and functional authority relationships. We will discuss the implications of these in Section 3 of this chapter. Now we will look at one of the major structural issues in personnel management: the extent to which it should be a specialist function, and whether it should therefore be centralised or decentralised within the organisation.

2   PERSONNEL AS A SPECIALIST FUNCTION

2.1   Centralisation or decentralisation?

Definition

> **Centralisation** and **decentralisation** refer to the degree to which control and authority to make decisions are organised and held centrally, by a particular (usually senior) group of people, *or* delegated and spread to a number of individuals and groups within the organisation

There are a number of benefits to be gained at each end of the continuum.

Pro centralisation	Pro decentralisation/delegation
1 Decisions are made at one point and so are easier to co-ordinate	1 Avoids overburdening top managers, in terms of workload and stress
2 Senior managers in an organisation can take a wider view of problems and consequences.	2 Improves motivation of more junior managers who are given responsibility since job challenge and entrepreneurial skills are highly valued in today's work environment
3 Senior management can keep a proper balance between different departments or functions – eg by deciding on the resources to allocate to each.	3 Greater awareness of local problems by decision makers. Geographically dispersed organisations should often be decentralised on a regional basis.
4 Quality of decisions is (theoretically) higher due to senior managers' skills and experience	4 Greater speed of decision making, and response to changing events, since no need to refer decisions upwards. This is valued by customers and is particularly important in rapidly changing markets

Pro centralisation	Pro decentralisation/delegation
5 Possibly cheaper, by reducing number of managers needed and so lowering cost of overheads.	5 Helps junior managers to develop and helps the process of transition from functional to general management. Centralised organisations tend to fill senior positions from external sources.
6 Crisis decisions are taken more quickly at the centre, without need to refer back, get authority etc.	6 Separate spheres of responsibility can be identified: control, performance measurement and accountability are better.
7 Policies, procedures and documentation can be standardised organisation-wide.	7 Communication technology allows decisions to be made locally, with information and input from head office if required.

Centralised control over personnel management would generally imply the existence of a personnel officer or department with authority over all personnel management tasks in the organisation.

Decentralised control over personnel management would generally imply the delegation to departmental managers and team leaders of the authority for personnel management tasks affecting their own staff and activities. In practice there is a need for a mix of both, in order to gain the benefits of co-ordination and consistency as well as flair and flexibility. This would commonly be achieved by:

(a) Decentralising tasks such as selection, reward negotiation, working hours management, and training and development to the units where the people work, and where such personnel management decisions have direct impact, while

(b) Centralising specialist and strategic functions such as HR planning, policy formation and culture creation in a dedicated HR department, which can have an organisation-wide perspective and specialist expertise

Activity 1   **(1 hour)**

You are a sales manager in Mpower Ltd, an organisation which develops and markets software and services for Internet users: web page design, internet connection, browser programs and so on. You are responsible for a team of 12 salespeople who work more or less 'independently' from home and 'on the road', and who service a remote rural area with a widely dispersed population.

What personnel management tasks would you wish to be **your** responsibility? What areas would you wish to have specialised or centralised help with? (You might like to do this activity with a fellow student who can take the role of Mpower's head office HR manager. See what conflicts of interest come up, and how they might be resolved.)

The arguments for centralisation and decentralisation of personnel management essentially boil down to the need for specialism on the one hand, and the need for managers to exercise line authority in the sphere of their own responsibilities on the other. We'll look at each of these in turn.

2.2 Specialism

In any organisation, there is a need for:

- Specialist advice on personnel matters (whether from within the organisation or outside); and/or

- Well defined personnel policies

Because

- Constant developments in personnel management require expertise – perhaps increasingly so (as discussed below); and

- Personnel management practice needs to be consistent, fair, efficient and in line with organisational goals.

Several factors have contributed to the perceived need for a specialised personnel function.

(a) The need to **comply with changing regulation and legislation** means that expert attention will have to be given to matters such as recruitment and selection (to avoid racial or sexual discrimination), termination of the employment contract (to avoid unfair dismissal), and health and safety at work.

(b) Constant **changes in the labour market** have required that policies be designed and implemented by individuals with current knowledge.

(c) There is continuing pressure for **social responsibility** towards employees, with new requirements for communication, involvement and working conditions – notably from Europe.

(d) **Behavioural sciences** (psychology, sociology and social psychology) are increasingly used to explain and predict how individuals operate and co-operate (or not) at work. Up to date research on such matters as motivation, stress, resistance to change, industrial fatigue and response to leadership style need to be monitored.

(e) Trade unions, Industrial Tribunals, the Advisory, Conciliation and Arbitration Service (ACAS) and others have a continuing role in **employee relations**: familiarity with legislation, best practice, liaison and negotiation techniques and so on will be required.

FOR DISCUSSION

'Managers, if one listens to the psychologists, will have to have insights into all kinds of people. They will have to be in command of all kinds of psychological techniques. They will have to understand an infinity of individual personality structures, individual psychological needs, and individual psychological problems... But most managers find it hard enough to know all they need to know about their own immediate area of expertise, be it heat-treating or cost accounting or scheduling.'

Drucker: *Management*

Do you think is an argument for:

(a) The irrelevance of all the 'psychological techniques' to day-to-day management; or

(b) The need for specialists who can explain to managers what lies behind people's behaviour at work?

2.3 Line authority

Definitions

> **'Authority'** is the 'right to do something'.
>
> **Line authority** refers to the direct authority a person has, by virtue of his or her position in the organisation structure of 'chain of command', to give orders and instructions, make decisions and manage resources: the authority of a 'superior' over a 'subordinate' in the organisation hierarchy. (In a culture of empowerment, the emphasis might be more on the **responsibility** to get things done and the authority to mobilise and manage human and other resources to that end.)

In an article in *The Administrator* (May 1985) entitled *'The Personnel Function: a shared responsibility'*, Laurie Mullins pointed out that line managers:

> 'have both the right and the duty to be concerned with the effective operation of their own department, including the management and well-being of their staff.'

After all, it is the line managers who are directly responsible for the impact on performance of poor personnel management: lateness, low morale, hostility, absenteeism, incapacity to perform to standard, or whatever.

Mullins suggests that: 'It is the job of the personnel manager to provide specialist knowledge and services to line managers, and **to support them in the performance of their jobs**. It is not the job of the personnel manager to manage people, other than (his or her own) direct subordinates. The personnel manager has no direct control over other staff except where a specific responsibility is delegated directly by top management, for example, if nominated as safety officer under the Health and Safety at Work Act 1974. The personnel manager has executive authority for such delegated responsibility and for the management of the personnel department and its staff... In all other respects the personnel manager's relationship with other managers, supervisors and staff of the organisation is **indirect**, that is an advisory or **'functional'** relationship.'

Definition

> **'Functional'** authority is the authority a person or department has by virtue of special expertise, knowledge or experience in a particular area. The experts have formally delegated to them the authority to influence specific areas (those in which they are specialists) of the work of other departments and their line managers. Personnel managers may thus have functional authority over employee relations negotiations and HR planning, in the same way that the Information Technology department may have functional authority to purchase, configure and maintain computer systems in other departments.

> **Activity 2** **(20 minutes)**
>
> List the aspects of personnel management which could be devolved to line departments. Where there is a particular advantage in doing so, state briefly what this is. (If you get stuck, look back over Figure 2.1, and consider whether each of the 'HRM activities' mentioned would best be centralised or devolved.)

2.4 What should be centralised and what should be devolved?

Areas which might be retained as the **responsibility of the HR function** include the following.

(a)   Strategic issues such as change management programmes and human resource planning, and all aspects of HR at the strategic level, including the formulation and communication of organisational policy. This is necessary to incorporate HR expertise at this level, ensuring that the impact of human factors on strategic plans (and vice versa) is taken into account.

(b)   Organisation-wide communication, employee-relations management and collective bargaining. Centralisation has the advantage both of special expertise and knowledge and a wider organisational viewpoint. Negotiating and implementing industrial agreements with trade unions is one area where the central HR function traditionally has clear-cut 'line' or executive authority.

(c)   Provision of specialist service and advice/consultancy, where required: for example, on compliance issues or the design and delivery of training services (where up-to-date specialist knowledge is required), or on grievance and disciplinary issues (where extra-departmental arbitration and conciliation is required).

(d)   Researching and auditing of HR systems (for selection, training, appraisal, reward and so on), such as job evaluation exercises, benchmarking or the local government review. This helps to co-ordinate and control HR functions across the organisation, to ensure that line departments are complying with policy and that policies are effective and relevant to the needs of line departments.

The above centralised functions would create a coherent and integrated framework of policies, plans, systems and (where necessary for compliance) rules, developed by HR specialists, which would maintain consistent practice and minimise redundant problem-solving and 're-inventing the wheel' by line managers. Within such a framework, a number of aspects of personnel management could be **devolved to line departments**.

Most commentators observe a trend toward greater decentralisation of personnel functions, in line with 'slimmer' head office staff, flatter management structures and flexibility through greater autonomy for local business units. The increase in the white-collar 'knowledge-based' workforce, with its mobility and higher expectations, has supported a move toward individualism in career development, reward-negotiation and so on which can be more flexibly managed by line managers and team leaders. Meanwhile, the sophistication of personnel information and administrative systems (as we will discuss in Chapter 9) has facilitated HR decision-making, on a day-to-day basis, by line managers.

Definition

> **Devolution** is the term used by Stephen Connock (*HR Vision: Managing a Quality Workforce*) to describe the shift of responsibilities away from personnel specialists back towards line management.

Connock suggests that devolution is not a **loss** for HR specialists, but will allow them to concentrate on longer term issues, on performance standards, on providing advice and guidance on more complex subjects'.

2.5 Personnel in the flat organisation

Organisations are tending to 'delayer': that is, to cut out superfluous levels of management, usually from the middle level of the organisation hierarchy.

'Tall' organisations, with lots of layers of management, tend to be inefficient and inflexible: communication up and down the organisation is slow, and responsibilities are narrower in scope and are tightly controlled.

The more power is delegated or decentralised in an organisation, the less tightly activities are supervised and controlled, the fewer layers of authority it will have. The resulting 'flat' organisation is often more efficient and flexible. In practice this has meant the disappearance of 'middle management', smaller head office staffs, and more extensive empowerment.

For personnel management this has contributed to the devolution of authority for people-management functions to line managers directly involved with team management, and the slimming down of centralised HR departments for activity at the strategic level.

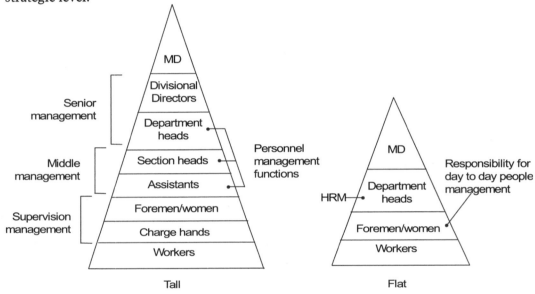

EXAMPLES

The September 1992 edition of *Accountancy* reported a decimation of middle managers – not just 'penpushers' but technicians as well – at a number of large British companies.

(a) In 1990, a new chairman at BP announced 1,000 job losses of which 160 were head office managers. This represented a 30% cut at head office.

(b) BT's Project Sovereign in 1990 involved a change in structure. Of a total cut in jobs of 19,000, 6,000 came from management ranks.

In his book *Once a customer, always a customer*, Chris Daffy quotes Jan Carlson who, when he was CEO for SAS Airlines, told his employees that 'If you're not directly serving customers, you need to be serving someone who is'. Daffy himself then goes on to argue that 'There should be just two roles in an organisation. Either directly serving customers, or serving the people who do, so that they can serve customers better'. The organisation with a customer-focused structure would therefore inevitably be very flat, with just two levels! This is, of course, a drastic over simplification but it does contain an underpinning principle with merit – nobody in an organisation should be far removed from customers.

> **Activity 3**   **(1 hour)**
>
> Make a list of twelve key activities that a personnel manager could be involved in (for example, advising a sales manager on how best to recruit new staff, negotiating with trade union representatives, or producing monthly figures on sickness and absenteeism).
>
> Now subdivide your list into three categories according to which of the following personnel staff would be more likely to be involved:
>
> (a)   A personnel/administrative officer
>
> (b)   A more senior qualified personnel manager whose main role is to provide specialist advice to other line managers
>
> (c)   A personnel director
>
> Are there any activities in which more than one of them would be involved?

The complexity of personnel's role raises the question: when it comes down to it, what power does the personnel function really have? What if – however expert the HR manager is – line managers choose not to heed his or her advice? What good is 'functional' authority without 'line authority'? Let us look at the kinds of power and control the HR manager can exercise.

3   THE AUTHORITY OF THE PERSONNEL MANAGEMENT

3.1   Line, staff and functional authority

Line and staff relationships

There are two ways of looking at the distinction between line and staff management.

(a)   Line and staff can be used to describe **functions** in the organisation. Line management consists of those managers **directly** involved in achieving the objectives of an organisation (usually production and sales managers, in a manufacturing company). Every other manager is staff (including accounting, research and development, and personnel).

(b)   Line and staff can be used to denote **relationships** of authority. A line manager is any manager who has been given (delegated) authority over a subordinate down the chain of command. Staff authority, on the other hand, resides in some knowledge or expertise, resources or other desirable qualities, that can be offered to support line management.

Staff functions and relationships exist in many organisations where there is a need for specialisation of management: accountants, personnel administrators, economists, data processing experts, and so on. Where this expertise is 'siphoned off' into a separate department, the problem naturally arises as to whether the experts:

(a)   Exist to **advise** line managers, who may accept or reject the advice given or

(b)   Can step in to **direct** the line managers in what to do – in other words, to assume authority themselves: that is, they have formal 'functional' authority, based on the recognition of expertise in areas which are vital to the achievement of line objectives

The ambiguities of line/staff relationships create a potential for conflict, where:

(a) Staff managers are held in low regard as overheads who contribute nothing to the bottom line but have considerable nuisance power in imposing rules and policies

(b) Staff managers **are** in fact divorced from the business objectives of line management, but impose rules and procedures in the interest of their profession or speciality, or to enhance their power

(c) Staff managers undermine the authority of line managers – intentionally or otherwise

(d) Staff managers report over the heads of line managers, as advisers to senior management

(e) Staff managers are not held accountable for the results of their advice – or **are** held accountable for such results, without having the authority to get it properly implemented

The solutions to these problems are easily stated, but not easy to implement in practice.

(a) Authority must be clearly defined, and distinctions between line authority and staff advice clearly set out (for example, in job descriptions).

(b) Senior management must encourage line managers to make positive efforts to discuss work problems with staff advisers, and be prepared to accept their advice. The use of experts should become an organisational way of life, part of the culture.

(c) Staff managers must be fully informed about the aspects of the business in which, as functional experts, they will become involved. They should then be less likely to offer impractical advice.

(d) When staff advisers are used to plan and implement changes in the running of the business, they must be kept involved during the implementation, monitoring and review of the project. Staff managers must be prepared to accept responsibility for their failures and this is only really possible if they advise during the implementation and monitoring stages.

The HRM approach may solve some of these ambiguities, because it both proposes a much fuller and clearer involvement for line managers, and transforms the role of the HRM professional into one of specialist consultant operating at the strategic centre of the organisation.

FOR DISCUSSION

Which 'side' do you naturally relate to: the line managers trying to get things done but hedged in by personnel rules and polices or the HR manager having to beat his or her head against a brick wall to convince line mangers of hard-won insights into people at work? Or do you feel that as a line manager, you would be glad of expert help with complex people issues? Or as an HT manager, would you be glad that line managers are prepared to get on with their jobs, leaving you to more 'global' perceptions of the organisation's needs?

Set up a discussion between line and staff: 'Why should we/you listen to the personnel department?'

3.2 Power and influence

The personnel specialist may lack 'positional' or 'legal power' in the organisation, in relation to line departments, but may possess:

(a)   'Resource' power – through control over manpower and pay

(b)   'Expert' power – where his /her specialist knowledge is recognised

In addition, he/she can 'influence' (direct and modify the behaviour of others) through:

(a)   Establishing rules and procedures

(b)   Bargaining and negotiation

(c)   Persuasion

(d)   'Ecology' or environmental control'

'The design of work, the work, the structure of reward and control systems, the structure of the organisation, the management of groups and the control of conflict are all ways of managing the environment in order to influence behaviour. Let us never forget that although the environment is all around us, it is not unalterable, that to change it is to influence people, that ecology is potent, the more so because it is often unnoticed.'

(Handy)

Activity 4   **(20 minutes)**

List **five mechanisms** through which the personnel function might shape the work environment in order to influence or control behaviour in an organisation, and suggest briefly **how** that influence is achieved.

According to Michael Armstrong (*A Handbook of Personnel Management Practice*):

'What in effect the personnel manager says is that "this is the personnel policy of the company, ignore it at your peril". He can seldom forbid anyone to do anything, except where it contravenes a law or negotiated procedure, but he can refuse to authorise something – say, a pay increase – if it is in his power to do so. And he can refer a matter to higher authority (the joint superior of the two managers concerned) and request that the action be delayed until a ruling is made.'

The establishment of policy and procedure can be an important source of influence for the personnel function but there are dangers in sticking to the rule-book too rigidly. Formal policies are helpful in terms of consistency, standardisation throughout the organisation, impartiality and clarity. On the other hand, if the policy is seen to be too far removed from practical reality it may lack credibility; if it is too rigid it will act as a barrier to flexibility. Fixed policies and rules may also reduce initiative and creative problem solving and may not allow junior managers, in particular, to develop if their activities are too closely prescribed and controlled.

3.3 Credibility and status

Whatever the range of the personnel function's formal responsibilities, it is important to remember that it operates largely by **consent** and the **perception of its authority** by line management. Personnel managers frequently suffer from lack of credibility related to:

(a)   Lack of definition of the personnel function and its contribution to business objectives

(b)   The perceived idealistic and/or theoretical basis of people-oriented activity

(c) The perceived ambiguity in personnel's 'clientele' – its 'internal customers' are employees *and* senior management – whereby its loyalty to the management position may be seen as suspect

(d) The traditionally administrative role of personnel lacking the creativity and proactivity expected of a management function.

'Sometimes it seems as though a great many very talented personnel specialists are wasting an awful lot of time. They carefully watch developments in the industrial relations, political and labour market environments; they develop sensible, well thought-out personnel policies that would make their company one of the most progressive and highly respected of employers. And then they see their efforts continually frustrated and subverted by a management team that seems determined to ignore most of what the personnel department does.'

Brewster and Richbell, *Getting Managers to Implement Personnel Policies*

Activity 5   **(30 minutes)**

Think about your job. Is it 'line' or 'staff' in the nature of its authority? What kinds of authority or power do you have personally in your job (whether or not formal authority is involved)? How do you influence other people, when you need them to do something for you at work?

Does the personnel function in your organisation have power, and if so what kind? What tactics does the personnel department use to 'get its way' in the organisation?

Then one of the implications of the 'internal customer concept' for personnel departments is that they may need to carry out some internal marketing and public relations in order to improve their status and credibility. This can be done by:

(a) Internal market research: conducting attitude surveys to determine the expectations and perceptions of other departments

(b) Informing and educating line managers about the personnel department's goals and values – and what it can and cannot do

(c) Emphasising that personnel shares line department goals for customer service and quality. (This may require substantiating, by training personnel staff in customer needs and encouraging contact with the customer: job rotations between the marketing and personnel departments may be possible.)

(d) Strategic integration of the personnel function

(e) Consultation with line departments when formulating and applying personnel policy

(f) User-friendly and professionally-presented communications to line departments, with minimal 'red tape'

(g) Expert briefings for line managers on specialist areas affecting their work

Having mentioned the influence that resides in the formulation and interpretation of policies, we will now offer a brief overview of personnel policies and how they are formulated.

4 PERSONNEL POLICY

4.1 Personnel policies

Policies might be formulated for any of the activities of the personnel function, in order to ensure:

(a) That people are treated fairly and consistently

(b) That people are treated in the way the organisation had defined as important and desirable to secure a required level of performance and which is consistent with the image it wishes to convey to its employees and to the outside world

(c) That laws and regulations are complied with

Here are some examples.

EXAMPLES

- A **multiskilling policy**. Jobs are not 'owned' by particular groups: instead, the most appropriate individual to do a particular job should be trained in the skills to do it.

- A **single status policy**. Salary and benefit systems should be common to all employees, breaking down barriers of status/reward between different grades or specialisms.

- An **equal opportunities policy**. Selection for vacancies, promotions or training opportunities should not be based on any discrimination of sex, race, age, marital status, or disability.

- A **succession/promotion policy**. Where possible, the organisation will seek to promote skilled individuals from within the organisation, in preference to external recruitment.

- An **employee communication policy**. Employees or their representatives will be given all information necessary to perform their tasks and to appreciate their role in the organisation's performance, and all information that will affect their working terms and conditions.

- A **disciplinary policy**. All employees are to be given oral warnings prior to disciplinary proceedings. All employees are to be given a fair hearing, accompanied by a representative, prior to disciplinary measure being taken.

- A **recruitment policy**. All vacancies are to be advertised internally. No discrimination shall be shown in the placement or wording of advertisements. All applicants will be treated fairly and clearly, and informed of the progress of their application.

- A **safety policy**. Training in safe use of all equipment and machinery, and in safety and emergency procedures, will be provided.

We will encounter further examples in the relevant chapters of this Course Book.

4.2 What are policies based on?

Personnel polices are based on:

(a) Employment legislation and regulations (including EU influences) in work-related areas such as health and safety and discrimination

BPP
PUBLISHING

(b) The values and philosophies of the organisation about how people should be treated and what kind of treatment will enable them to work most effectively on the organisation's behalf

(c) The needs, wants and rights of employees to be treated fairly and with dignity

(d) The organisation's need to attract and retain the kind of employees it wants, by its reputation and practice as an employer.

According to Cuming (*The Theory and Practice of Personnel Management*), there are three main principles on which personnel policies in British industry, commerce, and public service are based.

(a) All employees should be treated with **justice**: that is, fairly, without discrimination, and consistently (from one case to another and over time).

(b) The **needs** of employees must be **recognised**, particularly 'their desires for job satisfaction, for knowledge of what is going on within the organisation, and for consultation before changes affecting them take place'.

(c) A business will **function better democratically** than autocratically; success is more likely with employee co-operation in achieving objects than with the use of coercion.

A certain number of assumptions are inevitably being made here, about what 'a worker' is like, what his or her needs and desires are, and about what the organisation can hope to gain from satisfying those needs and desires. Social attitudes, psychological 'models' and theories of management all contribute to the framework within which personnel policies are formulated. Some of these assumptions and perspectives were discussed in Section 2, Chapter 1: we will encounter others as we proceed through this Course Book.

5 EVALUATING PERSONNEL

5.1 The problem of evaluation

If HRM is to be taken seriously at a strategic level as a contributor to bottom line business performance, it must be subject to evaluation. However, there are considerable difficulties attached to the evaluation of the personnel function.

(a) While some performance-based criteria (profitability, productivity, error reduction, compliance and so on) are relatively easy to measure and compare, having to do with units and monetary values, others are not (for example, innovation or flexibility)

(b) Effective personnel management should, over the long term, measurably impact on improved business performance. However:

(i) Its short-term activities may not show such effects

(ii) It is difficult to attribute these effects to HR activity alone: organisational performance involves many other variables, including technology, management effectiveness, market conditions, competitor initiatives and so on

(c) Subjective criteria such as the quality of working life, employee motivation, team spirit, openness to change, job satisfaction, the quality of employee relations and so on are notoriously difficult to measure, let alone to attach monetary values to, as a means of comparison

(d) Benchmarking, or standard-setting on the basis of best practice in other organisations, is difficult because of the wide differences in the environmental and internal variables affecting different organisations

(e) Personnel management itself is a wide-ranging activity, and therefore requires a wide range of criteria for evaluation

5.2 Cost-benefit analysis

Despite these difficulties, there are certain criteria, both quantitative and qualitative, which allow HR managers to demonstrate their effectiveness in the way that other managers do: by cost-benefit analysis. Assessing the costs of their activities against the benefits resulting from them, HR managers can determine:

(a) Whether the costs are justified by equal or greater benefits

(b) Whether costs and/or benefits are increasing or decreasing over time

(c) How the costs and/or benefits compare to competitor or benchmark organisations

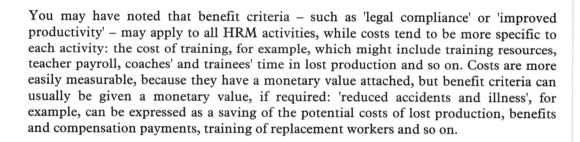

Activity 6 **(15 minutes)**

Before we proceed, see if you can brainstorm ten examples each of benefit criteria and cost criteria relevant to personnel management.

You may have noted that benefit criteria – such as 'legal compliance' or 'improved productivity' – may apply to all HRM activities, while costs tend to be more specific to each activity: the cost of training, for example, which might include training resources, teacher payroll, coaches' and trainees' time in lost production and so on. Costs are more easily measurable, because they have a monetary value attached, but benefit criteria can usually be given a monetary value, if required: 'reduced accidents and illness', for example, can be expressed as a saving of the potential costs of lost production, benefits and compensation payments, training of replacement workers and so on.

5.3 Quantitative measures

Quantitative or statistical indices of the HR function's activities may be available in relation to areas such as the following.

(a) Staff turnover/labour wastage (or labour stability) ratios

(b) Absenteeism rates

(c) Unit labour costs (useful in comparison to previous periods and/or competing businesses)

(d) Incidences of grievance procedures, disciplinary procedures, appeals to industrial tribunals, compensation claims, proceedings for non-compliance and so on

(e) Number of days production (and associated costs) lost through accidents, sickness, industrial disputes and so on

(f) Number of applications attracted by recruitment methods and/or lead time to recruit an employee

(g) Number of selected recruits remaining in the job, achieving performance targets, achieving promotion and so on

(h) Number of staff (including HR staff) achieving professional or other qualifications, or undertaking training programmes

(i) Success of training (and other) programmes in achieving their objectives

(j) Number of requests for information handled by the HR department, lead time in responding to requests, ability to answer technical personnel questions on demand and so on

(k) The costs of any and all of the above

We will look at means of evaluating specific HR activities, such as recruitment and training, in relevant chapters.

5.4 Qualitative measures

Qualitative, or subjective, criteria may be harder to measure, but may be equally important in the field of HRM. Examples include the following.

(a) Employee motivation, team spirit, job satisfaction, acceptance of change and so on – as gauged by attitude surveys, interviews, psychological testing and other tools of behavioural science, as well as presumed observed effects on productivity, communication, absenteeism and so on

(b) The extent to which HR proposals, policies, documentation and so on are accepted by line managers – as suggested by implementation rates, questions and objections

(c) The perception of the HR function's value, service, expertise, quality of advice, professionalism and so on by its internal customers: senior management, line managers and employees

5.5 The Four Cs

The Four Cs model was developed by researchers at the Harvard Business School as a means of investigating HRM issues. It suggests that the effectiveness of the outcomes of HRM should be evaluated under four headings.

(a) **Commitment** – that is, employees' identification with the organisation, loyalty and personal motivation in their work. This, like the qualitative criteria mentioned above, may be assessed through methods such as attitude surveys, exit interviews and analysis of presumed effects (such as absenteeism and labour turnover).

(b) **Competence** – that is, employees' skills and abilities, training needs and potential for performance improvement and career development. This may be measured through skill audits, competency testing and performance management systems.

(c) **Congruence** – that is, the harmonisation of the goals, values and efforts of management and employees (or at least the *perception* by employees that they have a mutual vision and purpose, to mutual benefit). This may be estimated by the quality of employee/industrial relations, the incidence of grievance and disciplinary action, conflict and communication and so on.

(d) **Cost-effectiveness** – that is, efficiency, whereby HRM objectives are met and benefits obtained at the lowest input cost.

The Harvard model does not solve the problems of the accurate measurement of qualitative criteria; nor of the incompatibility of varying criteria (cost-effectiveness achieved by downsizing, for example, might not encourage commitment or congruence); nor of the sheer variety of HR activity and contexts (since there are organisations and areas of organisational activity in which low-skilled monotonous jobs and authoritarian management styles, for example, are still possible and indeed appropriate). However, it does offer a simple framework for thinking about HR effectiveness.

Activity 7 (30 minutes)

Think about your own work organisation, or an organisation you know well.

(a) How would you go about assessing the effectiveness of its HRM, according to the Four Cs model?

(b) Without doing a detailed assessment, how do you estimate it would rate on each of the Four Cs?

Chapter roundup

- Centralised control over personnel management would generally imply the existence of a personnel officer/department with authority over all personnel management tasks in the organisation. Decentralised or devolved control over personnel management would imply the delegation to line managers the authority for personnel management tasks affecting their own staff.

- In practice, there is a tension between centralisation and decentralisation because of the need for specialism and a strategic perspective on the one hand, and for the flexibility and immediacy of control – such as is offered by line authority – on the other.

- The role of the personnel function is often ambiguous, as it carries responsibilities to **both** senior management (as prime customer) and employees (as prime users).

- A further ambiguity exists in the staff or 'advisory/support' role of the personnel function, which may be formally recognised by 'functional' authority – co-existing with unit managers' line authority – or may have to rely on indirect forms of power and influence.

- The influence of the personnel function consists of control over ecological factors such as policy, regulation, reward, career development, employee resourcing, expertise in law and behavioural sciences, and credibility.

- The personnel function can only establish credibility by systematic evaluation of its activities in the light of organisational objectives. While there are problems inherent in this process, there are qualitative and quantitative criteria available for measurement. Two possible approaches to evaluation are (a) cost benefit analysis and (b) the Four Cs model (Harvard).

Quick quiz

1   List Handy's five process activities of HR managers which create role ambiguity.

2   Give five reasons for centralising a function such as personnel management.

3   Suggest three reasons why specialised expertise might be valuable in the area of personnel management.

4   What is meant by the terms 'line manager' and 'staff manager' as functions? Give examples of each.

5   What is meant by the terms 'line' and 'staff' when used as relationships of authority? Give an example of each.

6   What is the implication of 'functional' authority?

7   The personnel specialist may possess:

(a)   'Resource' power
(b)   'Expert' power

Outline what is meant by each of these.

8   What can cause a lack of credibility for personnel managers?

9   What are the Four Cs of the Harvard model?

10   Give three examples of quantitative criteria for evaluating the HR function.

Answers to quick quiz

1   Executive (line management), adviser, service provider, auditor, planner/ co-ordinator.   (see paragraph 1.2)

2   For greater control and standardisation, for a broader organisational view, for greater experience and skill, for reasons of economy and speed of decision making.   (para 2.1)

3   Changing regulation/legislation; changing labour market; changing expectations/ requirements for social responsibility; changing findings of behavioural research; the need for advanced communication/negotiation skills for employee relations.   (para 2.2)

4   Line managers make a direct contribution to organisational objectives (eg production managers). Staff managers make an indirect contribution (eg personnel managers).   (para 3.1)

5   Line authority is endowed authority over a subordinate (eg financial accountant over cashier). Staff authority is acquired authority on the basis of expertise (eg legal expert over personnel generalist).   (para 3.1)

6   'Functional' authority formally recognises expert power and delegates authority for the area of expertise, even within the activities of line managers.   (para 2.3)

7   (a) Resource power: through control over people and pay.
     (b) Expert power: through recognition of specialist knowledge. (para 3.2)

8   Lack of contribution to business objectives, idealism, divided loyalty, administrative burden.   (para 3.3)

9   Commitment, congruence, competence, cost-effectiveness.   (para 5.5)

10   (a) Whether the costs are justified by equal or greater benefits.

     (b) Whether costs and/or benefits are increasing or decreasing over time.

     (c) How the costs and/or benefits compare to competitor or benchmark organisations.   (para 5.2)

Answers to activities

1   The answer to this activity is personal to you. However, the case scenario suggests some areas for consideration.

     (a)   As sales manager, you are responsible for staff who have particular **needs**; notably for motivation, encouragement and supervision while 'on the road'. You need to think about whether team-building would be best served by **your** maintaining contact with them on personnel management matters (such as appraisal, reward, development) or through a (possibly anonymous) personnel department. On the other hand, you might like some expert briefing on the effects of working alone, in an ever-changing technological environment, on sales workers.

(b) You have quite specific **requirements** for your staff. They need to be technically aware (in order to advise customers on highly technical matters), highly knowledgeable about the company's products, proactive sales people (since the customers are dispersed, and likely to be a bit traditional – although ideal candidates for the products). You might feel, given the difficulties of team-building, that you would like to retain responsibility for selection and training your own team – or you may prefer a more organisation-wide perspective; perhaps it would be good to have centrally selected/trained people who are close to the product and its technical possibilities – and then train them in sales?

These are just some suggestions to show you how widely and deeply an organisation needs to think through these issues.

2   Suggestions include the following.

(a) Recruitment and selection of department members, enabling the particular needs of the department (and its customers) to be taken into account more flexibly

(b) Administration of routine systems and maintenance of employee records (some of which may be centrally duplicated or databased for the purposes of statistical returns and management reporting)

(c) Intra-departmental disciplinary and grievance handling

(d) Issuing of employment contracts (perhaps using a standard computerised system, which protects the organisation's core values and service conditions)

(e) Objective-setting, monitoring and appraisal of subordinates' performance, and award of incremental rewards and incentives

(f) Determination of patterns of work, teamworking arrangements and so on

(g) Contract management and the deployment of part-time and contract workers

(h) Occupational health and safety and the maintenance of the working environment

(i) Welfare of departmental employees: counselling, absence management and so on

(j) On the job training and coaching of departmental staff

3   The list of activities which may be undertaken by personnel managers would include the following.

The Personnel/ administrative office (operational)	The specialist personnel manager (advisory)	The personnel director (strategy and policy making
Wages and salaries		
Record keeping	Employment law	Devising manpower plans
Recruitment and selection administration	Industrial relations issues	Policy making and personnel strategies
Job analysis		
Evaluation of jobs	Training	
Administration of grievance and disciplinary procedures	Recruitment and selection procedures	
Sickness and absenteeism statistics		

Many of the activities will involve more than one level. For example, the personnel manager may advise line management on recruitment and selection procedures and, in conjunction with the personnel officer, actually assist in carrying these out.

4   Control mechanisms include:

(i)   Organisation structure – constraining behaviour by job description

(ii)   Recruitment and training – employing people who 'fit', and encouraging conformity to technical and cultural standards and methods

(iii) Reward and punishment – conditioning behaviour through positive or negative reinforcement

(iv)   Policies and rules – constraining behaviour through guidance, training and prescription

(v)   Culture – guiding behaviour within a set of values, beliefs and norms

(vi)   Budgets – directing behaviour towards attainment of targets

(vii) Machinery – limiting behaviour to what the machinery requires or allows (known as 'negative discipline'). As an example, computer packages are set up so that information has to be input in a certain way

5   The answer to this activity is personal to you and your organisation. Don't let this put you off thinking about the questions posed, though, if you haven't already done so: the answers will highlight important points and areas for learning which will benefit you in any career.

6   Some examples are as follows.

(a)   Benefit criteria: increased productivity, increased quality/reduced error/wastage, reduced absenteeism, reduced labour turnover, increased job satisfaction, legal compliance, reduced accidents/illness, reduced employee stress, increased job involvement, increased innovation, reduced costs of fines, reduced grievance/disciplinary actions, reduced industrial disputes, enhanced response to recruitment, enhanced community goodwill

(b) Cost criteria: costs of health and safety activity, training, recruitment, consultancy, remuneration, HR department training, welfare provision, computerisation, HR salaries, ergonomic improvements, compliance

7 Suggested methodologies include attitude surveys, questionnaires, observation, interviews (eg exit interviews, counselling interviews, appraisal interviews), and analysis of the presumed effects of more or less 'C' factors (positive or negative labour stability, absenteeism rates, incidence of conflict and so on).

In terms of the evaluation of your chosen organisation's HRM function, you are on your own! Do attempt this exercise, however, even if it is just a brief mental survey of your college, your favourite fast food outlet or whatever. This will get you thinking not just about how to evaluate the success of HRM policy and practice, but about how HRM goes about fostering, maintaining and increasing the 'C' factors in the organisation.

Assignment 2 (2 hours)

Flyblown and Fudgett

You are the Human Resource Manager at Flyblown and Fudgett, chartered accountants and management consultants, which was formed a year ago as a result of a merger.

Fudgett was a medium sized firm of accountants employing around 1000 staff in its 12 regional offices around the country, the largest of which was in London. It had enjoyed a reputation of being a conservative but highly professional, patriarchal partnership with a large number of solid, if unspectacular clients.

The 'merger' was the result of a take-over by Flyblown, a larger, more aggressive, American-dominated practice who were interested in the merger only to acquire a presence in areas of the country where Fudgett had previously been pre-eminent. Their approach to clients was also very different, taking the opportunity to hard-sell other related services wherever possible. The newly merged firm now has over 3,300 staff in its 35 regional offices, together with 150 partners.

As a consequence of the dominance of Flyblown's approach to management, much of the work previously handled by the Personnel Department in Fudgetts was 'decentralised' to line managers, and there was much talk of 'empowerment', 'quality' and 'teamworking'.

However, all did not go too well as the two 'cultures' met head on. Labour turnover and absenteeism increased, and a number of senior staff threatened resignation under the pressures of 'Performance Management'. Despite being regrouped into 'mixed' open plan offices, the tensions among the two groups of staff became increasingly apparent, resulting in a rash of petty grievances and disciplinary issues.

Your task

As the newly appointed Human Resource Manager at Flyblown and Fudgett, propose some ways of retrieving the situation and achieving a happier blend of the two organisational cultures.

Chapter 3 :
HUMAN RESOURCE PLANNING

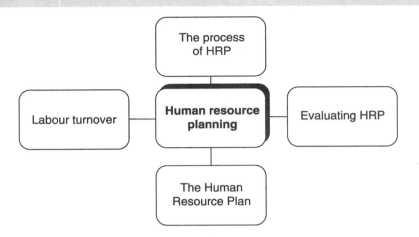

Introduction

As we saw in Chapters 1 and 2, human beings are one of the resources that a business must obtain and manage in pursuit of its objectives. Human resource (or 'manpower') planning is the task of assessing and anticipating the skill, knowledge and labour time requirements of the organisation, and initiating action to fulfil or 'source' those requirements. If the organisation (or a particular area of its activity) is declining, it may need to plan a reduction or redeployment of the labour force. If it is growing, or moving into new areas of activity, it will need to find and tap into a source of suitably skilled labour.

It may already have occurred to you that this cannot be as easy as it sounds! External factors – particular over the long term – create fluctuations in the demand for and supply of labour. So do internal factors, such as individual and team productivity, training, and labour turnover through retirements, resignations, maternity leaves and so on.

If anything, as we shall see, the uncertainties of human resource planning make it even more important – and certainly, it becomes more important to approach it systematically. In this chapter, we consider how this can be done. In the chapters that follow, we look at external and internal sources of labour.

Your objectives

In this chapter you will learn about the following

(a) The objectives of human resource planning

(b) The process of human resource planning

(c) The importance of human resource planning and the difficulties involved in accurately predicting manpower requirements

(d) The influence of the external environment, and changes in the external environment, on the human resource planning process

NOTES

1 HUMAN RESOURCE PLANNING

1.1 What is HRP?

Definition

> **Human resource planning** (also known as 'manpower planning') may be defined as 'a strategy for the acquisition, utilisation, improvement and retention of the human resources required by the enterprise in pursuit of its objectives.'

The process may be broadly outlined as follows.

   (a)   Forecast demand for each grade and/or skill of employee.

   (b)   Forecast supply of each grade and/or skill of employee, both within and outside the organisation.

   (c)   Plan to remove any discrepancy between demand and supply. If there is a shortage of labour, for example, you would need to reduce demand (say, through improved productivity), or improve supply (through training and retention of current staff, or recruitment from outside, for example).

The first thing you might notice is that when we consider fulfilling labour requirements, we are not merely talking about recruitment and selection, or 'getting people in to the organisation from outside'. We are talking about:

   (a)   **recruiting** the required number and type/quality of staff

   (b)   **retaining** the required number and type/quality of staff – and therefore letting go those who are not required (by natural labour turnover and/or by planned downsizing)

   (c)   **utilising** staff in the most efficient and effective manner: increasing productivity, introducing multi-skilling and so on

   (d)   **improving** the skills, capabilities and motivation of staff, so that they become a more flexible resource capable of fulfilling new requirements and filling higher level vacancies

It is arguable that forecasting staff requirements has become more *difficult* in recent times because of the increasing uncertainty and rate of change. However, it has also arguably become more *necessary*, because the risks of 'getting it wrong' are correspondingly greater.

Human resource planning (HRP) is a form of risk **management**. It involves realistically appraising the present and anticipating the future (as far as possible) in order to get the *right people* into the **right jobs** at the **right time**.

Activity 1   **(15 minutes)**

We have noted that the supply (and demand) of skilled human resources is subject to a number of factors outside and within the organisation. Suggest three possible reasons why a business might find itself experiencing a shortage of a particular skill/type of employee.

BPP PUBLISHING

1.2 HRP and corporate planning

Definition

> **Corporate planning** involves devising a picture of how the organisation will look in three or five years time, and how it can reach that state during that time period.
>
> *'Common items for consideration include: anticipated financial situation (turnover, gross and net profit, return on investment); intended product markets and market share; desired output and productivity; changes in location and opening of new plants or outlets; employee numbers.'*
>
> Penny Hackett, *Success in Personnel Management*

Thus human resources are one element of the overall corporate strategy or plan, and the two are mutually inter-dependent. If the corporate plan envisages a cut in output, for example, or the closure of a particular plant, then the human resource plan will need to consider redeployment of staff, redundancies and so on. If the corporate plan specifies a move into a new product market, the human resource plan will have to source the required labour from outside or within the organisation, through recruitment or training.

In turn, the availability of labour resources can act as a constraint on, or spur to, the achievement of corporate goals. If there are skill shortages and employees cannot be recruited, plans for expansion may have to be curtailed. The availability of multi-skilled or expert teams, on the other hand, my inspire innovative strategies for growth and change.

Some of the links between business strategy and human resource planning are illustrated in Table 3.1.

Business	HR implications
What business are we in?	What people do we need?
Culture and value system – appropriate – inappropriate	How do you change?
Strategic direction New businesses New markets	Who will we need in future? What systems and procedures might be developed?
Strengths Weaknesses Opportunities Threats	How far related to existing use of HR? (eg skills base) Demand and supply in the labour market?
Critical success factors	How far do these depend on employees, rather than other factors?

Table 3.1: *Business Strategy and HRP*

NOTES

Some people might still argue that proactive forward planning to meet human resource requirements is a waste of time, especially for small to medium-sized businesses. Why does it have to be so complicated? Surely, if you are short of staff, you hire some – or train or promote some of your existing staff? And if business declines and you find yourself with superfluous staff, you make some redundancies? In fact, it is not quite so simple. We will suggest why.

1.3   Why is HRP necessary?

An attempt to look beyond the present and short-term future, and to prepare for contingencies, is increasingly important. Some manifestations of this are outlined below.

> 'Manpower planning has maintained its imperatives for several reasons: (i) a growing awareness of the need to look into the future, (ii) a desire to exercise control over as many variables as possible which influence business success or failure, (iii) the development of techniques which make such planning possible.'
>
> Livy, *Corporate Personnel Management*

(a)   Jobs often require experience and skills which cannot easily be bought in the market place, and the more complex the organisation, the more difficult it will be to supply or replace highly specialised staff quickly. It takes time to train and develop technical or specialist personnel (say, an airline pilot or computer programmer), so there will be a lead time to fill any vacancy. The need will have to be anticipated in time to initiate the required development programmes.

(b)   Employment protection legislation and general expectations of 'social responsibility' in organisations make staff shedding a slow and costly process. The cost must be measured not just in financial terms (redundancy pay and so on) but in loss of reputation as a secure employer and socially responsible organisation. This in turn may make it more difficult to recruit labour in times or skill areas where it *is* required – and may even alienate customers and potential customers.

(c)   Rapid technological change is leading to a requirement for manpower which is both more highly skilled and more adaptable. Labour flexibility is a major issue, and means that the career and retraining **potential** of staff are at least as important as their actual qualifications and skills. They *must* be assessed in advance of requirements. (In fact, 'trainability' as a major criteria for selection is one of the most popular innovations of the HRM era of personnel management.)

(d)   The UK continues to suffer from specific skill shortages (with wide local variations), despite high unemployment levels. Skill shortages also create a tendency to greater career mobility, which complicates the manpower planners' assumptions about labour wastage rates (the number of people leaving an organisation for any reason).

(e)   The scope and variety of markets, competition and labour resources are continually increased by political and economic moves such as the unification of Germany, the opening of Eastern Europe and continuing progress towards European union.

(f)   Computer technology has made available techniques which facilitate the monitoring and planning of manpower over fairly long time spans: manipulation of manpower statistics, trend analysis, 'modelling' and so on.

BPP PUBLISHING

Activity 2	(15 minutes)

To what extent would HRP be possible and desirable for:

(a)   A company designing, manufacturing and selling personal computers?
(b)   A large local authority?
(c)   An international airline?

1.4   A contingency approach to HRP

We have suggested that **long-range, detailed human resource planning** is necessary as a form of risk management, preparing businesses for foreseeable contingencies. However, Kane and Stanton (1994) have suggested that HRP should itself be viewed in a more flexible or contingent way, in response to variables in the organisation's internal and external environments.

There has been some disillusionment about the possibility and value of long-range, detailed HR planning, given the rapidly evolving and uncertain business environment and the kinds of highly flexible organisational structures and cultures that have been designed to respond to it.

(a)   **'Horizontal structures'**. What Peters (*Liberation management*) calls 'going horizontal' is a recognition that functional versatility (through multi-functional project teams and multi-skilling, for example) is the key to flexibility. In the words (quoted by Peters) of a Motorola executive: 'The traditional job descriptions were barriers. We needed an organisation soft enough between the organisational disciplines so that... people would run freely across functional barriers or organisational barriers with the common goal of getting the job done, rather than just making certain that their specific part of the job was completed.'

(b)   **'Chunked' and 'unglued' structures.** So far, this has meant team working, decentralisation (or empowerment) and flexibly-structured workforces (discussed later in this Course Book) to facilitate flexible deployment of labour. Beyond 'flattening' organisational hierarchies, however, Peters advocates destroying them. He cites successful US businesses like McKinsey, CNN and Titeflex as examples of structures made up of small, functionally versatile units that come together and disband constantly, according to task requirements; that find their own customers, set up their own networks and generate their own projects; that continuously re-educate themselves to meet new demands. Such structures are entirely flat, output/customer-focused, business-generating, information-seeking, continuously learning and shifting. They sweep aside traditional barriers to innovation, customer service and creative problem-solving – but also effectively abolish 'jobs' and predictability of labour utilisation.

(c)   **De-jobbed workers.** Within flexible structures and markets, where manipulating information – not making things – is the primary business activity, the traditional concept of the 'job' is being eroded. According to William Bridges (*Job Shift: How to Prosper in a Workplace Without Jobs*, 1995) the 'job' is a historical artefact. Put simply, it was created about 200 years ago to carry out the tasks required by the emerging industrial and commercial sectors. These activities could easily be 'boxed up' and given to separate workers. It came to be expected that one would secure a job and rise through a sequence of jobs which increased in remuneration and complexity: the concept of the 'career'. Now, however, Bridges sees a workforce made up of 'vendor workers' who sell their services to a variety of clients and work for them on a project basis. Peters similarly notes that workers must become adept at 'résumé management', the development and marketing of a skill portfolio. This fundamentally changes the nature of 'job vacancies' and of the labour pool.

(d) **The learning organisation**. With new emphasis on continuous improvement, customer service and product innovation, organisations are striving to be more adaptive, visionary, fluid in their structures and holistic in their thinking. The' learning organisation' embraces learning at all levels and in all areas, focusing on the process of learning and adapting to what is learned: HRP is thus an opportunity to explore different scenarios without pre-conceived requirements or solutions.

In such environments, a different, less prescriptive approach to HRP may be required. Kane and Stanton suggest three alternatives.

(a) **The staff replacement approach**. Staff are recruited or promoted to fill a vacancy as and when it occurs – if it is still required – with little formal planning. While this is essentially reactive, and does not provide for much change in the knowledge and skill base of the organisation, it allows a degree of flexibility on an ad hoc basis. Organisations or organisational units with relatively stable environments and a very small organisation may have little difficulty filling vacancies as they arise while in volatile environments and organisations with high staff mobility and turnover, it may be recognised that longer range projections of labour requirements are in any case meaningless.

(b) **Short-term Human Resource Strategy.** In environments where long-term forecasting of future requirements is quickly rendered obsolete by change and uncertainty, yet the ability to adapt the skills and knowledge of the workforce is required, a short-term strategic model may be more suitable. This approach has a 'key issues' orientation: HR and line managers collaborate to determine what the organisation's key HR issues are in the short term, emphasising flexibility and speed of response to emerging threats and opportunities.

(c) **Vision-driven Human Resource Development.** This approach is long-term in its orientation, but is driven by organisational vision, mission and core values, rather than detailed staffing forecasts and targets. Such an approach is often employed where a major cultural shift is required, calling for corresponding shifts in employee attitudes, skills and behaviours.

The process of choosing the appropriate approach may be shown as follows (adapted from Kane and Stanton, *HRP in a Changing Environment*).

NOTES

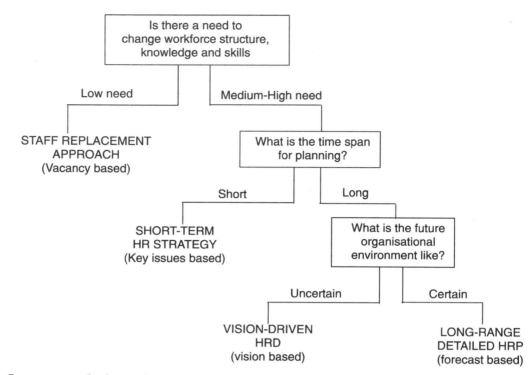

*Let us now look at the long-range, detailed **HRP** process in more detail. We have already suggested that it is a form of 'supply and demand management', aiming to minimise the risk of either surplus (and therefore inefficiency) or shortage (and therefore ineffectiveness) of the labour resource. We shall now see how that works in practice.*

2 THE PROCESS OF HRP

2.1 Forecasting demand

The **demand** for labour must be forecast by considering several factors.

(a) The **objectives** of the organisation, and the long and short-term plans in operation to achieve those objectives. Where plans are changed, the effect of the changes must be estimated: proposed expansion, contraction or diversification of the organisation's activities will obviously affect the demand for labour in general or for particular skills. This may be estimated by market research, competitive analysis, trends in technological advances and so on, (although sudden changes in market conditions complicate the process: the effect of the collapse of the Soviet Union on defence spending, for example).

(b) **Manpower utilisation** – how much labour will be required, given the expected productivity or work rate of different types of employee and the expected volume of business activity. Note that productivity will depend on capital expenditure, technology, work organisation, employee motivation and skills, negotiated productivity deals and a number of other factors.

(c) **The cost of labour** – including overtime, training, benefits and so on – and therefore what financial constraints there are on the organisation's manpower levels.

(d) **Environmental factors** and trends in technology and markets that will require organisational change, because of threats or opportunities. The recession in the early 1990s created conditions in which expectations of labour demand in the short term were low: downsizing of staffs and delayering of organisation structures were the trend.

EXAMPLES

(a)   The financial services sector in particular has undergone huge job losses, especially the banking industry. Lloyds Bank, for example, cut more than 15,000 jobs between 1990 and 1996.

(b)   Faced with falling profits, the chairman of Kodak has said that he will prune middle and senior management ranks by getting rid of one in five positions. Further down the ranks, 10,000 job losses are expected.

Kodak's return to cutting jobs not only reinforces the impression that downsizing has not just been a passing phase of the mid 1990s. It emphasises how Kodak is still struggling, as an older company, to compete with its nimbler rivals, especially in the digital market. The pressure to increase efficiency is relentless.

Activity 3	(15 minutes)

Think of as many occupations as you can that are currently in short supply in the job marketplace (and therefore in great demand). Then do the same for occupations where the supply is greater than the demand.

2.2   Forecasting supply

The available **supply** of labour will be forecast by considering the following factors.

(a)   The skill base, potential trainability and current and potential productivity level of the existing work force.

(b)   The structure of the existing workforce in terms of age distribution, skills, hours of work, rates of pay and so on.

(c)   The likelihood of changes to the productivity, size and structure of the workforce. Such changes may come through:

(i)   Wastage (turnover through resignations and retirements), promotions and transfers, absenteeism and other staff movements; this will require information on:

- The age structure of staff (forthcoming retirement or family start-up)
- Labour turnover for a comparable period
- The promotion potential and ambitions of staff

(ii)   Employee trainability and motivation which may increase productivity and flexibility

(iii)   Organisational, technological, cultural and other changes which may affect employee productivity, loyalty and so on

(d)   The present and potential future supply of relevant skilled labour in the environment – that is, the **external labour market**. The HR planner will have to assess and monitor factors such as:

(i)   Skill availability, nationally and locally and also internationally (for example, within the European Union)

NOTES

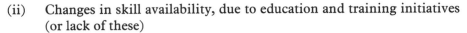

> (ii) Changes in skill availability, due to education and training initiatives (or lack of these)
>
> (iii) Competitor activity which may absorb more or less of the available skill pool
>
> (iv) Demographic changes: areas of population growth and decline, the proportion of younger or older people in the workforce in a particular region, the number of women in the workforce and so on
>
> (v) Wage and salary rates in the market for particular jobs. ('Supply' implies **availability**: labour resources may become more or less affordable by the organisation.)

FOR DISCUSSION

Select an organisation you are familiar with. Is its need for labour growing, shrinking, or perhaps moving into new skill areas? What , if anything, is the organisation doing about this?

2.3 Closing the gap between demand and supply

Shortages or surpluses of labour which emerge may be dealt with in various ways, in accordance with the organisation's specific HR and business objectives and policies (for example, equal opportunities), cultural values (for example about encouraging commitment, quality focus or developing people within the organisation) and available structures and technologies. Detailed action programmes may be drawn up for the following strategies.

A *deficiency* of labour may be met by:	A surplus of labour may be met by:
Internal transfers and promotions, training and development	Running down manning levels by natural wastage or 'accelerated wastage' (see below)
External recruitment or improvement of recruitment methods (eg diversity programmes to encourage more applicants)	Restricting or 'freezing' recruitment
The extension of temporary contracts, or the contracts of those about to retire	Redundancies (voluntary and/or compulsory)
	Early retirement incentives
Reducing labour turnover, by reviewing possible causes (including pay and conditions), improving induction/socialisation	A tougher stance on discipline, enabling more dismissals
The use of freelance/temporary/ agency staff	Part-time and short-contract working, or job sharing
The development of flexible working methods and structures	Eliminating overtime and 'peripheral' workforce groups
Encouraging overtime working	Redeployment of staff to areas of labour shortage. This may necessitate diversification by the organisation, to find new work for the labour force, and/or plans for multi-skilling, so that the workforce can be flexibly deployed in areas of labour shortage as and when they emerge
Productivity bargaining to increase productivity	
Automation (increasing productivity, and/or reducing the need for human labour)	

BPP
PUBLISHING

Definition

Accelerated wastage involves **encouraging** labour turnover, by withholding or retaining incentives to loyalty, for example by pay freezes or barriers to promotion.

Bear in mind that there are also external constraints on HR planners in considering any or all of the above: UK legislation and EU directives, regulations and court rulings, the employer brand or reputation and other factors must be taken into account when planning to hire, 'fire', or alter working terms and conditions.

Note that the sources of labour are both internal (the current workforce and its future potential) and external (people in the 'labour pool'). We will discuss the external labour market (including related issues such as pool (and related issues of promotion and succession) in Chapter 4. Another key issue of labour supply – flexibility – is discussed in Part B of this Course Book. We will now look at a major factor in forecasting the internal supply of labour turnover.

3   LABOUR TURNOVER

3.1   Measuring labour turnover

Definition

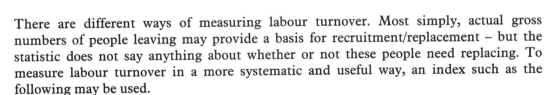

Labour turnover is the number of employees leaving an organisation and being replaced. The rate of turnover is often expressed as the number of people leaving as a percentage of the average number of people employed, in a given period. The term 'natural wastage' is used to describe a 'normal' flow of people out of an organisation through retirement, career or job change, relocation, illness and so on.

There are different ways of measuring labour turnover. Most simply, actual gross numbers of people leaving may provide a basis for recruitment/replacement – but the statistic does not say anything about whether or not these people need replacing. To measure labour turnover in a more systematic and useful way, an index such as the following may be used.

(a)   **Crude labour turnover rate** (*the BIM Index, British Institute of Management, 1949*)

Here we express turnover as a percentage of the number of people employed.

$$\frac{\text{Number of leavers in a period}}{\text{Average number of people employed in the period}} \times 100 = \% \; turnover$$

This is normally quoted as an annual rate and may be used to measure turnover per organisation, department or group of employees. The **advantage** of this index is that it can alert HR planners to unusually high percentages of the workforce leaving – compared with the HR plan, or with the industry average, say – which would suggest that something is wrong, or that more effort is needed to retain employees. The **disadvantage** of this index is that it does not indicate *who* is leaving the department or organisation: even a high turnover rate may not reflect any real instability if the core of experienced staff consistently remains. (In fact, most wastage occurs among young people and those in the early stages of their employment in an organisation: stability tends to increase with length of service.)

(b) **Labour stability**

Here we try to eliminate short-term employees from our analysis, thus obtaining a better picture of the significant movements in the workforce.

$$\frac{\text{Number of employees with one or more years' service}}{\text{Number of employees employed at the beginning of the year}} \times 100\% = \% \, stability$$

Particularly in times of rapid expansion, organisations should keep an eye on stability, as a meaningful measure.

(c) The labour stability index ignores new starts during the year but does not consider actual length of service, which may be added to the measurement via **length of service analysis**, or **survival rate analysis**. Here, the organisation calculates the proportion of employees who are engaged within a certain period who are still with the firm after various periods of time. There may be a survival rate of 70% after two years, for example, but only 50% in year three: the distribution of losses might be plotted on a survival curve to indicate trends.

Activity 4   **(20 minutes)**

Suppose a company has 20 employees at the beginning of 20X2, and 100 at the end of the year. Disliking the expansion, 18 of the original experienced labour force resign.

Calculate

(a)   The crude labour turnover rate
(b)   The stability rate

Comment on the significance of your results.

3.2   Causes of labour turnover

Some reasons for leaving will be largely unavoidable, or unforeseeable. '**Natural wastage**' occurs through:

(a) Illness or accident, although transfer to lighter duties, excusing the employee from shiftwork, or other accommodations might be possible

(b) A move from the locality for domestic, social or logistical reasons

(c) Changes to the family situation, for example, when an individual changes job or gives up work to accommodate child-rearing responsibilities

(d) Retirement

(e) Career change

Other causes of labour turnover, however, may be to do with the organisation, management, terms and conditions and so on: in other words **job dissatisfaction**.

NOTES

Activity 5 (15 minutes)

Suggest a number of factors that might contribute to labour turnover, which might broadly be grouped under the heading of 'job dissatisfaction'.

Which of these factors would be sufficient to make you leave an organisation: (a) in a market where you were reasonably sure of finding other employment and (b) in a market where other employment was scarce?

Labour turnover is also influenced by the following factors.

(a) **The economic climate and the state of the jobs market.** When unemployment is high and jobs are hard to find, labour turnover will be much lower.

(b) **The age structure and length of service of the work force.** An ageing workforce will have many people approaching retirement. However, it has been found in most companies that labour turnover is highest among:

   (i) Young people, especially unmarried people with no family responsibilities

   (ii) People who have been in the employment of the company for only a short time

   The employment life cycle usually shows a decision point shortly after joining, when things are still new and perhaps difficult. This is called the 'first induction crisis'. There is then a period of mutual accommodation and adjustment between employer and employee (called the 'differential transit' period): in the settling of areas of conflict, there may be further turnover. A second (less significant) induction crisis occurs as both parties come to terms with the new status quo. Finally, the period of 'settled connection' begins, and the likelihood of leaving is much less.

So far, you may have got the impression that 'labour turnover' equals 'instability', and that, since it is caused by job dissatisfaction, it must be a bad thing for the organisation. But remember: earlier in this Chapter we noted that an organisation may from time to time have a surplus of labour or particular skills, which it would like to be able to 'lose' through natural wastage instead of costly redundancies. So should organisations fight to retain employees – or not?

3.3   Is turnover a 'bad thing'?

The following table puts labour turnover in perspective.

Potential advantages of labour turnover	Potential disadvantages of labour turnover
(a) Opportunities to inject 'new blood' into the organisation: new people bringing new ideas and outlooks, new skills and experience in different situations.	(a) Broken continuity of culture and succession, where continuity could offer stability and predictability, which may be beneficial to efficiency.
(b) Balance in the age structure of the workforce. Absence of labour turnover would create an increasingly aged workforce, often accompanied by an increasing wage/salary cost.	(b) There is bound to be an hiatus while a replacement is found and brought 'on line' to the level of expertise of the previous job-holder.
(c) The creation of opportunities for promotion and succession which offers an important incentive to more junior employees.	(c) Morale problems. Turnover may be perceived by other employees as a symptom of job dissatisfaction, causing the problem to escalate.
(d) The ability to cope with labour surpluses, in some grades of job, without having to make redundancies.	(d) The costs of turnover, including: (i) **Replacement costs**: recruiting, selecting and training; loss of output or efficiency (ii) **Preventive costs**: the cost of retaining staff, through pay, benefits and welfare provisions, maintaining working conditions or whatever

It is common to hear that turnover is bad when it is high – but this cannot be assessed in isolation. What is an acceptable rate of turnover and what is excessive? There is no fixed percentage rate of turnover which is the borderline between acceptable and unacceptable. Labour turnover rates *may* be a signal that something is wrong when:

(a) They are higher than the turnover rates in another similar department of the organisation; for example, if the labour turnover rate is higher at branch A than at branches B, C and D in the same area, something might be wrong at branch A

(b) They are higher than they were in previous years or months; in other words, the situation might be deteriorating

(c) The costs of labour turnover are estimated and are considered too high – although they will be relative to the costs of *preventing* high turnover by offering employees rewards, facilities and services that will keep them in the organisation

Otherwise, the organisation may live with high rates because they are the norm for a particular industry or job, because the organisation culture accepts constant turnover, or because the cost of keeping employees is greater than the cost of replacing them.

So, if an organisation does decide that it needs to control or reduce its labour turnover rate, what can it do?

3.4 Retention planning

A systematic **investigation** into the causes of unusually or undesirably high turnover will have to be made, using various methods.

(a) Information given in **exit interviews** with leaving staff, which should be the first step after an employee announces his/her intention to leave. (It must be recognised, however, that the reasons given for leaving may not be complete, true, or those that would be most useful to the organisation. People may say they are 'going to a better job', while the real reason for the move is dissatisfaction with the level of interest in the current job.)

(b) **Attitude surveys**, to gauge the general climate of the organisation, and the response of the workforce as a whole to working conditions, management style and so on. Such surveys are notoriously unreliable, however.

(c) Information gathered on the number of (interrelated) variables which can be *assumed* to correlate with labour turnover – such as an ageing workforce, higher rates of pay outside the organisation and so on.

The causes of turnover should be addressed, where it is practical and cost-effective to do so.

(a) If particular managers' practices or styles are creating significant dissatisfaction, performance improvement measures may be implemented.

(b) Coherent policies may be introduced (or more consistently applied) with regard to training and development and promotion from within the organisation.

(c) Induction or orientation programmes for new recruits should address the issues that cause problems at the 'first induction crisis' stage.

(d) Selection programmes should be reviewed to ensure that future recruits are made aware of (and ideally are compatible with) the demands of the job and culture of the organisation.

(e) Problems with working conditions should be solved – especially if they concern health and safety.

(f) Pay levels and structures may be reviewed in the light of perceived fairness and/or market rates.

FOR DISCUSSION

'Accelerated wastage' is the practice of allowing (or using) job dissatisfaction to encourage people to leave in higher numbers than they would by 'natural wastage', in order to reduce a labour surplus.

How do you respond to this concept? Do you think it has a place in an ethical HRM policy? How would you justify it?

We have suggested that an organisation's continuity and stability partly depend on the retention of long-serving, experienced labour. Such people will often expect to rise through the organisation: to be developed and 'groomed' to fill vacancies which open up at higher levels of the organisation hierarchy. (Even in flat organisations, people may wish to be given greater responsibility, if not a fancier job title...) We will now go on to look at this area of succession and promotion which is 'in effect' a decision to utilise the internal labour market – rather than the external one – where possible.

The apparently simple 'supply and demand' equation discussed in Section 2 above makes HRP look scientific – but with so many 'messy' human factors involved, is it really? This is only one of the questions that arise when we consider how the success and value of HRP can be measured by the organisation. We will look at some of these questions below.

NOTES

4 EVALUATING HRP

4.1 How reliable is HRP?

Human resource planning is regarded as a scientific, statistical exercise, but it is important to remember that statistics in themselves are limited in value.

Forecasting is not an exact science. Few exponents of even the most sophisticated techniques would claim that they are wholly accurate, although:

(a) The element of guesswork has been substantially reduced by the use of computer models to test various assumptions and to indicate trends

(b) The general principles can still be applied to indicate problems and stimulate control action

---

Activity 6 **(15 minutes)**

Given that HR planners are human beings, and so are the 'HRs' themselves, what might be the major limitations on the reliability or objectivity of statistical methods in HR planning?

Statistical methods can be used to create a more accurate model of the future than simple subjective estimates. Computerisation has greatly enhanced the speed, ease and accuracy with which they can be applied. Even so, there are a number of assumptions involved, and the results are purely **quantitative** – for example, numbers of staff required – where **qualitative** information may be required for meaningful decision-making: the effects of change, re-staffing, or management style on the culture of the organisation and individual/group behaviour and so on.

Where end products are measurable, **work-study techniques** can offer a reasonably accurate forecast of staffing requirements. In service sectors and 'knowledge work', however, end products and output may not be easily subject to standard-setting. For example, the number of telephone calls, interviews, customers served, or ideas generated is likely to fluctuate widely with the flow of business and the nature of particular transactions.

Definition

Work study methods break down and measure the elements of a given task in order to define the standard number of staff hours per unit of output.

Managerial estimates form the simplest and cheapest method of assessment. As such, they may be the most appropriate – and are the most common – method for small organisations. At the best of times, however, this method has the disadvantage of a high degree of subjectivity, and although this can be controlled to an extent (by requiring managers to support their estimates with reasons and to reconcile their estimates with those of senior management), it is a source of potential risk.

A measure of flexibility will need to be built into any HR plan, so that it can be adapted to suit likely or even unforeseen contingencies. Above all, it should not be seen or communicated as an inflexible plan, as if it were based on certainty.

BPP
PUBLISHING

NOTES

'Clearly, the more precise the information available, the greater the probability that manpower plans will be accurate. But, in practice, they are subject to many imponderable factors, some completely outside an organisation's control... international trade, general technological advances, population movements, the human acceptance of or resistance to change, and the quality of leadership and its impact on morale. The environment, then, is uncertain, and so are the people whose activities are being planned. Manpower plans must therefore be accepted as being continuous, under constant review, and ever-changing. Since they concern people, they must also be negotiable.'

Cuming, Personnel Management

4.2 Is HRP working?

Definition

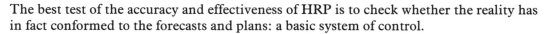

A **human resource audit** is an investigation designed to:

(a) Give a picture of the current structure, size and productivity of the organisation's labour force

(b) Check the HR plans, systems, policies and procedures have been and are being carried out

The best test of the accuracy and effectiveness of HRP is to check whether the reality has in fact conformed to the forecasts and plans: a basic system of control.

(a) Actual staffing levels and trends should be checked against budgets.

    (i) If HR planners have allowed for reductions in staffing levels through natural wastage, it is important to ensure that such wastage is allowed to happen. (It is a natural tendency for managers to seek replacements for any staff losses, even those which have been budgeted for.)

    (ii) The budgets themselves may be (or may have become) inappropriate. The HR plan must constantly be reviewed and revised in the light of changes and actual events (unanticipated).

(b) Personnel records should be checked to identify that each change (promotion, transfer, redundancy, recruitment, etc) has been properly approved, in line with the HR plan.

This process may uncover:

    (i) Inadequate authorisation of particular types of change; for example, it may be common to transfer employees within the same department without proper approval or reference to the overall staffing plan

    (ii) Unauthorised or unnecessary use of agency or temporary personnel

(c) Staff utilisation should be reviewed: how efficiently is the human resource employed? This process may uncover a need for some fundamental change (such as a complete restructuring of work practices). Apart from the satisfaction and development of employees, it should be clear that under-utilisation of a skill category is an inefficient use of the organisation's resources.

4.3 Is HRP cost-effective?

Labour can be a substantial cost to businesses. Although the labour costs in many manufacturing companies are falling as a proportion of total cost as more expensive technology is used, human resources costs are still significant and may form a large proportion of total costs in labour-intensive industries such as services.

The organisation should therefore assess the **cost** effect of any HR plan – recruitment drive, training initiative or indeed downsizing exercise – in proportion to the **expected benefits** to be derived from it.

Definition

> A **cost-benefit analysis** is a comparison of the cost of an actual or proposed measure with an evaluation or estimate of the benefits gained from it. This will indicate whether the measure has been, or is likely to be, cost-effective – or 'worthwhile'.

There are a number of reasons why a cost-benefit analysis of the HR plan might be useful.

(a) It emphasises the total cost of the plan, including wages and related costs, in relation to gains in efficiency or effectiveness.

(b) It allows costs of the plan to be compared with other options. For example, once the cost of recruitment has been evaluated in relation to gains in productivity, the organisation can assess the merits of alternative plans such as:

   (i) Contracting out the services or production to outsiders (eg getting a catering firm to run a canteen)

   (ii) Buying capital equipment or altering work processes in other ways to enhance productivity

(c) It emphasises that **cost-effectiveness** – not cost-minimalisation – is the aim. For example, temporary or part-time workers may be 'cheaper' for the organisation – but if long-term gains in stability, expertise, management succession and motivated output are lost (compared with employing full-time, permanent staff), this would be a false economy.

FOR DISCUSSION

Do a cost-benefit analysis of your HND qualification. Is education and training an investment – and if so, for whom?

You may have noticed that HRP, at the stage of closing the gap between supply and demand, actually involves planning in a number of areas of personnel management. We will end this chapter with a summary of the Human Resource Plan.

5 THE HUMAN RESOURCE PLAN

Once the analysis of human resource requirements has been carried out, and the various options for fulfilling them considered, the **human resource plan** will be drawn up. This may be done at a strategic level (and indeed, as we saw in section 1.2 above, it will have strategic impact). It will also involve tactical plans and action plans for various measures, according to the strategy that has been chosen. Typical elements might include the following.

(a) **The recruitment plan:** numbers and types of people, and when required, the recruitment programme

(b) **The training plan:** numbers of trainees required and/or existing staff who need training; training programme

(c) **The re-development plan:** programmes for transferring or retraining employees

(d) **The productivity plan:** programmes for improving productivity, or reducing manpower costs; setting productivity targets

(e) **The redundancy plan:** where and when redundancies are to occur; policies for selection and declaration of redundancies; redevelopment, retraining or relocation of redundant employees; policy on redundancy payments, union consultation and so on

(f) **The retention plan:** actions to reduce avoidable labour wastage

The plan should include budgets, targets and standards. It should allocate responsibilities for implementation and control (reporting, monitoring achievement against plan).

EXAMPLE

Chris Bottomley, of NatWest, described its approach to human resource planning, in an article in *People Management* (9/7/98). 'The knowledge and skills of the workforce are crucial and difficult to change quickly, so it is important to plan ahead to identify the skills required to deliver business plans (demand) compared with those that are currently available (supply), to find out where potential skill gaps may lie and how these might be filled.'

NatWest approached this process as follows.

(a) Demand for skills was assessed through a systematic, top-down approach, driven from the corporate centre. The central HR function held a series of meetings with line managers and HR leaders in each of five core businesses to consider the implications of their strategic plan in the light of their existing skills mix.

(b) A shared model was developed, which highlighted likely demand for skills, and provided an initial perspective on potential skill gaps, as a basis for exploring ways of filling gaps, and discussing the specific concerns of each business.

(c) A bottom-up skills audit was then implemented, to validate the findings of the top-down analysis, and to give a 'better feel' for the likely future supply of skills.

(i) Because of the size and variety of the workforce, NatWest 'needed to establish a common language between businesses to describe skills', and chose a broad-based 'job family' approach. An agreed set of job families (such as 'project manager') was drawn up: each family included characteristic competency profiles for different levels of staff. Gaining agreement on the families and profiles was the major challenge of the exercise, given 'the need to establish a common language and framework, while still recognising differences of interpretation between businesses'.

(ii) A range of different auditing techniques were used, such as sampling the performance of staff from each of the job families.

(d) Recognising the importance of flexibility to environmental factors, NatWest has, over the past two years, devolved responsibility for assessing demand for skills back to line managers in individual businesses, based on their own job family frameworks, tailored to their particular business environments. However, 'there is still a need to take an overview of the results of the business' analysis, to build an organisational picture of the changes in core or generic skills.'

(e) Such broad-based thinking has led to HR plans such as the introduction of annualised-hours contracts, thought to be the biggest arrangement of its kind for employees in a retail environment. The 'Hours by Design' system is based on what cover is required, which hours staff want to work and how long branches are open: managers set out the expected workflow demands and the staffing levels these require, and employees work out staffing rosters four weeks in advance (*People Management*, 28/1/99). In effect, this is on-going human resource planning at the micro-level.

NOTES

Chapter roundup

* HRP is a strategy for the acquisition or reduction, utilisation, improvement and retention of an enterprise's human resources.

* A systematic approach to HRP would be as shown in the diagram below.

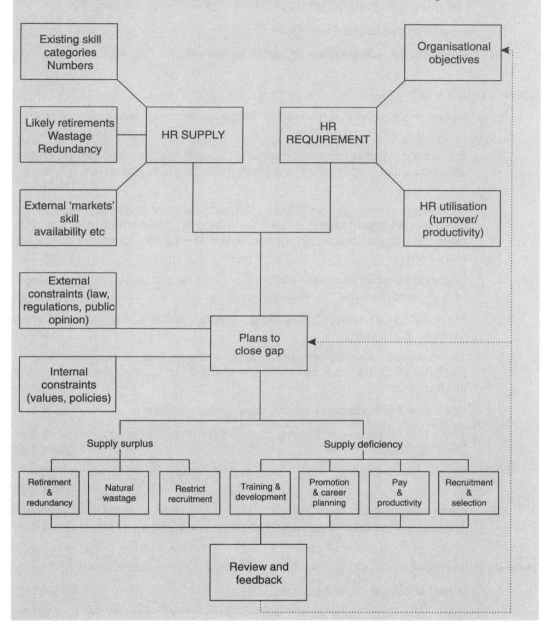

Quick quiz

1 List the elements of human resource planning.

2 Outline the items commonly contained in an organisation's corporate or strategic plan as they affect HRP.

3 List the reasons why human resource planning has increased in importance in recent years.

4 What are the major areas of information required by the human resource planner?

BPP
PUBLISHING

5   Outline the three major stages involved in the human resource planning process.

6   What is meant by the human resource audit?

7   List three methods used in forecasting for HRP.

8   List three basic approaches to HRP in a changing environment

9   How is labour turnover measured?

10   What are the **advantages** of labour turnover?

Answers to quick quiz

1   Recruitment, retention, utilisation, improvement and downsizing of staff.
(see paragraph 1.1)

2   Predicted financial situation; intended product markets and market share; desired output and productivity; changes in location; employee numbers.
(para 1.2)

3   Difficulty in replacing specialised staff; employment protection legislation; rapid technological change; need for effective utilisation of staff; national skills shortages in certain areas; international competition; computer technology.
(para 1.3)

4   Organisational objectives; staff utilisation; labour costs; environmental factors; staff turnover; production levels.
(para 2)

5   Forecasting demand; forecasting supply; closing the gap between demand and supply.
(para 2)

6   The process whereby an organisation ensures that its human resource planning systems work, and that the plans they incorporate are properly implemented.
(para 4.2)

7   Statistical methods; work study; managerial estimates.
(para 4.1)

8   The staff replacement approach; short-term; HR strategy; vision-driven HRD approach.
(para 1.4)

9   Crude labour turnover rate; labour stability index; survival rate analysis.
(para 3.1)

10   Opportunities for 'new blood'; balanced age structure; promotion/ succession opportunities; reduction of labour surplus.
(para 3.3)

Answers to activities

1   A skill shortage might be caused by:

(a)   long-term declines in education and training, or in population (nationally or in the local area)

(b)   the immediate effects of a competitor entering the market or area and employing some of the pool of skilled labour

(c)   increases in demand for the product or service for which the skill is required; or the relocation, resignation or demotivation of key skilled people – for all sorts of personal and circumstantial reasons

2   (a)   The computer company is operating in an extremely volatile and changing market, which will present HRP difficulties. The technology, and associated skills, are constantly changing, along with competitive pressures: an innovative competitor could 'steal'

the market. This is also a highly-skilled business, however, with skill shortages in the labour market, and long training times: despite the difficulties, long-term planning will be important.

(b) Some years ago, the local authority would have represented a fairly stable (not to say 'ponderous') bureaucratic structure, with fairly rigid, predictable HR plans. Reductions in funding, and the contracting out of services, have made HRP more difficult and desirable: workforce reduction and flexibility, and the use of HRP to change organisational culture, will be key issues.

(c) The airline is a business which is potentially volatile, and sensitive to barely controllable factors such as price wars. Political/terrorist action, industrial action, airspace restrictions, crashes affecting image and so on. At the same time it is dependent on several categories of employees (airline pilots, aerospace engineers) who are scarce and have long training cycles: planning ahead for selection and retention will be crucial.

3 Occupations in short supply/great demand might include: doctors, systems analysts, science teachers, surgeons. Occupations in surplus supply/short demand might include: actors, miners, unskilled labourers.

4 At the end of 20X2, the company works out that it has:

BIM Index: $\dfrac{18 \text{ leavers}}{60 \text{ (average) employees}} \times 100 = 30\%$ *turnover*

This is not uncommon, and would cause no undue worries. However:

Stability index: $\dfrac{2 \text{ year servers}}{20} \times 100 = 10\%$ *stability*

Only 10% of the labour force is stable (and therefore offering the benefits of experience and acclimatisation to the work and culture of the organisation). A crude turnover rate has disguised the significance of what has happened.

5 Common factors include the following.

(a) **Incompatibilities with the organisation climate or culture, or its style of leadership**. An organisation might be formal and bureaucratic, where employees are expected to work according to prescribed rules and procedures. Other organisations are more flexible, and allow more scope for individual expression and creativity. Individuals will prefer – and stay with – one system or the other.

(b) **Unsatisfactory pay and conditions of employment.** If these are not good enough according to people's needs (or in comparison with others), people will leave to find better terms elsewhere, or will use this as a catalyst to express their discontent in other areas.

(c) **Poor physical working conditions.** If working conditions are uncomfortable, unclean, unsafe, or noisy, say, people will be more inclined to leave.

(d) **Lack of career prospects and access to training.** If the chances of advancement before a certain age are low, an ambitious employee is likely to consider leaving to find a job where promotion is likely to come more quickly. The same may be true where an employee wants training for a qualification or skill development, and opportunities are limited in his/her current job.

The second part to this Activity is personal to you.

NOTES

6   (a)   Statistics are not the only element of the planning process, and are subject to interpretation and managerial judgements that are largely qualitative and even highly speculative (involving future growth, say, or potential for innovation).

(b)   Trends in statistics are the product of social processes, which are not readily quantifiable or predictable. Staff leave for various social reasons in (unpredictable) individual cases, to get married, relocate or whatever. The growth of the temporary and freelance workforce is a social trend, as are the buying patterns which dictate demand for goods and services.

Assignment 3   **(2 hours)**

Human Resource Planning at Quick-Send Ltd

Scenario

Quick-Send Ltd is a mail-order clothing company. They currently employ just over 200 people in their warehouse and packing section.

The need to be more competitive and productive has led to the planned introduction of new technology, and an update of the system and procedures used to process and despatch orders.

The personnel department at Quick-Send is currently carrying out its annual human resource planning exercise.

Table 1 shows the current age profile of staff (Year X).

Table 2 shows the number of orders dealt with over the year (Year X), the number of staff employed to deal with these orders, and the ratio of staff to orders – in other words, how many orders a single staff member will be expected to deal with.

Table 3 shows the predicted number of orders for the next five years, together with the new ratios proposed, which take into account the introduction of new technology and new systems.

Annual labour turnover for this group of staff is currently 5% and is predicted to stay at this level for each of the next five years.

TABLE 1	
Current age profile of staff in	
Warehouse and Packaging	
Age range	Staff numbers
Under 20	10
20–25	22
26–30	30
31–35	22
36–40	16
41–45	9
46–50	14
51–55	43
56–60	31
Over 60	20
Total	217

Cont'd

BPP
PUBLISHING

NOTES

Assignment 3 cont'd

TABLE 2

Current orders, staff numbers and ratio (Year X)		Ratios
	Number of staff	Staff:orders
Number of orders	217	1:1,705
370,000		

TABLE 3

Estimated orders and ratios for each of next five years

Year	Estimated orders	Number of staff	Estimated ratio
X + 1	380,000		1:2,000
X + 2	400,000		1:2,500
X + 3	500,000		1:2,500
X + 4	600,000		1:2,600
X + 5	640,000		1:2,700

Task

You are a personnel officer at Quick-Send

Produce a report for the attention of the Managing Director, covering the following:

1 (a) Decide upon the most appropriate illustration of the current age profile in Table 1.

   (b) Analyse the age profile and comment on the implications such a profile has for the resourcing of the department in the future.

2 (a) Using the ratios given in Table 3, calculate the estimated number of total staff numbers required in Warehouse and Packaging for each of the next five years.

   (b) Calculate the estimated surplus/shortage of staff numbers for each year.

3 What human resource implications has the plan got for Quick-Send?

   What action would you advise the company to take in order to meet their planned numbers for the next five years?

Chapter 4 :
RECRUITMENT

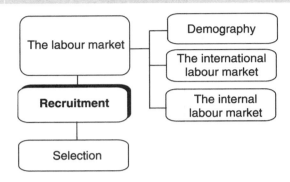

Introduction

In Chapter 3 we noted that there were sources of labour supply both **inside** the organisation and in its **environment**. In this chapter, we look at the labour market (one of the HR issues specified in Unit 22), both national and international. What does it consist of? How do employers access this market in order to identify and attract to the organisation the human resources it requires?

The process whereby an organisation goes into the labour market and communicates opportunities and information, seeking to attract the quantity and quality of potential employees it requires to fulfil its human resource plan is called **recruitment**. This chapter outlines a systematic approach to this task.

The process of deciding which of the potential employees attracted by recruitment are suitable and/or unsuitable for the organisation's need is called **selection**: this will be discussed in Chapter 5.

Your objectives

In this chapter you will learn about the following

(a)   The systematic approach to recruitment for a given organisation

(b)   The implementation of (recruitment) practice in the UK and in one other country

(c)   Factors influencing the labour market and their implications for human resource planning

(d)   Systematic procedures for recruitment

1 THE LABOUR MARKET

1.1 The pool of labour

Definition

> The **labour pool** consists of the group of potential employees, internal, local or otherwise, with the types of skill, knowledge and experience that the employer requires at a given time. It thus consists of people within the organisation, people who are out of work at that time, and also people in other organisations who may wish to change jobs or employers.

The size and composition (skill types and so on) of the external labour pool depends on factors such as the following.

(a) Government policies (on matters such as benefits, taxation or employment protection), legislation and regulation, relevant case law and European influences

(b) The level of activity in the economy (with associated unemployment levels) at the European, national, regional and local level

(c) Education/training standards and opportunities including government initiatives and cultural values about education

(d) Occupational choice trends among school leavers, women returners and other target groups

(e) Wage and salary levels: attracting skilled individuals (or not), influencing occupational choice, creating competition between employers for skills

(f) Competitor activity and employer branding in the market place, creating competition between organisations for particular skills

(g) The attitudes and the expectations of existing and potential employees (with regard to the quality of working life, wages, the role of technology, the adoption of flexible working methods and so on) which influence occupational (and job) choice, career mobility and self-employment opportunities

(h) The extent to which new technology replaces, or may replace, human skills in a given area

(i) Population changes affecting the number of people in an area, the age or sex distribution of the population and other factors (these are called 'demographic' factors: we will discuss them in detail later)

(j) The expansion of markets and organisations across national and cultural boundaries (for example, freedom of employment within the EU) which expands the potential labour pool and the need for particular skills such as languages

(k) The trend towards delayered/downsized organisations, widening the available labour pool

(l) The trend towards flexible structures and working methods, which has resulted in an increase in freelance, self-employed and contract working

1.2 The labour market

Definition

> The **labour market** is the sphere in which labour is 'bought' and 'sold', and in which market concepts such as supply and demand and price operate with regard to human resources.

The **labour market** has changed dramatically in the last few decades. Writers on manpower planning (as it was then called) in the 1970s suggested that a 'seller's market' had been established, as technology increased the skills and therefore scarcity value of employees in certain jobs, and as the scale of state benefits blunted the fear of unemployment: the initiative seemed to be with the employee, or with organised groups of employees.

The decline of manufacturing, the increase of women in employment and the more general application of technology, among other factors, have changed that situation. A 'buyer's market' for labour now gives employers considerable power, with a large pool of available labour created by unemployment and non-career labour.

On the other hand, even in conditions of high overall employment, particular skill shortages still exist and may indeed be more acute because of economic pressures on education and training. Engineers and software designers, among other specialist and highly trained groups, are the target of fierce competition among employers, forcing a re-evaluation of recruitment and retention policies.

Market intelligence will clearly have to be gathered by the personnel department in order to monitor fluctuations in the local, regional, national and international labour supply for the variety of skills the organisation requires.

1.3 Labour market trends in the UK

Flexibility is a major trend in the labour market.

The following table (drawn from the study *Labour Market Flexibility*, 1996) illustrates the composition of the UK labour force.

	1985 %	1995 %	2005 % (projected)
Part-time	21	24	25
Temporary	11	13	13.5
Self-employed	5	6	8
Permanent	84	82	79

In 1995, the combined percentage of the workforce *not* employed full-time within an organisation was 42% (or 51% if you add the 8% unemployed in that year). The comparable percentage in the USA (including unemployed) was 37%. Everywhere, the numbers of people in 'non-permanent' employment are growing.

Social Trends for the same period also indicated that:

  (a) The number of economically active people in the age group 16-24 is falling, whilst those aged 25-44 is rising

  (b) Women comprise a larger proportion of the labour force tan men

  (c) Nearly half of the women in work are in part-time jobs

(d)   Over half of those in temporary employment are women

(e)   Full-time workers average a 45 hour working week) the highest in Europe, especially since many EU countries have shorter legal maximum hours per week)

The 1998 *Labour Force Survey* estimated that there were well over one million foreign nationals working legally in the UK of whom 454,000 were EU citizens and 63,000 from the US.

Activity 1   **(30 minutes)**

(a)   Brainstorm a few sources of information on labour market statistics and trends (paragraph 1.4 may help you if you are stuck for ideas).

(b)   Select one or two sources (ideally, one published and one Internet) and locate the following information.

•   Percentage of the UK labour force in permanent employment in the current year.

•   Percentage of women in the UK labour force in the current year.

•   Percentage of women in part-time work in the current year.

1.4   Sources of information

Sources of information on the labour market include the following.

(a)   Other HR managers in the same business or local area

(b)   HRM professional organisations (like the CIPD) and publications (like *People Management* and *International Human Resource Management Journal*)

(c)   External agencies such as the Manpower Services Commission, Career Service and so on

(d)   Government publications, such as the *Department of Employment Gazette*, and *Monthly Abstract of Statistics* and *Social Trends*

(e)   The World Wide Web

(f)   HRP and recruitment consultants

We mentioned 'demographic factors' as one of the areas of interest to an HR planner. We will look briefly at demography here.

2   DEMOGRAPHY

2.1   What is demography?

Definition

Demography is an 'analysis of statistics on birth and death rates, age structures of populations, ethnic groups within communities etc' (Bennett, *Dictionary of Personnel and Human Resources Management*). The adjective **demographic** is sometimes used to denote the population-related aspects of an issue.

Many important facts about a country's demographic profile are collected by government to aid planning. Every ten years, the UK government conducts a census. Originally this was undertaken as a population count alone, but recently additional information about the population has been requested.

The UK government publishes various statistics every year, as a result of its different data collection exercises. Two examples are the *Annual Abstract of Statistics* and *Social Trends*. Both contain population data, although *Social Trends* goes into more detail about people's habits. Although *Social Trends* is published annually, some of the information it contains is, invariably, a projection.

> **Activity 2** (1 hour)
>
> Go to your college or local library (or HR department) and have a browse through a copy of the *Annual Abstract of Statistics* and *Social Trends*, just to familiarise yourself with the types of information they offer – for future reference!

To give you a flavour of how demography works, we will take a 'snapshot' of the UK at the end of the '90s, projecting the trends forward to 2011.

2.2 A demographic profile of the UK

The following are likely to be significant demographic indicators for HR planners.

(a) **Population size**. The population of the UK as a whole has grown by some 50% since 1901, but this growth is expected to level off. (The population of the world is growing much faster.)

(b) **Sex distribution**. There is a slightly greater number of women than men in the population: women generally have a longer life expectancy than men. There are, however, more men than women below the age of 65. While just over 70% of men of working age participate in the workforce (projected to fall slightly), over 50% of women of working age do – but this proportion is projected to rise slightly.

(c) **Age structure**. An increasing proportion of the UK population is over 65 years old, while falling birthrates after the post-war 'baby boom' mean that the number of people under 16 is falling.

An 'ageing' population has HRM implications because:

(i) It will be reflected in the working population;

(ii) It will be reflected in the market for the organisation's goods and services; and

(iii) There will be fewer skilled young people in the labour pool. In the late 1980s this was considered to be a 'demographic timebomb': organisations which had traditionally recruited heavily from among school leavers (like banks) had to readjust their HR plans to compete for the reduced young labour pool and/or to tap into non-traditional labour sources such as women returning to work after child-rearing. This demographic timebomb (or 'downturn') lost some of its importance as an HR issue with recessionary falls in the demand for labour: redundancies, rather than labour shortages, were the stories of the '90s.

NOTES

(d) **Regional distribution.** Different regions have different birth and death rates, and people move from one region to another for a variety of lifestyle and economic reasons. London has actually shown a slight decline in population in recent years, perhaps because of decentralisation to areas such as Cambridgeshire and Buckinghamshire, which have shown growth.

(e) **Ethnicity.** Ethnic minorities form around 5% of the UK population, heavily concentrated in London and the South-East. They are also younger than the average population.

Activity 3   **(30 minutes)**

What do you think might account for the **increasing** participation of women of working age in the workforce? Suggest five possible causes. (If you are stuck, ask some employed women in their 30s or 40s...)

You may already have realised the implications of the trends outlined above for the planners. Social Trends *itself notes:*

'Those employers who rely on young people as a significant source of their recruits face declining numbers over future years... . Better use must therefore be made of alternative recruits such as the unemployed, women returning to the labour market and older workers.'

Let us look more closely at some of the 'demographic timebombs' ticking away in HR offices...

2.3 Demography and HRP

Stephen Connock (*HR Vision*) identifies two main demographic variables for organisations to consider.

(a) **Long-term demographic trends.**

    (i) The fall in the number of young people

    (ii) The increase in overall labour force size because of increased female participation

    (iii) The increase in the proportion of the labour force in non-permanent (part-time, temporary) employment

    (iv) The increased mobility of the labour pool (at present, notably within EU countries)

(b) **Education trends.** The proportion of school leavers going into higher education is expected to increase, but with fewer school leavers in total.

    (i) This means that the base of potential recruits with the **right qualifications** will be **even smaller**. This is exaggerated by local variations. (1992 figures showed that 66% of 16 year olds remained in full-time post-compulsory education in the UK, compared to 80-95% in most other industrialised countries.

    (ii) It is government policy to increase the number of graduates. Employers will note trends towards:

        (1) More women

        (2) More mature students

        (3) More from 'non-conventional' backgrounds (eg increasing numbers of the unemployed doing Open University degrees)

(4)   A decline in engineering and technology graduates, unless trends are reversed

These are crucial influences on the **supply** of labour. However, even in times of high unemployment (when the 'supply of labour' should be larger) there may be a 'skills shortage'. This probably means that there is not the **right mix** of skills on supply to satisfy the demand. Stephen Connock believes that jobs will grow in IT services, health services, and multi-skilled occupations. It is currently suggested, however, that *too many* graduates are being produced in areas such as media and tourism, which were previously promoted as growth areas: supply has outstripped demand.

Activity 4	(45 minutes)

Outline a simple HRP procedure (refer to Section 2 of Chapter 3 if you need to) which will take into account demographic and educational trends.

FOR DISCUSSION

What can organisations do to attract:

(a)   Women
(b)   Older workers

into employment?

What effect do you think this will have on working life as a whole?

With an increasingly global economy, and continuing progress towards European Union, the labour market is no longer merely local or national in its scope. Obviously, we cannot cover the global world of work here. However, we can highlight some of the issues in European and global HRM. Others will be covered in Chapter 15.

3   THE INTERNATIONAL LABOUR MARKET

3.1   A global market?

You should be aware of the extent to which a **global labour market** is developing.

    (a)   The world is 'shrinking', because of technological developments in communications and travel. There is now talk of 'virtual teams', scattered geographically around the globe, but working together as a team via email, the Internet, video conferencing and so on.

        'A lawyer based in New York could now collaborate with another lawyer in Brussels – and five lawyers in London and a team leader in Singapore ... . Some international organisations now never sleep. When the European part of the virtual team stops work, the US collaborators have started ... ' (Ron Young, People Management, 5 February 98)

    (b)   Trade and communication barriers are breaking down (to an extent) with harmonisation of employment legislation, de-regulation etc (notably, at the moment, in Europe) and the opening of new markets (particularly in Eastern Europe and developing nations).

At the same time, geo-political 'chunking' (the separatist aspirations of political/ethnic/religious movements – notably, again, in Eastern Europe and the Balkan states) is creating new and more culturally complex markets.

Activity 5   **(15 minutes)**

What **barriers** to a common, global labour market can you foresee? What, for example, might prevent a UK organisation from recruiting in China?

3.2   The European labour market

Some of the key features of the European labour market are as follows.

(a)   **General and vocational education**

About 23% of the EU's population is currently in full-time education (comparable to Japan but slightly lower than in the USA) and 25% of people stay in education after the age of 19. Germany, Sweden and France have the highest percentage of 5-24 year olds in full-time education (around 83%), and Portugal and Britain the lowest (65%).

Vocational Education and Training (VET) varies widely in the extent of specialisation, financing, methods of testing competence and the status and role of VET in the national education system. VET begins at an earlier age in some nations than others, and in some EU countries vocational qualifications obtained at school offer equal access to higher education as 'academic' qualifications.

(b)   **An ageing workforce**

As in the UK, the EU workforce is ageing (and shrinking, due to accelerating retirements). By 2005, the bulk of the labour pool will be between 45 and 64 years of age – a group arguably lacking training and adaptability to new technologies and fast-evolving organisational forms.

(c)   **Non-permanent employment**

Some 15% of all EU workers are on part-time contracts, most of them women: the percentages of working women who are in part-time jobs varies from 10% (Italy, Portugal, Greece) to 80% (Netherlands). Some countries (Belgium, France, Germany, Netherlands, Portugal and Spain) have statutory restrictions on the use of temporary employees.

(d)   **The increased mobility of the labour pool**

Article 48 of the Treaty of Rome protects the free movement of 'workers' between EU member states: it applies to all citizens of the European Economic Area (EEA), which consists of all EU member states, plus Iceland, Norway and Liechtenstein. 'Workers' has been defined in the European court of Justice as 'someone who performs services for another during a certain period of time and is under the direction of another in return for remuneration'. *(Lowrie v Blum 1987):* part time and economically-active self-employed workers are included. As a result of a key decision by the Employment Appeals Tribunal in *Bossa v Nordstress Ltd* (*The Times*, 13 March 98), any EEA citizen can bring a claim under the UK Race Relations Act for discrimination by a UK employer on the grounds of nationality or national origin, where the work in question is within the EU. (This applies not just to recruitment, but to transfer, posting or promotion of existing employees.)

BPP PUBLISHING

NOTES

FOR DISCUSSION

As a result of the *Bossa* decision, a claim could be brought in the UK, under the Race Relations Act, by a German national living in Belgium who applied for a job advertised in a British national newspaper and who is refused employment on grounds of nationality by a decision made in the UK – even though the job might be based entirely in France. (*People Management*, 14 May 98).

Is European Union a nightmare or an opportunity for HRM?

EXAMPLE: INTERNATIONAL COMPARISONS

'In Japan, where the government forces people to care for their ageing relatives, between 60 and 70 per cent of men aged over 70 are in the workforce, because they do not want to be a burden on their children... In Australia, just 15 per cent of males aged over 70 are in the workforce.' (*Daily Telegraph*, Australia, Nov 22 2000)

3.3   Multinationals

Definition

> **Multinational companies** are groups of companies with a head office and parent company in one country, and subsidiaries in other countries.

There are particular challenges to the personnel function in multinational management structures.

(a)   HR factors might influence the **location** of subsidiary companies.

For example, a USA multinational might want to set up a new subsidiary in the EU, with the choice of any EU country as the base for the new operations. The choice of country would be influenced by various factors, including:

(i)   Relative costs, such as labour costs
(ii)   Infrastructure, such as roads and railways
(iii)   Access, eg to ports
(iv)   Government assistance, such as grants
(v)   Government policies and employment legislation
(vi)   Trade union power
(vii)   Language differences

(b)   Multinationals must develop a specific policy about whether to use 'local' labour, or labour from the 'home' (head office) country, especially in regard to:

(i)   Management

(ii)   Employees with specialist technical skills, which may not be available in all nations in which the company operates

Multinationals with subsidiaries in developing countries might have a deliberate policy of developing the skills of nationals in those countries. For example, a multinational with a subsidiary in West Africa might try to develop the technical skills of its West

African staff – in engineering, computers, accountancy or whatever – through a policy of education and training.

Over time, the personnel policy of multinationals is changing, from reliance on nationals of the 'head' country to fill skilled job vacancies, to reliance on the appointment and development of 'local' nationals.

The range of policies might be described as follows.

Policy		*Examples*
1	Key staff of subsidiaries are appointed from head office, and are nationals of the 'head' country.	A US multinational might recruit US employees for key positions in the US and in foreign subsidiaries.
2	Most key positions are held by nationals of the 'head' country. There are some exceptions, and talented 'foreigners' might be appointed.	A US multinational's key positions are staffed mainly by US employees, but some nationals from Europe or South America might be appointed from time to time.
3	As many management positions as possible are filled by nationals of the country in which the subsidiary operates, as a deliberate policy of development.	A US multinational has mainly North Americans in management at head office, but tries to appoint South American managers to run its South American subsidiaries, Italian managers to run its Italian subsidiary, etc.
4	Key vacancies are filled from any country in which the group operates and/or recruits.	A US multinational initially recruits a UK national as a manager in the UK then posts her to the Far East, Canada or the USA. Meanwhile, a German is recruited for the UK job.

4 THE INTERNAL LABOUR MARKET

When forecasting the supply of labour and skills available to the organisation to meet the demands of its activities and objectives, the HR planner must take into account:

- *the current skill base, size and structure of its existing workforce*
- *the potential for change in that skill base, size and structure.*

This constitutes an **internal labour market**

4.1 Internal sources of labour

If the organisation faces a demand for a particular skill, that demand may be satisfied from within the existing labour force by:

(a) **Retaining** skilled individuals, against the flow of labour turnover

(b) **Transferring** or deploying individuals with the relevant skills from their current job to the job where those skills can more effectively be utilised

(c) **Training, developing** and potentially **promoting** individuals in the required skills and abilities: this aspect of the internal labour market will be discussed in detail in Part C of this text

(d)   **Exploiting its contracts** with present employees, friends and family of employees, and former external applicants, who might be referred (and to en extent, pre-appraised) for vacancies

If the organisation experiences **fluctuating** demand for a particular skill or for numbers of workers, it may need to approach the above strategies somewhat differently, in order to be able to deploy labour flexibly. If a retail business requires extra sales people in the pre-Christmas period, for example, or a factory requires trained specialists in a particular field only at certain stages of a project – or in the event of problems – what do they do? Train, retain and transfer sufficient people for the busiest scenario? You should be able to see that this would be costly and inefficient – and unlikely to enhance the credibility of the HR planner! This is in essence what **labour flexibility** – in terms of numbers and skills deployed – is about.

Retention was discussed in Chapter 3. Training and development are covered in detail in Chapters 16 and 17 (Unit 23). Flexibility is discussed in Chapter 12 (Unit 22). Here we will briefly discuss promotion *as a form of internal 'recruitment'.*

4.2   Promotion

Definition

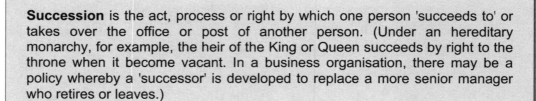

> **Succession** is the act, process or right by which one person 'succeeds to' or takes over the office or post of another person. (Under an hereditary monarchy, for example, the heir of the King or Queen succeeds by right to the throne when it become vacant. In a business organisation, there may be a policy whereby a 'successor' is developed to replace a more senior manager who retires or leaves.)

Promotion and succession policies are a vital part of the human resource plan, as a form of risk management associated with the internal supply of labour. The planned development of staff (not just skills training, but experience and growth in responsibility) is essential to ensure the **continuity** of performance in the organisation. This is particularly so for **management** planning. The departure of a senior manager with no planned or 'groomed' successor could leave a gap in the organisation structure: the lead time for training and developing a suitable replacement may be very long.

CASE STUDY: THE CAREER

A paper delivered to the British Psychological Society occupational psychology conference in January 1995 reported on a survey covering 1,600 managers in banking, insurance and building societies with an average length of service of nearly 18 years and an average age of 42. The survey found that the managers could be divided into four types.

(a)   Career lifers: those who do not think they will be made redundant and want to carry on with what they do with continuing recognition

(b)   Ambitious careerists: a younger group of ambitious managers who believe they will be promoted and want to get to the top

(c)   Flexible careerists: those who say they can accept they will not be promoted but who would appreciate a change of job or a new challenge

(d)   Career disengagers: mostly older people with no expectations of being promoted, bored with their job and willing to take early retirement or work part-time

---

A comprehensive **promotion programme**, as part of the overall manpower plan (for getting the right people into jobs at the right time) will include:

(a)   Establishing the relative significance of jobs by analysis, description and classification, so that the line and consequences of promotion are made clear

(b)   Establishing methods of assessing staff and their potential for fulfilling the requirements of more senior positions

(c)   Planning in advance for training where necessary to enhance potential and develop specific skills

(d)   Policy with regard to internal promotion or external recruitment and training

A coherent **promotion policy** may vary to include provisions such as the following.

(a)   All promotions, as far as possible, and all things being equal, are to be made from within the firm. (For the argument for this, see our answer to Activity 7.)

(b)   Merit and ability (systematically appraised) should be the principal basis of promotion, rather than seniority (age or years of service).

(c)   Vacancies should be advertised and open to all employees.

(d)   There should be full opportunities for all employees to be promoted to the highest grades.

(e)   Personnel and appraisal records should be kept and up-dated regularly.

(f)   Training should be offered to encourage and develop employees of ability and ambition in advance of promotion.

(g)   Scales of pay, areas of responsibility, duties and privileges of each post and so on should be clearly communicated so that employees know what promotion means – in other words, what they are being promoted *to*.

Activity 6   **(15 minutes)**

What problems with line/departmental managers can you foresee for a Personnel Manager who attempts to implement a policy such as the one outlined above?

4.3   Internal or external recruitment?

Promotion is useful from the firm's point of view, in establishing a management succession, filling more senior positions with proven, experienced and loyal employees. It is also one of the main forms of reward the organisation can offer its employees.

The decision of whether to promote from within or fill a position from outside will hinge on many factors. If there is simply no-one available on the current staff with the expertise or ability required (say, if the organisation is venturing into new areas of activity, or changing its methods by computerisation), the recruitment manager will obviously have to seek qualified people outside. If there is time, a person of particular potential in the organisation could be trained in the necessary skills, but that will require an analysis of the costs as compared to the possible (and probably less quantifiable) benefits.

Activity 7	(15 minutes)

Outline what you think would be the **advantages** of promoting from within the organisation, instead of recruiting someone from outside. What would be the main **disadvantages**?

5 RECRUITMENT

Definition

Recruitment is the part of the human resourcing process concerned with finding the applicants: it is a positive action by management, going into the labour market, communicating opportunities and information, and encouraging applications from suitable candidates.

5.1 A systematic approach

The overall aim of the recruitment process in an organisation is to obtain the quantity and quality of candidates required to fulfil the objectives of the organisation.

A systematic approach to recruitment will involve the following stages.

(a) Detailed **human resource planning** defining what resources the organisation needs to meet its objectives.

(b) **Job analysis,** so that for any given job there is:

    (i) A **job description**: a statement of the component tasks, duties, objectives and standards

    (ii) A **person specification**: a reworking of the job description in terms of the kind of person needed to perform the job

    If such documents exist, they may need to be updated or confirmed.

(c) An identification of vacancies, from the requirements of the human resource plan or by a **job requisition** from a department, branch or office which has a vacancy, and subsequent approval or **authorisation** for engagement. Seeking authorisation to refill a vacancy is a means of ensuring that the need for recruitment, and the criteria for recruitment, are in line with departmental and organisational requirements, timely and cost-effective. It may also provide an opportunity to review other options, such as redeploying existing staff, restructuring tasks, allowing natural wastage and so on.

(d) Evaluation of the **sources of staff,** which again should be forecast and in the human resource plan. Internal and external sources, and media (**job advertisement** or other means) for reaching both, will be considered.

(e) Preparation and publication of **information** (ie advertising copy), which will:

    (i) Attract the attention and interest of potentially suitable candidates

    (ii) Give a favourable (but accurate) impression of the job and the organisation

    (iii) Equip those interested to make an attractive and relevant application (how and to whom to apply, desired skills, qualifications and so on)

(f) **Processing applications** prior to the selection process. This may include:

    (i) Screening replies at the end of the specified period for application
    (ii) Short-listing candidates for initial consideration
    (iii) Advising applicants of the progress of their application
    (iv) Drawing up a programme for the selection process which follows

---

Activity 8   **(30 minutes)**

Which features of the recruitment process suggest that it might be most efficient and effective if *centralised* within the personnel function, rather than delegated to line managers in their own departments? (Refer back to Chapter 2 if you need some hints.) Suggest five advantages of centralised recruitment.

Movements towards flexibility and multi-skilling have encouraged a slightly different approach, which is oriented more towards 'fitting the job to the person' than 'fitting the person to the job'. In a highly innovative market, technological environment or organisational culture, for example, rigid job descriptions would not be suitable. In order to 'thrive on chaos' (Tom Peters' well-known phrase), organisations should be able to look at the skills and attributes of the people they employ, and those of gifted outsiders, and ask: 'What needs doing that this person would do best?' In a relatively informal environment, where all-round knowledge/skills and experience are highly valued and suitable external labour resources are scarce (say, in management consultancy), this approach would give much-needed flexibility. The organisation would try to recruit excellent, flexible, motivated and multi-skilled personnel, without reference to any specific job, as defined by a job description. They would form an available 'resource' for any tasks or requirement that arose.

However, the 'selection' approach ('fitting the person to the job') is still by far the most common, and is suitable for most organisations with fairly defined goals and structures.

5.2 Recruitment policy and procedure

Detailed procedures for recruitment should only be devised and implemented within the context of a coherent **policy**, or code of conduct.

A typical recruitment policy might deal with:

(a) Internal advertisement of vacancies

(b) Efficient and courteous processing of applications

(c) Fair and accurate provision of information to potential recruits

(d) Selection of candidates on the basis of qualification, without discrimination on any grounds

In 1994, the Institute of Personnel and Development issued a Recruitment Code that seeks to establish a model of good practice for recruitment.

Recruitment Code

1　Job advertisements should state clearly the form of reply desired, in particular, whether this should be by a formal application form or by curriculum vitae. Preferences should also be stated if handwritten replies are required.

2　An acknowledgement of reply should be made promptly to each applicant by the employing organisation or its agent. If it is likely to take some time before acknowledgements are made, this should be made clear in the advertisement.

3　Applicants should be informed of the progress of the selection procedures, what these will be (eg group selection, aptitude tests etc), the steps and time involved and the policy regarding expenses.

4　Detailed personal information (eg religion, medical history, place of birth, family background etc) should not be called for unless it is relevant to the selection process.

5　Before applying for references, potential employers must secure the permission of the applicant.

6　Applications must be treated as confidential.

7　The code also recommends certain courtesies and obligations on the part of the applicants.

Detailed **procedures** should be devised in order to make recruitment activity systematic and consistent throughout the organisation (especially where it is decentralised in the hands of line managers). Apart from the personnel resourcing requirements which need to be effectively and efficiently met, there is a **marketing** aspect to recruitment, as one 'interface' between the organisation and the outside world: applicants who feel they have been unfairly treated, or recruits who leave because they feel they have been misled, do not enhance the organisation's reputation in the labour market or the world at large.

Activity 9 (1 hour)

Find out, if you do not already know, what are the recruitment and selection procedures in your organisation, and who is responsible for each stage. The procedures manual should set this out, or you may need to ask someone in the personnel department.

Get hold of and examine some of the documentation your organisation uses. We show specimens in this chapter, but practice and terminology varies, so your own 'house style' will be invaluable. Try to find the job description for your job; the personnel specification for your job (if any); the application form(s) of the organisation; and an interview assessment form (if any).

5.3　Influences on recruitment policy

Recruitment policy will be influenced by the following considerations.

(a)　The organisation's image in the community, market-place and labour market: its 'employer brand' or image and identity as an employer. Recruitment advertising, in particular, is a public relations exercise: it must reflect the organisation's values and professionalism – and, where appropriate, its marketing message (quality, products/services and so on)

(b)　The human resource plan and subsidiary plans

NOTES

(c)   Fairness, courtesy and professionalism in dealing with applicants

(d)   Legislation and regulations affecting:

    (i)   Terms and conditions able to be offered to (or imposed on) potential employees (for example, minimal wage, working hours, holiday entitlements)

    (ii)   Equal opportunities – the prevention of direct and indirect discrimination by:

- The wording and placing of recruitment advertisements which imply or tend towards a preference for a particular group

- Indicating or implying **intention to discriminate** in internal planning, advertising or instructions to recruitment agencies

- Failing to state that the organisation is an equal opportunity employer

       This area will be discussed in detail in Part B of this Course Book.

    (iii)   Labour mobility – for example, discrimination on the basis of nationality or national origin against candidates from the European Economic Area

(e)   Cultural values of the organisation, as well as national culture. These are often reflected in the attributes considered essential or desirable in candidates: the importance attached to educational, vocational or professional qualifications; value attached to youth or maturity (and/or associated attributes); identification with the organisation's self-image (responsible, fun, fast-paced, flexible or whatever).

EXAMPLE: INTERNATIONAL COMPARISONS

The law on recruitment varies internationally. For example:

- In France and Belgium, the State Manpower Service has to be informed of all vacancies.

- In Italy, all employment should (in theory) be approved by the State placement service.

- A number of countries require consultation with workforce representatives (works council) before employment takes place.

- United States employment law and practice is based on the freedom of employers to hire (and fire) freely and without regulation: the concept of **employment at will** (subject to contract).

- Anti-discrimination legislation varies. Many countries in Europe have quota systems for employing disabled workers – although definitions of disability and size of quotas vary widely.

- Recruitment methods are variously regulated, as well will see in Paragraph 5.7 below.

We will now discuss some of the recruitment procedures listed in Paragraph 5.1 in more detail.

NOTES

5.4 Job analysis

Definition

> **Job analysis** is 'the determination of the essential characteristics of a job', the process of examining a job to identify its component parts and the circumstances in which it is performed (*British Standards Institute*).
>
> The product of the analysis is usually a **job specification** - a detailed statement of the activities (mental and physical) involved in the job, and other relevant factors in the social and physical environment.

Uses of job analysis

Job analysis, and the job specification resulting from it, may be used by managers:

(a) In recruitment and selection - for a detailed description of the vacant job to provide a source of information for the preparation of job descriptions and personnel specifications

(b) For appraisal - to assess how well an employee has fulfilled the requirements of the job

(c) In devising training programmes - to assess the knowledge and skills necessary in a job

(d) In establishing rates of pay - this will be discussed later in connection with job evaluation

(e) In eliminating risks - identifying hazards in the job

(f) In re-organisation of the organisational structure - by reappraising the purpose and necessity of jobs and their relationship to each other

Content of job analysis

Information which should be elicited from a job appraisal is both task-oriented information, and also worker-oriented information, including:

(a) **Initial requirements of the employee:** aptitudes, qualifications, experience, training required; personality and attitudinal considerations

(b) **Duties and responsibilities of the job:** physical aspects; mental effort; routine or requiring initiative; difficult and/or disagreeable features; degree of independence of discretion; responsibilities for staff, materials, equipment or cash etc; component tasks (where, when, how frequently, how carried out); standards of output and/or accuracy required; relative value of tasks and how they fit together

(c) **Environment and conditions of the job:** physical surroundings, with notable features such as temperature or noise; hazards; remuneration; other conditions such as hours, shifts, benefits, holidays; career prospects; provision of employee services - canteens, protective clothing etc

(d) **Social factors of the job:** size of the department; teamwork or isolation; sort of people dealt with - senior management, the public; amount of supervision; job status

Methods of job analysis

Opportunities for analyses occur when jobs fall vacant, when salaries are reviewed, or when targets are being set, and the personnel department should take advantage of such opportunities to review and revise existing job specifications.

Job analysis can be carried out by:

(a) **Observation of working practice**, where jobs are relatively routine and repetitive. The analyst watches and records the job holder's activity, task times and performance standards, working conditions and so on. A proforma question sheet listing the factors to be recorded would normally be used, incorporating range statements (circumstances in which each task is carried out and standards to which competence is required) and rating scales

(b) **Questionnaires and interviews**, for jobs with longer task cycles and invisible work (planning, relationship management and so on). The job holder would be asked to explain, describe and quantify (as far as possible) the job. His or her supervisor or manager, and other third parties, may be asked to complete the same exercise.

(c) **Diaries, time sheets and other self-recording techniques.** The job holder may be asked periodically to record activity, or may include **critical incidents** highlighting key aspects of the job.

Activity 10   **(15 minutes)**

The fact that a job analysis is being carried out may cause some concern among employees: they may fear that standards will be raised, rates cut, or that the job may be found to be redundant or require rationalisation.

How might the analyst need to carry out his or her work in order to gain their confidence?

5.5   Job description

Definition

A **job description** is a broad description of a job or position at a given time (since jobs are dynamic, subject to change and variation). 'It is a written statement of those facts which are important regarding the duties, responsibilities, and their organisational and operational interrelationships.' (Livy, *Corporate Personnel Management*)

Uses of job description

In **recruitment**, a job description can be used:

(a) To decide what skills (technical, human, conceptual, design or whatever) and qualifications are required of the job holder. When formulating recruitment advertisements, and interviewing an applicant for the job, the interviewer can use the resulting job specification to match the candidate against the job.

(b) To assess whether the job will efficiently utilise the abilities and provide scope for the aspirations of the prospective job holder

(c)   To determine a rate of pay which is fair for the job, if this has not already been decided by some other means

Job descriptions can also be used in other areas of personnel management.

(a)   For job evaluation (used in establishing wage rates)

   (i)   A standard format for analysing jobs makes it easier for evaluators to compare jobs

   (ii) Job descriptions focus attention on the job, not the job holder, which is important in the job evaluation process

   (iii) Job descriptions offer opportunities for the job holder and his manager to discuss any differences of opinion about what the job involves, allowing fairer and more accurate evaluation

(b)   In induction and training, to help new employees to understand the scope and functions of their jobs and to help managers to identify training needs of job holders on an ongoing basis

(c)   To pinpoint weaknesses in the organisation structure (such as overlapping areas of authority, where two or more managers are responsible for the same area of work; areas of work where no manager appears to accept responsibility; areas of work where authority appears to be too centralised or decentralised)

Townsend (*Up the Organisation*) suggested that job descriptions are of limited use.

(a)   They are only suited for jobs where the work is largely repetitive and therefore performed by low-grade employees: once the element of judgement comes into a job description it becomes a straitjacket.

(b)   Management jobs are likely to be constantly changing as external influences impact upon them, so a job description is constantly out of date.

(c)   Job descriptions encourage demarcation disputes, where people adhere strictly to the contents of the job description, rather than responding flexibly to task or organisational requirements: this in turn leads to costly overmanning practices. Many modern organisations are scrapping job descriptions for this reason.

Where job descriptions are used, it should be remembered that:

(a)   A job description is like a photograph, an image 'frozen' at one point in time

(b)   A job description needs constant and negotiated revision

(c)   A job description should be secondary in importance to a customer requirement, quality improvement or problems solved

The contents of a job description

A job description should be clear and to the point, and so ought not to be lengthy. Typically, a job description would show the following.

(a)   **Job title** and department and job code number; the person to whom the job holder is responsible; possibly, the grading of the job.

(b)   **Job summary** - showing in a few paragraphs the major functions and tools, machinery and special equipment used; possibly also a small organisation chart.

(c)   **Job content** - list of the sequence of operations that constitute the job, noting main levels of difficulty. In the case of management work there should be a list of the main duties of the job, indicating frequency of performance - typically between 5 and 15 main duties should be listed. This includes the degree of initiative involved, and the nature of responsibility (for other people, machinery and/or other resources).

(d)   The extent (and limits) of the jobholder's authority and responsibility.

(e)   Statement showing relation of job to other closely associated jobs, including superior and subordinate positions and liaison required with other departments.

(f)   Working hours, basis of pay and benefits, and conditions of employment, including location, special pressures, social isolation, physical conditions, or health hazards.

(g)   Opportunities for training, transfer and promotion.

(h)   Possibly, also, objectives and expected results, which will be compared against actual performance during employee appraisal - although this may be done as a separate exercise, as part of the appraisal process.

(i)   The names and positions of the people/person who has

  (i)   Prepared the job description
  (ii)   Agreed the job description

(j)   Date of preparation.

Two examples of job descriptions are shown below.

JOB DESCRIPTION

1   *Job title:* Baking Furnace Labourer

2   *Department:* 'B' Baking

3   *Date:* 20 November 20X0

4   *Prepared by:* H Crust, Baking Furnace Manager

5   *Responsible to:* Baking Furnace Chargehand

6   *Age range:* 20-40

7   *Supervises work of:* N/A

8   *Has regular co-operative contact with:* Slinger/Crane driver.

9   *Main duties/responsibilities:* Stacking formed electrodes in furnace, packing for stability. Subsequently unloads baked electrodes and prepares furnace for next load.

10   *Working conditions:* Stacking is heavy work and requires some manipulation of 100lb (45kg) electrodes. Unloading is hot (35° - 40°C) and very dusty.

11   *Employment conditions:*

   Wages £2.60 ph + group bonus (average earnings £158.50 pw)
   Hours: Continuous rotating three-shift working days, 6 days on, 2 days off. NB must remain on shift until relieved.
   Trade Union: National Union of Bread Bakers, optional.

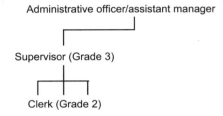

MIDWEST BANK PLC

1   *Job title*:   Clerk (Grade 2)

2   *Branch*:   All branches and administrative offices

3   *Job summary*:   To provide clerical support to activities within the bank

4   *Job content*:   Typical duties will include:

    (a)   Cashier's duties
    (b)   Processing of branch clearing
    (c)   Processing of standing orders
    (d)   Support to branch management

5   *Reporting structure*:

Administrative officer/assistant manager

Supervisor (Grade 3)

Clerk (Grade 2)

6   *Experience/Education*: Experience not required, minimum 3 GCSEs or equivalent.

7   *Training to be provided*: Initial on-the-job training plus regular formal courses and training.

8   *Hours*: 38 hours per week

9   *Objectives and appraisal*: Annual appraisal in line with objectives above.

10   *Salary*: Refer to separate standard salary structure.

Job description prepared by: Head office personnel department

5.6   Personnel specification

Definition

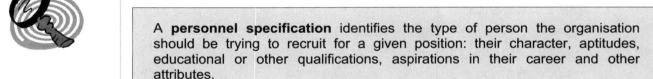

A **personnel specification** identifies the type of person the organisation should be trying to recruit for a given position: their character, aptitudes, educational or other qualifications, aspirations in their career and other attributes.

Professor Alec Rodger was a pioneer of the systematic approach to recruitment and selection in Britain. He suggested that:

> If matching *[ie of demands of the job and the person who is to perform it]* is to be done satisfactorily, the requirements of an occupation (or job) must be described in the same terms as the aptitudes of the people who are being considered for it.

This was the basis for the formulation of the personnel specification as a way of matching people to jobs on the basis of comparative sets of data: defining job requirements and personal suitability along the same lines.

The *Seven Point Plan* put forward by Professor Rodger in 1951 draws the selector's attention to seven points about the candidate:

(a)   Physical attributes (such as neat appearance, ability to speak clearly and without impediment)

(b)   Attainment (including educational qualifications)

(c)   General intelligence

    (d)   Special aptitudes (such as neat work, speed and accuracy)

    (e)   Interests (practical and social)

    (f)   Disposition (or manner: friendly, helpful and so on)

    (g)   Background circumstances

Munro Fraser's *Five Point Pattern of Personality* (1966) draws the selector's attention to:

    (a)   Impact on others, including physical attributes, speech and manner

    (b)   Acquired knowledge or qualifications⋆, including education, training and work experience

    (c)   Innate ability, including mental agility, aptitude for learning

    (d)   Motivation: individual goals, demonstrated effort and success at achieving them

    (e)   Adjustment: emotional stability, tolerance of stress, human relations skills

    ⋆Most personnel specifications include achievements in education, because there appears to be a strong correlation between management potential and higher education.

Note that the personnel specification includes job requirements in terms of a candidate's:

    (a)   Capacities - what he is *capable* of
    (b)   Inclinations - what he *will* do

In other words, behavioural versatility must be accounted for by considering not only the individual's mental and physical attributes, but his current attitudes, values, beliefs, goals and circumstances - all of which will influence his response to work demands.

Each feature in the specification should be classified as:

    (a)   **Essential**- for instance, honesty in a cashier is essential whilst a special aptitude for conceptual thought is not

    (b)   **Desirable** - for instance, a reasonably pleasant manner should ensure satisfactory standards in a person dealing with the public

    (c)   **Contra-indicated** - some features are actively disadvantageous, such as an inability to work in a team when acting as project leader

---

EXAMPLE

PERSONNEL SPECIFICATION: Customer Accounts Manager

	ESSENTIAL	DESIRABLE	CONTRA-INDICATED
Physical attributes	Clear speech Well-groomed Good health	Age 25-40	Age under 25 Chronic ill-health and absence
Attainments	2 'A' levels GCSE Maths and English Thorough knowledge of retail environment	Degree (any discipline) Marketing training 2 years' experience in supervisory post	No experience of supervision or retail environment

Intelligence	High verbal intelligence		
Aptitudes	Facility with numbers Attention to detail and accuracy Social skills for customer relations	Analytical abilities (problem solving) Understanding of systems and IT	No mathematical ability Low tolerance of technology
Interests	Social: team activity		Time-consuming hobbies 'Solo' interests only
Disposition	Team player Persuasive Tolerance of pressure and change	Initiative	Anti-social Low tolerance of responsibility
Circumstances	Able to work late, take work home	Located in area of office	

Limitations of personnel specifications

As our example suggests, a wide number of variables may be included in a personnel specification. If it is not used flexibly, however, and the specification fails to evolve as business and employment conditions change, it may swiftly lose its relevance. For example:

(a) Attainments are often focused on educational achievements, since there has traditionally been a strong correlation between management potential and higher education. However, as recent editions of *People Management* suggest, graduate recruitment is now in crisis, as more people enter higher education, with more diverse educational backgrounds, and more diverse educational standards.

(b) 'Physical attributes' and 'background circumstances' may suggest criteria which can now be interpreted as discriminatory, to the disabled (in the case of a speech impairment, say) or to women (for example, the ability of women with family responsibilities to undertake full-time employment). As Ted Johns notes: 'In the 1990s, employers and recruiters are much more sensitised to the damaging implications of such issues'.

(c) The category of 'general intelligence' has traditionally been based on 'IQ', a narrow definition of intelligence as mental dexterity. It is now accepted that there are at least seven different intelligences, not least of which (according to Charles Handy, *The Hungry Spirit*) are emotional, intuitive, practical and interpersonal intelligence, which are key factors in the new fluid, horizontal business world.

FOR DISCUSSION

'Forget loyalty and conformity. We can't afford narrow-skill people' (Rosabeth Moss Kantor). What does this say about the concept of the desirable **disposition** for an employee? What kind of characteristics may now take the place of loyalty and conformity?

In addition, personnel specifications were explicitly developed in order to match the aptitudes of job applicants to 'the requirements of an occupation (or job)' (Rodger). To the extent that 'the job' (let alone 'the occupation') no longer exists, meaningful personnel specifications will be difficult to devise. If employees are recruited and deployed on a project or consultancy basis, a different package of attributes will be required for each project in each organisation. The individual therefore needs a flexible, multi-functional résumé, as much as the organisation needs a flexible menu-driven way of assessing available labour (internal and external).

Competency profiles, based on key success factors in a given business or sector, offer one such approach. They can be linked directly to the organisation's strategic objectives. They are more readily adaptable to changing circumstances and requirements, since they are non-prescriptive about task specifics. William Bridges (*Jobshift*) suggests a 'portfolio' of competencies embracing skills in selling, negotiating and time management, as well as more specific task-related skills. Competencies can be made applicable to employees at all levels of the organisation hierarchy (although the specific behaviours expected will vary), which also helps to create an integrated organisation culture based on central values and attributes.

5.7 Recruitment methods and media:external

A number of methods are available to organisations to contract and market themselves to potential candidates. These can be summarised as follows.

Method	*Evaluation*	
(a) **Unsolicited requests:** Write-ins or walk-ins (Media: word-of mouth, recommendation, previous recruitment advertising, general employer branding	**Advantages:** **Disadvantages:**	Inexpensive. Pre-selected for enthusiasm, initiative Open **walk-in** policy may encourage application where job difficult to fill Needs control and systematic application handling
(b) **Existing contacts;** Previous (re-employable) em-ployees; retirees; career break; previous applicants of suitable general quality held on file.	**Advantages:** **Disadvantages:**	work behaviour/attributes known; may be amenable to part-time, temporary or flexible working Needs systematic database manage-ment
(c) **Referrals:** Registers of members seeking employment, kept eg by trade unions and professional bodies	**Advantages:** **Disadvantages:**	Pre-selection at low cost Indirectly discriminative
(d) **Agencies** **Job Centres:** Network of agencies provided by central government: particularly for manual and junior positions in admin/clerical/retail	**Advantages:** **Disadvantages:**	Free Local and national Socially responsible (not-for-profit) Register limited to unemployed Require relationship/selection management
Resettlement Services: Finding civilian positions for armed forces personnel at end of service	**Advantages:** **Disadvantages:**	Can be highly trained/experienced Inexperience in civilian culture?

Method	Evaluation	
Careers Services: Placing graduates of schools and training institutions	**Advantages:**	Potential for young unsocialised recruits Potential for preview through work placements Financial incentives (government schemes such as YT, Apex) Potential for strong relationship – selection preference, curriculum influence
	Disadvantages	Recruits may lack experience Administration of work-experience Possible indirect discrimination
Employment Agencies: Wide range of specialising agencies; temporary agencies for one-off requirements and short-term cover (eg of maternity or sick leave	**Advantages:**	May undertake pre-screening Temp agencies facilitate flexible working
	Disadvantages:	Quality can vary Cost
(e) **Consultancies** **Selection consultants:** Recruit and select for positions; may cover clerical/admin staff, specialist staff (media, financial etc), or managerial	**Advantages:**	Reduces administration for employer Specialist selection skills Wide-ranging contacts
	Disadvantages:	Cost May lack awareness of organisation's culture, values, detailed criteria Excludes internal applicants Lack of accountability
Outplacement consultants: Registers, retraining etc to help redundant and early-retired employees	**Advantages:**	Perceived socially responsible Provide some training
	Disadvantages:	Quality varies
Search consultants: 'Head hunters'. Networking to track highly employable individuals: candidates proactively approached	**Advantages:**	Selects for high employability networking, exploration opportunity
	Disadvantages:	Cost Limited range Organisation may be victim as well as beneficiary!
(f) **Direct to source:** Schools, colleges, universities (Media: advertisement, 'milk-round' presentation)	**Advantages:**	Networking relationships Opportunities to preview via work placement, 'gap' year etc Access to graduates in desirable (scarce) disciplines
	Disadvantages:	Local catchment area Tends to be annual 'season' Recruits lack experience Potential for indirect discrimination
(g) **The Internet:** Wide range of recruitment databases	**Advantages:**	IT-literate users Pre-selection through employer information database World-wide catchment
	Disadvantages:	Difficulty of verification Competition

EXAMPLE: INTERNATIONAL COMPARISONS

In some countries of the EU, recruitment consultants are used extensively. In other (eg Spain and Germany) they are banned, other than for the purposes of advising on recruitment methods and assisting in selection: they cannot actively place staff in organisations.

Activity 11   **(1 hour)**

We have already mentioned some of the 'media' by which an organisation can advertise or make known its staffing needs by the methods listed above. Brainstorm as a full list as you can of advertising/information media relevant to recruitment. For each of the media you mention, add any advantages or disadvantages you can think of.

The recruitment advertisement

The object of recruitment advertising is to home in on the target market of labour, and to attract interest in the organisation and the job.

In a way, it is already part of the **selection** process. The advertisement will be placed where suitable people are likely to see it (say, internally only - immediately pre-selecting members of the organisation - or in a specialist journal, pre-selecting those specialists). It will be worded in a way that further weeds out people who would not be suitable for the job (or for whom the job would not be suitable). Be aware however, that some such forms of pre-selection may be construed as discriminatory if it disadvantages some groups more than others. (Advertising internally only, where the current workforce is overwhelmingly male, may be construed as indirectly discriminatory to women, for example.)

The way in which a job is advertised will depend on the type of organisation and the type of job.

A factory is likely to advertise a vacancy for an unskilled worker in a different way to a company advertising for a CIPD-qualified person for a senior HR position. Managerial jobs may merit national advertisement, whereas semi- or un-skilled jobs may only warrant local coverage, depending on the supply of suitable candidates in the local area. Specific skills may be most appropriately reached through trade, technical or professional journals.

The advertisement, based on information set out in the job description, job and person specifications and recruitment policy, should contain information about:

(a)   The organisation: its main business and location, at least

(b)   The job: title, main duties and responsibilities and special features

(c)   Conditions: special factors affecting the job

(d)   Qualifications and experience (required, and preferred); other attributes, aptitudes and/or knowledge required

(e)   Rewards: salary, (**negotiable**, if appropriate) benefits, opportunities for training, career development, and so on

(f)   Application: how to apply, to whom, and by what date

The advertisement should encourage a degree of **self-selection,** so that the target population begins to narrow itself down. (The information contained in the advertisement should deter unsuitable applicants as well as encourage potentially suitable ones.) It should also reflect the desired image of the organisation in the outside world: its employer brand.

EXAMPLES

HR Generalist   £50,000

A high calibre generalist is sought by a leading investment bank. Duties include employee relations, performance management, compensation and benefits as well as recruitment. Suitable candidates need 5+ years' experience, ideally gained within financial services.

Email harrietguerrini@joslinrowe.com

HR Officer   to £35,000

A City based Bank requires seeks a HR officer with c3 years' experience. This generalist role includes recruitment and selection, employee relations and management reporting. Strong communication skills are essential, to undertake extensive internal liaison.

Email khadinebenkirane@joslinrowe.com

C&B Administrator   to £30,000

Leading European Bank requires an experienced C&B administrator with at least 2 years' experience. The successful candidate will have proven experience administering payroll and benefits. Strong organisational skills are essential.

Email khadinebenkirane@joslinrowe.com

Recruitment Officer   c£30,000

A prestigious financial institution seeks a recruiter with at least 3 years' experience to deliver a high quality recruitment services. Activities include screening CV's, interviewing applicants, liaising with client groups as well as writing job descriptions.

Email harrietguerrini@joslinrowe.com

Contact us for many further permanent and interim management vacancies.

AT MILTON KEYNES

'NO' ISN'T A WORD WE LIKE TO USE

We'd much rather give the thumbs up to new ideas and new innovations. And in our forward-thinking HR department, that's exactly what we're doing.

It's all part of the Council's wider aims to change the way local government operates. Embracing new legislation and bringing our services closer to internal and external clients alike, we're adopting a real business focus - and shaping some bold plans for the future. If you're MCIPD qualified, have a record of continued professional development and you're aware of the wider issues confronting a Council like ours, they're plans you could share in.

HUMAN RESOURCES OFFICER - OPERATIONS

£22,194 - £26,091 REF: R01331

You'll be part of our central HR operation, ensuring that all our services run smoothly and effectively - as well as contributing to the overall development of the department. We'll also look to you to provide Council-wide advice on everything from employment legislation to HR procedure, calling on at least 3 years' generalist human resources experience, a background in trade union liaison and proven communication skills. Requests for full/part-time or term-time only are welcome.

HUMAN RESOURCES OFFICER - EMPLOYEE RELATIONS

£22,194 - £26,091 REF: R01332

You'll be reviewing, developing and undertaking briefings on HR policies; advising managers and HR colleagues on policies and employment legislation; trade union consultation; reviewing and monitoring the Occupational Health contract. You will have at least 3 years' human resources experience.

CLOSING DATE: 16 OCTOBER 2000.

Further information and application forms are available by telephoning (01908) 253344 or 253462 (answerphone service available 24 hours per day) or by writing to HR Recruitment Team, Milton Keynes Council, Saxon Court, 502 Avebury Boulevard, Milton Keynes MK9 3HS. Minicom (01908) 252727 (office hours only) or e-mail: Helen.Davey@milton-keynes.gov.uk

PLEASE QUOTE THE APPROPRIATE REFERENCE.

MILTON KEYNES
COUNCIL

EXAMPLE: INTERNATIONAL COMPARISONS

The law on recruitment varies internationally. For example:

- In France and Belgium, it is illegal to use press advertisements for (non-existent) job vacancies for the purposes of corporate image advertising.

- In France, job advertisements cannot lawfully specify an upper age limit for applicants. ('Ageism' is still under voluntary self-regulation in the UK.)

- In Italy, job advertisements have to comply with the State Workers' Statute, forbidding criteria on grounds of political views, union membership or religion (as well as race).

- In Spain, the state employment service is (in theory) supposed to vet all job advertisements for discriminatory intentions.

5.8 Recruitment methods and media: internal

Internal advertising of vacancies may be a requirement for some organisations, under agreements negotiated with trade unions. Advertising media include noticeboards (paper and electronic – for example via corporate intranet), in-house journals, memoranda to supervisors/managers soliciting recommendations and observation and word-of-mouth (the **grapevine**).

Methods of **internal recruitment** include:

(a) Advertising for self-applicants

(b) Soliciting recommendations from supervisors/managers, training officers and so on

(c) Soliciting referrals by existing employees to family, friends and contacts

(d) Formal succession, promotion and transfer planning

Most of these methods incur little extra cost, being based on existing or easily accessible information about the candidate's abilities, attitudes and so on.

5.9 Recruitment within the EU

As we mentioned in Paragraph 3.2, the free mobility of labour within the European Economic Area raises the possibility of cross-border recruitment. Many of the methods and media discussed above (Paragraph 5.7) can be extended to European media, contacts, consultancies and educational institutions. The cross-border recruiter will, however need to be familiar with:

(a) Recruitment law and practice in EU countries

(b) The relative status and curriculum content of EU countries' educational, vocational and professional qualifications

(c) Levels of pay and conditions of service necessary to comply with relevant legislation and to attract suitable applicants

5.10 Evaluation of the process

An evaluation of recruitment and selection procedures will aim to determine whether the procedures succeeded in getting a *suitable* person into a job, at the *time* when the person was required and at an acceptable cost. At a more strategic level, it determines whether recruitment and selection procedures are succeeding in achieving the organisation's overall manpower plan.

Connock suggests that auditing the recruitment process can occur at four levels.

(a) **Performance indicators** should be established for each stage of the process. Data can be collected about actual performance and compared with the standards. As Connock says 'Significant variations from the established standards will need to be individually investigated, and remedial action initiated if necessary. Remedial action might include extra staffing for the recruitment section if turn-round times are not being met. One of the major causes of candidate demotivation is a slow turn round of applications'.

(b) **Cost-effectiveness** of the various methods used should be measured. It may be that a certain advertising medium is too costly for the number of worthwhile responses it generates. Advertising in the national press, for example, may generate a large number of responses, but few of the required quality; meanwhile an insertion in a professional journal may, with a smaller circulation, generate a higher proportion of potentially suitable candidates.

Activity 12   **(20 minutes)**

What kind of information would you need to record in order to appraise the cost-effectiveness of a recruitment method/medium? Aim to end up with a meaningful figure for the cost per person appointed (and actually entering employment).

(c) **Monitoring the make up of the workforce** and the impact on its constitution of new recruits is essential as part of an equal opportunities policy. This will identify areas where certain groups are under-represented, for example women, disabled people or ethnic minorities. The reasons for this should be investigated and eliminated.

(d) Finally, Connock suggests conducting an **attitude survey** amongst staff who have been recruited to find out whether they were satisfied with the various stages of their recruitment and selection – did they feel that the job advertisement they responded to gave them a fair idea of the nature of the job, were they frustrated by the length of time they had to wait for a decision and so on.

Other methods of evaluating recruitment and selection include 'benchmarking' – comparing the organisation's systems with known example of good practice used in other organisations.

Where a personnel department has adopted the notion of the 'internal customer', it can seek the views of its customers (line managers) and users (job applicants).

Some specific **performance indicators** for evaluating recruitment procedures are as follows.

(a) Total numbers of applications received
(b) Time taken to locate applicants
(c) Cost per applicant
(d) Time taken to process applications/per application
(e) Number of female/minority/disabled applicants
(f) Number of qualified applicants (matching advertised criteria)
(g) Number of qualified female/minority/disabled applicants

NOTES

These basically assess the effectiveness and cost-efficiency of recruitment advertising, equal opportunities policy in recruitment and recruitment administration. Post-entry criteria – such as number of offers extended per source/method or in relation to applications received, cost and time of training recruits, subsequent job performance and length of service of recruits and so on – may only be applied after the selection process. However, they also reflect on recruitment retrospectively.

Chapter roundup

- The labour market consists of potential employees, both internal and external to the organisation.
- Many important facts about a country's demographic profile are collected by government. These include population size, age structure, sex distribution, ethnicity and regional distribution.
- Demographic trends have important implications for personnel management, especially the falling number of young people in the workforce, the rising number of female and older workers, and national/regional education trends.
- The European labour scene and international situation are of increasing importance to personnel practitioners in the UK, particularly with the freedom of movement of labour guaranteed within the European Economic Area.
- Recruitment is concerned with defining job requirements and attracting suitable applicants. Selection is concerned with fitting the person to the job.

- The essential points in this chapter can be summarised in diagrammatic form.

Cont...

NOTES

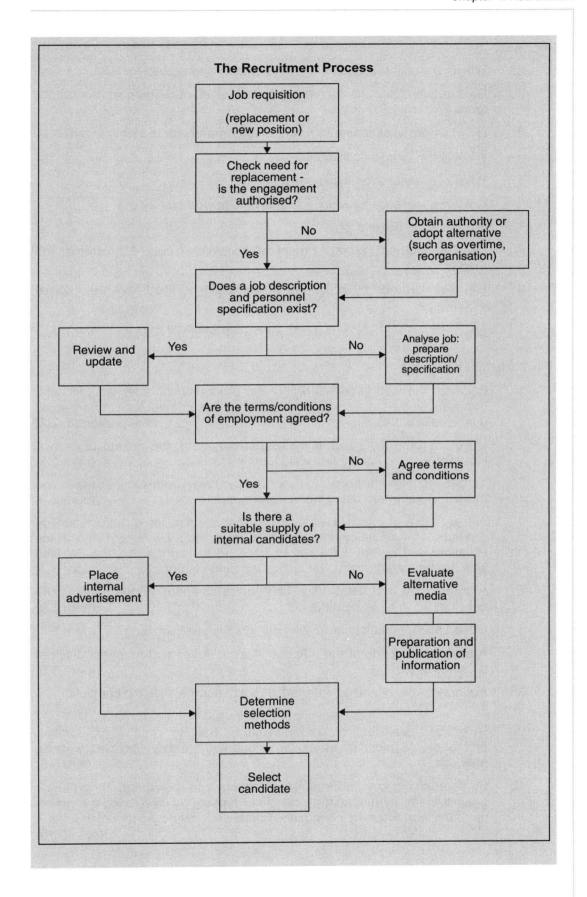

The Recruitment Process

Job requisition

(replacement or new position)

↓

Check need for replacement - is the engagement authorised?

No →

Obtain authority or adopt alternative (such as overtime, reorganisation)

Yes ↓

Does a job description and personnel specification exist?

Yes ← → No

Review and update

Analyse job: prepare description/ specification

↓

Are the terms/conditions of employment agreed?

No →

Agree terms and conditions

Yes ↓

Is there a suitable supply of internal candidates?

Yes ← → No

Place internal advertisement

Evaluate alternative media

↓

Preparation and publication of information

↓

Determine selection methods

↓

Select candidate

BPP
PUBLISHING

NOTES

Quick quiz

1 Why is the shift towards an ageing population important for HRP?

2 Give reasons for the increased participation of women in the labour force.

3 How can organisations make sure their demands for labour are met?

4 What is the '*Bossa* decision'?

5 What is a 'multinational company'?

6 List three methods by which job analysis may be carried out.

7 What is a job description?

8 List five methods of recruitment of candidates from the external job market.

9 List four methods by which vacancies could be filled from the internal labour pool.

10 List three methods by which recruitment procedures may be evaluated.

Answers to quick quiz

1 Because the workforce will reflect the proportion of older workers, and because of the corresponding decline in the number of young people available to work.   (see paragraph 2.2)

2 More part-time jobs, higher male unemployment, the growth of service industry, women having first child later in life.   (para 2.3)

3 Target recruitment more precisely, employ and train older workers, be more flexible on recruiting women workers.   (para 2.3)

4 A legal case in which it was shown that a claim for discrimination on grounds of nationality can be brought in the UK under the Race Relations Act by any EEA citizen applying for work within the EU who was discriminated against by a decision made in the UK.   (para 3.2)

5 A company with a head office and parent company in one country and subsidiaries in other countries.   (para 3.3)

6 Observation, questionnaire/interview, diaries/self-recording   (para 5.4)

7 A broad description of the purpose, scope, duties and responsibilities of a particular job.   (para 5.5)

8 Agencies, consultancies, Internet, direct to source, existing contacts.
                                                                    (para 5.7)

9 Retention, transfer or redeployment, training and development, promotion, exploiting employee contracts and/or flexible working methods.   (para 5.8)

10 By determining key performance indicators and monitoring performance against them; by measuring cost-effectiveness; by monitoring the make-up of the workforce; by conducting attitude surveys; by benchmarking.
                                                                    (para 5.10)

Answers to activities

1 The answer is: whatever your research led you to!

2 Again the answer is whatever you found!

3   The increasing participation of women may be related to:

    (a)   An increase in the availability of part time jobs (which are more accessible to women with family responsibilities)

    (b)   Male unemployment arising from the decline of traditional 'smokestack' industries (such as steel) which had a male workforce

    (c)   The growth of the service sector which offers non-manual labour

    (d)   An increase in the average age at which women have their first child

    (e)   Growing awareness of the need to recruit women, to compensate for the demographic downturn in other areas eg young people

    (f)   Growing initiatives aimed at enabling women to work: child care, term-time contracts; career break schemes; maternity leave; fast-tracking of women in management; education/training of women (in assertiveness, management etc as well as job skills) and so on

4   Stephen Connock suggests six steps by which organisations can cope with these demographic and educational trends.

    (1)   Establish what labour market the organisation is in (eg young people, part-time workers).

    (2)   Discover the organisation's catchment areas (ie location of potential recruits).

    (3)   Discern the supply side trends in the catchment area labour force. (For example, how many school leavers are expected? What is the rate of growth/decline of local population?)

    (4)   Examine education trends in the location.

    (5)   Assess the demand from other employers for the skills you need. (For example, if there is a large concentration of, say, electronics companies in the region, then they will be interested in hiring people with similar skills).

    (6)   Try to assess whether some of your demand can be satisfied by a supply from other sources.

5   Barriers to a global labour market include: language; culture (eg the fact that women are discouraged from certain jobs in some cultures); differences in employment law and practice; recognition of education/training qualifications; market rates of pay in different currencies (and cost of currency dealings); different expectations of working conditions; personal attachment of workers to family/home.

6   It is often difficult to persuade departmental managers to agree to the promotion of a subordinate out of the department, especially if he/she has been selected as having particular ability: the department will be losing an able member, and will have to find, induct and train a replacement. Moreover, if the manager's resistance were made known, there would be a motivational problem to contend with. The personnel manager will have to be able to back his/her recommendation with sound policies for providing and training a replacement with as little loss of the department's efficiency as possible.

7   Where the organisation has the choice, it should consider the following points.

(a) Management will be familiar with an internal promotee: there will be detailed appraisal information available from employee records. The outside recruit will to a greater extent be an unknown quantity – and the organisation will be taking a greater risk of unacceptable personality or performance emerging later.

(b) A promotee has already worked within the organisation and will be familiar with its:

   (i) Culture, or philosophy; informal rules and norms as well as stated policy

   (ii) Politics; power-structures and relationships

   (iii) Systems and procedures

   (iv) Objectives

   (v) Other personnel (who will likewise be familiar with him/her)

(c) Promotion of insiders is visible proof of the organisation's willingness to develop people's careers. This may well have an encouraging and motivating effect. Outsiders may well invite resentment.

(d) Internal advertisement of vacancies contributes to the implementation of equal opportunities policies. Many women are employed in secretarial and clerical jobs from which promotion is unlikely – and relatively few are in higher-graded roles. Internal advertising could become a route for opening up opportunities for women at junior levels.

(e) On the other hand, an organisation must retain its ability to adapt, grow and change, and this may well require new blood, wider views, fresh ideas. Insiders may be too socialised into the prevailing culture to see faults or be willing to 'upset the apple cart' where necessary for the organisation's health.

8 (a) The overall priorities and requirements of the organisation will be more clearly recognised and met, rather than the objectives of sub-systems such as individual departments.

   (b) There will be a control reference point for communication, queries and applications from outside the organisation.

   (c) Communication with the environment will also be more standardised, and will be more likely to reinforce the overall corporate image of the organisation.

   (d) Potential can be spotted in individuals and utilised in the optimum conditions – not necessarily in the post for which the individual has applied, if he or she might be better suited to another vacant post.

   (e) The volume of administration and the need for specialist knowledge (notably of changing legal and industrial relations requirements) may suggest a specialist function.

   (f) Standardisation and central control should be applied to, for example, equal opportunities, pay provisions and performance standards, where fairness must be seen to operate.

9 This is another task intended to develop your research skills and your awareness of HR practice in a specific organisation – starting with your own.

NOTES

10 The job analyst will need to gain their confidence by:

(a) Communicating: explaining the process, methods and purpose of the appraisal

(b) Being thorough and competent in carrying out the analysis

(c) Respecting the work flow of the department, which should not be disrupted

(d) Giving feedback on the results of the appraisal, and the achievement of its objectives. If staff are asked to co-operate in developing a framework for office training, and then never hear anything more about it, they are unlikely to be responsive on a later occasion

11 Some of the media you may have come up with include the following.

(a)	Newspapers and journals (trade, professional) – ie 'Press' media	• Journals better targeted, papers offer wider local or national coverage • Wider and more targeted coverage – higher cost: cost-effectiveness must be monitored, controlled • May offer opportunity to produce own artwork – may not (control required)
(b)	Cinema, radio, TV – ie 'broadcast' media	• Can offer general marketing opportunity • Powerful all-senses effect • Expensive (especially TV) • Mass coverage (option of local) • Appeal to young audience
(c)	Posters, leaflets, notices on notice boards (+ multi-media equivalents: cassettes, videos)	• Targeting through positioning only • Can be expensive, hit-and-miss, long timescale • Content/style controlled by organisation
(d)	Exhibitions, conferences, roadshows, open-days, presentations	• If well targeted location, can reach large number of relevant people • Opportunities for non-committal networking, exploration • Immediacy of face to face communication – but also a risk • Can be expensive to organise/delegate
(e)	Web-sites	• Untargeted (except to IT-literate) • Controllable • Relatively low-cost • Opportunity for general marketing

12 Connock suggests that a framework such as that shown below be used to determine the cost per person appointed for each method.

Source of application	Number of applications	Number of shortlisted candidates	Number offered job	Number commenced employment	Total cost	Cost per head appointed
Local press advert National press advert Specialist press advert Leaflet drop etc						
Total						

BPP
PUBLISHING

Activity 4 (1½ hours)

Rottenborough District Hospital

You are the Human Resources Manager at Rottenborough District Hospital, a major general hospital in Cambridgeshire. In spite of the recession you are finding it increasingly difficult as an organisation to recruit non-professional staff, namely auxiliary and care assistants. Staff recruited to these positions in the past have traditionally been women in their 30s and 40s. While your commitment to equal opportunities obviously means that you welcome applications from both sexes and all ages, you are aware that this is your target group and you must somehow make Rottenborough District Hospital a more attractive place to work in for these women.

You know that the NHS is suffering external pressures which impinge on staffing issues. For example, you are losing a considerable number of staff, both professional and non-professional, to NHS Trust status hospitals. You have also read a lot about the demographic timebomb, which leads you to believe that it won't be long before your target group becomes everybody's. Thirdly, and related to the second point, the country is faced with the task of dealing with an ageing population who will inevitably require more health care. This will have an obvious and powerful impact on any human resource planning you undertake. Indeed, you find yourself working in one of the very few growth industries in Britain: the NHS has predicted some 100,000 vacancies across the board by the turn of the century.

Your main problem, therefore, is to find ways to improve the 3Rs: the recruitment, retention and return of staff into your organisation. This is not easy because you already offer good maternity benefits, compassionate leave, sick pay, pensions and relocation packages. Write a report to your director of human resources outlining alternative ways in which you can attract, keep and encourage back your target group.

Chapter 5 :
SELECTION

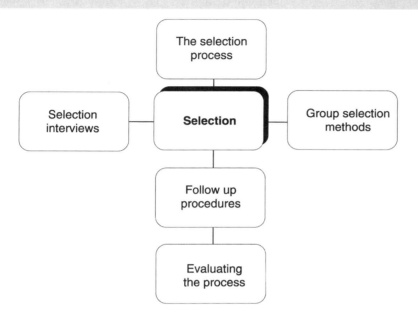

Introduction

As suggested in the Introduction to Chapter 4, selection is the part of the employee resourcing process which follows on from recruitment. It essentially involves the identifying of the most suitable of the potential employees attracted to the organisation by recruitment efforts. (In practice, this may be a negative process of weeding out people who are **unsuitable** for the job or organisation – or people for whom the job or organisation may be unsuitable.)

The selection of the right candidate(s) is of vital importance. No organisation wants to find that it has rejected out of hand someone who goes on to be a 'star' for another (possibly competing) organisation, any more than it wants to get 'stuck' with an employee who can't do the job and doesn't fit in – but who looked perfect in the interview! Various selection methods are used to try to reduce the risks by gathering as much relevant information about the candidate as possible, and we will evaluate some of the main approaches.

Your objectives

In this chapter you will learn about the following:

    (a)   The selection procedures used for two different organisations

    (b)   The implementation of selection practice in the UK and elsewhere

    (c)   A systematic approach to selection

    (d)   The limitations and strengths of a range of selection methods.

1 THE SELECTION PROCESS

1.1 A systematic approach

A typical selection system will include the following basic procedures.

(a) Take any **initial steps** required. If the decision to interview or reject cannot be made immediately, a standard letter of acknowledgement might be sent, as a courtesy, to each applicant. It may be that the job advertisement required applicants to write to the personnel manager with personal details and to request an application form: this would then be sent to applicants for completion and return.

(b) Set each application against **key criteria** in the job advertisement and specification. Critical factors may include age, qualifications, experience or whatever.

(c) **Sort applications** into 'possible', 'unsuitable' and 'marginal'.

(d) 'Possibles' will then be more closely scrutinised, and a **shortlist for interview** drawn up. Ideally, this should be done by both the HR specialist and the prospective manager of the successful candidate, who will have more immediate knowledge of the type of person that will fit into the culture and activities of his department.

(e) Invite candidates for **interviews** (requiring them to complete an application form, if this has not been done at an earlier stage). Again, if large numbers of interviewees are involved, standard letters should be used (pre-printed, or prepared on a word processor using the direct mail facility).

(f) Interview potentially qualified candidates.

(g) Reinforce interviews with **selection testing** if suitable.

(h) Check the **references** of short-listed candidates.

(i) Institute **follow-up procedures** for successful applicants.

    (i) Make an **offer of employment**, negotiating terms and conditions if appropriate.

    (ii) Draw up a **contract** or **written particulars of employment**.

    (iii) Arrange **work permits** and related issues of residency, if required by cross-border recruitment.

    (iv) Plan initial **induction** into the organisation and provide preparatory information if required.

(j) Review un-interviewed 'possibles', and 'marginals', and put potential future candidates on **hold** or in reserve

(k) Send standard letters to **unsuccessful applicants**, informing them simply that they have not been successful.

    (i) 'Rejects' should be briefly, but tactfully, dismissed: 'Thank you for your interest in the post of ... We have given your application careful consideration. I regret to inform you, however, that we have decided not to ask you to attend for an interview. The standard of application was very high...'.

    (ii) Reserves will be sent a holding letter: 'We will keep your details on file, and should any suitable vacancy arise in future...'.

The aim of the recruitment process, as we discussed in Chapter 4, is applications by suitably qualified candidates. What form might an application take, in order for it to be fed into the selection process?

1.2 Applications

Applications for a particular advertised (or unadvertised) vacancy, or for employment in the organisation as and when vacancies arise, may be received in various forms.

(a) **Unsolicited letter, e-mail, 'walk-in' or other enquiry**. This would normally be responded to with a request for the following.

(b) **Application form**

    (i) For lower-level, relatively standardised jobs, for which a high volume of applicants is expected, this may be a brief, directly targeted form (focusing on qualifications and experience considered essential to the job) in order to facilitate ruthless weeding out of unsuitable applicants, and requiring minimal discretion, self-expression and time in both completion and interpretation.

    (ii) For managerial, specialist or culturally-driven jobs, a more complex application form or package may be used, in order to elicit more complex responses: biographical/psychological ('biodata') questionnaires, guided self-expression, samples for hand-writing analysis, preliminary testing (an account of job problem-solving, or response to case-study scenarios, say) and so on. Such in-depth tools for pre-selection save time and effort at the interview stage, but are time-consuming to prepare and analyse, and should be subjected to cost-benefit considerations.

(c) **Curriculum vitae (CV)** or **resumé**, usually accompanied by a **covering letter** drawing the recruiter's attention to specific vacancy – or organisation - relevant aspects of the applicants' CV. The CV is essentially a brief, systematic summary of the applicant's qualifications, previous work experience and relevant skills/interests/requirements, plus details of individuals willing to vouch for his or her performance, character and employability (**referees**).

The application form or CV will be used to find out relevant information about the applicant, in order to decide, at the initial sifting stage:

(a) Whether the applicant is obviously unsuitable for the job or

(b) Whether the applicant might be of the right calibre, and worth inviting to interview

The application form will be designed by the organisation, and if it is to be useful in the sifting process, it should fulfil the following criteria.

(a) It should ask questions which will elicit information about the applicant and which can be directly compared with the requirements of the job. For example, if the personnel specification requires a minimum of 2 'A' Level passes the application form should ask for details of the applicant's educational qualifications. It should likewise discourage irrelevant and unnecessarily lengthy responses.

(b) For managerial, interpersonal and culturally-driven jobs – requiring particular values, orientations and attributes – it should also give applicants the opportunity to write about themselves, their career ambitions or why they want the job. It might be possible to obtain some information about their:

(i)   Organisational abilities

       (ii)   Intelligence

       (iii)   Ability to express themselves in writing

       (iv)   Motivation

       (v)   Self-image and values

(c)   It should convey a professional, accurate and favourable impression of the organisation, a public relations and employer branding tool.

(d)   It should elicit any information required to enable the organisation subsequently to monitor and evaluate the success of its recruitment procedures (in regard to numbers of female, minority and disabled applicants, number of applications per source and so on).

An example of a basic application form is given on the next page.

Activity 1　　　　　　　　　　　　　　　　　　　　　　　　**(20 minutes)**

Suggest four other ways in which an application form could be **badly** designed (both in appearance and content). You may be able to do this from personal experience.

1.3　Issues in selection

Some of the key HR issues arising in the selection process are as follows.

Discrimination

Detailed provisions in regard to equal opportunities will be discussed in Part B of this Course Book, since it is an area of relevance throughout the HR policy and practice. However, in regard to selection, you should be aware of the following.

NOTES

EXAMPLE

APPLICATION FORM

Post applied for: ....   Code: [Source in which advertised]

Surname: Mr/Mrs/Miss/Ms   First names:
Address:

Post Code: Telephone

Age: Date of birth: /   /
Nationality: Marital status:

EDUCATION AND TRAINING

Place of education (including schools after 11 years)	Dates	Examinations passed / qualifications

EXPERIENCE

Name of employer and main business	Position held	Main duties	From	To

OTHER INFORMATION

Please note your hobbies and interests, and any other information you would like to give about yourself or your experience

State of health (include any disability)

May we contact any of your previous employers?   Yes   No

If yes, please give the contact details of any referees to whom we may apply.

If selected, I would be able to from   /   /   .

I declare that the above information is correct to the best of my knowledge

Signed:_____   Date: _____

(a)   **Application forms** should include no questions which are not work-related (such as marital or domestic details) unless they are asked of all applicants/groups.

Medical references should not be required exclusively from older applicants (according to a 1999 Code of Practice on Age Diversity in Employment).

(b) **Interview procedures** and documentation should be carefully controlled to avoid discrimination. For example:

    (i) a non work-related question must be asked of all candidates, if any, and even then, should not imply discriminatory intent (by asking only women about care of dependants, or about hormonal influences on moods, say)

    (ii) at least one representative of both sexes and all races of applicants should be invited for interview

    (iii) detailed notes of proceedings, criteria and decisions should be made in order to furnish justification in the event of a claim of discrimination

(c) **Selection tests** should demonstrably avoid favouring particular groups (although this is a contentious area, as we will see in Paragraph 3.3 below).

Note that UK legislation outlaws discrimination on the grounds of sex, or change of sex, sexual orientation and marital status; colour, rate, nationality, ethnic or national origin; disability; and conviction for criminal offences (once the conviction is 'spent'). In addition, there is a voluntary Code of Practice seeking to discourage discrimination on the basis of age. In each case, there are strictly defined exceptions, such as:

(a) **'genuine occupational qualifications'** in relation to women, which include reasons of physiology (*not* strength), decency/privacy, special welfare consideration and international law or customs which would prevent a women operating effectively in a foreign context

(b) special welfare considerations and authenticity criteria (for example in dramatic or photographic roles), in the case of ethnic minorities

(c) size of the organisation, in relation to the duty to make reasonable adjustments for the employment of disabled persons

(d) the duty to disclose spent convictions of doctors, lawyers, teachers, accountants and police officers, and lengthy prison sentences

Note also that discrimination may be both **direct** (stating or implying or acting with the intention that one group is given preference over another) and **indirect** (whereby policy and practice are intended to be fair, but discriminate in practice). The issues of selection test design and the implications of interview questions address the potential for indirect discrimination.

EXAMPLE: INTERNATIONAL COMPARISONS

*   In France, it is unlawful to specify upper age limits in recruitment and selection literature. Application forms may not include questions concerning union membership, religion, politics or family situation.

*   In Northern Ireland, it is unlawful to discriminate on grounds of religious belief.

*   In Germany, selection methods are subject to approval by works councils and legislation, providing for the applicant's right to be treated with dignity, the reimbursement of interview expenses and the classification of 'improper' questions including political beliefs and family situation.

*   Questions regarding marriage and family plans and racial/religious criteria are generally unlawful within the EU countries.

NOTES

Activity 2 **(15 minutes)**

The following is a classic IQ test 'odd man out' question from an old '11+' paper.

'Which is the odd man out?

MEASLES, STEAMER, LEAVE, OMELETTE, COURAGE.'

(a)   What is the answer?
(b)   How might this question discriminate against certain tested groups?

Privacy and data protection

The gathering of data in the application and selection process is also a sensitive area. The Data Protection Act 1998 came into force in March 2000 and is being implemented in stages up to 2007 – but retrospectively, to affect all record systems set up on or after 24 October 1998. Major provisions include:

(a)   the right of employees to access their personnel files, to be informed of the purpose for which data is being collected about them and to approve the use of that data for other purposes)

(b)   requirements for the adequacy, up-to-dateness and security of information (particularly if it is to be exported outside the European Economic Area)

(c)   additional safeguards on the collection of data about race, ethnic origin, religious or political beliefs, union membership, health, sexual orientation or criminal activities (except for the purposes of monitoring racial equality).

EXAMPLE: INTERNATIONAL COMPARISONS

The law on recruitment varies internationally. For example:

*   In Spain, job applicants are legally guaranteed freedom from invasion of privacy.

*   In Belgium, job applicants are entitled to privacy during the selection process by a national agreement between unions and employer associations. Employers are required to return all application documentation to unsuccessful applicants.

EXAMPLE

A US employer that required applicants to answer intimate personal questions in a pre-employment psychological examination agrees to pay more than $2 million to settle a lawsuit over the test.

The employer, which operates a chain of retail stores in California, administered the test to about 2,500 applicants for security jobs. The test's 'true or false?' questions included the following.

*   I have never indulged in any unusual sexual practices
*   I have often wished I was a girl
*   I am very strongly attracted by members of my own sex
*   I believe my sins are unpardonable
*   I feel sure there is only one true religion

'Before settling the suit, the employer argued that the test was necessary to screen out applicants who are emotionally unstable, unreliable, undependable, and not inclined to follow directions or established rules, as well as applicants with addictive or violent tendencies who might put customers or other employees at risk.'

(From *Bulletin to Management*, 1993, cited by Shuler)

FOR DISCUSSION

Aside from the actual outcome of the case example cited above, how far do you think a test of this kind is:

(a)   useful or effective (and with what intention)? and

(b)   ethically reprehensible (and on what grounds)?

To the extent that the employer's concerns are genuine, what other means of screening might or should they employ?

We will now go on to outline some of the methods by which selection of/between applicants can be made.

1.4   Selection methods

Various techniques are available, depending on the policy and criteria of selection in each case.

(a)   **Interviews**. These may be variously structured (one-to-one, panel, sequential), and using various criteria of job relevance (application details, skills and competences, critical incident/situational questions) and scoring methods (general impressions, criteria ratings). As the most **popular** of methods, interviews will be considered in detail below.

(b)   **Evaluation of education and experience**, comparing application data to job requirements.

(c)   **Selection testing**. Written tests of ability and aptitude (cognitive and/or mechanical), personality and so on are increasingly used, alongside work sample tests (such as typing tests) which simulate job related activities. Tests are also discussed in more detail below.

(d)   **Background and reference checks**, in order to verify application claims as to qualifications, previous employment record and reasons for leaving and so on. References will be discussed in Section 5 of this chapter.

(e)   **Biodata analysis**. Biodata (biographical data) is gathered via multiple choice questions on family background, life experiences, attitudes and preferences. The results are compared against an 'ideal' profile based on correlations with effective job performance.

(f)   **Handwritten analysis,** or graphology. Handwriting is said to indicate up to 300 character traits of the individual. There is no scientific evidence of its predictive accuracy, but it is popular in Europe and to a lesser extent in the USA and Australia. (In general, handwritten covering letters are requested as a useful general indicator of orderly thinking, presentation and so on.)

(g)   **Group selection methods,** or 'assessment centres', allowing the assessment of team-working, leadership, problem-solving and communication skills through the use of group discussions, role plays, business games and 'in-tray' simulations. These are discussed below.

NOTES

(h) **Physical/medical testing**. Medical examinations are often one of the final steps in selection, to ensure fitness for work (and avoid compensation claims for pre-existing injuries or conditions). Specific tests – for example, testing for HIV/AIDS (subject to strict policy guidelines, and mindful of discrimination), or drug and/or alcohol abuse – may also be used for particular job categories: privacy and data protection principles will apply.

EXAMPLE: INTERNATIONAL COMPARISONS

The law on recruitment varies internationally. For example:

- The USA leads the way in several forms of selection testing, including **genetic screening** (analysis of blood samples to identify traits such as sensitivity to workplace chemicals) and **polygraph** or 'lie detector' tests (for example, where employees have access to financial control systems, pharmaceuticals or resaleable consumer items susceptible to theft). The US **Employee Polygraph Protection Act 1988** place restriction on the widespread use of such tests for selection purposes: in Australia, for example, lie detector tests were outlawed for employment purposes in 1983.

Activity 3   **(20 minutes)**

How accurate do you think these methods are?

Smith and Abrahamsen compiled data in 1994 to show how **popular** and how **effective** various techniques are. **Effectiveness** is measured according to the **'predictive validity'** scale, which ranges from 1 (the technique unfailingly predicts candidates' subsequent job performance) to 0 (the technique is no better than random chance at predicting candidates' subsequent job performance). **Popularity** is measured by the % of surveyed companies that use the technique.

(a) Rank the following techniques in order from most popular to least popular, from what you might anticipate.

(b) For each, add a number between 0.00 and 1.00 to indicate what you think their predictive validity might be.

Techniques: Personality tests, references, work sampling, interviews, assessment centres, cognitive tests, graphology, biodata.

We will now look at each of the three major techniques in turn.

2 SELECTION INTERVIEWS

2.1 Types of interview

Individual or **one-to-one interviews** are the most common selection method. They offer the advantages of direct face-to-face communication, and opportunity to establish **rapport** between the candidate and interviewer: each has to give his attention solely to the other, and there is potentially a relaxed atmosphere, if the interviewer is willing to establish an informal style.

The disadvantage of a one-to-one interview is the scope it allows for a biased or superficial decision.

(a) The candidate may be able to disguise lack of knowledge in a specialist area of which the interviewer himself knows little.

(b) The interviewer's perception may be selective or distorted (see Paragraph 2.4 below), and his lack of objectivity may go unnoticed and unchecked, since he is the sole arbiter.

(c) The greater opportunity for personal rapport with the candidate may cause a weakening of the interviewer's objective judgement: he may favour someone he got on with over someone who was unresponsive but better-qualified. Again, there will be no cross-check with another interviewer.

Panel interviews are designed to overcome the above disadvantages. A panel may consist of two or three people who together interview a single candidate: most commonly, a personnel manager and the departmental manager who will have responsibility for the successful candidate. This may be more daunting for the candidate (depending on the tone and conduct of the interview) but it has several advantages.

(a) The personnel and line specialists gather the information they need about the candidate at the same time, cutting down on the subsequent information-sharing stage, and making a separate subsequent interview with one or the other unnecessary.

(b) The questions each specialist wants to put to the interviewee (related to their own field of activity and expertise) will be included, and the answers will be assessed by the specialist concerned: each will also be able to give the interviewee the information he wants, both about the employment aspects of the position, and about the departmental task-related aspects.

(c) The interviewers can discuss their joint assessment of the candidate's abilities, and their impressions of his behaviour and personality at the interview. They can thus gain a more complete picture, and can modify any hasty or superficial judgements. Personal bias is more likely to be guarded against, and checked if it does emerge.

Large formal panels, or **selection boards,** may also be convened where there are a number of individuals or groups with an interest in the selection. This has the advantage of allowing a number of people to see the candidate, and to share information about him at a single meeting: similarly, they can compare their assessments on the spot, without a subsequent effort at liaison and communication.

Offsetting these administrative advantages, however, there are severe drawbacks to the effectiveness of the selection board as a means of assessment.

(a) Questions tend to be more varied, and more random, since there is no single guiding force behind the interview strategy. The candidate may have trouble switching from one topic to another so quickly, especially if questions are not led up to, and not clearly put - as may happen if they are unplanned. Candidates are also seldom allowed to expand their answers, and so may not be able to do justice to themselves.

(b) If there is a dominating member of the board, the interview may have greater continuity - but he may also 'force' the judgements of other members, and his prejudices may be allowed to dominate the assessment.

(c) Some candidates may not perform well in a formal, artificial situation such as a board interview, and may find such a situation extremely stressful. The interview will thus not show the best qualities of someone who might

NOTES

nevertheless be highly effective in the work context and in the face of work-related pressures.

(d)   The pressures of a board interview favour individuals who are confident, and who project an immediate and strong image: those who are articulate, dress well and so on. First impressions of such a candidate may cover underlying faults or shortcomings, while a quiet, overawed candidate may be dismissed, despite his strengths in other areas.

Activity 4   **(45 minutes)**

'In some cases, the option of sequential interviewing may be open to managers. Instead of, say, four people on a panel spending an hour with each of four candidates, the members might each spend an hour alone with each candidate. The panel could then take its selection decision in the light of the information obtained at the separate interviews.'

W David Rees, *The Skills of Management* (1991)

Weigh up the pros and cons of 'sequential interviewing'.

2.2   Preparing interviews

In brief, the factors to be considered with regard to conducting selection interviews are:

(a)   The impression of the organisation given by the interview arrangements

(b)   The psychological effects of the location of the interview, seating arrangements and manner of the interviewer(s)

(c)   The extent to which the candidate can be encouraged to talk freely (by asking open questions) and honestly (by asking probing questions), in accordance with the organisation's need for information

(d)   The opportunity for the candidate to learn about the job and organisation

(e)   The control of bias or hasty judgement by the interviewer

The interview is a two way process, but the interviewer must have a clear idea of what the interview is setting out to achieve, and must be in sufficient control of the interview to make sure that every candidate is asked questions which cover the same ground and obtain all the information required.

The agenda and questions will be based on:

(a)   The job description, and what abilities are required of the job holder

(b)   The personnel specification: the interviewer must be able to judge whether the applicant matches up to the personal qualities required from the job holder

(c)   The application form

(d)   More culture – or vision-focused criteria (such as flexibility or creativity), if a job-based approach is not appropriate

The interview process should be efficiently run to make a favourable impression on the candidates and to avoid unnecessary stress (unless ability to handle pressure is a selection criterion!). The interview room should be free from distraction and interruption.

NOTES

Activity 5 (30 minutes)

Think back to a selection interview you have had, for a job, school or place at your university/college.

(a) What sort of interview did you have: one-to-one, panel, formal or informal?

(b) What impression of the organisation did you get from the whole process?

(c) How well-conducted was the interview, looking back on it?

(d) What efforts (if any) were made to put you at your ease?

2.3 Conducting interviews

Questions should be paced and put carefully. The interviewer should not be trying to confuse the interviewee, plunging immediately into demanding questions or picking on isolated points; nor should he allow the interviewee to digress or gloss over important points. The interviewer must retain control over the information-gathering process.

A variety of question styles may be used, to different effects.

(a) **Open questions** or open-ended questions ('Who...? What...? Where...? When...? Why...?') force interviewees to put together their own responses in complete sentences. This encourages the interviewee to talk, keeps the interview flowing, and is most revealing ('Why do you want to be in Personnel?')

(b) **Probing questions** are similar to open questions in their phrasing but aim to discover the deeper significance of the candidate's experience or achievements. ('What was it about HRM that particularly appealed to you?')

In an article in *PM Plus* (August 1991) Alan Fowler describes the purpose of such questions as being 'to provide a clearer focus to too short or too generalised answers'. He adds that 'Poor interviewers too often let a candidate's general and fairly uninformative answer pass without a probe, simply because they are working through a list of prepared open questions.'

(c) **Closed questions** are the opposite, inviting only 'yes' or 'no' answers: ('Did you...?', 'Have you...?'). A closed question has the following effects.

    (i) It elicits answers only to the question asked by the interviewer. This may be useful where there are small points to be established ('Did you pass your exam?') but there may be other questions and issues that he has not anticipated but will emerge if the interviewee is given the chance to express himself ('How did you think your studies went?').

    (ii) It does not allow the interviewee to express his personality, so that interaction can take place on a deeper level.

    (iii) It makes it easier for interviewees to conceal things ('You never *asked* me....').

    (iv) It makes the interviewer work very hard.

(d) **Multiple questions** are just that: two or more questions are asked at once. ('Tell me about your last job? How did your knowledge of HRM help you there, and do you think you are up-to-date or will you need to spend time studying?') This type of question can be used to encourage the candidate to talk at some length, but not to stray too far from the point. It might also test the candidate's ability to listen and handle large amounts of information, but should be used judiciously in this case.

(e) **Problem solving or situational questions** present the candidate with a situation and ask him to explain how he would deal with it. ('How would you motivate your staff to do a task that they did not want to do?'). Such questions are used to establish whether the candidate will be able to deal with the sort of problems that are likely to arise in the job, or whether he has sufficient technical knowledge (in which case a line manager rather than the personnel manager might be the best person to ask the questions and judge the responses).

(f) **Leading questions** lead the interviewee to give a certain reply. ('We are looking for somebody who likes detailed figure work. How much do you enjoy dealing with numbers?' or 'Don't you agree that...?'. 'Surely...?')

The danger with this type of question is that the interviewee will give the answer that he thinks the interviewer wants to hear, but it might legitimately be used to deal with a highly reticent or nervous candidate, simply to encourage him to talk.

Activity 6   (20 minutes)

Identify the type of question used in the following examples, and discuss the opportunities and constraints they offer the interviewee who must answer them.

(a) 'So you're interested in a business studies degree, are you, Jo?

(b) 'Surely you're not interested in business studies, Jo?'

(c) 'How about a really useful qualification like a Business Studies degree Jo? Would you consider that?'

(d) 'Why are you interested in a Business studies degree, Jo?'

(e) 'Why particularly Business Studies, Jo?'

The interviewer *must* listen to and evaluate the responses, to judge what the interviewee:

(a)   Wants to say
(b)   Is trying *not* to say
(c)   Is saying - but doesn't mean, or is lying about
(d)   Is having difficulty saying

In addition, the interviewer will have to be aware when he:

(a)   Is hearing something he needs to know

(b)   Is hearing something he *doesn't* need to know

(c)   Is hearing only what he expects to hear

(d)   Is not hearing clearly - when his own attitudes, perhaps prejudices, are getting in the way of his response to the interviewee and his views

Candidates should be given the opportunity to ask questions. Indeed, well-prepared candidates should go into an interview knowing what questions they may want to ask. Their choice of questions might well have some influence on how the interviewers finally assess them. Moreover, there is information that the candidate will need to know about the organisation and the job, and about:

(a)   Terms and conditions of employment (although negotiations about detailed terms may not take place until a provisional offer has been made) and

(b)   The next step in the selection process - whether there are further interviews, when a decision might be made, or which references might be taken up

Having said all this, why did interviews score so badly on the predictive validity scale? (See our answer to Activity 3, if you have not already done so.) Despite their popularity, they have a number of limitations...

2.4   Limitations of interviews

Interviews are criticised because they fail to provide accurate predictions of how a person will perform in the job. The main reasons why this might be so are as follows.

(a)   Limited scope and relevance. An interview is necessarily too brief to 'get to know' candidates in the kind of depth required to make an accurate prediction of their behaviour in any given situation. In addition, an interview is an artificial situation: candidates may be 'on their best behaviour' or, conversely, so nervous that they do not do themselves justice. Neither situation reflects what the person is 'really like'.

(b)   Errors of judgement by interviewers. These might be:

(i)   The **halo effect** - a tendency for people to make an initial general judgement about a person based on a single obvious attribute, such as being neatly dressed, or well-spoken, or having a public school education. This single attribute will colour later perceptions, and might make an interviewer mark the person up or down on every other factor in their assessment

(ii)   **Contagious bias** - a process whereby an interviewer changes the behaviour of the applicant by suggestion. The applicant might be led by the wording of questions or non-verbal cues from the interviewer, and change what he is doing or saying in response

(iii)   A possible inclination by interviewers to **stereotype** candidates on the basis of insufficient evidence. Stereotyping groups together people who are assumed to share certain characteristics, then attributes certain traits to the group as a whole, and then (illogically) assumes that each individual member of the supposed group will possess that trait: all accountants are boring, or whatever

(iv)   **Incorrect assessment** of qualitative factors such as motivation, honesty or integrity. Abstract qualities are very difficult to assess in an interview

(v)   **Logical error**. For example, an interviewer might place too much emphasis on isolated strengths or weaknesses or draw unwarranted conclusions from facts (confusing career mobility with disloyalty, say).

(c)   Lack of skill and experience in interviewers. The problems with inexperienced interviewers are not only bias, but:

(i)   Inability to evaluate information about a candidate properly

(ii)   Inability to compare a candidate against the requirements for a job or a personnel specification

(iii)   Inability to take control of the direction and length of the interview

(iv)   A reluctance to probe into facts and challenge statements where necessary

While some interviewers will be experts from the personnel department of the organisation, it is usually thought desirable to include line managers in the interview team. They cannot be full-time interviewers, obviously: they have their other work to do. No matter how much training they are given in interview techniques, they will lack continuous experience, and probably not give interviewing as much thought or interest as they should. A simplified set of criteria, which does not use the terminology of the personnel specialist, is in non-personnel specialist's terminology, and is clearly related to relevant items on the job specification, may help.

3   SELECTION TESTING

3.1   Types of tests

In some job selection procedures, an interview is supplemented by some form of selection test. The interviewers must be certain that the results of such tests are reliable, and that a candidate who scores well in a test will be more likely to succeed in the job. The test will have no value unless there is a direct relationship between ability in the test and ability in the job.

Cushway (*Human Resource Management*) lists six criteria which such tests should satisfy.

    ' 1   A sensitive measuring instrument that discriminates between subjects.
      2   Standardised, so that an individual score can be related to others.
      3   Reliable, in that it always measures the same thing.
      4   Valid, in that the test measures what it is designed to measure.
      5   Acceptable to the candidate.
      6   Non-discriminatory.'

The science of measuring mental capacities and processes is called 'psychometrics'; hence the term 'psychometric testing'. There are five types of test commonly used in practice.

Intelligence or cognitive ability tests

Tests of **general** cognitive ability typically test memory, ability to think quickly (perceptual speed, verbal fluency and logically (inductive reasoning), and problem solving skills. An article in *Personnel Management* magazine in December 1993 referred to the continuing influence of cognitive ability tests and suggests that reliance on such measures may increase. This is because uncertainty in UK employers' minds about the validity of A-level and GCSE results and the wide variation in degree classes between higher educational institutions may lead them to seek alternative reassurance of general intellectual ability.

Most people have experience of IQ tests and so forth, and few would dispute their validity as good measures of **general** intellectual performance currently.

Aptitude tests

Aptitude tests are designed to predict an individual's potential for performing a job or learning new skills. There are various accepted areas of aptitude, as follows.

(a)   Reasoning - verbal, numerical and abstract/visual: (eg accuracy and speed in arithmetical calculations, naming or making words, identifying shapes)

(b) Spatio-visual ability - practical intelligence, non-verbal ability and creative ability (eg ability to solve mechanical puzzles)

(c) Perceptual speed and accuracy - clerical ability (identifying non-identical pairs of numbers)

(d) 'Manual' or 'psycho-motor' ability - mechanical, manual, musical and athletic: ability to respond accurately and rapidly to stimuli (eg pressing lighted buttons) using controlled muscular adjustments and/or finger dexterity

With a few possible exceptions most of the areas of aptitude mentioned above are fairly easily measurable and so long as it is possible to determine what particular aptitudes are required for a job it is likely that aptitude tests will be useful for selection.

Personality tests

Personality tests may measure a variety of characteristics, such as applicants' skill in dealing with other people, ambition, motivation or emotional stability. Probably the best known example is the 16PF, originally developed by Cattell in 1950. This is described as follows in *Personnel Management* (February 1994).

> The 16PF comprises 16 scales, each of which measures a factor that influences the way a person behaves.
>
> The factors are functionally different underlying personality characteristics, and each is associated with not just one single piece of behaviour but rather is the source of a relatively broad range of behaviours. For this reason the factors themselves are referred to as source traits and the behaviours associated with them are called surface traits.
>
> The advantage of measuring source traits, as the 16PF does, is that you end up with a much richer understanding of the person because you are not just describing what can be seen but also the characteristics underlying what can be seen.
>
> The 16PF analyses how a person is likely to behave generally, including, for example, contributions likely to be made to particular work contexts, aspects of the work environment to which the person is likely to be more or less suited, and how best to manage the person.

Other examples include the Myers-Briggs Type Indicator (mostly intended for self-development purposes) and the Minnesota Multiphasic Personality Inventory (MMPI). The validity of such tests has been much debated, but it seems that some have been shown by research to be valid predictors of job performance, so long as they are used and interpreted properly. A test may indicate that a candidate is introverted, has creative ability and is pragmatic, but this is only of use if this combination of characteristics can be linked to success or failure in the type of work for which the candidate is being considered.

Proficiency tests

Proficiency tests are perhaps the most closely related to an assessor's objectives, because they measure ability to do the work involved. An applicant for an audio typist's job, for example, might be given a dictation tape and asked to type it. This is a type of **attainment** test, in that it is designed to measure abilities or skills already acquired by the candidate.

Activity 7   **(30 minutes)**

What kind of work sample or proficiency tests would you devise for the following categories of employee? For each, state whether your test is a physical, verbal or mental test.

(a)   Administrative assistants
(b)   Construction supervisors
(c)   Pilots
(d)   Magazine editors
(e)   Telephone operators

3.2   Trends in the use of tests

In *Personnel Management*, Clive Fletcher identified the following six trends in the use and development of tests.

(a)   Continuing enthusiasm for personality measures

(b)   The continuing influence of cognitive ability tests

(c)   A focus on certain popular themes - sales ability or aptitude, customer orientation, motivation, teamworking and organisational culture are mentioned

(d)   The growing diversity of test producers and sources (meaning more choice, but also more poor quality measures)

(e)   Expanded packages of tests, including tapes, computer disks, workbooks and so on

(f)   A growing focus on fairness: the most recent edition of the 16PF test, for example has been scrutinised by expert psychologists 'to exclude certain types of content, such as dated material, content that might lead to bias, material that might be unacceptable in an organisational setting and anything considered to be strongly socially desirable or undesirable.

3.3   Limitations of psychometric testing

Psychometric testing has grown in popularity in recent years, but you should be aware of certain drawbacks.

(a)   There is not always a direct (let alone predictive) relationship between ability in the test and ability in the job: the job situation is very different from artificial test conditions.

(b)   The interpretation of test results is a skilled task, for which training and experience is essential. It is also highly subjective (particularly in the case of personality tests), which belies the apparent scientific nature of the approach.

(c)   Additional difficulties are experienced with particular kinds of test. For example:

        (i)   An aptitude test measuring arithmetical ability would need to be constantly revised or its content might become known to later applicants

        (ii)   Personality tests can often give misleading results because applicants seem able to guess which answers will be looked at most favourably

(iii) It is difficult to design intelligence tests which give a fair chance to people from different cultures and social groups and which test the *kind* of intelligence that the organisation wants from its employees: the ability to score highly in IQ tests does not necessarily correlate with desirable traits such as mature judgement or creativity, merely mental agility. In addition, 'practice makes perfect': most tests are subject to coaching and practice effects.

(d) It is difficult to exclude discrimination and bias from tests. Many tests (including personality tests) are tackled less successfully by women than by men, or by immigrants than by locally-born applicants because of the particular aspects chosen for testing. This may make their use indirectly discriminatory.

FOR DISCUSSION

'Among the qualities which neither the interview nor intelligence tests are able to assess accurately are the candidate's ability to get on with and influence his colleagues, to display qualities of spontaneous leadership and to produce ideas in a real-life situation.'

Plumbley

Why might this be a drawback? What can be done about it?

4 GROUP SELECTION METHODS

4.1 Techniques in group selection

Group selection methods or **assessment centres** might be used by an organisation as the final stage of a selection process for management jobs. They consist of a series of tests, interviews and group situations over a period of two days, involving a small number of candidates (typically six to eight) for a job.

Group selection methods are appropriate for assessing the following.

(a) **Social skills** such as sensitivity to the views and opinions of others, reaction to disagreement and criticism, and the ability to influence and persuade others

(b) **Intellectual skills** such as the consideration of the merits and demerits of other arguments put forward and the ability to think clearly (particularly at short notice), situational problem-solving and so on

(c) **Attitudes,** such as political, racial or religious views, and attitude to authority, particularly where these may be relevant to a potential employee's efficiency at work

Typical techniques used in group selection include:

(a) Group **role-play** exercises, in which they can explore (and hopefully display) interpersonal skills and/or work through simulated managerial tasks

(b) **Case studies**, where candidates' analytical and problem-solving abilities are tested in working through described situations/problems, as well as their interpersonal skills, in taking part in (or leading) group discussions of the case study

(c) **'In-tray' exercises,** simulating a typical work-load to be managed

(d) **Leaderless discussion groups** (LDGs), allowing leadership skills and issues to emerge freely

Often what are termed 'leaderless group activities' will be conducted. Such activities can be used to assess the leadership potential of job applicants in uncertain situations with no formal power structure. The group of applicants are presented with a topic for discussion, and are normally advised that they are expected to reach a conclusion within a defined period of time. The topic may be related to the job in question, and may either be of a problem-solving nature ('Should product X be developed given the following marketing and financial information?') or of a more general nature ('Is capital punishment an effective deterrent?'). The contribution made by individual candidates will be scored according to factors such as assertiveness, quality of thought and expression, analytical skill, and the ability to lead the group towards a decision.

Another method of assessment involves giving candidates a typical job problem to solve individually in a set time, at the end of which each candidate has to set out his solution to the problem to the other members of the group, and defend his views against the group's criticisms.

4.2 Purposes of group selection

Group sessions might be thought useful because:

(a) They give the organisation's selectors a longer opportunity to study the candidates.

(b) They reveal more than application forms, interviews and tests alone about the ability of candidates to persuade others, negotiate with others, and explain ideas to others and also to investigate problems efficiently. These are typically management skills.

(c) They reveal more about how the candidates' personalities and attributes will affect the work team and his own performance. Stamina, social interaction with others (ability to co-operate and compete), intelligence, energy, self confidence or outside interests will not necessarily be meaningful in themselves (as analysed from written tests), but may be shown to affect performance in the work context.

(d) They achieve some measure of comparability between candidates.

(e) The pooled judgement of the panel of assessors is likely to be more accurate than the judgement of a single interviewer.

(f) They provide information in situations where little historical information is known about the candidate in relation to the qualities to be assessed (such as when the candidate is an undergraduate or school leaver).

Since they are very suitable for selection of potential managers who have little or no previous experience and two days to spare for the sessions, group selection methods are often used for selecting university graduates for management trainee jobs.

Activity 8 (1 hour)

Think back to your own selection for your first job with your organisation. What procedures did you have to go through? What sort of interview did you have: was it well-conducted, looking back on it now? Did you have to take any tests?

Find out who does the selection interviewing in your office, what guidelines are laid down for them, and what training they get in interview technique.

Find out what selection tests (if any) are used in your organisation, and for what kinds of jobs.

We will now look at some of the later considerations in the selection process, bringing the candidate through to a contract of employment.

5 FOLLOW UP PROCEDURES

5.1 Checking references

References provide further confidential information about the prospective employee. This may be of varying value, as the reliability of all but the most factual information must be in question. A reference should contain:

(a) Straightforward factual information confirming the nature of the applicant's previous job(s), period of employment, pay, and circumstances of leaving.

(b) Opinions about the applicant's personality and other attributes. These should obviously be treated with some caution. Allowances should be made for prejudice (favourable or unfavourable), charity (withholding detrimental remarks), and possibly fear of being actionable for libel (although references are privileged, as long as they are factually correct and devoid of malice).

At least two **employer** references are desirable, providing necessary factual information, and comparison of personal views. **Personal** references tell the prospective employer little more than that the applicant has a friend or two.

Written references save time, especially if a standardised letter or form has been pre-prepared. A simple letter inviting the previous employer to reply with the basic information and judgement required may suffice. (If the recruiting officer wishes for a more detailed appraisal of the applicant's suitability, brief details of the post in question may be supplied but the previous employer's opinion will still be an ill-informed and subjective judgement.) A standard form to be completed by the referee may be more acceptable, and might pose a set of simple questions about:

(a) Job title
(b) Main duties and responsibilities
(c) Period of employment
(d) Pay/salary
(e) Attendance record

If a judgement of character and suitability is desired, it might be most tellingly formulated as the question: 'Would you re-employ this individual? (If not, why not?)'

Telephone references may be time-saving, if standard reference letters or forms are not available. They may also elicit a more honest opinion than a carefully prepared written statement. For this reasons, a telephone call may also be made to check or confirm a poor or grudging reference which the recruiter suspects may be prejudiced.

The pen is more double-edged than the sword!

'I am delighted to write a reference for X, now that I no longer employ him.'

'The person who gets Y to work for him will be fortunate indeed.'

'I cannot speak too highly of Z's ability.'

'I can honestly say that things have not been the same since P left.'

Note that when **giving** references, caution is also required.

NOTES

Activity 9   **(20 minutes)**

(a) At the end of a recent selection process one candidate was, in the view of everyone involved, outstanding. However, you have just received a very bad reference from her current employer. What do you do?

(b) For fun, rephrase the following comments in the way that you might expect to see them appear in a letter of reference.

  (i)   Mr Smith is habitually late
  (ii) Remains immature
  (iii) Socially unskilled with clients
  (iv) Is rather dull

EXAMPLE

'Mr Gary Rothville, a partner with law firm Phillips Fox, said:

'We are advising our clients against giving a reference which strays from the truth in overstating an employee's abilities or giving a false indication of their [sic] character.

'While it has been found that an employer owed a duty of care to a former employee when preparing a reference, it may not stop there.

'An employer could face civil liability from a company which suffered economic loss as a result of hiring an employee on the basis of a false reference.

'We sometimes get calls from ex-employees of our clients, raising concerns that their former manager has been making statements running them down.

'We strongly advise our clients in these circumstances not to go the other way and talk up a former employee. The best policy is to decline to comment, saying that the circumstances of the employment relationship are confidential.'

The concern about references arose after a landmark judgement last year in **Spring v Guardian Assurance plc**, where a four-to-one majority in Britain's House of Lords decided that an employer owes a duty of care to employees in relation to giving a reference, and in obtaining the information upon which the reference is based. This allows employers to sue for economic loss resulting from the reference, providing a wider potential remedy than a claim in defamation. Mr Spring, an insurance salesman, successfully sued for economic loss after Guardian Assurance supplied another firm, Scottish Amicable, with a reference which said that Spring was 'a man of little or no integrity who could not be regarded as honest'.

Guardian Assurance said Spring would give bad advice, deliberately or ignorantly, in the attempt to gain maximum commissions from insurance sales. Mr Spring was unemployable in the insurance industry when word was spread.'

Stephen Long, *Financial Review* 28.6.96

5.2   The offer of employment

Assuming that the 'right' candidate has by now been identified, an offer of employment can be made. Time may be sensitive, so it is common for an oral offer to be made, with a negotiated period for consideration and acceptance: this can then be followed up with a written offer, if appropriate.

(a)   All terms, conditions and circumstances of the offer must at this point be clearly stated.

(b)   Any provisos ('subject to... satisfactory references, medical examination, negotiation of contract terms', or whatever) must also be clearly set out.

(c)   Negotiable aspects of the offer and timetables for acceptance should be set out, in order to control the closing stages of the process.

The organisation should be prepared for its offer to be rejected at this stage. Applicants may have received and accepted other offers. They may not have been attracted by their first-hand view of the organisation, and may have changed their mind about applying; they may only have been testing the water in applying in the first place, gauging the market for their skills and experience for future reference, or seeking a position of strength from which to bargain with their present employers. A small number of eligible applicants should therefore be kept in reserve.

EXAMPLE: INTERNATIONAL COMPARISONS

- In Spain, the **Ley Basica de Empleo** (Basic Employment Law, 1980) regulates the commencement (and termination) of employment. Breach of contract and dismissal have become a contentious area of HRM, and it is provided that **probationary periods** be instituted (15 days for non-qualified workers, 6 months for graduates) within which either party can terminate the contract without prejudice. The state also defines a number of forms of 'standard' employment contracts, containing appropriate standard terms and conditions for full-time indefinite employment, temporary working, home working, workers over 45, apprentice/trainees and so on.

- In the USA, the doctrine of 'employment at will' – freedom to hire and fire – is subject to the individual's contract of employment, and terms and conditions determined by collective bargaining. Written terms and conditions are therefore key to the employment relationship and employee security: they are typically renegotiated every two or three years.

5.3   Work permits

A combination of new immigration rules and agreements within the EU have complicated the recruitment and selection of non-UK nationals.

(a)   The general principle is that people coming to the UK for employment require a work permit. 'Employment' includes paid and unpaid employment, self-employment and engagement in business or any professional activity. (This does not affect short 'business visits'.) Work permits are generally issued for 1 to 2 years and not more than 4 years.

(b)   Nationals from the European Economic Area (EEA) have a right to work anywhere in the EEA **without** permits (This covers the EU **plus** Austria, Finland, Norway, Sweden, Iceland and Switzerland.) However, member states can limit the length of time that nationals from other states can seek work (and claim benefits) within their territory: a minimum of 3 months according to a decision of the European Court of Justice in 1982; 6 months in the UK. Once a person has found work, (s)he has the right of residency: residency permits are issued for five-year periods (renewable). All residency rights apply to the worker's family members and dependants. Continuing residency rights may apply on retirement (after 3 years' residency), incapacity (after 2 years) and an incapacity by reason of industrial disease or accident (without qualification).

(c)   In order to get a work permit for a non-EEA overseas employee, the UK employer has to show:

   (i)   That there is no one in the EU who can fill the post in question, and that

   (ii)   The business requires the post to be filled by someone of the individual's particular calibre

(d)   Under Section 8 of the Asylum and Immigration Act 1996, it is a criminal office to employ someone who is subject to immigration control unless the person has valid permission to be in the UK which does not prevent them from taking the job in question. Employers are required to view one of a series of official documents provided by the recruit prior to the first day of employment (and should retain a copy for the whole period of employment and six months afterward. However, extensive background checks into the immigration status of foreign recruits lay employers open to claims of discrimination under the Race Relations Act 1976. The Commission for Racial Equality argued in 1999 that the Act led to discrimination against foreign nationals who were 'suspected' of being illegal immigrants. There is now a Draft Code of Practice to guide recruiters: *People Management* (28.9.2000) suggests that the best way to keep up with the codes is 'to treat all applicants alike, regardless of apparent nationality'.

(e)   The Employment Department tends to require less information where the post is a transfer within an international group; is at board level (or equivalent); is in a skill area recognised to be scarce in the EU; or is essential to a project which will bring investment and jobs into the UK.

5.4   Contracts of employment

Once the offer of employment has been confirmed and accepted, the contract of employment can be prepared and offered.

A contract of employment may be written, oral or a mixture of the two. At the one extreme, it may be a document drawn up by solicitors and signed by both parties; at the other extreme it may consist of a handshake and a 'See you on Monday'. Senior personnel may sign a contract specially drafted to include terms on confidentiality and restraint of trade. Other employees may sign a standard form contract, exchange letters with the new employer or supply agreed terms orally at interview. Each of these situations, subject to the requirements (outlined below) as to written particulars, will form a valid contract of employment, as long as there is agreement on essential terms such as hours and wages.

Written particulars of employment

Although the contract need not be made in writing, the employer must give an employee (who works at least eight hours a week) a written statement of certain particulars of his or her employment, within two months of the beginning of employment (*Employment Rights Act 1996*)

The statement should identify the following.

(a)   The names of **employer** and **employee**

(b)   The **date** on which employment began

(c) Whether any service with a previous employer forms part of the employee's **continuous period** of employment

(d) **Pay**

(e) **Hours** of work

(f) Any **holiday** and **holiday pay** entitlement

(g) **Sick leave** and **sick pay** entitlement (if any)

(h) **Pensions** and pension **schemes**

(i) Length of **notice** of termination to be given on either side (or the expiry date if employed for a fixed term)

(j) The **title** of the job which the employee is employed to do

(k) Details of **disciplinary procedures** and **grievance procedures,** works rules, union of staff association membership

(l) Rules on **health and safety at work** (by custom only)

It is sufficient to refer to separate booklets or notices (on pension schemes, disciplinary/grievance procedures and so on) where the relevant details can be found: not all the information needs to go in the written statement!

The purpose of these rules is to ensure that the employee has precise information of the terms on which he is employed. Some employers invite the employee to countersign and return a second copy of the particular as evidence that he has received them. But the statement is not the contract itself – it is merely written evidence, so if the particulars are found to contain an error, that does not bind either party to the erroneous terms: the true agreed terms of the 'contract' prevail.

Terms of a contract in the UK

Definition

> **Express terms** are those which are explicitly and specifically offered and accepted as part of the contract of employment.

Since it would not be practicable or desirable for all aspects of a contract of employment to be codified exhaustively into a written agreement, **common law** (made up of decisions in the courts which act as precedents for all later cases) 'implies' a number of terms. Even if no express terms have been agreed, the courts have nevertheless taken certain duties and entitlements to be implied by the nature of employment with regard to the following areas.

(a) **Employers' duties.** For example, on pay, provision of work, and health and safety.

(b) **Employees' duties.** The Employee has a basic duty of faithful service to the employer.

A severe breach of these common law implied duties can entitle the injured party to regard it as a breach of the contract of employment. In that case, the employer may dismiss the offending employee, or the employee may claim damages from the employer.

In addition, there may be **collective implied terms**. Terms of employment, such as wages and working conditions, are often negotiated on a collective basis by an employer (or employers' association) and trade unions. These collectively agreed terms are generally implied to be agreed between the individual employee and employer, even if they are not expressly stated in the contract between them, as long as the terms are reasonable, properly negotiated and known to the employee.

Definition

> **Statutory implied terms** are duties imposed on the parties by statute, or Act of Parliament.

Whatever the express terms of the employment contract, the law of the land overrides them; an employer cannot force employees to abide by a contract that denies their statutory rights with regard to:

(a)   Wage payments
(b)   Maternity leave
(c)   Time off work
(d)   Health and safety
(e)   Employment protection

This legislation will be discussed in relevant chapters of this book.

6   EVALUATING THE PROCESS

6.1   Evaluating selection

Much the same method can be used to evaluate selection as recruitment: see paragraph 5.10 of Chapter 4.

Selection procedures can further be evaluated by determining whether selection decisions seem to have been 'correct' in the light of subsequent job performance, cultural impact and service longevity of the successful candidate.

(a)   If tests were used to assess likely potential to perform certain tasks, the retained test results can be compared against actual performance in the job. Regular discrepancies may suggest that the tests are flawed.

(b)   Similar comparisons may be made using interview ratings and notes. Interviewers who consistently fall short in the accuracy of their judgements should be trained accordingly.

Other performance criteria for evaluating selection procedures include:

- Number of candidates (and/or minority/female/disabled candidates) interviewed in relation to applications

- Number of offers made in relation to number of interviews (especially to minority/female/disabled candidates)

- Number of acceptances in relation to offers made

- Number of successful applicants subsequently appraised as competent in the job

- Lead time for successful applicants to be trained to competence

- Number of starters still employed after 1 year (2 years etc)

- Cost of selection methods per starter employed 1 year later

Chapter roundup

- The contents of this chapter may again be summarised in diagrammatic form.

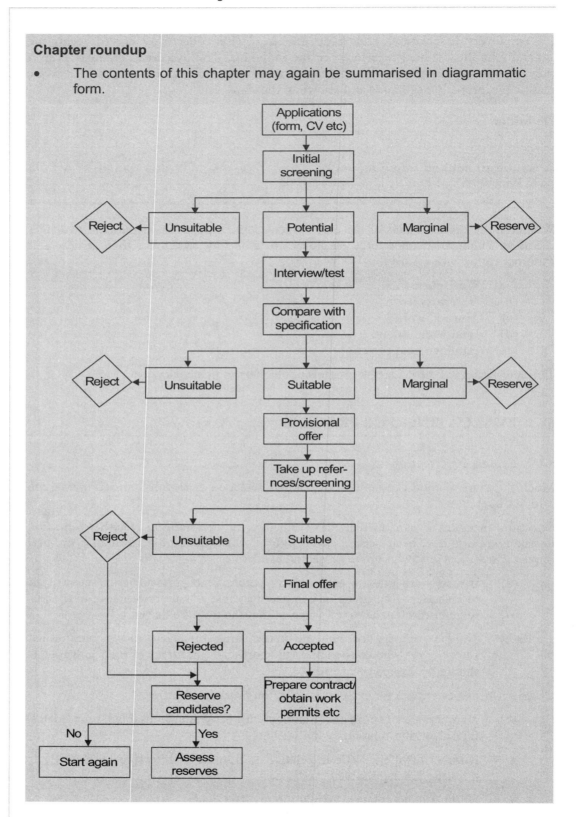

Quick quiz

1   What are the stages of the systematic approach to selection?

2   A job selection interview has several aims. If you were conducting one, though, you should **not** be concerned with:

A   Comparing the application against the job/personnel specification
B   Getting as much information as possible about the applicant
C   Giving the applicant information about the job and organisation
D   Making the applicant feel he has been treated fairly

3   Amon Leigh-Hewman is interviewing a candidate for a vacancy in his firm. He asks a question about the candidate's views on a work-related issue. The candidate starts to answer, and sees to his horror that Amon in pursing his lips and shaking his head slightly to himself. 'Of course, that's what some people say', continues the candidate, 'but I myself...' Amon smiles. His next question is 'Don't you think that...?

Amon is getting a distorted view of the candidate because of:

A   The halo effect
B   Contagious bias
C   Stereotyping
D   Logical error

4   Selection tests such as IQ tests and personality tests may not be effective in getting the right person for the job for several reasons. Which of the following criticisms is false, though?

A   Test results can be influenced by practice and coaching rather than genuine ability

B   Subjects are able (and tend) to deliberately falsify results

C   Tests do not eliminate bias and subjectivity

D   Test are generally less accurate predictors of success than interviews

5   What are two key issues in selection?

6   What can be done to improve the effectiveness of selection interviews?

7   What are the relative merits and drawbacks of the panel and one-to-one interviews in personnel selection?

8   What countries are included in the European Economic Area? Do members of these states require work permits for the UK?

9   What matters should be identified in the written particulars of employment supplied to employees?

10   Distinguish between:

(a)   Express terms
(b)   Implied terms in common law
(c)   Collective implied terms
(d)   Statutory implied terms

Answers to quick quiz

1   Set key criteria; compare applications (forms, CV) against criteria; sort and shortlist; acknowledge all responses; invite candidates to interview/selection testing or other methods; check references; issue offer of employment; draw up contract; obtain work permits (if necessary); plan induction; send standard letters to 'rejects' and 'reserves'.   (see paragraph 1.1)

2   B. Information needs to be relevant   (para 2)

3   B   (para 2.4)

4   D. Interviews are generally less accurate. (para 3)

5   Discrimination/equal opportunity and privacy/data protection   (para 6.1)

6   Planning; relevant criteria; interviewer training and appraisal; structured style of questioning; awareness of potential for bias. (para 2.4)

7   See Paragraph 2.1 for a detailed account.

8   EU countries plus Austria, Finland, Norway, Sweden, Iceland and Switzerland. They do not have to have work permits to seek work in the EU member states (subject to time limits). (para 5.3)

9   Identifying details, date of start, continuous period of employment (if any), pay, hours of work, holiday entitlement, sick leave/pay, pension, notice of termination or term of contract, title of job, details of employee relations mechanisms, health and safety rules (by custom). (para 5.4)

10 Express terms are explicitly offered and accepted as part of the contract. Implied terms at common law are those not explicitly stated but assumed by virtue of case law. Collective implied terms are those implied to be agreed between the individual and employer by virtue of collective agreement with trade unions. Statutory implied terms are those implied by virtue of legislation. (para 5.4)

Answers to activities

1   (a)   Boxes too small to contain the information asked for

    (b)   Forms which are (or look) so lengthy or complicated that prospective applicants either complete them perfunctorily or give up (and apply to another employer instead)

    (c)   Illegal (eg discriminatory) or offensive questions

    (d)   Lack of clarity as to what (and how much) information is required

2   (a)   'Steamer'. (The others share national connotations: German measles, French leave, Spanish omelette, Dutch courage.)

    (b)   The answer presupposes a knowledge of expressions which are rooted in a European context and, in some cases, are old-fashioned and dependent on a middle-class upbringing and education.

3

Method	% use	Predictive validity
Interviews	92	0.17
References	74	0.13
Work sampling	18	0.57
Assessment centres	14	0.40
Personality tests	13	0.40
Cognitive tests	11	0.54
Biodata	4	0.40
Graphology	3	0.00

The results are most revealing as they show a pattern of employers relying most heavily on the least valid selection methods for their recruitment purposes. Interviews in particular seem not much better than tossing a coin.

4   Rees suggests the following points. You may not agree with all of them.

    (a)   The method need take no more time for the organisation: in fact single interviews may turn out to take less than an hour.

(b) Candidates would have to spend more time being interviewed but 'might not mind this if they felt it was a more effective method of selection'.

(c) It is normally easier to create rapport and coax information out of a person when you are seeing him alone.

(d) However, inexperienced interviewers will be far more 'exposed' than they would have been in a panel interview. They may prefer merely to observe.

(e) The method is liable to create more argument about the final decision: the interviewee may be flagging by the end of the session and give a totally different impression to different interviewers.

5   This is personal to your experience: it will help you develop the evidence to show your competence in investigating selection procedures in organisations.

6   (a) Closed. (the only answer is 'yes' or 'no', unless Jo is prepared to expand on it, at his or her own initiative.)

(b) Leading. (Even if Jo was interested, (s)he would get the message that 'yes' would not be what the interviewer wanted, or expected, to hear.

(c) Leading closed multiple! ('Really useful' leads Jo to think that the 'correct' answer will be 'yes': there is not much opportunity for any other answer, without expanding on it unasked.)

(d) Open. (Jo has to explain, in his or her own words.)

7   Here are some suggestions:

Test

• Admin assistants	Word-processing on specific equipment (physical)
	Dictation (physical)
	Filing (physical)
	Letter proof-reading/correction (mental)
	Telephone answering (verbal)
• Construction supervisors	Plan error recognition (mental)
• Pilots	Rudder control, direction control (physical)
	Navigational reading (mental)
	Radio procedures (verbal)
• Magazine editors	Writing headlines (mental)
	Proof-reading/correction (mental)
	Page-layout (mental/physical)
• Telephone operators	Switchboard handling (physical/mental)
	Role play in-coming calls (verbal)

8   This is another investigation opportunity: use these same questions/skills on another organisation that you know, know someone in, or read about. Develop your findings into evidence for Assessment Criteria 21:2

9   (a) It is quite possible that her current employer is desperate to retain her. Disregard the reference, or question the referee by telephone, and seek another reference from a previous employer if possible.

(b) The phrases given are 'translations' by Adrian Furnham, (*Financial Times,* December 1991) of the following.

(i)   'Mr Smith was occasionally a little lax in time keeping'

NOTES

(ii) 'Clearly growing out of earlier irresponsibility'
(iii) 'At her best with close friends'
(iv) 'Got a well deserved lower second'

Assignment 5   **(2 hours)**

Task one

Use your knowledge of recruitment methods and media to locate and select a **job advertisement** which contains a reasonable amount of detail about the activities and culture of the employing organisation and about the job and candidate requirements.

Task two

From the information available, draft an interview agenda suitable for the job, which might be used as a structure for a personnel officer sorting applications and guiding a selection interview. Consider what information you would need to gather *and* give.

Task three

With the collaboration of a fellow student, colleague or family member, conduct a role-play interview, in which you are the interviewer ($^1/_2$ hour maximum)

Task four

Debrief. Discuss with your role-play partner (and observers, if any) how each of you felt the interview went; what information did not effectively come out of the interview; whether the interview was sufficient to make a decision; what further selection methods (if any) would be helpful; whether bias, discrimination or invasion of privacy were evident at any stage.

Chapter 6 :
PERFORMANCE APPRAISAL

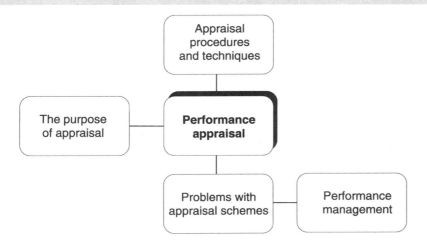

Introduction

The process of monitoring individual and group performance, and giving helpful feedback for improvement, is generally called **performance appraisal**. The purpose of appraisal was traditionally regarded as constructive criticism of the employee by his or her manager, but nowadays it tends to be more about:

(a) Helping the employee to overcome any problems or obstacles to performance

(b) Identifying where an employee's potential for improved performance and greater challenge could be better fulfilled

(c) Setting goals and priorities for further monitoring and development

Your objectives

In this chapter you will learn about the following:

(a) How to evaluate the application of appraisal procedures

(b) Systematic appraisal and reporting procedures, and some of their human relations problems

(c) How employee potential can be monitored and assessed

1 THE PURPOSE OF APPRAISAL

Definition

> **Performance appraisal** is the process whereby an individual's performance is reviewed against previously agreed goals, and where new goals are agreed which will develop the individual and improve performance over the forthcoming review period.

1.1 Uses of appraisal

Jeannie Brownlow has decided to leave Gold and Silver where she has worked for five years as a supervisor. When the personnel manager asked for her reasons she said, 'I'm fed up. You don't know where you are here. No one tells you if you're doing the job well, but they jump on you like a ton of bricks if anything goes wrong. Talk about "no news is good news" – that's the way it is here'.

Monitoring and evaluating the performance of individuals and groups is an essential part of people-management. It has several uses.

(a) Identifying the current level of performance to provide a basis for informing, training and developing team members to a higher level

(b) Identifying areas where improvement is needed in order to meet acceptable standards of performance

(c) Identifying people whose performance suggests that they might be suitable for promotion in future

(d) Measuring the individual's or team's level of performance against specific standards, to provide a basis for reward above the basic pay rate (in other words, individual or group bonuses)

(e) Measuring the performance of new team members against the organisation's (and team's) expectations, as a means of assessing whether selection procedures have been successful

(f) Improving communication about work tasks between managers and team members, as a result of discussing the assessment

(g) In the process of defining what performance should be, establishing what key results and standards must be reached for the unit to reach its objectives

It may be argued that a particular, deliberate stock-taking exercise is unnecessary, since managers are constantly monitoring and making judgements about their subordinates and (theoretically) giving their subordinates feedback information from day to day.

1.2 Why have a system?

It must be recognised that, if no system of formal appraisal is in place:

(a) Managers may obtain random impressions of subordinates' performance (perhaps from their more noticeable successes and failures), but not a coherent, complete and objective picture

(b) Managers may have a fair idea of their subordinates' shortcomings – but may not have devoted time and attention to the matter of improvement and development

(c) Judgements are easy to make, but less easy to justify in detail, in writing, or to the subject's face

(d) Different managers may be applying a different set of criteria, and varying standards of objectivity and judgement, which undermines the value of appraisal for comparison, as well as its credibility in the eyes of employees

(e) Managers rarely give their subordinates adequate feedback on their performance. Most people dislike giving criticism as much as receiving it

---

Activity 1   **(15 minutes)**

List four disadvantages to the individual of not having an appraisal system.

A typical system would therefore involve:

(a) Identification of **criteria** for assessment

(b) The preparation of an **appraisal report**

(c) An **appraisal interview**, for an exchange of views about the results of the assessment, targets for improvement, solutions to problems and so on

(d) The preparation and implementation of **action plans** to achieve improvements and changes agreed

(e) **Follow-up:** monitoring the progress of the action plan

Definition

A **criterion** (plural: criteria) is a factor or standard by which something can be judged or decided. For example, 'meeting output targets' is one criterion for judging work performance.

We will now look at each stage in turn. First of all, what is the basis of appraisal going to be?

1.3   What should be monitored and assessed?

Managers must broadly monitor and assess the same things, so that comparisons can be made between individuals. On the other hand, they need to take account of the fact that jobs are different, and make different demands on the jobholder. If every individual were rated on 'communication skills' and 'teamworking', for example, you might have a good basis for deciding who needed promoting or training – but what about a data inputter or research scientist who does not have to work in a team or communicate widely in your organisation?

Activity 2   **(20 minutes)**

Think of some other criteria which you would want to use in assessment of some jobs – but which would not be applicable in others.

There is also the important question of whether you assess **personality** or **performance**: in other words, do you assess what the individual is, or what (s)he does? Personal qualities like reliability or outgoingness have often been used as criteria for judging people. However, they are not necessarily relevant to job performance: you can be naturally outgoing, but still not good at communicating with customers, if your product knowledge or attitude is poor. Also, personality judgements are notoriously vague and unreliable: words like 'loyalty' and 'ambition' are full of ambiguity and moral connotations.

In practical terms, this has encouraged the use of competence or results-based appraisals, where performance is measured against specific, job-related performance criteria.

So how does a manager choose what criteria to base the assessment on? Most large organisations have a system in place, with pre-printed assessment forms setting out all the relevant criteria and the range of possible judgements. (We reproduce such a form later in this chapter). Even so, a team manager should critically evaluate such schemes to ensure that the criteria for assessment are relevant to his or her team and task – and that they remain so over time, as the team and task change.

Relevant criteria for assessment might be based on the following.

(a) **Job analysis:** the process of examining a job, to identify its component tasks and skill requirements, and the circumstances in which it is performed.

Analysis may be carried out by observation, if the job is routine and repetitive it will be easy to see what it involves. Irregular jobs, with lots of 'invisible' work (planning, thinking, relationship-building and so on) will require interviews and discussions with superiors and with the job holders themselves, to find out what the job involves.

The product of job analysis is usually a **job specification** which sets out the activities (mental and physical) involved in the job, and other factors in its social and physical environment. Many of the aspects covered – aptitudes and abilities required, duties and responsibilities, ability to work under particular conditions (pressure, noise, hazards), tolerance of teamwork or isolation and so on – will suggest criteria for assessment.

(b) **Job descriptions:** more general descriptions of a job or position at a given time, including its purpose and scope, duties and responsibilities, relationship with other jobs, and perhaps specific objectives and expected results. A job description offers a guide to what competences, responsibilities and results might be monitored and assessed.

(c) **Departmental or team plans, performance standards and targets**. These are the most clear-cut of all. If the plan specifies completion of a certain number of tasks, or production of a certain number of units, to a particular quality standard, assessment can be focused on whether (or how far) those targets have been achieved. (Personality and environmental factors may be relevant when investigating why performance has fallen short – but do not cloud the assessment of performance itself.)

Let us now look at some of the performance monitoring and reporting methods used in organisations.

2 APPRAISAL PROCEDURES AND TECHNIQUES

2.1 Monitoring and reporting

Overall assessment

This is much like a school report. The manager simply writes narrative judgements about the appraisee. The method is simple – but not always effective, since there is no guaranteed consistency of the criteria and areas of assessment from manager to manager (or appraisal to appraisal). In addition, managers may not be able to convey clear, precise or effective judgements in writing.

Guided assessment

Assessors are required to comment on a number of specified characteristics and performance elements, with guidelines as to how terms such as 'application', 'integrity'

and 'adaptability' are to be interpreted in the work context. This is a more precise, but still rather vague method.

Grading

Grading adds a comparative frame of reference to the general guidelines. Managers are asked to select one of a number of levels or degrees (Grades 1–5 say) which describe the extent to which an individual displays a given characteristic. These are also known as rating scales, and have been much used in standard appraisal forms (for example, see Figure 6.2 on the following page). Their effectiveness depends to a large extent on two things.

(a) **The relevance of the factors chosen for assessment.** These may be nebulous personality traits, for example, or clearly-defined work-related factors such as job knowledge, performance against targets, or decision-making.

(b) **The definition of the agreed standards or grades.** Grades A-D might simply be labelled 'Outstanding – Satisfactory – Fair – Poor', in which case assessments will be rather subjective and inconsistent. They may, on the other hand, be more closely related to work priorities and standards, using definitions such as 'Performance is good overall, and superior to that expected in some important areas', or 'Performance is broadly acceptable, but the employee needs training in several major areas and motivation is lacking'.

Numerical values may be added to gradings to give rating scores. Alternatively a less precise graphic scale may be used to indicate general position on a plus/minus scale, as in Figure 6.1.

Factor: job knowledge

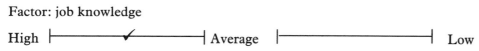

Behavioural incident methods

These concentrate on employee behaviour, which is measured against typical behaviour in each job, as defined by common '**critical incidents**' of successful and unsuccessful job behaviour reported by managers. Time and effort are required to collect and analyse reports and to develop the scheme, and it only really applies to large groups of people in broadly similar jobs. However, it is firmly rooted in observation of real-life job behaviour, and the important aspects of the job, since the analysis is carried out for **key tasks,** (those which are identified as critical to success in the job and for which specific standards of performance *must* be reached).

The behavioural equivalent of the graphic scale (Figure 6.1) for a manager's key task of 'marketing initiative' might appear as, for example:

Produces no new ideas for marketing. Appears apathetic to competitive challenge	Produces ideas when urged by head office. Ideas not clearly thought out nor enthusiastically applied	Produces ideas when urged by head office and gives full commitment to new programmes	Spontaneously generates new ideas for marketing and champions them through head office approval. Ideas related to identified needs and effective in practice

Figure 6.1: Critical incident scale

Results-orientated schemes

All the above techniques may be used with more or less results-orientated criteria. A wholly results-orientated approach sets out to review performance against specific targets and standards of performance, which are agreed – or even set – in advance by a manager and subordinate together. This is known as **performance management**. It will be discussed further in Section 4 of this chapter.

Performance Classification

Outstanding performance is characterised by high ability which leaves little or nothing to be desired.

Personnel rated as such are those who regularly make significant contributions to the organisation which are above the requirements of their position. Unusual and challenging assignments are consistently well handled.

Excellent performance is marked by above-average ability, with little supervision required.

Satisfactory Plus performance indicates fully adequate ability, without the need for excessive supervision. Personnel with this ratings are able to give proper consideration to normal assignments, which are generally well-handled. They will meet the requirements of the position. 'Satisfactory plus' performers may include those who lack the experience at their current level to demonstrate above-average ability.

Marginal performance is in instances where the ability demonstrated does not fully meet the requirements of the position, with excessive supervision and direction normally required.

Employees rated as such will show specific deficiencies in their performance which prevent them from performing at an acceptable level.

Unsatisfactory performance indicates an ability which falls clearly below the minimum requirements of the position.

'**Unsatisfactory**' performers will demonstrate market deficiencies in most of the major aspects of their responsibilities, and considerable improvement is required to permit retention of the employee in his current position.

Personal Characteristic Ratings

1.- Needs considerable improvement - substantial improvement required to meet acceptable standards.

2.- Needs improvement - some improvement required to meet acceptable standards

3.- Normal - meets acceptable standards

4.- Above normal - exceeds normally acceptable standards in most instances.

5.- Exceptional - displays rare and unusual personal characteristics.

4168B/1

Personnel Appraisal: Employees in Salary Grades 5-8

Date of review	Time on position		S.G.	Age		Name
	Yrs	Mths		Yrs		
Period of Review	Position Title					Area

Important : Read guide notes carefully before proceeding with the following sections

Section One

Performance Factors	NA	U	M	SP	E	O		Section Two	Performance Characteristics 1 2 3 4 5 6
Administrative Skills								Initiative	
Communications - Written								Persistence	
Communications - Oral								Ability to work with others	
Problem Analysis								Adaptability	
Decision making								Persuasiveness	
Delegation								Self-confidence	
Quantity of Work								Judgement	
Development of Personnel								Leadership	
Development of Quality Improvements								Creativity	

Section Three Highlight Performance Factors and particular strengths/weaknesses of employee which significantly affect Job Performance

Overall Performance Rating (Taking into account ratings given)

Prepared by: Signature _____ Date _____ Position Title _____

Section Four Comments by reviewing authority

IR Review Initial

Signature _____ Date _____ Position Title _____ Date

Section Five Supervisor's Notes on Counselling Interview

Signature _____ Date _____ Position Title _____

Section Six Employees Reactions and Comment

Signature _____ Date

NOTES

Activity 3   **(15 minutes)**

Give three advantages of a performance management approach to appraisal.

In introducing 'performance management', we have raised the possibility that an employee might be involved in monitoring and evaluating his or her own performance. If targets are clear, and the employee is able to be honest and objective, self-assessment may be both effective and satisfying.

2.2 Who does the appraising?

Organisations have begun to recognise that the employee's immediate boss is not the only (or necessarily the best) person to assess his or her performance. Other 'stakeholders' in the individual's performance might be better, including the people (s)he deals with on a day to day basis:

    (a)   The current (and perhaps previous) boss (including temporary supervisors)
    (b)   Peers and co-workers (**peer appraisal**)
    (c)   Subordinates; (**upward appraisal**)
    (d)   External customers
    (e)   The employee him or herself (**self appraisal**)

360 degree feedback

360 degree feedback also known as 'multi-rater instruments' and 'multi-source assessment' is based on the recognition that the employee's immediate boss is not the only (or necessarily the best) person to assess his or her performance. According to Peter Ward (who introduced the system at Tesco in 1987) in a feature in *People Management* (9 February 1995):

> Traditional performance measurement systems have rarely operated on more than one or two dimensions. However, 360-degree feedback is designed to enable all the stake-holders in a person's performance to comment and give feedback. This includes the current (and perhaps previous) boss (including temporary supervisors), peers and co-workers, subordinates and even external customers. Finally, the employee's own self-assessment is added and compared.

This information is usually collected (anonymously) through questionnaires, either on paper or on disk.

The advantages of 360 degree feedback are as follows.

    (a)   It offers the opportunity to build up a rounded picture of an employee's performance: the more relevant parties contribute, the more complete the picture.

    (b)   Multiple appraisal may reduce or at least balance the element of subjectivity which inevitably enters appraisal of one individual by another, particularly where there are interpersonal or political issues between the individual and his immediate superior.

    (c)   360 degree feedback increases the amount and openness of task and performance-related communication in the organisation, especially where inter-departmental colleagues are asked to participate. This in turn can lead to:

        (i)   Increased awareness and integration of overall and sub-unit objectives

(ii) Increased integration of plans for learning and performance improvement

(iii) Cross-fertilisation of ideas on performance and objectives, which may elicit innovations and creative solutions to problems

(d) The element of upward appraisal (of superior by subordinate) can overcome barriers to upward communication, and can encourage improvement of leadership through a better appreciation of the experience of the followers.

(e) It takes into account feedback from customers (external and internal) that is particularly valuable in:

(i) Encouraging and monitoring the customer care orientation of the organisation as a whole - in line with modern thinking about business processes, quality management and so on

(ii) Showing a commitment to respond meaningfully to customer feedback

(iii) Focusing areas of an employee's performance that are recognised to have real impact on the business

(iv) Encouraging the 'internal customer' concept within the organisation, as an aid to co-ordination

(f) The extensive information-gathering process, and feedback from key performance areas and contacts, signals the seriousness with which appraisal is regarded by the organisation, reinforcing commitment to performance management and improvement.

The approach has a number of disadvantages, however.

(a) Subjectivity is not eliminated by the process: a number of subjective viewpoints is arguably no fairer than just one.

(b) Suspicion and hostility may be aroused by being judged by one's peers: the appraiser may hesitate to give a critical appraisal that may be construed as 'disloyal'.

(c) Upward appraisal is notoriously difficult: there may be fears of reprisal by the superior for a critical appraisal, or vindictive appraisal for political reasons. Superiors may find it hard to adjust to learning from their subordinates.

(d) It is not easy to define performance criteria that will be meaningful and measurable for each appraiser, nor to weight the evaluations of the different appraisers, nor to reconcile or prioritise contradictory evaluations by different appraisers.

(e) There is extra organisation, paperwork and evaluation to be done. This has cost implications, as well as behavioural ones: some parties to the appraisal process may resent extra work.

Activity 4 (20 minutes)

Peter Ward gives an example of the kinds of questionnaire that might be used as the instrument of 360-degree feedback. 'A skill area like "communicating", for example, might be defined as "the ability to express oneself clearly and to listen effectively to others". Typical comments would include "Presents ideas or information in a well-organised manner" (followed by rating scale); or: "Allows you to finish what you have to say".'

Rate yourself on the two comments mentioned here, on a scale of 1–10. Get a group of friends, fellow-students, even a tutor or parent, to write down, **anonymously**, on a piece of paper **their** rating for you on the same two comments. Keep them in an envelope, unseen, until you have a few.

Compare them with your self-rating. If you dare... What drawbacks did you (and your respondents) find to such an approach?

Upward appraisal

A notable modern trend, adopted in the UK by companies such as BP and British Airways , is **upward** appraisal, whereby employees are rated not by their superiors but by their subordinates. The followers appraise the leader.

The advantages of this method might be as follows.

(a) Subordinates tend to know their (one) superior better than superiors know their (many) subordinates

(b) Instead of the possible bias of an individual manager's ratings, the various ratings of several employees may reflect a rounded view

(c) Subordinates' ratings have more impact, because it is less usual to receive feedback from below: a manager's view of good management may be rather different from a team's view of being managed

(d) Upward appraisal encourages subordinates to give feedback and raise problems they may have with their boss, which otherwise would be too difficult or risky for them

---

Activity 5 (15 minutes)

Imagine you had to do an upward appraisal on your boss, parent or teacher. Suggest the two major problems that might be experienced with upward appraisal.

Having reported on an individual's performance – whether in a written narrative comment, or on a prepared appraisal form – a manager must discuss the content of the report with the individual concerned.

2.3 The appraisal interview

There are basically three ways of approaching appraisal interviews.

(a) The **tell and sell** method. The manager tells the subordinate how (s)he has been assessed, and then tries to 'sell' (gain acceptance of) the evaluation and any improvement plans.

(b)   The **tell and listen** method. The manager tells the subordinate how (s)he has been assessed, and then invites comments. The manager therefore no longer dominates the interview throughout, and there is greater opportunity for counselling as opposed to pure direction. The employee is encouraged to participate in the assessment and the working out of improvement targets and methods; change in the employee may not be the sole key to improvement, and the manager may receive helpful feedback about job design, methods, environment or supervision.

(c)   The **problem-solving** approach. The manager abandons the role of critic altogether, and becomes a counsellor and helper. The discussion is centred not on assessment of past performance, but on future solutions of the employee's work problems. The employee is encouraged to recognise the problems, think solutions through, and commit himself to improvement. This approach is more involving and satisfying to the employee and may also stimulate creative problem-solving.

EXAMPLE

*   A survey of appraisal interviews given to 252 officers in a UK government department found that:

    (a)   Interviewers have difficulty with negative performance feedback (criticism), and tend to avoid it if possible

    (b)   Negative performance feedback (criticism) is, however, more likely to bring forth positive post-appraisal action, and is favourably received by appraisees, who feel it is the most useful function of the whole process, if handled frankly and constructively

    (c)   The most common fault of interviewers is talking too much

    The survey recorded the preference of appraisees for a 'problem-solving' style of participative interview, over a one-sided 'tell and sell' style.

*   In 1995, Saville and Holdsworth (the largest occupational psychology practice in the world) conducted a survey into attitude towards appraisal interviews in the UK. They found that 96% of their survey group had conventional appraisal systems. Of these, 31% had self-appraisal, 11% had upward appraisal, 7% included peer appraisal and 74% expressed an interest in finding out more about 360 degree feedback.

Many organisations waste the opportunity represented by appraisal for **upward communication**. If an organisation is working towards empowerment, it should harness the aspirations and abilities of its employees by asking positive and thought-provoking questions.

(a)   Do you fully understand your job? Are there any aspects you wish to be made clearer?

(b)   What parts of your job do you do best?

(c)   Could any changes be made in your job which might result in improved performance?

(d)   Have you any skills, knowledge, or aptitudes which could be made better use of in the organisation?

(e)   What are your career plans? How do you propose achieving your ambitions in terms of further training and broader experience?

Follow-up

After the appraisal interview, the manager may complete his or her report with an overall assessment and/or the jointly-reached conclusion of the interview, with recommendations for follow-up action. This may take the following forms.

(a)   Informing appraisees of the results of the appraisal, if this has not been central to the review interview. (Some people argue that there is no point making appraisals if they are not openly discussed, but unless managers are competent and committed to reveal results in a constructive, frank and objective manner, the negative reactions on all sides may outweigh the advantages.)

(b)   Carrying out agreed actions on training, promotion and so on

(c)   Monitoring the appraisee's progress and checking that (s)he has carried out agreed actions or improvements

(d)   Taking necessary steps to help the appraisee to attain improvement objectives, by guidance, providing feedback, upgrading equipment, altering work methods or whatever

If follow-up action is not taken, employees will feel that appraisal is all talk and just a waste of time, and that improvement action on their side will not be appreciated or worthwhile.

Activity 6   **(2 hours)**

Look up the procedures manual of your organisation, and read through your appraisal procedures. Also get hold of any documentation related to them; the appraisal report form and notes, in particular.

How effective do you think your appraisal procedures are? Measure them against the criteria given above. How do you **feel** about appraisal interviews?

If you can get hold of an appraisal report form, have a go at filling one out for yourself - a good exercise in self-awareness!

2.4   Dealing with problem performers

In most organisations, the overall level of performance can be assessed on a year-by-year basis through the appraisal system. The manager and the appraisee can agree on objectives to be set and targets to be reached. It should therefore be possible to track poor performance on a month-by-month basis.

There may be occasions where normal use of the appraisal system is not possible, however, or the poor performance is such that it cannot be dealt with by the normal methods. In this case, managers are required to take a more in-depth view of the situation.

(a)   The facts need to be established. What is the real nature of the job? Has it changed so much that the job no longer fits the job description for which the employee was recruited?

(b)   Are there particular issues arising from the employee's personality which are causing the poor performance?

(c)   Are there personality clashes between the employee and other team members? Is the employee being singled out unfairly for the poor performance of the team as a whole?

(d)   Are there factors outside the work situation leading to the poor performance, such as marital or financial problems?

(e)   Might the problem be less with the employee than with the actual job design, work layout and so forth? Changing these might improve performance.

(f)   Is the poor performance a reaction to management style? Managers have a responsibility for their own behaviour.

(g)   Is there a problem with the employee's ability? Is the poor performer fundamentally incapable of doing the job?

In order to deal with the issue, the following four-step process could be implemented.

(a)   Have a chat with the individual, and secure the individual's agreement as to the following.

   (i)   **The facts.** The individual and the manager should accept that there is a problem; this may not be obvious to the individual.

   (ii)   **The causes.** The individual and the manager should agree on the causes of the problem. If one of the causes is the manager's own leadership style, then this should be taken on board. A constructive, rather than punitive, atmosphere is needed. It may be that the individual has been given too much to do, or has not been trained properly.

   (iii)   **The remedies.** The individual and the manager should agree on the remedies to the problem. Some of these might relate to the individual, such as presentation, or completion of work by deadlines. The manager might have to take some of the remedies on board, such as re-designing the job. If the poor performance arises out of interpersonal problems in the group, the remedies will involve other people. As for temporary, personal problems, the individual might be encouraged to take leave entitlement or, in extreme circumstances, have a reduced workload for a short period.

   Of course, one aspect of the performance might be caused by a lack of training, and this can be identified easily.

(b)   Ensure the individual understands the consequences of persistent poor performance, where relevant. This might involve invoking the firm's disciplinary procedures.

(c)   Concentrate on issues of behaviour, not personality.

(d)   Agree a period of time over which performance is expected to improve.

It is vital that the manager provides the individual with relevant feedback, both good and bad.

The problems associated with dealing with poor performers should be reduced if an organisation implements an overall policy towards the issue.

(a)   The organisation's prime concern is the effectiveness in which it carries out its mission. Staff performance is crucial to such effectiveness.

(b)   As far as possible, there should be objective standards for measuring people's performance.

(c)   People should know what performance is expected of them.

(d)   Poor performance cannot be treated until its causes are found out.

(e)   The organisation should take all reasonable steps to enable the poor performer to improve his or her performance, but persistent failure to improve might require that the employee be given other duties or, where this is not possible, the employment can be terminated. This might unfortunately be the case if the poor performance arises out of lack of ability.

(f)   Where the poor performance arises from breaches of discipline, the firm's disciplinary procedures should be invoked. Most performance issues are not disciplinary matters, however.

2.5   Assessing potential

Definition

> **Potential review** is the use of appraisal to forecast where and how fast an individual is progressing.

Potential review can be used as feedback to the individual to indicate the opportunities open to him or her in the organisation in the future. It will also be vital to the organisation in determining its management promotion and succession plans.

Information for potential assessment will include:

(a)   Strengths and weaknesses in the employee's existing skills and qualities

(b)   Possibilities and strategies for improvement, correction and development

(c)   The employee's goals, aspirations and attitudes, with regard to career advancement, staying with the organisation and handling responsibility

(d)   The opportunities available in the organisation, including likely management vacancies, job rotation/enrichment plans and promotion policies for the future

No single review exercise will mark an employee down for life as 'promotable' or otherwise. The process tends to be on-going, with performance at each stage or level in the employee's career indicating whether (s)he might be able to progress to the next step. However, an approach based on performance in the current job is highly fallible. L J Peter pointed out that managers tend to be promoted from positions in which they have proved themselves competent, until one day they reach a level at which they are no longer competent – promoted 'to the level of their own incompetence'!

Moreover, the management succession plan of an organisation needs to be formulated in the long term. It takes a long time to equip a manager with the skills and experience needed at senior levels, and the organisation must develop people continuously if it is to fill the shoes of departing managers without crisis.

Some idea of **potential** must therefore be built into appraisal. It is impossible to predict with any certainty how successful an individual will be in what will, after all, be different circumstances from anything (s)he has experienced so far. However, some attempt can be made to:

(a) Determine **key indicators of potential**: in other words, elements believed to be essential to management success; these include past track record, and also administrative, interpersonal and analytical skills; leadership; orientation towards work, and a taste for making money; or a suitable mix of any of these

(b) **Simulate** the conditions of the position to which the individual would be promoted, to assess his or her performance. This may be achieved using case studies, 'in tray' exercises (to test workload management and problem solving) role plays, presentations or team discussions and so on. An alternative approach might be to offer some real experience (under controlled conditions) by appointing the individual to assistant or deputy positions or to committees or project teams, and assessing his or her performance. This is still no real predictor of his or her ability to handle the whole job, on a continuous basis and over time, however, and it may be risky, if the appraisee fails to cope with the situation.

Activity 7   **(20 minutes)**

What do you think 'key indicators' of potential to become a successful senior manager might be? Brainstorm some, alone or in a **group**.

In theory, systematic appraisal schemes may seem fair to the individual and worthwhile for the organisation, but in practice the system often goes wrong. Let's see how, and what can be done.

3 PROBLEMS WITH APPRAISAL SCHEMES

3.1 Crticisms of appraisal schemes

Even the best objective and systematic appraisal scheme is subject to personal and interpersonal problems!

(a) Appraisal is often **defensive on the part of the subordinate,** who believes that criticism may mean a low bonus or pay rise, or lost promotion opportunity.

(b) Appraisal is often **defensive on the part of the superior,** who cannot reconcile the role of judge and critic with the human relations aspect of interviewing and management. (S)he may in any case feel uncomfortable about 'playing God' with the employee's future.

(c) The superior might show **conscious or unconscious bias** in the appraisal or may be influenced by rapport (or lack of it) with the interviewee. Systems without clearly-defined standard criteria will be particularly prone to the subjectivity of the assessor's judgements.

(d) The manager and subordinate may both be **reluctant to devote time and attention to appraisal.** Their experience in the organisation may indicate that the exercise is a waste of time (especially if there is a lot of form-filling) with no relevance to the job, and no reliable follow-up action.

(e) The organisational culture may **simply not take appraisal seriously:** interviewers are not trained or given time to prepare, appraisees are not encouraged to contribute, or the exercise is perceived as a 'nod' to Human Relations with no practical results.

Lockett, in his book *Effective Performance Management,* lists a number of reasons why appraisal may not always be effective.

(a) **Appraisal as confrontation.** ' ... one must ask why it [the appraisal] is approached by both parties with all the enthusiasm of a French aristocrat inspecting a guillotine. The appraisal is often seen as a showdown, a good sorting out or a clearing of the air.' The reasons for such a dysfunctional conflict are clear.

  (i) Lack of agreement on levels of performance

  (ii) Subjective feedback on performance ineffectively delivered

  (iii) Appraisals based on yesterday's performance and not on the whole year

  (iv) Disagreement on long-term career prospects

An effective performance appraisal system should ensure that such issues are addressed.

(b) **Appraisal as judgement.** ' ... it is seen as a one-sided process in which the manager acts as judge, jury and counsel for the prosecution. The process of performance management, if it is to be effective, needs to be jointly operated in order to retain the commitment and develop the self-awareness of the individual.'

(c) **Appraisal as chat.** 'The other extreme to be avoided is the "chat around the coffee table" without either purpose or outcome. Performance management is a disciplined, structured process with clear objectives and joint ownership of any outcomes. Many managers, embarrassed by the need to give feedback and set stretching targets, reduce the appraisal to a few mumbled "well dones!" and leave the interview with a briefcase full of unresolved issues that they have felt ill-equipped to raise.'

(d) **Appraisal as bureaucracy.** In some organisations the appraisal becomes nothing more than a bureaucratic exercise, measured by the completion of the necessary documentation. Underpinning such an approach is a lack of understanding of the relevance of appraisal to both the appraiser, the appraisee and the organisation.

(e) **Appraisal as unfinished business.** Appraisals should not be a one-off event but rather should be part of a continuous and on-going process.

(f) **Appraisal as annual event.** 'In the current climate, to review performance once a year is ludicrously relaxed and undisciplined. Most targets set at appraisal become irrelevant and out of date within months or even weeks. Twelve months later both parties can hardly remember what was agreed and the whole process becomes a painful exercise in retrospective rationalisation rather than a stimulating exercise in forward thinking.'

Activity 8 (15 minutes)

What would you anticipate the effects of appraisal on employee motivation to be?

3.2 Improving the system

The appraisal scheme should itself be assessed (and regularly re-assessed). Here's a handy checklist.

(a) **Relevance**

    (i) Does the system have a useful purpose, relevant to the needs of the organisation and the individual?

    (ii) Is the purpose clearly expressed and widely understood by all concerned, both appraisers and appraisees?

    (iii) Are the appraisal criteria relevant to the purposes of the system?

(b) **Fairness**

    (i) Is there reasonable standardisation of criteria and objectivity throughout the organisation?

    (ii) Has attention been given to the potential for direct or indirect discrimination in the criteria and methods of appraisal?

(c) **Serious intent**

    (i) Are managers committed to the system – or is it just something the personnel department thrusts upon them?

    (ii) Who does the interviewing, and are they properly trained in interviewing and assessment techniques?

    (iii) Is reasonable time and attention given to the interviews – or is it a question of 'getting them over with'?

(d) **Co-operation**

    (i) Is the appraisal a participative, problem-solving activity – or a tool of management control?

    (ii) Is the appraisee given time and encouragement to prepare for the appraisal, so that he can make a constructive contribution?

    (iii) Does a jointly-agreed, concrete conclusion emerge from the process?

(e) **Efficiency** is all the above achieved with a justifiable investment of time and cost.

The HR function has a role to play in encouraging line management to carry out systematic appraisal, and in overcoming some of the causes of managerial reluctance to appraise.

(a) Education in the potential benefits of and constructive approaches to appraisal may help, starting to build a culture where appraisal is perceived to be a primary problem-solving tool and keystone of managerial effectiveness.

(b) HR should design, and instruct managers in the use of, workable procedures and documentation for appraisal.

    (i) Standard review forms, based on relevant and specific standards of assessment, might be provided

    (ii) Grades and ratings should be related to work priorities and standards and clearly defined

    (iii) Results-oriented schemes might be designed, relieving the manager to an extent of his role as critic and encouraging co-operative problem-solving and post-appraisal action

(iv) Training sessions may be organised to help assessors. Most large organisations with standard review forms also issue detailed guidance notes to aid assessors

However, a change in attitudes and practice such as would be required in many organisations will not be easy to achieve, particularly since part of the attitude problem is likely to be the feeling that appraisal is being imposed on line managers by the HR department, which does not understand the operational difficulties. Ultimately, the cultural change may have to come from the HR department's own practices: the HR manager will have to lead by example, to show that it can be done.

4 PERFORMANCE MANAGEMENT

4.1 Why performance management?

In an article in *Personnel Management* in September 1993, Clive Fletcher commented on 'the breakup of the traditional, monolithic approach' to performance appraisal.

Connock (*HR Vision*, 1991) agrees: 'In the late 1980s the emphasis moved from performance appraisal to performance management. Whilst setting clear and measurable objectives was always a major part of earlier schemes, the emphasis was more on the appraisal of past performances'.

Definition

Performance management is a form of management by objectives in which there is a dual emphasis: on setting key accountabilities, objectives, measures, priorities and time scales for the following review period *and* appraising performance at the end of the period'.

Connock suggests four reasons for this shift in emphasis.

(a) Competitive pressures mean that if organisations do not improve they will not survive.

(b) It is now widely realised that corporate missions and strategic objectives can be more effectively implemented by linking them to individual objectives.

(c) The new focus on quality in many companies mean that quality standards have to be set or refined and this has fed through to the performance management processes.

(d) Performance-related pay is being used more and more widely. If it is to be used effectively, 'clear objectives, measures and time scales are necessary from which judgements about the individual's contribution can be made'.

There are a number of advantages to this development.

(a) Fletcher identifies a major advantage of performance management as the separation of performance appraisal from performance related pay awards. This takes some of the fear and inhibition out of the appraisal part of the process.

(b) Objective-setting gives employees the security and satisfaction of both understanding their jobs and knowing exactly what is expected of them. (A 1995 report by the Audit Commission, entitled *'Calling the Tune'*, showed that local authorities who operated a comprehensive performance management system also scored highly in staff attitude surveys on 'know how' and 'feel good' factors. In other words, objective-setting and appraisal help staff to feel that they understand more about their work, and 'feel good' about it.)

(c) Joint-objective setting and a developmental approach are positive and participatory, encouraging regular and frequent dialogue between managers and individuals or teams, with a shared results focus, and helping employees' to accept and 'own' - commit to - change and improvement.

(d) Performance management 'focuses on future performance planning and improvement rather than retrospective performance appraisal' (Armstrong), so it contributes to an output, customer and flexibility focus.

FOR DISCUSSION

Armstrong (*A Handbook of Personnel Management Practice*, 1996) describes the purpose as follows.

'Performance management is a means of getting better results from the organisation, teams and individuals by understanding and managing performance within an agreed framework of planned goals, standards and competence requirements. It is a process for establishing shared understanding about what *is* to be achieved, and an approach to managing and developing people in a way which increases the probability that it *will* be achieved in the short and long term. It is owned and driven by line management.'

How is this different from performrance appraisal? What are its implications for the HR function: recuritment, reward, training and development and its own role?

How does this work in practice?

4.2 Performance management activities

There are four key performance management activities.

(a) **Preparation of performance agreements** (also known as performance contracts). These set out the individual's or team's objectives, how performance will be measured (ie the performance measures to be used), the knowledge, skills and behaviour needed to achieve the objectives and the organisation's core values.

    (i) Objectives may be either:

        (1) Work/operational (results to be achieved or contribution to be made to the accomplishment of team, departmental and/or organisational objectives) or

        (2) Developmental (personal or learning objectives)

    (ii) The following points should be borne in mind when performance measures are established.

        (1) Measures used should be objective and capable of being assessed

        (2) Appropriate data should be readily available

        (3) If possible, existing measures should be used or adapted

        (4) Measures should relate to results and not to effort

        (5) Those results should be within the individual's control

(iii) Discussions between managers and individuals should ensure that individuals fully understand what is expected of them and that if they fulfil those expectations they will be regarded as having performed well.

(iv) The organisation's core values might cover quality, customer service, equal opportunities and so on.

(b) **Preparation of performance and development plans**. These set out performance and personal development needs.

(c) **Management of performance throughout the year**. This involves the **continuous process** of providing feedback on performance, conducting informal progress reviews and dealing with performance problems as necessary.

(d) **Provision of performance reviews**. These involve both taking a view of an individual's progress to date *and* reaching an agreement about what should be done in the future. The performance review provides the means by which:

(i) Results can be **measured** against targets
(ii) The employee can be given **feedback** on how well he is doing
(iii) **Praise** and **constructive criticism** can be given as necessary
(iv) **Views can be exchanged**
(v) An **agreement can be reached**

Chapter roundup

The main points of an appraisal system can be conveyed diagrammatically as follows.

Performance appraisal

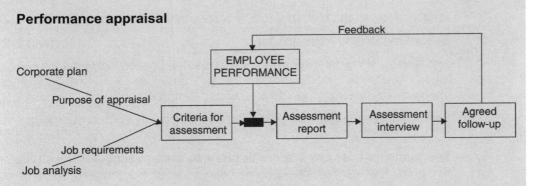

Potential appraisal indicates:

° the individual's promotability (present and likely future);

° the individual's training and development needs;

° the direction and rate of progress of the individual's development;

° the future (forecast) management resource of the organisation;

° the management recruitment, training and development needs of the organisation.

Performance management is a new approach which emphases **both** defining the knowledge, skills, behaviour and targets required to produce the desired results *and* the appraisal and comparison of performance against objectives for the purposes of on-going performance improvement. It is a forward-looking, on-going and collaborative approach.

Quick quiz

1   What are the purposes of appraisal?

2   What bases or criteria of assessment might an appraisal system use?

3   Outline a results-oriented approach to appraisal, and its advantages.

4   What is 360-degree feedback?

5   What is upward appraisal?

6   What follow-up should there be after an appraisal?

7   How can appraisal be made more positive and empowering to employees?

8   What kinds of criticism might be levelled at appraisal schemes by a manager who thought they were a waste of time?

9   What is the difference between performance appraisal and performance management?

10 What techniques might be used to measure an employee's potential to become a successful senior manager?

Answers to quick quiz

1   Identifying performance levels, improvements needed and promotion prospects; deciding on rewards; assessing team work and encouraging, communication between manager and employee.   (see paragraph 1.1)

2   Job analysis, job description, plans, targets and standards.   (para 1.3)

3   Performance against specific, mutually agreed targets and standards.
                                                                        (para 2.1)

4   Appraisal by all the stakeholders in a person's performance.   (para 2.2)

5   Subordinates appraise superiors.   (para 2.2)

6   Appraisees should be informed of the results, agreed activities should be taken, progress should be monitored and whatever resources or changes are needed should be provided or implemented.   (para 2.3)

7   Ensure the scheme is relevant, fair, taken seriously and co-operative.
                                                                        (para 3.2)

8   The manager may say that he or she has better things to do with his or her time, that appraisals have no relevance to the job and there is no reliable follow-up action, and that they involve too much paperwork.
                                                                        (para 3.2)

9   Appraisal is a backward-looking performance review. Performance management is a forward-looking results-orientated scheme.   (para 4.1)

10 Key indicators of performance should be determined and the employee should be assessed against them. The employee could be placed in positions simulating the responsibilities of senior management. (para 2.5)

Answers to Activities

1   Disadvantages to the individual of not having an appraisal system include of the following. The individual is not aware of progress or shortcomings, is unable to judge whether s/he would be considered for promotion, is unable to identify or correct weaknesses by training and there is a lack of communication with the manager.

NOTES

2   You will have come up with your own examples of criteria to assess some jobs but not others. You might have identified such things as:

(a)   Numerical ability (applicable to accounts staff, say, more than to customer contact staff or other non-numerical functions)

(b)   Ability to drive safely (essential for transport workers – not for desk-bound ones)

(c)   Report-writing (not applicable to manual labour, say)

(d)   Creativity and initiative (desirable in areas involving design and problem-solving not routine or repetitive jobs in mass production or bureaucratic organisations)

3   Advantages of performance management include the following.

(a)   The subordinate is more involved in appraisal of his or her own performance, because he or she is able to evaluate his or her success or progress in achieving specific, jointly-agreed targets. The sense of responsibility and independence may encourage job satisfaction and commitment.

(b)   The manager is therefore relieved of his or her role as judge, to an extent, and becomes a counsellor. A primarily problem-solving approach may be adopted (what does the employee require in order to do a better job?)

(c)   Learning and motivation theories suggest, as we have seen, that clear and known targets are important in determining behaviour.

4   Drawbacks to 360-degree appraisal include:

(a)   Respondents' reluctance to give negative feedback to a boss – or friend

(b)   The suspicion that management is passing the buck for negative feedback, getting people to 'rat' on their friends

(c)   The feeling that the appraisee is being picked on, if positive feedback is not carefully balanced with the negative

5   Problems with upward appraisal include fear of reprisals or vindictiveness (or extra form-processing). Some bosses in strong positions might feel able to refuse to act on results, even if a consensus of staff suggested that they should change their ways.

6   This research activity, if you tackle it systematically and record your answers (or prepare them as a presentation), will help you to gather evidence of your competence in Assessment Criteria 21.3

7   Various research studies (by employing organisations and by theorists) have been carried out into exactly what makes a successful senior manager (and could be identified in junior people to indicate that they might *become* successful senior managers).

The following are some of the factors identified. Some you may have guessed – others may be new.

(a)   General effectiveness (track record in task performance and co-worker satisfaction)

(b)   Administrative skills (planning and organising, making good decisions)

BPP PUBLISHING

(c)   Interpersonal skills or intelligence (being aware of others, making a good impression, persuading and motivating)

(d)   Intellectual ability or analytical skills (problem-solving, mental agility)

(e)   Control of feelings (tolerance of stress, ambiguity and so on)

(f)   Leadership (variously defined, but demonstrated in follower loyalty and commitment)

(g)   Imagination and intuition (for creative decision-making and innovation)

(h)   'Helicopter ability' (the ability to rise above the particulars of a situation, to see the whole picture, sift out key elements and conceive strategies - the ability to 'see the wood for the trees')

(i)   Orientation to work (being motivated by work rather than non-work satisfactions; self-starting, rather than needing to be motivated by others)

(j)   Team work (ability and willingness to co-operate with others)

(k)   Taste for making money (empathy with the profit motive: ambition for self and business)

(l)   'Fit' (having whatever mix of all the above skills, abilities and experience the business organisation needs - being in the right place at the right time)

8   The effects of appraisal on motivation are a tricky issue.

(a)   Feedback on performance is regarded as vital in motivation, because it enables an employee to make calculations about the amount of effort required in future to achieve objectives and rewards. Even negative feedback can have this effect – and is more likely to spur the employee on to post-appraisal action.

(b)   Agreement of challenging but attainable targets for performance or improvement also motivates employees by clarifying goals and the value (and 'cost' in terms of effort) of incentives offered.

(c)   A positive approach to appraisal allows employees to solve their work problems and apply creative thinking to their jobs.

However, people rarely react well to criticism – especially at work, where they may feel that their reward or even job security is on the line. In addition, much depends on the self-esteem of the appraisee. If s(he) has a high self-image, (s)he may be impervious to criticism. If s(he) has a low self-image, (s)he may be depressed rather than motivated by criticism.

Assignment 6   **(1¹/₂ hours)**

Biotherm plc

You are the Personnel Director for Biotherm PLC, a detergent and washing powder manufacturer based in Bootle, Merseyside. You have a staff of nine reporting to you, from junior clerks to senior managers, and you are just preparing for the annual round of appraisal interviews. One of your senior personnel officers, Alan Heath, has become a real problem child of late. You have never particularly warmed to this individual; he never really seems part of the team, his attendance record is poor and he never works beyond contracted hours. You know that Alan is not especially fit and healthy, but you rather feel he is playing on his physical condition.

You would describe yourself as a 'person-oriented' leader, although you acknowledge that with difficult staff you tend to become *laissez faire*. This has been the case with Alan: you have never tackled him on his absence record (29 days sickness in the past year) nor on his desire to work to contract. Apart from yourself, he is the only person with extensive and detailed knowledge of employment law, which is valuable in your organisational environment. You secretly admit that this is the main reason for your reticence in handling him: in spite of his difficult demeanour you would be lost without him.

However, you must now grasp the nettle and deal with the situation at his appraisal interview. Prepare a plan for the interview which not only reviews his past performance but also proposes a set of acceptable objectives for the forthcoming year. Remember that your meeting should not, if possible, degenerate into a disciplinary case! Your plan should be organised according to the following headings:

—   Assessment of performance

—   How to improve current performance

—   How to motivate Alan Heath

—   How to assess him for promotability

—   How to tackle unsatisfactory performance areas

Throughout this plan, you should anticipate questions, issues and objectives which he will raise, and resolve how to deal with them.

Chapter 7 :
REWARD MANAGEMENT

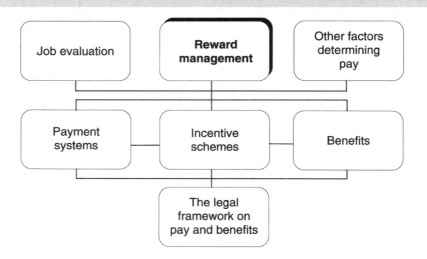

Introduction

In your studies for Core Unit 3: *Organisations and Behaviour*, you should have considered rewards and incentives in the context of employee motivation. You may have noted that pay has a central – although somewhat ambiguous - role in motivating employees to achieve and/or maintain a desired level of performance.

In this chapter we discuss how reward systems can be designed to fulfil the dual requirements of:

(a) **Equity** – to pay rates for the job that are fair in relation to others and that accurately reflect the relative value-adding potential of the job and

(b) **Incentive** – to be able to offer extra reward for extra effort and attainment in pursuit of the organisation's goals

We will look at: techniques for measuring the 'value' of jobs and other methods of determining levels of pay; structures designed to facilitate equity and incentive; and the components of a complete 'remuneration package'. We will also briefly consider the legislative framework of reward systems.

Your objectives

In this chapter you will learn about the following:

(a) Job evaluations

(b) The implementation of (reward) practice in the UK and in another country

(c) Other influences on pay levels

(d) Payment and incentive systems

(e) The legal framework on pay and benefits

1 JOB EVALUATION

1.1 Purpose of job evaluation

Job evaluation is a systematic method of arriving at a wage or salary structure, so that the rate of pay for a job is felt to be **fair** in comparison with other jobs in the organisation.

The Institute of Administrative Management's *Office Job Evaluation* (1976) describes its purpose in the following way.

> 'Any job for which a wage or salary is offered has been evaluated in some way or other in order to arrive at the amount of payment to be made. To this extent it might be said that all organisations which pay employees have job evaluation. However, the term 'job evaluation' is mostly used nowadays with greater precision to describe a formal standardised method for ranking jobs and grouping them into grades. Invariably, such systems are used primarily as the basis for a payment structure....'

Some have suggested that job evaluation is on the wane but a 1994 survey (described later) suggests otherwise.

Definition

> '**Job evaluation** is the process of analysing and assessing the content of jobs, in order to place them in an acceptable rank order which can then be used as a basis for a remuneration system.'
>
> The British Institute of Management *(Job Evaluation)*

Advantages of job-evaluated structures	Disadvantages/limitations of job-evaluated structures
• The reasons for salary levels, and differentials between jobs, has a rational basis that can be explained to employees.	• They pay a fair rate for a job only in the sense that differentials are set according to *relative* worth. Job evaluation alone does not make any recommendations about what the general level of pay ought to be, in money terms.
• The salary structure should be well balanced, even in an organisation that employs people with a wide range of skills.	• They pay a rate for the job irrespective of the personal merits of the job holder or fluctuations in his performance. If an organisation rewards individual merit with bonuses, evaluated differentials will again be distorted.
• The salary structure is based on job content, and not on the personal merit of the job-holder himself. The individual job-holder can be paid personal bonuses in reward for his efforts, and when he moves to another job in the organisation, his replacement on the job will be paid the rate for the job, and will not inherit any personal bonuses of his predecessor.	• Job definition for evaluation purposes supports rigid hierarchical organisation and concepts of status which (arguably) suppress employee motivation and creativity, under labour flexibility/multiskilling and may undermine attempts to foster a people-centred organisation culture: job evaluation assumes that people are commodities who can be made to fit defined roles (Murlis and Fitt, *Personnel Management*, May 1991).

Advantages of job-evaluated structures	Disadvantages/limitations of job-evaluated structures
• Regular job evaluation should ensure that the salary structure reflects change and flexibility.	• Many job evaluation methods suggest that job evaluation is a scientific and accurate technique, whereas in fact there is a large element of subjective judgement involved in awarding points or ratings, and evaluations can be unfair.
• A job-evaluated salary structure might prevent an employer from using discrimination: men and women should be paid the same rate for similar work or work of a similar value as judged under a job-evaluation exercise (1984 amendments to 1970 Equal Pay Act).	• Job evaluated salary structures can get out-of-date – particularly in fast-change environments. There ought to be periodic reviews, but in practice, an organisation might fail to review jobs often enough.
• Analysis of job content and worth are available for use in recruitment, selection, training and other HR contexts.	• Job evaluation only suits 'jobs': some highly flexible organisation structures/cultures are striving to abolish the job concept in favour of freewheeling entrepreneurial project management.

Activity 1   **(1 hour)**

Do you feel your salary is fair for the job you do, and in relation to others? Do you know how your job is evaluated? Do you know how your salary is worked out? What could the organisation do to make the system (a) clearer and (b) fairer?

Either answer these questions yourself, or ask them of an employed person who is willing to be interviewed by you on this topic.

1.2   Methods of job evaluation

In large organisations, it is impossible to evaluate every individual job, because the process would be too long and costly. Instead, selected key jobs are evaluated, and provide a benchmark for the evaluation of other similar jobs. Ideally, the key jobs chosen for analysis should be jobs comparable with jobs in other organisations, for which a market rate of pay is known. Some information for evaluation may already be available in the form of job descriptions. It may be said that, even in its more quantitative or analytical forms, job evaluation is 'systematic' rather than 'scientific'. The number of different inputs and environmental variables make an element of subjectivity inevitable, despite refinements aimed at minimising it.

- **Non-analytical** approaches to job evaluation make largely subjective judgements about the whole job, its difficulty, and its importance to the organisation relative to other jobs. (Ranking and classification are methods of this type.)

- **Analytical** methods of job evaluation identify the component factors or characteristics involved in the performance of each job, such as skill, responsibility, experience, mental and physical efforts required. Each component is separately analysed, evaluated and weighted: degrees of each factor, and the importance of the factor within the job, are quantified. (Examples of such methods include points rating and factor comparison.) These methods involve detailed analysis and a numerical basis for comparing jobs as like to like.

Activity 2   **(30 minutes)**

Can you see how an element of subjectivity may remain even in 'analytical' methods?

(a)   Suggest **three** ways in which such methods would remain subjective to an extent.

(b)   Why is objectivity desirable?

The revised Equal Pay Act clearly states that job evaluations must use analytical methods: they must examine '**in terms of the demands made on the worker** under various headings (for instance, effort, skill, decision) the jobs to be done by all or any of the employees in an undertaking'. Non-analytical systems are open to challenge in the courts, so we will not cover them here.

We shall describe four main methods of job evaluation.

(a)   *Factor comparison*
(b)   *Points rating*
(c)   *The HAY-MSL method*
(d)   *Competencies*

Factor comparison method

This is an analytical method of job evaluation. It begins with the selection of a number of qualitative factors on which each job will be evaluated. These qualitative factors might include, for example, technical knowledge, physical skill, mental skill, responsibility for other people, responsibility for assets or working conditions.

Key benchmark jobs are then taken, for which the rate of pay is considered to be fair (perhaps in comparison with similar jobs in other organisations). Each key job is analysed in turn, factor by factor, to decide how much of the total salary is being paid for each factor. So if technical skill is 50% of a benchmark job paying £10,000, the factor pay rate for technical skill (within that job) is £5,000. When this has been done for every benchmark job, all the different rates of pay for each factor are correlated, to formulate a ranking and pay scale for that factor.

Other (non-benchmark) jobs are then evaluated by analysing them factor by factor. In this way a salary or grading for the job can be built up. For example, analysis of a clerk's job factor by factor might be:

Factor	Proportion of job		Pay rate for factor (as established by analysis of benchmark jobs)	Job value £
Technical skills	50%	×	£12,000 pa	6,000
Mental ability	25%	×	£16,000 pa	4,000
Responsibility for others	15%	×	£10,000 pa	1,500
Other responsibilities	10%	×	£5,000 pa	500
				12,000

The Institute of Administrative Management comments about the factor comparison method that: 'the system links rates closely to existing levels for key benchmark jobs and depends heavily on careful allocation of money values to each factor of the benchmark jobs. It is not easy to explain to employees, and is best suited to situations where the range of jobs is limited and of a fairly simple nature.' It is not well-suited to the evaluation of office jobs.

Points rating method

Points rating is probably the most popular method of formal job evaluation. It begins with listing a number of factors which are thought to represent the aspects of jobs for which the organisation is willing to pay: these are called '**compensable factors**'. (Remember that jobs are being evaluated, not job holders themselves, and the qualities listed should relate to tasks or outcomes.) In a typical evaluation scheme, there might be about 8-12 factors listed. The factors will vary according to the type of organisation and can be adapted to its changing needs and key values.

A number of **points** is allocated to each compensable factor, as a maximum score, across a range of '**degrees**' which reflect the level and importance (or weighting) of the factors within a job. A comprehensive **points rating chart** is therefore established, covering a range of factors and degrees which can be applied to a variety of jobs. An example of such a chart is shown on the next page: Figure 7.1.

NOTES

	Compensable factor	DEGREE (Weighting)				
		1	*2*	*3*	*4*	*5*
G E N E R A L	Job knowledge	10	25	50	70	-
	Practical experience	15	30	50	70	-
	Physical effort	5	10	15	-	-
	Complexity	15	20	25	30	-
	Judgement/initiative	15	20	30	40	50
	Job conditions	5	10	15	-	-
	Contact with peers	5	10	20	40	-
	Contact with clients	10	20	30	40	50
	Attention to detail	5	10	15	20	-
	Potential for error	5	10	20	40	-
	Confidential data	5	10	15	20	30
	.....	...	...	...	...	...
S U P E V I S O R Y	Nature of supervision	5	10	20	-	-
	Scope of supervision	10	15	25	-	-
	Resource allocation	10	15	25	30	-
	Trust	15	20	30	40	50
	Management reporting	10	15	25	30	-
	Quality	15	30	90	50	60
	.....	...	...	...	...	...

Degree definitions

- **Job knowledge**
  1. Maintain basic procedures; operate and maintain basic machinery; undertake range of tasks under supervision; comply with rules and policies.

  2. Administer a routine area of worker, under supervision; operate and maintain basic machinery to proficient standard; understand purpose of rules and policies and be able to identify compliance issues.

  3. Supervise a small number of staff in routine and non-routine tasks; be responsible for checking of working; manage own routine and non-routine workload; control maintenance of range of machinery and compliance with rules and policies, including coaching/briefing of staff; certificate-level qualification in job-related area

  4. Supervise staff in routine and non-routine tasks; manage quality and customer service issues; plan and co-ordinate own and section workload; systematic view of rules and procedures, with ability to propose improvements; diploma-level qualification in job-related area

  5. -

- **Practical experience** 1. *et cetera*

Figure 7.1: Points rating chart

BPP PUBLISHING

Each **job** is then examined, analysed factor by factor according to the value chart, and a points score awarded for each factor, up to the maximum allowed. The total points score for each job is found by adding up its points score for each factor. The total points scored for each job provides the basis for ranking the jobs in order of importance, for grading jobs, if required, and for fixing a salary structure. An example of a job evaluation form for points rating is shown below: Figure 7.2

Job evaluation form

Key job code _____	Department _____
Job type _____	Job holder studied _____
Date _____	Employee number _____

Task number

Description

Factor	Rating			Comments
	Points	Weighting	Total	

Skills and knowledge
  Education/qualifications
  Experience
  Dexterity				

Skills sub-total				
Initiative				

Responsibility
  People
  Equipment
  Resources				

Responsibility sub-total				

Effort
  Mental
  Physical				

Effort sub-total				

Communication
  Oral
  Written				

Communication sub-total				
Interpersonal skills				

Conditions of work
  Hazards
  Isolation
  Monotony				

Conditions sub-total				
TOTAL				
RANKING				
COMMENTS				

Figure 7.2: Points rating form

'Points rating has the advantage of flexibility in that the factors selected are best suited for the particular types of job being evaluated, and the importance given to each factor is decided by the allocation of points. It also provides a rank order of jobs according to the numbers of points, without determining the money value of the job. This allows the pattern of grades and salary rates to be determined as separate operations. Like all systems, it has some disadvantages; the selection of factors, the points score allocated to a job, and the points weighting given each factor remain subjective judgements.'

The Institute of Administrative Management

HAY-MSL method

The HAY-MSL method is an 'off-the-shelf' job evaluation package which organisations can purchase. It is a points method, whereby points are awarded for significant elements of a job and the importance of individual jobs relative to others is measured by comparing their total points scores. The job elements by which jobs are compared are, in effect:

(a) **Know-how**: the amount of skill, knowledge and experience needed to do the job, including the ability to handle people

(b) **Problem solving**: this is concerned with the amount of discretion and judgement the job holder must exercise, the frequency of problems that call for decisions by the job-holder and the extent to which the job-holder is expected to contribute new ideas

(c) **Accountability**: this is the assessment of whether the job-holder is responsible and accountable for small or large areas of work, and whether the activities of the job holder affect the organisation to a larger or smaller extent in terms of money (revenues and expenditures)

The HAY-MSL system lends itself better to professional, supervisory, managerial and executive positions than to lower-ranking jobs.

Activity 3   **(No time limit)**

Find out now – if you do not already know – what system of job evaluation your organisation uses, and inspect the relevant supporting documentation if possible. Read any instructions or procedure manuals available.

Competencies

These methods are a fairly recent development. They use a scheme of 'competence'-related appraisal criteria, with degree or range statements – such as those developed for National Vocational Qualifications (NVQs) – integrated into a point-factor scheme. Many are associated with what is called 'broad-banding': retaining only four or five grades, for each of which the maximum level of pay may be 100% or more above the minimum pay level.

EXAMPLE

A survey by the CIPD found that 55% of responding organisations operate a formal job evaluation scheme. Most (68%) use a proprietary scheme devised by management consultants and others. Around 30% use point-factor rating, 20% job classification and 10% competencies or factor comparison.

'Job evaluation continues to flourish in one form or another because organisations dislike chaos. Job evaluation at least brings a semblance of order and equity to the process of pay determination. Our research did, however, reveal that some companies are establishing the relative value of roles quite effectively without the use of bureaucratic job-evaluation systems. A visit to the US confirmed that a number of organisations there are abandoning the point-factor schemes they developed in the 1970s and 1980s, and are adopting much more flexible, people-based approaches that use competencies and broad-banding.

'Traditional, rigid, bureaucratic and hierarchical approaches to job evaluation, which purport to be objective, scientific and rational and to represent job evaluation as a system that will deliver the "right answer", are inappropriate and are generally recognised as such. Many organisations are finding that traditional approaches cannot be used effectively to evaluate "knowledge" workers.

'Organisations that have gone through delayering and are team-, process- and project-based are eliminating artificial restrictions. This is prompting them to seek means of valuing jobs that are more congruent with the need for operational and role flexibility. They are turning to broad-banded or job-family pay structures, within which there is more scope to reward people for their capacity to adapt to new challenges as they develop their competencies and expand their roles - increased reward no longer depends on gaining extra points in order to be upgraded.'

People Management, September 1995

In practice, 'carrying out a job evaluation' (Assessment Criteria 21:3) will probably involve using an existing points rating chart and job analysis, according to the system used or developed by the organisation. (So do Activity 3 as soon as possible!) However, it is worth considering what issues are raised by the introduction of job evaluation.

1.3 Introducing a job evaluation scheme

Steps in introducing a job evaluation programme will include:

(a) Informing and involving staff - particularly where trade union attitudes need to be considered

(b) Selecting benchmark jobs as a sample for internal and external comparison

(c) Planning the programme itself, including:

   (i) Staffing - who is responsible? what training do they need?
   (ii) Information - to management, staff and unions
   (iii) Procedures, methods and timetable
   (iv) Techniques for pay comparison and job analysis as required

(d) Communicating and negotiating the results and structure

(e) Maintaining the scheme, including machinery for regradings and appeals

Job evaluation is a highly political exercise, and will require openness and communication - not to mention diplomacy - throughout.

(a) Staff will have to be informed of the overall purpose, objectives and potential benefits of the system. It will, in particular, have to be made clear that the employees themselves are not being judged or evaluated. Increasingly, job evaluation **committees** are used, to involve staff in setting up, conducting and maintaining the scheme, to take advantage of the job holders' knowledge, and to minimise suspicion and demoralisation.

(b) The degree of consultation and participation will depend heavily on union attitudes (where unionisation exists). Unions may consider that job evaluation should be the true basis for **job** structuring only - otherwise it undermines the traditional role of collective bargaining. Others may simply insist on full communication between management and unions throughout the programme, the active participation of union members, and the institution of revision/appeals procedures.

(c) If an evaluation committee is used, there may be a delicate balance of power between management nominees, trade union representatives, and specialists (from the personnel or, in larger organisations, salary administration department). This will have to be moulded into a team, by sorting out its collective responsibilities and its component interests.

(d) There are bound to be problems which will require appeal, and revision will in any case be necessary over time. Some of these situations may be sensitive, not only where unions are involved: managers may regard the grading of jobs in their jurisdiction to be part of their political power base, and may be sensitive to any perceived undervaluation. Appeal procedures will have to be negotiated, to involve:

    (i) The immediate superior, in the first instance

    (ii) The grading committee

    (iii) If the judgement is still unacceptable, union branch officials, or a higher organisational authority (according to normal grievance procedure for non-unionised workers) and

    (iv) A top management committee, for final judgement

FOR DISCUSSION

People Management (11/3/99) reported that employees at Vauxhall's Ellesmere Port plant have asked for their pay slips to show their pay in euros as well. 'The suggestion, if implemented, would allow the workforce to compare its pay with the higher-earning German employees ...'

What might the benefits and limitations of job evaluation be in this scenario?

As the above Discussion Topic suggests, rating alone cannot determine how much people are paid or want to be paid: other forces are at work. We will now consider what those may be.

2 OTHER FACTORS DETERMINING PAY

2.1 Equity

Definition

> **Equity** is 'the level of earnings for people in different occupations which is felt by society to be reasonably consistent with the importance of the work which is done, and which seems relatively fair to the individual.'   Wilfred Brown

In other words, pay must be **perceived** and felt to match the level of work, and the capacity of the individual to do it: it must be 'felt-fair'. Pay structures should allow individuals to feel that they are being rewarded in keeping with their skill, effort and contribution, and with the rewards received by others for their relative contributions.

Reward strategists should not under estimate employees' beliefs and cultural values about the worth or value of their job and contribution relative to others.

2.2 Negotiated pay scales.

Pay scales, differentials and minimum rates may have been negotiated at plant, local or national level, according to various environmental factors:

(a) Legislation and government policy (on equal pay, say, or anti-inflationary increases)

(b) The economy (levels of inflation; unemployment, affecting labour supply and demand, and therefore market rates)

(c) The relative bargaining strength of the employers and unions/staff associations in negotiation

2.3 Individual performance

'A growing number of organisations, commentators and academics assert that paying for individual skills, contribution and competence is more relevant to the needs of today than traditional job-based evaluation . . . Placing the heaviest emphasis on job requirements discounts the importance of other compensatable factors - particularly individual capability and performance.'

(Murlis and Fitt, *Personnel Management*, May 1991).

2.4 Market rates of pay

Thomason suggests that if an employer were free to pay what he liked, he would pay 'the lowest rate consistent with securing enough labour in quantity to satisfy his production needs and . . . to ensure . . . a sufficient contribution to the enterprise's tasks to allow it to survive.' This is the **market rate** for the given type of labour.

The market rate will vary with supply/demand factors, such as:

(a) the relative scarcity of particular skills; and

(b) the sensitivity of employers to pay levels or differentials and to the perceived inadequacies: the extent of labour mobility in response may dictate the need for higher rates of pay to retain employees, or to attract them from other organisations. Pay may or may not act as an incentive to change employers, depending on the availability of work elsewhere, the employee's loyalty, willingness to face risk and change, and the attractions of his present job which may not be measurable in financial terms: work relationships, conditions and so on.

Market rates of pay will have most influence on pay structures where there is a standard pattern of supply and demand in the open labour market. If an organisation's rates fall below the benchmark rates in the local or national labour market from which it recruits, it will have trouble attracting and holding employees.

The concept of the market rate, however, is not exact. Different employers are bound to pay a range of rates for theoretically identical jobs, especially in managerial jobs, where the scope and nature of the duties will vary according to the situation of each organisation.

Factors which distort or dilute the effect of the forces of supply and demand on labour pricing include:

(a)   The organisation's ability to pay.

(b)   The bargaining strength of unions (if any).

(c)   Government intervention, including incomes policies, equal pay legislation and anti-inflationary measures. The National Minimum Wage Regulations 1999, in particular, prevent outright exploitation of labour, even if employers wished to pursue it. In general, where there is no express agreement, the employee is entitled to 'reasonable remuneration'.

(d)   Internal differentials and equity existing in the organisation. Where there are established differentials, or a job-evaluated salary structure, it will be difficult for employers to justify a conspicuously low rate of pay for one type of job, or in response to market fluctuations.

(e)   The culture and value systems of the organisation, which will influence the attitude of management towards the market rate, and whether age, length of service, motivation, employee aspirations and/or other factors are taken into account in the determination of pay, rather than fluctuations in supply and demand.

Activity 4   **(10 minutes)**

What are the arguments *for* and *against* an organisation's offering above-market rates of pay?

EXAMPLE: INTERNATIONAL COMPARISONS

*   Reward policy in Germany is highly collectivised. Each union (organised on broad industry lines) negotiates with the employers federation on a state by state basis – allowing for the relative prosperity of the region. Companies (such as Volkswagen) which are not part of a trade association may negotiate separately with the relevant trade union. Many HR managers will therefore not be involved in wage negotiation at all, but will implement the agreement locally.

    The system of industrial democracy known as 'co-determination' gives a plant-level representative works council the right to co-determine company policy on matters including how wages and salaries are to be paid (method, time), the use of incentives (bonus schemes, piece work, performance-related pay) and so on. Traditionally popular elements of reward systems include holiday and long-service bonuses, suggestion schemes, incentive/merit pay (for manual grades) and profit-sharing (for managerial grades), with employee share ownership schemes attracting tax incentives.

*   In the US, non-unionism and a strong internal labour market have encouraged individualised and independent pay policy. Internalised wage structures sheltered employees in large US firms from external labour market forces, allowing a high degree of employment security, coupled with above-market pay and benefits (with profit-sharing and employee share ownership schemes adding up to 50% to the value of rewards). Observers note, however, that this is changing with downsizing and flexible working: wages are becoming more sensitive to local external conditions, and differentials are no longer driven by seniority or length of service. US firms are increasingly emphasising individual performance factors in

remuneration, and are reducing their pension obligations to employees. The culture of employment in the US, minimising artificial status distinctions between managerial and non-managerial grades, supports salaried status for all staff.

- A key feature of employment in Japan is the seniority system, which links reward with length of service rather than with job or performance factors. This is a subtler distinction than it may appear, since length of service is equated with commitment, skill development and status: 'older = more experienced = better worker'. 'It is a scale of 'person-related' payments – as opposed to 'job related' payments ... an intricate set of rules, based on the exponential principle that the higher you go the faster you rise, designed to give recognition to both seniority and merit. The seniority principle requires that everybody goes up a notch every year' (Dore, 1973, cited by Beardwell and Holdern). This concept of 'performance related pay' is very different from the Western concept of performance as individual achievement: it reflects the complexity of the relationship between the individual, the organisation, the job and socio-cultural values of status, commitment and belonging.

We will now look briefly at some of the issues of salary and wage systems and structures.

3 PAYMENT SYSTEMS

3.1 Salary administration

Salary administration is not to be confused with payroll administration, which is usually a financial function. It refers to the process by which levels of pay for staff employees are determined, monitored and controlled.

Definition

'**Salary administration** is an attempt to achieve the objectives formulated in a salary policy, which itself ought ideally to be a plan, not simply to pay fair and equitable salaries, but to relate and reconcile career aspirations in terms of current and potential earnings, and personal commitment to total organisation objectives. A host of variables is involved.'

Livy, *Corporate Personnel Management*

The aims of salary administration are therefore broadly concerned with:

(a) Obtaining, retaining and motivating suitable staff, within the requirements of the HR plan *by*

(b) Developing and maintaining a **salary structure** which:

    (i) Reflects the hierarchy of jobs and is felt to be **equitable** for jobs with similar responsibilities, and **consistent** in the differentials between differently valued jobs

    (ii) Takes market rates and cost of living increases into account

    (iii) Is flexible enough to accommodate changes in market rates, organisational structure and so on

(iv)   Reward performance commitment and other desired outcomes and creates **incentives** to such performance outcomes, by providing for incremental merit-based awards and progression over time

(c)   **Reviewing** salary levels and differentials

(d)   Operating the system so that it is easily understood and **seen to be fair** by staff

(e)   Controlling salary and administrative **costs** to the organisation

3.2   Salary structures

Armstrong identifies the main objectives in designing a coherent salary structure as being 'to provide for internal **equity** in grading and paying staff and to maintain **competitive rates** of pay' and notes that 'neither of those objectives can be achieved if a chaotic set of rates exists which have evolved over the years and is altered at whim or because of a panic reaction to difficulties in recruitment or retention.'

A salary structure may be designed using any, or a combination, of three main types:

(a)   A graded structure, based on job evaluation
(b)   Rate for age scales
(c)   Progression curves

Graded salary

A typical structure of this type consists of a series of salary grades, to which all jobs are allocated on the basis of job evaluation. For each grade, there is a salary **scale** or range: minimum and maximum salary levels for jobs in that grade.

The **range** and **overlap** of the scales between grades, will require careful thought because of the consequences for promotions, and transfers between grades. For example, the range must be wide enough to allow for progression: people in similarly-graded jobs may perform differently and should be rewarded accordingly. There should also be an overlap, in recognition that an experienced person performing well in a given job may be of more value than a new or poor performer in the next grade up.

The number of different scales in the structure will then depend on the number of distinct grades of jobs (according to job evaluation), the width and overlap of each scale, and the range of appropriate salaries in the organisation from the most junior to most senior job.

Flexibility must be built into the system. Changes in job content and/or market rates should prompt re-grading. Moreover, the main principal of the structure is that progression within a grade is **performance related**, with the assumption that a normally competent individual eventually reaches the scale maximum, unless he is promoted out of the grade first. Again flexibility may be required, for example in the case of an individual whose performance is outstanding, but for whom there are no immediate openings for promotion: discretionary payment of a salary **above** the grade maximum may be made, in order to maintain the individual's loyalty and motivation.

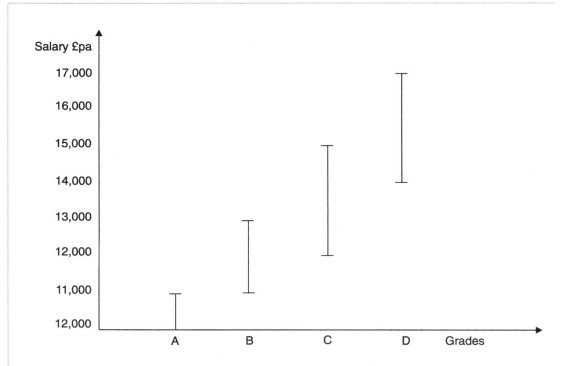

Figure 7.3: Salary structure

Rate for age systems

A rate for age system links the **age** of staff to defined scales or rates, for certain jobs, particularly where there are young employees who are being trained or carrying out junior, routine work. Incremental scales for age are based on the assumption that the value of staff to the organisation is directly related to greater experience and maturity.

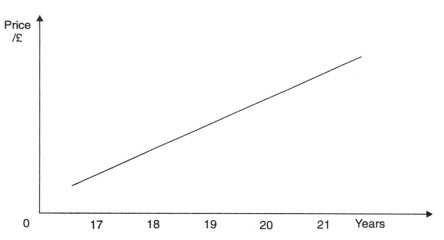

Figure 7.4: Simple incremented rate for age system

Such systems are, in their simplest form, easy to administer, because no evaluation of the relative merit of specific employees has to be made: they are, therefore, perceived to be entirely equitable, but may not have a motivating effect unless a system is used which relates pay to performance as well as age, by applying scales for merit at each age.

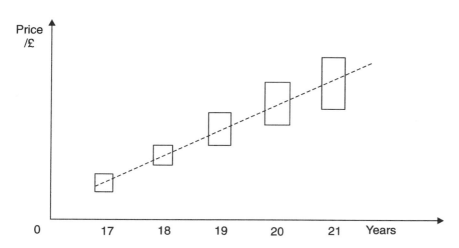

Figure 7.5: With added 'merit bands'

Salary progression curve

The salary progression or **maturity curve** also aims to relate salary increases to maturity and experience, but in the longer term. It is most relevant to staff whose value is measured in terms of their professional ability rather than pure job content: for example, scientific and professional jobs. It is assumed that salary starts at the market rate for the person's **qualifications**, and that he or she will subsequently develop as a result of experience at a standard rate. In fact, some will develop faster than others, so the curve is only a guideline.

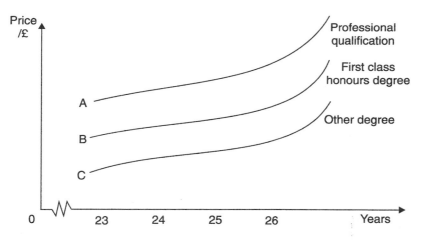

Figure 7.6: Salary progression curve

3.3 Salary review

Salary reviews may be carried out as a general exercise, when all or most salaries have to be increased to keep pace with market rates, cost of living increases or negotiated settlements. **General reviews** are often carried out annually (government regulations permitting) during inflationary periods: this may or may not create problems in financing individual merit awards as well.

Individual salary reviews are carried out to decide on merit awards. Again, these are usually held annually - with interim reviews, possibly for trainees and younger staff who are making fast progress. Some companies phase reviews throughout the year rather than hold them all at once; this is more difficult to administer but does diffuse the tension of a general review period.

Guidelines for salary review will be necessary to minimise the subjectivity of discretionary payments. The total cost of all merit increases, or minimum/maximum amounts for increases, might be specified.

A **salary review budget** will determine the increase that can be allocated for awards, as a percentage of payroll costs for the department. The size of the budget will depend on:

(a)   How average salaries in each grade differ from the target salary (the mid-point): ideally, they should correspond, but may be too high or low. A high ratio indicates that **earnings drift** has taken place, and salaries have moved towards the upper end of the scale – which may or may not correspond to the merits of the staff concerned

(b)   The amount the company estimates it will be able to pay, based on forecast revenue, profit, and labour cost savings elsewhere (perhaps from highly-paid employees leaving, and recruits entering at lower-paid levels: this is called **salary attrition**).

Activity 5   **(No time limit)**

(a)   Is there a salary **policy** and salary **structure** in your organisation? Find out and record their salient details.

(b)   If you had trouble finding out, what does this say about the political aspects of salary administration?

3.4   Wage systems

The terms 'wages' and 'salaries' are sometimes used interchangeably to refer to monetary rewards, but there are traditional distinctions between them.

Wages	Salaries
Manual/blue collar workers – historically on short terms	White-collar workers – historically with greater security of tenure
Paid weekly (traditionally in cash)	Paid monthly (traditionally by direct transfer to bank account
Based on a weekly or hourly rate for time worked, or on a piecework (unit output) rate	Based on an annual sum, of which monthly salary is merely one-twelfth: not directly related to hours worked or output
Paid for time/output – not for attributes, potential, seniority or other contribution to employment	Paid for age, seniority, qualifications, experience, performance; with progression over time
Hours of work strictly controlled ('clocking in and out') and financially penalised for lost time	Hours of work less strictly controlled
Comparatively low status	Comparatively high status: access to benefits and 'perks'

A typical wage structure will include:

   (a)   A basic (time or piecework) rate; *plus*

   (b)   Overtime premium rates ('time and a quarter', 'double time' etc) for work done outside normal hours varying according to time of day, weekends, holidays and so on

   (c)   Shift pay premium rates for employees who work unusual or socially disruptive hours or shift patterns: this is a form of **compensatory** pay

   (d)   Compensatory payments for abnormal working conditions (eg 'danger money', 'dirt money', 'wet money') – although these may be built into basic rates during job evaluation (if applicable)

   (e)   Allowances (eg to employees in high cost-of-living areas like London)

   (f)   Merit or length-of-service bonuses

   (g)   Payments by results bonuses and incentives (discussed in Section 4 of this chapter)

EXAMPLE: INTERNATIONAL COMPARISONS

Night-working and overtime working are legislatively controlled in some EU countries, including statutory minimum rates. Spain, Portugal and Greece have a statutory minimum rate of 125% for night work. French, Greek, German and Irish workers are entitled to 125% rates for overtime; Portuguese workers, 150% for the first hour, and 175% thereafter; Spanish workers typically also get 175% (formerly statutory, now negotiated).

You may have noticed that workplace change tends to make white-collar work more routine and blue-collar work more technologically skilled: the historical reasons for wage/salary distinctions, and associated differences in status (such as clocking on, separate canteens and facilities, different holiday and sick pay entitlements) are disappearing. This has led to the concept of 'harmonisation' or 'single status'.

3.5   Single status schemes

In fact, wage payment systems have been replaced by salaries in many organisations, as part of **single status** or **staff status** schemes. These represent an attempt to harmonise the payment systems operating in an organisation, mainly by removing the distinction between the treatment of manual and white-collar staff. Such agreements 'represent more than just a change of payment systems and an improvement in manual workers' conditions of work. The employers involved were consciously attempting to change the relationships between workers and management. They wanted to encourage responsibility, pride in work, and co-operation, and hoped thereby to increase efficiency.'   (Lupton and Bowey, *Wages and Salaries*).

Activity 6	**(10 minutes)**

What advantages and disadvantages for the organisation and workers can you see from single status schemes?

3.6 Three approaches to reward

There are three basic elements of, or approaches to, employee reward.

(a) **Payment by time**

The amount is paid at intervals of a week or month, and reflects 'hours of work': the amount of time spend at the workplace or on the job. This is appropriate as a basic pay component in jobs where output or effort are less meaningful or measurable (for example, where monitoring, supervising or cognitive activity is concerned). It also provides a relatively constant and predictable basic income.

(b) **Payment by results**

Either all or part of the employee's pay is directly linked to the quantity of the output produced by the individual (or team): for example, piecework, commission bonuses (based on sales, say), output – or target-based bonuses.

(c) **Pay as an incentive**

More sophisticated motivational links between performance and reward offer incentives to output, quality and a wide range of performance variable (customer service, teamworking, innovation and so on). Incentive payment schemes include bonus schemes based on output/productivity or profits generated (for example in profit-sharing and employee share ownership schemes). Individual performance-rated pay systems (where awards are determined by appraisal of individual achievement of objectives) are another incentive approach.

We will now go on to look at incentive schemes in more detail.

4 INCENTIVE SCHEMES

4.1 Performance-related pay (PRP)

In Section 3.6 above, we distinguished payment by results (PBR) from performance-related pay (PRP). PBR is based on work study techniques, establishing what output per hour/day (or time taken to produce a unit of output) should be: it is an approach traditionally applied to manual work, which has a steady and measurable flow of task and output. However, there has been a decline in PBR systems in recent years, as quality and flexibility issues (among others) have made output quantity a less valuable measurement criterion. Team-based PBR, in particular, was subject to inequity (due to necessary fluctuations in output between members) and the whole system was a source of shopfloor conflict around measurement, rate fixing and output norms.

Payment by results (PBR) is, on the other hand, on the increase, as it allows flexibility in determining key targets and results.

For managerial and other salaried jobs, a form of management by objectives will probably be applied so that:

(a) Key results can be identified and specified, for which merit awards (on top of basic salary) will be paid

(b) There will be a clear model for evaluating performance and knowing when or if targets have been reached and payments earned

(c) The exact conditions and amounts of awards can be made clear to the employee, to avoid uncertainty and later resentment

For service and other departments, a PRP scheme may involve **bonuses** for achievement of key results, or **points schemes**, where points are awarded for performance on various criteria (efficiency, cost savings, quality of service and so on) and certain points totals (or the highest points total in the unit, if a competitive system is used) win cash or other awards.

EXAMPLE

Personnel Management, November 1990, reported research into the benefits and problems of performance-related pay in a number of high-profile companies.

	Black & Decker	Komatsu UK	Birds Eye Walls
	1 Benefits of PRP cited		
Improves commitment and capability	Yes	Yes	Yes
Complements other HR initiatives	Yes	Yes	Yes
Improves business awareness	Yes	Yes	Yes
Better two-way communications	Yes	Yes	Yes
Greater supervisory responsibility		Yes	Yes
	2 Potential problems cited		
Subjectivity			Yes
Supervisors' commitment and ability	Yes	Yes	Yes
Translating appraisals into pay	Yes	Yes	Yes
Divisive/against team working			Yes
Union acceptance/employee attitudes			Yes

'In the wrong hands, PRP can do more harm than good, so organisations considering PRP should consider carefully whether it is appropriate for them ... Other payment systems which do not seek to directly link individual performance and reward may be more suited to the aims of the business.'

People Management (September 1997) reported that only a quarter of firms directly link pay and performance, according to a survey by the Industrial Society. Of 536 firms surveyed, nearly half made no link between performance and pay, even though more than 75% operated appraisal schemes.

4.2 Suggestion schemes

Another variant on performance-based pay is the **suggestion scheme,** where payments or prizes are offered to staff to come up with workable ideas on improving efficiency or quality, new marketing initiatives or solutions to production problems. The theory is that there is in any case motivational value in getting staff involved in problem-solving and planning, and that staff are often in the best position to provide practical and creative solutions to their work problems or the customer's needs - but that an added incentive will help to overcome any reluctance on the part of staff to put forward ideas (because it is seen as risky, or doing management's job for them, or whatever).

Wherever possible, the size of the payment should be related to the savings or value added as a result of the suggestion - either as a lump sum or percentage. Payments are often also made for a 'good try' - an idea which is rejected but considered to show initiative, effort and judgement on the part of the employee. *People Management* (9 February 1995) reported that British Gas had plans to offer 'scratch' cards with £1, £2, and £5 prizes to employees whose ideas were **rejected,** in a bid to encourage more people to put forward ideas.

Suggestion schemes usually apply only to lower grades of staff, on the grounds that thinking up improvements is part of the supervisor's or manager's normal job, but with the increase of worker empowerment and 'bottom up' quality initiatives, such as quality circles, they are becoming more widespread in various forms.

Whichever system is used, results-oriented payments should:

(a) Offer real incentives, sufficiently high after tax to make extraordinary effort worthwhile, perhaps 10-30% of basic salary

(b) Relate payments to criteria over which the individual has control (otherwise he will feel helpless to ensure his reward, and the expectancy element in motivation will be lacking)

(c) Make clear the basis on which payments are calculated, and all the conditions that apply, so that individuals can make the calculation of whether the reward is worth the extra level of effort

(d) Be flexible and sensitive enough to reward different levels of achievement in proportion, and with provision for regular review, and adaptation to the changing needs of the particular organisation

4.3 Bonus schemes

Bonus schemes are supplementary to basic salary, and have been found to be popular with entrepreneurial types, usually in marketing and sales. Bonuses are both incentives and rewards.

Group incentive schemes typically offer a bonus for a group (equally, or proportionately to the earnings or status of individuals) which achieves or exceeds specified targets. Offering bonuses to a whole team may be appropriate for tasks where individual contributions cannot be isolated, workers have little control over their individual output because tasks depend on each other, or where team-building is particularly required.

It may enhance team-spirit and co-operation as well as provide performance incentives, but it may also create pressures within the group if some individuals are seen to be 'not pulling their weight'.

Long-term, large-group schemes may be applied **factory-wide,** as an attempt to involve all employees in the organisation of production. Typically, bonuses would be calculated monthly on the basis of improvements in output per man per hour against standard, or value added (to the cost of raw materials and parts by the production process).

Value added schemes work on the basis that improvements in productivity (indicated by a fall in the ratio of employment costs to sales revenue) increases value added, and the benefit can be shared between employers and employees on an agreed formula. So if sales revenue increases and labour costs (after charges for materials, utilities and depreciation have been deducted) stay the same, or sales revenue remains constant but labour costs decrease, the balance becomes available. There has been an increase in such schemes in recent years (for example, at ICI).

Activity 7	(10 minutes)

What advantages and disadvantages can you see in a **factory-wide** bonus scheme?

Well-known collective incentive schemes from the past include:

(a) *The Scanlon Plan* (1947). This is based on collective bargaining, and operated by a joint management-union committee. It includes a suggestion plan, to stimulate, implement and monitor improvements in production and reductions in labour costs, the benefits of which are shared by union members and management

(b) *The Rucker Plan* (1955), which uses added value, and involves a joint productivity committee to achieve cost reductions, the savings again being shared.

4.4 Profit-sharing schemes and employee shareholders

Profit-sharing schemes offer employees (or selected groups of them) bonuses, perhaps in the form of shares in the company, related directly to profits. The formula for determining the amounts may vary, but in recent years, a straightforward distribution of a percentage of profits above a given target has given way to a value-added related concept. The profit formula itself is not easily calculated - profit levels being subject to accounting conventions - so care will have to be taken to publish and explain the calculations to employees if the scheme is not to be regarded with suspicion or as simply another fringe benefit.

Profit sharing is in general based on the belief that all employees can contribute to profitability, and that that contribution should be recognised. If it is, the argument runs, the effects may include profit-consciousness and motivation in employees, commitment to the future prosperity of the organisation and so on.

The value of the incentives to employees, and the effect on productivity will be greatest if the scheme is well designed.

(a) A perceivably significant sum should be made available to employees - once shareholders have received appropriate return on their investment - say, 10% of basic pay.

(b) There should be a clear, and not overly delayed, link between effort/performance and reward. Profit shares should be distributed as frequently as possible - consistent with the need for reliable information on profit forecasts and targets and the need to amass a significant pool for distribution.

(c) The scheme should only be introduced if profit forecasts indicate a reasonable chance of achieving the above: profit sharing is welcome when profits are high, but the potential for disappointment is great.

(d) The greatest effect on productivity arising from the scheme may in fact arise from its use as a focal point for discussion with employees, about the relationship between their performance and results, and areas and targets for improvement. Management must be seen to be committed to the principle.

EXAMPLE

(a) *Personnel Management*, May 1991, reported the results of a study of an employee share ownership scheme (operated as a voluntary Save as You Earn-related scheme) in a Midlands factory.

'In the event, we concluded there had been no change in attitudes which we felt should be attributed to the scheme,' they report. 'If this is correct, it is hard to see how it could have had any effect on the behaviour of the employees and any significant advantage to the firm.'

There were also very few joiners. Researchers say many workers on low incomes are unwilling to make a five-year or seven-year savings commitment. They warn that this could lead to such schemes becoming the preserve of higher-paid staff, intensifying the 'them and us' attitudes of British industry.

(b) Share ownership has little effect on class divisions, according to a survey of employees in two privatised utilities carried out by Leicester University. This revealed that only 10 per cent believed that 'them and us' attitudes were replaced with a sense of common purpose because of share ownership.

Although 80 per cent of the sample of nearly 450 employees were employee shareholders, 65 per cent said that it made no difference to how careful they were with the company's equipment, and 70 per cent felt it did not make people work harder.

The administration of employee share schemes is outside the scope of this syllabus, but you should be aware that the Finance Act 2000 contains legislation for a **New All-Employee Share Plan**. Articles in *Chartered Secretary* (January 2000) describe how this arose out of the Chancellor's concern that existing all-employee tax-approved schemes did not meet the objectives of linking employee share ownership with productivity. The SAYE scheme is highly popular, but did not appear to provide long-term employee share ownership – which would have an effect on productivity – because employees often sold their shares as soon as they exercised their option, and, with no risk to the employee, there was no real incentive to increased productivity. The Chancellor wanted employees to invest their own monies in shares and to risk those monies on business performance: this formed the basis of the new plan, which was subject to extensive consultation with companies, administrators and advisers.

The main features of the new plan are that:

(a) Employees can buy Partnership Shares in their employing company with pre-tax salary up to a limit of £1,500 per year

(b) The employer can give up to £3,000 of Free Shares to employees: this may be linked to performance on the basis of approved performance measures

(c) Employers can give additional free Matching Shares to employees to match their bought shares

(d) Income tax, National Insurance and Capital Gains Tax exemptions apply to shares held in trust for a specified period

(e) Free Shares can be awarded subject to performance

(f) Free and Matching shares are to be retained for a holding period of between three and five years (set by the employer). No holding period can be imposed on Partnership Shares

Keep an eye on the business press to see how the new plan develops, and whether it achieves its objectives!

Activity 8 (15 minutes)

Are you motivated by **monetary** incentives? At what point would the offer of more money **cease** to motivate you to longer hours, greater efforts (or whatever)? Try and identify three likely problems with, or limitations of, **cash**/monetary incentives

4.5 Non-cash incentives

Incentive and recognition schemes are increasingly focused not on cash, but on non-cash awards. According to a feature in *Personnel Management*, September 1992:

> 'Traditionally aimed at sales people, gifts and travel incentives have been spreading slowly to other areas and are now used to add interest to quality schemes and encourage money saving ideas... to enable managers to show gratitude to staff for such things as continuous improvement and teamwork...to lift morale'.

EXAMPLES

(a) British Telecom - in the wake of large scale voluntary redundancies - launched an up-beat 'Living our values' initiative, including the awarding of gifts to employees exemplifying the organisation's values and being role models to others.

(b) British Aerospace has preserved its quality awards, despite job losses. Teams receive gold pens, watches, ties or scarves for a PSB (Problem Solution Benefit).

(c) ICL used to offer symbolic awards of bronze, silver and gold medals, but has now replaced these with a gift catalogue (called the 'Excellence Collection') from which nominees choose rewards they value: 'Change is essential if recognition schemes are going to succeed... This is one of the problems with this kind of programme. If you don't update it from time to time, it just gets tired.'

(Personnel Management, September 1992).

(d) Abbey Life's top performers are given the opportunity to attend conventions in exotic foreign locations, with partners (and without an onerous work content): length of stay and luxury of location depend on performance.

(e) Trusthouse Forte 'has launched a drive to cut employee turnover through an incentive scheme which awards air mileage in return for staff loyalty ... In addition to the basic retention programme, THF is also offering further incentives to staff, including 500 miles for the employee of the month and 1,000 for employee of the year, with another 200 miles for staff receiving a complimentary letter from a guest.' *Personnel Management* (February 1991)

More recently, *People Management* (September 1995) cited other organisational examples, including the following.

(a) Taylor Walker has introduced a points-based incentive scheme for all its staff. Points are awarded for sales, customer care, progress in training and for general 'above and beyond' performance. Points can be exchanged for items from a catalogue of gifts.

(b) Midland Bank offers travel vouchers, at the discretion of the branch manager, for a variety of things, including referrals, balancing and exceptional effort, in order to recognise achievement within the branch.

Such schemes can be regarded by some staff as manipulative, irrelevant ('awards are being made for things that are part of normal duties: no special effort required') or just plain gimmicky. (The general secretary of the staff union at Sun Alliance has been quoted as saying: 'I have worked for a firm which rewarded its top salespeople with a cruise. I can't imagine anything worse than being trapped on a yacht with a lot of other life assurance salesmen'!) However, it is generally considered that such schemes can be effective as incentives, team-building exercises, and, perhaps more fundamentally, ways of expressing recognition of achievement - without which staff may feel isolated, undervalued or neglected.

FOR DISCUSSION

What is motivating you to study? What incentives are there to study to the best of your ability/effort? What kind of compensation is there for the hardships? What kind of reward and/or recognition do you receive for your efforts?

We will now move on to the related area of employee benefits. These will be discussed further in Chapter 14, insofar as they relate to employee welfare. Here we will discus their role in the remuneration package.

5 BENEFITS

5.1 The remuneration package

As we noted in Section 4 above, the rewards paid to an individual are frequently comprised of a fixed rate or amount of 'basic pay', plus additional compensatory, merit-based or incentive payments. Benefits are a further addition.

Many organisations now operate on the view that pay and benefits form a total 'remuneration package': Figure 7.7.

(a) Remuneration levels which take bonuses and benefits into account are helpful for comparisons of reward levels, and for determining the full cost of remuneration to the organisation.

(b) The package concept is flexible, allowing pay policy to be adapted to organisational needs and values by manipulating the performance-related and discretionary elements: some jobs may be more readily measured for performance-related payment than others.

(c) The package concept can be structured to allow employees to determine the make-up of their remuneration. ('Cafeteria' systems are discussed below.)

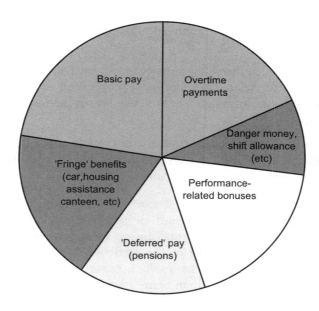

Figure 7.7: Total remuneration package

EXAMPLE: INTERNATIONAL COMPARISONS

Trevor Bolton reports that: 'Across Europe interest in flexible systems of pay is common. However, what is less common is the method by which flexibility is explored and developed. In the UK share schemes ... are common: they are rare elsewhere. In Sweden the use of group bonuses is the norm; profit sharing is popular in France and Germany; while performance-related pay is common in Italy and in the UK.

5.2 'Fringe' benefits

Benefits consist of items or awards which are supplementary to normal pay. Some – such as pensions and sick pay – are essential entitlements, so the common term 'fringe benefits' is perhaps misleading. Certain provisions of the maintenance of adequate standards of living have been underwritten by the state, which has legislated for employees and employers alike to bear some of the cost. They are awarded to anyone who meets certain qualifying conditions and as such are independent of the employer's discretion and performance considerations. Other benefits such as cars, medical insurance and 'perks', are more in the nature of optional extras and as such may be part of the recruitment, retention and incentives strategies of the organisation.

Entitlements include the following.

(a) **Pension provisions.** Pensions are generally regarded as the most important benefit after basic pay: they are a kind of deferred pay, building up rights to a guaranteed income on retirement (or to dependants, on death). They are financed by contributions from the company, with facilities for contribution by employees as well.

(b) **Sick pay.** It is understandable that sickness or other enforced absence from work would haunt workers with the prospect of lost earnings, unless there was some sort of provision for genuine sufferers. Many employers supplement the state benefit by additional sick pay schemes, which may be tailored to the organisation's particular objectives (looking after long-serving employees, or generosity from the outset to attract recruits).

(c) **Maternity leave and maternity pay**.

(d) **Holidays.** This is a benefit which is very much taken for granted, but it was only recently (Working Time Regulations 1998) that any formal entitlement to annual leave was formulated. Employees who have been continuously employed for 13 weeks are entitled to 15 days' leave per annum, rising to 20 days for leave commencing after November 1999. There is no statutory right to 'customary' holidays (public holidays, Christmas etc) although these may be granted by contract terms. Additional holiday entitlements may be regarded as a fringe benefit, including sabbaticals and long-service leaves.

Other benefits which may be offered include the following.

(a) **Company cars** are a highly-regarded benefit in the UK, especially among managerial staff for whom they have connotations of status – despite the reduction in tax incentives over the years – and those whose work requires extensive road travel (eg sales and service staff).

(b) **Transport assistance.** Examples may include loans for the purchase of annual season tickets, or bulk buying of tickets by employers for distribution to staff.

(c) **Housing assistance**, perhaps in the form of:

(i)   Allowances to staff who have been transferred or relocated – removal and travelling expenses, lodging, conveyancing fees and so on or

(ii)   Assistance with house purchase – bridging loan, preferential mortgage terms

(d)   **Medical benefits** – say private medical and/or dental insurance. Some medical services may also be provided at the workplace: for example eye and hearing tests (where relevant to the industrial context).

(e)   **Catering services** – most commonly, subsidised food and drink at the workplace or Luncheon Vouchers.

(f)   **Recreational facilities** – subsidy and organisation of social and sports clubs or provision of facilities such as a gymnasium or bar.

(g)   **Allowances** – for telephone costs, professional subscriptions or work-related reading matter.

(h)   **Discounts** or **preferential terms** on the organisation's own products/services. Bank employees, for example, may receive: a mortgage subsidy; discounts on unit trusts or insurance products; bonus interest on accounts or savings plans; or reduced interest rates on overdrafts and loans.

(i)   **Educational programmes**. In-house study opportunities, or sponsorship of external study (not necessarily work-related).

(j)   **Family-friendly policies** – such as workplace nurseries, term-time hours contracts, career break schemes.

There are a number of reasons why organisations offer benefits packages.

Activity 9   **(15 minutes)**

Which, of all the benefits mentioned, would you think were the most important to people?

(a)   To attract and retain staff by the generosity and/or relevance of benefits offered, and buy facilitating career longevity (eg by allowing career breaks and sabbaticals)

(b)   To encourage commitment to, and consumption of, the organisation's own products (at a discounted rate) by employees

(c)   To demonstrate care for people and social responsibility (by giving above-statutory sick pay, paternity leave, pensions and so on)

(d)   To encourage desirable behaviours/values in employees (by subsidising clothing, fitness programmes, education and so on)

(e)   To offer rewards of perceived high value to the employee, with discounted or marginal cost to the employer

'It must always be recognised, nevertheless, that, however generous they are, (benefits) can never be an adequate substitute for an inadequate base rate or an illogical salary structure or for tangible recognition of the effect of inflation.'

(Betty Ream, *Personnel Administration*)

5.3   Cafeteria systems

An organisation might run what has been called a **cafeteria system**, whereby a range of benefits are on offer, and employees can choose from among them up to their allowed budget. This offers the element of choice, and may increase the value of the benefit to the individual, since it answers his real needs or wants. According to an article in *Personnel Management* in December 1994, 'The number of firms offering their employees flexible benefits has risen by more than 50% in the last year, with perks ranging from childcare vouchers to personal pensions.' A scheme at Admiral Insurance, for example, allows employees to spend a sum worth up to 13% of the basic salary on benefits from a menu including an extra day's annual leave (valued at £9.32 per month), members of a sports club (£20 per month) or vouchers: 'unspent' allowance can be taken in cash. All staff receive 'care' benefits, including 20 days' holiday discounts on motor insurance, death-in-service and sickness benefits, interest-free seasons ticket loans and loans for work-related training.

We will now look at some of the legal requirements for pay and benefits (legal aspects of benefits such as sickness and maternity pay are discussed in Chapter 14 in the context of welfare.)

6 THE LEGAL FRAMEWORK ON PAY

6.1 Methods of payment

Employment Rights Act 1996

Every employee must receive a statement showing gross and net amounts payable to him, variable and fixed deceptions, and methods of calculation. If such an itemised pay statement is not provided, the employee may go to Industrial Tribunal to get repayment of the sum of unnotified deductions.

The employer must make deductions for income tax under Schedule E (known as PAYE: Pay As You Earn) from salary paid to employees under a contract of service.

Wages Act 1986

Under the Truck Acts (1831-1940), all manual employees had to be paid in cash. The Department of Employment released a statement in March 1987, saying that 'the Government ... foresee a steady growth in non-cash methods of wage payment, which should reduce opportunities for crime and end unfair distinctions between the terms and conditions of employment of blue-collar and white-collar workers'.

The Wages Act repealed former legislation, so that the method of wage payment for **all** workers will not be entirely a matter for negotiation and contractual agreement between them and their employers. The Act does not, however, remove any existing **contractual** rights an individual may have to payment in cash, nor does it require an employer to change over to non-cash methods of wage payment.

Part 1 of the Act also introduced an important new set of rights for all workers against unlawful deductions from wages or payments to employers. Deductions or payments will be unlawful unless provided for:

(a) In statute (such as income tax or national insurance) or by order of the courts (eg to settle a fine)

(b) In the contract of employment. This may cover agreed deductions for union subscriptions, lateness or poor work, or (for retail employees) cash or stock shortages (eg money missing from the till or pilfered items).

(c) With the prior written agreement or at the prior written request, of the worker, or

(d) To rectify previous overpayments

Any worker who believes that an employer has not followed the provisions of the Act has a right to complain to an industrial tribunal

6.2 Minimum wage

National Minimum Wage Regulations 1999

In 1999, the UK government accepted the findings of the Low Pay Commission and introduced a national minimum wage.

- (a) Over the age of 21: £3.70 per hour (from October 2000)
- (b) 18-21 year olds: £3.20 per hour (from June 2000)

16-17 year olds on formal apprenticeships, casual workers, agency workers and homeworkers are excluded.

Other guaranteed payments

Once terms and conditions have been agreed and set out in a contract of employment, the employer is legally bound to pay the wage or salary specified. There are further statutory entitlements:

- (a) For employees who have been laid off or put on short-time because of shortage of work to continue to receive pay for up to five days in any 90 day period (Employment Rights Act 1996)

- (b) For employees suspended under health and safety regulations to receive normal pay up to a maximum of 26 weeks (ditto)

- (c) For employees to receive Statutory Sick Pay (Social Security and Housing Benefits Act 1982)

- (d) For female employees to receive Statutory Maternity Pay for 18 weeks of maternity leave (Employment Relations Act 1999)

6.3 Equal pay

Equal Pay Act 1970 and amendments

The Equal Pay Act (effective from 1975) was the first major attempt 'to prevent discrimination as regards terms and conditions of employment between men and women'. Women were entitled to claim equal pay and conditions of service for:

- (a) Jobs rated as equivalent under a job evaluation scheme and

- (b) Work that was 'the same as or broadly similar' to the work of a man in the same establishment, where job evaluation was not used

The Equal Pay (Amendment) Regulations 1984 implementing the European Equal Pay Directive) established the right to equal pay and conditions for work of equal **value** (that is, not necessarily 'similar' work, but work of equivalent evaluation). If job evaluation was not used in the organisation, the employee could apply to an industrial tribunal for a (legally enforceable) order to have an evaluation carried out by an independent expert reporting to the tribunal.

The Equal Opportunities Commission issued a 1997 Code of Practice on Equal Pay, covering definitions, pay systems, methods of identifying discrimination, job evaluation recommendations and a model policy on equal pay.

European legislation

Article 119 of the Treaty of Rome explicitly demands 'the application of the principle that men and women should receive equal pay for equal work'. It encompasses areas such as equal pay for work of equal value (Equal Pay Directive 1975) and equal access to employment-related benefits (Equal Treatment Directive Occupational Social Security 1986). All provisions have now been implemented in UK law. Decisions in the European Court of Justice have further extended provisions to pension rights, resulting in the harmonisation of retirement ages, the equalising of pension scheme rules and the extension of access to occupational pension schemes to part-time workers.

Chapter roundup

- Job evaluation is the process of analysing and assessing the content of jobs, in order to place them in an acceptable rank order which can then be used as a basis for a remuneration system.

- The two most common analytical methods of job evaluation are as follows.

Scheme	Characteristics	Advantages	Disadvantages
Factor comparison method	Separate factors are identified as a proportion of the job and valued in comparison with benchmark jobs	Uses benchmark jobs which are considered to be fairly paid	Hard to explain. Depends on accuracy of benchmark rates. Limited applicability
Points rating methods	Separate factors are scored to produce an overall points score for the job	The analytical process of considering separate defined factors provides for objectivity and consistency in making judgements	Complex to install and maintain – judgement is still required to rate jobs in respect of different factors

- The constituents of a remuneration policy must embrace such crucial factors as the objectives of the organisation, its finances, cash flow and profitability, the state of the labour market, expected demand and supply of various types of labour, any government regulations on pay, anticipated contraction or expansion of the organisation, as well as the personal aspiration and inclination of the workforce.

- Salary structures most commonly consist of a graded structure, with a range (or scale) of salaries within each grade, and an overlap of pay scales between grades.

- Incentives are built into graded salary systems on a limited basis. In addition, many organisations operate incentive or Performance-Related-Pay (RPR) schemes, such as bonus schemes, suggestion schemes and profit-sharing.

- Remuneration can be seen as a whole package of pay and benefits, including

  ○ Pension, sick pay and maternity leave, as statutory entitlements

  ○ Expended holiday entitlement (and a range of other (potentially flexible) 'perks)

- There is a legislative framework covering methods of payment, deductions, minimum wage and other guaranteed payments, and equal pay.

Quick quiz

1   What are the advantages and disadvantages of job evaluation?

2   Distinguish between analytical and non-analytical approaches to job evaluation. What is a major drawback of non-analytical approaches?

3   What are the three job elements compared in the HAY-MSL points rating method?

4   What factors, other than job content, may be considered in setting remuneration levels?

5   List three examples of salary structure

6   What kinds of payment will typically be included in a wage structure?

7   What are the potential drawbacks or problems cited for Performance Related Pay (PRP)?

8   Give five examples of 'fringe' benefits

9   What categories of employee are protected by the minimum wage?

10 What was the effect of the 1984 Amendments to the 1970 Equal Pay Act?

Answers to quick quiz

1   See the table in paragraph 1.1 for a full account.

2   Analytical methods identify the components of the job and its characteristics, and give attention to the relative degree and importance of each factor in the job. Non-analytical methods make judgements about the relative worth of whole jobs. They may be subject to court challenge under equal pay legislation.   (see paragraph 1.2)

3   Know-how, problem-solving, accountability.   (para 1.2)

4   Equity, negotiated agreements, individual performance and performance incentives, market rates, organisational cultural values and policies, equal pay legislation.   (para 2)

5   Graded, rate for age, progression curve.   (para 3.2)

6   Basic (time or piecework) rate, plus overtime rates, shift rates, compensatory payments (eg danger money), allowances, merit or length-of-service bonuses; payment by results, bonuses/ incentives.   (para 3.4)

7   Subjectivity, reliance on supervisors' commitment/ability, difficulty translating appraisals into monetary values, divisive effect on team-working, problems of employee/union acceptance and attitudes.
                    (para 4.1)

8   Pension, sick pay, holidays, company car, transport assistance.(para 5.2)

9   Wage earners aged 18 upwards, excluding casual, agency and home workers.   (para 6.2)

10 Extending rights of equal pay and conditions from 'broadly similar' work to 'work of equal value', with the right to have the job independently analysed by job evaluation.   (para 6.3)

Answers to activities

1   This is a personal investigation and response activity. If you availed yourself of the opportunity to interview another person, make concise

notes of the answers: useful evidence of having considered the HR implications of this topic.

2   (a)   Subjectivity may take the following forms.

         (i)   The factors for analysis are themselves qualitative, not easy to define and measure. Mental ability and initiative are observable in job holders, but not easily quantifiable as an element of the job itself.

         (ii)   Assessment of the importance and difficulty of a job cannot objectively be divorced from the context of the organisation and job holder. The relative importance of a job is a function of the culture and politics of the organisation, the nature of the business and not least the personal power of the individual in the job. The difficulty of the job depends on the ability of the job holder and the favourability or otherwise of the environment/technology/work methods/management.

         (iii)   The selection of factors and the assignment of monetary values to factors remain subjective judgements.

    (b)   It is undoubtedly desirable to achieve objectivity, to reduce the resentment commonly felt at the apparent arbitrariness of pay decisions. If job evaluation were truly objective, it would be possible to justify differentials on a rational basis, the organisation would have a balanced and economical pay structure based on contribution, and employers would be safe from accusations of unfair pay decisions.

3   Another research activity, preparing you to demonstrate competence according to Assessment Criteria 21:3.

4   One may list the general arguments for paying over market rate as follows.

    (a)   The offer of a notably higher remuneration package than market rate may be assumed to generate greater interest in the labour market. The organisation will therefore have a wider field of selection for the given labour category, and will be more likely to have access to the most skilled/experienced individuals. If the organisation establishes a reputation as a 'wage leader' it may generate a consistent supply of high-calibre labour.

    (b)   There may be benefits of high pay offers for employee loyalty, and better performance resulting from the (theoretically) higher calibre and motivation of the workforce.

    (c)   Even if a cheap supply of labour were available, and the employer could get away with paying a low rate, its ideology or ethical code of an organisation may make reluctant to do so. A socially responsible employer may wish to avoid the exploitation of labour groups, such as immigrants, who may not be aware of general market rates.

    (d)   An employer might adopt a socially responsible position not purely for ethical reasons but to maintain a respected image and good relations with government, interest groups, employee representatives and the general public (potential customers/ consumers).

    (e)   Survival and immediate profit-maximisation are not necessarily the highest objective of any organisation. Employers in growth markets, or hoping to diversify into new markets, cannot afford a low-calibre, high-turnover workforce. Notably innovative organisations can be seen to be offering higher than market rate on salaries (eg Mars) or remuneration packages including profit-related bonuses (eg Sainsbury's): moreover, their financial performance bears out their view that pay is an investment. To an extent, this pay strategy stems from the culture or value system of the organisation, the importance it attaches to loyalty, innovation and initiative, and its willingness to pay more to attract and retain such higher-level attributes: quantity may not be the prime employment criterion.

On the other hand, there are substantial cost savings in paying lower rates. It cannot be assumed that high remuneration inevitably leads to higher motivation and better performance. Not everybody has an instrumental orientation to work: money may not be the prime incentive - and pay is often a source of dissatisfaction rather than satisfaction, whatever its level.

If the organisation's ability to maintain high rewards in the future is in doubt, management ought also to be aware that the disappointment and culture shock of reversing a high-remuneration policy is very great.

5   If you are not employed in a work organisation, ask a salaried acquaintance. Do not neglect to think about part (b) of this activity: research has shown that in the absence of information about salaries, people become dissatisfied by what they **think** they are earning in relation to others. Some people seem genuinely not to want to know how their salary is determined, as long as it progresses year on year: what might the consequences of such an attitude be for loyalty, motivation and the salary bill of the organisation

6   Single status schemes can save an organisation administrative and overtime costs, and may improve employee flexibility and industrial relations. For manual workers, there are clear advantages in receiving a wider range of benefits and an annual salary (which at least improves their borrowing position).

However, there may be an increase in labour costs overall. For the workers, too, there is a drawback, in monthly – instead of weekly – payments. There is also a perceived loss of status for salaried workers, in the achievement of parity by previous wage-earners: this may affect their morale, although the organisation culture will have a lot to do with whether harmonisation is perceived as threatening or equitable and exciting.

7   (a)   *Advantages* of factory-wide schemes

        (i)   Increasing employee identification with the organisation's objectives

        (ii)   Stimulating interest in productivity in general

        (iii)   Encouraging communication and consultation, which may be a source of job satisfaction, and may help overcome resistance to change

        (iv)   Facilitating equality of treatment for indirect as well as direct workers (cleaners, stores assistants and so on)

(b)   *Disadvantages*

    (i)   Need for detailed and comprehensive costing systems which must be communicated to all employees

    (ii)   Failure to provide direct incentives, since reward has become divorced from individual effort

8   There are a number of difficulties associated with incentive schemes based on monetary reward.

    (a)   Increased earnings simply may not be an incentive to some individuals. An individual who already enjoys a good income may be more concerned with increasing his leisure time, for example.

    (b)   Workers are unlikely to be in complete control of results. External factors, such as the general economic climate, interest rates and exchange rates may play a part in **profitability** in particular. In these cases, the relationship between an individual's efforts and his reward may be indistinct.

    (c)   Greater specialisation in production processes means that particular employees cannot be specifically credited with the success of their particular products. This may lead to frustration amongst employees who think their own profitable work is being adversely affected by inefficiencies elsewhere in the organisation.

    (d)   Even if employees *are* motivated by money, the effects may not be altogether desirable. An instrumental orientation may encourage self-interested performance at the expense of teamwork: it may encourage attention to output at the expense of quality, and the lowering of standards and targets (in order to make bonuses more accessible).

Workers remain suspicious that if they achieve high levels of output and earnings, management will alter the basis of the incentive rates to reduce future earnings. Work groups therefore tend to restrict output to a level that they feel is 'fair' and 'safe'.

9   In a survey of 2,000 people in full-time employment in France, Britain, Germany and Italy, it was discovered that:

    (a)   Most workers think a staff restaurant is a more important benefit than a company car (84% of workers, in 'cuisine-conscious' France!)

    (b)   Company cars were also rated less important than pensions or private health insurance

Personnel Management Plus, September 1992

Assignment 7 (1½ hours)

Ad Hoc Ltd is a small firm which manufactures highly fashionable computer mouse devices for sale through selected dealerships (such as Dixons and Apple Centres). It employs a 500-strong diverse team of:

(a) Designers, responsible for creating new models and 'packages' in response to user trends and endorsements (eg by Apple Macintosh)

(b) Customer support workers, responsible for responding to end-users installation and software inquiries via a 24-hour hotline and subscription Technical Support programme

(c) Technical hardware/software designers, carrying out technical research and product planning and development. These individuals are encouraged to spend 15% of work time on their own technical projects and interest (following the model of US giant 3M, which used this as a device to encourage innovation)

(d) Manufacturing controllers/co-ordinators who liase with management and staff at the technical manufacturing facility which Ad Hoc contracts to do its component manufacturing, assembly and packing

(e) Sales staff, responsible for selling on to dealerships, negotiation of promotions in-store, stock control and replenishment, and dealer relations and

(f) Support staff, including technical writers (for instruction manual development and related collaborative publishing projects), HR, finance and administrative departments

Addison Hoc, the young general manager and founder of the company, has strong attitudes about the kind of freewheeling, entrepreneurial, flexible, innovative organisation he wants to develop. Jobs are considered fluid and cross-department collaborations and 'deals' – like those with external partners – are encouraged. Individuals have always negotiated their remuneration packages on a one-to-one basis with the general manger and HR manger.

As a result, there is a wide-ranging disparity in the structure and amount of rewards. Recently, this has begun to cause problems. Salary costs have been spiralling: differentials are all over the place, to the disgruntlement of several senior staff members; commissions on sales frequently push sales salaries above those of the technical designers; and now, several female staff in the customer support department have threatened to bring appeals against the company, because they feel they are being paid less than the men in sales support.

Addison Hoc has been advised by his lawyers that he may need to consider introducing some form of job evaluation scheme, in order to prevent equal pay claims.

As HR manager, you have been asked your opinion: is job evolution worth doing? You will give a presentation to the senior management team.

Task

(a) Prepare notes, weighing up the pros and cons of job evaluation

(b) Anticipate objections on the basis of the cons, so that you can suggest how the scheme could be made to work effectively at Ad Hoc.

Chapter 8 :
DISCIPLINE AND GRIEVANCE PROCEDURES

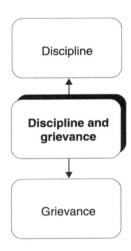

Introduction

In your studies for Core Unit 3: *Organisation and Behaviour*, you should have covered disciplinary action as an interpersonal management task focused on diagnosing and solving behavioural problems. In this chapter, we look at it from a slightly different point of view, within the framework of personnel policy. In this context, it sits alongside the complementary processes of grievance handling.

Disciplinary procedures broadly deal with the 'downward' process whereby a superior draws a subordinate's attention to a problem in the behaviour or performance of the subordinate which needs addressing in order for the organisation's requirement to be met. **Grievance** procedures, broadly, deal with the 'upward' process whereby a subordinate draws a superior's attention to a problem in the behaviour or performance of some other individual which needs addressing in order for the subordinate's needs to be met.

Your objectives

In this chapter you will learn about the following:

    (a)   The effectiveness of disciplinary and grievance procedures used by two organisations

    (b)   Model disciplinary and grievance procedures and policies

1 DISCIPLINE

1.1 What is discipline?

The word discipline brings to mind the use of authority or force, and to many people it primarily carries the disagreeable meaning of punishment. However, there is another way of thinking about discipline.

Definition

> **Discipline** can be considered as: 'a condition in an enterprise in which there is orderliness in which the members of the enterprise behave sensibly and conduct themselves according to the standards of acceptable behaviour as related to the goals of the organisation'.

'Negative' discipline is the threat of sanctions designed to make employees choose to behave in a desirable way, although this need not be a wholly negative matter. Disciplinary action may be **punitive** (punishing an offence), **deterrent** (warning people not to behave in that way) or **reformative** (calling attention to the nature of the offence so that it will not happen again).

The best discipline is **self-discipline**. Most mature people accept that following instructions and fair rules of conduct are part of any job. They believe in performing their work properly, coming to work on time, following their leader's instructions, and so on. If employees know what is expected of them and feel that the rules are reasonable, self-disciplined behaviour becomes a part of group norms.

Types of disciplinary situations

There are many types of disciplinary situations which require attention by the manager. The most frequently occurring are:

(a) Excessive absenteeism (not coming to work, perhaps giving the excuse of ill health)

(b) Excessive lateness in arriving at work

(c) Defective and/or inadequate work performance

(d) Poor attitudes which influence the work of others or which reflect on the public image of the firm

> **Activity 1** (15 minutes)
>
> Suggest five more reasons for management taking disciplinary action. (You might be able to draw on your own experience at work, school or college.)

In addition, managers might be confronted with disciplinary problems stemming from employee behaviour **off** the job: abuse of alcohol or drugs, or involvement in some form of law-breaking activity. If off-the-job conduct has an impact upon performance **on** the job, the manager must be prepared to deal with it.

In order to protect employees from unfair punishments or penalties, there needs to be a clear framework for discipline at work. The Advisory, Conciliation and Arbitration Service (ACAS), which was designed to promote good industrial relations, has laid down voluntary guidelines for disciplinary action. Let's look at what disciplinary procedures might involve.

1.2 Model disciplinary procedure

Any disciplinary action must be undertaken with sensitivity and sound judgement: its purpose is not punishment, or retribution, but improvement of the future behaviour of the employee and other members of the organisation, or the avoidance of similar occurrences in the future.

ACAS guidelines for disciplinary action suggest that an employee should not be dismissed from his or her job for a first offence, except in the case of gross misconduct (such as serious theft, or violence against another employee). Many enterprises have accepted the idea of **progressive discipline**, which provides for increasing severity of the penalty with each repeated offence: a bit like the yellow card (warning), red card (sent off) system used in football. The following are the suggested steps of progressive disciplinary action.

(a) **The informal talk**

If the offence is of a relatively minor nature and if the employee's record shows no previous discipline problems, an informal, friendly talk may clear up the situation. The manager simply discusses with the employee his or her behaviour in relation to the standards expected by the organisation, and tries to get a recognition that such behaviour is unacceptable, with a commitment that it will not be repeated.

(b) **Oral warning or reprimand**

The manager emphasises the undesirability of repeated violations, and warns the offender that it could lead to more serious penalties.

(c) **Written or official warning**

At this stage, the **ACAS Code of Practice** comes into effect. A written warning is a formal matter, and becomes a permanent part of the employee's record. (It may also serve as evidence in case of protest against the later dismissal of a repeated offender.)

(d) **Disciplinary lay-offs, or suspension**

Disciplinary lay-offs usually extend over several days or weeks. Some employees may not be very impressed with oral or written warnings, but they are likely to find a disciplinary layoff (without pay) a rude awakening.

(e) **Dismissal**

This should be reserved for the most serious offences. For the organisation it involves waste of a labour resource, the expense of training a replacement, and change in the work team. The threat of dismissal may be a sufficient deterrent, but in the last resort, a disruptive, violent or untrustworthy employee may simply have to be expelled from the workplace.

There is a right to **appeal** against disciplinary action; and a right to be accompanied to **disciplinary meetings** by a colleague or trade union representative.

FOR DISCUSSION

How (a) accessible and (b) clear are the rules and policies of your college: do people really know what they are and are not supposed to do? Have a look at the student regulations. How easy is it to see them – or were you referred elsewhere? Are they well-indexed and cross-referenced, and in language that all students will understand?

How (a) accessible and (b) clear are the disciplinary procedures? Who is responsible for discipline?

In addition to formal procedures, discipline raises a number of interpersonal issues.

1.3 Managing disciplinary situations

The following guidelines may help managers reduce the resentment that will be inevitable, to an extent, in all disciplinary actions.

- (a) **Immediacy**

    The manager should take disciplinary action as speedily as possible. However, (s)he should allow a brief 'cooling off' period in circumstances where on-the-spot emotion might lead to hasty judgements, and the **ACAS Code of Practice** requires investigation to be made, where possible, before action is taken.

- (b) **Advance warning**

    In order to encourage self-discipline, and ensure that disciplinary action is (and is seen to be) fair, it is essential that all employees know in advance what is expected of them and what the rules and regulations are. Policy provisions may be included in employee handbooks, recruitment literature or employment contracts.

- (c) **Consistency**

    Rules and penalties should apply equally to everyone and on every occasion. Inconsistency in application of discipline only creates uncertainty, and loss of respect. (Consistency does not mean imposing a standard penalty every time for a particular offence: there may be mitigating circumstances which partly excuse the offender's behaviour.)

- (d) **Impersonality**

    'Punishment' should be connected with the 'crime': based on clear rules and standards, *not* personalities. Once disciplinary action has been taken, the manager should not bear grudges or nurse suspicions. Impersonality is sometimes called the 'hot stove' rule (if you touch the stove, you get burnt – nothing personal ...).

- (e) **Privacy**

    As a general rule (unless the manager's authority is challenged directly and in public) disciplinary action should be taken in private, to avoid the spread of conflict and the humiliation – or martyrdom – of the employee concerned.

The crucial interpersonal event in disciplinary action will be the interview. The following advice takes into account both procedural guidelines and interpersonal issues.

1.4 Disciplinary interviews

Preparation

Preparation for the disciplinary interview will include the following.

- (a) Gathering facts about the alleged infringement.

- (b) Determination of the organisation's position: how valuable is the employee, potentially? How serious are his offences/lack of progress? How far is the organisation prepared to go to help him improve or discipline him further?

- (c) Identification of the aims of the interview: punishment? deterrent to others? problem-solving? Specific standards for future behaviour/performance need to be determined.

(d) Notification of the employee concerned, with time to prepare for the disciplinary interview. (The Employment Relations Act 1999 provides that employees involved in 'serious cases' may be represented by a fellow employee or trade union representative.

Content of the interview

The content of the interview should be as follows.

(a) The manager should explain the purpose of the interview, and state the charges against the employee, clearly and without personal emotion.

(b) The manager should explain the organisation's position: disappointment, concern, need for improvement, impact on others and so on. This should be done frankly – but tactfully, with as positive an emphasis as possible on the employee's capacity and responsibility to improve.

(c) The organisation's expectations with regard to future behaviour/ performance should be made clear.

(d) The employee or his/her trade union representative should be given the opportunity to comment, explain, justify or deny. If (s)he is to approach the following stage of the interview in a positive way, (s)he must not be made to feel hounded or hard done by.

(e) The organisation's expectations should be reiterated, or new standards of behaviour set for the employee. It will help him/her if:

    (i) They are specific, performance-related and realistic: increased output, improved timekeeping, or whatever

    (ii) They are related to a practical but reasonably short time period. A date should be set to review progress

    (iii) The manager agrees on appropriate measures to help the employee: mentoring, or counselling, say

(f) The manager should explain any penalties imposed, and issue a clear warning of the consequences of failure to meet improvement targets.

(g) The manager must inform the employee of his/her right to appeal.

Activity 2   **(20 minutes)**

Suppose that you, as the personnel manager, have been asked to introduce a new disciplinary procedure.

(a) What points would you have to consider initially?

(b) With whom would you consult before writing it?

(c) How would you communicate it to the workforce?

1.5 The ACAS Code of Practice

Disciplinary procedures should:

(a) be in written form (the ACAS code of practice does not extend to informal 'first' warnings);

(b) specify to whom they apply (all, or only some of the employees);

(c)   be capable of dealing speedily with disciplinary matters;

(d)   indicate the forms of disciplinary action which may be taken (such as dismissal, suspension or warning);

(e)   specify the appropriate levels of authority for the exercise of disciplinary actions;

(f)   provide for individuals to be informed of the nature of their alleged misconduct;

(g)   allow individuals to state their case, and to be accompanied by a fellow employee (or union representative);

(h)   ensure that every case is properly investigated before any disciplinary action is taken;

(i)   ensure that employees are informed of the reasons for any penalty they receive;

(j)   state that no employee will be dismissed for a first offence, except in cases of gross misconduct;

(k)   provide for a right of appeal against any disciplinary action, and specify the appeals procedure.

2   GRIEVANCE

2.1   What is grievance?

Grievance procedures are not the same as disciplinary procedures, although the two terms are often confused.

Definition

> A **grievance** occurs when an individual feels that (s)he is being wrongly treated by a colleague or supervisor: picked on, unfairly appraised or blocked for promotion, or discriminated against on grounds of race or sex.

Some grievances might be resolved informally by the individual's manager. However, there should also be a formal grievance procedure, to which employees at all levels can appeal.

2.2   Grievance procedures

Formal grievance procedures, like disciplinary procedures, should be set out in **writing** and made available to all staff. These procedures should do the following things.

(a)   State what **grades of employee** are entitled to pursue a particular type of grievance.

(b)   State the **rights of the employee** for each type of grievance. For example, an employee who is not invited to attend a promotion/selection panel might claim that he has been unfairly passed over. The grievance procedure must state what the individual would be entitled to claim. In our example, the employee who is overlooked for promotion might be entitled to a review of his annual appraisal report, or to attend a special appeals promotion/selection board if he has been in his current grade for at least a certain number of years.

(c)   State what the **procedures for pursuing a grievance** should be.

   Step 1.   The individual should discuss the grievance with a staff/union representative (or a colleague). If his case seems a good one, he should take the grievance to his immediate boss.

   Step 2.   The first interview will be between the immediate boss (unless he is the subject of the complaint, in which case it will be the next level up) and the employee, who has the right to be accompanied by a colleague or representative.

   Step 3.   If the immediate boss cannot resolve the matter, or the employee is otherwise dissatisfied with the first interview, the case should be referred to his own superior (and if necessary in some cases, to an even higher authority).

   Step 4.   Cases referred to a higher manager should also be reported to the personnel department. Line management might decide at some stage to ask for the assistance/advice of a personnel manager in resolving the problem.

(d)   **Distinguish between individual grievances and collective grievances.** Collective grievances might occur when a work group as a whole considers that it is being badly treated.

(e)   Allow for the **involvement of an individual's or group's trade union** or staff association representative. Indeed, many individuals and groups might prefer to initiate some grievance procedures through their union or association rather than through official grievance procedures. Involvement of a union representative from the beginning should mean that management and union will have a common view of what procedures should be taken to resolve the matter.

(f)   **State time limits** for initiating certain grievance procedures and subsequent stages of them. For example, a person who is passed over for promotion should be required to make his appeal within a certain time period of his review, and his appeal to higher authority (if any) within a given period after the first grievance interview. There should also be timescales for management to determine and communicate the outcome of the complaint to the employee.

(g)   **Require written records** of all meetings concerned with the case to be made and distributed to all the participants.

As with disciplinary action, the main job of conflict resolution will take place in an interview between the manager and the subordinate.

2.3   Grievance interviews

The dynamics of a grievance interview are broadly similar to a disciplinary interview, except that it is the **subordinate** who primarily wants a positive result or improvement in someone else's behaviour.

Prior to the interview, the manager should have some idea of the complaint and its possible source. The meeting itself can then proceed through the following stages.

(a)   **Exploration**. What is the problem: the background, the facts, the causes (obvious and hidden)? At this stage the manager should simply try to gather as much information as possible, without attempting to suggest solutions or interpretations: the situation must be seen to be open.

BPP PUBLISHING

(b) **Consideration**. The manager should:

    (i)   Check the facts

    (ii)   Analyse the causes – the problem of which the complaint may be only a symptom

    (iii)   Evaluate options for responding to the complaint, and the implication of any response made

It may be that information can be given to clear up a misunderstanding, or the employee will withdraw his complaint – having 'got it off his chest'. However, the meeting may have to be adjourned (say, for 48 hours) while the manager gets extra information and considers extra options.

(c) **Reply**. The manager, having reached and reviewed various conclusions, reconvenes the meeting to convey (and justify, if required) his or her decision, hear counter-arguments and appeals. The outcome (agreed or disagreed) should be recorded in writing.

Activity 3   (20 minutes)

Think of a complaint or grievance you have (or have had) at school or college. Have you done anything about it? If so, was it on your own, or through some kind of grievance procedure? If so, what happened: were you satisfied with the process and outcome? If not, why not? How could the procedure have been improved?

Chapter roundup

- Discipline has the same end as motivation: to secure desired behaviour from members of the organisation. Motivation may even be called a kind of self-discipline – because motivated individuals exercise choice to behave in the way that the organisation wishes. Discipline is more often related to negative motivation however, an appeal to the individual's need to avoid punishment, sanctions or unpleasantness.

- Grievance procedures embody the employee's right to appeal against unfair or otherwise prejudicial conduct or conditions that affect him and his work.

Quick quiz

1   Which organisation gives advice on disciplinary matters?

2   What is progressive discipline?

3   What factors should a manager bear in mind in trying to control the disciplinary situation?

4   What should a manager do or consider in preparation for a disciplinary interview?

5   Who may accompany an employee to a disciplinary interview?

6   Outline typical grievance procedures.

7   Name the three stages through which the grievance interview passes.

Answers to quick quiz

1   ACAS   (see paragraph 1.1)

2   Progressive discipline is characterised by increasing severity of penalty with each repeated offence.   (para 1.2)

3   Immediacy, advance warning, consistency, impersonality, privacy.

(para 1.3)

4   He or she should gather the facts and consider the organisation's position and the aims of the interview.   (para 1.4)

5   A fellow worker or trade union representative.   (para 1.5)

6   Discuss the grievance with a colleague; take the grievance to the immediate boss, and try to resolve it in an interview; refer the matter to a higher authority if it is not yet resolved. Written records of all meetings should be kept.   (para 2.2)

7   Exploration, consideration, reply.   (para 2.3)

Answers to Activities

1   Reasons for disciplinary action might include:

   (a)   Breaking rules regarding rest periods and other time schedules, such as leaving work to go home early.

   (b)   Improper personal appearance or dress.

   (c)   Breaking safety rules, such as failing to observe fire regulations, failing to wear protective clothing and so on.

   (d)   Other violations of rules, regulations and procedures, such as smoking in a non-smoking office, or abuse of expenses claims.

   (e)   Open insubordination: refusal to carry out a legitimate order.

   (f)   Fighting, sexual harassment, racial abuse or other forms of unacceptable conflict.

2   Having been asked to introduce a new disciplinary procedure, the following would have to be borne in mind.

   (a)   You would have to consider employment legislation with regard to warnings and dismissals, limits of authority as to who would be authorised to carry out which steps of the procedure. For example, section leaders may have the authority to issue verbal warnings but all further steps are carried out by managers.

   (b)   Other managers and trade union officials if a union is recognised within the organisation.

   (c)   Possibly by a general meeting so that everyone is told at once, but it must also be confirmed in writing to all employees.

3   Assuming you did do something about your grievance, you probably found there were various stages of the procedure. Hopefully the first and second stages were sufficient to solve the problem, but you may have felt that the procedure was too cumbersome or long-winded.

Assignment 8   **(1hour)**

You have been asked to devise a disciplinary procedure. You will have to consider the types of offence and the degree of discipline the offence will incur. Also think about progressive discipline and what action will be taken if the employee repeats the offence or breaches discipline in some other way.

Write a draft procedure.

Chapter 9 :
PERSONNEL ADMINISTRATIVE AND INFORMATION SYSTEMS

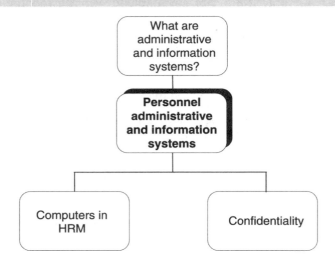

Introduction

As you may already have realised from the early chapters of this Course Book, personnel management depends on the gathering, processing and communication of **information**. Information is gathered from within the organisation (for example, about workforce size and structure, about labour turnover, accidents, absenteeism, employee performance, training and development progress and so on) and from its environment (for example, about market rates of pay, demographics, availability of skills, potential suppliers or training and other services, legislation and regulation, the practices of other employers and so on).

Some of this information is used in the routine administrative tasks of the personnel function: details of hours worked, for example, are used to prepare pay statements. Some information is used to help personnel, and other managers to make decisions and plans – as we have seen in the chapter on Human Resource Planning, for example.

In this chapter, we look at some of the elements of the administrative and information systems used by personnel departments, and how they can be used most effectively. We will not distinguish, in general, between 'administrative' and 'information' systems, since the data records used for administration are nowadays likely to become the raw material for management information.

Your objectives

In this chapter you will learn about the following

    (a)   The need for effective management of personnel records

    (b)   Criteria for an effective personnel information system

    (c)   The range of data required to be gathered, stored and communicated by the personnel function

    (d)   The benefits of a computerised personnel system, and the likely facilities of such a system

NOTES

(e)   The importance of confidentiality and the requirements of Data Protection legislation

1   WHAT ARE ADMINISTRATIVE AND INFORMATION SYSTEMS?

1.1   Information requirements

Information is the life blood of an organisation, flowing through it, prompting decisions and actions: without information, no-one in an organisation could take a single effective action.

The personnel function is responsible for gathering, storing, using and communicating information about the human resources of the organisation: who they are, what they do, how they behave, what they need, why they leave and so on.

Information of different types or levels is needed for different purposes.

Type of information	*Purpose*	*Example*	*Type of information system*
Records of past and current transactions and events	Storage for confirmation, later analysis, legal evidence	An employee's rate of pay and overtime pay are kept on record as a confirmation	Record system
Routine data on which current transactions and operations are based	Utilisation in relevant activities, procedures	The employee's hours worked and overtime hours, plus rates of pay, are used in payroll calculations and preparation of pay packets and statements	Administrative or transaction processing system
Feedback data on performance, results	Comparison with plans/budgets/ standards for control: identifying the need for corrective action to bring results in line with plan	Data on overtime hours worked is compared with budget: excessive hours/payments require investigation	Control information system (a type of management information system)
Information on results, trends and the 'bigger picture', derived from historical/routine data	Support for management decision-making and longer-range planning	A report showing escalating wage costs as a result of increasing overtime hours may suggest the need for flexible working hours, added staff numbers or reduced overtime rates	Decision-support or management information system

Data on organisational activities may also be required by external stakeholders in the organisation (shareholders, creditors, customers and suppliers), outside agencies who require it for their own activities (such as the Department of Trade and Industry and Inland Revenue) and regulatory bodies who monitor organisational practices (such as the Health and Safety Executive or Training Commission).

You may have noticed, from the examples given above, that the same raw data can be processed and used in different ways: it becomes **information** for control, decision-making, planning, reporting and so on. This is an important feature of information systems – and particularly personnel systems. Example records are **not** kept just for the sake of record-keeping (although that in itself is a legal requirement), nor even for routine administrative processing (payroll, holiday entitlements, sick pay and so on). They are essential to the wider role of HRM in the organisation: anticipating internal and environmental trends; managing the flow of labour through the organisation to meet its strategic objectives; managing change.

FOR DISCUSSION

Betty Ream (Personnel Administration) suggests: 'The importance of adequate personnel records, once seen as a peripheral, tedious and undemanding part of the personnel function, is becoming increasingly recognised.'

Despite the recognition of HRM as a planning – not just organising – function, however, the fact remains that the gathering, storing and updating of statistical information can be 'tedious and undemanding'. How can the personnel function lose its image as made up pen-pushers and filing clerks?

We will now look briefly at the main types of information system mentioned above. Nowadays, it is taken for granted that these will be computerised systems – but you should be able to see how the same types of information could be provided without the use of computers.

1.2 Types of information system

Definitions

> **Data** are the raw materials of information: facts and figures in an unprocessed state.
>
> **Information** is data that have been processed (selected, sorted, analysed, formatted) so as to:
>
> - Have meaning for the person who receives it
> - Be suitable for a particular purpose

Administrative or transaction processing systems

Transaction processing systems represent the 'operational' and 'administrative' level of the information system. Data are used to process transactions and update files as part of day-to-day operations.

Management information systems

Definition

> A **Management Information System (MIS)** is a system designed to collect data from all available sources and to convert them into information relevant to managers, for the purposes of planning and controlling the activities for which they are responsible.

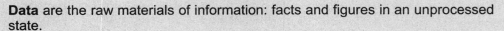

At a tactical level, the MIS will be concerned with how objectives are being achieved. Three types of formal MIS are often used at this level.

(a) **Control systems**, monitoring organisational performance and reporting on any variation from plans.

(b) **Database systems**, which store data records in a way which is flexible and accessible: managers can select and format data according to their needs. The data base may consist of the organisation's own records **plus** access to an external pool of data – for example, on the Internet.

(c) **Decision support systems** which store and process information for analysing problems and testing possible solutions. (We discuss this further below.)

At a strategic level, the MIS will be concerned with the longer-term plans and objectives of the organisation: its strengths and weaknesses, potential threats and opportunities in its environment, forecasts and trends. This information will be used to formulate strategies and policies; it is likely to be more subjective and less detailed than 'lower level' information.

Decision support systems

Definition

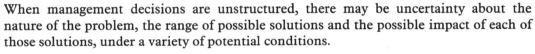
A **Decision Support System (DSS)** is a management information system (usually computerised) designed to produce information that will assist managers in making decisions which require analysis and problem-solving.

When management decisions are unstructured, there may be uncertainty about the nature of the problem, the range of possible solutions and the possible impact of each of those solutions, under a variety of potential conditions.

(a) **Modelling** is the term given to the techniques which represent a real situation, by depicting the interrelationships between relevant factors in the situation in a simplified and structured way. Models can be used to increase a manager's understanding of the situation in which a decision has to be made, and to help him or her evaluate alternative decisions. In effect, models allow managers to try out decisions and see what happens – without incurring any real risks.

(b) **Sensitivity analysis** is a technique which basically asks 'What if ...?': what if a particular piece of data in a decision model were changed? A manager can see what the alternative outcome of a decision would be if different assumptions were adopted. What would be the impact on the HR plan if a higher than planned pay rise were awarded to a particular group of staff, for example?

(c) **Spreadsheets** are simple models which allow a manager to input a range of interrelated variables into a matrix, and to see the effect of changing one or more of them on the others. You could instantly gauge, for example, how a day's slippage in the schedule for a process might affect your overall plans.

Note that the DSS does not *make* the decision: it merely gives the manager added information on which to base the decision.

NOTES

Expert systems

Definition

> **Expert systems** are computer programs which allow users to benefit from expert knowledge and information, and also advice.

The master/reference file holds a large amount of specialised data, for example on legal or medical issues, or tax matters. The system can give a factual answer to a specific query, from this data. However, it can also indicate to the user what a decision ought to be in a particular situation. The user keys in certain facts, and the program uses its information on file to produce a decision about something on which an expert's decision would normally be required.

(a) A user without a legal background can obtain guidance on the law without having to consult a solicitor – for example, on unfair dismissal or health and safety.

(b) A user with no financial background could consult an expert system for taxation, for guidance on particular matters of tax.

Activity 1   **(30 minutes)**

Suggest ways in which raw data on the names of all the workers recruited into the organisation in a given year could be used:

(a)   In an administrative/transaction processing system
(b)   In a management information system

1.3 Objectives of the system

The main purposes of a record/information system for personnel are as follows.

(a) The personal details of employees and their employment history must be stored and accessible for reference and updating.

(b) Data must be provided in returns to government and other agencies.

(c) Information must be gathered and processed for decision making in all areas of personnel management, as we have already seen, including:

    (i) Manpower forecasting and planning
    (ii) Recruitment and selection
    (iii) Employment: transfer, promotion, discipline, termination
    (iv) Training and development
    (v) The design and administration of remuneration systems
    (vi) Health, safety and welfare

Activity 2   **(45 minutes)**

Whether the information system is manual (paper files) or computerised, it needs to be designed so that items of information are easy to locate, identify, retrieve and use. Imagine that you need to find out when a particular employee last attended a training course. Your organisation uses a paper-based system, so the information will be in a file somewhere. Imagine what difficulties and frustration you might encounter.

Task:

Outline what you consider to be the three most important attributes or qualities of a good information/record-keeping system.

BPP
PUBLISHING

NOTES

So far, we have covered the basics of information systems, using personnel management examples. We now turn directly to the information requirements and information-handling responsibilities of the personnel function.

2   SYSTEMS FOR PERSONNEL ADMINISTRATION AND MANAGEMENT

2.1   Personnel records and statistics

Definition

> **Employee records** are those kept by an organisation about each of its employees. They are built up and added to as the employee's career with the organisation progresses.

The information kept in an employee's record will be:

(a)   His or her original application form, interview record and letters of reference

(b)   His or her contract of employment, giving details such as period of notice, conditions and terms of work

(c)   Standing details about the employee, such as:

    (i)   Age
    (ii)   Home address
    (iii)   Current position/grade in the organisation
    (iv)   Details of pay
    (v)   Details of holiday entitlement
    (vi)   Date of birth
    (vii)   Date of commencement of employment

(d)   Accumulated details, gathered over the employee's work history

> **Activity 3**   **(15 minutes)**
>
> From your knowledge of the role of the personnel function, suggest some of the information that it might gather about an employee throughout his/her career with the organisation.

These data will have to be kept continuously flowing in from the department where the employee works.

Figure 9.1 (which follows shortly) is an example of an employee record card in a paper-based system.

There will also be **collective** employee records, such as:

- Age and length of service distributions
- Total wage/salary bill; wage rates and salary levels
- Overtime statistics
- Absenteeism, labour turnover statistics
- Accident rates and costs
- Grievances, disciplinary action, disputes
- Training records

BPP
PUBLISHING

Records required by **statute** include the following.

- Hours of work: hours, breaks and overtime of young employees (16–18) on outside duties; hours of work of women and young persons employed in factories; hours of work of drivers

- Disabled employees: names of registered disabled persons

- Statutory Sick Pay: the Official Deductions Working Sheet.

- Safety: notifiable accidents, dangerous occurrences and illnesses (under RIDDOR 95); records and dates of first aiders' qualifications and training; records of first aid treatment given

- PAYE records, under the jurisdiction of the Inland Revenue: details of gross pay, taxable pay, tax due, tax deducted, National Insurance contributions, statutory sick pay and maternity pay (Form P11)

ACAS (1981) recommended that records should also show the following.

- The numbers and occupations of employees required for efficient production, including future production plans

- How well the age balance of the work force is being maintained

- The rate of labour turnover and retention of key workers

- How many and which employees have the potential for promotion within the organisation

2.2 Personnel returns

Personnel returns may be required in the UK by:

- (a) The Health and Safety Executive – health and safety statistics

- (b) Department of Employment or employers' associations – manpower and earnings statistics

- (c) Industrial training boards – training statistics

- (d) The Department of Social Security and Inland Revenue – manpower, earnings, pension and other benefit statistics

NAME:

EMPLOYEE RECORD CARD

Date of birth ______ Nationality ______ Sex ☐M ☐F

National Insurance No ______ No of dependants ______

☐ Single ☐ Engaged ☐ Married ☐ Separated ☐ Divorced ☐ Widowed

Job related physical disabilities ______ Registration No ______

Education ______

Higher education ______

Qualifications ______

Company training ______

Other skills (eg languages) ______ Driving licence ______

Pension scheme ______ Date eligible ______ Date joined ______

Address ______

Postcode ______

Telephone ______

1st CHANGE

Address ______

Postcode ______

Telephone ______

2nd CHANGE

Address ______

Postcode ______

Telephone ______

IN EMERGENCY INFORM

Name ______

Address ______

Tel (work) ______

(home) ______

Name ______

Address ______

Tel (work) ______

(home) ______

EMPLOYMENT HISTORY

Dates		Position	Pay	Reasons for change or termination
From	To		£	

TRAINING HISTORY

Dates		Courses attended
From	To	

Form ERC/1

Figure 9.1 Employee record card

2.3 Management information

Decision-making in a range of personnel activities will require statistical information, or data about individuals, for various reasons.

(a) **Human resource planning**. Forecasting the future demand for labour will require ratio-trend analysis, environmental information about the market and competitor action and so on. Forecasting the future supply of labour will require information about the labour market, as well as, for each category of labour within the organisation, turnover, age distribution, promotions etc.

(b) **Planning recruitment and selection.** Job and person specifications will be the basis of both activities. Study of past recruitment campaigns, the cost/success rate of advertising media and offered incentives will help in the design of new recruitment campaigns. Data on the success of interview and testing techniques in selection (did the high-scorers also do well in performance assessment on the job?) may likewise lead to improvements.

(c) **Planning training programmes.** Analyses of future manpower and job requirements and training specifications will determine needs for the subjects to be covered, types of course, numbers to be trained and so on.

(d) **Planning and reviewing remuneration systems.** Statistics of earnings fluctuations, average (as opposed to target) salaries, cost per unit of output, rates of pay in competitor organisations and the market in general, etc., will help in reviewing pay systems, structure and levels of pay.

(e) **Improving employee satisfaction and relations.** Work methods, supervision or disciplinary procedures may be improved by analysing disciplinary cases, causes of disputes, statistics on labour turnover, absenteeism or grievances.

(f) **Improving health, safety and fire precautions,** by analysing statistics on sickness, accidents and incidents in the organisation, and reports and returns on industrial disease, health hazards, inspection and audit methods and so on.

2.4 Information resources

Remember that there are sources of information **outside** the organisation, as well as within the organisation's files: we discussed some of them in Chapter 8.

The 'expert system' of the personnel function may include:

(a) Books and journals on personnel issues, demography and other statistics. In the UK, for example, there is the *Abstract of Statistics, People Management, Pay Magazine* (payroll issues), *European Update* (published by the CIPD) and many others; Eurostat provide statistics on the EU

(b) Consultants, personnel managers in other organisations, conferences and seminars

(c) The World Wide Web (if you are interested, check out the CIPD's website: www.cipd.co.uk) or *People Management* journal at www.peoplemanagement. co.uk.

FOR DISCUSSION

'It's all very well to say "work smarter, not harder". But we've got plenty of information. We don't need more information. What we need is the 'smarts' to use it more wisely and more effectively. Where can we buy that?'

Do you sympathise with this view? Or is 'more information', 'better information'?

Finally, we are ready to look at the use of computers in personnel administration and management, and how they have revolutionised the performance of information systems.

3 COMPUTERS IN HRM

3.1 Computers in personnel administration and management

The advantage of computers is that they are fast and accurate at storing, retrieving, transmitting, formatting and manipulating data. They can generate tailor-made management information in a wide variety of formats, and can store huge amounts of information in a very small space (on magnetic tape or disk) and with easy accessibility (since records can be updated or amended without the inconvenience of re-arranging or defacing a paper record).

The main general uses for computers in personnel administration and management are as follows.

(a) **Keeping records:** accessible, space-economical storage of all the records discussed above, on training, pay, employee history and so on. This facility may be used as a pure historical filing cabinet, or as a database for accessible information in constantly updated areas such as the administration of Statutory Sick and Maternity Pay, accident, disciplinary, absenteeism and turnover analysis.

(b) **Preparation of management information**. Computer programs can be used to provide statistics, lists (selecting and sorting data entries according to defined criteria of age, sex or grade), analyses, ratios, trends, forecasts and models. This will enable raw data in records to be interpreted and organised for manpower, succession and development planning. 'What if...?' questions can be asked in the evaluation of options with regard to salary increases, say, or reduction in manning levels. In particular, it allows routine administrative information, such as payroll records, to be converted into decision-support or management information – for example, to analyse the payroll costs of a range of manpower plans.

(c) **Analysis and comparison of different records** for recruitment, selection, job evaluation, employee appraisal, planning of workflow on the basis of workload distribution. Comparison of relevant details for different jobs, applicants and employees can be made accurately and almost instantaneously.

(d) **Calculation** – for example, of pay-roll costs and ratios, the effect of alterations to the structure or payments on the overall pay system and levels, budgets (and performance against them), or weightings of job evaluation factors. Computers are fast and accurate (given accurate inputs) in calculation.

(e) **Routine paperwork**, such as standard letters of acknowledgement or refusal in selection, notification and confirmation of job gradings or salary reviews, preparation of contracts or statements of employment. Word processing facilities can be used to merge new text and name/address files with standard skeleton documents. Time spent on typing and editing tasks (notices, advertising material, even in-house bulletins and journals, as well as correspondence) will be reduced, and output quality enhanced.

(f) **Graphics facilities,** used in the design of forms and documents where these still have to be used.

EXAMPLE: PERCEIVED NEED FOR COMPUTERISED SYSTEMS

A survey carried out in the UK by Richards-Carpenter found that the main reasons given for needing a system are:

NOTES

• Routine personnel reports	90%
• Manpower planning	80%
• Salary administration	72%
• **Ad hoc** reports	38%
• Industrial relations negotiations	38%

Brian Livy (*Corporate Personnel Management*) suggests that computers can have a major impact, not just on the effectiveness and efficiency with which the personnel function performs its information-related tasks, but on the function itself.

'Once the personnel function is freed from routine burdens, personnel specialists can be used more effectively... Decisions and actions can become proactive rather than delayed and reactive.'

An advertisement for Compel (Computers in Personnel) in *People Management* (14 May 1998) reads as follows.

'HR is now at the strategic heart of most successful organisations. But how can you do justice to your *strategic* role when your time is still so occupied with *routine* issues?

Compel can help you bring a more sensible balance to your life. To begin with we can ensure you always have instant access to the complete HR picture and the tools to generate tailored *strategic* reports within minutes.

Then, we can relieve you of most of the routine paperwork, for example by introducing once-only data entry across all your personnel, recruitment, training and payroll operations. We can even help you delegate many time-consuming, non-core HR tasks to line management level, where they belong, by harnessing Compel's Intranet options.'

Activity 4   **(15 minutes)**

You work for a medium-sized organisation that currently keeps paper-based employee record files. It is beginning to be a source of frustration that updating and analysing information seems slow and generates a lot of paper! Just from your own knowledge of computers, in general terms, see if you can anticipate the arguments for computerising such a record system.

Livy sounds a note of caution, however.

'The introduction of an electronic machine into the personnel system will not necessarily make that unit any more effective or automatically benefit the organisation. There is no guarantee. Information needs to be properly utilised.'

Activity 5   **(1½ hours)**

Get hold of a copy of People Management, the magazine of the CIPD, from your college, library or newsagent. Browse though it, making a note of all the advertisements for computerised personnel information systems software and consultancy. Note the benefits they claim, and the features and facilities offered.

3.2 Facilities of a computerised personnel information system (CPIS)

The basic building blocks of a computerised personnel information system are the employee records, ie the records kept by an organisation about its staff. Computerising the system enables more information to be stored, collated and analysed. Comprehensive reports can be extracted quickly. Some of the main uses of a CPIS are outlined below.

PUBLISHING

Employee records

Data, letters, forms and photos can all be scanned, filed and managed (without paper!) within the system, for ease of storage, retrieval and updating. Employee records can be sorted and analysed to show collective summaries and trends, breakdowns by age/gender and so on. They can also be linked with other applications (see below). The following is an example of a page from a computerised Employee Records System (ASR for Windows).

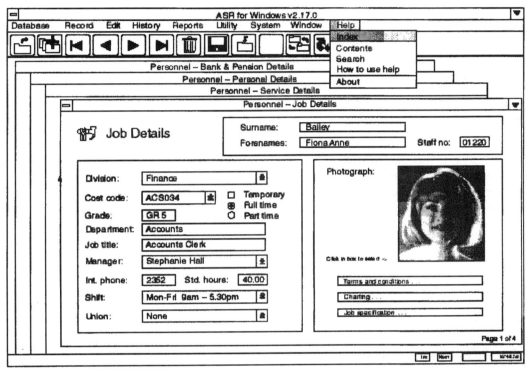

Figure 9.2 ASR for Windows

Time and attendance records

Details of staff absence can be categorised according to reason for absence, highlighting problem areas and calculating remaining holiday entitlements. The system can also be used to calculate statutory sick pay (SSP), and cross-linked (with other working hours data) to **payroll**.

Shift-work/flexitime co-ordinating

Shifts can be allocated based on (a) periods of highest demand and (b) applications from staff for time off, which are prioritised according to (c) the number of hours worked by the member of staff. Such a system (called Timecare) has just been introduced by the NHS to co-ordinate nurses' shifts (*People Management* 5 March 1998)

Human resource planning

The CPIS can be used to provide information for staffing planning purposes. Analysis of posts and vacancies, labour turnovers, age and service profiles of different grades of staff, plus information on qualifications, training, skills and experience of staff can be provided from routinely kept employee records.

Modelling and data analysis

Computerised models can play an important role in decision support. For example, wage and salary models can be developed using computer spreadsheets that can be

NOTES

manipulated to allow automatic calculations to be performed, to show the overall financial effects of, say, job evaluation or retraining.

More sophisticated manpower planning models can test the effects of trends on labour turnover, promotion and recruitment patterns.

Recruitment and selection

A computerised personnel information system, perhaps linked to the Internet, can be used to provide a database of applicants. It can be used to automate all the various stages involved in recruitment and selection, from sending application forms on request, to selection testing, to sending out acceptance and rejection letters.

The computerised system used for recruitment and selection can be linked to other areas of the personnel system to monitor the performance of successful candidates.

EXAMPLE

A firm of consultants wishing to employ a trainee marketing executive (*Guardian Careers*, 25 March 1995) was faced with over 800 applications. The consultancy devised a computer database with marks out of 10 awarded for key competences, combined with a weightings mark according to the importance of the competence. The resulting spreadsheet produced a rank order of candidates from which the short list was formed.

Training

CPIS can be used to automate training management. Academic achievement and educational qualifications can be logged in the system, along with information about training courses and resources, and details of who attended such courses. This information can be cross-referenced with other personnel data (performance appraisals, job vacancies and requirements) to provide a **skills matching service** (matching who is suitably skilled and qualified with a given task or vacancy), a **promotion planning service**, and an automatic **training needs analysis**.

The following is an example of a page from a computerised training record system (*HR Works*, by GAP Software Ltd).

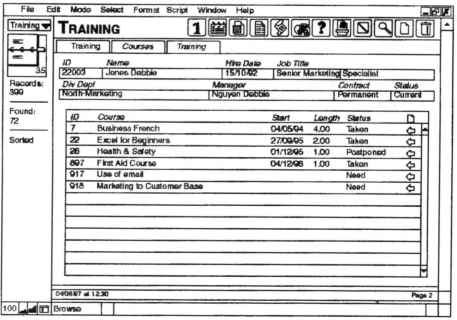

Figure 9.3: A computerised training record

PUBLISHING

EXAMPLE: IBM AND CPIS

IBM (UK) currently use a centralised main-line system for the personnel function. Sensitive information, such as references, confidential test results or welfare provisions, are kept in ordinary paper files, but most employment and salary data are computerised.

- On recruitment (and termination), starter (and termination) 'vouchers' containing basic details are completed by the manager responsible: duplicates are sent to the central personnel unit for entry into the computer. Other personal and career information is input straight from the application form, and added as the employee's career progresses. Every two years, a copy of the 'Personnel Information Survey' is sent to each employee for checking, to ensure that personal details are complete, up-to-date, accurate and relevant.

- Payroll is also computerised at Central Office. The system is updated every other day. The computer produces the payslip and organises credit transfers for payment. Vouchers ('employee profile – current information') are again used for changes to the record of individual salaries: the authorising manager forwards details on the voucher to the Central Payroll Group for input. Once the file has been amended, a copy of the new record is returned to the manager for confirmation, as an 'employee profile – history' voucher for the line manager's records.

- Salary planning is aided by modelling the cost effects of any given set of pay rises.

- Access to computer terminals is strictly limited, and areas of information in storage are also protected by passwords.

Activity 6   **(No time limit)**

Try and get access to a computer with a computerised personnel information system, and observe someone using it. Ask them to demonstrate it for you, or have a go yourself. (If this is in a work, rather than an educational, setting: ask **courteously** for access, and show a sensitivity to the **confidentiality** of records.) Just get an idea of how quickly information can be accessed and manipulated; how varied the records are; how easily and extensively records can be interlinked, and for what purpose; how user-friendly the record pages are. Have fun!

3.3 Selecting a CPIS

General criteria to be examined when selecting any computer system include: the extent and nature of envisaged use, flexibility, ease of use, costs and benefits. Particular questions may include the following.

(a) Is the system going to be required for routine text production and record-keeping tasks only (in which case a cheap PC and some off-the-shelf software may be sufficient) or is more complex management information required? If immediate access (on-line) facilities are required, for example, for swift interrogation of a huge database, or advanced graphics, a mini or mainframe computer may be necessary, with a powerful CPU and possibly special software for particular applications.

(b) Is an integrated system possible and desirable: for example, for operating payroll and personnel systems together? This avoids duplication of effort

and inconsistency in the up-to-dateness of different databases. However, the timescale for using information may be different for different users, and authority for entries and access will have to be clearly defined (and proscribed by the system itself if possible) to avoid confusion. The equivalent consideration in manual systems might be the use of multi-purpose forms or documents sets.

(c)   What are the costs and benefits? Costs include direct costs (hardware, software, peripherals, supplies, maintenance) and also development, accommodation, labour and training costs. Benefits will not be so readily quantifiable. Wille and Hammond pose the following four questions as a test of whether computerisation is economical.

1   How many people are required to run a manual system?

2   How many would be needed to maintain the desirable extra records a computer system would easily include?

3   How many people would be needed if a computer system were adopted?

4   What are the additional costs involved in using a computer system?

        If the cost of 1 + 2 is greater than 3 + 4, the organisation should computerise.

(d)   Should the organisation use its own hardware (with internally developed, or 'off-the-shelf' software) or use a computer bureau? Bureaux relieve the pressure on the client's system development and hardware resources, but the available package may not be entirely relevant to the company's needs. In the same way, commercial software packages are cheaper but not as tailor-made as in-house software.

As you have worked through this chapter so far, it may have occurred to you that quite a lot of personnel data is highly personal in nature! Perhaps more than any other function in the organisation, personnel deals with information which is private and which may have an impact on the reputation, livelihood and well-being of individuals. This raises the important issues of confidentiality and Data Protection.

4   CONFIDENTIALITY

4.1   Concerns about privacy

The Chartered Institute of Personnel and Development has produced a 'Code of Professional Practice in Personnel Management' which deals with confidentiality of information. It states that a personnel manager should:

(a)   'Respect the employer's requirements for confidentiality of information entrusted to him during the performance of his duties, including the safeguarding of information about individual employees' and

(b)   'Ensure the privacy and confidentiality of personnel information to which he has access or for which he is responsible, subject to any legal requirements and the best interests of the employee'.

Especially with the advent of computer records systems, fears have arisen with regard to:

(a)   Access to personal information by unauthorised parties

(b)   The likelihood that an individual could be harmed by the existence of computerised data about him or her which was inaccurate or misleading, and which could be transferred to unauthorised third parties at high speed and little cost

(c)   The possibility that personal information could be used for purposes other than those for which it was requested and disclosed

The Data Protection Acts 1984 and 1988 were passed to address these concerns.

FOR DISCUSSION

Do you know what details about you are held on file by your college, or employer? Consider who else might keep a file on you. Is there any type of information that might be on file that could be detrimental to you if it fell into the wrong (or even, the 'right') hands?

4.2   Data Protection Act 1998

The 1984 Act on which the most recent legislation builds was an initial an attempt to afford some measure of protection to the individual. The terms of the Act cover data about **individuals** – not corporate bodies – and data which are processed **mechanically** (which includes any 'equipment operated automatically in response to the instructions given for that purpose', not just computers). The 1998 Act came into force on 1 March 2000 and is being implemented in stage up to 2007 - but retrospectively, to effect all record systems set up on or after 24 October 1998. (Watch this space – and articles in the HR press!)

Definitions

> **Personal data** are information about a living individual, including facts and expressions of opinion about him or her. Data about other organisations are not personal, unless they contain data about their members. The individual must be identifiable from the data, whether by name, or by code number (say, an employment number) from which the user can identify the individual.
>
> **Data users** are organisations or individuals who control the contents of files of personal data and the use of personal data which are processed (or intended to be processed) automatically.
>
> Clearly, these two definitions put personnel administrators within the scope of the Act, unless a purely manual system of records is kept.

The Act provides that data users and computer bureaux have to register with the Data Protection Registrar. Data users must limit the use of personal data to the uses which are registered, and must abide by **Data Protection Principles** (discussed below).

The Act establishes the following rights for data subjects.

(a)   A data subject may seek compensation through the courts for damage and any associated distress caused by:

(i)   The loss, destruction or unauthorised disclosure of data about himself or herself or by

(ii)   Inaccurate data about himself or herself

(b)   A data subject may apply to the courts or to the Registrar for inaccurate data to be put right or even wiped off the file.

(c)   A data subject may obtain access to personal data of which he or she is the subject.

Data Protection Principles

Personal data held by data users

(1)   The information to be contained in personal data shall be obtained, and personal data shall be processed, fairly and lawfully. Processing means amending, adding to, deleting or rearranging the data, or extracting the information that forms the data (eg printing out).

(2)   Personal data shall be held only for one or more specified (registered) and lawful purposes. There are restrictions on the collection of data about race, ethnic origin, religious or political beliefs, union membership, health, sexual orientation and criminal activities (except for the lawful collection of data for the purposes of monitoring racial equality).

(3)   Personal data held for any purpose or purposes shall not be used or disclosed in any manner incompatible with that purpose or those purposes without the approval of the individual.

(4)   Personal data held for any purpose or purposes shall be adequate, relevant and not excessive in relation to that purpose or those purposes.

(5)   Personal data shall be accurate and, where necessary, kept up to date. 'Accurate' means correct and not misleading as to any matter of **fact**. An **opinion** cannot be challenged on the grounds of inaccuracy and breach of the fifth DP Principle. Additional safeguards on the security of information must be applied if it is to be exported outside the European Economic Area.

(6)   Personal data held for any purpose or purposes shall not be kept for longer than is necessary for that purpose or those purposes. Data users should therefore review their personal data regularly, and delete any data which no longer serve a purpose.

(7)   An individual shall be entitled:

(a)   At reasonable intervals, and without undue delay or expense:

(i)   To be informed by any data user whether he/she holds personal data of which that individual is the subject

(ii)   To access to any such data held by a data user

(b)   Where appropriate, to have such data corrected or erased

Personal data held by data users or in respect of which services are provided by persons carrying on computer bureaux

(8)   Appropriate security measures shall be taken against unauthorised access to, or alteration, disclosure or destruction of, personal data and against accidental loss or destruction of personal data. The prime responsibility for creating and putting into practice a security policy rests with the data user.

There are some important **exemptions** from the Act.

(a)   **Unconditional exemptions:** personal data which are essential to national security, required to be made public by law, or concerned only with the data user's personal, family or household affairs

(b)   **Conditional exemptions,** including:

(i)   Personal data held for payroll and pensions

(ii) Data held by unincorporated members' clubs, relating only to club members

(iii) Data held only for distribution of articles or information to the data subjects (say, for mailshot advertising) and consisting only of their names and addresses or other particulars necessary for the distribution)

(c) **Exemptions from the 'subject access' provisions only,** including: data held for the prevention or detection of crime assessment or collection of tax; data to which legal professional privilege could be claimed (for example, that held by a solicitor); data held solely for statistical or research purposes.

(d) **A special exemption for word processing operations** performed only for the purpose of preparing the text of documents. If a manager writes reports on his employees for disclosure to third parties using his computer as a word processor, he will not as a result become a data user. If he stores the text of his report on disk in order to be able to make further copies, he will still not necessarily become a data user. If, however, he intends to use the stored data as a source of information about the individual and can extract the information automatically, he must register as a data user.

The organisation will need to appoint a Data Protection Co-ordinator. He/she will arrange registration and set up systems: to monitor compliance with the Principles; meet subject access requirements; and alert him/her to any changes in the organisation which may require amendment in the registered entry. The entry should be amended whenever there is a change in the nature or purpose of data being held and used. The organisation's staff should be informed of the Act's implications and their rights as data subjects, as well as their duties as data users (if they work with computers).

Activity 7   **(10 minutes)**

Are the following examples permissible under the Act, or not?

(a) You demand your right to access any personal data held by the Inland Revenue on your tax affairs.

(b) Your personnel file contains an appraisal report by your supervisor which states: 'In my opinion, [your name] appears to display a negative attitude towards supervision, which may account for recent disciplinary proceedings?' You do not, in fact, have a negative attitude towards supervision: the disciplinary proceedings were caused by factors outside your control. You demand compensation for loss caused to you (since you were not promoted, as expected, following appraisal) as a result of this inaccurate data.

(c) You discover that your employee record contains a mention of a conviction for drink-driving – which you have never had. You had wondered why you were always refused access to the 'pool' car at work. You claim compensation for the loss caused as a result of this inaccurate data, and ask for it to be wiped from the file.

(d) As HR manager, you have compiled a recruitment file on the candidate for a senior management position. You hired a private investigation agency to search her home, access her bank records and tap her phone (all without her knowledge) in an effort to vet her character and circumstances, in the interest of the firm's security. The report is held on your database.

NOTES

4.3 The Criminal Justice and Public Order Act 1994

This Act created new offences in the field of data protection by amending Section 5 of the Data Protection Act 1984. The new offences are:

(a) Procuring the disclosure of computer-held information

(b) Selling computer-held information

(c) Offering to sell computer-held information

This is relevant to HR, because personnel information could be quite valuable to other organisations for the purposes of head-hunting; vetting prospective employees; marketing of products; and industrial espionage.

4.4 Data security measures

Confidentiality of paper records is reasonably easy to ensure, since withdrawal of files requires the physical presence of an individual. The file storage area should be restricted to authorised personnel only, and named individuals only should be allowed to consult or remove personnel files. Third party enquiries, for employee addresses or salary, say, should not be given without reference back to the employee.

Security measures in relation to computerised files include the following.

(a) Access to computer terminals should be strictly limited.

(b) Areas of information in storage should be protected with passwords, so that files cannot be called up by an unauthorised user of the VDU.

(c) Printouts of records, if done by a central computer department, should be made under the supervision of a member of staff responsible for records management. If such printouts are sent through internal mail to employees for checking, they should be properly sealed and marked 'Private and confidential'.

(d) Any disks used as back-up storage of personal data should also be protected with passwords and stored safely in a lockable container.

(e) Since data must be kept safe from loss or destruction as well as unauthorised access, there should be procedures for backing up stored records (keeping copies), fire-proof storage for disks and so on.

Chapter roundup

- Organisations need up-to-date and accurate personnel-related information. This is provided by personnel records and information systems.

- Information systems may be designed for administration/transaction processing or for the provision of management information and decision support.

- Information is kept on each individual employee to form an employee record. Collective employee records are also kept, and provide statistical information for the internal use of the company, and for returns to government and other agencies.

- Facilities of a computerised personnel information system include: employee records; time and attendance recording linked to payroll; modelling and data analysis for manpower planning, recruitment and selection, and training.

- Care must be taken to ensure the confidentiality and security of information and compliance with the Data Protection Act 1998 and the Criminal Justice and Public Order Act 1994.

NOTES

Quick quiz

1   What are the main purposes of a personnel record system?

2   What information will be contained in:

    (a)   An employee's personnel record?

    (b)   Collective records of the organisation's workforce?

3   Which government agencies require personnel returns?

4   Which personnel records must be kept by law?

5   In which areas can statistical information help personnel decision making?

6   Why would an organisation want to centralise its record system in a file registry or similar department?

7   List five general uses of computerised personnel information systems. Give a specific example for each case.

8   List four types of information system. Think of one example of how each of these types of system might be used.

9   What rights do data subjects have under the Data Protection Act 1998?

10 How can the security of computer files be ensured?

Answers to quick quiz

1   To store personal details of employees and their employment history, to provide returns to government agencies, to gather information for personnel decision making.   (see paragraph 1.3)

2   (a)   The original application form, reference letters, interview record, contract of employment, standing details (eg date of birth, starting date), accumulated details (eg training received, holidays taken).

    (b)   Age and length of service distributions, wage bill, pay rates, overtime records, absenteeism, labour turnover, accident rates, grievances, disciplinary action, disputes, training records. (para 2.1)

3   The Health and Safety Executive, Department of Employment, industrial training boards, Department of Social Security, Inland Revenue.

         (para 2.2)

4   Hours of work, disabled employees, statutory sick pay, safety.   (para 2.1)

5   Human resource planning, recruitment and selection, training programmes, reviewing remuneration systems, employee satisfaction and relations, improving health and safety matters.   (para 3.1)

6   Consistent procedures, control over access and accuracy, cost-effectiveness, reduction of duplication, control over whereabouts.

         (para 3.3)

7   Keeping records (training), management information (age profile), analysis and comparison (appraisal), calculation (budgets), routine paperwork (rejection letters), graphic facilities (application form).

         (para 3.1)

8   Transactions processing systems, decision support systems, management information systems, expert systems. Payroll items, promotion decisions, manpower planning, employment law.   (para 1)

9   Compensation for damages and distress caused by loss or inaccurate data, right to have inaccurate data corrected or removed, access to personal data.   (para 4.2)

10   Limited access to files, use of passwords, supervision of printouts, passwords for back-up disks, copies of stored records.   (para 4.4)

Answers to activities

1   (a)   Recruitment data might be used administratively: to update staff number records; to prepare returns to the Department of Trade and Industry on numbers employed; to prepare/update payroll records and other employee data files; to initiate induction/orientation training for new recruits.

(b)   Recruitment data might be used in decision support, planning and control: to monitor and adjust recruitment in light of the HR plan; to monitor recruits' performance as a way of evaluating selection procedures; to monitor labour cost and efficiency; to analyse changes and trends in the age/sex distribution of the workforce; to monitor equal opportunity in the organisation and so on!

2   Your three priorities may be slightly different from ours, but we would suggest attention to the following attributes.

(a)   **Simple to operate and easy to maintain.** Forms should be designed so as to be logical and easily read, understood, completed, and identified for retrieval. Relevant items should be capable of being immediately isolated and retrieved, without having to wade through complicated indexing systems or irrelevant data.

(b)   **Accurate and up to date.** Records should be clearly identified. The purpose and definition of entries should not be left ambiguous. Data on the record must be checked for accuracy, up-to-dateness, within tolerance levels dictated by the purpose and time/cost budget of the system. (If approximations are sufficient, it is not cost-effective to record data to a minute degree of accuracy – although correctness will always be essential).

(c)   **Comprehensive but not overloaded.** Information should be regularly reviewed for completeness (no gaps where information is required) but also, crucially, relevance (no information that is redundant or unnecessary to the system's purpose). This consideration may prohibit setting up a system in the first place: a one-off request for information should not inspire a permanent record or data collection system unless the information is likely to be a recurring need, and of significant benefit to the organisation (so as to justify the costs of maintaining the record).

3   Accumulated employment information includes:

(i)   Training

(ii)   Professional qualifications acquired

(iii)   Holidays taken

(iv)   Positions held previously in the organisation: transfers and promotions

(v)   History of accidents, sick leave and absence

(vi)   Appraisal forms

(vii)   Results of proficiency tests

(viii)   Disciplinary measures taken against him/her

4   System designs vary with the needs of organisations, but computerised systems are becoming more available, with benefits for:

  (a)   Secure and economical information storage

  (b)   Flexibility of processing functions for the preparation of management information

  (c)   Speed and accuracy of data manipulation

  (d)   Versatility for text editing and production, information storage, calculation etc

  (e)   Document design and production

5   The answer depends on what your research turned up. (We have incorporated some of the features and facilities currently available in Section 3.2 of this chapter.)

6   This was a purely experiential activity.

7   (a)   No: this is an exemption from the 'subject access' provisions
     (b)   No: an opinion cannot be challenged on these grounds
     (c)   Yes: this is your right
     (d)   No: data must be obtained fairly and lawfully

Assignment 9   **(1 hour)**

Novalux PLC

You have recently been appointed as personnel officer for Novalux PLC, a large engineering firm just outside Bristol. One of your key responsibilities is to produce regular management reports to all members of senior management. These reports should be interesting, succinct and valuable, and should present personnel information in a clear and digestible form. One of your other key tasks is to recruit and select new employees.

You are astonished at how many people seem to come and go from Novalux, suggesting you have some kind of retention problem. Therefore, you have decided to combine both issues and produce a management report on staff turnover. You have created the following table.

LENGTH OF SERVICE

Entry age	0–4 weeks Number of staff	5–26 weeks Number of staff	27–52 weeks Number of staff	53+ weeks Number of staff
16–24	25	14	13	10
25–34	10	16	25	15
35–49	6	20	18	9
50–64	8	16	13	11

Your task

Your task is to analyse these figures to see if age upon entry has an impact on length of service. What additional information would you require in order to draw other useful conclusions on the pattern of leavers from Novalux?

Chapter 10 :
EMPLOYEE EXIT

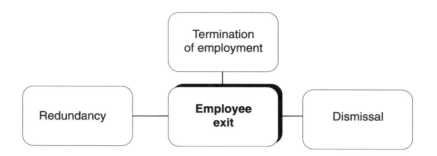

Introduction

So far, this Course Book has covered some of the processes by which the human resource is managed as it moves into and through or within the organisation. In this chapter, we look at some of the ways in which it must be managed on its way **out** of the organisation.

The exit of employees from the organisation requires careful management because of:

(a)   The need for compliance with the legal framework on employment protection (particularly in regard to dismissal and redundancy)

(b)   The need for sensitivity to the human issues involved (especially in regard to retirement, dismissal or redundancy)

(c)   The need for the organisation to gather feedback from departing employees in order to identify retention problems (especially in regard to resignation)

We will consider these aspects in the context of each type of exit.

As you read through this Course Book, which covers the law and regulations on various employment-related issues, remember: 'The law is a floor'. It sets minimum standards below which no organisational practice may fall without penalties. It does not set out 'best practice'. Personnel managers should ask themselves 'What *must* we do?' (compliance) – but also 'What *should* we do and what *can* we do to enhance business performance *and* employee satisfaction?'

Your objectives

In this chapter you will learn about the following:

(a)   Employee exit procedures used by different organisations

(b)   The need for effective management of employee dismissal

(c)   The selection criteria used for redundancy

(d)   Alternative approaches for dealing with redundancy

1 TERMINATION OF EMPLOYMENT

1.1 Termination of the employment contract

As we discussed in Chapter 5, the formation of a contract signals the beginning of an employment relationship. That relationship is **finite**: it comes to an end. This is obviously so of **fixed-term contracts**, where a person is employed for a certain period of time or the duration of a specific project. But even indefinite contracts, where a person is employed on an open-ended basis, come to an end sooner or later.

Contracts of employment can be 'terminated' in the following ways.

(a)   **By performance**

The employee does what he or she was hired to do, and the employer gives the agreed payment or consideration: the contract is fulfilled. This is common in fixed contracts and contracts for specific services. It may also be said to apply in the case of retirement.

(b)   **By mutual agreement**

Both parties can agree that they are entitled to terminate the contract at any time, say in the event of 'irreconcilable differences.'

(c)   **By notice**

One party can terminate the contract, but must give adequate notice or warning to the other. This happens in the case of:

(i)   Resignation by the employee
(ii)   Dismissal of the employee
(iii) Redundancy

There are strict rules on the periods of notice which must be given to protect both parties: we will cover them in this chapter.

(d)   **Breach of contract**

If one party 'breaks' or fails to fulfil the terms of the contract, the other party has the option of considering the contract to have been terminated. (In addition, he or she may seek legal remedies to compensate for, or minimise the effects of, the breach.) Failure by the employer to pay the agreed wage, or dishonest conduct by the employee, would be in breach of the implied terms of the employment contract, for example.

(e)   **Frustration**

A contract is 'frustrated' when it is prevented from being fulfilled – for example, because of the death, illness or imprisonment of one of the parties.

NOTES

| Activity 1 | (20 minutes) |

(a) Alan countersigns his employment contract and written statement with Sheerbrow Ltd but after two weeks is told that the holiday entitlement of four weeks per annum as stated in the particulars should have read three weeks, as was originally agreed. What can he do?

(b) Anita was engaged for a two-year period as sub-editor of a newspaper. Six months later, however, the publishers sold the newspaper and ceased to publish it. What has happened to Anita's contract?

(c) Ambrose attended a selection interview for a job due to begin on September 1. The interviewer said he was impressed with Ambrose's CV; he felt that Ambrose was an ideal candidate, and he would get back to him as soon as possible after the selection process was finished. Owing to confusion in the personnel department, no-one subsequently contacted Ambrose. Ambrose turned up to work on September 1, and (owing to further confusion in the personnel department) put in a day's work before it was realised that he was not, in fact, the successful candidate! The company told Ambrose to leave, and refused to pay him for the day's work. What can Ambrose do?

We will now go on to look at the HR department's role in managing the termination of employment contracts, looking in particular at the legislative and managerial frameworks that influence policy in this area. We will start by looking at employee-side reasons for leaving: retirement and resignation

1.2 Retirement

The average age of the working population has been steadily increasing, with higher standards of living and health care. The problems of older workers, and the difficulties of adjusting to retirement, are therefore commanding more attention. The time at which an individual will experience difficulties in obtaining or retaining jobs because of age will obviously vary according to the individual, his/her lifestyle and occupation, and the attitudes of his/her society and employers.

There are two basic approaches to retirement policy

(a) **Flexible retirement,** whereby a stated retirement age is a minimum age at which the contract can be ended for retirement purposes: fit and capable employees are allowed to continue to work after this age.

(b) **Fixed retirement,** whereby retirement is enforced at the stated age.

There are various arguments for delaying or enforcing the retirement of older workers.

BPP
PUBLISHING

Disadvantages of retaining older workers	Advantages of retaining older workers
• There is resistance to late retirement from younger workers, because it is felt that promotion opportunities are being blocked.	• Older workers are still capable of non-strenuous work, and may be particularly valuable in jobs requiring mature judgement, conscientiousness, attention to detail or experience.
• Younger employees with family responsibilities have a greater need for job security: in the event of downsizing, workers nearing retirement should be selected first for redundancy. So, when redundancies are proposed, it is common for pensioners and those nearing retirement to be discharged first.	• They may make a great contribution to the training and coaching of more junior staff.
• The age structure of an organisation may become unbalanced for future work requirements: there may have to be an injection of 'younger blood'.	• There is some evidence that older workers are less likely to move than younger workers, which is an advantage where labour stability is important.
• Engaging staff above middle age can be costly for the organisation: the cost of providing pensions rises according to the age at which the employee joins a superannuation scheme.	• Older workers are often more concerned with customer service and product quality.
• Individual mental and/or physical shortcomings may render an older individual unfit to carry out his or her duties efficiently, especially if they require agility or muscular strength.	• An organisation may perceive age to be an equal opportunity/ discrimination issue.

How far any of the above factors apply will depend to a large extent on the individual concerned, the type of work involved and the state of the local labour market. Retirement policies, and age limits on particular posts will have to be clearly communicated; and decisions regarding particular cases discussed confidentially and tactfully with the individual concerned. Written confirmation of the decision to retire an employee should likewise be tactful, with expressions of regret and appreciation as appropriate. Whatever is done should be done carefully, because the way an organisation treats its retiring workers sends powerful messages to its other employees.

Activity 2   **(10 minutes)**

Employers can give not only financial assistance to retiring employees, but also practical help and advice. Suggest three ways in which the HR department could help older employees.

It should be noted that the Sex Discrimination Act 1986 introduced an equal retirement age for men and women. **Employers** setting a compulsory retirement age must apply it to men and women alike: women made to retire earlier than male colleagues can claim both discrimination and unfair dismissal. At present the State retirement age (the age at

BPP
PUBLISHING

Part A: Unit 21 Human Resource Management

which the individual is entitled to a State pension) is still 65 for men and 60 for women, but it is to be equalised at 65 for both sexes by the year 2010.

1.3 Resignation

Definition

> **Resignation** is the process by which an employee gives notice of his or her intention to terminate the employment contract.

Employees may resign for any number of reasons, personal or occupational. Some or all of these reasons may well be a reflection on the structure, management style, culture or personnel policies of the organisation itself. Management should attempt to find the real reasons why an employee is leaving in an **exit interview,** which may provide helpful feedback on its policies and practices: note, however, that there is no legal requirement for the employee to give reasons for leaving.

The principal aspect of any policy formulated to deal with resignations must be the length to which the organisation will go to try to dissuade a person from leaving. In some cases, the organisation may decide to simply let the person go, but when an employee has been trained at considerable cost to the firm, or is particularly well qualified and experienced, or has knowledge of information or methods that should not fall into the hands of competitors, the organisation may try to keep him or her. Particular problems that the employee has been experiencing (eg salary) **may** sometimes be solved, but there are dangers in setting precedents by giving special treatment.

Various arrangements will have to be made when an employee decides to leave. There will have to be co-operation and full exchange of information between the HR function and the leaver's immediate superior, so that procedures can begin when notice is given of an intended departure.

(a) If attempts to make the employee stay have been unsuccessful, the exit interview will have to be arranged.

(b) The period of notice required for the employee to leave should be set out in his/her contract of employment, but some leeway may be negotiated on this, for example if the employee wishes to take up another position immediately. The statutory minimum notice period (Employment Rights Act 1996) is one week.

(c) Details of the departure have to be notified to the wages clerk, pension fund officer, social secretary, security officer and so on, so that the appropriate paperwork and other procedures can be completed by his/her date of leaving. The organisation may have a departure checklist to ensure that all procedures are completed.

(d) The departmental head and/or supervisor should complete a leaving report form: an overall assessment of the employee's performance in the organisation. This can then be used to provide references to his/her future employer(s).

It should be noted that during the notice period, all terms and conditions of the employment contract still apply: the employee still owes the employer duties of fidelity, obedience and care, while the employer still owes the employee duties of trust, care and provision of work. If there is any doubt that this kind of relationship will be possible during the notice period, due to the circumstances or feelings, surrounding the

234

resignation, it may be advisable to let the employee leave immediately with pay in lieu of notice: this may prevent loss of morale in the team from a disgruntled employee's behaviour, and indeed possible sabotage of work or customer relations by the outgoing employee, gathering of information for use by the new (competing) employer and so on.

Activity 3   **(30 minutes)**

Brainstorm:

(a)   Some reasons for resigning from a job

(b)   Some procedures that might be included on an Employee Departure Checklist

---

Of course, not everybody leaves their organisation on a 'voluntary' basis. Where employees are required *to leave employment, there is a clearer need to protect their rights and livelihoods against injustice or exploitation by employers. After all, people may be 'resources' and 'assets' – but they are not 'things'. This is where employment protection legislation comes into force. We will now look at the thorny issue of dismissal.*

2   DISMISSAL

Definition

Dismissal is the termination of an employee's contract by his/her employer with or without notice, including the ending of a fixed term contract without renewal on the same terms.

Constructive dismissal is resignation by the employee, in circumstances in which he/she is entitled to assume that the employer has in effect terminated the contract, by: 'Conduct [on the part of the employer] which is a significant breach of the contract of employment or which shows that the employer no longer intends to be bound by one or more of the essential terms of the contract ... '   *Western Excavating v Sharp 1978*

2.1   Dismissal by notice

If an employer terminates the contract of employment by giving notice:

(a)   The period of notice given must not be less than the statutory minimum – (Employment Rights Act 1996):

Employee's length of service	*Minimum notice to be given by the employer*
1 month–2 years	1 week
2–12 years	1 week for each year of 'continuous employment'
12 years and over	12 weeks

Longer periods may be written into the employment contract, and these then apply

(b)   Notice may be given without a specific reason being stated, unless the contract requires otherwise

(c)   Either party may waive their right to notice, or accept payment in lieu of notice

    (d)   Employees with two years' service are entitled to a written statement of the reasons for their dismissal within 14 days, on request. (Women dismissed during pregnancy or maternity leave are entitled to this statement irrespective of length of service.)

Many of the rights given to employees under the Employment Rights Act 1996, in areas such as redundancy and unfair dismissal, are only available if an employee has a specified period of **continuous employment.**

In calculating length of service (for all purposes including notice, redundancy pay and compensation for unfair dismissal) the following rules apply.

    (a)   A 'week' is a week during which the employee is employed for at least eight hours or in which his or her employment is subject to a contract which involves employment for eight hours or more. Employees attain continuous employment after two years. (A recent European Union directive gave equal rights to part-time workers, in this respect, as those given to full-time workers.)

    (b)   A period of *absence* (through sickness, injury, secondment or pregnancy) can be included in calculating length of service. Other absences (including strikes) do not break continuity of service, but are not counted in length of service.

    (c)   When an 'undertaking' – a business in the UK or a part of it – is transferred, the employees in the business are automatically transferred (on the same terms and with unbroken continuity of service) to the employment of the new owner.

2.2   Dismissal without notice

In most cases , the statutory and/or contractual minimum notice must be given to the employee. However, rare circumstances may justify 'summary dismissal' or instant dismissal without notice. The law protecting employees from unfair dismissal (discussed below) requires that summary dismissal be limited to cases of serious breach of contract, such as:

    (a)   Gross misconduct by the employee: theft, violence, serious refusal to obey reasonable instruction, endangerment of other staff

    (b)   Serious neglect of duties, or absence from work without permission or good cause

    (c)   Serious breaches of trust or conflicts of interest affecting the organisation's business

Even then, with the onus on employers to justify fair dismissal, an organisation may prefer to use temporary suspension and other disciplinary measures, or dismissal by notice (with pay in lieu of notice if the employee must be removed immediately from the workplace).

FOR DISCUSSION

Debate for and against the proposition.

'An employer should have the right to fire incompetent, incompatible and dishonest employees without costly restrictions and red tape.'

Dismissal is clearly a bit of a political, legal and interpersonal minefield! Fortunately there are two relatively clear definitions of circumstances in which an employee cannot legally be dismissed.

2.3 Wrongful dismissal

A claim for **wrongful dismissal** is open to employees at **common law**, if they can show they were dismissed without notice and without a reasonable cause. The employee must show that he or she was dismissed in breach of contract (for example, with less than the required notice) and that he or she thereby suffered loss. He/she may then be able to claim damages compensating for the amount lost: accrued wages, payment for an entitlement to notice, or the balance of wages due under a fixed-term contract. In practice, such claims are less common now that **unfair** dismissal provisions offer wider remedies, but the common law remedy is still useful for those who cannot claim unfair dismissal (for example, because they have not been continuously employed for long enough to qualify).

Wrongful dismissal is compensated under common law – but only to the amount lost by the employee. Employment protection legislation aimed to widen the scope of protection and to increase the range of remedies available. The concept of 'unfair dismissal' is an extremely important element of this legislation.

2.4 Unfair dismissal

Certain categories of employee are **excluded** from the statutory unfair dismissal code, under the Employment Rights Act 1996, including:

(a) Persons ordinarily employed **outside Great Britain**

(b) Employees dismissed while taking **unofficial strike** or other industrial actions

Subject to these exclusions, an employee has the right not to be unfairly dismissed if (s)he:

(a) is under the normal retiring age applicable to his/her job, or under 65

(b) has been continuously employed for 12 months (whether full-time or part-time). (This qualifying period was reduced by the Employment Relations Act 1999: it used to be two years.)

(c) has the statutory right not to be unfairly dismissed.

So what is a 'fair' dismissal or an 'unfair' dismissal?

Dismissal is fair and justified	Dismissal is unfair
(a) **Redundancy** (provided that the selection for redundancy was fair).	(a) **Redundancy** where the selection is unfair.
(b) **Legal impediment** – the employee could not continue to work in his/her present position without breaking a legal duty or restriction: for example, driving having lost his/her licence. (This is fair only if the employee was offered suitable alternative employment.)	(b) Dismissal for **Trade Union Membership** (actual or proposed) and activities, or **refusal** to join a trade union.
	(c) Dismissal for **pregnancy**, *unless* by reason of it the employee becomes incapable of doing her work adequately.

Dismissal is fair and justified	Dismissal is unfair
(c) **Lack of capability or qualifications to perform the work** (provided that adequate training and warnings had been given). In the case of incapacity due to ill-health, suitable alternative work should be offered. (d) **Misconduct** (provided that warnings suitable to the offence have been given and appeals procedures followed – so the disciplinary procedures of the organisation are vitally important). (e) Some other **'substantial' reason**: for example, the employee marries a competitor, or refuses to accept a reorganisation made in the interests of the business and with the agreement of other employees. (f) **Temporary** work comes to an end (provided its temporary notice was made clear at its commencement).	(d) Dismissal for a **spent conviction** under the Rehabilitation of Offenders Act 1974. (e) Dismissal on **transfer of the undertaking** (unless there are ETO – 'economic, technical or organisational' – reasons justifying it). (f) The employee was dismissed for taking steps to avert danger to health and safety at work. (g) The employee was dismissed for trying to enforce statutory employment rights (eg initiating proceedings against an employer for equal pay). (h) The employee was selected for dismissal from others, who were equally 'guilty' (for example, sacking some strikers and not others). (i) During the first eight weeks of a strike (Employment Relations Act 1999). (j) Based on a 'waiver' written into a fixed term contract of one year or more (ERA 1999 - previously permissible under ERA 1996). (k) The employee disclosed information which (s)he believed exposes malpractice, injustice or health and safety dangers ('whistle blowing') – under the Public Interest Disclosure Act 1998.

Dismissal will **automatically** be considered unfair (irrespective of eligibility criteria) in the case of pregnancy, trade union membership, transfer of undertakings and the enforcement of statutory rights: (b), (c), (e) and (g) above.

An employee who believes (s)he has been unfairly dismissed may present a complaint to an industrial tribunal, which will hear the case after an attempt to settle the dispute by conciliation.

To claim unfair dismissal, three issues have to be considered.

    (a)   The employee must show that he or she is a **qualifying employee** and that he or she has in fact been **dismissed**.

    (b)   Then the employer must show:

        (i)   What was the only or principal reason for dismissal and

        (ii)   That it was one of the justifiable reasons listed above, or was otherwise a **'substantial reason** of a kind such as to justify the dismissal of an employee' (rather than some lesser action) and

(iii)   That formal warnings were issued, training given, proper investigations and record keeping carried out, and fair dismissal procedures followed (with right of appeal etc)

 (c)   Application has to be made to the industrial tribunal within three months of dismissal.

Activity 4   **(20 minutes)**

All other criteria being met, would the following cases be fair or unfair?

(a)   Bernie is a van-driver for a carrier firm. After a number of driving infringements in his own car and in his own time – ie not on the job – Bernie has lost his driving licence. The carrier firm dismisses him.

(b)   Berenice is a shop manageress, but after an period when it has been observed that she leaves the shop dirty and untidy, fails to maintain cash registers and does not put stock away, the chain of shops dismisses her.

(c)   Bernadette worked in telecommunications. The global economy and internet usage requires increased staffing at night, and the company proposes a change in its shift-working, which is accepted by the trade union following a vote. Bernadette refuses to work night shifts. She is dismissed.

(d)   Benedict has noticed that he is not getting an itemised pay statement, and believes that he is entitled to one by law. The personnel department is evasive. Benedict consults the union representatives, who press the question. The personnel department stalls. Benedict starts putting up posters and holding meetings. He is told to stop 'being a trouble maker'. He refuses, and continues lobbying his colleagues. He is dismissed for persistent trouble-making.

The Conciliation Officer or employment tribunal to whom a complaint of unfair dismissal is made may order various remedies including:

 (a)   **Re-instatement** - giving the employee his old job back

 (b)   **Re-engagement** - giving him a job comparable to his old one

 (c)   **Compensation** - this may consist of:

     (i)   A **basic award** calculated on the same scale as redundancy pay. If the employee is also entitled to redundancy pay, the lesser is set off against the greater amount

     (ii)   A **compensatory award** (taking account of the basic award) for any additional loss (earnings, expenses, benefits) on common law principles of damages for breach of contract

     (iii)   A **punitive additional award** if the employer does not comply with an order for re-instatement or re-engagement and does not show that it was impracticable to do so

In deciding whether to exercise its powers to order re-instatement or re-engagement the tribunal must take into account whether the complainant wishes to be reinstated, whether it is practicable for the employer to comply with such an order and, if the complainant contributed to any extent to his dismissal, whether it would be just to make such an order. Such orders are very infrequent.

The Employment Relations Act 1999 raised the ceiling for unfair dismissal awards to £50,000. It also provided that there should be **no** limit on compensation payouts for employees dismissed as 'whistleblowers'.

2.5 Factors to consider

In an article in *The Administrator* (June 1985) John Muir wrote of the difficulties of 'firing' employees particularly in cases of incompetence.

> It is a fairly common experience to hear managers at all levels say of a subordinate, 'I wish I could get rid of him. He's really not up to the job and costs us money. But he's been here years and I really don't see how I can do it.' Behind such a statement there are usually two themes. One is about the **personal difficulty and the unpleasantness** involved in going to the individual and starting the process leading to dismissal; the other is the **fear of being taken to an industrial tribunal** and being found to have acted unfairly.

The solution to these difficulties lies partly in the hands of the personnel function, which may be responsible for designing the **procedures for dismissal**. These should include the following.

(a) Ensuring that **standards** of performance and conduct are set, clearly defined and communicated to all employees

(b) **Warning** employees where a gap is perceived between standard and performance

(c) Giving a clearly defined and reasonable **period for improvement** - with help and training where necessary, and clear improvement targets

(d) Ensuring that **disciplinary procedures** (including appeal procedures, rights to representation and so on) are made clear and meticulously followed

(e) Implementing **progressive discipline** procedures (ideally according to ACAS guidelines: see Chapter 8), so that dismissal is used as a last resort

(f) **Evaluating all disciplinary** decisions and actions in the light of policy, legislation and the requirement to 'act reasonably' at all times

If such procedures are formulated, the employer will not only feel that he has given the employee every chance to redeem himself, but will also be in a strong position at a tribunal in rebutting a complaint of unfair dismissal.

EXAMPLE: INTERNATIONAL COMPARISONS

- Italy and Portugal have no statutory provision on notice periods for dismissal. Other EU countries specify varying notice periods. Austria, Belgium and Greece distinguish between blue and white collar workers. In Sweden, notice periods are age-related, while in most other countries (like the UK) they are based on length of service.

- Compensation provisions for unfair dismissal vary within the EU. Greece makes no provision other than civil remedies. Most countries provide for reinstatement as an alternative to monetary award, but Belgium does not: in Sweden, damages are payable only if the employer refuses to reinstate the employee. Monetary awards vary: civil damages (Netherlands), minimum of six months wages (Belgium, France), maximum of 39 weeks' (Denmark), 18 months', (Germany), 24 months' (Ireland), 12 months' (Italy), 42 months' (Spain) pay, or an amount equal to the worker's earnings over the duration of the legal case (Austria).

- In the USA, there is a considerable freedom to hire and fire at any time, for any reason - subject to negotiated contract terms.

- In Japan, the employment culture has traditionally been based on lifetime 'commitment' (not necessarily lifetime 'employment' in the sense that employees remain in a particular job or plant). According to Beardwell and Holder, 'it would not be unusual for an employee to have to transfer ... or be lent ... to another associated firm in order to remain within the commitment system. It is estimated (1987) that over 30% of the employees over 45 years of age were 'lent' to other plants or even sub-contracting firms.'

FOR DISCUSSION

How would you handle the following 'cases'? Discuss the disciplinary issues, and the consequences of any courses of action you recommend.

(a) An employee is persistently 15 minutes late for work.

(b) An employee persistently uses the office telephone for personal calls, despite clear policies.

(c) An employee is found smoking in a chemical storage area, despite clear safety warnings.

(d) An employee slaps his supervisor in the course of an argument.

One of the fair and justified reasons for dismissal (listed earlier) is 'redundancy' – provided that selection of employees for redundancy is fair. We will now go on to look at redundancy in detail.

3 REDUNDANCY

Definition

Redundancy is defined by the Employment Protection legislation as dismissal:

(a) By reason that the employer has ceased to carry on the business

(b) By reason that the employer has ceased to carry on the business in the place where the employee was employed

(c) By reason that the requirements of the business for employees to carry out work of a particular kind have ceased or diminished, or are expected to

(d) For reasons 'not related to the individual concerned.' (The Trade Union Reform and Employment Rights Act 1993 says that all such dismissals shall be presumed to be for redundancy, for the purposes of statutory consultation with trade unions – not for redundancy pay. This complies with the EU directive on collective redundancy.)

3.1 Redundancy pay

Redundant employees are entitled to compensation, in the form of **redundancy pay**:

(a) For loss of security

(b)   To encourage them to accept redundancy without damage to industrial relations

The employee is **not** entitled to redundancy pay if:

(a)   The employer has made a 'suitable' offer of alternative employment and the employee has unreasonably rejected it. The offer must be of alternative employment in the same capacity, at the same place and on the same terms and conditions as the previous employment. It must be made before the end of the old employment, to take effect within four weeks of its end

(b)   The employee is of pension age or over, or has less than two years' continuous employment

(c)   The employee has resigned voluntarily, been dismissed for misconduct or has otherwise been dismissed for reasons not defined as redundancy

---

Activity 5   **(5 minutes)**

(a)   A's job is abolished, and A is transferred to B's job, and B is dismissed. Is this a case of redundancy?

(b)   An employer wishes to alter employees' contract terms in order to harmonise terms following a merger. It decides to do this by dismissing all employees and re-employing them all on new terms: no one effectively ceases to be employed, since everyone accepts the new terms. Has there been a redundancy?

Redundancy pay entitlement is half a week's pay for each year of employment between ages 18 and 21; one week's pay for each year of employment between 22 and 40; and one-and-a-half weeks' pay for each year of employment between ages 41 and 65. In practice this is often supplemented by voluntary payments by the employer.

3.2   Redundancy procedures

Consultation

From a purely humane point of view, it is obviously desirable to consult with employees or their representatives, and to give warning of impending redundancies. Beyond this, the employer has a statutory duty under the Employment Protection Act 1975, and the Collective Redundancies and Transfer of Undertakings (Protection of Employment) (Amendment) Regulations 1995 and 1999, to consult with any trade union which is independent and recognised (in collective bargaining) by the employer as representative of employees. The consultation must begin 'at the earliest opportunity', defined as:

(a)   A minimum of 90 days before the first dismissal, if 100 or more employees are to be dismissed at any one establishment

(b)   A minimum of 30 days before the first dismissal of 10–99 employees

(c)   At the earliest opportunity before even one (but not more than nine) employees are to be dismissed for redundancy

These rules are applied to the total number involved and cannot be evaded by making essential dismissals in small instalments. Failure to comply renders an employer liable to pay up to 90 days' wages to the employees concerned. The employer must, within the same periods, notify the Secretary of State in writing of proposed redundancies, with details of consultations with the trade union: a copy of this notice is given to the union representative.

Under the 1995 regulations, where there is no recognised trade union, an employer must invite elected employee representatives to receive information and be consulted with. Under the 1999 regulations employers have additional responsibilities for ensuring that employee representatives (where required) are fairly elected, trained and informed. The 1999 regulations also require employers to consult not only about the people who are going to be made redundant, but those affected by the dismissals - for example, those who may have to take on additional duties. The regulations refer not just to actual dismissals but to '**proposals to dismiss**', to close loop-holes such as dismissal for re-employment (see our answer to Activity 5) and the offer of voluntary redundancy without genuine intention to close or reduce jobs.

In giving notice to employee representatives, the employer must give certain details in writing, including the reasons for the dismissals, the numbers employed and the number to be dismissed, the method of selecting employees for dismissal and the period over which the dismissals will take place. Information should be accurate, clear, realistic and positive as far as possible. Ideas for retraining and redeployment, benefits and potential for voluntary redundancies or retirements should be far enough advanced for some good news to be mixed with the bad. The employer should allow the trade union time in which to consider what has been disclosed and to make representations or counter proposals. The purpose of consultation is to reach agreement with union representatives.

Failure to comply with consultation requirements entitles the union to bring a complaint before the industrial tribunal. If conciliation (facilitated by ACAS) is not possible, the tribunal will hear the complaint. If the complaint is upheld, the tribunal may postpone dismissal and order consultation to take place, or may make a 'protective award' of pay to employees concerned, based on the number of redundancies and the period over which they are carried out.

Activity 6	**(30 minutes)**

From our discussion of the internal labour market in Chapters 3 and 4, what measures might a personnel manager consider in order to avoid or reduce the numbers of **forced** redundancies that have to be made?

Employee rights

Redundant employees have rights in addition to redundancy pay and notice/ consultation, as follows.

(a)   The right to 'reasonable' time off with pay to look for another job or arrange training

(b)   The right to accept alternative work offered by the employer for an agreed trail period, and to refuse that work (if unsuitable) at the end of the trial period without prejudice to the right of redundancy pay

Softening the blow

Where enforced redundancies are necessary, the legal provisions discussed above come into force, together with such collective bargaining procedures as may exist. Where possible, procedures and benefit packages should be planned for well in advance as a contingency measure, rather than as a reactive measure in the context of cost-cutting and

BPP PUBLISHING

industrial conflict. (This also benefits the employee, since benefits are likely to be higher if they are set **before** the use of economy measures which commonly necessitate workforce reduction.)

Many large organisations provide services and benefits well in excess of the statutory minimum, with regard to consultation periods, terms, notice periods, counselling and aid with job search, outplacement training in job-search skills and so on.

Unemployment can represent not only an economic threat to lifestyle, but a source of insecurity, loss of self-esteem, extreme stress and hopelessness. The personnel function should therefore be concerned to **prevent** enforced redundancies where possible, and to **alleviate** the effects of unemployment where it is unavoidable, by:

(a)   Careful HR planning, so that foreseen seasonal or other contractions in demand for labour can be taken into account, and the organisation is not over-supplied with labour for its needs.

(b)   Planning redundancy terms and measures early, to safeguard the interests of those who may be made redundant.

(c)   Retraining and redeployment programmes. This may be a solution where alternative jobs are available, employees have some of the skills (or at least aptitudes) required and retraining facilities are available.

(d)   Liaison with other employers in the same industry or area, with a view to redeployment within the linked group of organisations.

(e)   Provision of unemployment services, (or time, during the notice period, to seek them) such as:

(i)   Counselling, to aid re-adjustment to the situation in which the newly-unemployed individual finds himself, to encourage a positive outlook

(ii)   Outplacement training in job-search skills: how to locate employment opportunities; how to carry out self-appraisal and communicate it attractively on a CV; how to use application forms, letters and phone calls to advantage; how to handle interviews

(ii)   Information on job opportunities and self-employment opportunities and funding. Individuals should be made aware of the role and accessibility of the Department of Employment's facilities and private sector services for careers counselling, recruitment and CV preparation.

EXAMPLE: THE BODY SHOP

'How does a firm that prides itself on its ethical approach to its "employees, customers, franchisees, suppliers and shareholders" negotiate the process of making redundancies?'

'At the start of 1999, (the Body Shop) found itself in the potentially embarrassing situation of having to cut jobs in order to press ahead with restructuring and fight off competition from cheap suppliers ... An ethical employer cannot be seen to hand out redundancy notices without any thought for the people involved...

'The entrepreneurs' club was set up to try and reduce the impact of impending redundancies on the local area. As well as loans, it also provided coaching and mentoring, opportunities for networking and access to an IT business centre. Other new

BPP
PUBLISHING

businesses set up by former staff included a payroll consultancy, a glass-staining business and a video and music soundtracking company...

'Mark Barrett, head of HR at Body Shop International, says ... "We're a young company. People leaving the Body Shop were well thought of, and so found it easier to get new roles ..."

'About 40 per cent of the redundancies were voluntary, although Barrett believes some of those who were made compulsorily redundant were also happy to leave. Outplacement support was provided ...

'Special treatment was given to staff aged over 50. This was partly a result of pressure from the consultation and representation committee, made up of employee representatives (the firm is non-unionised). People over 50 who had not found a job by the end of their redundancy period were entitled to an extra 25% on top of their original redundancy payment – although only 4 out of the eligible 25 applied for any additional cash. Employees leaving the firm were also offered £1,000 to spend on training ... matched by a further £1,000 from Sussex Enterprise, a local training and enterprise council.

'Only 37 out of the 200 staff show jobs were made redundant did not take up the training grant. It was later decided to extend the £1,000 offer to people who weren't leaving ... "There was a feeling at the time that people were leaving and being well supported, but that maybe those who were staying were not being given the same backing" ...

'Staff in the service centre (where the redundancies occurred) felt under pressure because of the length of time it took to decide who was going to be made redundant. Barrett admits that the consultations, which took up to three months in some cases, went on too long. Some managers failed to tell people what was happening ... These criticisms were initially made by ... a consultant on employee surveys who was asked to evaluate the consultation exercise.

'In an attempt to improve communication, the firm introduced a monthly newsletter for all employees, along with fortnightly meetings with managers from the service centre, so that people could be kept better informed ...

'An employee attitude survey, carried out among 390 staff who stayed at BSI and 220 who left or transferred to other parts of the Body Shop, clearly demonstrates some of the problems that occurred ... Leavers were the most dissatisfied with the support they received from the HR department, while employees who stayed also highlighted communications with managers as an area of concern ... 61% of those who took compulsory redundancy were satisfied with the outplacement support ... More than two thirds of all leavers said that they had enjoyed their time at the Body Shop and would consider working for the company again.'

Neil Merrick, *People Management*, 26 October 2000

Activity 7   **(1½ hours)**

Use your research skills to find one or more further accounts (written or oral) of a redundancy situation: HR journals, quality press and acquaintances who have experienced redundancy are good sources. The **redundancy policy** of a business organisation, including selection criteria and ethical aims, will also be useful if you can gain access to one (or more).

BPP
PUBLISHING

3.3 Selection for redundancy

There are various approaches to selection for redundancy. If demand for a particular type of work has disappeared completely, the situation is relatively clearcut: all those previously contracted to perform that work can be dismissed. Where management have to choose between individuals doing the same work, they may take the following approaches.

(a) Enforced or early **retirement**. This may be felt to be fair, if careers are seen to 'wind down' in any case, but may not be appropriate in a high loyalty/seniority culture such as that pertaining in Japan. It may also be a factor, in terms of social responsibility, that mature-aged employees will have greatest difficulty finding new employment if they wish to do so.

(b) Seeking **volunteers**, who would be willing to take their chances elsewhere on good redundancy terms.

(c) Value to the organisation, or **retention by merit** – keeping those who perform well (according to competence tests, appraisal ratings or similar criteria) and dismissing less effective workers. This may be harder to justify to individuals and their representatives. Criteria will have to be specific, realistic and clearly communicated. They should ideally be agreed with the relevant trade unions. From the organisation's point of view, selection criteria should ensure that the skills needed for organisational survival and regrowth are not lost through redundancy (a danger of voluntary schemes), and if possible that the best people are retained in the most value-adding jobs.

(d) 'Last in, first out' (LIFO). Newcomers are dismissed before long-serving employees. This may sound fair (especially in a seniority culture such as characterises Japanese big business), but may not meet the organisation's need for 'young blood' or for particular skills or merit in the individual. It may also be indirectly discriminatory, if the recruitment of women and ethnic minorities has only recently been encouraged.

3.4 Follow-up

Redundancy clearly has a human cost, not least in terms of the morale and sense of security of employees remaining in employment after redundancy programmes. 'Survivors' may suffer guilt and anxiety, insecurity about their own job security and a loss of reciprocal loyalty to the organisation: they may tend to identify more closely with fellow workers and less with the organisation as an 'impersonal' entity. Efforts will have to be made to reinforce survivors' loyalty and morale by acknowledging their worth to the employer – particularly since, despite the concept underlying 'redundancy', remaining workers may in fact have to shoulder an increased workload in downsized organisations.

Definition

> The **survivor syndrome** has been coined as a term for a psychological state which involves long-term anxiety about job loss, increased loyalty to co-workers and reduced loyalty to the employer.

'Survivor syndrome' can lead to increased labour turnover, deliberately restricted output, risk-averse behaviour (suppression of feedback, new ideas, innovation) and industrial conflict.

Management's motives and intentions must be transparent and true, and fairness (even generosity, if possible) demonstrated. Positive values (better chances of corporate survival and success, 'heroism' of the lean-mean workforce, importance of remaining employees) must be sold.

FOR DISCUSSION

A recent textbook on personnel management has argued that 'Personnel Management will become increasingly involved in getting rid of people instead of recruiting them.' Why might such a prediction be made? Do you think it is correct? Does it make good business sense to offer anything more than a basic redundancy package (as required by law) to affected employees?

Chapter roundup

- Exit from employment takes several forms, voluntary and involuntary, including:

  ○ Retirement: termination of contract at a fixed, statutory or negotiated retirement age

  ○ Resignation: voluntary termination by notice on the part of the employee

  ○ Dismissal: termination, with or without notice, on the part of the employer, or (constructive dismissal) on the part of the employee where (s)he is entitled to assume that the employer has terminated the contract by breach

  ○ Redundancy; dismissal; by reason of the ending of the work for which the employee was contracted, or for other reasons 'not related to the individual concerned' (collective redundancy: for the purposes of consultation only)

- Employment protection legislation and regulations set out employee rights with regard to:

  (a) Notice periods to be given for dismissal

  (b) Valid reasons for dismissal

  (c) Remedies in the event of dismissal being judged 'unfair'

  (d) Consultation with employee representatives over proposed redundancies

  (e) Redundancy pay

  (f) Time off to prepare for redundancy

  (g) Trial periods prior to acceptance of alternative employment

- In addition to statutory requirements, exit has ethical and employee relations implications. Attention is commonly given to:

  (a) Learning from resignations by means of exit interviews

  (b) Socially responsible polices surrounding progressive discipline, dismissal and redundancy

  (c) The motivation of 'surviving' employees

NOTES

Quick quiz

1 In what five basic ways may a contract (including a contract of employment) be terminated?

2 What are the arguments for enforcing retirement?

3 What are the benefits of retaining older workers?

4 What procedures should be carried out when an employee resigns from the organisation?

5 What is the difference between wrongful dismissal and unfair dismissal?

6 What reasons may an employer rely on in seeking to show that a dismissal was fair?

7 Why is it important for an organisation to follow a clear disciplinary procedure?

8 Describe circumstances when redundancy would be legal?

9 Explain the term 'survivor syndrome'.

Answers to quick quiz

1 Performance, mutual agreement, notice, breach or frustration.
(see paragraph 1.1)

2 To open up promotion opportunities; to offer security to younger employees; to inject 'young blood'; to save money; to enhance efficiency.
(para 1.2)

3 Better attendance; organisational loyalty; commitment to quality; customer service focus.
(para 1.2)

4 Persuade to stay (if appropriate); exit interview; negotiate notice period; notify key people; complete performance assessment.
(para 1.3)

5 Wrongful dismissal is where there are insufficient reasons to justify dismissal, whereas unfair dismissal is where law and internal policies have been breached.
(para 2.3, 2.4)

6 Redundancy; legal impediment; non-capability; misconduct; some other substantial reason.
(para 2.4)

7 Because the aim of a disciplinary procedure is to improve performance, and because adherence to such procedures will be taken into account in the event of the employee claiming unfair dismissal.
(para 2.5)

8 Cessation of the business; cessation of the business in a particular location; cessation of the need for work of a particular kind.
(para 3)

9 A psychological state suffered by employees who have survived redundancy programmes, characterised by long-term anxiety, increased loyalty to co-workers and decreased commitment to the organisation.
(para 3.4)

Answers to activities

1 (a) Alan's only option is to require Sheerbrow Ltd to provide him with an amended copy of the particulars (within one month). The written particulars are merely evidence of the employment contract's terms – they do not represent the contract itself, so an amendment of an error cannot be said to be a breach.

(b) The publisher has breached the contract, because of the **express** contract terms of two year's work in a particular post: the employer also had the implied duty to supply the work, and failed to do so.

(c)   Ambrose cannot claim that the company is in breach of contract for failure to provide work, or pay for work done, because no contract existed in the first place! There was no offer made – although Ambrose 'accepted' what he **thought** was an offer, by turning up to work.

2   (a)   The burden of work in late years can be eased by shortening hours or a transfer to lighter duties.

     (b)   The final stage of employee training and development may take the form of courses, commonly run by local technical colleges, intended to prepare employees for the transition to retirement and non-work.

     (c)   The organisation may have, or may be able to put employees in touch with, social/leisure clubs and other facilities for easing the shock of retirement.

3   (a)   Reasons for leaving are many and various, but some of the ones you may have thought of are: relocation to another city/area; dissatisfaction with work conditions (or location, or workmates or scope for responsibility or any number of work-related factors); finding another (preferred) job; being head-hunted; change of career (or return to full-time education, or move to self-employment, or change of domestic circumstances/family responsibilities); clash of culture/values with the employer; ill-health; to pre-empt dismissal in order to save face.

     (b)   Procedures may include: return of keys, security passes and so on; handing of files to department head; completion or transfer of work-in-progress; removal of personal data/passwords from computer files; collection of final pay and leaving information; removal of personal effects.

4   (a)   Bernie was fairly dismissed by reason of legal impediment.

     (b)   Berenice was fairly dismissed by reason of lack of 'capability': she is clearly incompetent compared to the standard of performance required by the job.

     (c)   Bernadette was fairly dismissed: failure to accept necessary reorganisation is a 'substantial' reason.

     (d)   Benedict was unfairly dismissed, because he was trying to enforce his employment rights in a reasonable manner.

5   (a)   Yes – but it is **B** who has been made redundant.

     (b)   Yes – for the purposes of consultation with trade unions, since this fits the TURER '93 definition of collective redundancy: the reasons for dismissal were not related to the individuals concerned. The consultation requirements refer to 'proposals to dismiss': the employer presumably proposed to dismiss any employee who did not accept the new terms – even if this did not eventuate. The employer bound to consult – and to pay penalties if it had failed to do so. (This is based on an actual case before the EAT: *GMBV v Man Truck and Bus UK Ltd, 2000*)

6   Alternatives to enforced redundancy include:

     (a)   Retirement of staff over the normal retirement age

     (b)   Offering early retirement to staff approaching normal retirement age

NOTES

(c) Restrictions or even a complete ban on recruitment, so as to reduce the workforce over time by natural wastage

(d) Dismissal of part-time or short-term contract staff, once contracts come to sensible break-off points or conclusions

(e) Offering retraining and/or redeployment within the organisation

(f) Seeking voluntary redundancies

7 The answer is up to you! Note that this is good preparation for demonstrating competence in Assessment Criteria 21.4: make orderly notes as you do your research, even if you are only recalling your own experience or discussing someone else's

---

Assignment 10   **(1½ hours)**

Q and R Ferries PLC

You are the newly-appointed Personnel Manager for Q and R Ferries PLC, a passenger and cargo-handling service operating out of East Anglia. Unusually for such a large company, Q and R had no personnel function until you were recruited two months ago. The culture of the company has been largely based around allowing line managers to 'do their own thing' so far as staff are concerned, provided, of course, that they work within general company guidelines and consult with department heads if in any doubt. Two claims for unfair dismissal (which have just landed on your desk) lead you to suspect that this notion of 'reasonable authority' has completely broken down.

Both claims concern sickness, though of a very different nature from each other, and both employees were dismissed under 'capability and qualifications'. In other words, the sickness record of both employees was considered sufficient grounds to question their ability to do their jobs to the required standard. Dismissal took place accordingly.

The first employee, Roger Price, was a maintenance man at Q and R's headquarters at Harwich. He had been off sick with a bad back for 3 weeks but, during this period, he was seen on a Q and R ferry doing a striptease in a karaoke evening. He was dismissed for contravention of the sick pay scheme.

The second employee, Mary Gardner, who is disabled, had been a satisfactory credit control clerk for many years. But in 1991 her health deteriorated and she was frequently absent. In 1993 she became part-time. In 1995 she was off for some time. Mrs Gardner believed she was improving, but her GP's report was that her health was not good; he considered she would not return to work in the near future. The company decided that a full time replacement was necessary. Mrs Gardner's manager did not consult with her about this because he thought it would be difficult as she believed she was improving. Instead, he wrote to her announcing his decision to terminate her employment.

Both employees have now submitted claims for unfair dismissal. Your task is to prepare a report to the Chief Executive, outlining whether you believe Q and R will win the cases, defining what you consider are the main points a tribunal will take into account when they go to trial. You must draw up a checklist of questions you wish to raise with the relevant department managers when you interview them shortly about Mr Price and Mrs Gardner.

PART B

UNIT 22: MANAGING HUMAN RESOURCES ISSUES

Chapter 11 :
PERSPECTIVES ON HRM

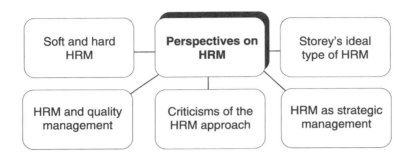

Introduction

In this chapter, we explore further some of the themes already discussed in Chapters 1 and 2, highlighting the ambiguities and dualities in the role of the personnel function and some of the issues that arise from the shift to an 'HRM' orientation.

One of the key assumptions of HRM is that the employment relationship can be managed so that the needs of both organisation and employees are met, to mutual benefit. Ethical, people-friendly HR policies are intended to facilitate efficient and effective working as well as employee health, welfare and satisfaction. This dual emphasis will be reflected in the following chapters as we look at some of the major issues facing HR managers in the 21st century workplace.

Your objectives

In this chapter you will learn about the following:

(a) Guest's model of hard-soft, loose-tight dimensions of HRM

(b) The differences between Storey's definitions of HRM and Personnel and IR Practices

(c) HRM from a strategic perspective and its implications for the role of the line manager and employees

(d) The internal customer concept and its implications for the role of Personnel in the organisation

BPP PUBLISHING

1 SOFT AND HARD HRM

In Chapter 1, we defined HRM as 'a strategic and coherent approach to the management of an organisation's most valued assets: the people working there who individually and collectively contribute to the achievement of its objectives for sustainable competitive advantage.' (Armstrong).

We have so far suggested that the role of HRM is twofold (leading to some ambiguity): both business-oriented (concerned with performance) and people-oriented (concerned with the motivation and quality of working life of employees). However, Storey (1989) and Guest (1999) identify two distinct versions of HRM, which they characterise as 'hard' and 'soft'.

1.1 Hard HRM

Definition

> Karen Legge defined the **'hard' model** of HRM as a process emphasising 'the close integration of human resource policies with business strategy which regards employees as a resource to be managed in the same rational way as any other resource being exploited for maximum return'.

The **hard model of HRM** may be summarised as follows.

(a) Its philosophy towards managing people is business-oriented: employees must be managed in such a way as to obtain value-adding performance, which will in turn give the organisation competitive advantage.

> The drive to adopt HRM is... based on the business case of a need to respond to an external threat from increasing competition. It is a philosophy that appeals to managements who are striving to increase competitive advantage and appreciate that to do this they must invest in human resources as well as new technology.
>
> (Guest)

(b) Following 'a long-standing capitalist tradition in which the worker is regarded as a commodity' (Guest), it regards employees as a resource of the organisation, to be managed (exploited) in as rational and strategic a manner as any other economic resource: human capital from which a return can be obtained by adding value, through judicious investment in performance management and employee development.

(c) It emphasises the interests, role and authority of management 'over' those of employees.

(d) It is essentially a pluralist viewpoint, which maintains that the interests of the owners and managers of a business are inherently different from those of the workers: organisations are therefore political systems, within which there is competition for scarce power and resources. Workers must be controlled in order to ensure that they perform in the organisation's interests.

Features of hard HRM include:

(a) A close matching or integration of the strategic objectives of the HR function with the business strategy of the organisation. 'Hard strategic

HRM' will emphasise the yield to be obtained by investing in human resources in the interests of the business (Storey)

(b)   A focus on quantitative, business-strategic objectives and criteria for management

(c)   An emphasis on the need for performance management and other forms of managerial control.

Activity 1   **(10 minutes)**
What HRM techniques would you expect to be adopted as a result of a hard HRM approach?

1.2   Soft HRM

Definition

> Legge defined the '**soft**' version of HRM as a process whereby employees are viewed as 'valued assets and as a source of competitive advantage through their commitment, adaptability and high level of skills and performance.'

The **soft model of HRM** may be summarised as follows.

(a)   Its philosophy towards managing people is based in the human relations school of management thought (described in Chapter 1), emphasising the influence of socio-psychological factors (relationships, attitudes, motivation, leadership, communication) on work behaviour.

(b)   It views employees as 'means rather than objects' (Guest): 'treating employees as valued assets, a source of competitive advantage through their commitment, adaptability and high quality (of skills, performance and so on)' (Storey).

(c)   It focuses on 'mutuality', a unitarist viewpoint which assumes that the interests of management and employees can and should coincide in shared organisational goals, working as members of an integrated team. Employees are viewed as 'stakeholders' in the organisation.

The main **features of soft HRM** are:

(a)   A complementary approach to strategic HRM in relation to the business strategies of the organisation. Brewster argues that a stakeholder perspective and environmental constraints (such as EU legislation) mean that HR strategies cannot be entirely governed by business strategy. 'Soft strategic HRM' (Storey) will place greater emphasis on the human relations aspect of people management, stressing security of employment, continuous development, communication, involvement and the quality of working life.

(b)   A focus on socio-psychological and cultural objectives and criteria for management.

(c)   An emphasis on the need to gain the trust and commitment of employees – not merely compliance with control mechanisms.

NOTES

Activity 2   **(10 minutes)**

What HRM techniques would you expect to be adopted as a result of a soft HRM approach?

We will now look at two models of HRM which reflect the soft and hard approaches respectively.

1.3 The Michigan model

The **matching model** of HRM was developed by the Michigan School in 1984. It held that HR systems and the organisational structure should be managed in such a way as to 'match', or be congruent with, the organisation's business strategy: an essentially hard orientation. The **human resource cycle** consists of four basic functions which are performed in all organisations:

(a) Selection: designed to match available human resources to jobs

(b) Performance management/appraisal: designed to match performance to objectives and standards

(c) Rewards: reinforcing short- and long-term achievements in order to 'drive organisational performance'

(d) Development: matching the skill quality of the human resource to future requirements

The school (Fombrun et al) suggests that the HR function should be linked to line management by:

(a) Providing good HR databases

(b) Ensuring that senior mangers give HR issues as much attention as they give to other functions

(c) Measuring the contribution of the HR function at the strategic (long-term policies designed to encourage organisational 'fit' to its environment in the future), managerial (medium-term activities ensuring the acquisition, retaining and development of people) and operational (daily support of business activities) levels

1.4 The Harvard model

The Harvard School model (Beer et al, 1985) was based on the belief that the problems of historical personnel management can only be solved

> when general managers develop a viewpoint of how they wish to see employees involved in and developed by the enterprise, and of what HRM policies and practices may achieve those goals... Today, many pressures are demanding... a longer-term perspective in managing people and consideration of people as potential assets rather than merely a variable cost.

The Harvard model was influential in emphasising the fact that:

(a) 'Human resource management involves all management decisions and actions that affect the nature of the relationship between the organisation and its employees'

(b) Organisations involve a variety of stakeholders who have an interest in the practice and outcomes of HR policies: there is a 'trade-off' between the interests of owners and employees, as well as other stakeholders, with a view to mutuality and commitment

BPP PUBLISHING

(c) Strategic HRM choices are influenced by a broad range of contextual factors, including both product-market and socio-cultural factors

(d) Line managers are at the interface between competitive strategy and personnel policies and must take more responsibility for their alignment

The Harvard framework can be illustrated as follows (Beer at all, 1985).

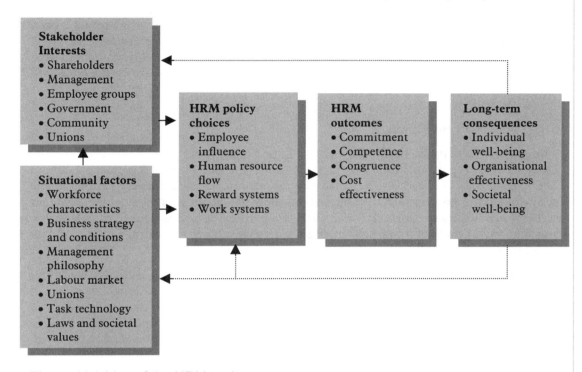

Figure 11.1 Map of the HRM territory

This is essentially a soft HRM model,

> composed of policies that promote mutuality – mutual goals, mutual influence, mutual respect, mutual rewards, mutual responsibility. The theory is that policies of mutuality will elicit commitment, which in turn will yield both better economic performance and greater human development
> (Walton, 1985)

FOR DISCUSSION

How do you respond intuitively to the 'hard' and 'soft' versions of HRM? What words and phrases connected with each strike you as positively or negatively loaded: where do you perceptions come from? Are 'soft' and 'hard' perspectives really as different as contrasting descriptions make them seem? Does your experience of organisations suggest that they operate under **either** one **or** the other?

1.5 Hard or soft?

In practice, there are likely to be times when a hard orientation (eg in the face of the need for organisational downsizing) directly conflicts with the more developmental and paternal philosophy of the soft approach. Many organisations operate a mix of soft-hard, loose-tight systems. One way of formalising this is to segment the labour force into a 'core' of permanent employees managed via soft HRM policies, and a 'periphery' of short-contract labour used as an exploitable commodity. (Another option is the out-sourcing of

all non-core activities.) As Kramer, McGraw and Shuler note, 'whether an organisation leans more towards the hard or soft version of HRM, or does not consider HRM to be relevant to its operation, depends very much on the values of the organisation.'

The broad 'achieve success through people' focus of HRM may therefore be approached from two different perspectives which imply very different techniques of management. These techniques have been classified, according to the amount of control each orientation assumes to be necessary to obtain job performance from workers, as 'tight' and 'loose'. Before we discuss the characteristics of tight and loose HRM, we will look at some early theories of how managerial philosophy and assumptions set up the hard-soft, tight-loose continuum.

1.6   Theory X and Theory Y

The distinction between hard/tight and soft/loose management control was suggested by **Douglas McGregor**, an influential contributor to the neo-human relations school. In *The Human Side of Enterprise*, he discussed the way in which managers handle people according to the assumptions they have about them and about what kind of management style will obtain their efforts. He identified two extreme sets of assumptions (Theory X and Theory Y) and explored how management style differs according to which set of assumptions is adopted.

(a)   **Theory X** holds that human beings have an inherent dislike of work and will avoid it if they can. People prefer to be directed, wishing to avoid responsibility. They have relatively little ambition and want security above all, resisting change. They are self-interested, and make little effort to identify with the organisation's goals. They must be coerced, controlled, directed, offered rewards or threatened with punishments in order to get them to put adequate effort into the achievement of organisation objectives: this is management's responsibility.

(b)   According to **Theory Y**, however, the expenditure of physical and mental effort in work is as natural as play or rest. The ordinary person does not inherently dislike work: according to the conditions, it may be a source of satisfaction or deprivation. A person will exercise self-direction and self-control in the service of objectives to which they are committed: they are not naturally passive or resistant to organisational objectives, but may have been made so by bad experience. The most significant reward that can be offered in order to obtain commitment is the satisfaction of the individual's personal growth and development needs. The average human being learns, under proper conditions, not only to accept but to seek responsibility. Management's responsibility is to create conditions and methods that will enable individuals to integrate their own and the organisation's goals.

You will have your own viewpoints on the validity of Theory X and Theory Y. In fact, McGregor intentionally polarised his theories as the extremes of a continuum along which most managers' attitudes fall at some point. However, he also recognised that the assumptions are self-perpetuating, even where the 'types' of employee described did not really exist. If people are treated according to Theory X (or Theory Y) assumptions, they will begin to act accordingly – thus confirming management in its beliefs and practices. Essentially, Theory X embodies the 'hard-tight' **control theory of management**, while Theory Y embodies the 'soft-loose' **commitment theory of management**.

> **Activity 3** (45 minutes)
>
> The following was sent to the letter page of *Personnel Management*.
>
> > Hark, I think I detect the first cuckoo of a recessionary spring on your pages ('Making time for productivity', March), with such an unashamed reassertion of Taylorism. Come on, all you personnel folk. Off with your HR nomenclature; away with all this nonsense about the 'success culture', 'employee involvement', 'maximising people power', 'establishing the right climate' and 'sharing gains' (all drawn from the CIPD's current national priorities). Get out your sticks and stopwatches, 'precisely time' those tea breaks, slash that overtime, enforce 'bell-to-bell working', put in a few more controls and 'disincentives'... Surely employee involvement is not just an illusion created by the 1980s boom which we can ignore now times are tough?
>
> What are the characteristics of the approach to HRM which the letter identifies? Why might economic recession lead managers to adopt such an approach?

A number of theories of '**leadership style**' were developed to reflect the continuum between Theory X and Theory Y. Some that you may have encountered in your studies include:

(a) The 'tells-sells-consults-joins' model of leadership developed by the Ashridge Management College

(b) The dictatorial – laissez-faire continuum of Tannenbaum and Schmidt

(c) The managerial grid developed by Blake and Mouton, in which one axis represents concern for people and the other concern for production

Charles Handy developed a contingency approach to leadership which suggests that there is a 'loose-tight' continuum of managerial control, and that a more or less loose or tight style will be appropriate depending on situational factors including: the leader's abilities, attitudes, preferred style and power; the team's abilities, attitudes and cultural values; and the extent to which the task requires close supervision, or initiative, flexibility and innovation.

What might a similar loose-tight continuum look like in the case of HRM policy and practice?

1.7 Tight and loose HRM

The distinction between tight and loose HRM may be characterised as the difference between a system based on compliance and a system based on commitment.

Definition

> **Compliance** means performing according to set rules and standards, according to what you are expected and asked to do.
>
> **Commitment** has been defined as 'the relative strength of an individual's identification with and involvement in a particular organisation. It is characterised by at least three factors:
>
> (a) A strong belief in and acceptance of an organisation's goals and values
>
> (b) A willingness to exert considerable effort on behalf of the organisation
>
> (c) A strong desire to maintain membership of the organisation
>
> (Mowday, Porter, Steers: *Employee-Organisation Linkages*)

Compliance based systems of control reflect a low level of trust and challenge: performance is expected to be no less than the set standard – but also no **more**, since there is little room for creative or exceptional input or effort, which may militate against tight managerial control. Such systems may be effective and efficient: in a highly stable market environment; where the task is low-tech and low-discretion, with little need to differentiate skills or abilities and little difference between compliant and committed performance; and where the managerial prerogative of superiority and control continue to have meaning because of cultural values to do with respect and conformity (eg in latino cultures and traditional family businesses).

Commitment based systems of control reflect a high level of trust and mutuality, based on Theory Y assumptions that the work relationship can offer employees opportunities to meet their needs and aspirations as well as the organisation's needs. Such systems are effective in environments where customer demands and technologies are varied and changing, and employees are required to be flexible, creative and positive in contributing to the organisation's goals.

David Guest (*Managing Employment Relations*) set out the differences in personnel policy in a compliance-based system of control and a commitment-based system of control, as follows.

Aspects of policy	Compliance	Commitment
Psychological contract of work	'Fair day's work for a fair day's pay'	Mutual/reciprocal commitment
Behavioural references	Norms, custom and practice	Values/mission
Source of control over workers' behaviour	External (rules, instructions)	Internal (goals, values, willingness)
Employee relations	Pluralist perspective ('Us' and 'Them')	Unitarist ('Us')
	Collective	Individual
	Low trust	Trust
Organising principles/ organisational design	Formal/defined roles	Flexible roles
	Top down	Bottom-up
	Centralised control	Decentralised control (delegation, empowerment)
	Hierarchy	Flat structures
	Division of labour	Team-work/autonomy
	Managerial control	Self control
Policy goals	Administrative/efficiency	Adaptive/effectiveness
	Performance to standard	Constantly improving performance
	Minimising cost	Maximising utilisation for added value

Guest also identified these contrasting dimensions as distinguishing 'traditional industrial relations' and 'HRM' approaches.

Activity 4   **(10 minutes)**

Would you say you were compliant in your attitude to your studies, or committed? Think about how you approach the assignments set for you, the classes you attend and so on.

(a) What are (or would be) the benefits to you if you are/were committed rather than compliant?

(b) What are/would be the benefits to your trainers?

(c) What could (1) you and (2) your trainers do to increase your commitment to your studies?

EXAMPLE

A survey (reported in *People Management* in September 1997) organised by the DTI and DFEE looked at how successful companies' approaches to people management enhance performance. The themes covered below are echoed throughout this Course Book. 90% of successful companies interviewed said that people management had become a higher priority in recent years. One managing director said: 'There is no other source of competitive advantage. Others can copy our investment, technology and scale, but not the quality of our people'.

The survey found common threads running through the people management policies of all the organisations which were examined:

- Shared goals: understanding the business
- Shared culture: agreed values binding people together
- Shared learning: commitment to continuous improvement
- Shared effort: one business driven by flexible teams
- Shared information: effective communication

The right culture takes a long time to develop and is extremely fragile. Behaviour of management speaks volumes. One company related the cautionary tale of a supervisor who, when a worker collapsed on the production line, rushed to get the line restarted before tending to the sick person. This act of 'culture betrayal' was a considerable setback.

'Empowerment' was a word almost universally disliked by those surveyed, although the concept itself was regarded as essential for creating the climate and structure in which people would take responsibility. This did not, however, mean giving people freedom without parameters.

When it came to training, 90% had formal training policy based on the business plan, and 97% said training was important or critical to success. By providing a development path, organisations significantly increase their chances of keeping good people.

All the companies spoken to used teams as the building blocks of their organisation. Leyland Trucks aims for 80% of its employees to be involved in multidisciplinary teams. Training is seen as the key to success of team working - 65% of the companies interviewed trained employees to work in teams. One MD commented: 'Our customers tell our teams what is required and my job as MD is to make sure they have the resources they need'.

2   STOREY'S 'IDEAL TYPE' OF HRM

2.1   Storey's definitions

John Storey regarded HRM as a 'set of interrelated policies with an ideological and philosophical underpinning'. A meaningful version of HRM involves:

(a)   A particular cluster of beliefs and assumptions

(b)   A strategic focus to decision-making about people management

(c)   A central role for line managers in delivering HR outcomes

(d)   The use of 'levers' to shape the employment relationship, which can be distinguished from those used under traditional industrial relations systems

In *Developments in the Management of Human Resources* (1992), Storey put forward a theoretical 'ideal type' description of what a fully implemented model of HRM might look like, in contrast to a similarly abstracted description of the traditional personnel/industrial relations model. As you consider the differences tabulated in Figure 11.2 below, remember that this is an 'ideal': it is not meant to describe the current, typical state of affairs – since, as we have seen, the definition of HRM, and its application in practice, is by no means clear cut. The model does, however, reflect the general direction of the shift in approach in recent decades.

DIMENSION		PERSONNEL/IR APPROACH	HRM APPROACH
Beliefs and assumptions			
1	Contract	Careful delineation of written contracts	Aim to go 'beyond contract'
2	Rules	Importance of devising clear rules/mutuality	'Can do' outlook; impatience with 'rule'
3	Guide to management action	Procedures	'Business-need'
4	Behaviour referent	Norms/custom and practice	Values/mission
5	Managerial task vis-à-vis labour	Monitoring	Nurturing
6	Nature of relations	Pluralist	Unitarist
7	Conflict	Institutionalised	De-emphasised
Strategic aspects			
8	Key relations	Labour-management	Customer
9	Initiatives	Piecemeal	Integrated
10	Corporate plan	Marginal to	Central to
11	Speed of decision	Slow	Fast
Line Management			
12	Management role	Transactional	Transformational leadership
13	Key managers	Personnel/IR specialists	General/business/line managers
14	Communication	Indirect	Direct
15	Standardisation	High	Low
16	Prized management skills	Negotiation	Facilitation
Key levers			
17	Selection	Separate, marginal task	Integrated, key task
18	Pay	Job evaluation (fixed grades)	Performance related
19	Conditions	Separately negotiated	Harmonisation
20	Labour management	Collective bargaining contracts	Towards individual contracts

DIMENSION	PERSONNEL/IR APPROACH	HRM APPROACH
21 Thrust of relations with union delegates	Regularised through facilities and training	Marginalised (with exception of some bargaining for change models)
22 Job categories and grades	Many	Few
23 Communication	Restricted flow	Increased flow
24 Job design	Division of labour	Teamwork
25 Conflict handling	Reach temporary truces	Manage climate and culture
26 Training and development	Controlled access to courses	Learning companies
27 Foci of attention for interventions	Personnel procedures	Wide ranging cultural, structural and personnel strategies

Figure 11.2: Twenty-seven points of difference

Activity 5   **(10 minutes)**

What kinds of personnel policies and practices might:

(a)   'Institutionalise' or 'de-emphasise' conflict?

(b)   'Restrict' or 'increase' the flow of communication?

2.2 Implications for the worker's role

The HRM viewpoint, as outlined above, is explicitly unitarist. It implies that employees can be willingly co-opted to the business task of competition, quality enhancement and problem-solving. Tight managerial control over workers is replaced by a culture of trust: performance is assumed to be largely self-regulating within a guiding framework of inspirational leadership and shared cultural values and aspirations.

Definition

Empowerment is the process of distributing authority through the organisation, of 'decentralising' control and responsibility to the workers for the achievement of work targets and organisational goals.

The purpose of empowerment is to free someone from vigorous control by instructions and orders and give them freedom to take responsibility for their ideas and actions, to release hidden resources which would otherwise remain inaccessible.

(Personnel Management, November 1993)

Empowerment is based on the belief that:

The people lower down the organisation possess the knowledge of what is going wrong within a process (or could be done better) but lack the authority to make changes. Those further up the structure have the authority to make changes but lack the profound knowledge required to identify the right solutions. The only solution is to change the culture of the organisation so that everyone can become involved in the process of improvement and work together to make the changes.

(Hand, *Management Accounting*, January 1991)

NOTES

EXAMPLE

The validity of this view and its relevance to modern trends appears to be borne out by the approach to empowerment adopted by Harvester restaurants, as described in *Personnel Management*. The management structure comprises a branch manager and a 'coach', while everyone else is a team member. Everyone within a team has one or more 'accountabilities' (these include recruitment, drawing up rotas, keeping track of sales targets and so on) which are shared out by the team members at their weekly team meetings. All the team members at different times act as 'co-ordinator' - the person responsible for taking the snap decisions that are frequently necessary in a busy restaurant. Apparently, all the staff involved agree that empowerment has made their jobs more interesting and had hugely increased their motivation and sense of involvement.

Instead of power being used from the top down to **control** workers' performance, power was used to **support** workers' performance: performance (including quality, customer satisfaction, innovation and so on) became the guiding force of the organisation, not the wishes of senior management.

This has implications for the personnel function, as illustrated in Figure 11.3

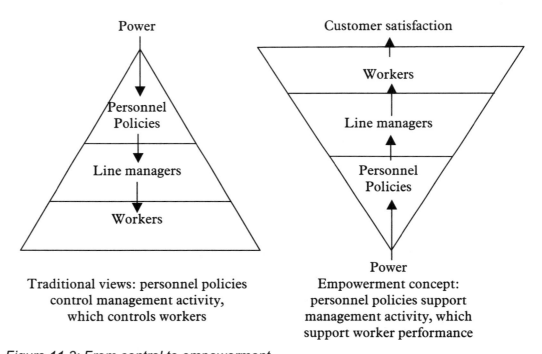

Figure 11.3: From control to empowerment

Activity 6   **(10 minutes)**

What might be the consequences of empowerment for personnel policy in the areas of (a) recruitment and selection and (b) training?

Implications for HR responsibilities

One of the key features of HRM, in Storey's view, is that 'its performance and delivery are integrated into line management'.

According to Armstrong (*Strategic HRM: a guide to action*) the hard HRM approach, in particular,

> is claimed to be a central, senior management-driven strategic activity that is developed, owned and delivered by management as a whole to promote the interests of the organisation that they serve. It purports to be an holistic approach concerned with the total interests of the organisation – the interests of the members of the organisation are recognised but subordinated to those of the enterprise. Hence the importance attached to strategic integration and strong cultures, which flow from top management's vision and leadership, and which require people who will be committed to the strategy, who will be adaptable to change, and who will fit the culture. By implication, as Guest (1991) says: 'HRM is too important to be left to personnel managers'.

Kramar, McGraw and Shuler note the ironic and paradoxical result:

> HRM has become more influential in company decision-making, yet has declined as a separate department within the organisation as HR tasks and decisions have been devolved to line managers. Many leading edge HR practitioners now see themselves more in an internal consultancy capacity assisting line managers to devise and implement more sophisticated ways of managing people, rather than implementing and managing those systems themselves. Such HR managers would also claim to be working towards the eventual removal of their own positions within the organisation.

HR specialists therefore increasingly share responsibility for delivering HR policy outcomes with:

(a)   Top management, who shape the aims, strategy and culture of the organisation.

(b)   Line managers, who take on a day-to-day leadership-oriented responsibility for people management.

(c)   Employees themselves. It is no longer uncommon for employees to appraise themselves (and their peers and superiors), write their own job descriptions, determine their own performance standards and improvement goals, and manage their own learning and career development.

The role of the HR specialist is therefore to establish guiding principles and policies designed to integrate top management aims and strategy with line management activity and individual aspirations.

David Guest suggested (see Chapter 1) that the four key policy goals of an authentic HRM approach are: high commitment, flexibility, strategic integration and high quality. We have discussed commitment (above), and will be covering flexibility in detail in Chapter 12. Here, we will look briefly at some models for the strategic integration of HRM, and then at HRM as a quality issue.

3   HRM AS STRATEGIC MANAGEMENT

3.1   Strategic HRM

The term 'strategic human resource management' emerged in the 1980s to describe a variety of models which attempt to explain how human resource policies can be integrated with business strategy.

NOTES

Definition

> **Strategy** is the determination of the basic long-term goals and objectives of an enterprise, and the adoption of courses of action and the allocation of resources necessary for carrying out the goals.
>
> **Strategic HRM** is 'the pattern of planned human resource deployments and activities intended to enable the firm to achieve its goals'. (Wright, McMahan)

According to Armstrong,

> the fundamental aim of strategic HRM is to generate strategic capability by ensuring that the organisation has the skilled, committed and well-motivated employees it needs to achieve sustained competitive advantage. Its objective is to provide a sense of direction in an often turbulent environment so that the business needs of the organisation, and the individual and collective needs of its employees can be met by the development and implementation of coherent and practical HR policies.

Strategic HRM can have either a soft or hard orientation, as the Michigan and Harvard models suggest.

3.2 Strategic integration or fit

The concept of strategic fit suggests that to maximise competitive advantage, a firm must:

(a) Match its capabilities and resources to the opportunities and constraints of the external environment (external fit)

(b) Match the macro features of the organisation: its mission, strategy, structure, technology, products and services, culture and workforce (internal fit)

For Guest, there are three aspects to strategic fit in HRM terms:

(a) Developing HR strategies that are integrated with the business strategy and support its achievement (vertical integration or fit)

(b) Developing integrated HR practices (resourcing, reward, development and so on) so that they complement and mutually reinforce one another (horizontal integration or fit), so that they consistently encourage quality, flexibility and commitment

(c) Encouraging line managers to realise and internalise the importance of human resources

As one of the key policy goals of HRM specified by Guest, strategic integration ensures that HRM 'is fully integrated into strategic planning so that HRM policies cohere both across policy areas and across hierarchies and HRM practices are used by line managers as part of their everyday work.'

3.3 Approaches to developing HR strategy

Guest has identified various types of fit, which represent different approaches to the development of HR strategy.

(a) **Fit as strategic integration**: linking HR practices to the external context. HR strategies are congruent with, or aligned to, the thrust of business competitive strategies (classified by Porter as innovation strategy, quality

PUBLISHING

266

enhancement strategy and cost leadership strategy); appropriate to the stage of the business life-cycle reached by the business (start-up, growth, maturity, decline); adapted to organisational dynamics and characteristics and so on. Employee expectations should also be aligned with strategic direction, by communication of the organisational vision, translating strategy into performance management, and developing a corresponding organisational culture.

(b) **Fit as contingency**: ensuring that internal practices respond to particular contextual factors and changes. Contingency theory states that 'it all depends'. The 'best fit' approach seeks to align practice to specific needs identified by analysis of the firm's context, both external (opportunities, threats and constraints) and internal (culture, structure, technology and processes). This requires attention to both the flexibility/adaptability and coherence/consistency of HR policy and practice.

(c) **Fit as an ideal set of practices**: ensuring that internal practices reflect 'best practice', as determined by benchmarking. The best practice approach is based on the belief that adopting certain HRM practices will lead to superior organisational performance. This is contrary to contingency theory, which emphasises the need to take into account the many differences between organisations and their environments. Nevertheless, several sets of best practices have been put forward, including: employment security, selective hiring, self-managed teams, high compensation contingent on performance, training, reduction of status differentials and sharing information (Pfeffer).

(d) **Fit as 'bundles'**: developing and implementing distinct configurations or 'bundles' of HR practices (such as the use of performance management, or competence frameworks) which creates coherence across a range of activities, ensuring that they complement and mutually reinforce each other.

Activity 7   **(10 minutes)**

What do you think might be the key HR policy issues and approaches of an organisation:

(a) Pursuing an innovation strategy
(b) Pursuing a cost leadership strategy
(c) In the growth stage of its life-cycle
(d) In the decline stage of its life-cycle

---

4 HRM AS QUALITY MANAGEMENT

4.1 'Customer care' and HR policy

Values to do with the **customer** ('the customer is king', 'know your customer') and his needs have been a major feature of the perception of quality, and the achievement of success, in the 1980s and 1990s. Strategically, there has been a move away from a technical or production orientation, to a marketing orientation: the objectives of a business can best be met by identifying the market, its needs and wants, and by fulfilling those needs and wants in the most efficient way possible.

'Customer care' initiatives have been a feature of this orientation, since it has been recognised that:

(a) Customers have an ever-widening choice of products and services available to them

(b) Service (including sales service, delivery, after-sales service and, in general, communication and contact between the customer and the organisation) is of major importance in winning and retaining customers

One consequence of a customer orientation for the HR function is that it must identify with the organisation's objectives of winning and retaining **external customers**, in order to achieve business success. So, for example, if the organisation establishes a service improvement or customer care policy, HRM objectives will be to staff the organisation (and particularly those units which deal directly with customers) with people who have a strong service ethic, good communication skills and so on - whether through recruitment and transfer, training or retraining.

One conspicuous example might be in banks, which have hitherto been regarded as non-responsive bureaucratic organisations. They are currently making particular efforts to establish a customer-friendly culture at branch level. Staff are being trained in complaint handling, face-to-face transactions ('personal banking'), explaining bank procedures and technology and so on. Quality/service surveys are being used to find out what customers think of the service they get from staff.

4.2 The internal customer

An equally important concept for the HR function, however, is that of the **internal customer**.

Market forces can be a useful way of compelling departments or functions in an organisation to reappraise their performance, and their relationship to each other. Personnel - like any other unit - may focus on its activity for its own sake, as if it had no objective, no purpose outside the department. It may take for granted its relationship to other units, having a 'take it or leave it' attitude to the service it provides, being complacent about quality because it appears to have an effective monopoly on that service or task ('if we don't do it - it doesn't get done'). The concept of the internal customer aims to change all that.

As the term suggests, the internal customer concept implies the following.

(a) Any unit of the organisation whose task contributes to the task of other units (whether as part of a process, or in a 'staff' or 'service' relationship) can be regarded as a supplier of services like any other supplier used by the organisation. The receiving units are thus **customers** of that unit.

(b) The concept of **customer choice** operates within the organisation as well as in the external market environment. If an internal service unit fails to provide the right service at the right time and cost, it cannot expect customer loyalty: it is in **competition** with other internal and external providers of the service. Although there are logistical and control advantages to retaining the provision of services within the organisation, there is no room for complacency.

(c) The service unit's objective thus becomes the efficient and effective **identification of** and **satisfaction of customer needs** - as much within the organisation as outside it. This has the effect of integrating the objectives of service and customer units throughout the organisation. (It also makes units look at the **costs** of providing their services and what **added value** they are able to offer.)

The internal customers of personnel therefore include:

(a) Primarily the senior management and shareholders of the organisation, who expect the strategic objectives of the organisation to be met through human resource management

(b) Line managers, who expect the right quality and quantity of labour resources, HRM policies and systems, and specialist advice to be able to meet their own objectives

(c) Employees, who expect their contract of employment to be fulfilled, and to have their interests preserved (insofar as they do not conflict with those of the other internal customers)

Activity 8 **(10 minutes)**

Who might be the 'competitors' of the HR function?

In his book *Perfect Customer Care* (1994) Ted Johns makes the distinction between 'customers' as people who use a product or service and **pay** for it, as opposed to 'users' who benefit from a product or service without paying.

> Applying this framework to the personnel department of a major pharmaceutical company, and asking them to list all their customers and users, it turns out that they only have one customer in the strict sense of the term: the Board - or, even more precisely, the CEO. On the other hand, the personnel function has plenty of users, both inside and outside the organisation.

4.3 HR vision: a quality workforce

Stephen Connock (*HR Vision: Managing a Quality Workforce*) suggests that there is a renewed focus on the need for a 'productive, trained, flexible and innovative workforce', which he sums up as 'a **quality** workforce'. He suggests that human resource managers should use vision and strategies to create and maintain this quality workforce in support of business objectives: this is the source of perceived added value for the HR function.

Connock lists what he considers the dimensions of quality for employers.

(a) A customer services orientation

(b) Taking personal responsibility for quality output

(c) Well trained and developed staff to meet quality requirements

(d) Employee involvement in all aspects of quality

(e) Maintaining quality standards

(f) Communication and recognition programmes which reinforce quality

(g) Searching for continuous improvement

(h) Knowledge of and identification with quality from staff at all levels

EXAMPLE

Four Square (suppliers of Klix drinks systems, among others) have strong quality principles, communicated from Mars.

(a) The concept of the 'internal customer' is highly developed and considerable time has been devoted to the 'Putting customers first' campaign, involving both internal and external customers. Each associate in the company has to have a company service objective included in his/her annual standards of performance.

(b) There is a seven-step programme - including communication and training - to develop all suppliers to be suppliers of excellence.

(c)   On the customer side, drinks system distributors' staff are not only given technical training in servicing, fault finding and learning but also a lot of sales and customer-care training.

Personnel Management, September 1992

In discussing some of the theoretical and ideal models of HRM, and its advances on the traditional personnel/industrial relations model, you may have got the impression that HRM is universally regarded as the greatest thing since sliced bread. But this is not so. We will look briefly at some of the reservations people have about HRM.

5   CRITICISMS OF THE HRM APPROACH

5.1   A deficient theory

Some writers have noticed that HRM does not really hold up as a theory of management because:

(a)   It is based on philosophies, concepts and propositions rather than measurable variables and testable hypotheses. Even the basic definition of the term is ambiguous and under debate.

(b)   Because of the complexity of the variables, attempts at a workable model tend to be simplistic, focusing on context at the expense of content and technique.

(c)   It has not been demonstrated to have widespread application, either in different types of organisation or in different national contexts.

(d)   It contains internal contradictions, torn between individualism and teamwork; employee involvement and the inevitable balance of power in favour of the owners and managers of the business; strong corporate culture and individualism/flexibility.

5.2   An over-optimistic idea

HRM has probably been over-hyped, and in the process has become unrealistic. Armstrong quotes the comment of Mabey *et al* that

The heralded outcomes [of HRM] are almost without exception unrealistically high', with the implication that 'management has either been conned by consultants offering quick-fix solutions or is indulging in rhetoric influenced by 'extra-organisational' values such as excellence, flexibility, quality and customer focus.

Armstrong himself notes that

To put the concept of HRM into practice involves strategic integration, developing a coherent and consistent set of employment policies, and gaining commitment. This requires high levels of determination and competence at all levels of management and a strong and effective HR function staffed by business-oriented people. It may be difficult to meet these criteria, especially when the proposed HRM culture conflicts with the established corporate culture and traditional managerial attitudes and behaviour.

5.3   An immoral method

Armstrong notes that

In spite of all their protestations to the contrary, the advocates of HRM could be seen to be introducing alternative and more insidious forms of 'control by compliance' when they emphasise the need for employees to be committed to do what the organisation wants them to do.' He quotes Karen Legge, who sums up her own reservations about the morality of HRM as follows: 'Sadly, in a world of intensified competition and scarce resources, it seems inevitable that, as employees are used as a means to an end, there will be some who will lose out. They may even be in the majority. For these people, the soft version of HRM may be an irrelevancy, while the hard version is likely to be an uncomfortable experience.

Many academics accuse HRM of regarding employees as means to an end – which is perhaps fair enough, since organisations do have 'ends' or aims, which can only be achieved through people: this is the reason organisations are formed in the first place. However, the core of the accusation is the element of manipulation that HRM suggests: the rhetoric of mutuality, united effort and shared values, with the underlying reality that the mutuality is directed at the organisation's interests, the shared effort is unequally remunerated and the shared values are those selected and sanctioned by senior management.

FOR DISCUSSION

After all this, what do you think of the HRM concept? Do you agree with any of the criticisms mentioned above?

Chapter roundup

- While HRM is about 'success through people', there are two different orientations of this view.

    ° 'Hard' HRM emphasises the close integration of human resource policies with business strategy, and regards employees as a resource to be managed in the same rational way as any other resource being exploited for maximum returns.

    ° 'Soft' HRM views employees as valued assets and as a source of competitive advantage through their commitment, adaptability and high level of skills and performance.

- The Michigan model stressed the matching of HR policy to business strategy (hard), while the Harvard model stressed development and neutrality (soft).

- HR policies may be categorised as tight or loose according to the extent of managerial control which they assume to be necessary to achieve performance goals. Guest identifies the contrast between (tight) systems of compliance and (loose) systems of commitment.

- Storey developed an ideal type model or HRM contrasted to the traditional personnel/industrial relations model of labour management. 27 points of difference (expressed as extremes) were identified in the areas of beliefs and assumptions, strategy, the line management role and key levers used to shape the employment relationship.

- Strategic HRM is the direction of HR policy in such a way as to achieve the strategic goals of the business. HR strategy may be developed using business strategy, 'best fit', 'best practice' or 'configuration/bundling' approaches.

- Quality is one of the key policy goals of HRM (Guest), and should be directed to internal and external customer needs.

Quick quiz

1   What are the features of hard HRM?

2   What are the philosophical underpinnings of HRM?

3   What are the four stages of the human resource cycle in the Michigan model?

4   What levels of management should HR be involved in, according to the Michigan model?

5   List four key ideas of the Harvard model.

6   Distinguish between:

(a) Theory X and Theory Y
(b) Compliance and Commitment

7   What is the difference between a personnel/IR approach and an HRM approach in the dimensions of:

(a)   The role of rules
(b)   The nature of relations
(c)   Prized managerial skills
(d)   The focus of attention for interventions

8   What is empowerment?

9   What does 'strategic fit' involve as applied to HRM?

10   On what grounds has the HRM concept been criticised?

Answers to quick quiz

1   Matching of HR and business strategy; focus on yield on human resources; focus on quantitative measures of management effectiveness; emphasis on the need for performance management and managerial control.   (see paragraph 1.1)

2   Human relations school of management; socio-psychology; view of employees as assets/means rather than costs/objects; unitarist ideology; stakeholder perspective.   (para 1.2)

3   Selection, performance management, reward, development.   (para 1.3)

4   Strategic (long-term, focus on future 'fit'), managerial (medium-term, focus on acquisition, retention and development), operational day-to-day, focus on supporting business activities.   (para 1.3)

5   HRM involves all management decisions affecting the employment relationship. Organisations are made up of stakeholders and there is a trade-off between their interests. HRM is influenced by a range of contextual factors. Line managers take responsibility for aligning HR policy and competitive strategy.   (para 1.4)

6   See paragraphs 1.6 and 1.7 for a full account.

7   (a)   Importance of rules v 'can do' outlook creating impatience with rules
       (b)   Pluralist v unitarist
       (c)   Negotiation v facilitation
       (d)   Personnel procedures v wide-ranging cultural, structural and personnel strategies.   (para 2.1)

8   The process of distributing authority through the organisation so that employees share responsibility for the achievement of work targets and organisational goals.   (para 2.2)

9   HR strategies integrated with business strategy to support its achievement (vertical fit). HR practices developed to complement and mutually reinforce one another with consistent results (horizontal fit). Line managers internalising the importance of human resources.

(para 3.2)

10   Not rigorous, complex or transferable enough as a theory. Over-hyped and unrealistic in its expectations. Manipulative, as a form of disguised control.   (para 5)

Answers to Activities

1   **Tight:** high levels of rules, procedures and instructions, and appropriate training; strong corporate culture/values for the purposes of selection, socialisation and 'weeding out'; selection on the basis of pre-determined job criteria; close supervision and work inspection; administrative controls on time-keeping, absence, hours worked and so on; performance management focused on monitoring of performance against imposed standards and targets; job descriptions; job evaluation based on standard measures of performance; payment by results (narrowly defined); short-term cost-benefit evaluation of HR policies; centralised control over HR functions; adversarial mechanisms for dealing with discipline, grievance and relationships with trade unions; 'need to know' communication policies; welfare to minimise costs/lost production; managerial status symbols and tiered terms and conditions.

2   **Loose:** articulation of goals and values; strong corporate culture/values for the purposes of inspiration – especially quality; flexible working methods; emphasis on teamwork; self-managed time-keeping and attendance; consultation and agreement on work targets and criteria; values- and outputs-driven criteria; consultation and agreement on issues affecting the workforce; delegation and empowerment; HR fulfilling and enabling rather than controlling role; training for development, employability, flexibility; personal development and improvement plans; employee relations based on communication and involvement; welfare based on well-being and enabled performance; reward systems and performance management based on collaboratively agreed criteria; harmonised terms and conditions.

3   The writer is describing a Theory X, tight-control approach. In a recession, organisations are likely to be faced with pressures to cut costs and improve productivity in order to remain competitive: managers may be tempted to adopt this approach towards HR issues to achieve these goals. Remember that 'loose-tight' is a continuum. According to a contingency view of strategic 'fit', there is nothing inherently right or wrong about loose or tight control strategies: the chosen approach must suit the business needs of the organisation and respond to changes in its environment.

4   This answer will be highly individual to you and your situation (which may indicate why commitment is not easy to pin down or foster in practice). Benefits to **you** (analogous to the employee) may have included enjoyment, sense of purpose, possibly extra effort resulting in better results, which in turn may lead to further satisfaction and opportunities for development. Benefits for your **trainers** (analogous to employers) may have included the same, perhaps defined in different ways: better

attendance and time keeping, more creative ideas put forward to improve the course, encouragement to other students from your positive attitude, better results. Ways of **increasing commitment** may have included: clearer instructions, linking your studies to your goals in HRM, more enjoyable or challenging teaching methods and activities, and perhaps your willingness to put effort in now for rewards later.

5 Some examples you may have thought of are:

    (a) **Institutionalise conflict** through strict procedures for disciplinary action, grievance handling, appeals mechanisms, conflict resolution, negotiation with union representatives. (These are all good and helpful in the event of conflict – but they do assume that conflict is going to occur...) **De-emphasise conflict:** interpersonal conflict resolution handled on a contingency basis by management; win-win approach (assuming mutuality of interests); emphasise and reward teamworking and co-operation.

    (b) **Restrict communication:** institutionalised communication avenues (eg house journal or bulletin); managerial control over in-house communication; hierarchical, functional channels of communication; 'need to know' policies; lack of training in communication skills; centralised information storage and retrieval; discouragement of social networking among employees (by job and work environment design). **Increase communication:** training in communication; cultural reinforcement of communication (management example, reward and appraisal on communication skills); encouragement of multi-functional teamworking and/or briefings; encouragement of informal networking; focus on quality/customer overriding procedure.

6 Empowerment might influence recruitment/selection in the following ways.

    (a) Empowered workers may wish to take over responsibility for recruiting new members of their teams.

    (b) Jobs (and therefore job descriptions and selection criteria) would need to reflect new ways of working such as multi-skilling, team-working and so on.

    (c) Communication, leadership and facilitation skills would become key selection criteria for managers.

Empowerment might influence training as follows.

    (a) Training would be initiated and shaped by the job needs of empowered workers: relevant to the job, focused on areas such as responsibility, planning, teamworking and communication.

    (b) The trainer's role would be that of 'coach', reflecting the empowering/equipping philosophy towards training.

    (c) The manager may well take on the coaching/facilitating role: training will be seen to be a continuous on-the-job process and part of personal development by employees.

7 (a) For innovation, the organisation will require creative behaviour, long-term thinking, collaborative working, willingness to take risks and tolerance of unpredictability. HR practices that may help foster these qualities include: teamworking, high communication flow, multi-skilling and flexible working; broader career/development

paths allowing flexibility; longer-term, team-based performance appraisal; selection and reward for innovation values.

(b) For cost leadership, the organisation will need a focus on output quantity (with less concern for quality), a relatively short-term outlook, and controlled/low-risk performance. HR practices that may help foster these qualities include: narrow job design and explicit job descriptions; short-term, output-focused appraisal and reward; close monitoring of employee activities; little investment in training and development; focus on cost minimisation.

(c) In the growth stage, the organisation will require more progressive and sophisticated recruitment and selection (compared to start-up), training and development, performance management processes and reward systems, a focus on achieving high commitment and emphasis on developing stable employee relations. (Storey and Sisson)

(d) In decline, the organisation may have to shift to rationalisation, down-sizing by accelerated wastage or redundancy, curtailing of HR programmes (especially employee development) in order to cut costs, the attempt to marginalise or de-recognise trade unions.

8   Depending on the nature of the task concerned, the competitors of the HR function may be:

(a) External service providers, including training providers, recruitment and selection consultants, industrial relations conciliation services like ACAS, computer bureaux, or indeed the HR departments of organisations to which non-core activities are outsourced

(b) Internal service providers – notably, line managers and employees themselves

NOTES

Assignment 11 (1½ hours)

You are the HR assistant in a chain of retail outlets. It manages its real estate, positioning and buying policies well, resulting in steady growth, but it also has a somewhat variable reputation for customer service. There is a high turnover of staff, and frequent representations from staff for better pay and conditions, which your department constantly has to handle. HR policies have been introduced to try and improve staff morale, but these tend to be piecemeal and reactive to problems. Attention has recently been paid to tighter selection criteria according to specific job descriptions, to try and recruit staff who will be more amenable to the highly developed norms, rules and procedures laid down for the floor staff. Additional training has also been offered to supervisors, so that they will be able to monitor staff behaviour and operate disciplinary measures where necessary.

The HR Manager has been trying to convince the Board of Directors that HR should be represented on the Board, and that it should completely review the role of personnel policy and practice in the organisation. 'We don't pay enough attention to the people aspects of our business – and that includes the customers as well as the staff!' she has said to you on several occasions. 'We're not doing HRM – we're doing personnel management! And it isn't working, so they think HRM makes no contribution to the bottom line. It's a vicious circle.'

The HR Manager asks you to prepare some notes for a forthcoming presentation to the Board of Directors. 'I want a good clear summary of the difference between personnel management and HRM, which will show that our current approach is not really HRM...They're still bound to say that HRM is too 'soft' and people-focused. We need to emphasise that business success is central to its aims – that there are 'hard' aspects to it as well as 'soft'... Pick out a couple of good punchy theories, will you, and do me up something that will come across well on visual aids.

Your task: summarise (a) Storey's points of difference between personnel/IR and HRM, and (b) hard and soft HRM in a format suitable for presentation (via a medium of your choice: presentation software, flip chart, overhead slides, written handouts and so on).

Chapter 12 :
FLEXIBILITY IN THE WORKPLACE

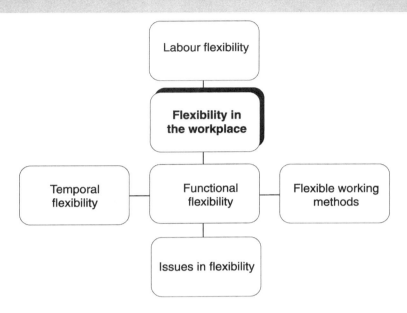

Introduction

In Chapters 3 and 4, we noted that sourcing labour requirements may be achieved from **within** the organisation as well as from the external labour market (listed within this unit, but covered in Chapter 4). The efficiency with which labour resources can be deployed and redeployed, at need, within the organisation depends on a measure of flexibility. Employees who are functionally versatile (or multi-skilled) and culturally flexible may be redeployed across the functional boundaries previously set by job descriptions and occupational demarcation zones. A flexible workforce may be deployed at periods of peak workloads. Given the pace of change in technologies and market places, and the 'ungluing' of traditional organisational structures to meet changing customer demands, flexibility is one of **the** Hot Topics in HRM!

Your objectives

In this chapter you will learn about the following

(a) The types of flexibility which may be developed by an organisation and give examples of how they can be implemented

(b) The advantages and disadvantages of flexible working practices from both the employee and the employer perspective

(c) The implications of flexibility for HR policy and practice

1 LABOUR FLEXIBILITY

1.1 Why flexibility?

Flexibility emerged as a major issue in the 1980s, as the Western European economies were forced to respond to change. Increased competition (particularly from the newly-industrialised Pacific Rim), international recession, uncertainty about future markets and the effects of new technology undermined expectations of stable economic growth.

(a) Increased competition has placed emphasis on quality, innovation and reducing the unit costs of production: job design and the organisation of work must both mobilise employees' energies for quality/innovation and secure productivity.

(b) Increased market uncertainty means that organisations need to be more adaptable to changes in demand: able to vary the size and deployment of their workforces to meet demand as effectively and efficiently as possible.

(c) Technological change, particularly in the automation and computerisation of work processes, has eroded traditional demarcation boundaries between jobs: job design and the organisation of work must fit the new technology in order to secure its benefits for efficiency.

The need for flexibility therefore suggested two key objectives:

- Increasing managerial ability to adapt the size and deployment of the workforce in line with changing demand

- Raising the quality and/or quantity of workforce output

This is clearly in line with the HRM approach to making the most effective and efficient use of the human resource.

As we saw in Chapter 11, however, there are two ways of looking at HR issues: from a 'hard' perspective and from a 'soft' perspective. What does flexibility look like from each of these.

1.2 Hard or soft HRM?

There are two distinct orientations to flexibility, in accordance with the hard and soft views of HRM.

(a) Flexibility is a key goal of strategic HRM, with its hard emphasis on meeting business needs through efficient deployment of the labour resources. 'Hard' flexibility, in the words of Beardwell and Holden, means 'the ability to adjust the size and mix of labour inputs in response to changes in product demand so that excess labour is not carried out by the organisation'. This approach has been popularised as **'lean production'**: minimising overhead labour costs by reducing jobs not directly contributing to production, and minimising the cost of directly productive labour by raising productivity.

(b) Flexibility is consistent with the soft HRM emphasis on empowerment and involvement of employees for increased commitment, motivation and development. 'Soft' flexibility means creating an adaptable workforce, by involving employees in decision-making, broadening their skills individually and through teamworking and creating a culture of continuous learning and improvement focused on outcomes rather than inputs or procedures.

1.3 Mutual benefits

Depending whether a hard or soft flexibility approach is used, flexibility may have benefits for the employing organisation and for employees. We will discuss the advantages and disadvantages of specific flexible working practices, from both points of view, as we proceed through this chapter. In general, however, the intended benefits are as follows.

(a) For the **organisation**, it offers a cost-effective, efficient way of utilising the labour resource. Under competitive pressure, technological innovation and a variety of other changes, organisations need a flexible, 'lean' workforce for efficiency, control and predictability. The stability of the organisation in a volatile environment depends on its ability to adapt swiftly to meet changes, without incurring cost penalties or suffering waste. If employee flexibility can be achieved with the co-operation of the employees and their representatives, there may be an end to demarcation disputes, costly redundancy packages and other consequences of apparently rational organisation design.

(b) From the point of view of the **employee**, the erosion of rigid specialisation, the micro-division of labour and the inflexible working week can also offer benefits. For example, a higher quality of working life; an accommodation with non-work interests and demands; greater job satisfaction, through variety of work; and perhaps job security and material benefits, since a versatile, mobile, flexible employee is likely to be more attractive to employers and have a higher value in the current labour market climate.

FOR DISCUSSION

Eli Lilly, winner of the 1996 Parents at Work award, is having to re-evaluate its family-friendly culture after its employees complained that, as a result of high workloads and line management indifference, they were unable to take the breaks on offer.

> Despite the fact that the pharmaceutical firm has a wide range of flexible working policies, its HR department is having to conduct a survey to find out how many employees are being allowed to take advantage of them…
>
> We have quite a macho management culture,' said …, the firm's corporate communications manager. We have changing shift patterns, longer hours, an unwillingness to delegate and a culture that encourages people to stay late …"
>
> You cannot simply pop (a policy) in and think: "Ooh, that will be wonderful" (he) added.

Why might line managers in a 'macho culture' fail to appreciate HR policies for flexibility, accommodating working parents, and balancing life and work goals?

You may have noticed from the preceding paragraph that there are a number of different types of flexibility, including not only the employer's ability to change the size of the workforce in response to demand, but the broadening of employees' skills and task variety, and the re-structuring of the working day or week. We will now summarise the flexibility approaches.

NOTES

1.4 Types of flexibility

A 1984 paper for the Institute of Manpower Studies (*Flexible Manning: the way ahead*) suggested that there are four different types of flexibility to which we have added a fifth.

Type of flexibility	Responding to:	Personnel management approach
• Numerical	Fluctuations in demand for staff numbers (seasonal, cyclical, task-related and so on)	Use of non-permanent, non-career labour: temporary staff, part-time staff, short-contract staff, consultants, sub-contractors
• Temporal	Fluctuations in working patterns, over 24 hours/ week/year: fluctuations in demand for labour at particular times	Use of 'flexi-time' and variations: overtime, shift-working, annualised hours
• Functional	Fluctuations in demand for particular skills - not necessarily related to staff numbers (since one person can be multi-skilled)	Deployment of staff across job/skill boundaries ('demarcation lines'): multi-skilling, multi-disciplinary teams, fewer or broader job descriptions
• Financial	Functional/temporal flexibility of staff. (They need to be rewarded flexibly and fairly - since 'the job' is no longer a fixed basis for reward.)	Performance - and/or profit-related pay: individual negotiation of pay according to market rates; single status policy (organisation-wide salary/benefit system)
• Cultural (our addition)	The need for a change of traditional attitudes towards jobs, careers, occupational identify: the need for a culture which embraces flexibility, variety, change, entrepreneurship	Recruitment and reward systems geared to employ and advance culturally flexible and versatile people; communication of flexibility as key value; counselling to help overcome fear of change

---

Activity 1   **(No time limit)**

Observe staff at a local supermarket and talk to friends who might work for one of the big supermarket chains. What evidence of flexibility can you see within organisations such as these? Which 'type' of flexibility is suggested by each of your examples?

We will now look in more detail at some of the approaches mentioned above.

PUBLISHING

2   FLEXIBLE WORKING METHODS

2.1   The core and periphery model

Fluctuations in the demand for workers may be foreseeable: regular peaks due to daily, weekly or seasonal cycles (such as lunch and dinner times at an all-day restaurant, Saturdays at supermarkets, or Easter at a chocolate factory) or irregular peaks due to organisational activity (such as a product launch). Other fluctuations may be unforeseeable: industrial action affecting competitors; events or reports in the media which stimulate or 'kill' demand for the product/service and so on.

The organisation cannot afford to employ a full-time workforce based on the best-case scenario or greatest demand. Indeed, in times of pressure to downsize the workforce (or at least, not to expand it), organisations prefer to increase their proportion of non-permanent labour, to avoid redundancies and/or seasonal layoffs.

The 'flexible firm' model was developed at the Institute of Employment Studies (Atkinson et al, 1984 – 1986). It suggested 'a reorganisation of firms' internal labour markets and their division into separate components, in which the worker's experience and the employer's expectation of him/her are increasingly differentiated'.

A model was developed which divided the workforce in 'core' and 'peripheral' groups of workers.

The core

The **core** group is permanent and stable, and is based on:

(a)   The lowest number of employees required by work activity at any time throughout the year and

(b)   Key tasks which require firm-specific skills and experience

The core group offers **functional** flexibility by virtue of re- or multi-skilling: training, retraining and redeployment within core tasks.
HR implications include:

(a)   The need for training in core skills

(b)   The need to offer employment security/continuity in order to facilitate skill/experience build-up and in order to protect the firm's investment in core workers' training

(c)   The need for reward structures which reflect and support flexibility and multi-skilling by removing rigid grade or functional barriers

(d)   The need to secure the commitment of the core workforce: this would usually foster commitment-based 'soft' HRM policies

The periphery

The **peripheral** group is designed to offer numerical flexibility: the ability to meet short-term peaks in demand through hiring, layoff and re-hiring, and variations in working hours. It may consist of:

(a)   Full-time employees in areas where there is a high level of mobility and wastage/turnover (clerical/secretarial and so on), creating a relatively numerically flexible internal labour market

(b)   Workers on non-standard contracts:

(i)   Short-contract or temporary workers

    (ii)   Job-share workers

    (iii)   Part-time workers

    (iv)   Work-placement trainees

    (v)   Casual workers

(c)   'Distance' workers not employed by the organisation but contracted to supply services:

    (i)   Self-employed individuals and other organisations from whom work might be outsourced

    (ii)   Sub-contractors

    (iii)   Agency temporary workers

Core-periphery

By acting as a 'buffer' against the need to downsize the organisation in the face of fluctuating demand, the core-periphery model allows for:

(a)   Relatively 'hard' HR policies aimed at reducing labour costs, and avoiding labour excesses and shortages, applied at the periphery and

(b)   Relatively 'soft' HR policies aimed at increasing productivity and commitment, providing employment security and organisational stability, applied at the core

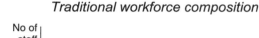

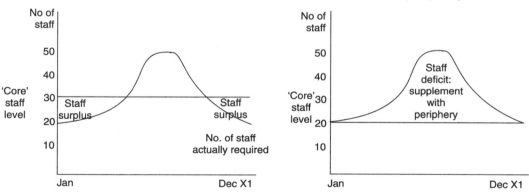

Figure 12.1 Atkinson's core and peripheral groups

EXAMPLE: CALOR GAS

In *Personnel Management Plus* (September 1992) it was reported that:

Calor Gas has replaced more than a third of its hourly paid workers with temporary staff on lower rates of pay, after terminating the contracts of the entire manual workforce.

Two-thirds of the group have been re-employed on new contracts, including 500 drivers, and 100 skilled workers and supervisors, whose pay levels have been maintained. But they are now working more flexibly under a new agreement with the Transport and General Workers Union.

The temporary workers... have replaced full-time operatives who cleaned and filled gas bottles at nine depots around the country.

John Harris, operations and personnel director, said the company needed to cut costs, increase productivity and change its culture.

The market was seasonal and Calor Gas had always used temporary workers in the winter. The difference now was that there was a core of temps, many of whom he expected would work for the company on a long-term basis, as well as a fluctuating periphery.

The company had also replaced its single national pay rate with varying regional rates for the contract workers. 'We have fewer people, paid less and they are very much more productive,' said Harris.

A different 'shaped' model

Handy, *The Age of Unreason* puts forward the idea of the shamrock (or clover-leaf) organisation, giving examples such as Rank Xerox and IBM.

(a)   The first leaf is made up of the steadily reducing inner core of qualified professionals, technicians and managers.

(b)   The second leaf represents work which is contracted out.

(c)   The third leaf is the flexible workforce - temporary or fixed contract workers. This is the fastest growing group in the UK and now includes managerial staff as well as lower-skilled workers.

2.2   Part-time and temporary working

Part-time working has been gaining popularity over the last 20 years.

Between 1984 and 1997, the number of male part-timers in the UK more than doubled to 1.3 million while women part-timers rose from 4.4 to 5.4 million. Some 80% of part-time workers are women and this has added impetus to the drive for equal treatment of part-time workers, under EU directives: less favourable terms and conditions have been construed as indirect sexual discrimination.

Definition

> Under the EU directive on part-time work, a **part-time employee** is someone with a contract or employment relationship whose normal hours of work, averaged over a period of up to a year, are less than the normal hours of comparable full-timers.

> **Activity 2**   **(45 minutes)**
> Why do you think there has been an increase in part-time working?
> Consider the employer and employee points of view.

The legal framework on part-time and temporary working

The thrust of legislation and court decisions has been to protect 'peripheral' employees from exploitation by 'hard' flexibility policies.

EU directives on part-time and temporary work were incorporated into UK law by regulations and a Code of Practice under the Employment Relations Act 1999. Part-time and temporary or fixed-contract employees are now entitled to the same employment and health and safety protection as permanent full-time staff.

(a)   Part-timers (who work 8 hours or more per week) may not be treated less favourably because they work part time. This applies to access to training, proportional entitlement to benefits (paid holiday, sick pay and access to pensions and parental leave etc), selection for promotion, protection from unfair dismissal, rights to written particulars of employment, and so on.

(b)   Obstacles to part-time work should be removed: there should be opportunities for part-time work at all levels, and for transfer between full-time, part-time and job-sharing arrangements (part-time (and temporary) workers should be informed of permanent full-time vacancies, for example).

(c)   The Working Time Regulations (discussed in Chapter 14) give equal rights to part-time and temporary workers in respect of night working, minimum rest periods and Health and Safety protection services, since they are held to be particularly at risk.

(d)   Temporary and fixed-contract workers are also entitled to the same social security benefits as permanent employees.

(e)   Individuals engaged under temporary contracts must be informed of the reasons for their being employed on a temporary rather than a permanent contract.

(f)   Health and safety legislation applies equally to full-time, part-time and temporary workers.

DISCUSSION

Does the protection and extension of part-time and temporary workers' rights defeat the object of the core-periphery model? What does it suggest about the perceived advantages of the model to employers and its perceived disadvantages to peripheral employees?

EXAMPLE: INTERNATIONAL COMPARISONS

*   Temporary work has traditionally been more highly regulated in other member states of the EU than in the UK, including the obligation to justify temporary work, provide a contract, limit the duration of the contract and provide comparable pay and conditions. Fixed-term contracts automatically became permanent in most states if they over-run. Some countries (Belgium, France, Portugal, Spain) have placed restrictions on the use of temporary workers, specifying their use only to cover absences, and for seasonal and exceptional workloads: Italy banned temp agencies, while Germany and the Netherlands specified that agency temps not work for more than six months in any one establishment. (These provisions may change as directives come into effect.)

*   The USA has a free approach to part-time and temporary workers. Beardwell and Holden suggest that 'there are grounds for thinking that workers employed by temporary help agencies or contracting firms in the USA are denied the benefits of employment security, job progression and benefits such as pensions that go with internal labour markets.

2.3   Job-sharing

Job-sharing is an approach to part-time job creation in which an existing full-time position is split in two, so that two people can share it, working part-time and paid pro-rata.

NOTES

So far, we have mainly considered numerical flexibility. An alternative approach to flexibility, combining numerical, geographical and working-hours flexibility, is tele- or home-working.

2.4 Tele-working and home-working

Definition

> '**Telecommuting** describes the process of working from home, or from a satellite office close to home, with the aid of computers, facsimile machines, modems or other forms of telecommunication equipment.' (*The Administrator*, August 1992)

Telecommuting offers:

(a)   Savings on overheads, particularly premises costs, in view of rising rents in many of the major cities in the UK

(b)   The opportunity to bring into employment skilled and experienced people for whom traditional working practices have hitherto been impracticable: single parents, mothers, the disabled, carers and so on; (the greatest impact of this may be increased opportunities for the disabled, according to the article in *The Administrator*)

(c)   Elimination of the need to commute - with consequent reductions in traffic congestion, fuel consumption, travel costs, pollution etc

(d)   Potential reduction in stress, since there is less conflict with non-work goals and needs, and a more congenial environment (with no commuting to undergo)

In addition to 'telecommuters', home workers may be:

(a)   Traditional **outworkers**, such as home typists or work processors and envelope fillers (for mailshots), writers and editors, tele-canvassers and market-researchers; these may be employed by the firm or subcontracted (freelance)

(b)   **Itinerants** such as salespeople, who do not have a permanent presence in the office, and use their home (and even car) for 'working on the move'; these people may be employed by the firm, or self-employed

(c)   Those in personal services, such as ironing and mending clothes, out-of-salon hairdressing, music teaching and so on

EXAMPLE: SELF-EMPLOYED CONTRACTORS AT HOME

Rank Xerox launched a successful networking scheme as long ago as 1981. They closed down a central London office costing them £300,000 a year, 'fired' the staff and then re-engaged them on networking contracts: each became a **separate company** working from home, linked direct to HQ, and guaranteed income if they supplied work on time.

The advantages seemed to be that:

(a)   As 'self-employed' workers, the networkers developed the discipline and motivation to work conscientiously

BPP
PUBLISHING

(b)   The more they did, the more they earned, and the firm encouraged them to use their spare time to take on contracts outside Rank Xerox itself

(c)   Networkers travelled in to Head Office only one day per week

(d)   Some banded together to form multiple units, or shared office premises near their homes, thus overcoming any sense of isolation

EXAMPLE: EMPLOYEES ON THE MOVE

The following appeared in *People Management*, 12 October 2000: note that it is an advertisement feature for BT's 'workstyle consultancy'.

> BT's Flexible Working 2000 survey reports that an enviable advantage is increased productivity, in some cases by as much has 40 per cent. By way of example, at BT flexible working has saved £180 million in property overheads since 1993, 20 million car miles a year in travel and boosted productivity by 20 per cent.

> It is no surprise that more and more companies are introducing flexible working programmes. The BT survey reveals that flexible workers make up more than 5 per cent of Britain's total workforce and that this number is growing by between 15 and 20 per cent a year.

> The flexible working executives are the latest corporate status symbol - known as corporate nomads, they can spend more time with their customers unencumbered by thoughts of having to get back to the office. The results are happier customers and more business done ...

> Employees who treat home as their work base or corporate nomads, who are constantly on the move, can keep in touch with colleagues and managers with good communications technology such as mobiles, the company intranet, e-mail and audio conferencing providing the means ...

> The cost of office space can be frightening when calculated per employee. Across the country the annual cost of the area taken up by an individual averages between £2,5000 and £7,000. A special case is London, where a permanent desk is estimated to cost a company up to £10,000 a year and sometimes as much as £15,000. The bill takes account of rent, business rates, cleaning ser/ices and information technology support. In contrast, a flexible worker costs the company between £500 and £1,000 a year.

> The big changes are due to a switch in corporate attitudes. Only three years ago companies regarded cultural perceptions and the lack of technological awareness as the major barriers to flexible working. In 2000, the survey shows that nearly 43 per cent of the 200 leading companies approached see no obstacles to introducing flexible working and 25 per cent are now providing the technology for this purpose.

> At the same time, however, BT finds it a little alarming that only 8 per cent intend to implement any change management and training for their people when they introduce the technology to support flexible working.

> Employers must take account of the adjustments that have to be made by employees working away from the office and realise that if people are going through this change to flexible working the employers who do not help them are storing up problems for themselves.

> BY supports all of its people in the change to a flexible way of working via an intranet based education and training package and has in the past involved the employees' families in a day of familiarisation with what flexible working can mean for the whole family ...

> BT practises what it preaches. It has 4,000 staff registered as home-based workers and a further 40,000 are flexible workers with the ability to work anywhere.

> The policy seems to be well received. Last year's annual survey of employees' attitudes showed that the flexible workers were 7 per cent more satisfied with the management support they were given and with their work-life balance than their office based colleagues.

> **Activity 3**   **(20 minutes)**
>
> The BT example (above) comes across as entirely positive, as befits an advertisement. Can you see any problems for personnel management, arising from home-working?
>
> (a)   Suggest four major areas where policy will need adjustment.
>
> (b)   Brainstorm some problems for **employees** with the homeworking concept.

In an article in the May 1997 edition of *Chartered Secretary*, Peter Barnes suggests how teleworking might be most effectively managed.

> Proper management of teleworking will go a long way to ensuring its success and reducing the fear of loss of control which is the major employer preoccupation. Some pointers for good practice are:
>
> - Develop relationships of trust
>
> - Have policies covering operational issues such as insurance, confidentiality, taxation (possible capital gains tax liability arising from the use of domestic property for business purpose), security and health safety
>
> - Use criteria when recruiting which enables the selection of those with self-discipline, good self-management skills and other attributes of effective teleworkers
>
> - Have formal and informal channels of communication (social isolation is the major disadvantage of teleworking as reported by the workers themselves) with visits by supervisors, regular meetings at the office, use of telephone, newsletters, informal gatherings etc
>
> - Clearly define quantitative and qualitative targets to "manage-by-results" and give thought to monitoring performance making use of electronics whenever possible
>
> - Have performance appraisal, career management and training policies which meet the needs of teleworkers
>
> - Be open to part-time home and part-time office working and even 'occasional' teleworking if appropriate
>
> - Maintain the voluntary principle and have a "revolving door" policy whereby as circumstances change workers can return to full-time office working
>
> - Evaluate outcomes against objective measures in productivity, quality of output, accommodation cost etc.

We will now go on to examine functional flexibility, or 'versatility': the ability to move employees from one task to another.

3   FUNCTIONAL FLEXIBILITY

3.1   Multi-skilling

Jobs are changing from simple, well-defined tasks (set out in job descriptions) to more flexible, multi-dimensional work. This new approach recognises that:

(a)   Performing a whole meaningful job is more satisfying to a worker than performing only one of its component tasks (as in 'scientific' job design)

(b)   Allowing workers to see the big picture enables and encourages them to contribute information and ideas for improvements, which might not otherwise have come to light

(c)   The focus on the task and overall objectives reduces the need for tight managerial control and supervision over work processes and practices

Definition

Multi-skilling is versatility: the opposite of specialisation, with its tendency towards rigid job descriptions and demarcation lines between one job and another. It involves the development of versatility in the labour force, so that individuals can perform more than one task if required to do so: workers are being encouraged, trained and organised to work across the boundaries of traditional jobs and crafts.

Multi-skilling has been difficult to achieve historically, because craft and occupational groups (such as trade unions) have supported demarcation in order to protect jobs and maintain special skills, standards and pay differentials. This situation is changing now that multi-skilled, flexible labour is highly prized in today's labour market.

EXAMPLE: SMITHKLINE BEECHAM

SmithKline Beecham introduced multi-skilling at its factory in Irvine in 1995 . This was accomplished across a great 'divide' of strict demarcation between **operators** (belonging to the Transport and General Workers' Union, TGWU) and **craftsmen** (represented by the Amalgamated Electrical and Engineering Union, AEEU). Further problems were posed by deeply-entrenched working practices, and the strong trade union traditions of western Scotland.

In the past, process operators faced with a blockage in the pipes (carrying materials from one stage of the process to another) have had to tell their supervisor, who would tell the engineering foreman, who would send a fitter to deal with it: meanwhile, production would grind to a halt. After multi-skilling, the job could be done by whoever was best placed to do it: craftsman or - more often - operator.

Analysis of such situations by working parties resulted in the concept of the 'best person': instead of jobs being 'owned' by particular groups, the most appropriate individual to do a particular job should be trained and skilled to do it!

'The intention was to increase efficiency across the whole site by cross-skilling electrical, mechanical and instrument engineers, while at the same time equipping operators with basic engineering, materials movement and analytical skills'.

Agreement was achieved after three years' consultation and negotiation with the unions. Support was added by a grant from the European Commission, under the 'Force' programme (since superseded). Force aimed to promote employee development by encouraging the sharing of information about good practice and successful initiatives like multi-skilling at SmithKline Beecham. (*People Management*, 9 February 1995)

The benefits of multi-skilling to the organisation are as follows.

(a) It is an efficient use of manpower.

(i) It smoothes out fluctuations in demand for different skills or categories of worker. As a simple example, take a secretarial services department. If audio typing, say, was in high demand one week, while shorthand dictation was going through a slack period, you would have a problem with specialised staff: there would be a bottleneck in audio typing, while shorthand staff were under-utilised. If the secretaries could both type and take shorthand, the inefficiency would not arise.

(ii)   It may be possible to maintain a smaller staff, because you would not need specialists in each skill area.

(b)   It puts an end to potentially costly demarcation disputes, where one category of worker objects to others 'invading' their area of work, as defined by narrow job descriptions.

(c)   On the other hand, it is less likely that a task will be left undone because it does not explicitly appear on anybody's job description.

Activity 4   **(15 minutes)**

What does multi-skilling offer the employee?

An alternative range of approaches to functional flexibility was put forward by Frederick Heizberg, an American psychologist who developed the concept of job satisfaction. Heizberg suggested that motivation and lasting satisfaction can only come by increasing the task variety and challenge of the job. He devised three methods of re-designing work for job satisfaction: job rotation, enlargement and enrichment. We will look at each these is turn.

3.2   Job rotation

Definition

Job rotation is a means of increasing task variety and skill acquisition by transferring employees from job to job on a rotational basis.

Job rotation might take two forms.

(a)   An employee might be transferred to another job after a period in an existing job, in order to give him new interest and challenge.

(b)   Job rotation might be regarded as a form of training. Trainees might be expected to develop broader skills and experience by spending 6 months or 1 year in each job before being moved on. The employee is regarded as a trainee, rather than as an experienced person holding down a demanding job.

No doubt you will have your own views about the value of job rotation as a method of training or career development. It is interesting to note Drucker's view: 'The whole idea of training jobs is contrary to all rules and experience. A man should never be given a job that is not a real job, that does not require performance from him.'

3.3   Job enlargement

Definition

Job enlargement is the attempt to widen job scope and task variety by increasing the number of operations or tasks in which the job holder is involved.

Job enlargement is a 'horizontal' extension of the job into more areas at a similar level of skill and responsibility. This has the effect of lengthening the time cycle of repeated operations: by reducing the number of repetitions of the same work, the dullness of the job should also be reduced. Job enlargement is therefore a 'horizontal' extension of an individual's work.

Arguably, job enlargement is limited in its ability to improve motivation since, as Herzberg points out, to ask a worker to complete three separate, tedious, unchallenging tasks is unlikely to motivate him more than asking him to fulfil one single tedious, unchallenging task ...

3.4 Job enrichment

Definition

> **Job enrichment** is a planned, deliberate action to build greater responsibility, breadth and challenge of work into a job.

Job enrichment is, in effect, a form of empowerment: a 'vertical' extension of the job design, which might include:

(a) Removing controls
(b) Increasing accountability
(c) Creating natural work units
(d) Providing direct feedback
(e) Introducing new tasks
(f) Allocating special assignments

FOR DISCUSSION

Even those who want their jobs enriched will expect to be rewarded with more than job satisfaction. Job enrichment is not a cheaper way to greater productivity. Its pay-off will come in the less visible costs of morale, climate and working relationships.   Handy

Who really gains from job enrichment?

3.5 Flexible working groups

The basic work units of organisations have traditionally been specialised functional departments. In recent decades, organisations have moved towards small, functionally flexible working groups or teams. Teamworking allows work to be shared among a number of individuals, without the requirement for complex and lengthy co-ordination and communication mechanisms.

Teams may be:

(a) Temporally flexible: called together to achieve specific task objectives and then disbanded (project management) and/or

(b) Numerically flexible: co-opting members and advisers as different skills, attributes and expertise are required

In terms of functional flexibility, there are two basic types of flexible working groups.

(a) **Multi-disciplinary teams**, which bring together individuals with different skills and specialisms, so that their skills, experience and knowledge can be pooled or exchanged (like different pieces making up a jigsaw puzzle).

This is regarded as a useful mechanism for organisational communication and co-ordination. It is particularly useful in problem-solving and creative ideas generation, since it fosters awareness of overall objectives, allows the airing of wide-ranging organisational issues, and accesses different ideas which can 'hitchhike' or 'leapfrog' on one another.

(b) **Multi-skilled teams** which bring together a number of multi-skilled individuals who can each perform any of the group's tasks. These tasks can therefore be shared out in a more flexible way between group members, according to who is available and best placed to do a given job at the time it is required. (See the Smithkline Beecham example above.)

Activity 5   **(45 minutes)**

What may be the drawbacks to teamworking? (Your earlier studies in Organisations and Behaviour should furnish some ideas ...)

We will now proceed to the third major form of flexible working: temporal flexibility.

4 TEMPORAL FLEXIBILITY

4.1 Flexible contracts

Forms of flexible contracted hours of work include the following.

(a) **Overtime**: premium rates of pay for hours worked in excess of standard hours. A business may ask employees to work overtime:

    (i) To increase production to meet seasonal or ad hoc peaks in demand, without increasing the labour force

    (ii) To maintain production (eg machine running) despite temporary shortages of labour. (Covering colleague absence is an example of this in the service section.)

    Overtime can militate **against** efficiency where it is employee-driven, as a means of increasing outcome. Salaried workers are often not paid overtime, and some businesses negotiate higher basic pay rates for wage earners in lieu of overtime.

(b) **Zero hour contracts**: no guarantee of work (or pay) is given for the week. Staff may be called upon as and when required, on a full- or part-time basis, effectively imposing self-employed status. This is obviously highly flexible from the employer's point of view, but has been identified by the National Association of Citizens' Advice Bureaux (NACAB) as potentially abusive, since it creates financial insecurity and inability to plan commitments.

(c) **Annualised hours contracts**: agreeing a number of hours' work per year, rather than per week or month. Some or all of these hours may be committed to a rota schedule or roster while additional 'bank hours' may be held in reserve for unforeseen fluctuations (such as the need to cover for absences) plus 'reserve hours' designated for specific purposes other than normal working (such as training). Intensive hours can be called on during seasonal peaks in labour demand via longer working days or shifts, with time off in periods of low demand. This offers high flexibility for the employer, with employment security for the employee, although there is the danger of overwork during peak hours.

In an annualised hours scheme, workers may be paid a basic annual salary in monthly instalments. A system of 'credits' for hours worked, hours 'on call' for work but not called, and hours spent at work but not needed (and so on) minimises the effect of fluctuations in work load and allows for positive or negative balances to be rolled over into the following year. Detailed planning of rosters, monitoring of hours and recording of credits is clearly required.

(d) **Term-time contracts**: similar to annualised-hours but allowing parents to maximise hours during school terms, so that family responsibilities can be met during holidays.

4.2 Flexi-time

There are many 'flexi-time' systems in operation providing freedom from the restriction of a '9 to 5' work-hours routine. The concept of flexi-time is that predetermined fixed times of arrival and departure at work are replaced by a working day split into two different time zones.

(a) The main part of the day is called 'core time' and is the only period when employees must be at their job (this is commonly 10.00 to 16.00 hours).

(b) The flexible time is at the beginning and the end of each day and during this time it is up to the individual to choose when he arrives and leaves. Arrival and departure times would be recorded by some form of 'clocking in' system. The total working week or month for each employee must add up to the prescribed number of hours, though he may go into 'debit' or 'credit' for hours from day to day, in some systems.

A flexi-time system can be as flexible as the company wishes.

(a) The most basic version involves flexibility only within the day, with no possibility of carrying forward debit or credit hours into other days, so if you arrive late, you work late. This type of system is used in some factories where transport difficulties make arrivals and departures difficult.

(b) Another system is flexible hours within the span of the week. Hours can be carried forward to the next day. This enables an employee to cope with a fluctuating work load without overtime and gives him some control over his work and leisure time.

(c) Finally, flexi-time may be operated by the month. Each employee will have a coded key which can also serve as an identity card, and this will be used on arrival and departure by insertion into a key acceptor, which records hours worked on a 24 hour clock.

Activity 6 (20 minutes)

Suggest three advantages to

(a) the organisation, and
(b) the worker,

of implementing a flexi-time system.

NOTES

4.3 Some limits on working hours

Note that under the Working Time Regulations 1998 (implementing EU directives), working hours have been regulated in the UK.

(a) Working hours are limited to 48 hours per week, averaged over a standard reference period of 17 weeks (or 26 weeks, where continuity of work is necessary, as in health or essential services, 24-hour production or seasonal work). This **can** be extended to a year by collective workplace agreement - to preserve annual hours schemes, for example.

(b) An employee may agree individually, in writing, to work more than 48 hours per week, and a record of hours should be retained in case the Health and Safety Commission requires it.

(c) All employees are entitled to a daily rest of 11 consecutive hours in every 24, and a 24-hour rest in every seven days (averaged over 2 weeks) - subject to adjustment by collective agreement.

(d) If the working day exceeds six hours, the employee is entitled to a minimum of 20 minutes' break.

4.4 Shift work

Shift-working allows a longer production/service day. This is important for the efficiency of production (minimising machine down-time and set-up) and increasingly important with consumer demands for 24-7 (24 hour, 7 day) service, available over the Internet.

There are three main systems in operation.

(a) **Double-day system** - ie two standard working day (eight hour) shifts, say from 6am - 2pm, and 2pm - 10pm. The physical and social problems of such a system are much less acute than where night-work is required - although the hours may seem somewhat 'anti-social' and hard on the evening social life.

(b) **Three-shift system** - ie three eight-hour shifts covering the twenty-four hour day (say 6am - 2pm, 2pm - 10pm, 10pm - 6am). The main problem here is the 'unnaturalness' of night-time work, on the third shift. There are physiological, psychological and social effects - which we will discuss below. Most complaints are directed at the so-called 'dead fortnight', when the pattern of afternoon and nigh shifts interfere most with normal social life.

(c) **Continental or 3-2-2 system**. This entails more frequent changes than the traditional system, enabling employees to have 'normal' leisure time at least two or three times per week! Over a four-week cycle, shifts rotate so that workers to 3 mornings, 2 afternoons, 2 nights, 3 rest days, 2 mornings, 2 afternoons etc (see table below). This gets away from the 'dead fortnight', but it may cause confusion initially, and also means that there are no entirely free weekends - which may be important to families.

3-2-2 system (using 24-hour clock times)

Week	Mon	Tue	Wed	Thur	Fri	Sat	Sun
1	6-14 hrs	6-14	14-22	14-22	22-6	22-6	-
2	-	-	6-14	6-14	14-22	14-22	22-6
3	22-6	22-6	-	-	6-14	6-14	14-22
4	14-22	14-22	22-6	22-6	-	-	6-14

Average 42 hours per week

BPP PUBLISHING

The 3-2-2 system is becoming increasingly popular - and is already established in the chemical and iron and steel industries. ICI operate it in two factories, and surveys show 80% of the workforce in favour because:

(a) Shorter, though more frequent, spells on each shift were found to be less fatiguing than longer periods on, say, the nigh shift

(b) The variety was more enjoyable

(c) Employees felt that they had more time off for social and family life

(d) Senior staff found it easier to keep in touch with the shiftworkers

A study by Folkard and Monk suggests that the best way of adapting to hours which are not normal for the human body is to work permanently on one shift, allowing the body to develop a 'revised schedule'. This is, however, unlikely to be widely implemented because of the anti-social nature of evening and night work.

Activity 7   **(1 hour)**

What do you think would be the effects of shift-working on an employee's life? Think about:

(a) Physiological/medical effects
(b) Psychological effects
(c) Social effects and
(d) Economic effects

The Working Time Regulations 1998 laid down restrictions and entitlements for workers involved in 'nightwork' (defined as a period of at least seven hours commencing between midnight and 5am).

We have already covered some of the HR implications of flexible working on a method-by-method basis. Here, we will draw together some of the threads.

5 ISSUES IN FLEXIBILITY

5.1 HR issues

Some of the HR policy choices to be considered are as follows.

(a) **Recruitment and selection**. Flexibility will need to be reinforced by selection criteria, both in terms of temperament (adaptability, willingness to adopt flexible working) and skills (trainability, existing multiple skills). In return, flexible working practices may act as a boost to the recruitment and retention of staff (especially women returners, say).

(b) **Training and development**. Performance management, training needs analysis and career planning will have to be tailored to flexible working in terms of: broadening skills, fostering flexible attitudes, teamworking (where relevant: criteria may be different for isolated homeworkers), opportunities for promotion (with equal access for part-time and temporary workers).

(c) **Supervision and control**. Flexibility militates against the supervisor's traditional role as monitor/controller of performance - especially where outworking and/or self-managing teams are used. The supervisor is increasingly becoming a coach/mentor/facilitator to empowered teams and/

or a co-ordinator/facilitator ensuring that communication is maintained with distant or part-time workers. (This change in role may itself require HR interventions in training and counselling support.) Control mechanisms must be developed to retain cohesion without rigidity: performance management, communication of cultural values, commitment-based policies and so on.

(d) **Motivation and reward.** Flexible payment structures will be required to reflect multi-skilling and team-working, while detailed administrative systems will have to support flexi-time and its variants. Attention will need to be given to employee morale and esprit-de-corps, particularly where people are only part-time or external members of the team: team-building will have to be broadened to include geographically separated 'virtual' teams.

(e) **Health and safety and other compliance aspects.** The employment environment is more highly regulated than ever before in terms of the protection of flexible workers. It places planning, administrative and employee relations duties on HR departments. In addition to compliance, there are the issues of social responsibility and employer branding/reputation, which dictate that 'soft' flexibility approaches may be more favourably regarded than 'hard' approaches such as zero hours contracting.

(f) **Cultural reinforcement.** HRM will have an important role in developing a culture which accepts and celebrates flexibility in general, through integrated systems for recruiting, rewarding, promoting, developing and facilitating flexibility, change, innovation and so on.

(g) **Problem-solving.** As we have seen, there are a number of drawbacks to flexibility from the point of view of the employee. HRM as a welfare function will have the task of minimising the impact of uncertainty, fluctuating earnings, isolation and so on, through supportive systems, compensations, safeguards and benefits.

Activity 8   **(2 hours)**

Pick an organisation that you have worked for, or are familiar with, or can find out about. How flexible is the workforce in this organisation? Is it versatile, multi-skilled and happy to work unorthodox hours or without a strict job description? What does the human resource department in this organisation do to encourage, or to discourage, flexibility of labour? (Think about job descriptions, training and development, working hours and so on.)

5.2 New psychological contracts

In our discussion of the labour market in Chapter 4, we noted that, according to the concept of 'job shift' (Bridges, 1995), the workforce is increasingly made up of 'skill vendors' who sell their services to a variety of clients on a project basis, and who take responsibility for their own résumé management: skill development, experience, self-marketing and so on.

This amounts to the re-writing of the traditional psychological contract of employment. Many organisations are making this explicit, by spelling out the new contract, in which concepts such as 'lifetime employment' or even a 'career' within a company are no longer valid. There are compelling reasons why an organisation may wish to repudiate responsibility for the job security and career development of its employees, even where it is offering 'permanent' employment.

(a) It may wish to discourage a culture of complacent performance based on job security and the fulfilment of job descriptions, and instead encourage the perception that competitive, value-adding performance is required in order to keep one's position.

(b) It may genuinely be unable to guarantee long-term, secure employment: in making this explicit, it is being socially responsible in encouraging employees to take ownership of their careers.

(c) It may wish to establish an attractive employer brand as an honest, open and realistic employer, in a market where educated employees are cynical about unrealistic recruitment offers.

On the other hand, there are risks to such an approach.

(a) There may be some loss of morale and performance, as the effects of newly-articulated insecurity are felt.

(b) There may be some loss of skilled labour, where individuals are alienated by the implication that they are not doing enough, or made uncomfortable by the uncertainty and responsibility of having to manage their own careers.

(c) There may be some loss of skilled labour, where individuals embrace the 'skill vendor' approach and career mobility to the point where they leave the organisation in order to develop their career portfolio.

One concept arising from the de-jobbing of employment is 'employability': a term which describes a portfolio of knowledge, skills and attributes that enhances an individual's marketability in the labour pool. Companies which have spelled out the new psychological contract may offer employability training in order to be socially responsible in facilitating employees' transition (if necessary) to other employment – while simultaneously benefiting from the resulting flexibility and versatility of employable individuals. (Employability and employability training are discussed further in Chapter 17.)

EXAMPLE

People Management (28 September 2000) reported how King's Healthcare NHS Trust, London, used an innovative package of flexible working practices – called Kingsflex - to meet a serious shortage of nursing and midwifery professionals.

The Kingsflex 10-point package

- Part-time working.

- Job-sharing.

- Temporary reductions in hours for specific periods to help employees deal with special circumstances.

- Staggered working hours. Staff can determine their working patterns on a planned, weekly basis. Hours can be staggered - for example, 10am to 6pm instead of the standard 9am to 5pm - for the whole week or for one or two days.

- Annual hours. Work can be spread unevenly over the year, giving employees scope for reducing their hours during school holidays, for example.

- A phased return to work. Staff can build up the number of weekly hours over a period after an absence such as sickness or maternity leave.

- Special and parental leave. Staff can take paid time off for specific needs - fostering, for example.

- Working from home - an occasional option as long as normal work is fulfilled.

- Career breaks. Employees can take unpaid leave for up to two years in order to travel, pursue further education or fulfil their caring responsibilities.

- 'Personalised' annual leave. Individuals can buy or sell days of annual leave, adjusting their entitlement by up to 10 days and increasing or decreasing their salaries accordingly.

Although these options are open to everyone, they were recognised as offering a better work-life balance for working mothers in particular. The Trust was overall champion in the 2000 Parents at work/Employer of the year awards.

Chapter roundup

- Labour flexibility can be approached from a 'hard' HRM orientation (focused on reducing labour costs and unit costs of production and on minimising the organisation's exposure to 'excess' labour: an approach called 'lean production') or from a 'soft' HRM orientation (focused on enhancing the quality and adaptability of the labour resource through broadening skills and commitment).

- Flexibility may be numerical, temporal and/or functional, and must be supported by cultural flexibility through integrated HRM systems. (A number of specific methods and techniques of flexibility were discussed in detail.)

- Flexibility poses key HR issues for recruitment and selection, training and development, control and the role of the supervisor, motivation and reward and compliance with legal requirements.

- 'Flexible working arrangements used positively can benefit employees as well as being in the interests of the business ... but abusing them could make it more difficult to recruit people and could damage competitiveness in the long run.' (CIPD).

- The nature of the 'job' and the psychological contract of employment have changed with the emphasis on flexible working.

Quick quiz

1   What are the pressures that have led organisations to develop flexible working?

2   What are the five types of flexibility?

3   Outline the core-periphery model.

4   What are the rights of part-time workers under the Employment Rights Act 1999?

5   List three advantages of teleworking.

6   List five methods of allowing flexibility in working hours.

7   Distinguish between job rotation, enlargement and enrichment.

8   What are the two basic approaches to flexible group working?

9   How does flexibility affect the supervisor's role?

10   What is 'employability'?

Answers to quick quiz

1   Increased market uncertainty, increased competition, technological change.   (see paragraph 1.1)

2   Numerical, temporal, functional, financial, cultural.   (para 1.4)

3   For a full account, see paragraph 2.1.

4   Rights to equal treatment in respect to access to training, selection for promotion, protection from unfair dismissal (and other statutory requirements); proportional entitlement to benefits (paid holiday, sick pay, maternity pay); access to pension schemes and parental leave, protection under all health and safety legislation.   (para 2.2)

5   Savings on overheads; employment access for home-bound workers; elimination of commuting; reduction in stress through better work/life balance.   (para 2.4)

6   Zero hours, annualised hours, overtime, shift-working, flexi-time, term-time contracts.   (para 4.1)

7   Rotation: moving the worker from one job to another.   (para 3.2)

Enlargement: horizontal extension of the job to increase task variety and number of operations.   (para 3.3)

Enrichment: vertical extension of the job to increase responsibility and challenge - ie empowerment.   (para 3.4)

8   Multi-disciplinary teams, multi-skilled teams.   (para 3.5)

9   Shift from monitor/controller to coach/facilitator and/or co-ordinator.   (para 5.1)

10   The development of a portfolio of knowledge, skills and experience that enhances a worker's marketability and mobility in the labour pool.   (whole chapter)

Answers to Activities

1   Examples of flexibility in a supermarket might include:

(a)   Extra staff employed for Christmas (numerical)

(b)   Adult staff with family responsibilities employed just during school term-times numerical/temporal)

(c)   School-age staff employed just during school holidays (numerical/temporal)

(d)   Staff on zero hours contracts (only called in to work when needed) (numerical/temporal)

(e)   Staff paid according to their performance (financial)

(f)   All staff trained to use checkouts (functional)

(g)   Staff skilled enough to work in more than one department (functional)

NOTES

2   Stephen Connock *(HR Vision)* gives seven main reasons for the increase in part-time working.

    (a)   Employers can match working hours to operational requirements better.

    (b)   The personal circumstances of key staff can be accommodated through part-time working. This will be particularly relevant to women returners.

    (c)   The productivity of part-timers is generally higher than that of full-timers (hardly surprising, since work is undertaken in more concentrated time periods).

    (d)   The absence levels of part-timers are generally lower: domestic requirements can more easily be fitted into the free periods in the part-time schedule.

    (e)   A pool of trained employees is available for switching to full-time work, or extending working time temporarily.

    (f)   Difficulties in recruiting full-time staff have prompted organisations to recruit and train part-time staff. Women returners are more likely to be attracted to an organisation if the hours of work are suitable, which will generally mean working part-time.

    (g)   Part-time working can cut overtime costs, since it makes it possible to avoid paying premium rates.

3   (a)   **Control**. There needs to be a shift of emphasis from managing the work process and methods - since supervision on a day-to-day basis is impossible - towards monitoring and controlling work output or results. This will apply to performance appraisal and rewards as well.

        Communication. Communication for planning, control and co-ordination - as well as morale, motivation and team-building - will need to be constantly pursued.

        Co-ordination. Employing outworkers increases the project management aspects of a task. Integrated plans, communication and control will be required to ensure that the outworkers' output fits into the overall operation in which they are involved.

        Health and safety. Housing is not always well adapted to work. There may be problems with electrical wiring, fire precautions and other matters which can be more closely controlled at a central office.

    (b)   Some of the drawbacks you may have identified include: isolation/lack of work relationships, uncertainty from lack of supervision, stress (for example, if not used to or trained in self-management), lack of 'change of scene', have home turned into a workplace environment, potential lack of communication (resulting in loss of identification with the organisation, loss of access to services and opportunities), health and safety concerns, distractions from work leading to poor performance. If on a self-employed contract basis - insecurity, possible lost earnings.

4   The erosion of rigid specialisation and fragmented job design can offer:

    (a)   A higher degree of job satisfaction, through variety of work and a greater understanding of its purpose and importance.

(b)   Job security and material benefits, since a versatile, flexible employee is likely to be more attractive to employers, and have a higher value in the current labour market; and

(c)   Personal skill development.

5   (a)   Teamworking is **not suitable for all jobs**: it does not always lead to superior or faster decision-making or performance than individuals working alone.

    (b)   Teams can delay decision-making in search of consensus (although consensus decisions do offer commitment and a rounded perspective).

    (c)   Social relationships might be maintained at the expense of other aspects of performance.

    (d)   **Group norms** may **restrict individual personality** and flair.

    (e)   **Group think**, or self-maintaining consensus, may prevent consideration of alternatives or constructive criticism.

    (f)   Personality clashes and political behaviour can get in the way of effective working.

6   Benefits to the organisation include: improved staff morale (because of flexibility); less stressed/distracted staff (because problems outside work can be solved without the guilt attached to lateness); less absenteeism (because of the 'I'm late for work: I'd better not go at all' syndrome).

Benefits to the workers include: less frustration in rush-hour commuting; less pressure over needs like the dentist or school sports days; time to shop, socialise etc in off-peak times; satisfaction of choice.

7   (a)   **Physiological or medical effects** - a disruption of body-temperature, disturbance of digestion, inability to sleep during the day resulting from the disorientation of the body's 'clock', its regular cycle of meals, sleep and energy expenditure. Shiftwork tends to conflict with the body's 'circadian rhythms', or 24-hour body cycles. Stress-related ill-health may also be caused. Some people suffer more from the physical disruption than others: in particular, diabetics, epileptics and those prone to digestive disorders should be screened by management, and excluded from shiftwork for health reasons.

    (b)   **Psychological effects**. The experience of variety can be stimulating. On the other hand, the fatigue and sense of physical disorientation can be stressful. Those with strong security or structure needs may feel threatened by a lack of 'rhythm' in working life. A sense of isolation and lack of variety arising from the social problems of shiftwork may also be threatening - particularly if strain is being put on non-work relationships and roles.

    (c)   **Social effects**. Some forms of shiftwork involve high social costs, though others - in particular double-day working, very little. In some systems, the normal hours of socialising - afternoon and evening - are taken up at work, which may isolate the individual from his non-work social circle. Family problems may be acute - especially where weekends are lost: not only is the worker absent, leaving a role gap in the family, but the routine of the whole family will be disrupted by his sleeping and eating patterns.

(d) **Economic effects**. Overtime is not necessarily eliminated by shiftwork: premiums for double-shift and Sundays are common in practice. Shiftworking itself is inherently unpopular, and its appeal will largely depend on financial incentives.

8   This allowed some space for your own research and reflection on your own experience. Plenty of sources of information: the HRM journals regularly report on flexibility initiatives, the currency of which is constantly reviewed by fresh considerations like family-friendly policies for recruitment, EU directives on worker rights and so on.

Assignment 12   **(1 hour)**

Flexconsult

You are a human resources consultant for Flexconsult, a consultancy which specialised in advising businesses on the best way to utilise their labour force, and on using flexible organisation structures and mechanisms to ensure that they have a labour force capable of fluctuating numerically in response to short term and/or seasonal changes in demand for their products and services.

You have just been handed a memo by your managing partner, which reads as follows.

Flexconsult

MEMO

To: (Your name)
From: Ed Hon Cho, Managing Partner
Date: (Today)
Re: New clients briefing

The partners have just met to discuss leads to prospective new clients. We are having preliminary discussions in two weeks with:

- A seaside holiday hotel

- A manufacturer of domestic appliances and

- A firm of management consultants

We would like to go into these meetings with an initial report, just to demonstrate our understanding of the HRM/labour demand issues involved in these businesses.

Please brief the Research Team on what you think those issues are, and what flexibility measures we might initially invite each business to consider.

EHC

Task

Compile some brief notes for yourself for the briefing of the Research Team. Include the supply/demand issues and some possible flexibility mechanisms for each of the three prospective clients.

Chapter 13 :
EQUAL OPPORTUNITIES IN THE WORKPLACE

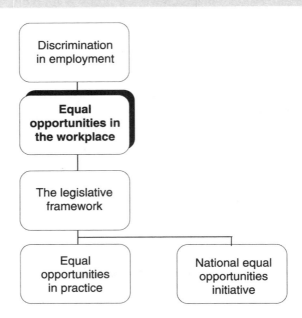

Discrimination in employment

Equal opportunities in the workplace

The legislative framework

Equal opportunities in practice

National equal opportunities initiative

Introduction

In this chapter, we look at discrimination at work and the legal framework shaping personnel policy in this area. As you read, be aware that while the law defines certain 'groups' against whom discrimination is illegal, discrimination can result from bias and prejudice of any kind: 'ageism' is one current area of debate. An ethical and cultural framework for justice and equality is as important as legislation and codes of practice: the 'management of diversity' concept is one development of this line of thought.

You may also note that discrimination can take subtle forms - classified as 'indirect' in current legislation: 'sexual harassment' is perhaps the most high-profile example of an issue which has emerged and been recognised as a form of discrimination.

Your objectives

At the end of this chapter you should:

(a) Be able to describe the forms of discrimination that take place

(b) Be able to discuss the implications of equal opportunities for human resource management

(c) Be able to discuss how the legislative framework relating to discrimination in the workplace can be applied by an organisation

(d) Be able to describe the role of the Equal Opportunities Commission, and Commission for Racial Equality

(e) Be able to compare the implementation of (equal opportunities) practice in the UK with that of one other country

1   DISCRIMINATION IN EMPLOYMENT

1.1   Equal opportunities

Definition

> **Equal opportunities** is an approach to the management of people at work based on equal access and fair treatment irrespective of gender, race, ethnicity, age, disability and sexual orientation.

Equal opportunities employers will seek to redress imbalances based around differences, where they have no relevance to work performance. Certain aspects of equal opportunities are enshrined in law, others rely upon models of good practice and have no legislative foundation.

1.2   Women in employment

Despite the fact that women have contributed directly to the national product since medieval times - on the land and in home-based industries such as textiles - the acceptance of women in paid employment has been a slow process, which is even now having to be enforced by law.

The distribution of women in the UK workforce today is still heavily concentrated in categories such as textiles, footwear, clothing and leather, hotel and catering, retail distribution and repairs, professional and scientific services, and miscellaneous services. A significant percentage of the women employed in these categories work part-time.

Only in recent decades has there been a widespread challenge to sex segregation in employment - the idea that there are 'men's jobs' and 'women's jobs', with only a few genuinely 'unisex' categories of work.

> **Activity 1**   **(30 minutes)**
>
> Why do you think women have been regarded as 'second-class citizens' in the work place? Consider social values, educational influences; the changing nature of work; the historical composition of the workforce and so on.

Many assumptions about women's attitudes to work, and capabilities for various types of work are being re-examined, and we will look a bit later at some of the measures being taken to remove the barriers to women in employment. The role of women in employment is currently being reassessed: forecasts predict that women will soon outnumber men in the workforce, although they may still be concentrated in lower-level, temporary and part-time positions.

1.3   Ethnic minorities in employment

The Commission for Racial Equality has noted that the level of unemployment for black people in the UK is nearly twice as high as that for white people. The Home Office Research Unit listed five causes of high minority unemployment.

(a)   Because immigration has mainly occurred in the last thirty years, the ethnic minority population is much younger than the population as a whole: young people find it particularly hard to get jobs when vacancies are scarce.

(b) Again because of fairly recent arrival, minority workers may not have UK-accepted occupational skills and qualifications, and may perhaps have poor English as well.

(c) Direct racial prejudice in favour of white labour when this is in ample supply.

(d) Indirect discrimination via selective recruitment methods. In 1982 the Commission for Racial Equality found that failure to advertise jobs or use Job Centres - relying on word of mouth among existing (predominantly white employees) was a major cause of the under-representation of blacks, for example.

(e) Concentration of minorities in certain industrial sectors, types of firm and occupations (perhaps as a result of discrimination) which are contracting (hitherto mainly in the manufacturing sector), insecure or low-status.

The Research Unit concluded that the first two factors will diminish with time, highlighting further need to address the issue of racial prejudice.

Additional issues in ethnic employment have been raised by UK skill shortages and immigration policy. In September 2000, the UK government announced that it would tackle skill shortages (particularly in the information technology and health service sectors) by relaxing immigration laws to attract foreign workers. The immigration minister pointed out that nearly a third of the UK's doctors were born outside the country and nearly a third of all nurses in inner London were trained outside the UK. Agencies working with refugees in the UK point out, however, that overseas-qualified refugees waiting to have their asylum appeals heard are not allowed to work, and are not being helped to qualify under UK education and training systems: a waste of an available resource.

There are also discrimination issues in employing developing-world immigrants because of the Asylum and Immigration Act 1996. UK employers are required under the Act to check the immigration and work-permit status of foreign workers - and yet are not permitted to discriminate on grounds of race, colour, ethnic origin or nationality, under race relations law. (Discussed in Chapter 5.)

Activity 2	(5 minutes)

Have you ever felt discriminated against (at school, work or training institution)? On what grounds: your sex, colour, age, social background./ beliefs/attitudes? What was the effect of the discrimination on your plans and attitudes?

Reasons for adopting positive action plans on racial equality include:

(a) Good HR practice, in attracting and retaining the best people (not just ethnic minority employees, but all those who care about discrimination)

(b) Compliance with the CRE's Code of Practice (1984), which is used by industrial tribunals

(c) Widening the recruitment pool for access to more labour

(d) Other potential benefits to the business through its image as a good employer, and through the loyalty of customers, particularly in geographical areas of ethnic diversity

1.4   Disabled people in employment

Definition

> **Disability** is 'a physical or mental impairment which has a substantial and long-term adverse effect on a person's ability to carry out normal day-to-day activities' (*Disability Discrimination Act 1995.*)

Disability covers a wide range of impairments, including restricted mobility, speech impediment, poor hearing or eyesight, learning disability and disfigurement. Despite this variety, attitudes towards the disabled in the workplace have been extremely negative, tending to focus on generalised and stereotypical problems such as:

(a)   Long periods off work for medical causes

(b)   Accident-proneness

(c)   Poor skill levels

(d)   Difficulties of adjusting the work environment for wheelchair access and other disability needs

(e)   Negative image to customers, who allegedly felt awkward in the presence of disabled people

(f)   The 'positive' association of certain jobs with disabled workers (eg lift attendants, switchboard operators, simple assembly tasks) stereotyping disabled roles and capabilities

(g)   Dislike of imposed recruitment and employment quotas

The Disabled Persons (Employment) Act 1944 established a Quota Scheme, which required that every employer with 20 or more workers should employ at least 3% registered disabled workers. This undoubtedly raised employment levels among disabled persons, but public as well as private organisations frequently failed to meet quota requirements - many protected by bulk exemption permits. Problems with the Quota Scheme included:

(a)   Failure of disabled people to put themselves on the register, which represents a segregative rather than integrative approach

(b)   Lack of incentives for employers actively to re-examine job specifications so as to employ more disabled people. (The scheme merely gave priority to disabled applicants with equal qualifications up to the quota)

(c)   Lack of legal provision for access and other facilities for disabled people in the workplace

(d)   Lack of attention to factors such as vocational training and career guidance for disabled people, which would improve their employability.

Some of these issues were finally addressed in the Disability Discrimination Act 1995, discussed in Section 2.

FOR DISCUSSION

The Employers' Forum on Disability (*Personnel Management* Feb 1991) suggested that plans to 'beef up' the Quota Scheme implied that employers were refusing to employ disabled people (a 'demand-side' problem), whereas the real problem was 'supply-side': a

NOTES

lack of suitable disabled candidates, due to poor skills training and career guidance ... 'We see a refreshed and broadened voluntary code of practice as a more realistic and effective alternative to quota system.'

Why should employers take on more disabled workers? Debate the question from a 'hard' and 'soft' HRM perspective.

1.5 Ageism

Despite demographic and educational changes and associated skill shortages among the younger population, a certain amount of discrimination is still directed at more mature workers. Age discrimination is not currently illegal in the UK: the government has preferred to develop a voluntary Code of Conduct. (However, see Section 2.6 below.)

Many organisations are unwilling to recruit staff over whatever they consider the 'normal' age for the job. The following extracts are taken from job advertisements in the *Chartered Secretary*.

'Aged 38 - 45 years, you are qualified ACIS or ACA ...'

'The appointee, probably aged 30 - 40 ...'

Research has found that almost a third of job advertisers specify an age bar, with the barrier being between 40 and 45. The Employers' Forum On Age estimated (*People Management* 28/1/99) that age discrimination is costing the UK economy up to £26 billion per year.

Activity 3	**(10 minutes)**

List some reasons - perhaps based on your own experience or prejudices! - why organisations might practise age discrimination.

The fact is that older workers:

- (a) Have developed expertise and skills that may be valuable in the job.

- (b) Tend to stay in the job, reducing turnover and associated costs and have better attendance and disciplinary records.

- (c) Do experience some loss of strength and stamina. However, this is unlikely to be relevant to performance in most modern jobs, and older workers typically understand and work within their physical limitations.

- (d) Do experience some loss of mental functioning (short term memory, for example) but retain - or even gain - in other cognitive functions.

- (e) Are no more likely to be flexible or inflexible in relation to learning and change than younger employees.

- (f) Do not necessarily cost the organisation more, as age-based reward systems are being replaced by performance-related ones.

EXAMPLE: INTERNATIONAL COMPARISONS

- In the Far-East, great value is placed on 'the wisdom of age'. In Japan, age is equated with long service, the acquisition of skill and experience, and hence the quality of the worker.

- In the USA, Congress enacted the Age Discrimination in Employment Act (AEDA) in 1967, stating that no employee aged 40-65 could be discriminated against in employment practices due to his or her age. A 1986 amendment extended this to all workers 'over 40'.

We will now look at the laws passed to protect the rights of typically disadvantaged groups, as well as some of the issues which are currently being worked out in European courts and professional Codes of Practice.

2   THE LEGISLATIVE FRAMEWORK

2.1   Sex Discrimination and Race Relations Acts

In Britain, two main pieces of legislation deal with inequality of opportunity by reason of sexual and racial discrimination.

- The Sex Discrimination Acts 1975 and 1986 (SDA) outlaw certain types of discrimination on the grounds of sex or marital status.

- The Race Relations Acts 1976 and 1996 (RRA) outlaw certain types of discrimination on the grounds of colour, race, nationality, or ethnic or national origin.

There are two types of discrimination, under the Acts.

Definition

> **Direct discrimination** occurs when one interested group is treated less favourably than another (except for exempted cases).
>
> For example, advertising for barmaids rather than barstaff. It is unlikely that a prospective employer will practise direct discrimination unawares.
>
> **Indirect discrimination** occurs when requirements or conditions are imposed, with which a substantial proportion of the interested group could not comply, to their detriment. For example, 'all applicants must be over six feet tall' (this would prohibit more women than men from applying). The employer must, if challenged, justify the conditions on non-racial or non-sexual grounds. It is often the case that employers are not aware that they are discriminating in this way.

The obligation of non-discrimination applies to all aspects of employment, including advertisements, recruitment and selection programmes, access to training, promotion, disciplinary procedures, redundancy and dismissal. The 1986 SDA also provides that companies with a compulsory retirement age must abolish different retirement ages for men and women.

> **Activity 4**   **(15 minutes)**
>
> Suggest four examples that would constitute **indirect** discrimination on the grounds of sex.

BPP
PUBLISHING

NOTES

In each of the Acts, however, there are certain exceptions, in which discrimination of a sort may be permitted.

Permissible reasons for discriminating on grounds of gender (*genuine occupational qualifications*)	Permissible reasons for discriminating on racial grounds
• Physiology (not physical strength) • Decency or privacy (closely defined) • Special welfare consideration • Provision of personal services promoting welfare or education • Legal restrictions, particularly jobs likely to involve work outside the UK, where 'laws or customs are such that the duties could not, or could not effectively, be performed by a woman' • Employment carried out wholly or mainly outside the UK	• Dramatic performances, where the *dramatis personae* requires a person of a particular racial group • Artists or photographic models for advertising purposes, for reasons of authenticity • Personal services rendered for the **welfare** of the particular group • Employment carried out wholly outside the UK

Activity 5 (15 minutes)

Think of examples of **each** of the categories of exception listed above.

In addition, the Employment Act 1989 laid down some restrictions on employing women, particularly while pregnant, to avoid exposing them to substances (lead, radiation) and work situations (aircraft) that might damage their health.

Despite these 'special cases', the legislation does **not** (except with regard to training) permit **positive discrimination** - actions which give preference to a protected person, regardless of genuine suitability and qualification for the job.

Training may be given to particular groups exclusively, if the group has in the preceding year been substantially under-represented. It is also permissible to encourage such groups to:

(a) Apply for jobs where such exclusive training is offered

(b) Apply for jobs in which they are under-represented

A training body (other than the employer) running such a positively discriminating scheme must be either permitted by the Acts or specially designated by application to the Secretary of State for Employment.

Complaints

Complaints of discrimination may be made to an industrial tribunal within three months of the alleged offence. If conciliation is unsuccessful, the tribunal will hear the case, with the power to award:

(a) An order declaiming the rights of both parties

(b) A recommendation for action to redress discriminatory practices within a specified time and

(c)   An order requiring the discriminating employer to pay compensatory damages

The **Sex Discrimination and Equal Pay (Miscellaneous Amendments) Regulations 1996** extended the remedies available for sex discrimination.

In addition, **EU Reversal of Burden of Proof in Sex Discrimination Cases Directive** establishes the assumption that employers accused of sexual discrimination are guilty unless they can prove the contrary: a reversal of the previous system whereby the complainant had to prove that discrimination took place. (This has caused huge controversy in the UK: watch the business press to see how the situation develops.)

EXAMPLES

- *Case: Ms B M Price v Civil Service Commission and Another (1977).* Ms Price applied for a post in the Civil Service. She was not considered, as she was over the age limit of 28. She contended that this was indirectly discriminatory to women, since many women in their twenties were hampered by domestic duties. It was held that this constituted indirect discrimination. The Civil Service was required to raise its age limit.

- 'An advertisement asking 18- to 25-year-old 'attractive' females to apply for jobs as camel racers has fallen foul of Australia's minister for the status of women, Judi Moylan. The Australian Camel Racing Association told an anti-discrimination tribunal that it wanted exemption from equal opportunities laws because an all-female camel racing league would broaden the appeal of the sport. But Moylan accused the association of judging applicants more by their looks than by their ability to race camels. The tribunal has reserved its decision.' (*People Management*, 19 February 98.)

The Equal Opportunities Commission and Commission for Racial Equality

The **Equal Opportunities Commission** and **Commission for Racial Equality** (set up under the Acts) have powers, subject to certain safeguards: to investigate alleged breach of the Acts; to serve a 'non-discrimination notice' on employers found guilty of contraventions; and to follow-up the investigation until satisfied that undertakings given (with regard to compliance and information of persons concerned) are carried out. In cases of persistent discrimination they might institute legal proceedings. Both bodies also publish **Codes of Practice** giving detailed guidance on how personnel policies can be developed to avoid discrimination, how staff should be informed and trained, how practices should be monitored and so on.

Sexual orientation

The European Commission recently announced a package of proposals in the area of discrimination to eliminate anomalies and gaps in the current legislation, including the issue of sexual orientation. A recent amendment to the Sex Discrimination Acts also extends protection to those discriminated against on grounds of a **change of sex.**

Marital status

The Sex Discrimination Acts make it unlawful to discriminate against married people, for example where an employer believes that a single man will be able to devote more time to the job than a married one. The Act permits discrimination against one partner because of the particular employment circumstances of the other (eg there is a conflict of interest, where the partner works for a competitor). There is, curiously, no protection for single workers.

Related issues

Some issues which have arisen as potential causes of indirect sexual discrimination include:

(a) Unequal treatment of part-time workers, who are mostly women (see Chapter 12)

(b) Sexual harassment (see below)

Equivalent issues in racial discrimination include nationality and immigration status, and religious beliefs (see Chapter 4).

EXAMPLE: INTERNATIONAL COMPARISONS

A report by the Australian Human Rights and Equal Opportunities Commission (Daily Telegraph (Australia) 26/8/99) revealed that, fifteen years after pregnancy discrimination was outlawed in Australia (Sex Discrimination Act 1984) there was still widespread and significant discrimination against pregnant women in the workplace. The report cited the following 'horror stories'.

- **Case 1**. A manufacturing company refused to provide seating for a pregnant woman who suffered bleeding. She eventually miscarried.

- **Case 2**. A woman in her first trimester of pregnancy was in hospital to save the child. Her employer sacked her at her bedside because it was her last day of sick leave.

- **Case 3**. An employer dismissed a pregnant bar attendant on the basis that she might fall on the slippery floors and injure her unborn child.

- **Case 4**. An employer refused to employ women of child-bearing age because they might become pregnant.

- **Case 5**. A woman who worked in a male-dominated workplace said that during the course of her first pregnancy the organisation embarked upon a selection process of 'downsizing'. Male managers used criteria such as 'who might be pregnant; who is pregnant' to identify the positions that would be made redundant.

- **Case 6**. A government employee aged between 20 and 30 told her department of her pregnancy one week before her contract was due for renewal. The department advised her they would not be renewing her contract and hired someone else for her position.

- **Case 7**. A first-year cabinet-making apprentice, who moved to the city after her pre-vocational course, was told directly by employers that they would not take her as an apprentice because she was a girl and she might get pregnant.

- **Case 8**. A boss who did not like the physical appearance of a pregnant woman, moved her from the front desk and reduced her hours from 30 hours a week (which she had been doing for four to five years) to four hours a week.

2.2 Equal Pay Act

The Equal Pay Act 1970 was the first major attempt to tackle sexual discrimination. It was intended 'to prevent discrimination as regards terms and conditions of employment between men and women'.

The Equal (Amendment) Regulations 1984 established the right to equal pay for 'work of **equal value**', so that a woman would no longer have to compare her work with that of a man in the same or broadly similar work, but could establish that her work had equal value to that of a man in the same establishment. These provisions were discussed in detail in Chapter 7.

A study published in 1999 in the *Australian Economic Review* suggested that:

(a) There was still an overall wage gap between men and women, of between 10-15%. 'One explanation is that it has been difficult to implement the principle of equal pay for work of equal value in female-dominated occupations.'

(b) There is a new gap widening between high- and low-paid female workers. Women have made inroads into higher-paying occupations, but the wages of low-paid women have not increased significantly relative to the male median. Moves towards decentralised pay setting may be exacerbating the problem: 'Women in low-paying jobs are often those least equipped to negotiate their own pay and conditions.'

2.3 Sexual harassment (Code of Conduct)

Definition

Sexual harassment as set out in the 1991 EU Code of Conduct is:

(a) 'Unwanted conduct of a sexual nature, or other conduct based on sex affecting the dignity of women and men at work'

(b) 'Unwelcome physical, verbal or non-verbal conduct'

(c) 'Conduct that denigrates or ridicules or is intimidatory or physically abusive of an employee because of his or her sex, such as derogatory or degrading abuse or insults which are gender-related and offensive comments about appearance or dress'

Compliance with the EU Code of Conduct on sexual harassment is only voluntary, and there is no specific law against sexual harassment in Europe: indeed, it is not mentioned in law at all. However, it has been ruled by the courts that proven sexual harassment is **unlawful sex discrimination**, under the Sex Discrimination Act.

Recommendations to organisations for handling sexual harassment in the EU Code of Conduct - and the CPD statement on sexual harassment - include the following.

(a) The issuing of a clear policy statement or corporate Code of Conduct, with communication and awareness training (especially for managers) to highlight the seriousness of the offence.

(b) The implementation of counselling procedures, giving advice to victims, and hopefully resolving problems by informal means, but - if not - also planning further proceedings.

(c)   The design of complaints procedures.

        (i)   Informal procedures would include person-to-person reproof (a clear statement by the victim to the offender that the conduct is unwelcome) and intervention by a trusted third party.

        (ii)   Formal procedures should exist for confidentiality to be guaranteed, and for an investigator of the same sex as the victim to be available to follow up complaints.

    (d)   The implementation of disciplinary action. Rules should be defined, including protection of the complainant from further victimisation as a result of the action.

FOR DISCUSSION

Come up with some examples of what might be defined as 'sexual harassment': you may even have experienced some. Are these examples clear-cut? What issues are involved? How are your examples discriminatory? Consider how male and homosexual workers might also be harassed.

2.4 Disability

Previous legislation on disability focused narrowly on securing employment for disabled people (see paragraph 1.4 above), without addressing the issue of discrimination. This shortcoming was addressed when the **Disability Discrimination Act 1995** came into force in December 1996.

Definition

A **disabled person** is defined as a person who has a physical or mental impairment that has a substantial and long-term (more than 12 months) adverse effect on his ability to carry out normal day to day activities. The effect includes mobility, manual dexterity, physical co-ordination, and lack of ability to lift or speak, hear, see, remember, concentrate, learn or understand or to perceive the risk of physical danger. Severe disfigurement is included, as are progressive conditions such as HIV even though the current effect may not be substantial.

The Act contains provisions for disabled access to services, transport facilities and education and training opportunities. In the sphere of employment, it makes it unlawful to discriminate against a disabled person/employee:

    (a)   In deciding who to interview or who to employ or in the terms of an employment offer

    (b)   In the terms of employment and the opportunities for promotion, transfer, training or other benefits, or by refusing the same

    (c)   By dismissal or any other disadvantage

The employer also has a duty to make reasonable adjustments to working arrangements or to the physical features of premises where these constitute a disadvantage to a disabled job applicant or employee. Examples of changes to working arrangements given in the Government's Code of Practice include the following.

    (a)   Altering working hours
    (b)   Acquiring or making changes to equipment

(c)   Allocating some duties to another employee
(d)   Providing supervision
(e)   Making adjustments to premises
(f)   Assigning the employee to a different place of work
(g)   Training
(h)   Providing a reader or interpreter

A number of factors will be relevant in deciding whether a change is reasonable, chiefly its effectiveness, cost (both financially and in terms of disruption), and practicability in the light of the employer's resources and the availability of financial or other help.

The provisions regarding employment do not apply to an employer who has fewer than 20 employees.

A **Disability Rights Commission** was established to ensure that employers and disabled people are informed of their respective rights and duties.

The Government has issued a Code of Practice on disability which gives advice to employers on how to avoid disability discrimination in employment. It does not itself impose legal obligations, but will be taken into account by Industrial Tribunals. The Code provides many examples of good practice, as well as general principles.

(a)   Be flexible
(b)   Do not make assumptions
(c)   Consider whether expert advice is needed
(d)   Plan ahead
(e)   Promote equal opportunities.

Activity 6   **(30 minutes)**

What arguments would you put forward as to why an organisation should consider employing people with disabilities?

2.5   Rehabilitation of Offenders Act

Under the 1974 Act, a conviction for criminal offences is 'spent' after a period of time (which varies according to the severity of the offence). After this period, an offender is 'rehabilitated' and is not obliged to disclose the nature of his offence or details of his conviction. Failure to disclose a previous conviction (eg answering 'no' to a question in section interview) is therefore not justifiable grounds for non-engagement (or dismissal). There are exceptions, however, including life imprisonment, prison sentences over 30 months, and convictions for doctors, lawyers, teachers, accountants and police officers.

The Police Act 1997 makes it easier for recruiters to screen out applicants who have a criminal record by making available 'conviction certificates' (covering unspent convictions).

The CIPD conducted a survey on diversity in 1996, and reported the opinions of recruitment consultancies around the UK. Typical views included:

'Of all the things to put off a client, a criminal record is the worst.'

'As far as I am concerned, if they've done it once, they might do it again.'

2.6   Ageism (Code of Practice)

Discriminatory practices are not currently illegal in the UK. However, there is already some redress for employees treated unfairly on the grounds of age. Age is **not** one of the reasons for dismissal acknowledged as potentially fair under the Employment Rights Act

1996, except on grounds of ill-health. Ageism has also successfully been challenged in terms of indirect sex and race discrimination, on the grounds that fewer women are able to comply with age requirements because of childbearing, and fewer ethnic minorities because of adult immigration.

The government has not ruled out legislation on ageism, but has so far preferred to tackle the problem by means of a voluntary Code of Practice, published in June 1999. The Code is intended to set a standard of 'reasonable behaviour' for decisions by tribunals, on a par with ACAS codes and those used in other types of discrimination cases. The Code of Practice on Age Diversity in Employment states that employers should:

(a) Recruit on the basis of the skills and abilities; refrain from using age limits or phrases that imply restrictions (such as 'newly qualified' or 'recent graduate') in job advertisements; refrain from asking for medical references only from older applicants

(b) Select on merit and use, where possible, a mixed age panel of interviewers, trained to avoid decisions based on prejudices and stereotypes

(c) Promote on the basis of ability, having openly advertised opportunities

(d) Train and develop all employees and regularly review training to avoid age being a barrier

(e) Base redundancy decisions on objective, job-related criteria, and ensure that retirement schemes are applied fairly. 'Last in first out' policies may be construed as discrimination to young people

Meanwhile, others have led the way in changing policy.

- The Employment Service vowed to turn away ageist recruitment ads in April 1998

- *People Management* refused to carry ageist ads

- Recruitment agency Jefferson Lloyd offered a 25% discount to firms taking on applicants over the age of 50

2.7 Where next?

In October 2000, the EU member states agreed a directive (known as 'Article 13') which will outlaw discrimination on the grounds of sexual orientation, disability, religion and age.

This will be the first time ageism has been outlawed in the UK (though not in other EU member states).

- Article 13 provisions on sexual orientation and religion must be introduced by 2003.

- Article 13 provisions on age must be enacted in UK law by 2006.

- Disability provisions are already covered by the Disability Discrimination Act 1995 and will not be altered by Article 14.

Watch the HRM and business press for further debate!

3 EQUAL OPPORTUNITIES IN PRACTICE

3.1 Formulating effective policies

In an article in *The Administrator* (June 1992), John Green suggested that many organisations make minimal efforts to avoid discrimination. They pay lip-service to the idea, to the extent of claiming 'We are an Equal Opportunities Employer' on advertising literature! He goes on to explore the factors necessary to turn such a claim into reality.

(a) **Support** from the top of the organisation for the formulation of a practical policy.

(b) A working party drawn from - for example - management, unions, minority groups, the HRM department and staff representatives. This group's brief will be to produce a draft Policy and Code of Practice, which will be approved at senior level.

(c) **Action plans and resources** (including staff) in order to implement and monitor the policy, publicise it to staff, arrange training and so on. These may be based on the range of Codes of Practice published by interested statutory bodies (the Commission for Racial Equality, Equal Opportunities Commission and Disability Rights Commission) and others (such as the CIPD).

(d) **Monitoring**. The numbers of female, disabled and ethnic minority staff can easily be monitored using 'Equal Opportunity Monitoring Forms' filled out by employees:

(i) On entering (and applying to enter) the organisation
(ii) On leaving the organisation
(iii) On applying for transfers, promotions or training schemes

(e) **Positive action**: the process of taking active steps to encourage people from disadvantaged groups to apply for jobs and training, and to compete for vacancies. Examples might be: using ethnic languages in job advertisements, or implementing training for women in management skills. (see Paragraph 3.2 following.)

An area of particular sensitivity is recruitment and selection. There is always a risk that a disappointed job applicant, for example, will attribute his or her lack of success to discrimination, especially if the recruiting organisation's workforce is conspicuously lacking in representatives of the same ethnic minority, sex or group.

Activity 7(1½ hours)

From your knowledge of direct and indirect discrimination on grounds of sex and race, outline a set of antidiscrimination policy points for the recruitment manager, covering:

(a) Job advertising
(b) Use of recruitment agencies
(c) Job application forms
(d) Job interviews
(e) Selection tests
(f) Record keeping

Bear in mind the need to avoid both discrimination and **allegations of discrimination**.

3.2 Positive action approaches

In addition to responding to legislative provisions, some employers have begun voluntarily to address the underlying problems of equal opportunities, with measures such as the following.

(a) Putting equal opportunities higher on the agenda by appointing Equal Opportunities Managers (and even Directors) reporting directly to the Personnel Director.

(b) Flexible hours or part-time work, 'term-time' or annual hours contracts (to allow for school holidays) to help women to combine careers with family responsibilities. Terms and conditions, however, must not be less favourable.

(c) Career-break or return-to-work schemes for women.

(d) Fast-tracking school-leavers, as well as graduates, and posting managerial vacancies internally, giving more opportunities for movement up the ladder for women currently at lower levels of the organisation.

(e) Training for women returners or women in management to help women to manage their career potential. Assertiveness training may also be offered as part of such an initiative.

(f) Awareness training for managers, to encourage them to think about equal opportunity policy.

(g) The provision of workplace nurseries and other family friendly policies, to help working mothers.

(h) Positive action to encourage job and training applications from minority groups: using ethnic languages and pictures showing a racial/ethnic mix of people in advertisements, for example. Another example is pre-recruitment or pre-training training for minority groups: the metropolitan police piloted a scheme of such courses, covering literacy, numeracy, current affairs, physical fitness and interpersonal skills, to allow ethnic minority applicants to compete on an equal basis for training places.

(i) Alteration of premises to accommodate wheelchair users: supplying braille or large-print versions of documentation; supplying computerised text-based telephones or interpreters for hearing impaired people and so on.

(j) Extending benefit schemes and incentives to gay partners as well as heterosexual married partners. (For example, British Airways' extension of its concessionary travel scheme to partners of gay employees. Entitlement to a dead partner's pension is another big issue for partners in homosexual and even heterosexual partnerships: most schemes only recognise husbands or wives as beneficiaries.)

4 NATIONAL EQUAL OPPORTUNITY INITIATIVES

4.1 Opportunity 2000

The Opportunity 2000 campaign (led by the voluntary organisation, Business in the Community) was launched on 28 October 1991, with an initial 62 organisations - mostly household names. Each set out and published its goals for employing and promoting women during the years up to 2000. Highlights include:

- **J Sainsbury**: More than 95,000 staff, about two-thirds women, are employed in more than 320 supermarkets and 60 DIY stores. At the end of last financial year 40 per cent of management were women.

New measures included scholarships to female weekend employees who are going on to higher education to take courses in areas in which women are traditionally under-represented, such as retailing, information technology, transport studies and engineering.

- **IBM (UK)**: The computer group set four goals: 'To contribute externally to the advancement of women in the national workforce; ensure that the company takes full advantages of the economic potential of women in the workforce; encourage women employees to realise their full potential; and increase the representation of women in senior management positions.' To achieve these IBM aimed for 30 per cent of graduate intake to be female.

- **BBC**: The BBC has been one of the leading organisations in setting numerical targets for the promotion of women. Existing targets are for the following female/male ratios: 30:80 for senior executive grades: 40:60 senior management; 40:60 management.

  These targets were reviewed in 1996 and further targets set for the year 2000. It intends to introduce more sophisticated monitoring procedures, further flexible working arrangements, and a policy to tackle harassment at work.

- **British Airways**: Of 50,000 British Airways staff worldwide, 32 per cent are women. Principle goals are: for women employed at all levels to reflect the proportion of women in the total UK workforce. (1991: 32 per cent; 2000: 42 per cent.) Women managers in the UK workforce to reflect the proportion of women in full-time employment in the total UK workforce. (1991: 20 per cent; 2000: 27 per cent.)

  An equality steering group is to decide and implement recommendations for action. Departmental equal opportunity objects are to be incorporated into the performance appraisal system for managers.

People Management (1995) reported on the experience of the 293 member organisations who had signed up for the initiative. The number of women directors had doubled in the previous year (from 8% to 16%), while the number of women in middle and senior management positions had also increased by some 4-5% (to 28% and 17% respectively).

4.2 Other positive action initiatives

Similar national initiatives have been introduced to improve employment opportunities for members of ethnic minority groups.

In January 1995, the Commission for Racial Equality (CRE) launched a new initiative in the drive for equal opportunities with its bench marking standard for employers, **Racial Equality Means Business**, or **Race for Opportunity**. This aims to move the issue beyond compliance with legislation, and even beyond commitment to the moral principle of equality to a recognition of its business benefits. Companies which have implemented practical policies and action plans on racial equality - including Midland Bank, Littlewoods and WH Smith - claim to have found measurable benefits in terms of staff morale and performance, and customer loyalty.

Perhaps it is unfair to expect legislation to change deep-seated attitudes towards individual differences. Law may only change people's behaviour; to change how we feel and what we know (ie our attitudes) requires long term education and actual experience of working with the affected groups. A new approach to the management of individual differences has recently emerged in the USA and is beginning to capture the imagination of British employers.

NOTES

4.3 Managing diversity

Definition

> **Managing diversity** is based on the belief that the individual differences we currently focus on under equal opportunities (gender, race, age etc) are crude and irrelevant classifications of the most obvious differences between people, and should be replaced by a genuine understanding of the ways in which individuals differ.

The ways in which people are **meaningfully** different in the workplace include personality, preferred working style and individual needs and drives. These things do not necessarily correlate with racial or gender differences in any way. For example, it would be a gross oversimplification to say that all women in your organisation require assertiveness training: it may be less appropriate for many women than for some men. Thus, effective managers seek to understand the job-relevant ways in which their staff differ and should seek to manage their performance in ways which recognise those differences as far as possible. Managers need to understand the unique contribution each person - not each 'category or person' - can make to the organisation.

A 'managing diversity' orientation implies the need to be proactive in managing the needs of a diverse workforce in areas (beyond equal opportunity and discrimination) such as:

(a) Tolerance of individual differences

(b) Communicating effectively with (and motivating) ethnically diverse workforces

(c) Managing workers with diverse family structures and responsibility

(d) Managing the adjustments to be made by the ageing workforce

(e) Managing diverse career aspirations and paths

(f) Confronting literacy, numeracy and qualifications issues in an international workforce

(g) Managing co-operative working in ethnically diverse teams

EXAMPLE

Kramer, McGraw and Schuler describe the award-winning diversity strategy of USA multi-national, Pitney Bowes.

The vision statement on diversity reads

> Pitney Bowes will provide an open, flexible and supportive work environment that values the uniqueness of each of its employees. Through leadership, communication and training programs, Pitney Bowes will aggressively promote an understanding of individual difference, including (but not limited to) age, gender, race, religion, ethnicity, disability, sexual orientation and family circumstances.

The five goals of the Pitney Bowes strategic plan on diversity and examples of the action the company has taken to achieve these are set out below.

• **Goal 1: Communications**: 'Our vision of diversity and its implications for the organisation will be clearly communicated to all of us'. Action:

BPP

PUBLISHING

- Formed diversity councils throughout the company

- Engaged in widespread promotional activity to promote the diversity agenda

- Development of diversity marketing guidelines for Pitney Bowes products and services.

- **Goal 2: Education and training**: 'We will become sensitive to and demonstrate an understanding of the value of differences through education and training'. Action:

    - Provided multiple training opportunities for the stimulation of diversity awareness.

    - Identified high profile minority customers to address employees on diversity issues.

- **Goal 3: Career development:** 'We will create a culture that enables and encourages the development and upward mobility of all of us'. Action:

    - Introduced new succession planning process based on 'assessing competencies for tomorrow'

    - Published career networking directory

    - Increased opportunities for rotational assignments and cross-training

    - Increased participation in employee mentoring programme.

- **Goal 4: Recruitment and hiring:** 'We will further increase the diversity of our employees so that our organisation reflects the demographic changes in our labour force'. Action:

    - Developed new minority recruitment campaigns including new promotional material and specific recruitment from schools with diverse populations

    - Supported minority scholarships and intern programs

    - Increased funding support for external organisations promoting the diversity agenda

    - Tied management bonuses to diversity recruitment goals.

- **Goal 5: Work/life balance:** 'We will provide a flexible and supportive work environment for employees in achieving a balance of work/life issues'. Action:

    - Developed training to enhance flexible work environment for all employees
    - Expanded child care, elderly care and school referral programs
    - Supported emergency sick child care
    - Conducted employee surveys on work/life balance
    - Piloted telecommuting program.

In order to achieve the five goals of diversity, the business units at Pitney Bowes have tied the concept of diversity to management performance ratings. Part of the incentive compensation plan for the corporate management committee, for instance, includes a diversity component directly linked to the business unit's diversity action plan, and all managers are held accountable for diversity through the performance appraisal system.

Chapter roundup

- Discrimination at work affects a number of different groups, including women and ethnic minorities, the disabled and ex-offenders (who are protected by law) and homosexuals, transsexuals, and older workers (subject to Article 13, to be enacted in UK law by 2006).

- Discrimination can be both direct and indirect, or by implication. In addition, issues such as sexual harassment and the treatment of part-time workers fall within the scope of sexual discrimination.

- Equal opportunities is concerned with access to employment and also the whole employment life cycle: training and development, appraisal, promotion, reward, employment protection and so on.

- Managing diversity means managing people according to the meaningful individual ways in which people differ, instead of crude classifications.

Quick quiz

1   List the major forms of discrimination that may occur.

2   What is meant by:

    (a)   Direct discrimination and
    (b)   Indirect discrimination?

3   What are the three main provisions of the Disability Discrimination Act 1995?

4   What is sexual harassment?

5   What are the main aims of the Opportunity 2000 campaign?

6   Why can't laws change attitudes?

7   What is managing diversity?

Answers to quick quiz

1   Direct and indirect discrimination, against women, ethnic minorities, older workers, disabled workers and ex-offenders.   (see paragraph 1)

2   (a)   Direct discrimination is where one group is treated less favourably than another.

    (b)   Indirect discrimination is where a condition is applied which is not relevant to the job and which serves to disadvantage one group disproportionately.   (para 2.1)

3   (a)   A 'disabled person' is defined as one who has a physical or mental impairment that has a substantial and long-term effect on his/her ability to carry out normal activity.

    (b)   It is unlawful to discriminate against a disabled person in selection, and employment terms and conditions.

    (c)   The employer must make reasonable adjustments to working arrangements and premises which disadvantage the disabled person.   (para 2.4)

4   Sexual harassment is unwanted physical or verbal conduct with sexual connotations.   (para 2.3)

5   To increase the presence of women at all levels within the member
     organisations.   (para 4.1)

6   Because they can only force people to comply (ie act in a certain way).
     They cannot change more deep-seated beliefs and attitudes.   (para 4.2)

7   It is an alternative to equal opportunities which seeks better performance
     from employees based on their individual differences in personality, style
     and needs, rather than cruder distinctions such as gender and ethnicity.
                                                                    (para 4.3)

Answers to Activities

1   Reasons for discrimination against women at work include the following.

   (a)   Social pressures on the woman to bear and rear children, and on
         the man to make a lifetime commitment to paid work as the
         'breadwinner'. Employers assumed - and sometimes still assume -
         that women's paid work would be short term or interrupted, and
         that training and development was therefore hardly worthwhile.

   (b)   The nature of earlier industrial work, which was physically heavy:
         legal restrictions were placed on women's employment in areas
         such as mines, night work in factories etc.

   (c)   Lack of organisation of women at work and influence in trade
         unions (except in industries like textiles), up until 1980s.

   (d)   The reinforcing of segregation at home and at school: for example,
         lack of encouragement to girls to study mathematical and scientific
         subjects.

   (e)   Career ladders which fail to fast-track women. Apprenticeships, for
         example, are rarely held by girls. A woman graduate starting as a
         secretary is less likely to advance than a male graduate who starts as
         a management trainee. In addition, organisations like banks, which
         have traditionally developed staff on the assumption of a lifetime
         career with the one employer, have tended to assume that women
         are unlikely to want a lifetime career. Commitments to geographical
         mobility are similarly assumed to be undesirable to women.

   (f)   Child-bearing and family responsibilities. Part-time work has
         enabled many women to continue in paid employment, but tends to
         apply to jobs which carry little prospect for promotion.

2   This is personal to you. Note, however, how pervasive, subtle and
     influential discrimination can be.

3   Organisations offer a variety of excuses for doing this:

   (a)   Cost (although performance-based pay systems are taking over
         from age-based ones in many companies).

   (b)   Fear that the pay-back period on training will be too short.

   (c)   A young customer base (on the supposition of an affinity between
         people of a common age).

   (d)   A 'young' organisational culture.

   (e)   In IT recruitment, lack of relevant experience among older workers.

   (f)   Stereotypes about older workers' assumed resistance to change,
         inability to learn (and 'unlearn') skills and reduced motivation.

BPP PUBLISHING

NOTES

(g)   'Image' - if this is the right word! Middle managers will often go for very young glamorous secretaries, particularly if they are recruiting themselves.

In addition, one of the principle reasons for discriminatory practices is that they are not currently illegal in the UK.

4   (a)   Advertising a vacancy in a primarily male environment, where women would be less likely to see it.

      (b)   Offering less favourable terms to part-time workers (given that most of them are women).

      (c)   Specifying age limits which would tend to exclude women who had taken time out of work for child-rearing.

      (d)   Asking in selection interviews about plans to have a family (since this might be to the detriment of a woman, but not a man).

5   (a)   Examples of gender exception to the discrimination laws include:

              (i)   Specification of a male artist's model where male anatomy is required

              (ii)   Specification of a female changing room attendant for a women's lingerie shop

              (iii)   Specification of a same-sex employee in a private household, where the degree of contact and knowledge of intimate details may infringe privacy

              (iv)   Specification of women-only access to free breast cancer screening services

              (v)   Specification of women-only access to 'well women' clinics promoting women's health, or open days at college to encourage vocational education

              (vi)   Specifying a male driver in some Muslim countries

      (b)   Examples of ethnic minority exceptions include:

              (i)   A white actress to play the part of Queen Elizabeth

              (ii)   Specifying an Afro-Caribbean model for the advertisement of Afro-Caribbean cosmetic products

              (iii)   Inviting ethnic minority applicants only for a training course

6   (a)   Most people with disabilities have the same skills and abilities to offer as able-bodied people and are effective as employees without the need for any special help.

      (b)   Many other people with disabilities have as much to offer as able-bodied people, given the use of appropriate help which is readily available.

      (c)   When the abilities of workers with disabilities are overlooked, companies are missing out on the contribution of potentially valuable employees.

      (d)   Employers have obligations, along with the rest of the society, to ensure that people with disabilities are treated fairly.

(*Code of Good Practice on the Employment of Disabled People*, Employment Service, 1984)

BPP
PUBLISHING

NOTES

7   (a)   **Advertising**

        (i)   Any wording that suggests preference for a particular group should be avoided (except for genuine occupational qualifications).

        (ii)   Employers must not indicate or imply any 'intention to discriminate'.

        (iii)   Recruitment literature should state that the organisation is an Equal Opportunities Employer.

        (iv)   The placing of advertisements only where the readership is predominantly of one race or sex is construed as indirect discrimination.

    (b)   **Recruitment agencies.** Instructions to an agency should not suggest any preference.

    (c)   **Application forms**. These should include no questions which are not work-related (such as domestic details) and which only one group is asked to complete.

    (d)   **Interviews**

        (i)   Any non-work-related question must be asked of all interviewees, if any. Even then, some types of question may be construed as discriminatory. (You cannot, for example, ask only women about plans to have a family or care of dependants, or ask - in the worst case - about 'the pill' or PMT.)

        (ii)   It may be advisable to have a witness at interviews, or at least to take detailed notes, in the event that a claim of discrimination is made.

    (e)   **Selection tests**. These must be wholly relevant, and should not favour any particular group. (Even personality tests have shown to favour white male applicants.)

    (f)   **Records**. Reasons for rejection, and interview notes, should be carefully recorded, so that in the event of investigation the details will be available.

Assignment 13 (1½ hours)

Glamour Products

You have recently been appointed as Personnel and Training Officer at Glamour Products, which employs 250 staff manufacturing cosmetics at its plant in the West Midlands. Your post is a new initiative for this very 'traditional' company, and it is your first job since leaving university and qualifying as Grad.CIPD. so you are very much 'on probation'.

Previously, staff management was the responsibility of line managers and supervisors, who seem to resent your appointment. You do have the goodwill of the Managing Director, however, who has sent the following memorandum to you. You found it in your post this morning.

MEMO

To: P Jones (Personnel and Training Officer)
From: G Bull (Managing Director)
Date: 1 June 20XX
Re: **Equal Opportunities Training**

Please arrange a short training course within the next two weeks on equal opportunities for all our 18 supervisors. Book the Works Canteen.

As you've probably discovered, they are a good bunch of blokes, but a bit conservative. Most of them have worked for us for most of their lives. But the recent complaints we've been receiving alleging racial discrimination are embarrassing, and have given rise to some adverse publicity in the local press, probably whipped up by troublemakers.

Relations with the ethnic minority workforce have been pretty good until recently, so we don't need the paraphernalia of an Equal Opportunities policy etc. But Patel's IT case alleging unfair dismissal on grounds of race - though preposterous - is bad news, not least because it gives the Union ammunition to fire at us, after we defeated them over pay last year. I want to get the shop stewards off our backs by showing we're putting a stop to any alleged race problems.

The main objectives of the course must be to get the supervisors to realise they've got to be more diplomatic, and obey the letter of the law. Make it clear to them they can't use 'racist' language, even in light-hearted banter.

I'll leave this with you, but I want a draft programme for approval quickly. I'll be at HQ in Dagenham all this week. Fax your proposals to me by Thursday, with any comments you want to make.

Task

Draft your reply to the Managing Director's memo.

Chapter 14 :
WELFARE PROVISION

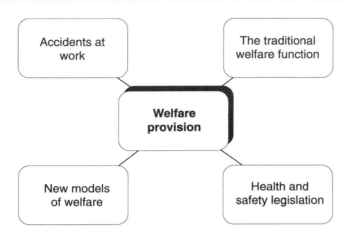

Introduction

Health, safety and well-being at work may be considered important for several reasons.

(a)   Employees should be protected from needless pain and suffering (obvious - we hope!)

(b)   Employers have legal obligations to take reasonable measures to protect the health and safety of their employees.

(c)   Accidents, illness and other causes of employee absence and/or impaired performance cost the employer money.

(d)   A business's image in the market place (to which it sells goods and services and from which it recruits labour and purchases other resources) may suffer if its health and safety record is bad.

This chapter looks at the law and best practice relating to health and safety at work, as well as broader welfare issues.

Your objectives

In this chapter you will learn about the following:

(a)   The traditional welfare function and the models of welfare within organisations

(b)   The implications of policy and practices of a welfare provision within an organisation

(c)   How to prepare a programme to introduce new welfare provision within a given organisation

(d)   How UK organisations have modified health and safety practice in response to EU employment legislation

1 THE TRADITIONAL WELFARE FUNCTION

1.1 What is welfare

Definition

> **Welfare** is 'a state of faring or doing well, freedom from calamity, enjoyment of health'. In HRM terms, this implies 'efforts to improve conditions of living for a group of employees or workers'.

In Chapter 1 of this Course Book, we described how the personnel/HR function grew out of industrial welfare work.

There is quite a long history in the UK of employers providing welfare to their employees. The Quaker Cadbury family used to provide housing for its employees at Bourneville. Similarly, coal mining employers, such as the mine owners of Lanarkshire, provided cottages for miners and their families, although they did not assist retired miners or bereaved families of miners. Other employers provided company stores, and schools for educating employees' children.

The 'welfare tradition' of HR was basically at the extreme of 'soft' HRM:

(a) Focused primarily on alleviating employee problems, such as illness, injury, bereavement or financial hardship, through welfare benefits and services such as:

    (i) Counselling/advice on work-related, personal or domestic issues

    (ii) Sick club, benevolent and savings schemes

    (iii) Pension or superannuation funds and retirement grants

    (iv) The granting of loans

    (v) Assistance with transport, housing, schooling or other difficulties

    (vi) Legal aid

    (vii) Training and counselling for redundancy and retirement

    (viii) Providing convalescence facilities or pensions for employees affected by long-term illness or injury (especially if work-related)

    (ix) Relocation assistance for employees posted to other sites

(b) Relatively independent of the business's management; counsellors, welfare visitors, pension/legal advisers and so on were usually contracted or employed by the organisation with the employee as end-user client. Professional rules of confidentiality prevented detailed disclosure of the process or results of this work, other than in a generalised or aggregated manner: reporting to management on trends, common problems identified and so on

(c) Based on non-strategic rationales, which were either:

    (i) Legalistic/reactive: complying with minimal standards required by law, regulation and labour demands or

    (ii) Paternalistic: socially responsible but also reforming philanthropy, designed to encourage improvement in the moral and social behaviour of workers (as defined by the philanthropist's religious and cultural beliefs

(d) Employers might want to provide welfare:

    (i)   Because of a genuine concern for the lives of their employees

    (ii)   To improve the morale and loyalty of employees or

    (iii)   Because other companies and organisations are offering similar services/benefits, and they need to do the same in order to attract and retain the calibre of staff they require

FOR DISCUSSION

'Suppose a 20-year old person enters the company at £10,000 per year, works there for 30 years, receives an eight percent per year increase, retires at half salary and lives to the age of 75. That person represents a £2.5 million investment to the company and the number just goes up from there. For a person who reaches top management, the figure can easily hit five to ten times that figure.

If that corporation had a machine worth this kind of money, they'd build a fence around it, polish it, show it off and have someone specially trained to provide whatever it needed to remain productive. We really think people need to be treated with the same level of respect for the investment they represent.

Administrator, October 1985

Is this a 'soft' or a 'hard' HRM view? Is it a convincing argument for welfare?

A case can, however, be made **against** the provision of discretionary welfare.

    (i)   Welfare is provided for by the state: why should other organisations duplicate services?

    (ii)   Welfare is irrelevant or even counter to the strategic objectives of the business (notably, profit maximisation).

    (iii)   Welfare services have not been shown to increase loyalty or motivation: they are largely taken for granted, and as such are more likely to be a source of disappointment and dissatisfaction at any shortcomings than a source of satisfaction. Even gratitude/or appreciation is not a prime motivator. Any positive effects are hard to measure: the whole concept is relentlessly 'soft'.

    (iv)   The non-work affairs and interests of employees are not the business of employers. If this attitude prevails in some situations (so that if the employee commits an offence outside work, this is not sufficient grounds for dismissal) it should prevail in others.

(e) Business organisations are not equipped to deal with welfare issues. Line managers are not trained to do so, and cannot devote sufficient time to follow-up. Centralising welfare responsibilities places a burden on HR specialists who are struggling to get away from the 'nursemaid' role and into strategic management.

The personnel management fraternity has spent many years trying to shake off its association with what it, and others, like to think of as at best peripheral and at worst redundant welfare activities

(Armstrong)

The case **for** welfare rests mainly on the concept of the social responsibility of organisations towards their employees. Martin (*Welfare at Work*) suggested that:

Staff spend at least half their waking time at work or in getting to it or leaving it. They know they contribute to the organisation when they are reasonably free from worry, and they feel, perhaps inarticulately, that when they are in trouble they are due to get something back from the organisation. People are entitled to be treated as full human beings with personal needs, hopes and anxieties; they are employed as **people**, they bring themselves to work, not just their hands, and they cannot readily leave their troubles at home.

In addition, it may be noted that employees 'cannot ... leave their troubles at home'. Whether a problem is work-related (sickness from exposure to workplace chemicals, stress from shift-working or whatever) or non-work-related (relationship breakdown, alcohol abuse, bereavement), it will inevitably impact on the employee's 'steady-state' performance. Once performance is affected, the employee's physical or mental state arguably becomes the 'business' of his or her employers.

Welfare may not demonstrably have a **positive** effect on morale and productivity - but anxiety, stress and distress invariably have a **negative** effect which should be alleviated where possible in the interests of effectiveness. In other words, welfare is a hygiene factor.

The more recent orientation of HRM towards welfare is that the health of the individual (in the broadest sense) represents the health of the organisation: if employees can be proactively helped not just to avoid accidents and illnesses, but to become more resilient to stress, healthier, physically fitter, mentally more flexible, emotionally more stable, they are more likely to perform at a consistent and high level on behalf of the organisation. We will examine this orientation and its implications in Section 3 below. Here, we will look at some of the concerns of traditional welfare.

1.2 Occupational health

Occupational health programmes are concerned largely with the effects of the working environment on workers. This may involve:

(a) Identifying substances, conditions or processes which are actually or potentially hazardous, and in what circumstances

(b) Identifying the effect of methods and processes of work on the human body and mind

(c) Exercising control over the working environment and substances used in the course of work, so as to minimise risk

Thus, occupational health is concerned with toxic substances (such as lead oxide, chlorine, asbestos, and radiation) and with protective measures against all of these, as well as less obvious sources of ill health at work, including noise, fatigue and physical and mental stress (excessive demands on the body and mind). Increasingly, it is also concerned with personal substance abuse (such as smoking and alcoholism) and other fitness and mental well-being factors that might have a direct or indirect affect on the workplace and work performance. We will discuss these factors in Section 3 below.

Activity 1	**(30 minutes)**

What aspects of your work or study environment (if any) do you think are:

(a)   A hindrance to your work?
(b)   A source of stress or dissatisfaction?
(c)   A hazard to your health?

Some of the key 'traditional' causes of ill-health at work, and the regulations applying to them, are as follows:

(a)   **Noise**

Industrial hearing impairment has long been recognised as a problem for factory workers and machine operators, but the stressful and distracting effects of noise have more recently been identified. Continuous loud noise can be protected against by sound-proofing and personal ear protection equipment for affected employees. Sharp intermittent noises, elusive meaningful noises (such as soft speech) and variations in noise level can be irritating and cause 'mental blinking', which may in turn be a source of accidents as well as impaired performance. Sound-proofing (eg acoustic hoods over noisy office printers) and broadcast 'white noise' (soft, constant, featureless sound) are often used in office environments to reduce noise irritation. Where the risks are high, employees should be given regular hearing checks. (Noise at Work Regulation 1989.)

(b)   **General environmental 'hygiene'**

The EU workplace directive provided for many specific controls on the work environment, most of which were already part of UK law. The Workplace (Health, Safety and Welfare) Regulations 1992 provides for health and hygiene in areas such as the following:

(i)   **Ventilation**. Air should be fresh or purified.

(ii)   **Temperature** levels must be 'reasonable' inside buildings during working hours: not less than 16°C where people are seated, or 13°C if moving about.

(iii) **Lighting** should be suitable and sufficient, and natural if practicable. Windows should be clear and unobstructed.

(iv)   **Cleaning and decoration**. Premises must be kept clean.

(v)   **Space**. Each person should have at least 11 cubic metres of space.

(vi)   **Sanitary conveniences and washing facilities** must be suitable and sufficient: properly ventilated and lit, properly cleaned, separate for men and women - and enough of them to avoid undue delay!

(vii) **Drinking water** should be available in adequate supply, with suitable drinking vessels.c

(viii) **Rest facilities and eating facilities** must be provided unless the employees' work stations are suitable.

(ix)   **First aid** equipment should be provided, under the charge of a responsible person who should be trained in first aid (150+ employees). The Health and Safety (First Aid) Regulations 1981 require employers to provide adequate equipment, facilities and personnel to enable first aid to be given to employees if they are injured or become ill at work.

(c)   Hazardous substances and work-related diseases

Procedures will need to be in place for: warning signs and labels identifying toxic or hazardous chemicals and other substances; training of staff in handling and storing substances and in first aid treatment and reporting mechanisms in the event of exposure; secure storage of substances; protective clothing and equipment for handling substances and so on. (Control of Substances Hazardous to Health Regulations 1994.) Hazards include not only burning, blinding, respiratory dysfunction, poisoning and other 'immediate' effects of substances, but also **work-related diseases**.

Several federal agencies in the USA have studied the workplace environment and identified the following hazards: arsenic, asbestos, benzene, coal dust, cotton dust, lead, radiation and vinyl chloride. These

329

have been linked to various cancers, leukaemia, lung diseases, central nervous system disorders and reproductive disorders (sterility, miscarriage, birth defects).

(d)   Manual handling operations

Back injuries due to the incorrect lifting and carrying of heavy objects accounts for more than a quarter of the accidents reported each year in the UK. Employers should, as far as is reasonably practical, avoid the need for employees to undertake risky manual handling activity. All remaining operations must be assessed, and steps taken to reduce risks to the lowest level reasonably practicable: providing properly maintained equipment and procedures (back braces, conveyer belts etc) and training in their use. Employees must report any injury or prior condition that may affect their ability to safely undertake manual handling operations. (Manual Handling Operations Regulations 1992.)

(e)   Use of computer workstations

The workstation has become one of the potentially toxic hazards of the workplace. If you have ever worked for a long period at a VDU you may personally have experienced some discomfort: back ache, stiffness, eye-strain, muscular disorders and so on are common effects. Referred to collectively as 'Repetitive Strain Injury' or RSI, they now account for more than half of all work-related injuries in the USA and have reached epidemic proportions in Australia. Problems are due both to the ergonomics of the workstation and to working practices: poor posture, insufficient breaks for movement and so on. The Health and Safety (Display Screen Equipment) Regulations 1992 provide for the adaptation of computer workstations and equipment so that: VDU screens do not flicker, are free from glare and are able to swivel and tilt; radiation is reduced to negligible levels; and desk, chair and keyboard arrangement allows for forearm rest and adjustment for improved posture. Additional policies should emphasise education in posture, stretching exercises and so on, and the provision of regular work breaks or changes in activity for VDU users.

Definition

> **Repetitive strain injury** (RSI) is the term for various complaints associated with sustained computer use, frequently including back ache, eye strain and stiffness or muscular problems of the neck, shoulders, hand or arms.

(f)   **Pregnancy/maternity**

Pregnant women, those who have recently given birth and those who are breastfeeding are traditionally recognised as a special at-risk group by occupational health regulation and policy. The EC directive on pregnancy and maternity was incorporated into the Management of Health and Safety at Work (Amendment) Regulations 1994.

Provisions include the following.

(i)   Every employer must undertake a **risk assessment**, if the workforce includes women of child-bearing age (c.20-35), and if the work is of a kind that could involve risk to women. (Risks already specifically mentioned in legislation, regulations and codes include working with lead, lifting objects, excessive use of VDUs, exposure to radiation, changes in air pressure and so on.) Heat, stress, exhaustion and mental stress are also potential hazards.

(ii) The work of pregnant women must be adjusted to remove the risk. This may involve transferring night workers to day work, removing the need to lift heavy objects, or reducing travel in the job.

(iii) If the work hours or conditions cannot be made safer, alternative safer work must be offered.

(iv) If no safer alternative work exists, the woman must be suspended on full terms and conditions, for the period of risk.

(v) The woman has the right to refuse night work on medical grounds.

Activity 2   **(30 minutes)**

Reassess your appraisal of the health of your workplace in answer to Activity 1 above, in the light of the specific issues and provisions discussed. Were any of the health hazards mentioned new to you - or easily overlooked in the course of work? If so, what does this say about the need for occupational health policies?

There will be several elements to occupational health policy in any given area.

(a) Hazard minimisation: removing hazards where possible. Assessing and reducing employees' exposure to risk.

(b) Information about hazards: education, warning signs and labels, consultation with employees and safety experts.

(c) Equipment; protective clothing, ergonomically-designed work-stations, sound-proofing, safety equipment, maintenance.

(d) Training in the use of equipment: systems and procedures for safe and healthy working, compulsory use of safety/protective equipment and clothing.

(e) Employee responsibilities: to co-operate with health and safety policies, use systems responsibly, inform the employer of conditions placing them at risk, inform the employer or health and safety officer of identified hazards.

(f) Monitoring of occupational health: reporting of illness and injury, identification of emerging health issues.

'Ill-health' and 'injury' are obviously closely related, and occupational health policies would consider issues relating to both. We will consider accidents as a particular workplace risk, in Section 2 of this chapter.

1.3 Absenteeism and employee absence

Employee absence

An article in *Chartered Secretary* (September 1997) suggested that 'absence from work is the single most important contributor to lost production'. CBI surveys suggest that 187 million working days were lost in 1996, with an average 8.4 days' absence for sickness per employee. Ill-health and injury are major causes of long- and short-term employee absence from work.

Only 14% of respondents to the CBI survey believed that all short-term sickness absence was genuine. There has been an increase in stress-related illnesses, and short-term absence due to ill health shows an upward trend in non-manual workers, especially those in government agencies. This suggests that absence may also be a cultural issue, influenced by factors such as management practices, work organisation, job design, motivation and employee relations. Since **statutory sick pay** is payable for the first eight weeks of absence through illness (reclaimed by the employer from national insurance payments), it has been claimed that workers frequently see sickness absence as a paid entitlement to be 'used up' in much the same way as holiday entitlement. (Some employment contracts now include clauses which provide that sick pay is to be treated as a 'loan' to employees, which is repayable to the employer if the employee recovers damages from a third party for any related accident or injury).

Some other reasons for absence are covered by employment protection legislation, such as pregnancy, redundancy preparation and trade union activities.

The Employment Relations Act 1999 provides for:

(a) 'Ordinary' maternity leave (18 weeks, irrespective of length of service), without loss of entitlement to the accrual of seniority and pension rights. Maternity leave is compulsory in the two-week period following the birth (four weeks, for factory workers).

(b) 'Additional' maternity leave (a further 29 weeks, after a qualifying period of one year's service) during which seniority may be suspended, but pension rights may be accrued if the woman is receiving maternity pay from the employer).

(c) Mothers, fathers and adoptive parents with one year's continuous service will have the right to 13 weeks' unpaid leave during a child's first five years in order to care for that child. It applies to children born after 15 December 1999. This criterion is being challenged by employment lawyers as discriminatory against parents who have children under 5 before that date. The time off in any one year is limited to four weeks, and leave has to be taken in blocks of at least one week.

(d) Prospective fathers' right to unpaid leave to be present at the birth of their child (as part of the paternity leave).

(e) Right of return, following maternity and paternity leave, to the same job on equivalent terms, provided that written notice of intention to return has been given prior to the absence.

(f) 'Reasonable' time off, unpaid, to deal with 'family emergencies' involving a dependent, including sickness, accident, death, serious problems at a child's school and so on.

Absence procedure

People Management (6/5/99) suggests that an absence procedure should do the following.

(a) Require all employees absent with prior consent to complete an absence form on their return to work.

(b) Discuss absences with employees and keep in touch with them, alerting them to the possibility of dismissal where appropriate. Meetings should be recorded and employees informed in writing.

(c) Ensure access to medical information and check this is up to date, prior to any disciplinary action being considered.

(d) Look for suitable work within the organisation for employees no longer able to perform their duties.

(e) Check employees' entitlements to relevant benefits.

EXAMPLE

The state government of New South Wales, Australia, has found a radical way of cutting 'sickies' (sick days) among ferry deckhands, with a deal which obliges fellow team-members to work extra shifts - unpaid - to cover for absent colleagues! Introduced as part of a wages package, the agreement is based on the 'mateship concept', applying peer pressure within the team. A recent report by Morgan and Banks revealed that most Australians took an average of six days' sick leave a year - with 12.4% admitting none of their 'sickies' were genuine! The new State Transit deal, however, has seen the average number of sick days per employee per year plunge from 13.13 to 5.56.

(Australian *Daily Telegraph*, 6/9/99)

'Absence' raises issues such as ill-health and injury, domestic problems and pregnancy. What might the organisation do to help its employees in such times?

1.4 Welfare benefits and services

We have already mentioned some of the welfare benefits and services traditionally offered to employees (see paragraph 1.1 above).

Some of the key issues (from the traditional welfare perspective) are as follows.

(a) **Pension schemes**

Many firms set up occupational pension schemes for their employees, either as:

(i) Self-administered funds, where the firms' contributions (and the employees', if it is a contributing pension scheme) are invested by fund managers and controlled by trustees or

(ii) Life office schemes, conducted through a contract with a life assurance office

Tight controls have been placed over the operation of pension funds, particularly with regard to the accountability of trustees, fund managers, auditors and advisers. Employees in occupational schemes which are contracted out of the State Earnings-Related Pension Scheme (SERPS) lose their future entitlements under the state scheme: occupational schemes are required to ensure that they provide adequate benefits, however, and are in practice much more generous than the state scheme.

(b) **Sick pay and procedures**

Statutory Sick Pay is paid under the Social Security and Housing Benefit Act 1982. It is related to annually-reviewed earnings bands, and is payable for eight weeks in any tax year, or in any single spell of illness. Payment is made only on the fourth successive qualifying day of illness, unless illnesses are separated by less than 14 days.

DSS advice and literature (the *Employers' Guide to Sick Pay*) is available to help in the details of administering the scheme.

For motivational reasons, claims of sickness might be taken on trust as far as possible (unless there is positive proof of malingering). An illness or

BPP PUBLISHING

diagnosis may be confirmed by referring the employee to a company-approved doctor - but disciplinary action cannot be taken against an employee who refuses to be examined (unless there is a contractual agreement).

A common sickness procedure would require the employee to:

(i) Notify the office as soon as possible on the first day of absence

(ii) Give as much information as possible about the nature and likely duration of the illness

(iii) Record the illness absence, on return to work

(iv) Arrange for a medical certificate to be sent to the office for absences of seven days or more

(v) Notify management if the illness is infectious or dangerous (since other staff may need to be warned or checked and quarantined)

Welfare calls and visits may also be made during prolonged absence, in order to identify financial or practical help that may be offered, alleviate anxiety, offer counselling and so on.

(c) **Maternity**

Maternity leave and health and safety provisions for pregnant workers have already been discussed above.

Statutory maternity pay is payable at any time from the 11th week before the estimated week of confinement (EWC), for 18 weeks. If a woman is absent with a pregnancy-related illness, statutory (or occupational) sick pay will apply until the 6th week before the EWC, at which time statutory maternity pay is triggered. Women with less than 26 weeks' continuous service are not eligible for payment, but may receive a maternity allowance from the DSS.

(d) **Domestic problems**

Situations such as marital breakdown or bereavement are essentially private, but their effects are likely to carry over into the workplace. The Employment Relations Act 1999 provides for what used to be called 'compassionate leave' (unpaid) to deal with 'family emergencies', but organisations may develop a policy on:

(i) What constitutes 'reasonable' time off
(ii) Whether time off will be paid to some degree
(iii) Whether additional welfare interventions will be offered

Welfare services may include: access to the firm's own counsellors or referral to other support organisations; help with financial, legal and funeral arrangements arising from bereavement; and so on.

(e) **Retirement/redundancy**

As discussed in Chapter 10, retirement and redundancy may be regarded as major adjustment crises in the lives of employees, and a variety of counselling, training and other services may be offered.

Activity 3   **(45 minutes)**

Does your college or workplace have provision for welfare services? What are they? How well publicised are they? Ask for information, if it is not available in the Student/Employee Handbook or on notice boards. List the issues which are highlighted by the counselling or welfare programme

We will now look at a major health and safety issue: workplace accidents.

2   ACCIDENTS AT WORK

2.1   Incidence of industrial accident

Newspapers frequently quote statistics showing large numbers of employee hours lost through accident, and the associated cost to businesses. However, it should be noted that:

(a)   Accident rates vary substantially by industry. (Firms in the construction and manufacturing industries have higher rates than service firms, for example.)

(b)   Small and large organisations have lower incidence rates than medium-sized organisations (perhaps because supervision is closer in small organisations and investment in safety/accident prevention staff and systems is greater in large ones).

(c)   Working conditions (outdoor v indoor) and tools and technology (heavy machinery v PC) have the greatest impact on incident rates, followed by ...

(d)   The 'accident proneness' of individual workers. There are suggestions that some people are more prone to accidents than others (due to poor vision, stress, depression, alertness, immaturity and so on). However, accident proneness is also related to the working patterns, responsibility and safety-awareness of individual employees: horseplay, practical jokes, cutting corners on safety measures and so on are frequent causes of accident.

(e)   Death by homicide is, in fact, the biggest cause of death in the workplace in the USA (Filipczale, 1993).

Activity 4   **(10 minutes)**

A scene from everyday life is shown below. Note down anything that strikes you as being dangerous about this working environment.

2.2 Workplace hazards

Apart from obviously dangerous equipment in factories, construction sites and even offices, there are many hazards to be found in the modern working environment. Many accidents could be avoided by the simple application of common sense and consideration by employer and employee, and by safety consciousness encouraged or enforced by a widely acceptable and well published **safety policy**.

2.3 Cost of accidents

The **cost** of accidents to the employer consists of:

(a) Time lost by the injured employee

(b) Time lost by other employees whose work is interrupted by the accident

(c) Time lost by supervision, management and technical staff as a result of the accident

(d) A proportion of the cost of first aid materials, or even medical staff

(e) The cost of disruption to operations at work

(f) The cost of any damage and repairs and modification to the equipment

(g) The cost of any compensation payments or fines resulting from legal action

(h) The costs associated with increased insurance premiums

(i) Reduced output from the injured employee on return to work

(j) The cost of possible reduced morale, increased absenteeism, increased labour turnover among employees

(k) The cost of recruiting and training a replacement for the injured worker

An employer may also be liable to an employee in tort if the employee is injured as a result of either:

NOTES

(a) The employer's failure to take reasonable care in providing safe premises and plant, a safe system of work and competent fellow employees, or

(b) The employer's breach of a statutory duty - say, to fence dangerous machinery. Although the injured employee's damages may be reduced if the injury was partly a consequence of his/her own contributory negligence, due allowance is made for ordinary human failings, such as inattentiveness, tiredness and so on.

2.4 Accident prevention

The prevention of illness or accidents requires efforts on the part of employers, including workplace design, communication of health and safety policies and procedures, training and so on. Some of the steps which might be taken to reduce the frequency and severity of accidents are as follows.

(a) Developing safety awareness among staff and workers and encouraging departmental pride in a good safety record.

(b) Developing effective consultative participation between management, workers and unions so that safety and health rules can be accepted and followed.

(c) Giving adequate instruction in safety rules and measures as part of the training of new and transferred workers, or where working methods or speeds of operation are changed.

(d) Materials handling, a major cause of accidents, should be minimised and designed as far as possible for safe working and operation.

(e) Ensuring a satisfactory standard from the safety angle for both basic plant and auxiliary fittings such as guards and other devices.

(f) Good maintenance - apart from making sound job repairs, temporary expedients to keep production going should not prejudice safety.

(g) In general, the appropriate code of practice for the industry/work environment should be implemented in full.

2.5 Accident reporting

Safety inspections should be carried out to locate and define faults in the system that allows accidents to occur. They may be carried out as a comprehensive audit, working through a checklist; or by using random spot checks, regular checks of particular risk points, or statutory inspections of particular areas, such as lifts, hoists, boilers or pipe-lines. It is essential that checklists used in the inspection process should identify corrective action to be taken, and allocate responsibility for that action. There should be reporting systems and control procedures to ensure that inspections are taking place and that findings are being acted on.

An accident report is a management tool, designed to:

(a) Identify problems and

(b) Indicate corrective action

Recurring accidents may suggest the need for special investigation, but only more serious incidents will have to be followed-up in depth. Follow-up should be clearly aimed at preventing recurrence - not placing blame.

The drawing below shows the format of a **typical accident book,** which should by law be kept by any organisation which employs more than 10 people. (The one used by your organisation may be laid out differently, or it might consist of loose-leaf sheets.)

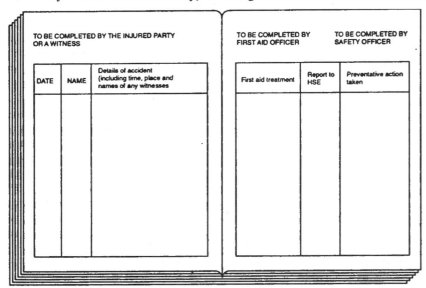

The **Reporting of Injuries, Diseases and Dangerous Occurrences Regulations 1995 (RIDDOR 95)** require employers to do the following.

(a) Notify the environmental health authority or the Health and Safety Executive **immediately** if one of the following occurs.

    (i) There is an accident connected with work and either an employee or self-employed person working on the premises is killed or suffers a major injury (including as a result of physical violence) or a member of the public is killed or taken to hospital.

    (ii) There is a dangerous occurrence.

(b) Send a completed **Accident report form** (see next page) to do the following.

    (i) Confirm within ten days a telephone report of an accident or dangerous occurrence (as described in (a) above).

    (ii) Notify, within ten days of the accident, any injury which stops someone doing their normal job for more than three days.

    (iii) Report certain work-related diseases.

Definitions

Major injuries include things like fractures other than to fingers, thumbs or toes, amputation, temporary or permanent loss of sight and any other injury which results in the person being admitted to hospital for more than 24 hours.

Dangerous occurrences are 'near misses' that might well have caused major injuries. They include the collapse of a load bearing part of a lift, electrical short circuit or overload causing fire or explosion, the malfunction of breathing apparatus while in use or during testing immediately before use, and many others.

Notifiable diseases include certain poisonings, occupational asthma, asbestos, hepatitis and many others.

The standard for the notification of injuries and dangerous occurrences is reproduced below.

Health and Safety at Work etc Act 1974
The Reporting of Injuries, Diseases and Dangerous Occurrences Regulations 1995

HSE
Health & Safety
Executive

Report of an injury or dangerous occurrence

Filling in this form
This form must be filled in by an employer or other responsible person.

Part A

About you
1 What is your full name?

2 What is your job title?

3 What is your telephone number?

About your organisation
4 What is the name of your organisation?

5 What is its address and postcode?

6 What type of work does your organisation do?

Part B

About the incident
1 On what date did the incident happen?

  / /

2 At what time did the incident happen?
(Please use the 24-hour clock eg 0600)

3 Did the incident happen at the above address?

Yes ☐ Go to question 4

No ☐ Where did the incident happen?

☐ elsewhere in your organisation - give the name, address and postcode

☐ at someone else's premises - give the name, address and postcode

☐ in a public place - give the details of where it happened

If you do not know the postcode, what is the name of the local authority?

4 In which department, or where on the premises, did the incident happen?

Part C

About the injured person
If you are reporting a dangerous occurrence, go to Part F.
If more than one person was injured in the same incident, please attach the details asked for in Part C and Part D for each injured person.

1 What is their full name?

2 What is their home address and postcode?

3 What is their home phone number?

4 How old are they?

5 Are they
☐ male?
☐ female?

6 What is their job title?

7 Was the injured person (tick only one box)
☐ one of your employees?

☐ on a training scheme? Give details:

☐ on work experience?

☐ employed by someone else? Give details of the employer:

☐ self-employed and at work?

☐ a member of the public?

Part D

About the injury
1 What was the injury? (eg fracture, laceration)

2 What part of the body was injured?

---

3 Was the injury (tick the one box that applies)

☐ a fatality?

☐ a major injury or condition? (see accompanying notes)

☐ an injury to an employee or self-employed person which prevented them doing their normal work for more than 3 days?

☐ an injury to a member of the public which meant they had to be taken from the scene of the accident to a hospital for treatment?

4 Did the injured person (tick all the boxes that apply)

☐ became unconscious?

☐ need resuscitation?

☐ remain in hospital for more than 24 hours?

☐ none of the above?

Part E

About the kind of accident

Please tick the one box that best describes what happened, then go to part G.

☐ Contact with moving machinery or material being machined

☐ Hit by a moving, flying or falling object

☐ Hit by a moving vehicle

☐ Hit by something fixed or stationary

☐ Injured while handling, lifting or carrying

☐ Slipped, tripped or fell on the same level

☐ Fell from a height
How high was the fall?

☐ [_____] metres

☐ Trapped by something collapsing

☐ Drowned or asphyxiated

☐ Exposed to, or in contact with, a harmful substance

☐ Exposed to fire

☐ Exposed to an explosion

☐ Contact with electricity or an electrical discharge

☐ Injured by an animal

☐ Physically assaulted by a person

☐ Another kind of accident (describe it in part G)

Part F

Dangerous occurrences

Enter the number of the dangerous occurrence you are reporting. (The numbers are given in the Regulations and in the notes which accompany this form.)

[_____]

Part G

Describing what happened

Give as much detail as you can. For instance
- the name of any substance involved
- the name and type of any machinery involved
- the events that led to the incident
- the part played by any people.

If it was a personal injury, give details of what the person was doing. Describe any action that has since been taken to prevent a similar incident. Use a separate piece of paper if you need to.

[_____]

☐☐☐☐ [_____]

Part H

Your signature

[_____]

Date

[___] / [___] / [___]

Where to send the form
Please send it to the Enforcing Authority for the place where it happened. If you do not know the Enforcing Authority, send it to the nearest HSE office.

For official use

Client number	Location number	Event number	
[_____]	[_____]	[_____]	☐ INV REP ☐ Y ☐ N

Activity 5   (30 minutes)

Invent (or *carefully* role-play) your own scenario for a typical (or unusual) workplace accident causing injury. Invent as many relevant details as you can. Now complete the specimen RIDDOR report reproduced here.

Health and Safety at Work etc Act 1974
The Reporting of Injuries, Diseases and Dangerous Occurrences Regulations 1995

HSE
Health & Safety
Executive

Report of an injury or dangerous occurrence

Filling in this form
This form must be filled in by an employer or other responsible person.

Part A

About you
1 What is your full name?

2 What is your job title?

3 What is your telephone number?

About your organisation
4 What is the name of your organisation?

5 What is its address and postcode?

6 What type of work does your organisation do?

Part B

About the incident
1 On what date did the incident happen?

/   /

2 At what time did the incident happen?
(Please use the 24-hour clock eg 0600)

3 Did the incident happen at the above address?

Yes ☐ Go to question 4

No ☐ Where did the incident happen?

☐ elsewhere in your organisation - give the name, address and postcode

☐ at someone else's premises - give the name, address and postcode

☐ in a public place - give the details of where it happened

If you do not know the postcode, what is the name of the local authority?

4 In which department, or where on the premises, did the incident happen?

Part C

About the injured person
If you are reporting a dangerous occurrence, go to Part F.
If more than one person was injured in the same incident, please attach the details asked for in Part C and Part D for each injured person.
1 What is their full name?

2 What is their home address and postcode?

3 What is their home phone number?

4 How old are they?

5 Are they
☐ male?
☐ female?

6 What is their job title?
☐☐☐

7 Was the injured person (tick only one box)
☐ one of your employees?
☐ on a training scheme? Give details:

☐ on work experience?
☐ employed by someone else? Give details of the employer:

☐ self-employed and at work?
☐ a member of the public?

Part D

About the injury
1 What was the injury? (eg fracture, laceration)
☐☐

2 What part of the body was injured?
☐☐

BPP
PUBLISHING

3 Was the injury (tick the one box that applies)

☐ a fatality?

☐ a major injury or condition? (see accompanying notes)

☐ an injury to an employee or self-employed person which prevented them doing their normal work for more than 3 days?

☐ an injury to a member of the public which meant they had to be taken from the scene of the accident to a hospital for treatment?

4 Did the injured person (tick all the boxes that apply)

☐ became unconscious?

☐ need resuscitation?

☐ remain in hospital for more than 24 hours?

☐ none of the above?

Part E

About the kind of accident
Please tick the one box that best describes what happened, then go to part G.

☐ Contact with moving machinery or material being machined

☐ Hit by a moving, flying or falling object

☐ Hit by a moving vehicle

☐ Hit by something fixed or stationary

☐ Injured while handling, lifting or carrying

☐ Slipped, tripped or fell on the same level

☐ Fell from a height
How high was the fall?

☐ [metres]

☐ Trapped by something collapsing

☐ Drowned or asphyxiated

☐ Exposed to, or in contact with, a harmful substance

☐ Exposed to fire

☐ Exposed to an explosion

☐ Contact with electricity or an electrical discharge

☐ Injured by an animal

☐ Physically assaulted by a person

☐ Another kind of accident (describe it in part G)

Part F

Dangerous occurrences
Enter the number of the dangerous occurrence you are reporting. (The numbers are given in the Regulations and in the notes which accompany this form.)

[ ]

Part G

Describing what happened
Give as much detail as you can. For instance
• the name of any substance involved
• the name and type of any machinery involved
• the events that led to the incident
• the part played by any people.
If it was a personal injury, give details of what the person was doing. Describe any action that has since been taken to prevent a similar incident. Use a separate piece of paper if you need to.

[   ]

☐☐☐☐ [   ]

Part H

Your signature

[   ]

Date

[/   /   ]

Where to send the form
Please send it to the Enforcing Authority for the place where it happened. If you do not know the Enforcing Authority, send it to the nearest HSE office.

For official use
Client number   Location number   Event number
[   ]   [   ]   [   ]   ☐ INV   REP ☐ Y ☐ N

We will now look at some of the main legislation on Health and Safety at work. Much of it is refreshingly practical, with lots of measures to be taken and procedures to be put in place: we will only be able to summarise. Like other legal provisions we have discussed in this Course Book, the 'law is a floor': remember that these are minimum standards - not 'best practice'!

3 HEALTH AND SAFETY LEGISLATION

3.1 The legal framework

In 1972, a Royal Commission on Safety and Health at Work reported that unnecessarily large numbers of days are lost each year through industrial accidents, injuries and diseases, because of the 'attitudes, capabilities and performance of people and the efficiency of the organisational systems within which they work'. Since then, major legislation has been brought into effect in the UK, most notably:

(a)   Health and Safety at Work Act 1974

(b)   The regulations introduced in January 1993 implementing EU directives on Health and Safety

Some of the most important regulations are as follows.

- The Reporting of Injuries, Diseases and Dangerous Occurrences Regulations 1995

- The Health and Safety (First Aid) Regulations 1981

- The Noise at Work Regulations 1989

- The Control of Substances Hazardous to Health Regulations 1994

- The Manual Handling Operations Regulations 1992

- The Workplace (Health, Safety and Welfare, Regulations 1992

- The Provision and Use of Work Equipment Regulations 1992

- The Health and Safety (Display Screen Equipment) Regulations 1992

- Management of Health and Safety at Work Regulations 1992

- The Personal Protective Equipment at Work Regulations 1992

We will not be able to cover their provisions in detail here. Just be aware that the framework for personnel policy in the area of health and safety is extensive and detailed!

3.2 The Health and Safety at Work Act 1974

In the UK, the Health and Safety at Work Act 1974 provides for the introduction of a system of approved Codes of Practice, prepared in consultation with industry. Thus an employee, whatever his/her employment, should fund that his/her work is covered by an appropriate code of practice.

Employers also have **specific** duties under the 1974 Act.

(a)   All systems (work practices) must be safe.

(b)   The work environment must be safe and healthy (well-lit, warm, ventilated and hygienic).

(c)   All plant and equipment must be kept up to the necessary standard (with guards on machines and so on).

In addition, information, instruction, training and supervision should be directed towards safe working practices. Employees must consult with **safety representatives** appointed by a recognised trade union, and appoint a **safety committee** to monitor safety policy, if asked to do so. Safety policy and measures should be clearly **communicated in writing** to all staff.

The **employee** also has a duty:

(a)   To take reasonable care of himself/herself and others

(b)   To allow the employer to carry out his or her duties (including enforcing safety rules)

(c)   Not to interfere intentionally or recklessly with any machinery or equipment

FOR DISCUSSION

'A baby was put on a social services at risk register', reported *The Times* in February 1992, 'after his father, a roofer, rook him to work up ladders in a sling fixed to his back.' The story continues:

After a two-hour hearing it was decided to place the boy in his godparents' care while his father goes to work. Putting (the child) on a register will allow social workers to ensure the child remains grounded. (The roofer) said that his wife ... a bank clerk ... was happy with the outcome.

'But I intend to fight this decision in the European Court', he said 'I should be allowed to raise my son as I want to.'

Who do you think is responsible for a person's safety? Should people be allowed to take risks if they 'want to'? Or should measures be taken to protect them 'for their own good'?

3.3   The Management of Health and Safety at Work Regulations 1992

Under the Management of Health and Safety at Work Regulations 1992 **employers** now have the following additional general duties.

(a)   They must carry out risk assessment, generally in writing, of all work hazards. Assessment should be continuous.

(b)   They must introduce controls to reduce risks.

(c)   They must assess the risks to anyone else affected by their work activities.

(d)   They must share hazard and risk information with other employers, including those on adjoining premises, other site occupiers and all subcontractors coming onto the premises.

(e)   They should revise safety policies in the light of the above, or initiate safety policies if none were in place previously.

(f)   They must identify employees who are especially at risk.

(g)   They must provide fresh and appropriate training in safety matters.

(h)   They must provide information to employees (including temps) about health and safety.

(i)   They must employ competent safety and health advisers.

Employees are also given an additional duty under the 1992 regulations to inform their employer of any situation which may be a danger. This does not reduce the employer's responsibilities in any way, however, because his/her risk assessment programme should have spotted the hazard in any case.

Under the **Health and Safety (Consultation with Employees) Regulations 1996**, employers must consult all of their employees on health and safety matters (such as the planning of health and safety training, any change in equipment or procedures which may substantially affect their health and safety at work or the health and safety consequences of introducing new technology). This involves giving information to employees **and** listening to and taking account of what they say before any health and safety decisions are taken.

3.4 The Workplace (Health, Safety and Welfare) Regulations 1992

The workplace regulations deal with matters that have been statutory requirements for many years in the UK under legislation such as the Offices, Shops and Railway Premises Act 1963, although in some cases the requirements have been more clearly defined. We mentioned many of the provisions in paragraph 1.2 above, dealing with general environmental hygiene. Additional safety provisions include the following.

(a) **Machinery and equipment**. All equipment should be properly maintained and fenced if dangerous.

(b) **Floors, passages and stairs** must be properly constructed and maintained (without holes, not slippery, properly drained and so on).

(c) **Falls or falling objects**. These should be prevented by erecting effective physical safeguards (fences, safety nets, ground rails and so on).

(d) **Glazing**. Windows should be made of safe materials and if they are openable it should be possible to do this safely.

(e) **Traffic routes**. These should have regard to the safety of pedestrians and vehicles alike.

(f) **Doors and gates**. These should be suitably constructed and fitted with any necessary safety devises (especially sliding doors and powered doors and doors opening in either direction).

(g) **Lifts, escalators and travelators** should function safely and be regularly maintained.

(h) **Fire precautions** should be taken, and appropriate firefighting equipment and clearly marked and unobstructed escape route should be provided. Fire alarms should be installed and tested.

The **Health and Safety (Young Persons) Regulations 1997** require employers to take into account the lack of experience, absence of awareness of existing or potential risks and/or the relative immaturity of young employees (aged under 18) when assessing the risks to their health and safety.

In addition to legislation, you need to be aware of helpful guidance on health and safety from other sources. The instruction manual to a piece of equipment or machinery, for example, makes all the difference between a help and a hazard. The Health and Safety Commission issues helpful booklets on matters such as working with VDUs, smoking and alcohol. But there is no substitute for common sense: care in handling chemicals, lifting heavy objects, operating machinery, moving around the workplace (and playing practical jokes) is part of every employee's own 'Safety Policy'.

Activity 6   **(15 minutes)**

Do you think the Royal Commission's 1972 findings on poor attitudes to health and safety are 'dated'? Suggest four reasons why society as a whole may have become more aware of health and safety since 1972.

EXAMPLE: INTERNATIONAL COMPARISONS

- Following the notorious leakage of lethal gas at Union Carbide's pesticide plant in Bhophal, India - which killed over 2,000 people, India formed committees in every state to identify potential hazards in factories. New regulations require environmental impact studies for all new plants.

- In Mexico, a disaster at Pemex (a state-owned gas monopoly) which killed over 500 people and wounded thousands more, had no noticeable effect on regulations.

- 'Developing countries are often so in need of economic development that they may accept any industry, even those that have the potential for significant harm ... Health hazards are still ignored: by having lax safety standards, developing countries can lure large multinational firms to their shores.'

(Kramer, McGraw Shuler)

3.5 Health and Safety authorities

The **Health and Safety Commission** was set up under the Health and Safety at Work Act 1974 to develop health and safety policies. It is made up of representatives of employers, employees, local government and relevant professional bodies. Responsibility for communicating, monitoring and enforcing the Commission's policies and relevant legislation falls to the Health and Safety Executive, which has powers of inspection and enforcement by:

(a) **Prohibition notice** requiring the shut down of hazardous processes until remedial action has been taken

(b) **Improvement notice** requiring compliance with a statutory provision within a certain time (subject to appeal to an industrial tribunal)

(c) **Seizure** of hazardous articles for destruction or rendering harmless, and /or

(d) **Prosecution** of offenders, who are liable to fine and even imprisonment in serious cases

3.6 Working hours

You should be aware that working hours are also a health and safety issue, under the Health and Safety (Young Persons) Regulations 1997 and the Working Time Regulations 1998 (implementing the EU Working Time Directive). These regulations make detailed provision for maximum working hours per week, entitlement to days off and rest periods, and safeguards for night workers.

Activity 7   **(15 minutes)**

Since we have broadened our awareness of what constitutes threat to health and safety, take some time to think about what other issues personnel policies might cover? Suggest five areas for consideration. (If you are currently employed, check you organisation's manual on health and safety.)

3.7 Health and safety policy

In order to enhance safety awareness, promote good practice and comply with legal obligations, many employers have a health and safety policy for their staff. Such a policy might have the following features.

(a) Statement of principles.

(b) Detail of safety procedures.

(c) Compliance with the law (eg in siting of fire extinguishers, fire exits) should be enforced.

(d) Detailed instructions should be made available as to how to use equipment.

(e) Training requirements should be identified (eg no person who has not been on a particular training course can use the equipment), as part of the context of human resource planning.

(f) Committees of safety experts, line managers and employees can discuss issues of health and safety. There is no reason for example why safety issues should not be brought up for discussion in a firm's quality circles.

Safety policy must be implemented in detailed practice (such as fire drills and equipment checking) but it is less likely to be consistently observed if senior managers fail to set a good example, to discipline breaches of policy, or to reward health and safety suggestions. The aim is to create a culture in which health and safety are key values.

3.8 A culture of health and safety

Charles Hampden-Turner (in his book *Corporate Culture*) notes that attitudes to safety can be part of a corporate **culture**. He quotes the example of a firm called (for reasons of confidentiality) **Western Oil**.

EXAMPLE : WESTERN OIL

Western Oil had a bad safety record. 'Initially, safety was totally at odds with the main cultural values of productivity (management's interests) and maintenance of a macho image (the worker's culture) ... . Western Oil had a culture which put safety in conflict with other corporate values.' In particular, the problem was with its long-distance drivers (who in the USA have a culture of solitary independence and self reliance). They sometimes drove recklessly with loads large enough to inundate a small town. The company instituted **Operation Integrity** to improve safety in a lasting way, changing the policies and drawing on the existing features of the culture but using them in a different way.

The culture had five dilemmas.

(a) **Safety-first versus macho-individualism.** Truckers see themselves as 'fearless pioneers of the unconventional lifestyle... . 'Be careful boys!' is hardly a plea likely to go down well with this particular group.' Instead of trying to control the drivers, the firm recommended that they became **road safety consultants**(or design consultants). Their advice was sought on improving the system. This had the advantage that 'by making drivers critics of the system, their roles as outsiders were preserved and promoted'. It tried to tap their heroism as promoters of public safety.

(b) **Safety everywhere versus safety specialists.** Western Oil could have hired more specialist staff. However, instead, the company promoted cross-functional safety teams from existing parts of the business, for example to help in designing depots and thinking of ways to reduce hazards.

(c) **Safety as cost versus productivity as benefit.** 'If the drivers raced from station to station to win their bonus, accidents were bound to occur... . The safety engineers rarely spoke to the line manager in charge of the delivery schedules. The unreconciled dilemma between safety and productivity had been evaded at management level and passed down the hierarchy until drivers were subjected to two incompatible injunctions: work fast and work safely.' To deal with this problem, safety would be built into the reward system.

(d)   **Long-term safety versus short-term steering**. The device of recording 'unsafe' acts in operations enabled them to be monitored by cross-functional teams, so that the causes of accidents could be identified and reduced.

(e)   **Personal responsibility versus collective protection**. It was felt that if 'safety' was seen as a form of management policing it would never be accepted. The habit of management 'blaming the victim' had to stop. Instead, if one employee reported another to the safety teams, the person who was reported would be free of official sanction. Peer pressure was seen to be a better enforcer of safety than the management hierarchy.

FOR DISCUSSION

What are the cultural values in your nation, local community and organisation that:

(a)   Promote health and safety?
(b)   Promote risk-taking and ill-health?

Now let's look at the 'new' welfare role of HRM, and some of the hazards of the new workplace.

4   NEW MODELS OF WELFARE

4.1   A shift in perspective

As suggested in paragraph 1.1, HRM specialists have tried to distance themselves from the traditional welfare tag with its legalistic/reactive and paternalistic associations.

The new orientation to welfare activities is based on the recognition that healthy and focused individuals are likely to perform better at work, to be more flexible (physically, mentally and emotionally) and adaptable to change: in short, that it is possible to take a business-strategic view of employee health and wellbeing.

The new model of welfare is therefore:

(a)   **Pro-active** in its attempt to address potential health and safety issues, rather than reacting to regulation, complaint or crisis

(b)   **Positive** in its attempt to promote health and well-being rather than focusing solely on ill-health, injury and crisis

(c)   **Holistic** in its definition of health and well-being, including emotional and even spiritual factors

(d)   **Wide-ranging** in its attention to diverse issues, rather than being led by legislative agendas

Goss (*Principles of HRM* 1994) summarised this new perspective as 'tough love': a hard-soft policy aimed at offering benefits and services which employees need and value, 'linked strategically with the needs of the organisation by enhancing performance'.

Issues in the new welfare model include:

(a)   Work-life balance and the management of stress

(b)   Promotion of positive health and fitness

(c)   Control/treatment of substance abuse

(d)   Confrontation of emerging workplace hazards (such as RSI, sick building syndrome)

(e)   Confrontation of emerging health issues (such as HIV/AIDS and passive smoking) and other sources of distress

(f)   Workplace counselling

(g)   Employee Assistance Programmes (EAPs)

We will discuss each of these issues, briefly, in turn.

4.2   Work-life balance and control of stress

Overwork is frequently associated with poor diet, lack of exercise, inadequate relaxation, stress and relationship difficulties.

Despite the desire to increase productivity or enhance performance, many companies are realising that increasing workloads and working hours is in fact counter-productive, potentially encouraging absenteeism, ill-health, accidents and poor-quality work.

Elements in a work-life balance programme may include:

(a)   In-house or consultant-led awareness training: clarification of values and priorities and so on

(b)   In-house or consultant-led skills training: in time-management, delegation, work organisation, relaxation techniques and, say,

(c)   Flexible working arrangements to allow time for family and social activities within the working week

Stress

Stress is a term which is often loosely used to describe feelings of tension - usually associated with too much, or overly demanding, work. In fact, stress is the product of demands made on an individual's physical **and mental** energies: monotony and feelings of failure or insecurity are sources of stress, as much as the conventionally-considered factors of pressure, overwork and so on.

It is worth remembering, too, that demands on an individual's energies may be stimulating as well as harmful: many people, especially those suited to managerial jobs, work well under pressure, and even require some form of stress to bring out their best performance. (It is excessive stress that can be damaging: this may be called **strain.**) This is why we talk about the management of stress, not about its elimination: it is a question of keeping stress to helpful proportions and avenues.

Harmful stress can be identified in symptoms such as nervous tension, irritability, sensitivity, sleeplessness, withdrawal (reluctance to communicate, absenteeism), depression, substance abuse and a variety of physical symptoms (such as skin and digestive disorders, tension headaches). Some symptoms of stress - say, absenteeism - may or may not be **correctly** identified with stress: there are many other possible causes of such problems, both at work (lack of motivation) and outside (personal problems).

All these things can, however, adversely affect performance, which is why stress management has become a major workplace issue.

Stress can be caused or aggravated by:

(a) **Personality**. Competitive, sensitive and insecure people feel stress more acutely

(b) Ambiguity or conflict in the **roles** required of an individual

(c) Insecurity, risk and change

(d) Management style including:

    (i) Unpredictability
    (ii) Destruction of workers' self esteem
    (iii) Setting up win/lose situations

Activity 8   **(30 minutes)**

What sources of stress are there in your own lifestyle? Are you aware of the symptoms of stress in yourself? What do you do (if anything) to control your stress?

Greater **awareness** of the nature and control of stress is a feature of the modern work environment. **Stress management techniques** are increasingly taught and encouraged by organisations, and include:

(a) Counselling

(b) Time off or regular rest breaks

(c) Relaxatio 1 techniques (breathing exercises, mediation)

(d) Physical exercise and self-expression as a safety valve for tension

(e) Delegation and planning (to avoid work-loan related stress)

(f) Assertiveness (to control stress related to insecurity in personal relations)

In addition, **job** training can increase the individual's sense of competence and security and **ecological** control can be brought to bear on the problem of stress, creating conditions in which stress is less likely to be a problem: well designed jobs and environments, and an organisation culture built on meaningful work, mutual support, communication and teamwork.

EXAMPLE

Here are some 'sound-bites' from a feature on stress in *People Management*.

In extreme cases, stress is a killer. The Japanese, who work longer hours than people in the US and the UK, experience **karoshi** (death from overwork). This is a documented ailment in which people develop illnesses and die from high stress and the pressures of overtime. **Karoshi** was officially registered as a fatal illness in 1989.

Findings show that the lowest grades - messengers and support staff - are three times more likely to die over a 10-year period than senior administrators, and they take six times more sick leave. Part of the reason for this is lack of control over work, less variety and less opportunity to develop new skills.

Effect on leadership. Studies have shown that, under stress, managers resort to experience and what has worked in the past rather than using their judgement. This is far less likely to be successful.

New research by Demos, an independent think-tank, has revealed the following statistics about British workers.

- 44 per cent of the workforce report coming home exhausted.
- Time off for stress-related illnesses has increased by 500 per cent since the 1950s.

So what is the best way forward for organisations? Many are already demonstrating best practice. Unipart, for example, tries to ensure the well-being of its employees through a fitness centre which also offers alternative therapies. Glaxo, Marks and Spencer, Sainsbury's, Grand Metropolitan and other organisations have joined the Wellness Forum, which promotes a healthy workforce. Marks and Spencer has also conducted programmes on managing pressure. Others, such as Threshers, the Post Office, BP and Laura Ashley, have embarked on employee counselling. Staff exposed to violence, such as police officers and employees in banks and off-licences, have undertaken post-traumatic stress counselling.

4.3 Promoting positive health and fitness

Ergonomics

Definition

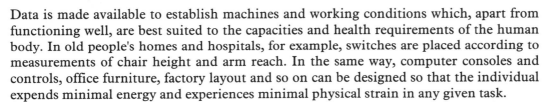

Ergonomics (Greek: **ergos** (work) + **nomos** (natural laws) is the scientific study of the relationship between man and his working environment. This sphere of scientific research explores the demands that can arise from a working environment and the capabilities of people to meet these demands.

Data is made available to establish machines and working conditions which, apart from functioning well, are best suited to the capacities and health requirements of the human body. In old people's homes and hospitals, for example, switches are placed according to measurements of chair height and arm reach. In the same way, computer consoles and controls, office furniture, factory layout and so on can be designed so that the individual expends minimal energy and experiences minimal physical strain in any given task.

More recently ergonomics has developed into a field that embraces the whole range of psychological factors that affect people at work. Apart from purely mechanical considerations - in what position should a worker be sitting in order to exert maximum force over a long period of time without physical strain or fatigue? - the ergonomist must now take into account the increasing problems of the worker as information processor. The perceptual limitations of the worker can also be measured, and systems designed which do not make unreasonable demands on the worker's attention span or capacity to absorb information - for example, the use of sound signals to attract attention to visual displays or equipment.

As Alan Fowler, the author of the above piece puts it, 'It is as important for work systems to be "people-shaped" in terms of mental and behavioural demands as it is for chairs and desks to fit people's physical dimensions.'

Health promotion services

Approaches to health promotion include the following.

(a) **Health monitoring and awareness campaigns**

Employees may be given regular health checks under occupational health regulations (hearing and eye tests, for example): this may be extended to heart and cholesterol checks, general fitness checks, skin cancer checks and so on, as part of a campaign to increase health awareness. Campaigns may be run to educate employees on nutritional guidelines, smoking and substance abuse hazards, the need for exercise and so on.

NOTES

(b) Nutritional support

The link between motivation and health is well-documented. Employers can encourage healthy eating habits through education programmes and through access to nutritionally balanced food in staff canteens, voucher schemes linked to health food outlets or products, sponsorship of weight-loss (or gain) programmes and so on.

(c) Anti-smoking programmes

Many organisations now operate smoke-free workplaces (as discussed in paragraph 4.6 below), but there is still a need to promote and support 'quit' campaigns because of smokers' health and time/environment in 'popping out (or elsewhere) for a smoke'. Information packs are available from health agencies, and incentives and encouragement may be offered.

(d) Fitness promotion

Sedentary occupations erode physical strength, stamina and flexibility, interfere with sleep patterns and metabolic rate, reduce alertness and contribute to the long-term consequences of all the above in stress, heart disease and other serious ailments. Fitness promotion in the workplace may range from educating employees in basic stretching exercises during work breaks to extensive sporting and gymnasium facilities. These have generally had a higher uptake among the young and already active: swimming, aerobics, yoga and other non-competitive activities and classes may make the provision more inclusive. Facilities may be accessed via discounted membership at public or private health clubs and sports centres. Staff may be sponsored and encouraged to participate in charity sporting events. In radical cases (considered the norm in Japan), whole staff exercise may be held at the start of each day.

EXAMPLE

Bonne Bell, a beauty-aids company in the USA, bends office rules and adds financial incentives' to promote good health among its employees. It started out encouraging employees to ride bikes to work, and arranged for them to purchase bikes at cost: the company now sponsors major charity races. In 1976, the company built tennis and volleyball courts, an athletics track, shower and locker facilities and exercise rooms at its office locations. Workers can use the facilities for free, with an extra 30 minutes free at lunch time if they exercise; they can purchase running shoes and suits at discount prices and workout clothes are permitted in the office after lunch. $250 was offered to employees who exercised four days a week during a given 6-month period. A $250 reward was paid to employees who stopped smoking for six months, and $5 per pound to employees who lost weight: if they relapsed, employees had to pay double those amounts, donated to charity. 'Early-bird' runs are held on Wednesday mornings. 'We've seen people start to take care of themselves', said a spokesperson. Sick days are down. Morale is high.

(Psychology Today, 1989)

(e) Private health care

Private health care or medical insurance packages can be tailored to suit the needs of individual employers and employees. They may include eye-wear, dental care, chiropody, in- and out-patient treatment in hospitals, health checks and screens and so on, for the employees and often their families. (There may be advantages in terms of prompter treatment than is available under the NHS system, thus avoiding both unnecessary suffering and periods of sub-optimal work performance.) Packages may also include broader health services: nutritional advice, alternative and sports medicine, stress control training, membership of sports facilities and so on.

The provision of private health care may be primarily welfare-based, or may be part of the remuneration package of the organisation and hence reward-based. Either way, it will be expected to reap benefits for employee performance.

4.4 Substance abuse

Substance abuse has become a major work-place issue, according to 1992 IRS Employment Trends Survey.

> It is estimated that one in 10 employees in Britain has an alcohol problem, and absences from work due to hangovers and other alcohol-related complaints account for an estimated 8 million days lost a year, three times the number lost through industrial action. In terms of lost production, this is costing the British economy around £1,700 million a year.
>
> The less quantifiable costs associated with alcohol misuse in terms of accidents at work are likely to inflate the figure significantly. Employees with alcohol problems also pay heavily in terms of their own health and, in extreme cases, their jobs.
>
> *IRS Employment Trends* 517

Most estimates place the numbers of drug users slightly below these levels, taking into account the sheer variety of prescription and non-prescription drugs used, and the difficulties of gathering user information given the illegality of most drug use.

Alcohol policy

A 1981 study in *Supervisory Management* suggests that:

(a) Workers who suffer from job stress and organisational frustration frequently turn to alcohol as a tool for unwinding.

(b) Many organisations continue to encourage social drinking, despite the known effects of physical/psychological dependency. Company celebrations frequently revolve around alcohol, and little concern is shown for the heavy drinker until his or her work is adversely affected, which may not be for some time after the onset of dependency.

Activity 9   **(30 minutes)**

What would you expect to be the symptoms of alcohol abuse that might alert a supervisor or manager to the problem?

Most alcohol policies embrace the following areas.

(a) **Positive aims and objectives** - including statistics on alcohol-related harm and affirmation of successful treatment.

(b) Restrictions on alcohol possession or consumption. These may be:

(i) A total ban on alcohol consumption on and/or off the premises during the working hours

(ii) Restriction of alcohol consumption to certain areas of the premises (say, visitors' dining rooms or a licensed canteen) and/or hours (usually special occasions)

(iii) Selective restrictions on certain employees - usually for health and safety reasons

(c) **The links between the policy and disciplinary procedure**. This is a sensitive area. Violent or illegal behaviour under the influence of alcohol would clearly trigger disciplinary action. Instances of random drunkenness and bad behaviour are usually treated under the heading of 'gross misconduct'. Deterioration in work performance or behaviour may, however, be better handled under the terms of the counselling and referral provisions of the alcohol policy - unless counselling and treatment are refused or ineffective. These fine lines will need to be clearly set out.

(d) **Confidentiality** of all measures undertaken in relation to alcohol problems of individual employees.

(e) **The roles of line and other managers in identifying and helping individuals with alcohol problems**. There should be detailed provisions on dealing with the problem drinker at work, from the initial identification of deteriorating work performance to assessing appropriate treatments and how to deal with the return to work.

(f) **Internal and external counselling services available**. Counselling is one of the central objectives of most alcohol policies. They should specify provisions for time off for counselling, the right of the individual to return to his job, any 'rehabilitation' requirements and a period of monitoring.

Drugs policy

Drug abuse policies are much more difficult to implement because:

(a) A significant number of workers may be legitimate short- or long-term users of prescription drugs and over the counter medicines which may impair performance in various ways (for example, by causing drowsiness)

(b) The illegality of the use of many drugs makes it difficult to gather information, and places drug use firmly within disciplinary as well as welfare policy frameworks

(c) Harm minimisation approaches (restricted use, risk avoidance and so on) may be interpreted as condoning drug use, although they do address the major workplace issues of safety risk and impaired performance

(d) It is difficult to distinguish fairly between 'acceptable' recreational drug use (of ecstasy or cannabis, say) and 'hard' drug use

(e) Random drug testing is fraught with industrial relations and legal issues (for example, under the Human Rights Act 1998), particularly since there are major problems of test reliability and privacy

Counselling, harm-minimisation (avoiding heavy machinery, driving and so on if affected) and voluntary supported rehabilitation programmes may be used judiciously as the basis of a policy. Entry into a company treatment programme should not be compulsory, where an employee can show that (s)he is undertaking independent treatment. The disciplinary issues will (as with alcohol) have to be worked out in detail.

4.5 Sick building syndrome

SBS is an illness (comparatively recently identified) associated with the workplace. Symptoms include lethargy, stuffy nose, dry throat, headache and itching eyes: once away from the workplace, staff are free from these problems. Factors in the workplace suspected to contribute to SBS include air-conditioning, and open-plan office space where there is perceived to be little control over the indoor environment. A report by the Health and Safety Executive (reported in *Personnel Management*, September 1992) found that 30-50% of new or refurbished buildings may affect people in this way, but that the causes (and therefore the cure) are uncertain.

Activity 10   **(20 minutes)**

The US Government estimates that between 30 and 75 million American workers are at risk of becoming ill because of the buildings in which they work. It sees indoor air pollution as one of the five most urgent environmental issues in the US, and its occupational health agency has studied more than 1,000 cases of suspected sick building syndrome.

In more than 50 percent of cases it identified inadequate ventilation, followed by chemical contamination and problems related to microbiological agents such as moulds, bacteria and fungi.

Personnel Management Plus, March 1993

In your role as office manager, a number of employees have recently complained to you that they feel below par after an hour or two in the building, but seem to recover when they pop out at lunch time and on the way home in the evening. What do you do?

4.6 Emerging health issues

Passive smoking

Recent case law has demonstrated that the employer has a duty to protect his/her employees from the effects of passive smoking, which means breathing in tobacco smoke from co-workers even though your don't smoke yourself. Thus, all employers are encouraged to devise smoking policies and procedures at work.

The CIPD have produced a code of practice in this area, which recommends that any smoking policy should aim to provide smoke-free air in most areas where smokers and non-smokers meet. The issue should not be about whether people smoke but about **where** they smoke. Some smokers might wish to cut down or give up smoking, though others will not welcome a smoking policy. A clear written policy should minimise conflict and misunderstanding between employees so that those who wish to smoke are aware of where and when they are free to do so.

After a long period of consultation and lobbying, the Health and Safety Commission introduced its own draft Code of Practice in September 2000: watch this space for approval and implementation.

HIV/AIDS

The fear and prejudice surrounding the Acquired Immune Deficiency Syndrome and the Human Immunodeficiency Virus require positive policy commitments from employers. Guidelines on policy, followed by many major employers, include the following.

(a) People with AIDS or who are HIV positive are entitled to the same employment rights and quality of working life as people with other serious diseases.

(b) Employment policies should be based on the scientific evidence that people with AIDS or HIV do not pose a risk of transmitting the virus through normal workplace contact.

(c) Employers should provide all workers with up-to-date, sensitively-handled information about AIDS/HIV, safe practices and risk reduction.

(d) Employers must protect the confidentiality of employees' medical histories, test results and so on.

(e) Employers should not require HIV screening ('AIDS testing') as part of general pre-employment or workplace physical examinations; nor should particular groups (eg gay men) be unfairly targeted for screening (discriminatory practice).

(f) Education and counselling programmes are considered helpful, but should not replace rigorous equal opportunities policies.

The Health and Safety Executive has issued a booklet (*AIDS and the Workplace*, 1990) with policy guidelines.

EXAMPLE

The Body Shop runs an education and counselling programme on HIV and AIDS. Its purpose is to give support to HIV-positive employees and employees with HIV-positive partners, and to prevent fear and discrimination by other employees, while promoting safe practices.

Other causes of disease

Some other issues of concern in the workplace, which may be the subject of policy guidelines, include the following:

(a) **Bullying at work**

Workplace intimidation, harassment and physical violence have been the subject of recent studies, suggesting that bullying is every bit as prevalent - and painful - in the workplace as it is in the school playground!

Policies should take into account victim-side factors (grievance procedures, confidentiality, counselling, transfer) and perpetrator-side factors (disciplinary procedures, counselling, transfer, cultural change): see the sexual harassment guidelines in Chapter 13 for a good model.

Activity 11 **(15 minutes)**

Brainstorm a list of behaviours you would consider 'bullying' in the workplace.

(b) **Recognition of religious practices**

Extending anti-discrimination policy in the area of religion, with a 'managing diversity' orientation, it has been recognised that freedom to observe strongly-held religious beliefs and practices is an important factor in employee well-being. Accommodating diversity in this area may include: flexible working to allow religious holidays and observances (prayer times); provision of meals in corporate canteens which offer choices to cover religious dietary laws (kosher, halal); permission to wear articles of clothing and adornment in accordance with religious custom; provision of 'chapel' facilities for private prayer and meditation; flexibility in work rules, by agreement, to allow for religious objection.

We have already suggested 'counselling' as part of many welfare policies. We will now go on to discuss counselling itself.

4.7 Workplace counselling

Definition

> '**Counselling** can be defined as a purposeful relationship in which one person helps another to help himself. It is a way of relating and responding to another person so that that person is helped to explore his thoughts, feelings and behaviour with the aim of reaching a clearer understanding. The clearer understanding may be of himself or of a problem, or of the one in relation to the other.' (Rees)

> **Activity 12**   **(10 minutes)**
>
> Suggest five situations, already mentioned in this Course Book, in which workplace counselling may be helpful.

The CIPD's 1994 *Statement on Counselling in the Workplace* makes it clear that effective counselling is not merely a matter of pastoral care for individuals, but is very much in the organisation's interests.

(a) Appropriate use of counselling tools can prevent under performance, reduce labour turnover and absenteeism and increase commitment from employees. Unhappy employees are far more likely to seek employment elsewhere.

(b) Effective counselling demonstrates an organisation's commitment to and concern for its employees and so is liable to improve loyalty and enthusiasm among the workforce.

(c) The development of employees is of value to the organisation, and counselling can give employees the confidence and encouragement necessary to take responsibility for self and career development.

(d) Workplace counselling recognises that the organisation may be contributing to the employees' problems and therefore it provides an opportunity to reassess organisational policy and practice.

The counselling process has three stages.

(a) **Recognition and understanding.** Often it is the employee who takes the initiative, but managers should be aware that the problem raised initially may be just the tip of the iceberg. (*Personnel Management Plus*, February 1993, cites a case where an employee came forward with a problem about pension contributions, and mentioned, as he was about to leave 'By the way – my wife wants a divorce'.)

(b) **Empowering.** This means enabling the employee to recognise their own problem or situation and encouraging them to express it.

(c) **Resourcing.** The problem must then be managed, and this includes the decision as to who is best able to act as counsellor. A specialist or outside resource may be better than the employee's manager.

Confidentiality is central to the counselling process. There will be situations when an employee cannot be completely open unless he is sure that his comments will be treated confidentially. However, certain information, once obtained by the organisation (for example about fraud or sexual harassment) calls for action. In spite of the drawbacks, therefore, the CIPD statement is clear that employees must be made aware when their comments will be passed on to the relevant authority, and when they will be treated completely confidentially.

The CIPD checklist below contains much useful advice for meeting and interviewing people generally, not merely in counselling situations.

Counselling checklist

Preparation

- choose a place to talk which is quiet, free from interruption and not open to view
- research as much as you can before the meeting and have any necessary papers readily available
- make sure you know whether the need for counselling has been properly identified or whether you will have to carefully probe to establish if a problem exists
- allow sufficient time for the session. (If you know you must end at a particular time, inform the individual of this)
- decide if it is necessary for the individual's department head to be aware of the counselling and its purpose
- give the individual the option of being accompanied by a supportive colleague
- if you are approaching the individual following information received from a colleague, decide in advance the extent to which you can reveal your source
- consider how you are going to introduce and discuss your perceptions of the situation
- be prepared for the individual to have different expectations of the discussion, eg the individual may expect you to solve the problem - rather than come to terms with it himself/herself
- understand that the individual's view of the facts of the situation will be more important than the facts themselves and that their behaviour may not reflect their true feelings

Format of discussion

- welcome the individual and clarify the general purpose of the meeting
- assure the individual that matters of confidentiality will be treated as such
- the individual may be reticent through fear of being considered somewhat of a risk in future and you will need to give appropriate reassurances in this regard
- be ready to prompt or encourage the individual to move into areas he/she might be hesitant about
- encourage the individual to look more deeply into statements
- ask the individual to clarify statements you do not quite understand
- try to take the initiative in probing important areas which may be embarrassing/emotional to the individual and which you both might prefer to avoid
- recognise that some issues may be so important to the individual that they will have to be discussed over and over again, even though this may seem repetitious to you
- if you sense that the individual is becoming defensive, try to identify the reason and relax the pressure by changing your approach
- occasionally summarise the conversation as it goes along, reflecting back in your own words (not paraphrasing) what you understand the individual to say
- sometimes emotions may be more important than the words being spoken, so it may be necessary to reflect back what you see the individual feeling
- at the close of the meeting, clarify any decisions reached and agree what follow-up support would be helpful

Overcoming dangers

- if you take notes at an inappropriate moment, you may set up a barrier between yourself and the individual
- realise you may not like the individual and be on guard against this
- recognise that repeating problems does not solve them
- be careful to avoid taking sides

- overcome internal and external distractions. Concentrate on the individual and try to understand the situation with him/her
- the greater the perceived level of listening, the more likely the individual will be to accept comments and contributions from you
- resist the temptation to talk about your own problems, even though these may seem similar to those of the individual

Source: *CIPD Statement on Counselling in the Workplace*

4.8 Employee assistance programmes (EAPs)

Recognising the difficulty of providing an effective counselling service in-house and also the special skills involved, a notable modern trend is to use outsiders for employee support.

Companies such as EAR, Focus, and ICAS provide Employee Assistance Programmes (EAPs), offering a 24-hour telephone line with instant access to a trained counsellor. Meetings can be face-to-face if the employee wants, and their immediate families are also covered by the scheme. The providers offer thorough briefing on the scheme for all employees, and management information and consultancy for the employers.

About 80% of the top 500 US companies use such schemes, and around 150 UK companies are estimated to have taken them up since the late 1980s. The cost on average is between £15 and £30 per employee, and companies such as Mobil Oil, Whitbread, and Glaxo report considerable benefits.

(*Personnel Management Plus*, February 1993; *Financial Times*, June 1993.)

An article in *People Management* (12 October 2000) laid out how to get the best from an EAP.

What to look for in an EAP

- Effective promotion of services
- Easy access - normally through a round-the-clock operations centre
- Expert consultation and training for managers, HR and occupational health professionals
- Confidential, appropriate and timely assessment of problems
- 'Brief-focused' professional counselling
- Referrals to long-term treatment
- Follow-up and monitoring of employees who access clinical services
- Crisis support after critical incidents

Dos and don'ts for the HR manager

Do   use the programme yourself

press for a dedicated EAP account manager

insist that complaints are fully investigated

check take-up figures each year

check the capabilities of the operations centre

check up on clinical procedures, counsellors' qualifications and supervision processes

intervene quickly during critical incidents and bigger crises

encourage managers and supervisors to use the EAP

Don't   expect your EAP provider to be proactive on all of these issues;

Imagine that your firm is receiving a high-quality EAP - verify it yourself.

NOTES

Chapter roundup

- The traditional welfare function was legalistic/reactive or paternalist in its orientation, and regarded as entirely 'soft'. The new welfare model, while meeting its legal obligations (in traditional health and safety and welfare benefits and services) is more positive, pro-active, holistic, flexible and strategic in aiming to improve employee performance.

- Occupational health and safety are key areas of legislation and regulation. The Health and Safety at Work Act and regulations implementing EU directives cover many areas of policy and practice.

- The modern workplace contains many potential hazards and particular attention must be given to accident prevention and reporting.

- Issues in the new welfare model include: work-life balance and stress control; ergonomics and 'well buildings'; positive health promotion; meeting emerging health issues such as substance abuse, passive smoking and HIV/AIDS; and meeting psycho-spiritual concerns such as bullying and religious freedom. Counselling in the workplace and Employee Assistance Programmes are two ways of accessing help.

Quick quiz

1   Give reasons for the importance of health and safety at work.

2   What are the duties placed on an employee by the HASAW Act 1974?

3   What additional duties have been placed on employers by recent regulations?

4   Explain the term Repetitive Strain Injury.

5   What does the cost of accidents to an employer consist of?

6   What preventative action could be taken to reduce the possibility of illness or accidents at the workplace?

7   What are the main objectives of a smoking policy?

8   What are the major work-related causes of stress?

9   What might be the components of an HIV/AIDS policy?

10 What is an Employee Assistance Programme?

Answers to quick quiz

1   To protect employees from pain and suffering; legal obligations; the cost of workplace accidents; to improve the company's image.

(see paragraph 1.1)

2   To take reasonable care of self and others; to allow employers to carry out their duties; not to interfere with machinery/equipment.   (para 3.2)

3   Risk assessment; risk control; information on risks and hazards; revise and initiate safety policies; identify 'at risk' employees; training; competence of advisers.   (para 3)

4   A syndrome involving back ache, eye strain, stiffness in the neck, shoulders, arms and hands.   (para 1.2)

5   Time lost by employees and management; cost of first aid and staff; cost of disrupted work.   (para 2.3)

6   Safety consciousness; consultation and participation; adequate instruction; minimal materials handling; safety devices on machines; good maintenance; codes of practice.   (para 2.4)

BPP
PUBLISHING

7   To provide smoke-free air in most areas where smokers and non-smokers meet; to identify areas where people can smoke; to minimise conflict between smokers and non-smokers.   (para 4.6)

8   Job demands; role conflict; role ambiguity; role overload and underload; responsibility for others; lack of social support; non-participation in decision making.   (para 4.2)

9   Equal opportunities for employees with HIV/AIDS; emphasis on low risk of infection; education on safe practices; counselling of employees with HIV (or HIV positive partners).   (para 4.6)

10   A contract for counselling services with an external service provider.
                                                                              (para 4.8)

Answers to Activities

1,2   Your own environment and experience - but the text in paragraph 1.2 should give you some ideas. If you spot any hazards: make a report and submit it to the relevant person in authority!

3   Again, your own research: learn to use the real-life resources you have available to you!

4   You should have spotted the following hazards

      (a)   Heavy object on high shelf
      (b)   Standing on swivel chair
      (c)   Lifting heavy object incorrectly
      (d)   Open drawers blocking passageway
      (e)   Trailing wires
      (f)   Electric bar fire
      (g)   Smouldering cigarette unattended
      (h)   Overfull waste bin
      (i)   Overloaded socket
      (j)   Carrying too many cups of hot liquid
      (k)   Dangerous invoice 'spike'

      If you can see others you are probably right.

5   Up to you: have fun!

6   Since 1972, society as a whole has become more aware of health and safety, through:

      (a)   Legislation requiring health warnings and descriptions of contents of goods

      (b)   The raising of issues such as unsafe toys, food labelling, flammable materials in furniture, and asbestos poisoning

      (c)   Experience of notorious disasters including the Kings Cross Station fire, the Piper Alpha oil rig explosion, Chernobyl and so on

      (d)   Improvements in the general quality of life and environments

7   Some areas you might have thought of include:

      (a)   Alcohol on the premises

      (b)   Drug taking (including prescription drugs) on the premises

      (c)   Horse play and practical jokes

      (d)   Noise (or 'acoustic shock'), particularly from headset use. (In a recent case, 20 BT telephone operators claimed that faulty equipment damaged their hearing: *PM* 15 May 98)

(e) Workplace behaviour: running, throwing things, etc

  (f) Tiredness (dangerous objects, dust, slippery objects etc)

8 Your own experience. Be as honest as you can. If you aren't doing much to control your stress, consider doing some further research on the list of techniques following the Activity.

9 Symptoms typically include: avoidance of supervisors and workmates; uncharacteristic aggression, mood swings and variations in work pace; sloppy appearance, signs of hangover; hand tremors, gastric upsets, insomnia; financial difficulties and relationship problems; bizarre excuses for work deficiencies; increased accidents and absences for ill health. (Similar symptoms apply to drug abuse, with the addition of: dilated or contracted pupils in the eyes; sudden 'nodding off'; slurred speech; uncontrolled laughter or tears; sloppy appearance and unsteady movements but without the smell of alcohol).

10 Dr Aric Sigman, the author of the above piece in *Personnel Management Plus*, suggests the following.

'If employees suspect they are working in a sick building and they have eliminated their boss and their job as potential causes of their condition, they should act as follows.

- Document the symptoms - who gets what, where and when. All doctor's visits should be recorded. Liaise with the occupational health unit.

- Check out the building - staff must take responsibility for looking around for sources of concern. Contact the Health and Safety Executive for advice on what to look for.

- Suggest action - clearly and in writing.

- Seek expert assistance.'

11 Some suggestions are: shouting, swearing; persistent public criticism; ridicule and name-calling; threats; physical intimidation (use of threatening body language or actual violence); sexual harassment; racial vilification; victimisation in applying work rules; deliberately allocating difficult or unpleasant tasks to an individual; sabotaging the individual's work complaining to other staff or supervisors about the individual; multiple grievance or disciplinary actions and so on.

12 The need for workplace counselling can arise in many different situations, including the following.

  (a) During appraisal

  (b) In grievance or disciplinary situations

  (c) Following change, such as promotion or relocation

  (d) On redundancy or dismissal

  (e) As a result of domestic or personal difficulties, alcoholism, drug abuse, HIV/AIDS

  (f) In cases of sexual harassment or violence at work

NOTES

Assignment 14   (1½ hours)

Duntoiling Nursing Homes

You are the personnel officer for Duntoiling Nursing and Retirement Homes PLC, a chain of residential complexes for senior citizens in the West Midlands region. Recently, Gareth Cheeseman, the bullish, entrepreneurial director, sent a brief memorandum to all staff informing them that all premises now constitute 'No Smoking' areas for patients, visitors and staff alike. Notices to this effect have gone up round the homes. Duntoiling is also declaring its 'No Smoking' policy in recruitment advertisements.

The abruptness with which Cheeseman introduced this policy is now causing problems. It seems that some staff are continuing to smoke 'behind closed doors', and visitors and patients are flouting the ban in the corridors and toilets. Staff rebuking them have been subject to verbal abuse. Some staff also complain of suffering from stress because they cannot give up the craving.

The crunch came last week, when one supervisor issued a formal oral warning to a member of his staff caught 'red-handed' smoking in her office, and stated that if she repeated the offence she would be dismissed. The employee in question resigned in a fit of pique and is now claiming constructive dismissal, with union support.

Cheeseman has asked you to brief him on what action needs to be taken:

(a) To deal with the disciplinary case and
(b) To ensure that the policy is complied with in the future

What advice will you give? Present your answer in the form of a memorandum to Gareth Cheeseman.

Chapter 15 :
INTERNATIONAL COMPARISONS

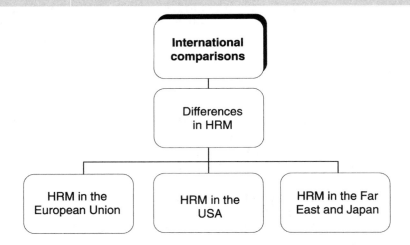

Introduction

We have already made international comparisons in the context of specific HR practices, in earlier chapters: similar comparisons will be made in Parts C and D of this Course Book with reference to employment development and employee relations.

In this chapter, we draw together the threads of the international perspective on HRM. We begin by considering why differences in the policies and practices of different nations arise, and whether there can genuinely be a global model of HRM from which to investigate or attempt to harmonise these differences.

We then discuss the impact of European Union on UK HRM policy and practice. (Again, we have already mentioned many specific examples - for example, in Chapter 14 covering health and safety.)

Finally, we survey in turn the key issues and distinctive features of HRM in various European Countries, the USA and the Far East.

This is clearly a vast area of study: you would need a Course Book such as this one for each country, in order to do it justice! We recommend that you use this overview to identify your own areas of interest and to guide you in follow-up reading (in the Press, International HR Journals and so on) as you proceed through your studies.

Your objectives

In this chapter you will learn about the following:

(a) The implementation of human resource practices in the UK and in other countries

(b) How UK organisations have modified employment practice in response to EU employment legislation

(c) The impact of increasing European social and employment legislation and the response of organisations within the UK

1 DIFFERENCES IN HRM

1.1 Why are there differences?

It may be argued that the 'activities' of HRM – HR planning, recruitment and selection, appraisal and reward, training and development, welfare, discipline, employee exit and employee relations – are common to organisations everywhere. The need to attract, retain, motivate and develop employees (the 'aims' of HRM) are universal. The globalisation of business and communications has also encouraged the exchange and sharing of certain technical terms, theories and practices (for example, the adoption of Japanese-style quality circles or Swedish-style autonomous working groups), and the standardisation of certain HR techniques such as job evaluation and staff appraisal. In this sense, there seems to be a 'convergence' of HR policy and practice.

Observers note, however, that while structures and technologies may converge, there is still enough diversity to encourage 'divergence'. The fact is that although everybody 'does' HRM – they seem to do it differently!

Throughout this Course Book, we have identified disparities in HRM policy and practice from one country to another (even within the EU, which is supposed to be on the road to 'harmonisation' of its employment conditions and practices). A number of factors might contribute to these variations.

(a) **Cultural factors**, arising from the history, traditions, language, social development and values and religious beliefs of different countries and ethnic groups. Culture amounts to a national way of doing and perceiving things. Cultural factors influence management/worker models, career expectations, perceptions and attitudes to work, education and training needs and so on, and are reflected in the culture of the organisation.

(b) **National legal frameworks.** As we discuss below, specific laws and regulations, and the systems by which they are derived, vary markedly from state to state. The extent of political/legal intervention in employment underscores the cultural dimension.

(c) **Structural factors.** Education and training systems influence the skills available in the labour pool, and therefore HRP, recruitment and development policies. Demographic factors likewise affect the structure of the labour market. Technological and communication infrastructures affect the way in which work is performed and structured, since work organisation and employment policies are different (as the UK experience has shown) in a fast-changing high-tech market than in a low-tech industrial market. Political factors also influence HRM via government intervention.

(d) **Employee relations traditions and ideologies**: the degree of state involvement in industrial conflict and regulation; government support for the unionisation or anti-unionisation of the workforce; collectivisation or individualisation of employment relationships; traditions of co-operation or conflict in industrial relations.

(e) **National economic development**: unemployment levels, rates of inflation, rate of economic growth, balance of trade: the extent of competition in the local product markets (encouraging HRM for competitive edge) and labour markets (encouraging HRM for attracting and retaining skills).

> **Activity 1** (30 minutes)
>
> Brainstorm a number of cultural dimensions or values on which societies might differ. (Think about all aspects of life that might impact on attitudes in employment.) Suggest examples where possible.

There have been a number of models of how cultural difference 'works'. We will look at two useful frameworks.

1.2 High and low context cultures

Hall (1976) suggested that one dimension of difference is the extent to which the content and understanding of communication is influenced by its context, in terms of non-verbal aspects, underlying implications, interpersonal dynamics and so on.

> Low context people take the content of a communication at its face value (words say what they mean). They therefore prefer clear, explicit, written forms of communication.
>
> High context people exchange and interpret messages at a more complex level. They tend to divulge less information officially in written forms, but are better at developing informal networks for information exchange face-to-face or by oral means (such as the telephone). They are also better at giving and interpreting non-verbal signals, unspoken implications, emotional undertones and so on.

Research has placed various cultures on the high-low context continuum as follows (Figure 15.1).

	4	3	2	1	0	1	2	3	4	
Low context										*High context*
	West Germany German Swiss	Scandinavia North America		Belgium Nether- lands Denmark		France	UK	Southern Europe Middle East Asia Africa Latin America	Japan	

Figure 15.1: Hall's high-context, low-context model

> **Activity 2** (30 minutes)
>
> (a) What might be some of the problems of a person from a low-context culture working in a high-context culture?
>
> (b) Imagine (or role-play) a discussion between a low-context manager and a high-context worker who has approached him or her informally because (s)he is having relationship problems with a colleague.

1.3 The Hofstede Model

Hofstede (1980) carried out research at 66 national offices of IBM and suggested that managers and employees vary on four primary dimensions.

(a) **Power distance:** the extent to which unequal distribution of power is accepted. High PD cultures accept a top-down hierarchy of authority and chain of command, and have little expectation of influencing decision-making: low PD cultures expect involvement and participation in decision-making.

(b) **Uncertainty avoidance:** the extent to which security, order and control is preferred to ambiguity, uncertainty and change. High UA cultures feel a greater need for rules and regulations than low UA cultures, in which 'rules are made to be broken' in the interests of flexibility and creativity.

(c) **Individualism:** the extent to which people prefer to live and work in individualist ways (looking after self and immediate family) or collectivist ways (tight-knit connections to extended family, group, organisation, community). High individuality cultures emphasise individual achievement, while low individuality cultures emphasise the interests of the group.

(d) **Masculinity:** the extent to which social gender roles are distinct. In high masculinity cultures, men are expected be assertive, ambitious and focused on material success, while women are expected to be modest, tender and focused on relationships and the quality of life. In low masculinity cultures, feminine values apply also to men.

Hofstede placed various cultures on these dimensions as follows.

Cultural group	*Power distance*	*Uncertainty avoidance*	*Individualism*	*Masculinity*
I More developed Latin *(Belgium, France, Argentina, Brazil, Spain)*	High	High	Medium to high	Medium
II Less developed Latin *(Portugal, Mexico, Peru)*	High	High	Low	Whole range
III More developed Asian *(Japan)*	Medium	High	Medium	High
IV Less developed Asian *(India, Taiwan, Thailand)*	High	Low to medium	Low	Medium
V Near Eastern *(Greece, Iran, Turkey)*	High	High	Low	Medium
VI Germanic *(Germany, Austria, German Swiss)*	Low	Medium to high	Medium	Medium to high
VII Anglo *(UK, US, Australia)*	Low to medium	Low to medium	High	High
VIII Nordic *(Scandinavia, Netherlands)*	Low	Low to medium	Medium to high	Low

Figure 15.2: The Hofstede Model

Activity 3   **(20 minutes)**

According to the Hofstede model, what issues might arise in the following cases?

(a) A Swedish company sets up a subsidiary in Brazil under a Swedish general manager, who wishes to import Scandinavian decision-making styles.

(b) The newly appointed Spanish HR manager of a UK firm asks to see the Rules and Procedures Manual for the HR department.

(c) A US-trained HR manager attempts to implement a system of Management By Objectives in Thailand.

(d) A Dutch HR manager of a US subsidiary in the Netherlands is instructed to implement downsizing measures.

FOR DISCUSSION

A French manager working in a subsidiary of an American corporation that insisted upon an open-door policy may well leave his office door open – thus adjusting to the behavioural requirements of the corporate culture – without any modification whatsoever to his basic concept of managerial authority.

(Laurent, cited by Beardwell and Holden)

What does this suggest about the 'transferability' of HRM approaches? Do you think there is any possibility of a truly international model of HRM – or is the model too hard to pin down even within one country?

Having noted some areas of convergence and divergence in HRM policy and practice, we will now go on to survey three contexts: Europe, the USA and the Far East (as represented by Japan). We will not be comparing specific HR policy and practice here: for detailed comparisons, see the 'International Comparison' features in relevant chapters of this Course Book – and also paragraph 2.3 below for a guide to following up your own specific research interests. What follows is a broad 'tour' of the key HR issues in these major contexts.

2 HRM IN THE EUROPEAN UNION

2.1 The legal framework

European law and policy are developed through the four main institutions of the EU.

(a) The **Council of the European Union**, the decision-making body which negotiates and approves measures put forward by the European Commission. It consists of:

    (i) The **European Council**: twice yearly meetings of the heads of the member states, the presidency of which rotates on a 6 monthly basis

    (ii) The **Council of Ministers**: meetings of ministers of the member states holding common portfolios (employment, education and so on): the main decision-making body which acts on proposals by the Commission

    (iii) The **Committees of Permanent Representatives** (COREPER) of the various member states, based in Brussels, preparing national positions on proposals

    (iv) **Working Groups** representing national government departments and COREPER, which hold preliminary negotiations on proposals

(b) The **European Commission**, the executive body which proposes policy measures and monitors their implementation. It consists of a President and nineteen Commissioners nominated by the members states (the largest states send two), each responsible for an area of policy (Transport, External Trade Relations, Social Policy and so on). The Commission has the power to bring legal action via the Court of Justice against member states which it deems have violated EU laws.

(c) The **European Parliament**, with Members (MEPs) elected by the citizens of the member states, in proportion to national population. Twenty specialist Committees investigate and report on Commission proposals prior to monthly parliamentary sessions: proposals are debated, amended (if required) and presented as the official response to the Commission. There is on-going controversy about the parliament's limited powers, given that this is the only elected body in the European system.

NOTES

(d)   The **European Court of Justice** is the final interpreter of the Treaties and Articles upon which the Union of Europe is based, and the court of arbitration and appeal in all disputes concerning European law and legislation enacted under it. It consists of sixteen judges and six Advocates General, appointed by member states in rotation. The Court gives preliminary rulings for the benefit of national courts and may also take proceedings against members states which fail to meet legal obligations.

EU law is therefore developed as follows (Figure 15.3)

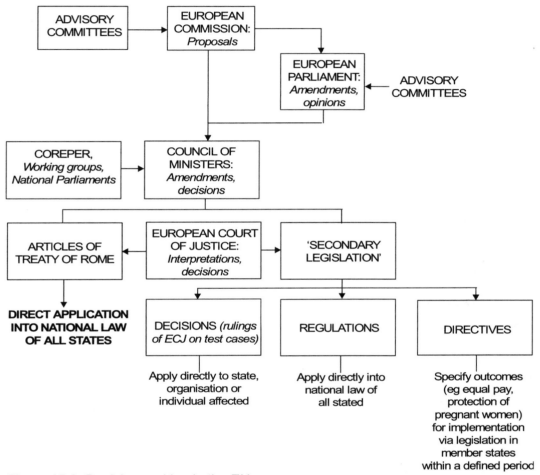

Figure 15.3: Decision-making in the EU

Draft Directives are proposals by the European Commission which have been accepted in principle but not yet implemented, because of opposition by one or more member states. There are a number of employment-related directives still under negotiation, and the situation changes regularly: make sure you monitor *People Management, International Human Resource Management* and the business section of the quality press for developments.

In addition, there are a number of **recommendations** and **opinions** which are not legally binding but are intended to encourage particular policy responses in member states.

2.2   The UK response

The UK has held an ambivalent position on EU law over the years, partly because:

(a)   UK law is based on case law (decisions in the courts) as well as statute, and EU law is by contrast highly codified and prescriptive: the UK has been forced to legislate in areas previously left to the courts' discretion

(b)   The UK has traditionally preferred to rely on voluntary self-regulation of employment policy (as can be seen in government's refusal to legislate on age discrimination until forced to do so by a 2000 EU Directive)

(c)   The cost implications of implementing directives can be high and may damage competitiveness (particularly in relation to the USA and Pacific Rim, where there is little regulation of wages, conditions or working hours)

(d)   Implementation encourages the development of large bureaucracies within government, and a corresponding administrative burden on enterprises

(e)   The overriding of UK law by EU law, and suspicions of EU social engineering, raise issues of sovereignty, particularly since the executive and decision-making bodies of the EU are not democratically elected, and since the spirit of 'free enterprise' is the supposed basis of the Single Market

(f)   Current social protection is greatest in the more affluent EU states: harmonisation of conditions may place an unfair burden on poorer EU countries

> **Activity 4**   **(45 minutes)**
> Can you think of counter-arguments to some of the above objections?

The UK has (successfully and unsuccessfully) opposed several measures over the years: most of the measures discussed below are now enacted in UK law and regulation.

2.3   EU Directives

The EU has developed an extensive framework for employment-related policy and practice within member states. Directives already encountered in this Course Book (mostly in the form in which they have been enacted in UK law) cover the following areas.

(a)   **Health and safety**: Display Screen Equipment (VDU) Directive 1990, Personal Protective Equipment Directive 1989, Workplace Directive 1989, Heavy Loads Directive 1990, Protection of Pregnant Workers Directive 1992, Working Time Directive 1994

(b)   **Equal opportunity and discrimination**: Equal Pay Directive 1975, Equal Treatment Directive 1976, Equal Treatment Directive (State Social Security) 1978, Equal Treatment Directive (Occupational Social Security) 1986, and Equal Treatment (Self-Employed) Directive 1986, plus the new 'Article 13' proposals on age, sexual orientation and disability

(c)   **Employment contracts**: Part-time and Temporary Workers Directive; Transfer of Undertakings Directive

(d)   **Working hours**: Working Time Directive, Young Workers Directive 1996, Parental Leave Directive

(e)   **Employment protection**: Collective Redundancy Directive 1975

(f)   **Free movement of workers**: Directives and agreements dealing with abolition of passport controls and work permits, mutual recognition of professional and vocational qualifications, application of employment law to posted workers and so on

(g)   **Employment relations**: the European Works Council Directive

Some matters are still work in progress, notably the 'Vredeling Directive' on information and consultation (discussed in Chapter 19 of this text) which would force companies with more than 50 employees to inform and consult staff on changes that might affect their jobs: the UK opposes implementation of the directive at the national level. After the sudden cancellation of a debate by the Council of Ministers, *People Management* (26 October 2000) suggested that the directive was unlikely to make swift progress: watch this space!

2.4   The Social Charter/Chapter

The European Union was partly developed as a 'Single Market' or trading bloc, removing barriers to trade and competitive bias, standardising technical regulations and creating a convergence of conditions between European markets. However, it also has a socio-political dimension which embraces employment issues, since it is believed that the success of the Single Market depends on the united efforts of employers and labour.

The main statement of European social policy is the 'Community Charter of the Fundamental Social Rights of Workers'– commonly known as the 'Social Charter' – which was ratified by 11 of the (then) 12 member states: the UK opted out. The Charter is based on the desire to improve living and working conditions and to ensure effective use of human resources across the EU. It is a statement of intent to guarantee individual rights in the following areas.

(a)   **Freedom of movement.** All workers should be able to move freely within the community.

(b)   **Employment and remuneration.** Workers should be paid a fair wage.

(c)   **Improvement of living and working conditions.** This provision covers the organisation of working time and holidays, and procedures for dealing with redundancy and insolvency.

(d)   **Social protection.** Workers in the community must have access to adequate social benefits and those outside the labour market must receive adequate financial assistance.

(e)   **Freedom of association and collective bargaining.** This includes the right to join, or not to join, a trade union; the right to negotiate and conclude collective agreements and the right to collective action such as strikes.

(f)   **Vocational training.** Every worker should have access to suitable vocational training.

(g)   **Equal treatment for men and women.** This covers access to employment, remuneration, working conditions, social protection, education and training and career development.

(h)   **Information, consultation and participation of workers.** Changes that affect the workforce such as new technology, working practices, mergers, restructuring and collective redundancy should involve prior consultation with employees.

(i)   **Health protection and safety in the workplace.** Every employee has the right to a safe and healthy working environment and moves must be taken to ensure harmonisation of conditions in this area.

(j)   **Protection of children and adolescents in employment.** The minimum employment age must not be lower than the school leaving age and neither of these must be lower than fifteen years of age. Duration of work must be limited and night work prohibited under eighteen years of age. Adequate remuneration and training must be made available.

(k) **Elderly persons.** At the age of retirement, every worker should be entitled to a decent standard of living and have recourse to social assistance where necessary.

(l) **Disabled persons.** Additional measures should be taken to improve the social and professional integration of disabled people. These include transport, housing, training and mobility.

This was subsequently developed as the Social Charter Action Programme, then the proposed 'Social Chapter' of the Treaty on European Union (the Maastricht Treaty). The treaty was signed in 1992 (and the European Community was renamed the European Union), although the UK insisted on a separate protocol for the Social Charter/Chapter. All 15 members of the EU have since agreed that the Charter be implemented by directive: member states will be bound to legislate and 'mobilise all the resources necessary' to implement its provisions. Some have already been covered by EU Directives, while others are still subject to negotiation and amendment.

The social policy of the European Union and its implementation in European law clearly impact on HRM policy and practice. However, the Single Market raises other issues for HR managers. We will briefly raise some of them here.

2.5 HR implications of European Union

The implications for European HRM are still being worked out in detail, but HR specialists will clearly need to be aware of the following issues.

(a) **Compliance with EU law** across a wide range of employment issues (as discussed above).

(b) **Differences in specific law and practice** in countries where the organisation may intend to recruit. The Posted Worker Directive provides that any employee posted to a foreign country for more than three months is entitled to the protection of the employment laws of the host country (minimum wage, working hours, notice periods and so on) rather than those of his or her home country, so that organisations cannot cut corners on employment protection by contracting labour from countries where the law is weaker.

(c) **The need for workers to be cross-educated in the languages and cultures of other states**: language is not an area amenable to harmonisation!

(d) **The mobility of labour within the EU**, allowing residence and permit-free working for full-time, part-time and economically active self-employed workers from all member states of the European Economic Area. **The recognition and comparison of qualifications** is a key related issue for recruitment, reward and development: harmonised standards for Higher Educational Diplomas (HEDs) in specific professions and industry-based 'Certificates of Experience' are designed to facilitate mobility of qualified workers.

(e) **Implications of European Monetary Union.** Although the UK has not joined the EMU, the 'euro' has been the accepted currency of business in the EU since 1999, and national currencies are scheduled to be phased out. A 1998 report *'EMU: Risk or Opportunity'* highlighted: the prospect of pan-European pay bargaining and settlements; the increased importance of European Works Councils for such pay bargaining; the need to reassess corporate structures in view of their potential for mergers and acquisitions, and opportunities for central payroll administrations created by EMU; and the need for employee communication and training to prepare for the change.

(f) **Potential pan-European HRM:** cross-border head-hunting and recruitment advertising, choice of international education and training avenues, management of expatriate management and staff, training in relevant EU markets (and product standards and other differences), management of diversity, welfare for dislocated staff and families, pan-European reward harmonisation and so on.

EXAMPLE

A feature in *People Management* (3 June 1999) described the Eurofighter programme, a four-nation exercise in political, technical, cultural and management integration between British Aerospace, Daimler Chrysler Aerospace (Dasa) of Germany, Alenia Aerospazio of Italy and Construcciones Aeronauticas of Spain, run by a German management company in Germany. Here are some soundbites on the HR issues (as identified by the German HR director) and the techniques used.

> The project's official language is English, and all the teams are multi-national, so fluency is essential. "The southern Europeans feel disadvantaged... The Spanish especially will not admit that they haven't understood something – they simply agree. And you have to be sensitive to varying language skills." Eurofighter has an open learning centre with language facilities...
>
> But cultural differences go deeper. "The decision-making process is different... The Latins need consensus and aren't empowered to make decisions. The Germans come closer to the Anglo-Saxon model of responsibility, but the Latins need more social contact, which develops trust. It's something we can learn from them"...
>
> There is a handover period for new employees, who are coached by the previous incumbents. They are briefed on local law, including the formalities of registering with the town hall, their entitlement to state benefits, the availability of local services, and – vital to the British contingent, according to [the German HR director] – the fact that cycling drunk in Bavaria is an offence that could cost you your driving licence. Each partner company has a sponsor – a senior manager in Eurofighter – who looks after the welfare of its employees and their families while in Germany...
>
> Managers need extra training to comply with German employment laws such as the rigid agreements on working hours and the role of the works council. "You can't do overtime without authorisation." Through the "right of co-determination" legislation, works councils have the right to negotiate on all terms and conditions. Everyone has to comply, right up to the managing director. Yet it's not a confrontational relationship. "This is a nightmare for British managers, who are used to the union system."
>
> "People here are very experienced. If the organisation is limiting them, they need to be given permission to act. We threw away all the terms of reference from the old days. Job descriptions, for example, were sometimes years old and did not reflect reality... Managers were given responsibility for designing their own jobs, and the works council backed the changes... "Everyone now has a dynamic job description that is updated twice a year. It is job enlargement. This does frighten people, but we try to support them."
>
> Appraisals are a tradition familiar to BAe staff, but other people have had less experience of implementing them successfully. Dasa had an appraisal programme, but it had not provided effective feedback for junior staff. The Spanish had appraisals only for senior managers, while the Italians had no comparable system at all...'

2.6 Harmonisation and divergence between states

The intention of EU policy appears to be the convergence or harmonisation of employment law and practice in member states. However, the protection of common minimum standards and principles does not in itself create a 'pan-European' model for HRM. As we have seen throughout this Course Book, member states still vary widely from each other (and from the UK) in:

(a) Their culture (as discussed in Section 1 above), which may dictate different approaches to motivation and reward, employee relations (industrial democracy), discrimination issues and so on

(b) The extent of State intervention in employment practices, according to political ideology, and the extent to which regulation, prescription and bureaucratisation is accepted in national culture and systems

(c) Their economic, technical and social development: standard of living, rates of unemployment, pressures on public sector expenditure, communication systems and other infrastructures, taxation incentives and disincentives to particular practices and so on

(d) The specific issues that affect their labour markets: for example, the unification of Germany, the extent of immigration from non-EU countries, their trade agreements with other trading blocs and so on and hence

(e) Their specific national laws and practices (some of which have been compared, in context, throughout this Course Book) in areas such as: terms and conditions of employment (overtime and night rates, holiday entitlements); the extent of the casualisation of national workforces (part-time and temporary working); family-friendly policies (maternity/paternity/parental leave, career breaks and so on); recruitment procedures; dismissal notices and compensation; anti-discrimination provisions and so on.

As we have noted repeatedly in this chapter, European HRM and harmonisation of law and policy within the EU is very much 'work in progress'. Debates about 'union' in general, and specific proposals in particular, are constantly in the news. You must take responsibility for your own on-going research in order to keep up-to-date with this area of the course. The following are some suggestions to help you to deepen your knowledge of particular EU countries (for the purposes of comparison) and to stay abreast of developments.

2.7 On-going research

Information structure

Decide whether you would prefer to organise your information by HR-related topic (recruitment, training, employee relations) or by country (EU general, Germany, France, Spain). Whichever you choose as your main file classification system, you can use the other method to create subsections within each file:

(a) Recruitment (Germany, France, Spain), Training (Germany, France, Spain) and so on, *or*

(b) Germany (Recruitment, Training, Employee Relations), France (Recruitment, Training, Employee Relations) and so on.

If you decide to use the second method, you may wish to select a small number of countries on which to concentrate your research. (This may help you to target relevant information as you 'scan' the daily press and HR journals.) Select countries that interest you: your research may help you live or work there one day. Select countries that present contrasts in culture and economic development: Germany (or France), Spain (or Portugal), and Sweden (or Denmark), say.

Information strategy

Compile a list of useful sources of information, cross-referencing or indexing them by your chosen method. The following may get you started.

(a) **Commission of the European Communities** (in the phone book) provide free publications, guides, factsheets etc.

(b) **DTI factsheets, bulletins and guides.**

(c) HRM publications (*People Management, International Human Resource Management Journal, Human Resource Management Journal*).

(d) **Quality and financial press:** business and management sections. Back issues are archived and indexed in local libraries: ask for help if you don't yet know how to locate specific articles or topics.

(e) **The World Wide Web**. The site of *People Management Journal* may be useful: (www.peoplemanagement.co.uk). Also check out the new 'Web Link' feature in the Journal's news pages.

(f) **Business and tourism offices** of the various EU (and other) countries.

Information storage

Open files in line with your information structure: ring binder files with subdividers would ideally suit the kind of classification structure outlined above. This will allow you immediately and flexibly to store any cuttings, notes, printouts of web pages and so on that you collect over time.

Ensure that you note each item of information with its **source** (so you can add it to your Source List and go back to it for details if necessary) and its **date**. Items will probably be added in chronological order as you find them: dating will allow you to identify when a piece of information has been outdated by subsequent events.

Activity 5   **(No time limit)**

Start the first steps of the 3S research strategy outlined above. Once you've got these steps set up, it will be much easier to spot interesting items of information – and know what to do with them!

If you think 'HRM in the USA' is another whole new topic, remember that the theories, concepts and prescriptions underlying the HRM approach originated in the USA. We have already discussed some of them (including the models of the Harvard and Michigan business schools) in Chapter 11. We will now look at some of the implications for US management.

3   HRM IN THE USA

3.1   The orientation of HRM in the USA

Beardwell and Holden identify the main dimensions of HRM in US management literature as follows.

(a) Emphasis on strategic integration: linking external strategies for competing in the product market to internal strategies for the management of organisational resources. This became particularly important with increased international competition (particularly from Japan and the Pacific Rim) in key US sectors such as the automobile industry.

(b) A unitarist perspective on employee relations, based on the belief that conflicts of interest are not inherent in the employment relationship and that effective management can integrate managerial and worker goals. (The pluralist, stakeholder perspective of the Harvard model has not been widely adopted – despite a long tradition of more or less adversarial employee relations.)

(c) Focus on developing individual workers' commitment to the organisation: loyalty and motivation to deliver high levels of performance. Methods of achieving this (previously founded on promotion channels and employment security) have became more complex as economic growth has slowed.

(d) The importance of developing strong organisational cultures, supportive of commitment-based HRM policies, centred on 'key guiding values' (often reflecting the vision of business founders).

Activity 6   **(15 minutes)**

Look back at Hofstede's cultural model (paragraph 1.3 above). From the USA's 'score' on the various cultural dimensions, what would you expect its culture of employment to be like? Consider the implications of each dimension, and give examples of associated techniques if you can.

3.2 The US workforce

The workforce is structurally diverse, comprising 43% white male, 35% white female and 22% racial/ethnic groups: in 2005, this is projected to be 32%, 33% and 35% respectively (Timm and Peterson, 2000). Despite falling birth rates, immigration has continued to supplement the skilled workforce, while unemployment is still heavily concentrated among African Americans. In addition, the sheer size of the USA means that there is a wide variety of geographical and cultural characteristics, from highly urbanised/industrialised to oil-rich wastes and rural-agricultural heartlands.

The US has a younger workforce than either Europe or Japan.

As in other Western economies, there has been a shift of employment from manual to non-manual, from manufacturing to service industries (and in the USA, from north to south). There has been a rise in temporary and part-time working (slightly lower than in the UK, at 26% of the workforce) and in self-employment (significantly less than in the UK at 6%).

Under the federal structure of the USA, each of the 51 states has its own laws and regulations, in addition to federal law. Some key issues in US HRM, however, are as follows.

3.3 HR policy issues

Diversity

> From its early days, the United States has depended on the inexpensive labor [sic] of newly arrived people to build its businesses. Black slaves worked on southern plantations; Irish and Chinese workers built the railroads; Polish, Italian and other groups filled factory, domestic and other unskilled jobs. Yet the door to better opportunities was often posted with signs such as "Whites Only" and "No Irish Need Apply". While the past century has seen many European immigrants assimilated into the American "melting pot"... for others, especially visible ethnic and racial groups such as African Americans, Hispanic Americans, and Asian and Pacific Island Americans, the problems of exclusion from opportunity persist.

(Timm and Peterson, *People at Work*, 2000)

The Civil Rights Act 1964 supported equal employment opportunities, requiring companies with 15 or more employees, labour unions and employment agencies not to discriminate on the basis of 'colour, religion, sex or national origin'. The Civil Rights Act

1991 strengthened the law and provided damages in cases of intentional employment discrimination. In addition, the US federal government established the Equal Employment Opportunity Commission (EEOC) to carry out 'affirmative action programmes' promoting diversity. Under the **Bakke decision** in the US Supreme Court, however, it is illegal to carry out 'reverse discrimination' by setting up rigid preferential systems in favour of ethnic minorities.

Employment security and internal labour markets

The doctrine of 'employment at will' stresses the free market imperative for employers to be able to hire and fire as they wish, subject to contract terms. Security of employment therefore rests on the employment contract determined by negotiation with the individual or by collective bargaining in unionised firms, and typically renegotiated on a regular basis.

At the same time, major US companies have been characterised by strong internal labour markets, supported by independent internally-structured rewards (largely independent of external market rates), and offering motivation and employment security through clear internal promotion channels. There is some evidence that this has been eroded in recent years. Strategic workforce reductions or 'downsizing' (rather than 'layoffs' as responses to short-term economic fluctuations) are more prevalent: groups previously insulated (managers and skilled workers) are increasingly likely to lose their jobs. Meanwhile, the use of flexible (temporary, part-time) labour has increased, particularly since their rights are not protected in the same way as their European equivalents.

Labour relations

There has been a steady decline in trade union membership since the mid 1960s, largely due to the structural changes in the labour force mentioned above, but hastened by a long history of anti-union values among employers. During the 1970s the differential between non-union and union wages rose to 20-30%: a powerful incentive to de-unionise, given global recession and intensifying competition. Anti-union measures have included:

(a)   The physical intimidation of union supporters and representatives, and the breaking of strikes by 'union busters'. Violent confrontations are still a feature of industrial relations, especially in the southern states.

(b)   State and federal legislation curbing the power of unions (equivalent to that introduced in the UK during the 1980s), including 'right to work' laws outlawing the 'closed shop' (agreements under which union membership is made a condition of employment); the outlawing of secondary strike action (in support of other disputes); the imposition of ballot procedures on disputes regarded as a potential threat to national health and safety; and the right to hire 'temporary replacements' during lock-outs in the course of a dispute.

(c)   Cutbacks to investment and production in (and/or closures of) unionised sites, to be replaced by new plants set up on a non-unionised basis.

Where union avoidance proved impossible, managements have sought to loosen the hold of unions through:

(a)   Limited partnership agreements, aimed at raising productivity and quality. These are generally based on negotiating greater flexibility of work rules and job roles, in return for the increased participation of workers through 'quality of working life' programmes (typically involving quality circles, briefing groups and so on).

(b)   Proactive attempts to marginalise unions by forestalling their demands, offering favourable rates of pay and fringe benefits, operating direct information and consultation (outside the collective bargaining framework) and so on.

FOR DISCUSSION

Is the HRM approach, with its psychology-based, individual-oriented personnel policies, just another (more subtle) way of marginalising trade unions?

There is no industrial democracy legislation in the USA, such as has been developed in Europe, requiring employee directors, work councils or equivalents. However, there has been some increase during the 1990s in management-initiated employee involvement schemes: self-managed (or 'empowered') teamworking, total quality management systems, quality circles, think tanks and so on.

EXAMPLE

The clash of culture between the USA and the EU was illustrated in a feature in *People Management* (28 September 2000) by Tony Royle. Here are some thought-provoking snippets.

> The McDonald's Corporation's stance on unions is well documented. As [the company's US labour relations chief in the 1970s] put it: "Unions are inimical to what we stand for and how we operate." In Canada and the US, McDonald's still routinely resists any bid to unionise its restaurants. For example, in April 1998 a group of about 20 workers in Macedonia, Ohio, staged the company's first strike in the US. After negotiations, the strike organisers were dismissed, but later they made out-of-court settlements with the company. The remaining employees made no further unionisation attempts...

> It is perhaps not surprising that McDonald's UK was one of the companies that recently attended union-busting seminars presented by Alan Lips, a US employment lawyer. Lips encouraged delegates to adopt confrontational tactics if they were concerned about the new union recognition procedures brought in by the Employment Relations Act 1999. (Discussed in Chapter 20)

> In mainland Europe, McDonald's faces a somewhat different situation. A variety of national legislative systems already give people rights to worker representation. These often involve unions, sometimes at both local and company level, and rights to collective bargaining...

> In recent years McDonald's has tried to avoid making outspoken anti-union pronouncements in Europe, because it is only too aware of the detrimental effect they have on sales... But the reality appears to be different...

The article proceeds to detail McDonald's persistent refusals to enter into collective agreements and sectoral negotiations, resistance to statutory works councils, alleged interference in works council elections and so on.

A reply from McDonald's is appended.

> The company has... made significant progress in locally implementing its worldwide policy to value people. We want to address three key issues: representation, diversity and opportunity. A diverse team of motivated, well-trained individuals working in partnership with the company is key to business success.

> We reject the anti-union tag. Employees are free to join trade unions. McDonald's consults directly with all staff. Examples of this include quarterly staff meetings in each restaurant and independently conducted employee satisfaction surveys... Managers operate an open-door policy, and staff publications rely on employee input. A commitment is made to each employee on working conditions, benefits, training and communications, with an emphasis on a 'psychological contract' model of employee relations based on trust, fairness and delivery on commitments.

McDonald's is the leading provider of opportunities for young people. In the UK, more than half the restaurant managers started as hourly paid staff. Many are promoted further, or become franchisees. Training for all is a McDonald's maxim, expressed as: "Everyone's job, every day".'

If 'HRM' originated in the USA, it did so partly in response to the competitive success of Japanese business in worldwide markets following post-war reconstruction: many HRM techniques were derived from the almost mythically perceived effectiveness of Japanese management techniques. Once again, therefore, there is a grey area between convergence and divergence! We will now go on to look briefly at Japan.

4 HRM IN THE FAR EAST: JAPAN

4.1 Cultural context and HR practice

Key cultural values in Japanese management practice have traditionally been as follows.

'Commitment'

This goes further than the idea of secure or guaranteed 'lifetime employment', which only ever applied to certain categories of staff and has in any case been eroded by the slowing of economic growth. Historically based in a feudal social system, it embodies a complex of ideas.

(a) Loyalty, expressed in conformity to company rules and cultural norms as well as low labour mobility.

(b) The identification of workers with the corporate entity ('family'), achieved through HR policies such as:

    (i) Careful selection and socialisation of workers into corporate philosophy and objectives

    (ii) The paternalistic, 'holistic' role of the corporate family in its workers' lives and welfare (traditionally including social activities and the housing and education of workers' families)

    (iii) Supporting mechanisms of organisation culture, such as corporate songs and factory morning exercises

(c) Seniority- or service-based appraisal and reward systems, on the basis that age implies more loyalty and experience and hence better quality of work and decisions. (We noted in Chapter 7 how alien this 'person-related' payment system seems to Western 'job-related' systems.)

(d) Long-term, slow-progression career paths which (since opportunities for upward mobility are scarce) encourage exposure and development in many areas, for 'well-rounded' management skills and personality.

'Harmony' ('wa')

This underpins the Japanese preference for consensus decision-making: involving all stakeholders in a decision; focusing on exploring the question rather than giving an answer; considering different perspectives and encouraging argument prior to seeking consensus on the basis of a synthesis of opposite views. (You may recognise this as a high 'Confucian dynamism' factor.) This may take longer than the Western model of 'rational' decision-making, but it allows a high degree of acceptability of and commitment to the decision once taken (Drucker).

It is also expressive of the Japanese approach to labour relations, characterised by participative decision-making, communication and co-operation on the basis of shared commitment. Although there is a deeply-ingrained hierarchy of authority and seniority (reflected in the Japanese language's complex levels of terms of respect and 'upward' and 'downward' relationship), there are no artificial barriers between management and workers: single status applies in terms of workplace dress, access to facilities (washrooms, canteens), participation in social activities and so on.

Tasks tend to be assigned to groups or teams rather than individuals, which are often given a measure of responsibility for determining their own work organisation and deployment, within productivity and quality targets. (This has been a model for Western 'self-managed teamworking' approaches.)

'Continuous improvement' ('kaizen')

The notion of 'quality' is open-ended: there are no conceptual limits to possible improvement, and therefore more attention is paid to quality processes than specific quality targets. Japanese manufacturing systems and work organisation techniques (which perhaps more than any other aspect have attracted the attention and emulation of Western businesses) are founded on this process-centred approach: Just-in-Time (JIT) manufacturing, for example, was an innovative Japanese technique for increasing the flexibility of systems and workforce deployment. Quality is regarded as part of all production processes, not merely an add-on monitoring and control system: this is often expressed as 'Total Quality Management' (TQM).

Individuals and groups are integrated into the improvement process, for example by means of quality circles (which have been widely imported to the West).

Definitions

> **Total Quality Management (TQM)** is an approach which extends the principles of quality control and continuous improvement throughout the strategic and tactical management of the firm, to create a quality orientation or culture.
>
> **Quality Circles** are multi-disciplinary participative working groups which meet periodically to discuss quality issues, with varying degrees of responsibility for implementation of quality improvements.

> **Activity 7**   **(30 minutes)**
>
> From the above discussion, draw up a table summarising the differences between Japanese and American employment in the areas of:
>
> (a) Length of employment
> (b) Career path/employee development
> (c) Personnel appraisal and reward
> (d) Decision making
> (e) Responsibility
> (f) Degree of the enterprise's concern for the employee

4.2 Emerging HR issues

The traditional values discussed above have been eroded in recent years, with the increasing influence of Western management practices and increasing economic pressures on Japanese business. We noted in Chapter 10 that it is now not unusual for employees to be transferred or lent to associated firms, thus remaining within the 'commitment' system without necessarily remaining in a particular work situation. The majority of Japanese workers are subject to the less regulated labour market made up of 'satellite' suppliers and subcontractors to the major enterprises: there is no expectation of lifetime employment security.

EXAMPLE

Japan is looking to exorcise the "wa", or harmony, from its system of government with a huge shake-up of the monolithic bureaucracy that will vest more power in politicians.

This morning, hundreds of thousands of public servants will make the crowded commute to newly named departments after... the number of government ministries has been pared down from 23 to 13... A quarter of the country's 540,000 civil servants will lose their jobs over the next 10 years...

The public service was credited with Japan's post-war economic recovery, but after the bubble burst in the 1990s it was recognised that the bureaucracy was not reacting fast enough to combat the decline. The problem was associated with its tradition of making policy decisions only by consensus to ensure the desired **wa** was achieved...

The new Cabinet Office... will appoint go-getters from the private sector to help the politicians determine policy, rather than look to those who have taken decades to rise through the civil service ranks.

The Australian (January 8, 2001)

Other issues have arisen from exposure to Western markets and cultures, notably:

(a) The position of women in business: you may recall that Japan scores high on Hofstede's 'masculinity' index, meaning that women are expected to adopt traditional gender roles

(b) Other diversity issues, given the cultural barriers to employing an ethnically diverse workforce

(c) The aspirations of young Japanese workers, who may be frustrated by the seniority culture, given the opportunities for swift advancement and reward in other accessible labour markets (such as Australia)

4.3 Other Asian economies

We have focused on Japan here as a study in contrast which has also been very influential on US and European management practices over recent decades. You should be aware, however, that Japan is by no means typical of Far Eastern economies and employment practices. China and Korea, for example, have booming export economies, partly because of their notoriously low wages and poor working conditions ('sweat shops') in some sectors, with paternalistic seniority cultures in others (such as finance), and close intervention by the centralised state bureaucracy.

EXAMPLE: PEOPLE'S REPUBLIC OF CHINA

People Management described in October 2000 how 'a British HR-led initiative [FIST] has kicked off a revolution in working practices across China'. In preparation for China's entry into the World Trade Organisation, 225 high-flyers from China's finance sector were funded by the UK government to work for British firms for three to ten months, in order to help Chinese firms to adopt more western practices. The culture shock was summed up as follows by the HR consultant running the scheme: 'People can't believe how collaborative our decision-making is or the opportunities that people have to share ideas. They also find it surprising that staff can develop according to ability and not how long they have been in the organisation.'

With the opening up of China to global markets and Western capitalism, management training has become a key HRM issue. However, the Western model of management development (based on group discussion, experiential learning and the free and open exchange of ideas) clashes with Chinese cultural focus on conformity, social status, the need to preserve 'face' and the authority of the 'expert': the preference is for formal, taught courses.

Chapter roundup

- Despite some convergence in (or harmonisation of) the structure, technology and terminology of HRM across the 'global village', there is still enough diversity to support the idea of divergence. Certain aims and activities of HRM are international – but they are 'done' differently.

- Differences in approaches may arise from cultural factors (such as those identified by the High-Low Context and Hofstede models), national law and regulation, structural factors (such as education, demographics, infrastructure, politics), employee relations traditions and ideologies, and economic and social development.

- EU law consists of regulations (applying directly into national law of member states), directives (stating objectives, to be implemented via legislation and regulation in each of the member states) and decisions of the European Court of Justice (binding on the nation, organisation or individual concerned). Many of the objectives of EU law were laid out in the Social Charter/Chapter, which states 12 principles of social policy relating to living and working conditions.

- In addition to the implementation of the Social Charter/Chapter and directives, there are HR issues related to the mobility of labour, European Monetary Union, cultural and language differences and continuing differences in national law and practice for companies exploring the possibilities of pan-European HRM.

- Key HRM issues in the USA include: individualism, cultural 'unitarism', diversity, 'employment at will', lean production, the weakening of internal labour markets and associated reward structures, an adversarial history of labour relations and union-avoidance, and less adversarial labour relations approaches (employee involvement and so on).

- Key values underpinning HRM in Japan include commitment, harmony and continuous improvement, with techniques such as long-term career planning, seniority-based appraisal and reward, paternalistic welfare policies, high cultural identification, consensus decision-making, self-managed team working, and quality circles.

Quick quiz

1 What aspects of HRM can be said to show 'convergence' across national boundaries?

2 Distinguish between High-Context and Low-Context cultures.

3 All European countries are low context cultures: true or false?

4 Explain the terms 'power distance', 'uncertainty avoidance', 'individualism', 'masculinity' and 'Confucian dynamism' as they are used in the Hofstede model.

NOTES

5   What is the main decision-making body of the European Union, which acts on proposals to institute EU secondary legislation.

6   Distinguish between regulations, directives and decisions in EU law.

7   What trends can be identified in the structure of the US workforce?

8   List four approaches to reducing trade union power used in the USA.

9   List three HR techniques related to the concept of 'commitment' in Japanese work culture.

10 Outline the features of Japanese decision-making.

Answers to quick quiz

1   Basic HR activities (HRP, recruitment, selection, appraisal, training and so on); the broad aims of HRM (attract, retain, motivate, develop); technical terms and techniques (job evaluation, quality circles).

(see paragraph 1.1)

2   High-Context people exchange and interpret messages with an appreciation of contextual factors such as non-verbal cues, attitudes, timing, emotional undertones, social differences and so on: they prefer face-to-face and oral communication and are good at developing informal information networks. Low-Context people take communication at its face value and prefer clear, explicit, written forms of communication.

(para 1.2)

3   False: southern Europeans (Spain, Italy) are high context; France and UK are on the high side of the scale, with Belgium, Netherlands and Denmark just on the low side: only West Germany and German Switzerland are very low.

(para 1.2)

4   See paragraph 1.3 for a full account.

5   The Council of Ministers.

(para 2.1)

6   Regulations apply directly into national law of member states; directives state objectives, to be implemented via legislation and regulation in each of the member states; decisions of the European Court of Justice (binding on the nation, organisation or individual concerned.

(para 2.1)

7   Increasing ethnic diversity (from immigration and affirmative action) and gender distribution; shift from manual to non-manual, manufacturing to service; rise in temporary, part-time and self-employed working.

(para 3.2)

8   Violent confrontation and intimidation; disinvesting in unionised plants; legislative controls on union activity and disputes; limited partnership agreements; 'enlightened' HRM policies, marginalising union roles.

(para 3.3)

9   Strong selection on/socialisation into cultural norms and values of the organisation; seniority-based appraisal and reward; paternalistic welfare orientation; long-term, slow-progression, generalist development plans.

(para 4.1)

10 Involving all parties in a decision; focusing on defining and exploring the question, rather than defining the answer; considering different perspectives and encouraging argument; consensus by synthesis of views; time-consuming but high acceptance.

(para 4.1)

Answers to Activities

1   Here are just some of the many dimensions you may have come up with.

   (a) Attitudes to the balance of work, leisure and family life ('work ethic': traditionally more pronounced in northern/protestant countries of Europe than in Mediterranean cultures)

   (b) The importance attached to the individual vis-à-vis the group or society as a whole (individualistic like the USA; family-oriented like Latino cultures; team/organisation-oriented like Japan)

   (c) Concepts of justice, fairness and ethical dealing (definitions of 'gifts' and 'bribes', for example are fluid in eastern cultures)

   (d) The relative value of different forms of reward and incentive (money is high-value in the US: respect and belonging have high value in Asian cultures)

   (e) Attitudes towards gender roles (women in business are less accepted in Islamic and, to a lesser extent, Asian and 'macho' Latino cultures), age (the seniority culture of Asia or the youth culture of the US and Western Europe), diversity: attitude to disabled, ethnic minorities, sexual orientation, religious beliefs (including specific traditional conflicts eg in Northern Ireland and Islamic states)

   (f) Valued personal attributes and attainments (status attached to education; different styles of education and training)

   (g) Perceptions of continuity/stability/security (Japanese 'commitment' system) v mobility/risk/change (Western 'flexibility' model)

   (h) Styles of interpersonal communication and decision-making (formality, reticence, consensus and hierarchy in Japan: informality, directness, authority in US: differences in eye contact and body language)

   And so on...

2   Problems may include: frustration at expecting to find information clearly written down and on file when it isn't; being 'left out of the loop' (not being part of informal networks and therefore missing out on information everyone else seems to know); confusion or causing offence by misinterpreting tones of voice and gestures, or taking expressions literally; failing to approach discussions and meetings with sufficient attention to protocol, courtesies, small talk and so on.

   Your role play or imaginary scenario may have highlighted some of the above on an interpersonal level. The high-context worker may have tried to raise his or her problems subtly, using innuendo or ambiguous words with meaningful non-verbal signals: the low-context manager may have failed to realise that there was a problem. Alternatively, the high-context worker, enjoying the 'drama' of the communication context, may have cheerfully exaggerated ('I have this terrible problem... I can't stand it...') and the low-context manager may have taken this at face value and overestimated the problem.

3   (a) A low-PD manager is likely to attempt consultative joint decision-making: high PD workers will be inexperienced and uncomfortable with such styles, preferring authoritative instruction.

   (b) A high-UA manager, expecting to find detailed and generally adhered-to rules for everything, may be horrified by the ad hocracy of a low-UA organisation: if (s)he attempts to impose a high-UA culture, there may be resistance from low-UA employees and management.

(c)   A high-individuality manager may implement MBO on the basis of individual performance targets, results and rewards: this may fail to motivate low-individuality workers, for whom group processes and performance is more important.

(d)   A low-masculinity manager may try to shelter the workforce from the effects of downsizing, taking time for consultation, retraining, voluntary measures and so on: this may seem unacceptably 'soft' to a high-masculinity parent firm.

4   Directives are designed to create a partnership between employers and workers. This will improve general social cohesion within the EU, with the effect of raising living standards, skill levels and worker performance. Without harmonisation of minimum social and employment conditions, there will be social inequity between poor and affluent nations. In addition, it may encourage 'social dumping': the unfair undercutting of the price of labour by certain countries (enabled by low wages, long working hours, lack of employment protection for part-time and casual labour and so on) for unfair competitive advantage.

5   Just do it!

6   The culture of employment in the USA tends to emphasises the following values.

(a)   Open vertical and horizontal communication, informal personal relationships and the minimisation of artificial status distinctions between managers and different grades of employee (eg single/salaried status schemes). Low power distance also accounts for the high ratio of managers to managed employees (flat organisation), linked to employee involvement through joint healthy and safety committees, briefing groups, quality circles and so on.

(b)   Openness to flexibility and change (expressed in US-led management theories such as 'excellence' and 'chaos', for example). Graham and Bennett note that 'Vigorous competition and the regular business shut-downs/start-ups that it implies have led perhaps to a greater willingness to accept change than in some other countries, and to a workforce that is prepared, on the whole, to move to areas and industries where jobs are available.'

(c)   High individualism: over and above the rhetoric of teamworking, the system prizes individual initiative and responsibility, selection and development on merit, upwardly mobile aspirations and anti-unionism.

(d)   High 'masculinity': vigorous competition; the (relative) freedom of the organisation to fire employees at will; HR planning based on 'lean production'; motivation based on (relatively high) rewards and penalties; strong 'gung ho' cultures (such as those associated with McDonald's, Disney, IBM)

7   WG Ouchi *(Theory Z: How American Business Can Meet the Japanese Challenge)* analysed the cultural values of Japanese and American businesses in order to formulate an 'ideal' style (an advance on McGregor's Theory Y, which he called Theory Z) incorporating the best elements of both. Ouchi outlined the Japanese business model (in comparison to the American model) as follows.

BPP
PUBLISHING

	Theory J (Japanese)	Theory A (American)
Length of employment	Lifetime	Varies, but typically short
Career path/employee development	Progression upward (slowly) and laterally; exposure in many areas, development of well-rounded management skills/personalities.	Progression upward (rapidly): specialised in chosen area
Personnel appraisal/reward	Based on loyalty/'commitment' to the firm (seniority)	Based on performance
Decision-making	Consensus by many; communication upward as well as downward	Individual, by managers
Responsibility	Collective (as a result of decision-making)	Individual (as a result of decision-making)
Degree of corporate concern with the employee	Total: all aspects of life, including housing, family, schooling	Focused on work performance only

Assignment 15 (2 hours)

Kaizen Tomorrow Ltd is a large UK manufacturing company. The Production Director approaches you, the HR assistant, and asks your advice about a new idea he has had. He has heard about the success in 'similar' Japanese companies of something called 'quality circles', and he wants to introduce them into KT's factories as soon as possible. 'They're great,' he enthuses. 'You can arrive at decisions for change in product designs and production methods – and get a maximum degree of acceptance from the workers. Quality Circles improve quality, productivity, interdepartmental communication, teamwork and team spirit. They reduce costs and absenteeism. I want them.'

You wonder if you should point out to the Production Director that there is currently very little 'teamworking' as such (although the company sometimes refers to its workers as 'the team'), and even less interdepartmental communication. Worker acceptance of decisions is largely a matter of negotiated compromises between management and the trade unions which represent the various occupational groups involved in production. Previous attempts by management to impose high quality targets were met with suspicion, defensiveness and increased pay claims.

'I'd like to discuss this again,' continues the Production Director 'to hear your suggestions for introducing Quality Circles. I don't foresee any problems – after all, they work fine for the Japanese - but if you think there may be difficulties, you'd better put that in the report as well.'

Your task: Use your research skills to find an article or other account of the experience of a UK company in introducing Japanese management techniques, including Quality Circles.

Make notes in preparation for the meeting. Consider the difficulties of getting this company to work in the way that a Japanese company would, and what could be done to facilitate the process (taking into account current attitudes and structures).

PART C

UNIT 23: HUMAN RESOURCE DEVELOPMENT

Chapter 16 :
LEARNING AND THE LEARNING ORGANISATION

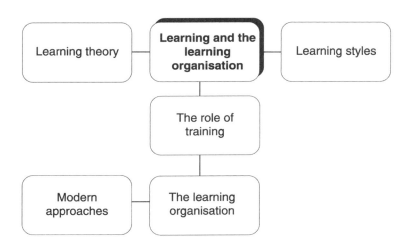

Introduction

Providing the organisation with the most suitable human resources for the task and environment is an on-going process. It involves not only recruitment and selection, as discussed in Chapters 3 – 5, but the training and development of employees in order to help them meet the requirements of their current and potential future job.

Training may be defined as helping individuals to learn how to carry out satisfactorily the work required of them in their present job. (**Development** discussed in Chapter 17, may be defined as preparing individuals for a **future** job). The main purpose of training is to raise competence and therefore performance standards. From the perspective of HR management, however, it is also concerned with personal development, helping individuals to expand and fulfil their potential (also motivating them to higher performance through the opportunity for personal growth).

In this chapter we examine how people learn, and how learning might be built into organisational culture and practice. In the next chapter, we examine and evaluate more specific types and methods of training and development.

Your objectives

In this chapter you will learn about the following:

(a)   Different types of learning styles

(b)   The types of learning cycle and learning curve

(c)   How training contributes to the achievement of business objectives

1 LEARNING THEORY

1.1 Three theoretical approaches

It is not possible to put forward a simple definition of learning, because despite intensive scientific and practical work on the subject, there are different ways of understanding how the process works, what it involves, and what we mean when we say that a person 'knows' something (epistemology).

There are three basic theories of how learning works.

(a) **The behaviourist (or stimulus-response) approach.** Behaviourist psychology is based on 'empirical' epistemology (the belief that the human mind operates purely on information gained from the senses by experience) and concentrates on observable behaviour, since 'thought processes' are not amenable to scientific study. It therefore concentrates on the relationship between stimuli (input through the senses) and the organism's responses to those stimuli. The work of Pavlov (on dogs) and Skinner (on rats) suggested that learning is the formation of new connections between stimulus and response on the basis of experience, which they called **conditioning.** According to this theory, we modify our responses to a given stimulus according to whether the feedback on the results of our previous responses was good or bad: an incentive (positive reinforcement) or deterrent (negative reinforcement) to similar behaviour in future. Repetition of the stimulus-response sequence strengthens the conditioning, making us more likely to respond in the same way in future.

(b) **The cognitive (or information-processing) approach.** Cognitive psychology is based on 'rationalist' epistemology (the belief that the human mind imposes organisation and meaning on sensory raw material) and assumes that it is possible to make inferences about those thought processes. According to this theory, our behaviour is 'purposive': we make plans of action in pursuit of goals that we value. Learning is the way in which we process and interpret feedback on the results of past behaviour/experience, and make decisions about whether to maintain successful behaviours or modify unsuccessful behaviours in future, in pursuit of our goals. (You may recognise this as a typical planning and control cycle: the use of feedback to compare performance with plan and adjust either or both accordingly.) We do not simply learn new habits (as conditioning theories suggest) but ways of dealing with information and choosing alternative methods of reaching our goals: we learn to learn.

(c) **The social learning approach.** Studies of child development suggest that human beings are designed to learn by imitating other people who are significant to us: our behavioural and role models (who shift over time from our parents and caregivers in childhood, to peers in adolescence, to selected experts and mentors in adulthood. We define our social identity and behaviour by reflection from other people: how they respond to us. We learn to perform actions by 'modelling': watching and analysing the way others do them, and imitating the successful aspects of their performance.

The learning strategies and styles we discuss below are essentially based on one or more of these theoretical approaches, incorporating elements of behaviourism (trial and error, repetition and positive/negative reinforcement), cognitive psychology (goal articulation, reflection and interpretation, testing, feedback and adjustment), and social learning (modelling and mentoring).

NOTES

Activity 1   **(10 minutes)**

Before reading what follows, see if you can pick out the aspects of the above theoretical approaches which might be important for the design of training programmes. (Think about the kind of training/learning techniques – which you may have experienced – that occur to you as you read about each theory...)

Implications for training design

Whichever approach it is based on, learning theory offers certain useful propositions for the design of effective training programmes.

(a) The individual should be **motivated** to learn. The advantages of training (to the trainee) should be made clear, according to the individual's motives or goals: reward, challenge, status, competence or whatever.

(b) Clear **goals and objectives** should be set, so that each task has some meaning. This will help trainees in the control process that leads to learning, providing targets against which performance will constantly be measured and adjusted accordingly.

(c) Learning should be **structured** and **paced** to allow learning processes to take place effectively and progressively. Each stage of learning should present a challenge (motivation), without overloading trainees so that they lose confidence and the ability to assimilate information/experience.

    (i) Tasks may be broken down and taught and practised stage by stage ('part learning') in order to build up stimulus-response associations, habits or memory: stages are then progressively put together into larger and larger chunks of practice. Alternatively, tasks may be taught or modelled in their entirety ('whole learning') in order to enhance perceived meaning and motivation.

    (ii) Stimulus-response associations and mental processes (especially memory) are subject to pacing effects. The most effective strategy is one which allows for short sessions with frequent rest/assimilation pauses, and which uses repetition (revision/practice) frequently at first and then at increasing intervals.

(d) There should be timely, relevant **feedback** on performance and progress. This will usually be provided by the trainer, and should be concurrent – or not long delayed. If progress reports or appraisals are given only at the course end, for example, there will be no opportunity for progressive behavioural adjustment.

(e) Positive and negative **reinforcement** should be judiciously used. Recognition and encouragement embeds correct learning and motivates further effort. Constructive criticism of errors is essential for learning, but must be used sensitively: 'punishing' error or slow progress may simply discourage the learner and create a culture of failure. (Even behaviourism notes that negative reinforcement merely conditions people to avoid error and punishment – not to find more constructive behaviours.) 'Failure' should be redefined as 'opportunity for learning'.

(f) Active **participation** in the learning experience (for example in action learning or discovery learning) is generally more effective than passive reception (for example in lectures or reading), because it enhances concentration and conditioning. Practice and repetition can be used to reinforce passive learning, but participation has the added effect of encouraging 'ownership' of the goals and process of change.

1.2 Stages of learning

The 'stages of learning' comprise a simple, intuitive model of the evolution of learned behaviour.

Stage 1. **Unconscious incompetence**. You aren't aware of what you don't know: you simply act in the way that seems best with the knowledge you have at the time.

Stage 2. **Conscious incompetence**. You become aware that you don't know. New information, feedback from others, or the results of your behaviour, suggest that there is something missing.

Stage 3. **Conscious competence**. You work at knowing. You research, analyse, practise, repeat, monitor, adjust. You may be competent – but it requires conscious thought and application.

Stage 4. **Unconscious competence**. You don't have to think about knowing. You have internalised the knowledge or skill and use it without having to think about it.

Think about the way a baby learns to walk, for example, and you will find that it corresponds to these four stages. The same goes for learning to type or to drive a car (remember how laborious the 'conscious competence' stage seemed?).

Activity 2   (15 minutes)

Illustrate the Stages of Learning with another example of learning a work-related skill.

1.3 The learning curve

Definition

A **learning curve** is a graph showing the relationship between the time spent in learning and the level of competence attained. Hence, it describes the progress and variable pace of learning. (It is common for people to say (or complain) that they are 'on a steep learning curve' when they have to acquire a lot of new knowledge or skills in a short period of time.)

A learning curve may be used:

(a)   To illustrate the improvement in a given trainee's competence (or output, or whatever measure of proficiency is relevant) during the training process, in order to monitor the progress and pace of training

(b)   To suggest typical patterns in the acquisition of a given skill or type of skill: the pace of skill acquisition, the standard at which performance 'levels out' (does not improve further); the point at which performance 'plateaus' (levels out for a while and then improves further)

The curve for the acquisition of skills typically shows a slow start (the trainee has a lot to take in – including contextual factors not directly related to the task), then gains upward momentum. There may be one or more plateaus, reflecting the trainee's need to consolidate what (s)he has learned so far, to correct some aspects of performance, to regain motivation and focus after the initial effort, or to establish habitual or

NOTES

unconscious competence in one skill prior to moving on to a new area. Momentum then gathers again, until the trainee reaches proficiency level, where the curve will level off – unless there is an injection of new equipment or methods, or fresh motivation, to lift output again. Such a learning curve is illustrated in Figure 16.1.

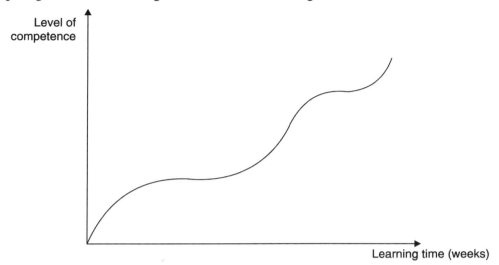

Figure 16.1: Learning curve (showing plateau)

Note that learning curves can be quite complex, going down as well as up: for example, if the trainee is unable to practise or apply newly acquired skills and forgets, or refuses to accept new areas of conscious incompetence which emerge in the course of training. An up-and-down 'transition curve' is common in cases where an individual changes jobs or work methods, or makes the transition from a non-managerial to a managerial position.

Activity 3   **(20 minutes)**

Draw a learning curve for:

(a)   An easy task that takes two weeks to learn

(b)   A complex task that takes eight weeks to learn, but for which the training programme has been 'paced' to include consolidation and problem-solving time, so that no plateau is evident

---

You may have noticed that the stages of learning and the learning curve appear to be linear or progressive, but in fact form part of an on-going cycle or control system: discovering further areas of conscious incompetence, starting further learning curves in order to adjust performance in response to feedback. This aspect of learning has been formulated as 'the learning cycle'.

1.4   The learning cycle

The best known model is the **experiential learning cycle** devised by David Kolb. He suggested that effective learning could start from concrete experience, as well as from abstract concepts. It should not be 'a special activity cut off from the real world and unrelated to one's life', but should integrate concrete (involvement) and abstract (detachment), active (doing) and reflective (observing) elements. This could be conceived as a simple cyclical process, as follows: Figure 16.2

BPP
PUBLISHING

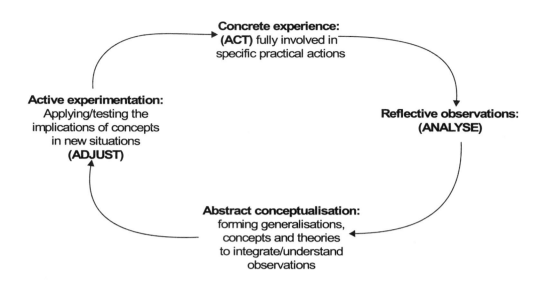

Figure 16.2 Experiential learning cycle

Say an employee interviews a customer for the first time (concrete experience). He observes his own performance and the dynamics of the situation (observation) and afterwards, having failed to convince the customer to buy his product, the employee analyses what he did right and wrong (reflection). He comes to the conclusion that he failed to listen to what the customer really wanted and was concerned about, underneath his general reluctance: he realises that the key to communication is listening (abstract conceptualisation). In his next interview he applies this strategy to the new set of circumstances (active experimentation). This provides him with a new experience with which to start the cycle over again.

FOR DISCUSSION

Can you trace the phases of the learning cycle in the way your studies are structured? What phases are well provided for – and which might you require more opportunity for? Do some phases(s) of the cycle naturally appeal to you more than others?

Kolb recognised that people tend to have a preference for a particular phase of the cycle, which he identified as a preferred 'learning style'. We will discuss this aspect of learning theory in Section 2 of this chapter. Meanwhile, we will look at another issue raised by the experiential learning cycle: what is the relationship between theory and practice in learning? If you have read a book on how a car works, should you be able to drive it? If you can drive a car, do you need to be able to explain how it works? And if you have grasped both theory and practice of driving a car, should you also be able to drive a truck? The idea that we can learn something in one context and 'carry it across' to another context is called the transfer of learning.

1.5 Transfer of learning

Definition

> **Transfer of learning** refers to the extent to which newly learned information or skills have been transferred from the learning context to the application of a specific task.

Positive transfer refers to a situation in which learning has been successfully transferred to a task: negative transfer refers to a situation in which learning has not been transferred to the application of a task.

There are two basic approaches to the transfer of learning.

(a) **Transfer by specific correspondence of elements.**

If you were learning French, for example, you might listen to language tapes which feature the repetition and rehearsal of phrases in specific useful contexts: 'I would like a hamburger, please', say. This would facilitate transfer of learning when you found yourself in those specific contexts: you would know how to order a hamburger in a Paris McDonald's. The workplace equivalent might be hands-on training in a specific procedure or piece of equipment which corresponds to those used in your employing organisation.

The advantage of this approach, when the correspondences are strong, is that learning can be swiftly and effectively applied in the work context, where it will be further embedded and adapted. The danger with this approach is that if the context, procedure or equipment are not quite the same as the models used in your learning, you might not be able to 'generalise' in order to transfer learning to the new situation. (You might not know the French for chicken nuggets, and this would result in negative transfer when you find yourself in the Paris KFC.)

Indeed, the attempt to transfer learning may have a detrimental effect on its application, if the techniques learned in one context are actively 'wrong' in another and have to be unlearned. This often happens where people who have learned computer skills on one operating system (say, PC) switch to another (Macintosh): much of what they have learned may be inapplicable, may confuse attempts to learn the new system, and may put them into a risky state of unconscious incompetence, where errors are made unawares.

(b) **Transfer by principle.**

If you were learning French, for example, you might use a method which went through the grammatical rules of the language and began to give you some vocabulary, so that you learned how to ask for things in general, including hamburgers. This might facilitate transfer of learning to a range of situations, since you could more easily pick up the French words for 'chicken nuggets' (from menus or by asking) if you knew how the rest of the question worked than the other way around. The workplace equivalent would be training which covered:

(i) The desired outcomes of performing a procedure (why it is performed)

(ii) Under what conditions this procedure is likely to be the most appropriate strategy among available alternatives

(iii) How to perform the procedure

(iv) How the stages of the procedure follow and depend on one another and what other variables influence performance

(v) Possible problems during a procedure and how to 'troubleshoot'

(vi) Sources of information and help, should they be required

The advantage of this approach is that it generalises learning and facilitates its transfer across a wider range of contexts. The danger, however, is that it may be too generalised to allow immediate application to a particular work context, and the knowledge may be forgotten if it is not immediately applied.

There is no right or wrong approach to transfer of learning. The nature of the task and the uniqueness or otherwise of the organisation's systems and 'house style' may dictate one or the other. In addition, some people have a preference for learning exactly what they need to do, by doing it: others prefer to work through a conceptual framework and then to apply what they know to a specific context. ('Learning styles' again: we will discuss them below.)

Whichever approach is used, organisations must take into account the transferability of learning if they are not to waste their training efforts and budgets. The range of contexts and variables, and the preferences of trainees, should be taken into account where possible, to ensure positive transfer. Modern approaches to training (such as competency definition, employability training and attitude and awareness training) are designed to be widely transferable within the organisational context and in the personal lives of trainees.

> **Activity 4**   **(30 minutes)**
>
> We have already mentioned some situations in which the learning curve levels out or even goes downwards: loss of motivation and negative transfer, for example. Can you think of other factors that might hinder or block learning? (Consider your work or study situation. What factors – cultural, emotional, intellectual, motivational, situational, physical – make it more difficult for you to learn than it needs to be?)

The various theories we have discussed so far encourage a contingency approach to learning: the appropriate strategy and techniques will depend on (among other things) the preferences of the individual for active or reflective, concrete or abstract learning experiences. Several theorists have classified these preferences as distinct 'learning styles': we will discuss them now.

2 LEARNING STYLES

2.1 Honey and Mumford

Peter Honey and Alan Mumford have drawn up a popular classification of four learning styles.

Learning style	Way of learning	Training preference	Training problems
(a) **Theorist**	This person seeks to understand underlying concepts and to take an intellectual, 'hands off' approach based on logical argument.	Such a person prefers training: (i) To be programmed and structured (ii) To allow time for analysis and (iii) To be provided by teachers who share his/her preference for concepts and analysis	Theorists find learning difficult if they have a teacher with a different style(particularly an activist style); material which skims over basic principles; and a programme which is hurried and unstructured.

NOTES

Learning style	Way of learning	Training preference	Training problems
(b) **Reflector**	People who observe phenomena, think about them and then choose how to act are called reflectors.	Such a person needs to work at his/her own pace and would find learning difficult if forced into a hurried programme with little notice or information.	Reflectors are able to produce carefully thought-out conclusions after research and reflection, but tend to be fairly slow, non-participative (unless to ask questions) and cautious.
(c) **Activist**	These are people who like to deal with practical, active problems and who do not have much patience with theory.	They require training based on hands-on experience.	Activists are excited by participation and pressure, such as making presentations and new projects. Although they are flexible and optimistic they tend to rush at something without due preparation, take risks and then get bored.
(d) **Pragmatist**	These people only like to study if they can see its direct link to practical problems – they are not interested in theory for its own sake.	They are particularly good at learning new techniques in on-the-job training which they see as useful improvements. Their aim is to implement action plans and/or do the task better.	Such a person is business-like and realistic, but may discard as being impractical good ideas which only require some development.

Training should ideally be designed to accommodate the preferences of all four styles. This can often be overlooked, especially as the majority of training staff are activists!

Activity 5   **(15 minutes)**

John, Paula, Ringo and Georgette are learning French, as part of their firm's initiative to develop staff in European market.

(a) John reckons that since he does not actually speak to clients, the whole scheme is a waste of time. He claims to be too busy to attend classes.

(b) Paula loves the classes, because they simulate real conversational situations. The trainees have to use whatever vocabulary they have to get their meaning across guided and corrected by the tutor: Paula doesn't like learning grammatical rules, she's happy to pick up the phrases to fit the situations.

(c) Ringo doesn't mind the teaching method either. He doesn't say anything for the first few minutes, though, just picks up what he can, gets it straight (allowing Paula to make the mistakes) and then comes out with a fluent response.

(d) Georgette is lost. She feels frustrated because, although she has learned the phrases for a given situation she is not sure it will apply in other contexts. She takes home a book of grammar at night, to bone up on the general principles and rules.

Who represents which learning style? What style has the course been designed for?

2.2 Kolb's Learning Styles Inventory

Kolb's Learning Styles Inventory is designed to identify the preferences of learners for particular phases of his experiential learning cycle (see 1.4 above).

For copyright reasons, the inventory cannot be reproduced here, but the broad categories of preference identified by Kolb are as follows.

    (a) The **'converger'** (Abstract Conceptualisation and Active Experimentation) prefer applying abstract generalisations in practical and specific ways

    (b) The **'diverger'** (Concrete Experience and Reflective Observation) prefer to reflect 'laterally' on specific experience from different points of view

    (c) The **'assimilator'** (Abstract Conceptualisation and Reflective Observation) is comfortable with concepts and abstract ideas

    (d) The **'accommodator'** (Concrete Experience and Active Experimentation) prefers to learn primarily from doing

Now that we have surveyed some of the theoretical framework of training, let's move on to its organisational framework.

3 THE ROLE OF TRAINING

3.1 Outcomes of training

We have talked about learning in terms of acquiring the knowledge or ability to do something. In fact, training may be directed towards a number of different outcomes.

Skill

Definition

Skill may be defined as a learned pattern of operations, or responses to stimuli, which allow the successful, rapid and apparently confident performance of a complex task.

Manual work is often divided into categories according to varying degrees of perceptual-motor skill required: 'skilled' (like electricians and vehicle mechanics), 'semi-skilled' (like machine operators) and 'unskilled' (like road sweepers and canteen assistants). The degree of skill attributed to these jobs is clearly associated with:

(a) The amount of learning required to master the necessary actions, techniques and methods

(b) The sophistication of perception and response required (diagnosing a fault and repairing a machine is more skilled work than simply operating it in accordance with learned methods)

Non-manual work involves a wide range of what are classified as 'higher order' thinking skills: cognitive (including information-processing and decision-making), creative, perceptual, linguistic/expressive, social/interpersonal and so on.

Knowledge

Knowledge is a very complex concept, but in the training context may be divided into two areas which Gardner calls 'know-that' and 'know-how'.

(a) 'Know-that' is knowledge **about** something or 'propositional knowledge': awareness of ideas, concepts, theories, methodologies and so on.

(b) 'Know-how' is knowledge **of** something, or the ability to do something: 'practical knowledge'. This may be based on underlying, unverbalised, untaught knowledge ('tacit knowledge'), but is typically acquired through imitation and experience.

Propositional knowledge is commonly associated with formal education, and has traditionally attracted high status in the social hierarchy of skills – while at the same time attracting the suspicion of those with practical knowledge, who see it as divorced from real-world competence. At the end of this course, you may know how HRM 'should' be done – but actually doing it in an organisational setting may be something else again! An organisation clearly needs to acquire and develop both propositional knowledge (understanding of management and technical processes) and practical knowledge (ability to make those processes work in practice).

FOR DISCUSSION

Which is more useful to an organisation: 'know-that' (propositional knowledge) or 'know-how?' (practical knowledge)? Do you agree that 'those who can, do: those who can't, teach'?

Competence

Definition

Competence may be defined in the context of industrial training as 'the ability to perform the activities within an occupational area to the levels of performance expected in employment' (Training Commission)

Competence is a relatively new concept for the purposes of selection, training and appraisal, but it represents one of the 'bundles' of practice which may contribute to the 'fit' or integration of HRM policies in an organisation. (See Chapter 11 if this does not ring a bell.) There are two key elements in the concept.

(a)   It integrates knowledge, skills and other attributes into the notion of overall ability.

    (b)   It defines and assesses ability in the context of performance.

Competency definition and testing have become a major element in the design of training and development in the UK.

Attitudes and awareness

Another recently-recognised area of training is aimed at encouraging trainees to gain insight into their own behaviour and to try to change the negative or restricting attitudes that prevent the individual from attaining more effective performance. Examples of training outcomes include:

    (a)   Assertiveness (the ability to assert one's rights, wishes and opinions in a straightforward, non-aggressive manner)

    (b)   Insight into the style and effectiveness of interpersonal relations and group dynamics

    (c)   Insight into the motives underlying undesirable attitudes (racism, sexism, sexual harassment, bullying and so on)

    (d)   Self-awareness and ability to manage emotional responses (sometimes called 'emotional intelligence')

Employability

Definition

Employability describes a portfolio of knowledge, skills, competences and attributes that enhances an individual's mobility and power in the labour marketplace. Employability training aims to equip employees with such a portfolio.

Traditionally, training has been seen as a way of improving an employee's performance in a particular job or career path for the benefit of the employing organisation. However, many organisations are no longer in a position to offer long-term job security to their employees. Socially responsible employers wish to facilitate employees' transition to other jobs – while simultaneously benefiting from the creation of a more flexible multi-skilled labour force.

We will be discussing competency and awareness/attitude training in Section 5 below, as modern approaches towards the so-called 'learning organisation' (discussed in Section 4). First we will look at what benefits the organisation can expect to gain from achieving the above outcomes through training.

3.2 Benefits of training

In so far as training increases competency, skills, versatility, confidence, awareness and/or knowledge among employees, it may contribute to the organisation in a number of ways.

    (a)   Increased efficiency and productivity, through faster, more skilled work

(b)   Reduction in costs, associated with the above, and with less wastage and fewer errors

(c)   Reduction in interpersonal and performance-related problems with supervisors and managers – both because of enhanced competence and greater confidence

(d)   Improved quality of work/service

(e)   Fewer accidents and problems with equipment and machinery

(f)   Improved job satisfaction, motivation and morale among trained employees, which may further increase productivity and quality

(g)   Greater communication between employees on job-related issues, with potential for quality improvements and innovations

(h)   Greater potential for increased empowerment and involvement of employees, as they become more aware and more skilled (particularly if training goes beyond technical skills to embrace communication and interpersonal skills, delegation skills for managers, problem-solving and decision-making skills and so on)

(i)   The fostering of a culture of continuous learning and improvement, which promotes adaptability to change and organisational flexibility

(j)   Compliance with legislation and regulation (where training is given in health and safety measures, non-discrimination and so on)

'Training is to some extent a management reaction to change, eg changes in equipment and design, methods of work, new tools and machines, control systems, or in response to changes dictated by new products, services, or markets. On the other hand, training also induces change. A capable workforce will bring about new initiatives, developments and improvements – in an organic way, and of its own accord. Training is both a cause and an effect of change.'

Livy: Corporate Personnel Management

Arguably, the more education and training an organisation makes available to its employees, the more flexible and versatile its workforce will be, and the more potential there will be for innovative ideas and new ways of working that will help the organisation adapt to changing demands.

EXAMPLE: MOTOROLA

Motorola found themselves trying to compete globally in a market of new technologies and changing demands, with people who, in many cases, had difficulty with reading and basic mathematics. It launched a wide-ranging scheme of education and training (its own 'University') for its employees – and for the employees of suppliers and key customers. Training was designed to develop the person, not just the company and the job. It was aimed at 'creating an environment for learning, a continuous openness to new ideas... We not only teach skills, we try to breathe the very spirit of creativity and flexibility into manufacturing and management.'

(Quoted by Pedler, Burgoyne, Boydell: *The Learning Company*)

Activity 6	**(20 minutes)**

What might be the benefits of training to the trainee? (Think what you are getting out of doing this course, for example.)

List at least five benefits.

BPP PUBLISHING

You might by now be thinking that training is obviously such a good thing that an organisation could not go wrong by simply providing some. If performance is poor: do some training! If morale is low: do some training! If empowerment is a foreign concept in your organisation: do some training! Let's get things into perspective ...

Realistic expectations

The personnel function must recognise – and emphasise to line managers – that:

- training and development programs can improve performance
  but

- there are many variables in job performance (see Figure 16.3), not all of which may be addressed by training alone
  and

- even in areas susceptible to training, the training programme must be designed and implemented appropriately for the needs of the organisation and the specific group of trainees – or it will not be effective

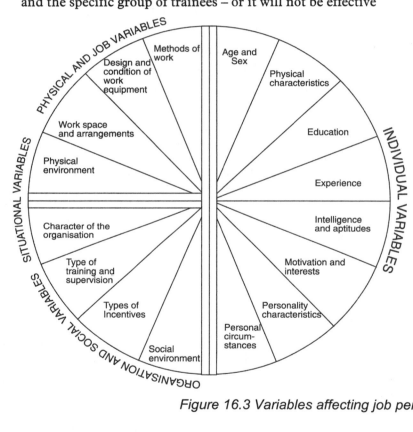

Figure 16.3 Variables affecting job performance

Let's examine unrealistic expectations and some of the other assumptions that might be made about the role of training in an organisation.

3.3 Attitudes to training

Easy assumptions about training and, within each organisation, specific training programmes, should constantly be challenged if the desired outcome from training is to be achieved.

(a) **'Training is a matter for the HR department.'** Yes it is - but not exclusively. Line managers are conversant with the requirements of the job, and the individuals concerned; they are also responsible for the performance of those individuals. They should be involved in:

(i)   The identification of training needs and priorities

(ii)   Training itself. A specialist trainer may be used as a catalyst, but the experience of line personnel, supervisors and senior operatives will be invaluable in ensuring a practical and participative approach

(iii) Follow-up of performance, for the validation of training methods

In addition, experience and learning opportunities in the job itself are very important, and the individual employee should be encouraged in self-learning, and in the 'ownership' of his own development at work.

(b)   **'The important thing is to have a training programme.'** The view that training in itself is such a Good Thing that an organisation can't go wrong by providing some is a source of inefficiency.

(i)   The individual needs and expectations of trainees must be taken into account. The purpose of training must be clear, to the organisation (so that it can direct training effort and resources accordingly) and to the individual (so that he feels it to be worthwhile and meaningful - without which the motivation to learn will be lost). If individuals feel that they are training in order to grow and develop, to find better ways of working, or to become more a part of the organisation culture, they will commit themselves to learning more thoroughly than if they feel they are only doing it to show willing, to fulfil the human resource plan, or whatever.

(ii)   It is too easy to run old or standard programmes, without considering that:

(1)   The learning needs of current trainees may be different from past ones

(2)   The requirements of the job may not all be susceptible to classroom or study methods: are the most relevant needs being met?

(3)   The training group may not be uniform in its needs: the training package may be off-target for some members.

(c)   **'Training will improve performance.'** It **might** - and **should,** all other things being equal - but a training course is not a simple remedy for poor performance. Contingency theory ('It all depends') must be applied to situations where employee performance is below the desired standard. An employee who is adequately **trained** to perform may still not be **able** or **willing** to do so, because of badly designed working methods or environment, faulty equipment, inappropriate supervision, poor motivation, lack of incentive, or non-work factors, such as health, domestic circumstances and so on. In particular, it must be remembered that performance is not just a product of The System, but a product, and manifestation, of human behaviour. Training methods, and their expected results, must take into account human attitudes, values, emotions and relationships.

3.4 Training policy

Training policy will therefore need to address the following issues.

- Why does the organisation train and develop people: how is training envisaged as contributing to strategic objectives and the HR plan?

- What are the desired outcomes of training: skills, knowledge, competence, awareness/attitudes, employability?

- How will training needs and objectives be determined?

- Who does the organisation intend to train and develop? What grades of employee will have access to training, of what type and at what level? What equal opportunity commitments should be made?

- Who will be responsible for the initiation and control of training: HR specialists, line managers, employees themselves? What value is placed on the concept of 'self-development'?

- When, where and how will training activity take place?

- How much investment is the organisation prepared to put into training and development?

- How is training and development to be monitored and evaluated?

We will discuss training policy issues in detail in Chapter 17. First, we will look at the emerging concept of the 'learning organisation' and at some of the approaches associated with it.

4 THE LEARNING ORGANISATION

4.1 The learning organisation

Definition

> A **learning organisation** is one that facilitates the acquisition and sharing of knowledge, and the learning of all its members, in order continuously and strategically to transform itself in response to a rapidly changing and uncertain environment.

A learning organisation values the process of learning – not just its specific outcomes. It learns how to learn: how to be open to new information; how to use feedback to adjust performance; how to view mistakes and failed experiments as opportunities for change; how to make decision-making flexible in order to accommodate learning.

Garvin defines a learning organisation as one that is 'skilled at creating, acquiring and transferring knowledge, and at modifying its behaviour to reflect new knowledge and insights.'

This implies an underlying vision for organisational learning and flexibility, and the creation of a culture conducive to learning, via an integrated and mutually-reinforcing set of policies, processes and techniques.

4.2 Learning culture

The cultural mechanisms and characteristics of a learning organisation are as follows.

(a) Decision-making procedures are continuously modified in the light of experience, avoiding rigid plans and procedures.

(b) Problem-solving is systematic and based on scientific method rather than guesswork: insisting on data rather than assumptions, generating and testing hypotheses.

(c) Experimentation – the systematic search for and testing of new knowledge - is encouraged, in order to generate new insights. Continuous improvement programmes (based on the Japanese concept of 'kaizen') are a feature of learning organisation.

(d) Risk-taking, failures and mistakes are regarded as useful input to the learning process, to avoid problems in future. (This has been called the 'Santayana principle' after the philosopher who said: 'Those who cannot remember the past are condemned to repeat it'.) In any case it is better to experiment with something new than stick with what you know for fear of failure.

(e) Information and feedback is encouraged from all possible sources (notably customers and competitors): opportunities to learn from others should be sought out. This includes the process of benchmarking: identifying best practice in other organisations and transferring appropriately adapted elements of their practice to one's own organisation. (Also known as 'SIS' – 'steal ideas shamelessly'!)

(f) Knowledge is disseminated throughout the organisation by formal communication and informal networking. Everyone operates with the knowledge of environmental changes and challenges and customer demands. Open-channel upward, downward and lateral communication is encouraged.

(g) Everything is open to challenge and questioning: no body of knowledge or procedure becomes 'enshrined' by habitual acceptance. Management actively supports questioning by subordinates.

(h) Selection, training and development, appraisal and reward are based not on existing goals and attainments but on flexibility, continuous improvement, initiative and ability to identify and exploit new areas of activity.

(i) Flexibility of decision-making is supported by self-managed team-working and the role of the manager/supervisor as coach/facilitator.

(j) Training focuses on 'learning how to learn': how to obtain, use and adapt to new information.

Activity 7   **(45 minutes)**

From what you know of how organisational culture is developed and reinforced, and building on the characteristics listed above, what would you expect to be the potential barriers to the creation of a successful learning culture?

According to the New Learning for New Work Consortium's report *Managing Learning for Added Value* (as summarised in *People Management,* March 1999) the goal of the new learning paradigm is a workforce capable of taking responsibility for adding value. This amounts to a new learning cycle, which may be illustrated as follows (Figure 16.4)

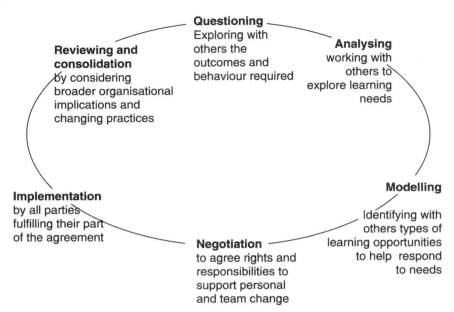

Figure 16.4: A new learning cycle – managing learning to add value

You may have noticed that the 'new learning cycle' emphasises collaboration and shared responsibility for learning goals and outcomes. We will look briefly at mechanisms aimed at encouraging employees to take responsibility for their own self-development.

4.3 Personal development plans (PDPs) and employee development programmes (EDPs)

Definition

> **Personal development plans** are action plans for individuals' skill and career development which put the onus on the individuals themselves to seek out and organise training and development opportunities.

A 1995 report by the Institute for Employment Studies suggested that the number of large employees implementing PDPs is increasing. 'Organisations no longer feel they can take prime responsibility for the future careers and development of their employees, and the PDP approach clearly places the development ball in the employee's court.'

The most popular PDP schemes take account of people's wider needs and aspirations, rather than focusing on skills required for present job performance.

This trend is also reflected in **employee development programmes** which offer employees a wide range or 'menu' of development opportunities, not necessarily related to the job. The effect of such schemes is to develop a culture in which learning and adaptability is valued, as well as to attract, retain and motivate skilled employees.

EXAMPLES

- A National Health Service development programme for unit general managers includes a budget for each individual to spend – as he or she wishes – on personal development. This can be spent on courses, seminars or books, or on 'buying in' a coach or instructor, or visiting other organisations to observe their methods – whatever. This approach empowers would-be learners, and encourages creative thinking about development needs and opportunities.

- In 1990, the Rover Car Group launched a multi-million pound 'internal business', dedicated to providing learning and development opportunities to all employees: the Rover Learning Business. Employees are encouraged to formulate individual development plans, with the opportunity to learn management skills.

FOR DISCUSSION

Why might an organisation wish to give control of the development agenda to the individual employees? What might the drawbacks be? Who controls your learning objectives and opportunities?

4.4   Investors in People

The scheme 'Investors in People (launched in 1991) set a standard for investment in employee development. Organisations seeking accreditation as an 'Investors in People' organisation must audit their current training practice and provision (with the aid of survey instruments provided) and bring them into line with the published standards. The organisation will be required to produce evidence of its training objectives and standards, which will be assessed by the Training and Enterprise Councils (TECs) in the UK. Organisations which achieve the required standards are entitled to display the 'Investors in People' logo on their publications.

EXAMPLE: INVESTORS IN PEOPLE

'Few companies are prepared to broaden the skills base of the team just to help employees get another job. Most, understandably, want to see some bottom line benefit. So it is important to develop acceptable ways of evaluating the return from expenditure on training and developing people.

The benchmarking process "Investors in People" offers a way forward. The aim is to encourage management to treat people as key assets, not simply controllable costs. Launched in 1991 by the Confederation of British Industry, together with some blue chip companies and the National Training Task Force, the scheme has a national standard based on proven best practice in human resource management, training and development.

Companies as diverse as WH Smith, Kwik Fit, KPMG, United Engineering Steels, and a host of smaller firms which have applied the philosophies of "Investors", claim to have achieved improved performance in customer service, sales, profitability and productivity. Their employees – whether full or part-time – have become highly motivated leading to higher quality work to the advantage of customers, employers and staff.

But achieving the set standards for Investors in People companies does require considerable effort and investment on the part of the organisation.

Basic requirements are:

- Make a public commitment from the top to develop all employees to achieve your business objectives
- Regularly review the training and development needs of all employees
- Take action to train and develop individuals on recruitment and throughout their employment
- Evaluate the investment in training and development to assess achievement and improve effectiveness

407

But the programme is not intended to be a prescriptive set of bureaucratic procedures and bulky manuals. Organisations are encouraged to develop their own solutions and methods but to use the national standards as benchmarks against which to evaluate their achievements. Key elements of the process are: analysis/diagnostics, commitment and action, evaluation and assessment.

To be effective, the scheme must have full support of the very top management of the business. No matter how professionally the organisation handles human resources, it will be embarking on a rigorous evaluation of policies and procedures and facing up to the views and opinions of everyone – from cleaners to chairperson – on its effectiveness.

The benefits of using "Investors in People" are enormous. Some of the more important ones include knowing that employees at all levels are convinced of the value and importance the company attaches to training and developing people to assure business success in the future.

The knock-on effect is that customers will have further evidence of a company's commitment to quality in all aspects of its operations.'

Phil McMahon, *Accountancy Age,* April 1994

5   MODERN APPROACHES

5.1   Competency training

We have so far used the word 'competence' in its general sense of 'capability', but you should be aware that it now carries more technical connotations, as part of a revolution in the approach to vocational and professional qualifications and training.

Competence-based education and training focuses on the output of the learning process (what the trainee should be able to do at the end of it) rather than its input (a scheme of learning, or a syllabus of topics to be covered). The idea has been around for some time, having its roots in teacher education in the US, but only gained currency in the UK in the 1980s. In 1986, the Manpower Services Commission launched a Standards Development Programme, while a review of vocational qualifications led to the establishment of the National Council for Vocational Qualifications (NCVQ) (now the Qualification and Curriculum Authority). This has responsibility for developing criteria for a new qualification framework based on **standards of competence**, against which candidates are assessed, rather than a syllabus, or body of knowledge, tested by examinations.

In practice, this has involved analysing real jobs in a given occupational area in order to find out what acceptable performance in the job entails. Standards of competence identify the key roles of the occupation and break them down into areas or units of competence. These in turn are formulated as statements describing what the job holder should be able to do.

- The specific activities concerned (**elements of competence**)
- How well (**performance criteria**)
- In what contexts and conditions (listed in a **range statement**)
- With what underpinning **knowledge and understanding**

The NCVQ **accredits** suitably (re)structured qualifications, awarded by bodies such as training councils and professional bodies such as Qualification and Curriculum Authority at a range of levels (1-5). Among the professional bodies, the Association of Accounting Technicians (AAT) for example, has already implemented a competence-based training and assessment scheme, leading to NVQ Levels 2, 3 and 4 in progressive stages. NVQs are designed to be vocationally relevant and nationally recognised, since the standards of competence being assessed are devised by lead bodies made up of highly qualified representatives of the occupation or profession nationwide. There are over 160 lead bodies: some are industry-specific (retail, construction and so on); some are more broadly occupational (training and development, accountancy and administration, marketing and so on).

In general terms, Connock (*HR Vision*) suggests that competence definition and analysis may be a useful approach within an organisation, as a way of assessing its future requirements, and providing data to underpin recruitment, training, appraisal, potential assessment, succession planning and reward strategies. Connock suggests that, being systematic and based on real-life observable behaviour, competence analysis provides a thorough and objective picture of job requirements at different levels, and one that is relevant to the circumstances and values of the organisation. He does recognise, however, that achieving definitions of competence is a long and complex task, and tends therefore to be over-simplistic and quickly outdated.

EXAMPLE

Guinness

According to *People Management*, 11 September 1997, in May 1996 Guinness Brewing Great Britain introduced a new pay system based on competences.

Restrictive job definitions, lengthy job descriptions and a 24-grade structure were replaced by broad role profiles and three pay bands. Roles are now specified in terms of 'need to know' (primary accountabilities), 'need to know' (experience and knowledge requirements) and 'need to be' (levels of competence).

Competences are defined as 'the skill, knowledge and behaviours that need to be applied for effective performance'. There are seven of them, including commitment to results and interpersonal effectiveness. Roles are profiled against each relevant competence and individuals' actual competences are compared with the requirements through the performance management process.

5.2 Attitude and awareness training

As discussed in section 3.1 above, the definition of ability and suitability may now include desirable awareness and attitudes which facilitate interpersonal relationships, customer awareness, leadership style and so on. The following are just four of the major approaches to training in these areas.

T-groups

Group training is based on the 'encounter group' principle, which allows people to analyse and practise their interpersonal skills in a controlled group, guided by a facilitator.

The purpose of group learning is to:

(a) Give each individual in a training group (or T group) a greater insight into their own behaviour

(b) Teach an individual how they appear to other people, as a result of responses from other members of the group

(c) Teach an understanding of intra-group processes, and how people inter-relate

(d) Develop an individual's skills in taking action to control such intra-group processes

Group learning can also be used to help people overcome prejudices about age, race, gender and so on, and to encourage people to learn from each other.

Assertiveness training

Definition

Assertiveness may be described as clear, honest and direct communication. It is not to be confused with 'bossiness' or aggression. Aggressive behaviour is competitive and directed at 'beating' someone else: assertion is based on equality and co-operation. Assertion is a simple affirmation that every individual has certain rights and can stand by them in the face of pressures from other people.

In practice assertive behaviour means:

(a) Not being dependent on the approval of others

(b) Not feeling guilty if you do not put other people's needs first all the time (being able to say 'no')

(c) Having the confidence to receive criticism openly and give it constructively

(d) Avoiding conflict without having to give up your own values and wants

(e) Being able to express your own values and feelings without guilt or fear

(f) Making clear requests for what you want

You can see that much of this is to do with awareness of one's own feelings, and attitudes about one's role and rights as a person. Training is therefore partly a matter of identifying, challenging and changing attitudes.

Assertiveness training commonly uses group role-play exercises to:

(a) Test individuals' natural reactions in situations.

(b) Analyse what the assertive alternative would be.

(c) Allow individuals to practise being assertive without the pressures of real-life scenarios. There are practical techniques and skills which can be taught – as well as habits of mind which can be developed – in order to achieve an assertive approach to situations such as asking for what you want, saying 'no', and giving and receiving criticism.

Activity 8   **(10 minutes)**

Who do you think would benefit most from assertiveness training, and for what purpose?

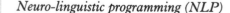

Neuro-linguistic programming (NLP)

Definition

NLP is a technique which emerged in the USA in the 1970s. It is based on two processes.

(a) Identifying and breaking down the behaviour patterns found in excellent performers

(b) Communicating these patterns to people who wish to emulate their performance in a way that overcomes the restricted thinking processes and limiting self-beliefs that typically hold those people back

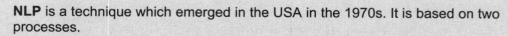

Typical NLP techniques include the following.

(a) The development of detached self-awareness or self-consciousness, so that trainees become able to monitor their own behaviour constantly and objectively. This is achieved through 'disassociation' - the attainment of a detached state in which they can observe and evaluate themselves dispassionately, as if from 'outside' the situation.

(b) Conditioning, such as that used by behaviourist psychologists. Positive and negative responses can be evoked by stimuli with which they have become associated in the mind. If you have spent many happy times with friends, for example, the stimulus (the sight of them) will become associated with the response (happiness), and you will tend thereafter to feel happy at the sight of your friends, or even thinking about them, or visualising their faces. A trainee can thus be conditioned to recall a 'trigger' stimulus (a person, image, place or event) in order to summon up associated feelings (of confidence, calmness or energy, say) which may be useful. This technique is called 'anchoring'.

(c) Developing the ability to establish rapport with others through 'matching' behaviour. The principle of rapport is that people feel comfortable with people who are like themselves in some way. 'Matching' is a technique of observing the behaviour of others and adapting your behaviour to theirs in some way - say, in the amount of gesturing they use, the volume of their voice, or the heartiness of their manner.

(d) Developing the ability to shift perspectives - to view things from another person's point of view - using 'mental mapping' and visualisation techniques. This can be used to help people with work relationships.

(e) The 'mental rehearsal' of events and plans. This operates as a form of practice, and also gives the mind positive suggestions (as if the event has already successfully taken place), giving confidence and therefore - usually - enhanced actual performance.

(f) Using words as powerful tools of suggestion and understanding.

FOR DISCUSSION

NLP, Training Breakthrough

Staff trained by NLP techniques acquire flexibility of thinking, choice of behaviour and control over their feelings; they are better equipped to handle themselves and others and to produce operational results. NLP also enables people to measure their results through sensory processes, giving them a very real sense of what they are achieving.

Deception?

This raises ... questions about the extent to which people should appear to be something they are not in order to achieve a particular result. Much the same question could be levelled at job applicants; how far should they go at a selection interview to persuade the interviewer they are an appropriate choice and would fit into the organisation?

NLP does not aim to resolve people's ethical problems; it aims to give them better quality information and more flexibility so they may make their own choices about behaviour.

Or manipulation?

Possibly because of the speed with which NLP produces results, some people have regarded it warily and are concerned that it is potentially manipulative. In reality these fears are unfounded; of course, NLP could be misused, but so could any other technique you might consider. The concern tends to arise when there is a confusion between influencing and manipulation. We all influence others all the time; it is not possible to exist and not exert an influence on those around us.

Carol Harris - director of the Association for NLP, *Personnel Management*, July 1992

NOTES

Emotional intelligence

Definition

> **Emotional intelligence** is 'the capacity for recognising our own feelings and those of others, for motivating ourselves, for managing emotions well in ourselves and in our relationships'. (Daniel Goleman)

The key components of emotional intelligence identified by Goleman are as follows.

Component	Comments	Associated competencies
Self-management	The ability to manage impulses and moods in order to regulate our own behaviour in pursuit of our goals	Self-control, integrity, initiative, adaptability, openness to change and desire to achieve
Self-awareness	The ability to recognise and understand our moods, emotions and impulses, and their effect on others	Self-confidence, realistic self-assessment and emotional self-awareness
Social awareness	The ability to understand the emotions of other people and respond to them accordingly	Empathy, organisational awareness, cross-cultural sensitivity, valuing diversity and client/customer service
Social skills	The ability to build networks, establish rapport and manage relationships in order to achieve desired outcomes through others	Leadership, effectiveness in leading change, conflict management, influence and team-building

Steps required to develop emotional intelligence include:

(a) Analysing jobs in terms of emotional intelligence competencies

(b) Appraising individuals to identify their level of emotional intelligence (for example, using 360° feedback)

(c) Motivating people to believe that learning in this area will be beneficial: overcoming fear and resistance

(d) Encouraging people to develop their own (self-directed) learning plan that fits their needs and goals

(e) Focusing on clear, manageable goals, bearing in mind that emotions and attitudes are hard to change and relapses will inevitably occur: use relapses as feedback for further learning

(f) Provide models of desired behaviour

(g) Encourage and reinforce practice and improvement

5.3 Training for quality

The British Standard for Quality Systems BS EN ISO 9000 (formerly BS 5750), which many UK organisations are working towards (often at the request of customers, who perceive it to be a guarantee that high standards of quality control are being achieved) includes training requirements. As the following extract shows, the Standard identifies training needs for those organisations registering for assessment, and also shows the importance of a systematic approach to ensure adequate control.

The training, both by specific training to perform assigned tasks and general training to heighten quality awareness and to mould attitudes of all personnel in an organisation, is central to the achievement of quality.

The comprehensiveness of such training varies with the complexity of the organisation.

The following steps should be taken:

1   Identifying the way tasks and operations influence quality in total

2   Identifying individuals' training needs against those required for satisfactory performance of the task

3   Planning and carrying out appropriate specific training

4   Planning and organising general quality awareness programmes

5   Recording training and achievement in an easily retrievable form so that records can be updated and gaps in training can be readily identified.

BSI, 1990

Chapter roundup

- There are three basic theoretical approaches to learning: the behaviourist, cognitive and social learning approaches.

- Learning has been modelled as:

  ○ Four stages (unconscious incompetence, conscious incompetence, conscious competence, unconscious competence

  ○ A curve, showing the relationship between learning time and level of competence

  ○ A cycle, such as the experiential learning cycle of David Kolb (concrete experience, reflective observation, abstract conceptualisation, active experimentation)

- Honey and Mumford identified four learning styles: theorist, reflector, activist, pragmatist.

- Training may be directed at the acquisition of skill, knowledge, competence, attitudes/awareness or employability.

- The learning organisation is one that is skilled at creating, acquiring and transferring knowledge, and at modifying its behaviour to reflect new knowledge and insights.

- Some of the approaches implied by the 'learning organisation' concept include self-directed development, commitment to investment in people, competence training, training of attitudes/awareness and training for quality.

Quick Quiz

1   What is an 'empirical' epistemology and a 'rational' epistemology?

2   What are 'whole' and 'part' learning?

3   Define the four stages of learning.

4   What is a 'plateau' in a learning curve?

5   What are the two approaches to transfer of learning.

6   Distinguish between skill, 'know-that', 'know-how' and competence.

7   List two 'antidotes' to unrealistic expectations of training benefits.

8   List five methods of creating a learning organisation/culture.

9   What do 'PDP', 'EDP' and 'IIP' stand for?

10   What are the four components of emotional intelligence?

Answers to Quick Quiz

1   'Empirical': a theory of how people know things based on the belief that the human mind operates purely on information gained from the senses by experience. 'Rational': a theory of how people know things based on the belief that the human mind imposes organisation and meaning on sensory raw material.   (see paragraph 1.1)

2   Whole learning: tasks are taught or modelled in their entirety. Part learning: tasks are broken down and taught and practised stage by stage, building up to the whole task.   (para 1.1)

3   See paragraph 1.2.

4   The point at which progress levels off, due to the trainee's need to consolidate, correct, regain motivation or establish unconscious competence before moving on further.   (para 1.3)

5   Correspondence of elements between the learning situation and applied context **or** transfer by principle, which allows general learning to be transferred to specific contexts.   (para 1.5)

6   See paragraph 3.1 for a full account.

7   Not all factors in work performance are amenable to training; training courses must be well designed (taking into account desired outcomes, learning styles etc) if they are to be effective.   (para 3.2)

8   See paragraph 4.2 for a full account.

9   Personal development plan; employee development programme; Investors in People.   (para 4.3, 4.4)

10   Self-management, self-awareness, social awareness, social skills.
                                                                                (para 5.2)

Answers to Activities

1   For a full account of the implications of learning theory for training design, see the text following the exercise.

2   We have used the example of assertiveness training: you may have come up with others.

Stage 1.   You have not heard of assertiveness, so you are not aware that you relate to people in a way that is either aggressive or passive: you simply relate in the way that seems natural to you.

Stage 2.   You read about assertiveness, or someone feeds back to you that your style of relating is unhelpfully unassertive, or you realise that you hardly ever get your needs met without damaging relationships: you realise that your behaviour is unassertive.

NOTES

Stage 3. You research and think about the principles of assertiveness, and remind yourself of them by sticking positive affirmation messages around your home and office. You apply the techniques of assertion consciously, having to remind yourself of the principles, using scripted responses, monitoring their effectiveness.

Stage 4. You naturally react in an assertive manner, without having to remind yourself or plan to do so.

3

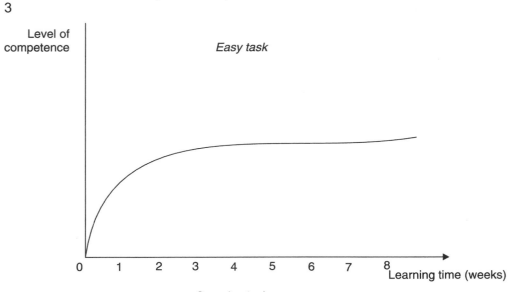

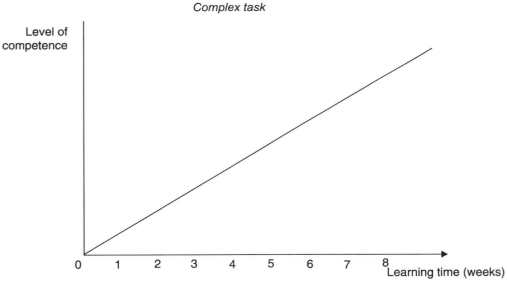

4   Some of the factors you may have identified include the following.

   (a)   Perceptual factors: unconscious incompetence, not seeing that there is a need; not receiving honest feedback from others

   (b)   Emotional factors: fear or insecurity about performance (not wanting to be a 'beginner' or 'learner'), fear of being judged, discomfort of conscious incompetence, frustration

   (c)   Motivational factors: lack of goals/incentives, unwillingness to take risks or make mistakes, no positive reinforcement for progress, previous bad experience with training

BPP
PUBLISHING

(d)   Cultural factors: values about 'not getting above yourself', 'the way we do things here' frustrating application of learning; boss/colleagues/family unsupportive

      (e)   Physical factors: no suitable space or time to study, practise

      (f)   Situational factors: lack of training opportunities; poorly designed training courses (negative transfer, unsuited to learning styles of trainees)

      (g)   Skill factors: poor learning skills (never learned to learn), limited learning styles, poor communication skills

5   John is a pragmatist: Paula an activist: Ringo a reflector: Georgette a theorist. The course seems tailored to activists: reflectors would probably cope, but might not contribute enough to keep the classes going.

6   (a)   It demonstrates that the individual is valued and believed to have potential.

      (b)   It gives the individual an enhanced sense of security (that he or she is and will be useful to the organisation).

      (c)   It can enhance a person's portfolio of skills, and hence a person's ability to take responsibility.

      (d)   It can motivate employees, because they see opportunities for advancement, or to make a difference to quality or innovation.

      (e)   Training and development sessions enable employees to mix with people from other business functions, and so develop networks and contacts.

      (f)   Training in areas such as assertiveness, communication or interpersonal skills can enhance personal effectiveness and self-esteem outside the work context.

7   Some problems you may have identified include the following.

      (a)   Inadequate organisation mechanisms for multi-directional communication, training in learning, selection according to flexibility etc: these will have to be established, and old machinery (reporting channels, job descriptions etc) dismantled or adapted

      (b)   Lack of commitment and example-setting by top management (essential to the development of culture)

      (c)   Poor communication and/or learning skills in some existing employees: they would need to be developed or the employees would need to be 'weeded out'. (This may happen through 'accelerated wastage', since the learning culture would be highly uncomfortable for them.)

      (d)   Organisational politics, discouraging the open sharing of information and acceptance of challenge.

      (e)   Fear/insecurity on the part of managers (required to open their decision-making to challenge) and all employees (fear of risk-taking, never secure in sense of competence under continuous improvement).

      (f)   Previous management style: punishing mistakes, avoiding risks etc.

(g)   Lack of motivation to learn at all levels: inadequate perception of the need to be constantly learning, flexible – when it would be much easier to settle into established routines.

8   Assertiveness training is popularly seen as a prime means of remedying under-achievement in women, or of helping women to avoid exploitation at work. It is likely to be part of a 'Women Into Management' programme. The techniques and insights involved are likely to be of benefit to men as well, but it has been recognised that it is primarily women who are disadvantaged in western society by the failure to distinguish between assertion and aggression, submission and conflict-avoidance. Assertiveness training may help women to criticise, confront and direct male subordinates and colleagues non-aggressively. The failure of victims of sexual harassment to come forward may indicate another area in which assertiveness could be of value.

Assignment 16   **(2 hours)**

Draw up your own 'Personal Development Plan'.

Include:

(a)   areas of knowledge/skill/competence/attitude /awareness that you want to attain;

(b)   qualifications or standards that you wish to attain as evidence of learning;

(c)   potential sources of learning in each of your chosen areas;

(d)   areas of organisational experience that you wish to try (jobs, functions, postings?);

(e)   potential sources of mentorship or guidance within the organisation who could help you attain your learning/experience goals;

(f)   an initial timetable or sequence according to which you might aim to acquire the relevant learning/experience.

There is no suggested answer to this Assignment: consult your own goals, aspirations, preferences and organisational opportunities. (Don't be limited to the latter, however: think 'employability' if appropriate.)

If you have studied for Unit 16 of the Business and Management module, the concept of a personal development plan will be very familiar to you.

Chapter 17 :

APPROACHES TO TRAINING AND DEVELOPMENT

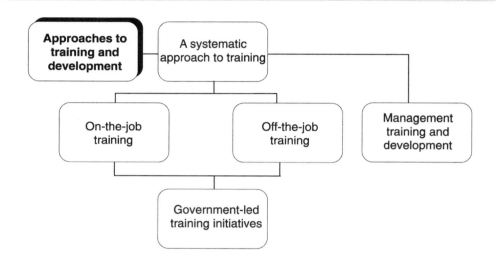

Introduction

In this chapter, we examine the practical application of the principles discussed in Chapter 16, starting with a systematic approach to training.

We evaluate various training options and resources available to organisations. We distinguish between 'education', 'training' and 'development', and discuss why and how development should be offered to employees, particularly at the management level.

Finally, we survey a range of initiatives by the UK government to facilitate vocational education and training.

Your objectives

In this chapter you will learn about the following:

- (a) The systematic approach to training

- (b) A range of different training methods

- (c) The effectiveness of on-the-job training and off-the-job training

- (d) How to devise on-the-job and off-the-job training programmes to meet the need of a given organisation

- (e) How to evaluate an organisation's approach to training

- (f) The purpose of management development and how to evaluate its effectiveness for a given organisation

- (g) The range of contemporary training initiatives introduced by the UK government

- (h) The role of the Training and Enterprise Councils

(i)   How to investigate a vocational training scheme

(j)   Implementation of (training) practice in the UK and one other country

1   A SYSTEMATIC APPROACH TO TRAINING

1.1   A training system

If training is to make a impact on performance at an individual level, let alone at a strategic level, it must be carefully designed to suit the **need for training** and the **needs of the trainee.**

Definition

> According to the Department of Employment, **training** is 'the systematic development of the attitude/knowledge/skill/behaviour pattern required by an individual in order to perform adequately a given task or job.'

The application of systems theory to the design of training has gained currency in the West in recent years. A **training system**, Figure 17.1, uses rational methods to programme learning, from:

(a)   **The identification of training needs:** by comparing the requirements of the job with an assessment of the present capacities and inclinations of the individuals available to do it; (this is called their 'pre-entry' behaviour since they have not yet entered the training system); via

(b)   **The design of courses,** selection of methods and media, to

(c)   **The measurement of trained performance** – the 'terminal behaviour' resulting from the training system – and its comparison against pre-determined performance targets

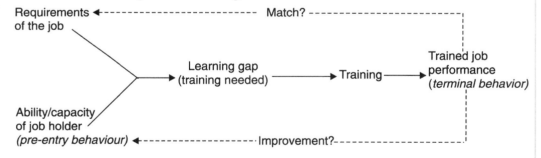

Figure 17.1 A training system

We will now look at each of the components of the training system: identification of training needs and objectives; design of training media and methods; and assessing the effectiveness of the training.

1.2   Training needs analysis

Whose needs and objectives

Training needs and outcomes should be evaluated in terms of their potential contribution to the key objectives of the organisation, including:

(a)   Profitability; by increasing productivity/revenue or reducing costs

(b)   The cost-effective provision of services, customer retention, ethical compliance, technical innovation, market standing and other measures of added value

(c)   The survival or growth of the business, which may be based on profitability, return on investment for shareholders, retention of market share and so on

(d)   Increased employee loyalty (with a knock-on effect in decreased labour turnover and smoother management succession)

(e)   Enhanced corporate image (which may impact favourably on consumer attitudes and the ability to attract skilled labour)

(f)   Enhanced potential for quality, innovation, flexibility in the face of change and acceptable risk-taking, through a culture of broad-based competence and support of learning

There is no intrinsic incompatibility between a **business's** strategic goals for training, and the developmental aspirations of **individuals**. The desire for learning, skill development and self-actualisation by the individual have long been recognised (Maslow, Herzberg) as incentives to motivated performance at work, as well as offering personal satisfaction.

Activity 1	(20 minutes)

When might fulfilling employee aspirations become incompatible with business objectives?

The training needs of individuals and groups vary enormously, according to the nature of the job and particular tasks, and the abilities and experience of the employees.

Training needs recognition

Some training requirements will be obvious and 'automatic'.

(a)   If a piece of legislation is enacted which affects the organisation's operations, training in its provisions will automatically be indicated. Thus, for example, personnel staff will need to be trained as and when various EU Directives are enacted in UK law.

(b)   The introduction of new technology similarly implies a training need: for relevant employees to learn how to use it.

(c)   An organisation seeking accreditation for its training scheme, or seeking a British Standard or International Standard (say, for quality systems, ISO 9000), will have certain training requirements imposed on it by the approving body.

Other training requirements may emerge in response to **critical incidents**: problems or events which affect a key area of the organisation's activity and effectiveness. A service organisation may, for example, receive bad press coverage because of a number of complaints about the rudeness of its customer service staff on the telephone. This might prompt an investigation which might in turn highlight the need for training in telephone skills, customer care, scheduling (for the team manager, if the rudeness was a result not of lack of skill but pressure of unmanageable workloads) and so on.

Some **qualitative indicators** might be taken as symptoms of a need for training: absenteeism, high labour turnover, grievance and disciplinary actions, crises, conflict, poor motivation and performance. Such factors will need to be investigated to see what the root causes are, and whether training will solve the problem.

Another alternative is **self-assessment** by the employee. This may be highly informal (a list of in-house or sponsored courses is posted on the notice board or intranet and interested employees are invited to apply) or more systematic (employees complete surveys on training needs). An example of a self-administered needs survey for managerial staff (suggested by Kramer, McGraw and Schuler) is as follows.

Self assessment of training needs

Please indicate in the blanks the extent to which you have a training need in each specific area. Use the following scale

Scale

1 ————— 2 ————— 3 ————— 4 ————— 5

(To no extent)   (To a very large extent)

To what extent do you need training in the following areas?

Basic management skills (organising, planning, delegating, problem-solving)

_____ A   Setting goals and objectives
_____ B   Developing realistic time schedules to meet work requirements
_____ C   Identifying and weighing alternative solutions
_____ D   Organising work activities

Interpersonal skills

_____ A   Resolving interpersonal conflicts
_____ B   Creating a development plan for employees
_____ C   Identifying and understanding individual employee needs
_____ D   Conducting performance appraisal reviews
_____ E   Conducting a disciplinary interview

Administrative skills

_____ A   Maintaining equipment, tools and safety controls
_____ B   Understanding local agreements and shop rules
_____ C   Preparing work flowcharts
_____ D   Developing departmental budgets

Quality control

_____ A   Analysing and interpreting statistical data
_____ B   Constructing and analysing charts, tables and graphs
_____ C   Using statistical software on the computer

The advantage of self-assessment, or self-nomination for training, is that it pre-supposes motivation on the part of the trainee and harnesses employees' knowledge of their own job requirements and skill weaknesses. The drawback, however, is that employees may be reluctant to admit to performance deficiencies.

A further alternative, therefore, is the use of **attitude surveys** and **360° feedback appraisal reports,** since the employee's superiors, subordinates, colleagues and customer contacts will be in a good position to identify performance deficiencies in areas that affect them: this will be particularly important in the case of customers.

Activity 2   **(15 minutes)**

Complete the above self-assessment for yourself. For any areas which are not applicable to your job, put NA (not applicable).

NOTES

FOR DISCUSSION

What alerted you to a training need, to encourage you to undertake this course? What was the training need: what could you not yet do, or what did you not yet know, that you thought you needed? What help did you get in identifying your training needs? Have you defined them (or had them defined for you) in a helpful way?

Other training requirements may only emerge as a result of the kind of learning gap (or training need) analysis shown in Figure 17.1.

Training needs analysis

Definition

> **Training needs** may be defined as the gap between what people should be achieving and what they actually are achieving. In other words:
>
> Required level of competence **minus** present level of competence = training need.

The **required level of competence for the job** can be determined by:

(a) **Job analysis,** identifying the elements of the task

(b) **Skills analysis,** identifying the skill elements of the task, such as:

    (i) What senses (vision, touch, hearing etc) are involved?
    (ii) What left-hand/right-hand/foot operations are required?
    (iii) What interactions with other operatives are required?

(c) **Role analysis,** for managerial and administrative jobs requiring a high degree of co-ordination and interaction with others

(d) **Existing records,** such as job specifications and descriptions, person specifications, the organisation chart (depicting roles and relationships) and so on

(e) **Competence analysis** or existing competence frameworks, such as NVQs relevant to the job

The **present level of employees' competence** (which includes not only skill and knowledge, but the employee's inclination or willingness to work competently as well) can be measured by an appropriate **pre-training test** of skills, knowledge, performance, attitude and so on. The ongoing system of performance appraisal (discussed in Chapter 6) will furnish some of this information. A **human resources audit** or **skills audit** may also be conducted for a more comprehensive account of the current level of competence, skill, knowledge (and so on) in the workforce.

The training manager will have to investigate the gap between current and required performance/competence to see whether training might be the solution. (Remember, there are alternative solutions: machinery may need repairing or upgrading, poor motivation might need to be addressed through pay and incentives, and so on.) If training is identified as the way to close the gap, specific objectives will need to be formulated.

PUBLISHING

1.3 Training objectives

Objectives should be clear, specific and related to observable, measurable targets. Ideally, there should be detailed definitions of:

(a) **Behaviour** – what the trainee should be able to do
(b) **Standard** – to what level of performance
(c) **Environment** – under what conditions

The advantage of **competency** frameworks is that they typically define competent performance in exactly this specific and quantifiable way.

Objectives are the yardsticks that will allow the trainer (and trainees) to see clearly whether and how far training has been successful. They are usually best expressed in terms of active verbs: at the end of the course the trainee should be able to describe... , or identify... or distinguish X from Y... or calculate... or assemble... and so on.

It is insufficient to define the objectives of training as 'to give trainees a grounding in... or 'to encourage trainees in a better appreciation of...': this offers no target achievement which can be objectively measured. Where possible, a **quantifiable** measure should be added: time taken to perform a task, percentage of questions answered correctly, percentage of errors acceptable, and so on.

Activity 3	(30 minutes)

Translate the following training needs into specific learning objectives. Begin each objective with the words: 'the employee will...'

Training need

(a) To know more about the Data Protection Act
(b) To establish a better rapport with customers
(c) To assemble clocks more quickly

Having defined what a training programme should be able to do, the training manager needs to evaluate different options for **how** *training is to be delivered, and* **how** *the desired outcomes are to be achieved. We will outline some of the methods and media available in Sections 2 and 3 below. Here, we will just highlight some of the decisions to be made.*

1.4 Training design and provision

The choices to be made in designing and implementing a training programme include the following.

(a) **Location of training.** This is commonly divided into:

   (i) on-the-job training in the workplace, and

   (ii) off-the-job training, which may be conducted in-house (in training/education facilities) or at the premises of external training providers (university, college, training centre) or at other locations (outdoor training areas, tours of other sites, use of computer- or video-based training packages at home and so on).

(b) **Methods of training.** These will vary according to the training needs and locations (as discussed later).

NOTES

(i) On-the-job training methods include: working with an experienced colleague or trainer ('sitting with Nellie'); systematic job instruction training; job rotation; apprenticeship or traineeship; coaching and mentoring.

(ii) Off-the-job training methods include: formal courses (self-trained by computer-based training or distance learning, or other-trained by lectures, workshops etc); induction training (orientation training when a new recruit joins the organisation); simulation exercises (in-tray exercises, case studies etc); role plays; group discussion; outdoor training; visits and tours; research assignments and so on.

(c) **Training technologies.** Any of the above methods may incorporate recent innovations in training delivery, including: video, interactive video, computer-assisted learning (CAL), computer-assisted instruction (CAI) and computer-managed learning (CML)

In an article in *People Management* (14 May 1998), Alan Mumford asks how trainers can decide on the most suitable means of delivering a learning programme. He notes, in particular, that training is all too susceptible to 'flavours of the month': training gurus constantly seem to develop or espouse a 'more modern' or 'more appropriate' method than whatever the training manager has done before.

Mumford suggests that trainers should ask the following questions of any method proposed.

- What is the contribution of the method to the development of knowledge, skills and insight?

- What is the impact of individual learning-style preferences on the acceptability of the method?

- What are the particular features of this method that make it more appropriate than a method I have used previously?

- In what way is the method more appropriate than any other method for a particular need?

In addition, there is the need for cost-benefit analysis on any given method: are the outcomes to be gained **worth** the cost involved?

1.5 Evaluation and validation of training

Validation

Definition

> **Validation** means observing the results of a process (in this case, a training scheme) and measuring whether its objectives have been achieved.

There are various ways of validating a training scheme.

(a) **Trainee reactions to the experience:** using Feedback Forms and Attitude Surveys to ask the trainees whether they thought the training programme was relevant to their work, and whether they found it useful. This form of monitoring is rather inexact, and it does not allow the training manager to measure the results, for comparison against specific training objectives.

PUBLISHING

(b)   **Trainee learning:** measuring what the trainees have learned on the course, by means of a test or assessment of competence at the end.

(c)   **Changes in job behaviour following training:** studying the subsequent behaviour of the trainees in their jobs, to measure how the training scheme has altered the way they do their work. This is possible, for example, where the purpose of the course was to learn a particular skill.

(d)   **Impact of training on organisational goals:** seeing whether the training scheme has contributed to the overall objectives of the organisation. This is a form of monitoring reserved for senior management.

Validation is thus the measurement of terminal behaviour (trained work performance) in relation to training objectives.

It should be noted, however, that many of the benefits of training programmes are qualitative, rather than quantitative, and hence difficult to identify and measure in financial terms.

(a)   Benefits may consist of long-term paradigm shifts and cultural changes (within the workforce, management and customer base) which take time to 'emerge' to the point where they offer a measurable return on investment.

(b)   Training tends to have 'knock on' effects on *esprit de corps*, technological change, communication, ideas generation and so on. Added value may accrue in unanticipated areas, which are not being monitored as part of the training validation system, and which may be overlooked as training effects.

(c)   Benefits accruing from 'soft' training outcomes such as the enhanced motivation, satisfaction and loyalty of employees are difficult to predict and measure accurately, since their connection to job performance has not been conclusively proven, and the dynamics of such factors in any case vary from individual to individual and over time.

(d)   There are many variables in job performance and performance improvement. It may be difficult to attribute quantifiable post-training added value (such as reduced costs of labour turnover, increased output or quality measures, reduced staffing costs, higher degree of product innovation and so on) to training effects alone.

Evaluation

Definition

> **Evaluation** means comparing the costs of a process (in this case a training scheme) against the benefits which are being obtained.

A training programme should only go ahead in the first place if the likely benefits are expected to exceed the costs of designing and running it. The problem here is not so much in estimating the costs as in estimating the potential **benefits**.

(a)   Costs will be those of the training establishment, training materials, the time (usually with pay) of the staff attending training courses, their travelling expenses, the salaries or fees of training staff, and so on.

BPP PUBLISHING

(b) Benefits might be measured in terms of:

   (i) Quicker working and therefore reductions in overtime or staff numbers

   (ii) Greater accuracy of work

   (iii) More extensive skills and versatility, offering greater labour flexibility

   (iv) Enhanced job satisfaction and reduced labour turnover

As you will appreciate, the benefits are more easily stated in general terms than quantified in money terms.

Activity 4   **(20 minutes)**

What technique of training validation is employed in the following cases?

(a) You fill out a Lecturer Assessment Form at the end of term.

(b) You sit an assessment at the end of this module.

(c) You write an essay on 'Human Resource Planning'.

(d) You fill out a questionnaire on how you feel about prejudice at work.

(e) A university asks new applicants to state why they chose the particular course and provider: was it by recommendation?

(f) You fill out a report for the Careers Office (in several years' time) on your career progress.

We will now go back and look at some of the available training methods and media in more detail. We will classify these under on-the-job training (Section 2) and off-the-job training (Section 3), but you should be aware that some methods may be used in either setting.

2 ON-THE-JOB TRAINING

2.1 Training methods

There are a number of different approaches to on-the-job training.

'Sitting with Nellie'

This is the traditional method of skill training. The trainee is placed beside an experienced worker (Nellie) and learns by observing him or her work and by imitating his or her operations and methods under close instruction and supervision, working with the actual materials and equipment that are involved in the job.

Advantages

- High transfer of learning (because learning in context)
- Effective and economical (where task amenable to observation-imitation)
- Immediate feedback and adjustment
- Establishes working relationships as well as skills

Disadvantages

- Ineffective if 'Nellie' uses poor work technique, or skill not amenable to observation

- Ineffective if 'Nellie' lacks training/instruction skills and job requires explanation

- Trainee socialised into shop floor culture of work: not necessarily methods or attitudes desired by management

Job instruction training

This is a technique which can be added to the 'sitting with Nellie' approach to minimise the disadvantages cited above. It was developed as a guide to systematic on-the-job training.

(a) Careful selection and preparation of trainer/'Nellie' and trainee: goals and objectives of learning outlined etc.

(b) Full explanation and demonstration of skill/task by the trainer/'Nellie'.

(c) Trial on-the-job practice/performance by the trainee.

(d) Thorough feedback session between trainer/'Nellie' and trainee to appraise and adjust trainee's performance and set further improvement goals. (Repeat (b) – (d) as required.)

Coaching

Coaching is one element of the 'sitting with Nellie' approach, but may be used flexibly in a wide range of training situations, and at any time during performance on an on-going basis.

Coaching is on-the-job guidance, advice, correction and teaching with a view to improving performance. A coach should:

(a) Demonstrate how areas of a job are performed, and guide the trainee's own performance of the same tasks, by advice and correction

(b) Help the trainee to identify problems or development needs in his or her work

(c) Seek out or identify opportunities for the trainee to develop, through doing new things at work

(d) Help the trainee plan the solutions to problems, or approaches to new challenges at work

(e) Be patient and tolerant of the trainee's initial mistakes, seeing them as necessary learning and problem-solving opportunities

(f) Encourage the trainee to assess his or her own progress and performance, and to formulate further plans for improvement

Essentially, coaching is a **collaboration** between the coach and the trainee, in which the coach's special role is encouragement and guidance as the trainee develops on the job.

Advantages

- Flexible and interactive: pace and content of learning suited to trainee needs and trainer analysis

- Collaborative: involves trainee in problem-solving

- High transfer of learning (connected to live job performance)

Disadvantage

- Requires coaching skills

Mentoring

Definition

> A **mentor** is a guide, ideally both more experienced and more powerful in the organisation, whose concern is the trainee's long-term personal development. (S)he may occupy a role as the trainee's teacher/coach, counsellor, role model, protector and/or champion/sponsor in the organisation, spur to action or improvement, critic, encourager and so on, as appropriate to the situation at a given time.

A mentor should:

(a) Help the trainee to greater self-awareness, by listening to, questioning and challenging his or her ideas, and feeding back on his or her behaviour

(b) Help the trainee to formulate and clarify his or her needs and ambitions in life, and to identify where events and opportunities at work fit into those plans

(c) Encourage the trainee to take responsibility for his or her development, while offering support – personally and within the organisation – if required

(d) Help the trainee to reconcile his or her non-work needs, interests and circumstances with the demands of work (or vice versa)

(e) Help the trainee to plan specific development and career paths or directions, offering opportunities where appropriate and possible

A similar approach is **action learning**, where a group of employees (often managers) meet together regularly to act as a mentoring, consulting, problem-solving and support group.

So far we have looked at ways in which employees can acquire and improve skills in a particular job or task through guided imitation and practice. A slightly different approach is to give employees a 'taste' of different jobs and functions.

Training by switching or 'shadowing' roles

This may be accomplished by a number of methods.

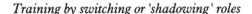

(a) **Job rotation** or 'shadowing': the trainee is given several jobs in succession, to gain experience of a wide range of activities and departments. (Even experienced managers may rotate their jobs to gain wider experience; this method is commonly applied in the Civil Service.)

(b) **Temporary promotion:** an individual is promoted into a superior's position while the superior is absent. This gives the individual a chance to experience the demands of a more senior position.

(c) **'Assistant to' positions:** an individual with management potential may be appointed as assistant to a manager. In this way, the individual gains experience of management, without a risky level of responsibility.

(d) **Project or committee work:** trainees might be included in the membership of a project team or committee, to obtain an understanding of inter-departmental relationships, problem-solving and particular areas of the organisation's activity.

NOTES

(e) **Assignment:** trainees may be delegated to a particular task or project by a superior.

Advantages

- Employees gain experience without risking immediate responsibility.

- Task/role variety may increase job satisfaction and awareness of organisational processes.

- Aids career/management/succession planning.

Disadvantages

- May be perceived as perpetual traineeship: not real work
- May be perceived as a 'nuisance' in departments having to 'carry' trainees

Apprenticeship and traineeship training

Apprenticeships and traineeships involve a combination of on-the-job training (using any of the above methods) and off-the-job training (one or two days a week, or a number of weeks in the year, at a college or university). The trainees earn while they learn, but at a lesser rate than full-time employees of the organisation in which they are placed to gain their work experience.

2.2 Advantages and disadvantages: summary

On-the-job training is very common, especially when the work involved is not complex. It will generally only be successful if:

(a) **Assignments have a specific purpose** from which the trainee can learn and gain experience; otherwise, it can be unfocused and overwhelming

(b) **The trainee is a practical type,** who prefers to learn by doing and can tolerate the process of trial and error; (other people might need to get away from the pressures of the workplace to think through issues and understand the underlying principles before applying new techniques)

(c) **Trainers are themselves trained** in instruction and coaching techniques (as well as modelling efficient and effective work practices)

(d) **The organisation is tolerant of mistakes.** Mistakes are an inevitable part of on-the-job learning, and if they are punished or frowned on, the trainee will be reluctant to take further risks and will be de-motivated to learn.

There may be real risks involved in throwing people in at the deep-end: the cost of mistakes or inefficiencies may be high and the pressure on learners great. (Would you want to learn medical procedures, or air traffic control procedures, on-the-job?)

An important **advantage** of on-the-job training, however, is that it takes place in the environment of the job itself, and in the context of the work group in which the trainee will have to operate. The style of supervision, personal relations with colleagues, working conditions and pressures, the culture of the office/shop floor and so on will be absorbed as part of the training process.

Activity 5   **(20 minutes)**

If you have had work experience, list the advantages you experienced through on-the-job training. If you have not worked, think about this course and list the disadvantages of the different methods of study you are given.

NOTES

We will now look briefly at a particular kind of training programme, involving both off- and on-the-job elements: **induction.**

2.3 Induction training

From his first day in a job, a new recruit must be helped to find his bearings. There are limits to what any person can pick up in a short time, so the process of 'getting one's feet under the table' will be a gradual one. Induction is an ongoing process.

On the first day, a manager or HR officer should welcome the new recruit. The manager might discuss in broad terms what he requires from people at work, working conditions, pay and benefits, training opportunities and career opportunities. He should then introduce the new recruit to the person who will be his immediate supervisor.

The immediate supervisor should then take over the process of induction. Here is a general checklist.

(a) Pinpoint the areas that the recruit will have to learn about in order to start work. Some things (such as detailed technical knowledge) may be identified as areas for later study or training, while others (say, some of the procedures and systems with which the recruit will have to deal) will have to be explained immediately. A list of learning priorities should be drawn up, so that the recruit, and the supervisor, are clear about the rate and direction of progress required.

(b) Explain first of all the nature of the job, and the goals of each task, of the recruit's job and of the department as a whole. This will help the recruit to work to specific targets and to understand how each task relates to the overall objectives of the department - or even the organisation as a whole.

(c) Explain about hours of work and stress the importance of time-keeping. If flexitime is operated, explain how it works. Any other work practices, customs and rules should be explained clearly.

(d) Explain the structure of the department: to whom the recruit will report, to whom (s)he can go with complaints or queries and so on.

(e) Introduce the recruit to people in the workplace. (S)he should meet the departmental manager and all the members of the immediate work team (and perhaps be given the opportunity to get to know them informally). One particular colleague may be assigned to the recruit as a *mentor* for the first few days, to answer routine queries and 'show him (or her) the ropes'. The layout of the premises, procedures for lunch hours or holidays, rules about smoking or eating at work and so on will then be taught informally.

(f) Plan and implement an appropriate training programme for whatever technical or practical knowledge is required. Again, the programme should have a clear schedule and set of goals so that the recruit has a sense of purpose, and so that the programme can be efficiently organised to fit in with the activities of the department.

(g) Coach and/or train the recruit; check regularly on his progress, as demonstrated by performance, reported by the mentor, and/or as perceived by the recruit. Feedback information will be essential to the learning process, correcting any faults at an early stage and building the confidence of the recruit.

(h) Integrate the recruit into the culture of the workplace. Much of this may be done informally: (s)he will pick up the prevailing norms of dress, degree of formality, attitude to customers etc. However, the supervisor should try to 'sell' the values and style of the organisation and should reinforce commitment to those values by rewarding evidence of loyalty, hard work and desired behaviour.

After three months, six months and/or one year the performance of a new recruit should be formally appraised and discussed. This should dovetail into a regular employee appraisal programme.

EXAMPLE

'McDonald's Restaurants typically employs young people - known as "crew" - who are often students working their way through college. Hours are variable, shift patterns differ and there is a relatively high labour turnover. But the fast-food chain's reputation for consistent quality needs to be maintained, so great emphasis is put on OJT [on-the-job training].

All new recruits receive a crew handbook: a description of their terms and conditions of employment, including general information about training, its importance and how it is to be carried out. Each crew member also gets a training handbook and a personal training card, in which particular jobs are ticked off when he or she is judged to be competent in them. In addition, a training log is kept in restaurants as a record of progress. Crew members are asked to check with managers that their development is properly recorded and to remind themselves of areas in which they have not worked.

After a three-hour induction covering health and safety, uniform and hygiene, new entrants are partnered with a "buddy", who is a member of the training squad. These individuals are competent in all areas and have received training off the job in half-hour sessions from restaurant managers in how to use the training manual and handbook. In a typical restaurant employing a crew of 50, about 5 will be members of the training squad.

Competence is assessed by observation and by questioning. Thus, a trainee being assessed will be observed for 30 minutes or more by a manager. Usually the crew member will be unaware that the observation is taking place on the first occasion, but not on the second. Two observations must be passed before the individual is assessed as competent. The training handbook contains a checklist of about 10 questions such as: "How long do fries cook for?" and "How do we salt fries?".

Managers who carry out these observations are themselves checked by area managers to ensure consistency. There is also a check in audits on restaurants' comparative performance.'
People Management, March 1997

Activity 6   **(5 minutes)**

Did you have any form of induction into student life?

Compare your experience to the checklist given above. How effective did you feel your induction was? What difference did it make to your confidence in your studies?'

We will now move on to off-the-job training.

BPP
PUBLISHING

3 OFF-THE-JOB TRAINING

3.1 Training providers

Off-the-job training providers include:

(a) Universities and colleges

(b) Private-sector colleges and training organisations including assessment centres for group training exercises

(c) Training consultancies, which may help the organisation locate or develop courses to meet its needs

(d) Publishers of training materials (texts and workbooks, videos, computer-based training packages) or

(e) The in-house education and training department of the organisation itself (large organisations)

Internal courses are sometimes run by the training departments of larger organisations. Skills may be taught at a technical level, related to the organisation's particular product and market, or to aspects such as marketing, teambuilding, interviewing or information technology management. Some organisations also encourage the wider development of staff by offering opportunities to learn languages or other skills.

One convenient and popular method of in-house education is computer-based training (CBT) or Interactive Video (IV), using equipment in offices or even trainees' homes. Training programmes may be developed by the organisation or by outside consultants – or bought 'off the shelf': the software (or 'courseware') can then be distributed, so that large numbers of dispersed staff can learn about new products or procedures quickly and simultaneously.

External courses vary, and may involve:

(a) Day-release, which means that the employee attends a local college on one day of the week

(b) Evening classes, or 'distance learning' (a home study or correspondence course, plus limited face-to-face teaching) which make demands on the individual's time outside work

(c) Full-time but brief introductory or revision courses preparing trainees for the examinations of vocational or professional qualifications

(d) A sponsored full-time course at a university for 1 or 2 years

EXAMPLE

'For years universities have been urged to become more businesslike. But the boot, it seems, is on the other foot as a growing number of employers attempt to emulate academia by setting up in-house 'universities'

'Corporate universities take a variety of forms. While some are little more than revamped training departments, others represent ambitious attempts to co-ordinate learning and share knowledge across organisations. A few have even begun to imitate real universities to the extent of investing in academic research. But a common feature of many of these institutions is their use of academic terminology to describe, and raise the status of, corporate training and development activities.

BPP
PUBLISHING

'Lloyds TSB, for example, runs its training function just as if it were a higher education institution, complete with "facilities" covering information technology, operations, management and other areas of the business. It even talks of "corporate governance of the curriculum" and about "the syllabus" – terminology that would not have been used in the past.

'Overseen by a strategy group of senior business leaders, the University for Lloyds TSB, as it is called, aims to align training and development with business strategy while also sending out a clear message to employees that the organisation is prepared to invest in them.

'It has given a strong, tangible focus to all of the learning that's provided, both by courses and multimedia-based distance learning. Our latest round of employee attitude surveys has shown a marked improvement in perceptions of our investment in training and development.'

'Although the University for Lloyds TSB was launched only last year, the corporate university concept is far from new. Pioneered in the US in the 1950s, it was not widely known in this country until the arrival of McDonalds's Hamburger University.

'The fast-food giant has now quietly dropped this title in the UK and these days refers – more accurately – to its nationwide network of "training centres". But the Hamburger University is still going strong on the other side of the Atlantic, where corporate universities are set to outnumber traditional higher educational establishments by the year 2010, according to a report by the US Department of Labor.

'In the UK, the first homegrown corporate university was set up in 1993 by Unipart, followed two years later by Anglian Water's University of Water. But it is only in the past couple of years that the idea has really taken off. According to research by Ray Wild and Colin Carnall of Henley Management College, there are around 200 corporate universities in the UK, and this number is likely to increase over the next few years.'

Anat Arkin, *People Management* (12 October 2000)

3.2 Training methods

Some methods of off-the-job training include the following.

(a) **Training room instruction.** Similar to on-the-job job instruction training (see paragraph 2.1 above), but in a dedicated training environment. Instruction is given using presentation techniques and/or a simulation of workplace equipment and methods.

(b) **Lectures** or **taught classes.** These are useful for knowledge or theory/principle-based learning. They may incorporate elements of instruction, case-study, role-play and other techniques to overcome the limitations of passive learning. They suit large numbers of trainees requiring the same basic body of knowledge. Drawbacks include their passivity and the difficulty of absorbing more than three or four key points per session, and their relative inflexibility to individual trainees' learning styles and needs.

(c) **Case study.** Using a description of a real-life scenario or example for analysis, providing insights and opportunities to exercise problem-solving skills, which can be transferred to the work context. Case-studies are a kind of on-paper simulation of work scenarios, allowing experimentation and exploration without risk. They are particularly useful for problem-solving and decision-making in a wide rage of specific contexts.

NOTES

(d) **Role play.** The simulation of an interpersonal scenario, allowing trainees to experiment with learned behaviours and skills and to observe their effects in interpersonal encounters. This is particularly helpful in training for customer service, interviewing, conflict resolution and so on. It suits small groups, allowing for all-member participation.

(e) **Simulation.** In technical training, this may involve the mocking-up of equipment and environments so that trainees can experiment with technical skills and observe results in a safe, progressively-staged and controlled manner. (Flight simulators for pilots is one example.) In other forms of training, simulation may involve case studies, role plays, assignments of 'in-tray' exercises, which mock up typical tasks and scenarios to test trainees' organisational and problem-solving skills.

(f) **Open** or **distance learning.** Employees access technology-assisted instruction where and when it suits them, using training manuals, workbooks, video (and video conferencing for group sessions), tapes, computer-based packages and so on. Some face-to-face tuition may be used periodically to assess or reinforce learning, or to add more interactive and group work. This can be a highly economical method, especially where trainees are geographically dispersed.

(g) **Discovery learning.** A method by which trainees explore a task or concept for themselves, with relatively little initial instruction or demonstration. Trainees are thus encouraged to find out the key principles, constraints and methods of the task, and to ask the questions that are relevant to them. This is a highly trainee-centred technique which is tailored to the learning styles and needs of the trainees and fosters problem-solving and learning skills alongside specific technical competencies. It is, however, time-, labour- and cost-intensive.

(h) **Programmed learning.** A structure of learning by which a trainee, working at his or her own pace, works through a carefully ordered sequence of units or operations, each with objectives, instruction, testing and consolidation which allow the trainee to master one unit before progressing to the next. This is a feature of many distance learning and computer-based learning programmes.

(i) **Visits and tours.** Trainees are given opportunities to observe other sites, departments, operations and so on. This may be helpful in demonstrating: how skills learned in the classroom are applied in practice; different types of machinery and work organisation; stages of operation before and after that in which the trainee will be involved; application of products/services by customers or end users; and so on.

(j) **Outdoor training.** Physical tasks and activities in challenging environments, designed to help trainees learn about themselves and their motivations, leadership skills, group dynamics and co-operation and so on. This is increasingly used in team-building and leadership training. Learning takes place through the process of working out a group solution to a problem or challenge, with a facilitator aiding reflection and analysis afterwards.

(k) **Computer-based training.** Using computer software for instruction and assessment. (This will be discussed further below.)

NOTES

> **Activity 7**   **(20 minutes)**
>
> Suggest a suitable training method for each of the following situations.
>
> (a)   A worker is transferred onto a new machine and needs to learn its operation.
>
> (b)   An accounts clerk wishes to work towards becoming qualified with the relevant professional body.
>
> (c)   An organisation decides that its supervisors would benefit from 'picking up some ideas' on participative management and democratic leadership.
>
> (d)   A new member of staff is about to join the organisation.
>
> (e)   A supervisor allows himself to be intimidated by his workteam and ends up carrying most of the workload himself. Occasionally, he tries to throw his weight around, but this never lasts.

3.3   Training technologies

Three major developments in training technology include the following.

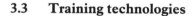

(a)   **Video.** Video presentations compare favourably with training films and live lectures in that they are less expensive, easily distributed for individual and group use, and flexible in use (being 'pausable' at any time, to allow for questions or discussion). Video allows the standardisation of training among widely-dispersed staff. (Video training can also be highly entertaining, using sophisticated communication techniques.)

(b)   **Interactive video** is a combination of video instruction and programmed learning: presenting a segment of tuition and then inviting response (via computer terminal or class discussion/exercise).

(c)   **Computer-based training,** using tailored software to:

     (i)   Control and manage the training process (Computer Managed Instruction, or CMI): feeding student records, session logs, test results and progress reports back to the training manager

     (ii)   Take the role of instructor/assessor (Computer Aided Instructions or CAI) providing tuition, drill and practice programmes, such as those used to teach typing skills and administer typing tests

     (iii)   Facilitate self-learning (Computer Assisted Learning or CAL), by offering simulations, business games, case studies and so on. Integrated computerised 'in tray' exercises, for example, can be used to simulate the business environment and the effect of changing one variable on a series of others.

EXAMPLE

Jooli Atkins (*People Management,* 14 September 2000) reported on the difficulties of embarking on ambitious knowledge management initiatives and CBT courses in organisations where employees can barely use a computer... such as the Sandwell Healthcare NHS Trust.

A wealth of high-quality information is available on the Internet and various medical databases, but on-line learning is possible only when people have learned to access it. It's all very well talking about the wealth of information that is available online, but how does someone who can't switch on a PC find it? ...

The problem at Sandwell was that the staff were career health professionals, not IT experts. Their morale was low in this area. Often, their children were skilled in IT in a way that they were not, which made them feel uncomfortable. The way that we as trainers approached the issue was therefore crucial.

First, we talked. We held three focus groups asking them how they felt about their access to knowledge and how they would like to get hold of it in the future, including how training should be delivered. It is difficult for a doctor who is regularly on call to be attentive to IT training for very long. Equally, nurses rarely have time to stand still, let alone attend training. So it was important that the programme took account of the way they worked.

The course was delivered in training rooms, on the wards and in surgeries where staff could give their attention for short periods while remaining available to their patients in case of an emergency. It was a somewhat surreal experience training A&E doctors and nurses in 10-minute bursts while the activities of the busy casualty department carried on all around.

Timing was equally important. Staff found it easier to give their attention to training when their patients were asleep or when the work of the ward was quieter. This meant providing it at either end of the day – for example, at 6.30 am and 10.30pm.

We started by teaching basic IT skills that would enable them to move on to database querying.

The training activities ranged from a 10 minute stint at one computer, where people were invited to watch a colleague's trainer-facilitated demonstration of a brief topic such as logging on to the network, to two hours of training and testing the process in a hands-on session. This flexibility allowed us to develop a training programme that would meet the needs of the diverse range of users.

Once they had the basic skills necessary to use a computer, the nurses were encouraged to obtain training in the West Midlands Information Service for Health (Wish) project, a collection of Internet databases accessible via one web address. The doctors were offered training in how to surf the World Wide Web and given information about specialist web sites such as Doctors.net.uk.'

3.4 Advantages and disadvantages: summary

Advantages of off-the-job training	Disadvantages of off-the-job training
• It allows exploration and experimentation by inexperienced employees without risking negative consequences for live performance	• If the subject matter of the training course is not felt to relate directly to the individual's job and organisation culture, the learning will not be applied afterwards, and will quickly be forgotten.
• It allows trainees to be away from the work environment where interruptions, distractions and performance pressure may interfere with learning.	• Individuals may feel that courses are, in general, a waste of time. They will not benefit from the training unless they are motivated to learn.
• It allows training to be standardised and distributed across a geographically dispersed workforce (eg via video, CBT or distance learning).	• Immediate and relevant **feedback** on performance and progress may not be available from the learning process, especially if knowledge is tested by unrealistic methods (such as exams) or at wide intervals. This will lower the learner's incentive and sense of direction.

NOTES

Advantages of off-the-job training	Disadvantages of off-the-job training
• It allows for self-study at the trainee's own pace (eg via distance learning).	• It does not suit some people, who may not have much experience of (or taste for) classroom learning since school. Some people simply prefer a 'hands-on' type of learning: learning by doing.
• It may have organisational status as a reward or peak: being sent on a course is a sign of potential.	• Some organisational cultures encourage fear and insecurity around training courses, with the perception that a person sent on a course must be performing inadequately.

FOR DISCUSSION

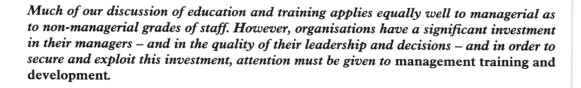

Beardwell and Holden quote Fairbairn's 'sad but familiar story of Del the Delegate, who returns from a course full of new ideas, anxious to implement them. He is confronted with scepticism and cynicism from both his bosses and fellow employees. 'The friction set up between Del and his company undermines his enthusiasm and exhausts all his energy. Del's behaviour reverts to what is (and always was) reinforced by the company.''

Is there an alternative ending to this tragic parable?

Much of our discussion of education and training applies equally well to managerial as to non-managerial grades of staff. However, organisations have a significant investment in their managers – and in the quality of their leadership and decisions – and in order to secure and exploit this investment, attention must be given to **management training and development.**

4 MANAGEMENT TRAINING AND DEVELOPMENT

4.1 What is 'development'?

You might subscribe to the trait theory of leadership, that some individuals are born with the personal qualities to be a good manager, and others aren't. There might be some truth in this view, but very few individuals, if any, can walk into a management job and do it well without some guidance, experience or training.

In every organisation, there should be a system of management development.

(a) Managers gain **experience**, which will enable them to do another more senior job in due course of time.

(b) Subordinate managers must be given **guidance** and **counselling**.

(c) Managers are given suitable **training** and **education** to develop their skills' and knowledge.

(d) Managers are enabled to plan their future and the opportunities open to them in the organisation.

If there is a planned programme for developing managers, it is called a **management development programme**. Note, however, that a 'programme' is no substitute for the individual's own commitment to **self-development**: the support of creating and using learning opportunities in the job.

Definition

> **Management development** is 'an attempt to improve managerial effectiveness through a planned and deliberate learning process'.   (Mumford)

4.2   Management training in the UK

Constable and McCormick reported in 1987 that:

The total scale of management training is currently at a very low level. The general situation will only improve when many more companies conscientiously embrace a positive plan for management development. This needs to be accompanied by strong demand on the part of individual managers for continuing training and development throughout their careers.

Recommendations of the report *The Making of British Managers* included the following.

'Senior management

1   Create an **atmosphere** within the organisation where continuing management training and development is the norm.

2   Utilise **appraisal procedures** which encourage management training and development.

3   Encourage individual managers, especially by **making time available** for training.

4   Provide **support** to local educational institutes to provide management education and training (E & T).

5   Integrate in-house training courses into a wider system of management E & T. **Make the subject matter of in-house courses relevant to managers' needs.** Work closely with academic institutions and professional institutions to ensure that the 'right' programmes are provided.

Individual managers

1   Actively want and seek training and development and to 'own' their own career.

2   Recognise what new skills they require, and seek them out positively

3   Where appropriate, join a professional institute and seek to qualify as a professional member.'

4.3   The Management Charter Initiative

The concerns expressed in Constable and McCormick's report led to the setting up of the Management Charter Initiative (MCI) with the aim of:

(a)   Defining a body of knowledge and skills that could be identified as 'management' so that generic standards of assessment could be developed

(b)   Improving the levels of training in management

(c)   Developing professional standards of behaviour (professional ethics) and qualifications with a view to the eventual 'professionalising' of management under a chartered body

The approach taken was that of competency development: an outcomes-based model similar to the NVQ (see Chapter 16).

There are four key areas of activity in which managers are expected to demonstrate competence:

(a)   Managing operations
(b)   Managing finance
(c)   Managing people
(d)   Managing information

Within each of these areas, there are **units of competence**, broken down into **elements of competence** which must be demonstrated according to defined **performance criteria** with a number of variables set out in an accompanying **range statement**.

There are national standards of competence in supervision and management equating to NVQ level 3, level 4 (Certificate in Management – replacing the old certificate in Management Studies) and level 5 (Diploma in Management – replacing the old Diploma in Management Studies or DMS), plus a respecified Masters degree in Business Administration (MBA). Awarding bodies for the CIM and DIM include BTEC, the Open University and a consortium of universities called the Management Verification Consortium. The Management Lead Body is now the National Training Organisation for Management and Enterprise (METO).

The competency-based approach to management development appears to have taken hold in the UK, replacing the traditional approach based on academic management education and/or short training courses. Some observers, however, note that organisations are beginning to move away from the MIC model (perceived to be bureaucratic, prescriptive and rigid in its standardisation, with associated costs) and towards:

(a)   In-house competence frameworks, reflecting the specific organisational culture and context

(b)   The use of competencies in performance management, to reinforce desired managerial behaviours

(c)   The use of more 'holistic' forms of development, underpinning specific competencies with a wider skill base, employability training, mentoring, self-managed and experiential learning, learning to learn and so on

EXAMPLE: INTERNATIONAL COMPARISONS

Beardwell and Holden suggest that:

- The UK and USA share the approach to management development outlined above.

- European approaches have traditionally been less concerned with management development as a discrete activity. In France, the making of a manager begins within the higher education institutions and forms part of the development of a historical social elite. In Germany, the approach is more functional: managers tend to stay in functional roles longer, and specialist expertise is pre-developed within the vocational education system. Where there is training, it tends to be highly structured and specified. Despite this 'relatively weak tradition in explicitly

focused forms of management', there has been an upsurge of interest in management education since European Union: the emergence of business schools, MBA activity, and EU-led initiatives promoting the exchange of European business and management students between nations.

- The development of managers in Japan, based on the commitment system (discussed in Chapter 15), is long-term, slow-progression, carefully planned and generalist in its scope. 'Whereas Anglo-Saxon models stress individualism and development through short, intensive bursts of training to prepare managers for assignments characterised by challenge and risk, Japanese development programmes are longer and more culturally reflective in focusing on collectivism and group/team effort ... Unlike the US/UK where management development is in the hands of specialists, the Japanese view the relationship between the individual and the boss as a significant factor in developing the manager.'

FOR DISCUSSION

Are good managers born – or made?

4.4 Methods of management development

A useful distinction between management education, training and development was given by Constable and McCormick.

(a) **'Education** is that process which results in formal qualifications up to and including post-graduate degrees.'

(b) **Training** is 'the formal learning activities which may not lead to qualifications, and which may be received at any time in a working career'; for example, a course in manpower forecasting or counselling skills.

(c) **'Development** is broader again: job experience and learning from other managers, particularly one's immediate superior, are integral parts of the development process.'

It is important to realise that 'education and training' no longer implies bookwork, academic and theory-based studies. W A G Braddick (Management for Bankers) suggests the kind of shift in focus that has occurred in management development methods in recent years. (The notes are ours.)

From	To	Notes
Principles	Specifics	(Every organisation is unique)
Precepts	Analysis/diagnosis	(Address the issues)
Theory-based	Action-centred	(Understand it - and do it)
Academic	Real time problems	(Tackle 'live' problems)
Functional focus	Issue and problem focus	(Deal with 'whole' activities)
Excellent individual	Team members and leaders	(Develop people – together)
Patient	Agent	(Learn actively, take control)
One-off	Continuous	(Keep learning)

Thus management education and training now tends to focus on the real needs of specific organisations, and to be grounded in practical skills. In-house programmes and on-the-job techniques have flourished, as have techniques of off-the-job learning which simulate real issues and problems: case study, role play, desk-top exercises, leadership exercises and so on.

Activity 8   **(5 minutes)**

'Does getting wet, cold and generally miserable in the countryside help you to become a better manager?' Supporters of outward bound courses believe it does, but critics question the value of having highly-paid and specialised executives tramping around the woods honing boy scout-level skills.

Is outdoor training not just a way of keeping ageing physical exercise teachers, sadistic ex-corporals and overpaid consultants employed? And is it just an expensive fad in training, no better or worse than classroom teaching?'

Financial Times, January 1993

What do you think?

4.5 Career development and succession planning

Note that management development includes career development and succession planning by the organisation. This will require attention to a number of matters outside the scope of education and training courses.

(a)   The types of **experience** a potential senior manager will have to acquire. It may be desirable for a senior manager, for example, to have experience of:

    (i)   Both line and staff/specialist management - in order to understand how authority is effectively exercised in both situations, and the potentially conflicting cultures/objectives of the two fields

    (ii)   Running a whole business unit (of whatever size) in order to develop a business, rather than a functional or sub-unit perspective. This is likely to be a vital transition in a manager's career, from functional to general management

    (iii)   Dealing with head office, from a subsidiary management position - in order to understand the dynamics of centralised/decentralised control and politics

---

Activity 9   **(5 minutes)**

See if you can suggest two more areas of experience that might be useful for a manager to acquire in order to enhance his or her prospects.

(b)   The individual's **guides and role models** in the organisation. It is important that individuals with potential should measure themselves against peers - assessing weaknesses and strengths - and emulate role models, usually superiors who have already 'got what it takes' and proved it. Potential high fliers can be fast-tracked by putting them under the guidance of effective motivators, teachers and power sources in the organisation.

    At any stage in a career, a **mentor** will be important. The mentor may occupy a role as the employee's teacher/coach/trainer, counsellor, role model, protector or sponsor/ champion, spur to action or improvement, critic and encourager. In May 1993 the FT reported that 40% of British companies now have a mentoring scheme, and a further 20% are thinking about creating one.

(c) The level of **opportunities and challenges** offered to the developing employee. Too much responsibility too early can be damagingly stressful, but if there is not some degree of difficulty, the employee may never explore his full potential and capacity.

EXAMPLE

'When Jack Welch steps down next April as chairman and chief executive of General Electric after 20 years, one of three senior GE managers is expected to take his place.

The board of the US group has been interviewing Mr Welch's possible successors – Jeffrey Immelt, chief executive of the GE Medical Systems, Bob Nardelli who runs GE Power Systems, and James McNerney, head of GE Aircraft Engines.

The directors have also been talking to the staff of the three front-runners and visiting their businesses. The company has appointed chief operating officers for each of their divisions. This is so that, when the successor is appointed head of GE, someone can swiftly step into his shoes in his old job. The other two chief operating officers are widely seen as necessary in case the disappointed executives resign.

Few large companies approach their succession planning with such care.

When Sir Richard Greenbury stepped down as chairman of Marks and Spencer last year, it took the retailer months to find a successor. Other companies that have struggled to find new leaders include Barclays and Reed Elsevier, the publisher.

When Bob Ayling was sacked as chief executive of British Airways earlier this year, one of the many criticisms directed at him was that he had sidelined any rivals and failed to groom a successor.

The heads of companies often do not want to think about who should come after them. But the directors need to insist on developing a plan for appointing a new chief executive, even if the present incumbent is years away from retirement.

Because the directors do not know when they might need the successor, there is no point in settling on a particular individual. Instead, the directors need to be aware of who the leading figures in the sector are, so that they can approach them as soon as the need arises.'

Financial Times, 13 July 2000

4.6 Continuing professional development

In 1995, the UK Institute of Management launched a new policy on Continuous Professional Development (CPD), as a framework for managers to keep their skills up to date. This reflects the professionalisation of management emulating the practice of other professional bodies. CPD is envisaged as a self-managed process, with the individual manager continually reassessing his or her learning needs (in the light of technological, legislative, social and market changes) and seeking to meet those needs via available avenues. CPD is essentially a recognition that 'qualification' – like getting a driver's licence – is only the start of the development process.

The Chartered Institute of Personnel and Development has – fittingly enough – introduced CPD requirements for its members, undertaken through engagement in professional activities, formal learning, and self-directed and informal learning.

An article in the **Financial Times** *noted the huge industry that has sprung up around management training. 'But do these courses work? Can they be measured in some way and be shown to have a desirable effect? A lot of sweat, tears and ink has been spilled*

over this apparently simple question. Hard-headed types want evidence that the expense is justified by increased productivity and revenue. On the other hand, human resources managers seem happy enough if they get the feeling, through ratings on a feedback form, 'that participants have 'enjoyed' the course.'

Unfair to HR managers, perhaps. But how useful is management development?

4.7 The value of management development

Drucker has suggested that management development should be provided for all managers, not just the ones who are considered promotable material (and not just men, though this direct quote does seem to suggest this!)

The promotable man concept focuses on one man out of ten - at best one man out of five. It assigns the other nine to limbo. But the men who need management development the most are not the balls of fire who are the ... promotable people. They are those managers who are not good enough to be promoted but not poor enough to be fired. Unless they have grown up to the demands of tomorrow's jobs, the whole management group will be inadequate, no matter how good ... the promotable people. The first principle of manager development must therefore be the development of the entire management group.

On the other hand, Handy noted that '... it remains true that career planning in many organisations is not a development process so much as a weeding-out process'.

The *Financial Times*, 13 November 1991, put forward four possible views of management training. (Note: these are extreme 'types' - not real people!)

(a) **Cynics** believe that it is a waste of time, and despise the resulting Smart-Alecs and 'course junkies'. They believe that management practices are either learnt through experience, or cannot be taught. Many believe that people are basically untrainable anyway: 'They certainly do not take seriously the proof that training works, arguing that what can be taught is not ... relevant.' Moreover, they subscribe to the view that: 'Those who can, manage; those who can't, become management trainers.'

(b) **Sceptics** are less hostile but not entirely convinced. They believe that training can help - but that not all training courses are clear or helpful in practice, and even if they are, the benefits tend to wear off. 'Back in the work place, the idealistic practices are ignored or even punished and hence discontinued. Most believe the solution lies in selecting people who are already well-trained or at least trainable.'

(c) **Enthusiasts** 'simply cannot see how people are expected to manage without being explicitly taught and trained'. They both reward training attendance, and use it as a reward. They take training needs audits, course appraisal and follow up very seriously.

(d) **Naive proponents** 'are proselytisers of the near miraculous benefits of such-and-such a course, test, guru or concept. If only, they argue, people were to go on a course, understand and live its message, all would be well with the organisation.' They innocently embrace personal testimony and glossy brochure claims for courses.

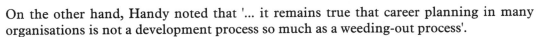

Activity 10   **(5 minutes)**

Suggest three reasons why an organisation should give attention to management training and development.

NOTES

We will now look at various UK government initiatives in VET: Vocational Education and Training. Note that this area is constantly changing: some of the schemes mentioned in the Guidelines are already being phased out! We will give you a brief overview: use your research skills to stay on top of developments.

5 GOVERNMENT-LED TRAINING INITIATIVES

5.1 Vocational Education and Training in the UK

Trevor Bolton (*HRM: An Introduction*) summarises the position of VET in the UK as follows.

> Study after study ... have [sic] repeated the assertion that at the top end of training and education, the United Kingdom does as well as any other nation with, for instance, the proportion of young people achieving university degrees. It is at the intermediate level of qualification, the technician, the apprenticeship, secretarial and clerical training, that we do so poorly. It is generally recognised that the UK trains about half the number of young people with these skills as do many of our competitors.

Concerns have been raised in the areas of:

(a) The competitiveness of British business, given a comparatively unskilled workforce

(b) The social costs of having a rising proportion of the potential labour force condemned to long-term economic inactivity because of inadequate skills (including literacy and numeracy)

(c) The difficulties of recruiting in certain skill areas: skill shortages, despite recession and high unemployment

Some of the characteristics of VET practice and culture in the UK and other nations are as follows.

EXAMPLE: INTERNATIONAL COMPARISONS

	UK	Germany	US	Japan
Extent of State intervention	Voluntarist (left to employers)	Directed (laws and guidelines require employers to provide training funding and resources)	Voluntarist (anti-federalist, with wide variation	Voluntarist/directed (voluntary, provision, but strong directives setting and enforcing high-quality training standards)
Orientation to development	Finance (rather than industry) oriented. Individualist development. Development largely extraneous to corporate culture: seen in context of performance improvement or management succession	Industry oriented (eg engineering) functionally specific	Individualist: trainee aspirations, effort, reward. Excellent training by leading companies – other wise uncoordinated.	Collectivist view of development. On-going long-term training within employment: structured development for individual/organisation benefit. Development embedded in corporate culture, open to all employees

BPP PUBLISHING

	UK	Germany	US	Japan
Training avenues and initiatives	Colleges of further and higher education and business schools Training for work schemes for unemployed Encouragement of business to train employees (eg TECs, LECs Investors in People) National Vocational Qualifications (and managerial competencies) Apprenticeships: declining (c. 13,000 places	**Dual system**: in-company (practical) training under supervision of meister-worker (skilled craftsman) and vocational school (theoretical) training concurrent. Partnership between government (funding vocational colleges), business (funding on-the-job training) and trainees. Apprenticeships: c. 300,000 places Technical colleges Universities	University courses Technical institutes Vocational, trade and business schools Private schools and colleges Community colleges Apprenticeships: declining	Two-year college: vocationally specific training University courses (4 years) College of technology courses (5 years) On-going - company training

UK government initiatives have therefore focused on:

(a)   Schemes to equip unemployed people to enter or re-enter the active workforce (eg Youth Training, Training for Work)

(b)   Schemes to encourage employers to train and develop employees (eg TECs, Investors in People)

(c)   Schemes to integrate vocational education and training into the education system via a comprehensive national framework of qualifications (National Vocational Qualifications, GNVQs as an alternative to academic 'A' levels, management competencies) and various schemes for the accreditation of prior learning and experiential learning)

(d)   Schemes to establish national training targets

We will look at some of the major initiatives that affect organisational training and development.

5.2   Training and Enterprise Councils

Training and Enterprise councils (TECs) in England and Wales and Local Enterprise Councils (LECs) in Scotland were set up in 1991. They are private companies, formed by local business people, under contract to the government to manage public investment in training and to regulate the local training market. TECs do not provide training, but:

(a)   Help businesses to analyse staff training needs and prepare actions plans

(b)   Commission subsidised courses and provide grants (especially towards the training of long-term unemployed people), and advice on training loans for small businesses

NOTES

(c)   Advise businesses on available training services, college/university courses and entrance requirements, Training Access Points (database of local courses) and so on

(d)   Advise on career-planning and development

(e)   Provide on-going support for training initiatives

TECs have also sponsored the Investors in People scheme, 'New Horizons' initiatives for young people (modern apprenticeships), after-school care schemes for children whose parents are at work and so on.

TECs and LECs have been the main point of delivery of training initiatives by the Department for Education and Employment, and the first point of contact for HR managers concerned with training and development

There has been on-going criticism of TECs and LECs from political opponents, commerce and industry – and their own administrators – because of:

(a)   Their voluntary nature. Critics claimed that business organisations, left to themselves, trained to meet their own needs rather than investing in closing the skills gap for the benefit of the economy as a whole.

(b)   Insufficient government funding to meet their aims, given the recessionary pressure on firms to cut their training budgets.

(c)   The gearing of funding to outcomes such as numbers trained and gaining jobs, rather than to the training needs of individuals and organisations for the future.

(d)   The variable quality of training commissioned by TECs from suppliers (linked to accusations of collusion with private training providers, misuse of funds, skimping on training funding in order to retain a surplus for their own initiatives and activities, and so on).

In March 1999, a long-awaited review of the TEC system was ditched on the eve of expected publication, in favour of a new review designed to examine all aspects of the government's plans to reform the education and training system. However, the report had highlighted incoherence, duplication and variable standards. TEC leaders were told to concentrate on raising standards in commissioned training, with future funding to be related more to quality and less to the number of trainees attaining qualifications.

The **Learning and Skills Act 2000** instituted a radical shakeup of responsibility for education and training in the UK, including the foundation of:

(a)   Learning and Skills Councils, which replace TECs from April 2001, and

(b)   The Adult Learning Inspectorate (ALI) which will be responsible for the standard of provision of training for adults in FE colleges, community and adult education

At the time of writing, this is all in the process of development. Watch this space!

5.3   The National Training Framework

In 1986, the National Council for Vocational Qualifications (NCVR) was set up to develop a national system of competence-based vocational qualifications, enabling the standardisation of occupational competence on a national scale. The National Training Framework is designed to harmonise and compare standards of a range of academic and vocational qualifications.

Representatives of professional bodies, industry, commerce and the public service, gathered into 'Industry Lead Bodies', jointly agree occupational standards for their industry (with the NCVQ/QCA and awarding bodies, in accordance with the National Framework

(a)   Competence-based National Vocational Qualifications (NVQs)and Scottish Vocational Qualifications (SVQs) are available at five levels. They are delivered through various training centres (eg local colleges) which are approved by awarding bodies (eg EdExcel (formerly BTEC), City and Guilds, the Association of Accounting Technicians) which in turn must be accredited by the Qualifications Curriculum Authority or the Scottish Qualification Authority.

(b)   General National Vocational Qualifications (GNVQs) have been developed in a number of work-related areas as an alternative to academic A-levels, for delivery via full-time education.

Many awarding and professional bodies are developing their various qualifications for harmonisation within the framework. Meanwhile, the nature of the Industry Lead Bodies has been evolving: some formed themselves into Occupational Standards Councils (OSCs) for particular sectors of employment. There is now a network of renamed National Training Organisations (such as METO – see paragraph 4.3 above), set up by the Department of Education and Employment. The Qualifications and Curriculum Authority issues guidelines on the definition and assessment of competence for NVQs.

While uptake of the competence-based model of VET has gained momentum, the uptake of specific NVQs has been comparatively low. There has been considerable debate and criticism about the National Framework, including accusations of:

(a)   Excessive bureaucracy in assessment, and complexity in standards

(b)   'Jargon-ridden' language in the standards

(c)   Lack of relevance to real-life requirements; the inflexibility of competence as a measure of success in changing organisational environments and different cultures

(d)   The weakness of work-based assessment: accrediting existing competence rather than encouraging learning; variable standards, requiring external quality checks by National Training Organisations

(e)   'Quick fix' qualifications without addressing underlying issues in education and training: difficulties of defining higher-level competences (eg creative conceptual skills) within a prescriptive, demonstration-based system; reluctance of UK employers to invest in training and so on

5.4   The Modern Apprenticeship Scheme

The UK government launched this scheme in 1994 in an attempt to involve industry more closely in the process of vocational training. The apprenticeships (traditionally available in crafts and engineering sectors) are available in childcare, tourism, travel and other industries.

The apprenticeship combines vocational education (towards NVQ level 3) including core skills development (literacy, numeracy communication and so on) with hands-on experience in a sponsoring organisation. Apprentices are attached to a particular employer (as contracted, currently, between the administering TEC and the employer) for the purposes of training: there is no guarantee of employment at the end of the training period (envisaged as two to three years).

BPP PUBLISHING

NOTES

The Labour government 2000 consultation document on modern apprenticeships proposed overhauling the scheme, following a report by the National Skills Task Force, by:

(a)   Increasing the taught element of the programme (setting a minimum time that should be allocated to off-the-job study)

(b)   Specifying that training should take place at a college or other training provider, and

(c)   Providing guaranteed apprenticeships to all those capable of completing it

The Task Force chairperson and Confederation of British Industry opposed these proposals, suggesting that the Department for Education and Employment had misinterpreted the Task Force's recommendation that knowledge and understanding should be assessed separately from on-the-job performance, and turned it into a prescription for training in external colleges: apprentices would, however, be equally well served by on-site training or distance learning.

Half of all apprentices, according to the CBI, fail to complete their courses and gain a qualification. (*People Management* 14 September 2000). The government has, at the time of writing, yet to finalise its revised plans for the scheme: watch this space!

5.5   Watch this space

The Labour government in the UK has extensively overhauled VET policy and initiatives in areas such as:

(a)   The funding of VET through 'learning accounts'
(b)   The establishment of Learning and Skills Councils to replace TECs
(c)   The setting up of a technology-based 'University of Industry'

Much of this is still work-in-progress, as is the shifting picture of European initiatives.

You will need to use your research skills and awareness to keep up-to-date on developments, name-changes, new proposals and so on.

Some useful information sources include:

(a)   Local colleges, universities and school link officers

(b)   Local TECs (or LSCs) and their publications

(c)   The European Centre for the Development of Vocational Training (CEDEFOP)

(d)   *People Management* and other HRD journals

(e)   The quality press

(f)   The World Wide Web or email

- enquiry@city-and-guilds.co.uk   (City and Guilds)
- info@dfe.gov.uk   (Department of Education and Employment)
- enquiries@edexcel.org.uk   (EdExcel – formerly BTEC)
- information@iipuk.co.uk   (Investors in People)
- info@qca.org   (Qualifications and Curriculum Authority)

NOTES

Activity 11 **(No time limit)**

Identify and investigate a vocational training scheme of your choice, relevant to your area of study or work. Compile a dossier or report of information you find as to the scheme's:

(a) Aims and objectives
(b) Entry/access qualifications and commitments
(c) Funding
(d) Delivery methods and locations
(e) Assessment methods and standards
(f) Managing bodies and accountabilities
(g) Qualifications offered
(h) Routes to further qualifications or employment opportunities (if any)

Chapter roundup

A systematic approach to training can be illustrated as follows.

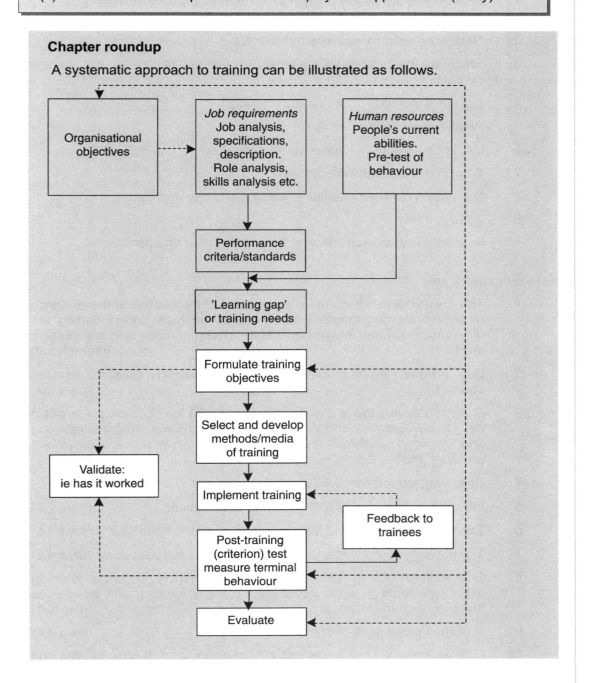

Chapter roundup (cont'd)

Quick quiz

1. How do 'training needs' arise in an organisation and how would you carry out a 'training needs analysis' if required to do so?

2. Give three examples of external courses.

3. What are the advantages and disadvantages of 'on-the job' training methods?

4. List three methods of 'on-the-job' training.

5. What is induction?

6. List three ways to validate a training scheme.

7. What is management succession?

8. Distinguish between education, training and development.

9. What is a mentor?

10. How can an individual enhance his or her career prospects?

Answers to quick quiz

1. The answer depends on the job or tasks and the abilities and experience of individuals or groups. Training needs analysis entails finding the difference between the required level of competence and the present level. (see paragraph 1.2)

2. Day release, evening classes, distance learning, revision, full-time courses. (para 3.2)

3. The main advantage is that it is relevant to the job. It takes place within the job environment, so that the style of supervision, personal relations and working conditions are absorbed. The main disadvantages are pressure and the cost of mistakes. (para 2.1)

4. Coaching, job rotation, 'assistant to' positions. (para 2.1)

5. Introducing new recruits to the job and environment. (para 2.3)

6. Trainee reactions, trainee learning, changes in job behaviour. (para 1.5)

7. The movement of suitable people into management positions. (para 4.5)

8. Education results in formal qualifications; training is formal learning activities related to work; development is any learning and experience that prepares an individual for future work requirements. (para 4.1)

9. An experienced guide within the organisation. (para 2.1)

10. Gain experience in all areas and with all levels, accept opportunities and challenges. (para 4.5)

NOTES

Answers to Activities

1   Fulfilling such aspirations may become incompatible with business objectives if:

    (a)   Specific training outcomes become divorced from the strategic aims of the business, and become focused on purely personal development for its own sake

    (b)   Training outcomes serve to increase employee mobility, by giving them transferable skills and self-confidence

    (c)   Training outcomes encourage the employee to 'outgrow' the organisation's culture and leadership style, creating expectations and capabilities that the organisation may not (yet) be in a position to utilise or even tolerate

2   Your own needs assessment: you might make this the basis for Activity 11, later.

3   The answer offered by Torrington and Hall (*Personnel Management, A New Approach*) is as follows.

Training needs	**Learning objectives**
(a) To know more about the Data Protection Act	The employee will be able to answer four out of every five queries about the Data Protection Act without having to search for details.
(b) To establish a better rapport with customers	The employee will immediately attend to a customer unless already engaged with another customer.
	The employee will greet each customer using the customer's name where known.
	The employee will apologise to every customer who has had to wait to be attended to.
(c) To assemble clocks more quickly	The employee will be able to assemble each clock correctly within thirty minutes.

4   Techniques of training validation used in the given examples are as follows.

    (a)   Trainee reaction
    (b)   Trainee learning
    (c)   Trainee learning
    (d)   Change in behaviour (attitude) following training
    (e)   Impact of training on the organisation's goals
    (f)   Impact of training on your goals.

5   You have probably covered most of the following points.

Advantages include working for a specific purpose, carrying out practical work, the feeling of achievement when a task is completed successfully, knowing you have made a contribution to the organisation's objectives, learning to work with others. If mistakes are made they are rectified and do not affect your overall performance (unless you make too many or keep making the same mistakes).

Disadvantages could include the difficulty of relating exercises or assignments to the 'real work' situation, working mainly on your own and the few practical applications for your studies. Unlike work, you only have one chance to get things right: the marking system means that if you make a mistake there is little you can do once the work is handed in and marked.

6   Your own experience (NB: important source of learning!)

7   Training methods for the various workers indicated are as follows.

(a)   Worker on a new machine: on-the-job training, coaching.

(b)   Accounts clerk working for professional qualification: external course – evening class or day-release.

(c)   Supervisors wishing to benefit from participative management and democratic leadership: internal or external seminar, or group training exercise. Careful attention will need to be given to how these 'ideas' will be integrated into practice on the job.

(d)   New staff: induction training.

(e)   Intimidated supervisor: assertiveness training.

8   The *FT* article goes onto give three arguments in favour of this type of training.

(a)   Experimental versus theoretical learning. Since the 1960s, when encounter groups thrived, trainers have claimed that real learning occurs when people are put in difficult, novel and problematic situations and not when they study elaborate theories or abstract ideas.

(b)   Emotions not ideas. Most training courses are about ideas, concepts, skills and models. They involve brain work and traditional classroom activities. But outdoor trainers claim that modern management is as much about self-confidence and courage.

(c)   Team membership not leadership. There are plenty of leadership courses but not too many for those who have to follow. Despite mouthing platitudes about teams and team work, Anglo-Americans come from an individualistic, not a collective, culture. Team work does not come easily or naturally.

9   (a)   International operations - if the organisation is in (or moving into) the international arena. Understanding of cultural differences is crucial to effective strategic and people management.

(b)   Other disciplines and organisations. Some consultancies and banks, for example, offer secondment with business organisations, development agencies or the civil service. Organisations often encourage potential high-fliers (and sometimes HR specialists) to gain experience in different areas of the business.

10   (a)   The prime objective of management development is improved performance capacity - both from the managers *and* from those they manage.

(b)   Management development secures management succession: a pool of promotable individuals in the organisation.

(c)   The organisation's showing an interest in the career development of staff may motivate them and encourage loyalty. (This will be especially important if the firm intends to rely on management succession to fill senior management positions.)

11 Up to you. (The Assessment Criteria in this area specifies that you should be able to '**investigate**' a vocational training scheme'...)

Assignment 17   **(2 hours)**

Price-U-Like Stores

You are a recently appointed Personnel and Training Manager for Price-U-Like Stores. As a result of the increasing cut throat competition in the retail grocery sector, you launched a new initiative in customer care in the firm, some eight weeks ago.

You arrive at work this morning, to find the following e-mail message waiting for you.

Memo: Personnel and Training Manager

From: A Smith – Chief Executive

Re: 'Customer Care' programme

Despite the publicity and financial backing given to this project, I was very concerned to learn from Public Relations that there has been an increase in complaints from customers about staff; particularly about the ways in which they have been treated by check-out staff and supervisors. Comments range from 'unhelpful' to 'surly', 'rude', 'bloody-minded'. On one occasion a customer referred to obscene gestures from one particular check-out operator.

Whilst I acknowledge that these issues cannot be laid solely at the door of the 'Customer Care' programme, they clearly stand in stark contrast to the objectives of the programme and what we are trying to achieve.

Please put together a training programme for all front line store staff (currently 100 across 10 stores) to put across the message of 'Customer Care' more effectively.

Task:

Produce an outline full-day training programme on Customer Care in Price-U-Like Stores. The programme should indicate current problem areas and a rationale for the Customer Care initiative and why you have chosen to run the programme in the way you decide.

UNIT 24: EMPLOYEE RELATIONS

Chapter 18 :
THE FRAMEWORK OF EMPLOYEE RELATIONS

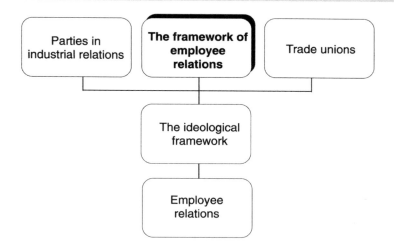

Introduction

Thanks largely to its turbulent history and tainting with political colours, industrial relations is an emotive subject which requires careful handling in study and professional contexts: as you read, try to appreciate both sides of the debate.

Traditionally, industrial relations are the dealings and co-operation (or lack of it) between management and workers, usually via their representatives in a trade union or staff association. However, trade unionism has been on the decline in the UK (and USA) and a high proportion of employees do not now belong to unions. Nevertheless, industrial relations still exist in organisations. A shift to the term 'employee relations' reflects a broader orientation towards communication with and involvement of employees, and a more unitarist perspective in which co-operation is regarded as both possible and desirable in order for business' and employees' needs to be met.

In this chapter we will consider the players and ideologies involved in industrial relations and the shift towards 'employee relations'. In Chapter 19 we will examine more closely some of the processes involved in the management of employee relations.

Your objectives

In this chapter you will learn about the following

(a)   The unitary and pluralistic frames of reference

(b)   The development of trade unions and the nature of industrial relations

(c)   The role of a trade union and its contribution to effective industrial relations

(d)   The ideological framework of industrial relations

BPP PUBLISHING

(e)   Industrial relations and employee relations

    (f)   The effectiveness of employee involvement techniques

    (g)   The impact of HR on employee relations

1   PARTIES IN INDUSTRIAL RELATIONS

1.1   What are industrial relations?

Definition

> **Industrial relations (IR)** comprises 'all the rules, practices and conventions governing interactions between managements and their workforces, normally involving collective employee representation and bargaining.'
>
>   (Graham and Bennett)

Industrial relations policy and practice covers areas such as:

    (a)   Procedures for setting terms and conditions of work, profit-sharing, training targets, equal opportunities policy and so on

    (b)   Disciplinary and grievance procedures, both individual and collective, including external arbitration and conciliation

    (c)   Recognition of trade unions (if applicable) to represent worker interests through the processes of collective bargaining and consultation

    (d)   Development of added or alternative mechanisms for employee representation and consultation (such as works councils, joint consultation committees and employee forums)

    (e)   Determination of the structure and scope of consultation and employee involvement in decision-making, within the framework of collective bargaining, partnership agreements, works councils, general HRM policies and so on

1.2   Workers and their organisations

Trade unions

Definitions

> A **trade union** is an organised association of employees who 'consist wholly or mainly of workers of one or more description and whose principal purposes include the regulation of relations between workers and employers' (Trade Unions and Labour Relations (Consolidation) Act.
>
> An **independent trade union** is one which has been certified as being autonomous and financially self-supporting: not dominated by an employer because of the provision or withdrawal of financial or other support.

A single trade union might include members from different organisations in the same industry, and a single organisation might employ workers who belong to a number of different trade unions. Employees may be members of various unions, but the employer is not compelled to deal with a union unless it is 'recognised' for the purposes of collective bargaining or negotiation. Until recently, there was no statutory provision for obtaining or enforcing recognition: that was changed by the Employment Relations Act 1999 (see below).

A firm may recognise a number of different unions in the workplace, to represent different categories of employees. Multi-unionism has significant drawbacks: encouraging demarcation disputes and the proliferation of work rules; competitive and therefore escalating pay settlements; and the cost and complexity of multiple bargaining time and machinery.

Firms desiring to simplify bargaining arrangements and secure greater flexibility and integration will often seek to negotiate a **sole recognition** or **single union agreement**, whereby only one union is recognised for the purpose of collective bargaining: workers who want representation must join this union. Sole recognition – and even more, the de-recognition of one union in favour of another – is, however, fraught with inter-union competition, and may not be perceived as genuinely representative of the interests of all staff. It is frequently achieved by a 'beauty contest approach', which arguably creates a situation in which unions must offer to fulfil the expectations of management in order to be granted recognition (and access to a fresh pool of members) rather than fulfilling the expectations of their members.

The primary functions carried out by a trade union are directly related to its objectives of improving the collective pay, conditions and job security of its members: collective bargaining and negotiation, representation of employees in formal discussions with management (say, as part of disciplinary procedures), consultation in the event of business changes which will affect members (say, redundancies or transfer of the undertaking) and so on.

Activity 1   **(15 minutes)**

What other activities of unions are you aware of, which are not directly connected to the achievement of its goals, but which might indirectly be effective in protecting members' rights?

The Trades Union Congress (TUC)

The TUC is a voluntary association of unions. It holds an annual week-long congress or conference, for the purpose of debate, policy formation and the election of its general council. The TUC's purpose is:

(a)   To formulate and express policy for the trade union movement as a whole

(b)   To consult with industry and government bodies on issues affecting the trade union movement, and to lobby for relevant legislation

(c)   To manage inter-union disputes

We will discuss trade unions in more detail in Section 2 below. However, trade unions are not the only employee representatives with whom management may deal, formally or informally. There has been a trend towards non-unionised forums for consultation and participation. Again, these will be discussed in detail later (in Chapter 19), but we will survey some of the possibilities briefly here.

Staff associations

Staff associations represent the employees of a particular organisation. They have been particularly popular among white-collar workers, for whom trade unionism was less socially acceptable. Management generally prefer to deal with staff associations because they are less subject to third-party external interests: mutuality of interests may therefore be expected to be easier to achieve, with less external exposure, and staff associations may offer sufficient representation to head off demands for unionisation. Most staff associations, however, are independent of the employer and provide a genuine alternative to trade unions in terms of employee representation, despite lack of militancy, narrow membership base and lack of funding.

1.3 Managers and their organisations

Employers' associations and federations

Employers' associations are voluntary private groups of employers founded to facilitate trade, communication and representation in areas of common interest. Some are national bodies covering a whole industry (for example, the Engineering Employers Federation or the Publishers Association), while others are regional or specialised in their scope. They were initially developed on an ad hoc basis in response to specific industrial disputes with the early trade unions, but by the end of the nineteenth century, in response to the growing influence of unionism, adopted the federated approach to organisation at an industry/national level. The role of the associations has declined with the increasing decentralisation of industrial relations processes: the growth in company- or plant-level bargaining, for example, and the decline of industry-wide agreements.

The main purposes of employers associations are:

(a) To give general help and advice on employee relations issues

(b) To represent members' views to political influencers (eg lobbying parliament)

(c) To assist member firms in the resolution of disputes (including representation at Employment Tribunals)

(d) To negotiate sectoral collective agreements (where applicable) with trade unions

The Confederation of British Industry (CBI)

The Confederation of British Industry (CBI) was formed in 1965 as the main national federation of employers' associations in the UK, with the purpose of promoting British industry through political lobbying. Its main function is to influence policy on industry-related issues: it is not directly involved in employee relations processes, although it does maintain working relationships with the TUC, ACAS and other bodies.

1.4 Third parties

Third parties, such as government, arbitrators and judges (now including the European Court of Justice) have an important bearing on industrial relations, because they set a framework for what employers and employees can and cannot do.

The government has established agencies such as the Advisory, Conciliation and Arbitration Service (ACAS) and Employment Tribunals, to assist or act as go-betweens in employment and industrial relations matters.

ACAS

According to the Employment Protection Act 1975, ACAS was designed to 'promote the improvement of industrial relations'. It is an independent body, governed by a Council whose members are appointed after consultation with worker and employer organisations.

ACAS has the ability to intervene at the request of employers and/or trade unions in the event of a possible or actual trade dispute. It may enquire into a complaint by a recognised trade union that insufficient information has been disclosed for collective bargaining purposes. It may also enquire on its own initiative into any industrial relations matter and publish its findings. It prepares and publishes Codes of Practice giving guidance for improving industrial relations (in areas such as disciplinary procedure).

ACAS may also be involved in individual conciliation cases, prior to hearing by tribunal. (It is frequently called in, for example, over equal opportunity and unfair dismissal complaints.)

Activity 2   **(10 minutes)**

Look up some definitions: what is the meaning of (a) conciliation (b) mediation and (c) arbitration. (Add the ways in which ACAS accomplishes these things, briefly, if you know.)

In 1993, 47% of ACAS' completed collective conciliation cases related to disputes over pay and employment conditions, 20% to redundancy and 9% to union recognition. ACAS hit the headlines in 1994 owing to its successful intervention in the Railtrack dispute with rail union RMT.

The Central Arbitration Committee

This body acts as arbitrator in disputes referred to it by ACAS. Under the Employment Relations Act 1999, it is called upon to make a ruling in cases where a union and an employer fail to reach agreement on union recognition or on the conduct of collective bargaining.

Employment Tribunals

Employment Tribunals (formed under the Employment Tribunals Act 1996) deal with most cases brought under employment law. They consist of an independent, legally-qualified chairperson, and two representative members, from the employer and the union. Their constitution is informal, but their decisions are legally binding. Evidence is given on oath, witnesses are called and legal representation is permitted as in a court of law. Appeals may be made (on points of law only) to the Employment Appeals Tribunal: this is a formal court, consisting of a judge and lay members representing both sides of industry, and its decisions establish legal precedent.

ACAS has prepared plans for an arbitration-based alternative to employment tribunals (*People Management* September 2000), but their publication has been repeatedly delayed: watch this space!

EXAMPLE: INTERNATIONAL COMPARISONS

In the USA, although the government plays a limited role in influencing collective agreements, third party intervention in negotiation and mediation (eg via the Federal Mediation and Conciliation Service) is widespread.

1.5 The role of the HR department

As in many other areas of HRM, it is often the line managers who have responsibility on a day-to-day basis for the implementation of industrial relations policy in regard to:

(a) Exchanging information with office representatives – say, to discuss changes in work procedures or newly-introduced rules

(b) Conducting disciplinary and grievance measures

(c) Implementing collective agreements on working procedures and conditions

(d) Managing interpersonal and team relations in such a way as to minimise potential conflict and preserve organisational authority in the face of collective labour strength

However, there is a continuing role of HR specialists in developing policies which promote consistent decisions on industrial relations issues, especially since line managers may resist employee relations techniques in the belief that they will hamper their work and limit their flexibility.

FOR DISCUSSION

Clegg argues that: 'If line managers are left to handle industrial relations issues for themselves, the pressures of production are likely to lead to ad hoc and contradictory decisions ... If a personnel policy is introduced to promote consistent decisions on industrial relations issues, its effectiveness may depend on granting authority to the personnel department to override the natural priorities of the line managers.'

How can the HR function overcome the 'natural priorities' of line managers in the sphere of employee relations?

We will discuss in Section 4 below how HR policy affects industrial relations, and how the HRM approach ('employee relations') differs from the traditional approach ('industrial relations'). Here, we will look in more detail at the major player in traditional industrial relations: the trade unions.

2 TRADE UNIONS

2.1 Types of trade union

Unions are often distinguished as follows.

(a) **Craft and occupational unions,** which recruit employees who perform certain jobs. These include:

(i) White collar unions (employees in office work or desk jobs), and
(ii) Craft unions (manual workers skilled at a particular craft)

Examples include the British Airline Pilots Association (Balpa) and the Professional Footballers Association.

(b) **Industrial unions,** which recruit all grades of employees employed in a particular industry. Examples include the National Union of Mineworkers and the Iron and Steel Trades Confederation.

(c)   **General unions,** which organise workers from a variety of different jobs and industries. Examples include the Transport and General Workers Union (T&G).

Despite these different types, the UK system is essentially 'job-centred': the job an individual performs largely determines which union (s)he will join.

EXAMPLE: INTERNATIONAL COMPARISONS

- In Germany, trade unions are organised on industrial lines: one trade union represents all organised employees at a workplace, irrespective of their individual occupation. The German Trade Union Federation (DGB) is a non-political affiliation based on industrial unionism.

- In Japan, unions are mostly organised by company or establishment: an enterprise union consists of regular employees of a single firm, both white- and blue-collar. This has traditionally been supported by long-term career stability.

- In France, unions are mostly general unions, organised into five major confederations with broad divisions along politico-religious lines: socialist, communist, social democratic, Christian.

- Job- or occupation-centred unionism is a feature of Anglo-Saxon countries such as the UK, USA and Australasia.

2.2   Trade union representatives

Trade union representatives include:

(a)   Full-time paid officials: 'organisers' or 'officers', employed by the union at district or regional level to carry out its policies under the direction of its national executive committee; and headquarters staff (financial, legal and administrative, under a 'general secretary').

(b)   Part-time voluntary officials, elected to be branch officers of the union in a particular area.

(c)   Workplace representatives (shop stewards or staff representatives) who are employed by the organisation, but act on behalf of their fellow employees as their recognised representative. (Some very large firms with sensitive industrial relations may retain one or two employees on full pay to act in their union capacity full time.) Shop Stewards are the link between the work group, the union officials and management: they require extensive knowledge of the union's service, employment and industrial relations law, ACAS and tribunal machinery, the policies and practices of the organisation, the role of managers and so on.

The structure of a union is democratic: local branch members elect representatives to a district or regional committee, which elect a national committee. The policy of the union is (theoretically) representative of the views of members, not of its leadership. However, the potential divergence between the goals and values of individual members and those of the organisation is just as great for a trade union as for a business. This view was given a political edge by the Conservative government's legislative support for the rights of individual union members (for example, secret balloting on use of union funds and industrial action). Its Industrial Relations Code of Practice stated that it should be the responsibility of the union to ensure that:

(a)   Its members understand the organisation, policy and rules of the union

(b)   Its members understand the powers and duties of the members themselves and those of their union representatives

(c)   Its officials are adequately trained to look after their members' interest in an efficient and responsible way

EXAMPLE

The MSF, the general technical union, applied in 1992 for accreditation under the BS 5750 (now BS EN SIO 9000) quality assurance scheme, as part of a programme to make the union 'user friendly'. Members were given guarantees on servicing, representation and voting rights, backed by a clear set of service standards.

2.3   The rise, fall and rise of trade unionism

Early development

The UK trade union movement is the oldest in the world. Trade unions developed in the mid-nineteenth century, mainly as organisations of skilled workers in craft-dominated industries seeking to secure employment. In the latter half of the century, labourers and other unskilled workers also organised.

The local craftsman's clubs were initially suppressed by the Combination Acts (1799, 1800), which made illegal any combination of working men for the purpose of improving their work conditions: the government of the day feared the spread of revolutionary ideas from France.

The Acts were repealed in 1824. An outbreak of strikes followed, and a further Act was passed in 1825 allowing trade unions to exist, but limiting their right to strike.

The first attempt to unite skilled and unskilled worker was Robert Owen's Grand National Consolidated Trades Union (1834). This collapsed following the transportation to Australia of the so-called 'Tolpuddle Martyrs': six members of the Friendly Society of Agricultural Labourers of Tolpuddle, Dorset, founded in 1833 to secure fair wages for its members, who were charged with administering unlawful oaths, and became the founding heroes of the trades union movement.

In 1851, the first successful national trade union, the Amalgamated Society of Engineers, was formed, and the Trades Union Congress (TUC) met for the first time in 1868.

Trade unions were finally granted legal status in 1871.

Rise...

Following legal status, more trades unions began to be formed, particularly by unskilled workers. The London dockers successfully struck in 1889 (for a wage of sixpence, ie 2 ½ pence, per hour!), encouraging others.

During the 1890s, the trades union movement supported the formation of the Labour Party, supplying funding (as it continues to do today). The Labour Representation Committee was formed in 1900 and renamed the Labour Party in 1906. In that same year, unions in the UK finally became secure: the Trade Disputes Act (1906) prevented employers form suing unions for damages following a strike.

The Labour Party grew in influence until in 1922 it replaced the divided Liberal party as one of the two major UK parties: in 1924 and 1929/31 it was able to form a minority government (under Ramsay MacDonald).

1926 saw a national strike by workers in Britain's major industries, lasting from 3-12 May: The General Strike. The TUC called out its members in support of the miners, who had refused to accept a reduction in wages. The strike involved over two million workers in transport, iron and steel, building, printing, gas and electricity. However, the government was able to keep essential services going, and the strike was forced to fold. This was a blow to the trades union movement, and the subsequent Trade Disputes Act (1927) made general strikes illegal.

In 1945, however, Labour won a huge majority in the first post-war general election, and was able to introduce a programme of radical policies under Clement Attlee: this included widespread nationalisation of industries, the setting up of the social security system – and the repeal of the Trade Disputes Act.

The unions became increasingly powerful during the Labour term(s) in government. The Industrial Relations Act (1971) was enacted by a Conservative government, introducing strike ballots and cooling-off periods, but this was repealed by the following Labour government in 1974.

In 1975, ACAS was set up to assist in settling industrial disputes.

Trade union membership in the UK reached a peak of 13.29 million in 1979, also the year in which the number, duration and severity of strike actions reached their peak.

And fall…

During the 1980s and early '90s, the power of trade unions in the UK was affected by a number of factors.

(a)   Declining membership and the increase in non-unionised organisations. Total union membership, for example, peaked at 13.2 million in 1979 and fell to 7.8 million in 1997. This is partly due to the decline in manufacturing, the traditional heartland of unionism, and the growth in the service sector where membership has traditionally been low. Meanwhile, competitive pressures resulted in employers' de-recognising of trade unions in order to end restrictive work rules and collective bargaining. Falling membership creates a vicious circle: weakening union effectiveness, which further depresses membership, and so on.

(b)   Conditions of employment, levels of pay and HRM policies were in general terms becoming more favourable to employees and 'softer' in orientation (if only because of employer self-interest, in the face of skill shortages and consumer expectations of social responsibility). This marginalised the role of trade unions as protectors of employee interests.

(c)   Union concerns such as collective negotiation, occupational demarcations and work rules were being marginalised by HRM trends such as: negotiation of individual contracts; individual performance management and performance- or merit-related pay awards; multi-skilling and flexible working; direct communication policies; worker empowerment, involvement and participation schemes; the introduction of Japanese management and production techniques (collectivist, participative, low-conflict) and so on. The whole trend towards 'commitment'-based HRM, with a unitary perspective, suggested that the adversarial industrial relations model, associated with unionism, could be by-passed.

(d)   The unions' power was intentionally weakened by Conservative governments from 1979 – 1997, through legislation such as:

   (i)   The abolition of the 'closed shop', under which membership of a union could be made a condition of employment

BPP
PUBLISHING

(ii)   The requirement for secret balloting of union members when electing voting members of a union's governing body, and when proposing industrial action, which gave support to the more moderate elements of the trade union movement

(iii)   The protection of individual union members' rights (including the right to refuse to participate in or support a strike), assisted by a Commissioner for the Rights of Trade Union Members

(iv)   The right of employers to dismiss employees taking unofficial strike or other industrial action

(v)   The curbing of secondary picketing

(vi)   The prevention of the use of union funds to compensate a member for the consequences of unlawful conduct during a strike (eg paying fines)

And rise...?

Gregor Gall (*People Management,* September 2000) suggests that there has been a significant turnaround in the last few years in the number of union recognition agreements in force in the UK and the number and proportion of workers covered by such agreements.

This has been accelerated by:

(a)   New recognition laws (see paragraph 2.6 below)

(b)   The Labour government's support for an industrial relations climate in which employers are less inclined to behave unilaterally, thus legitimising the union role in organisations

(c)   Employer recognition that there is a positive business case for dealing with the workforce through unions, as a more efficient, positive and democratic method

(d)   Concerted recruitment drives, often supported by employers who have signed voluntary and partnership agreements with a union

The picture for unions is not all rosy, however. American anti-union consultants have been advertising for business in the UK, advising on 'union-busting' strategies (see Chapter 15). Lingering anti-union strategies include:

(a)   Substitution, including company councils or forums and open-management techniques, and

(b)   Suppression, by dismissal, victimisation, harassment and spying

In addition, union leaders are also concerned that the new recognition law has sparked inter-union disputes and competition for single-union recognition deals, wasting union resources and distracting from the key task of recruitment. The TUC conference 2000, for example, highlighted two long-running disputes over single-union deals signed by the Transport and General Workers Union (T&G): at the JVC Kilbride factory, squeezing out the Iron and Steel Trades Confederation (ISTC), and at Eurotunnel, squeezing out the train drivers' union, Aslef.

2.4   The sources of trade union power

The power of a given trade union in bargaining and negotiating with employers will depend on a complex of factors.

(a) The degree of support for union actions from its members, and its ability to attract and maintain membership. This in turn may depend on a number of factors:

    (i) The conditions pertaining in the industry or organisation, the aspirations of members and hence the perceived advantages of trade union membership.

    (ii) Employment issues such as recessionary downsizing, or the introduction of new technology, which enhance the perceived importance of worker representation.

    (iii) Competition for members between unions, or between a union and a staff association: for example, the split in representation for miners in the UK after the 1984 miners' strike. *People Management* (9 February 1995) noted a trend of union mergers with other unions and staff associations, in a bid for what it called 'safety in numbers': for example, the merger between the National Communications Union (NCU) and the Union of Communication Workers (UCW) to form the new Communication Workers Union (CWU)!

(b) The perceived success or failure of the union in obtaining beneficial agreements for its members.

(c) The bargaining environment, including:

    (i) The employer's HRM policies. If terms and conditions are felt to be fair, good in comparison to market rates and so on, there will be little impetus for bargaining.

    (ii) The local labour market. If there is a local shortage of the skill groups represented by the union, it will have greater bargaining power, but the reverse is also true: in time of high unemployment, the union movement is weakened. (There is less talk about the quality of working life when there is little work to be had.)

(d) The culture of the union, and in particular its willingness to use industrial muscle. This resides primarily in the threat of withdrawal of labour in disputes (discussed in Chapter 18).

Activity 3   **(5 minutes)**

Why do you think size of the union (number of members) has been left out of our account?

2.5 The law on trade union membership and activities

The **closed shop** (whereby an employee had to be a member of a relevant union in order to obtain or retain a job) was stripped of all legal protection under the Employment Acts 1988: dismissal for non-membership of a union was automatically to be deemed unfair, and industrial action to create or maintain closed shop practices lost its legal immunity. On the other hand, further legislation has protected the freedom of individuals to join the union of their choice. No action may be taken to compel people to be members of a union, nor to deter them. Nor can employees be prevented from participation in union activities at an appropriate time: if the union is both independent and recognised by the employer, there is a further right to reasonable time off for union activities.

Individual union members' rights (Employment Act 1988) include:

(a)   The right not to be unjustifiably disciplined by a union (eg by fines, expulsion, withdrawal of benefits or blacklisting) for refusing to strike, for crossing a picket line or for initiating or inciting legal actions against the union

(b)   The right to a postal vote in union elections and ballots on the use of union funds for political purposes (with the assurance that such elections and ballots will be subject to proper standards of independent scrutiny)

(c)   The right to inspect the union's accounting records

The **Employment Relations Act 1999** reinforced these rights.

- Individuals not currently included in collective contracts can have these rights extended to them by decision of the Secretary of State for Trade and Industry.

- Employees covered by a collective workplace agreement cannot be forced to sign an individual contract.

- Blacklisting of, or discrimination against, trade union members is outlawed.

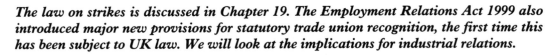

Activity 4   **(15 minutes)**

Why do you think the closed shop existed, and why was it abolished?

The law on strikes is discussed in Chapter 19. The Employment Relations Act 1999 also introduced major new provisions for statutory trade union recognition, the first time this has been subject to UK law. We will look at the implications for industrial relations.

2.6   Trade union recognition

Under the Employment Relations Act 1999, independent trade unions can apply in writing to an employer to be granted recognition. Recognition may be:

(a)   Voluntary, if a ballot (triggered by 10% union membership within the proposed bargaining unit) returned a 40% 'yes' vote, or

(b)   Automatic, if more than 50% (plus one person) of the bargaining unit are 'full and conscious' members of the union

If the union and the employer fail to reach agreement on recognition or on the conduct of collective bargaining, the Central Arbitration Committee (CAC) can make a ruling.

Initial reports from the CAC suggest that trade unions are using applications for statutory recognition as bargaining tools to win voluntary agreements from employers. Several hundred new recognition deals per year have been signed since 1999. High-profile 'scalps' include Virgin Atlantic, which after many years of refusal entered discussions on recognition with the pilots' union Balpa.

Of the 748 recognition agreements listed on Gregor Gall's database in September 2000, most are standard recognition agreements covering rights of information, consultation, representation and negotiation. 'Sweetheart' agreements (negotiated with a single union and featuring 'no disruption' clauses and compulsory arbitration) are uncommon. There are also a small but significant number of non-traditional deals stipulating that bargaining should be conducted through company councils or staff forums, on which there may also be representation for union members. This usually happens where union recognition is added to existing consultation procedures: examples include Monarch

Airlines' agreement with the AEEU and Eurotunnel's with the T&G. These may or may not be described as 'partnership' agreements. (Gall notes that partnership is in vogue at the moment and that there is some pressure to sign such deals.)

Elia Rana, appraising the effect of the new recognition law (*People Management*, September 2000) suggests that it appears to have brought about a surprising (if not necessarily lasting) amiability between management and unions. The chief executive of the Employers' Forum on Statute and Practice is quoted as follows.

> The proposition unions are putting to employers is different from what it was a generation ago. More are approaching companies with an offer that seeks to provide workforce representation in a way that's not necessarily going to make life disruptive for the employer. They are asking: "How can we work with you?" We've been surprised at the extent to which the voluntary approach seems to be the dominant one."

2.7 Concerns about the return of unionisation

The benefits expected to accrue from non-union workforces will vary from organisation to organisation, depending on the nature of the task, environment and workforce. In a changing environment, the organisation may only survive through flexibility and the creation of a culture where changes, innovation and risk are welcomed: organised resistance to corporate plans, and insistence on inflexible work rules and agreements, are obviously undesirable from management's point of view. Some managers have feared that the Employment Relations Act 1999 will re-establish the industrial relations atmosphere of the 1970s.

FOR DISCUSSION

The following views were expressed in *People Management* in September 2000.

The ERA has brought no return to the closed shop, no permission for industrial action without ballots, no return to "semi-corrupt" union election systems and no secondary picketing.... The reactionaries focus on the recognition provision, implying that it is being forced on unwilling employers with disastrous economic results. But most mainstream HR commentators accept that employers are under growing pressure to motivate and enthuse their people. They need to build trust and constantly improve their communication methods so that their appeals for flexibility do not fall on deaf ears.

Sir Ken Jackson, general secretary of the Amalgamated Engineering and Electrical Union

While many managers have become more democratic and inclusive in their approach to employee relations, too many union reps are still resistant to change.

Employers are genuinely fearful that, if they had to revert to collective bargaining and the sorts of practices involved with union recognition, they could not act fast enough to anticipate and respond to changing customer needs.

Geoff Armstrong (director-general of the CIPD)

What is your view of the new legislation, from what you hear in the press from both sides?

The views quoted in the 'For Discussion' exercise above highlight the extent to which industrial relations can be contentious, with both legitimate differences and ingrained prejudices on either side. We will now look briefly at the ideological framework underlying industrial relations.

BPP PUBLISHING

3. THE IDEOLOGICAL FRAMEWORK

3.1 Unitary and pluralist frames of reference

Alan Fox (*Industrial Relations and a Wider Society: Aspects of Interaction,* 1975) identified three broad ideologies which are involved in industrial relations.

(a) **Unitary ideology**. All members of the organisation, despite their different roles, have common objectives and values which unite their efforts. Workers are loyal, and the prerogative of management is accepted as paternal, and in everyone's best interests. Unions are a useful channel of communication, but are no longer strictly necessary: they can indeed be counterproductive in offering support to potentially disruptive elements.

> Any business must mould a true team and weld individual efforts into a common effort. Each member of the enterprise contributes something different, but they must all contribute towards a common goal. Their efforts must all pull in the same direction, without friction, without unnecessary duplication of effort'

(Drucker)

(b) **Pluralist ideology**. Organisations are political coalitions of individuals and groups which have their own interests. Management has to create a workable structure for collaboration, taking into account the objectives of all the various interest groups or stakeholders in the organisation. A mutual survival strategy, involving the control of conflict through compromise, can be made acceptable in varying degrees to all concerned.

(c) **Radical ideology**. This primarily Marxist ideology argues that there is an inequality of power between the controllers of economic resources (shareholders and managers) and those who depend on access to those resources (wage earners). Those in power exploit the others by indoctrinating them to accept the legitimacy of their rights to power, and thus perpetuate the system. Conflict between these strata of society – the proletariat and the bourgeoisie – does not aim for mutual survival, but for revolutionary change: bringing down the system.

> The history of all societies hitherto is the history of class struggles. Freeman and slave, patrician and plebeian, lord and serf, guildmaster and journeyman, in a word, oppressor and oppressed, stood in constant opposition to one another, carried on an uninterrupted, now hidden, now open fight.

(Marx and Engels, *The Communist Manifesto,* 1888)

3.2 Different interests

'Them and us' attitudes have traditionally been ingrained in UK industry, partly because of class-consciousness. You should be aware that they are to an extent inevitable, given the tendency of people to draw boundaries round any group they are in. It should be remembered that there are different interest groups **within** both management and employees as well as **between** them. For example, there may be a clash of interests between HR managers aiming for the stability, quality and flexibility of the workforce, in accordance with ethical HR practice, and production operations managers aiming for immediate efficiency gains through 'lean production'. The interests of white-collar, craft and unskilled workers may clash over differentials, status and demarcation boundaries.

However, the root of union-management conflict, as we have seen, frequently lies in genuine inequities and artificial status distinctions. We have already discussed ways in which less divisive systems (such as single status agreements, salaried status for all grades and Japanese management practices) are available to emphasise a unitary rather than a pluralistic perspective.

According to Gennard and Judge *(Employee relations)*, 'the rationale for employee relations is to solve the problem that in a labour market the buyers (employers) and sellers (employees) have an endemic conflict of interests over the 'prices' at which they wish to exchange their services.' In this view, there is a perpetual trade off between what the employer wants (productivity, quality, functional flexibility, numerical flexibility and/or labour stability according to circumstance and so on) and what the employee wants in return (a certain level of pay and incentives, family-friendly policies, opportunities for development, job security and/or mobility according to circumstances and so on).

Employee relations therefore recognises differences (if not conflicts) of interest. Gennard and Judge quote a Recognition Procedural Agreement involving the Scottish Carpet Workers Union which includes the following general principles.

> The union recognise management's responsibility to plan, organise and manage the company's operation.

> The company recognises the union's responsibility to represent the interests of their [sic] members and to maintain or improve their terms and conditions of employment and work within the constraints imposed on the plant by corporate policy and finance.

3.3 Shared interests

Trade unions have a vested interest in the success of the organisation to which their members belong because unless the organisation prospers, the job security, pay and benefits of their members will be compromised. Likewise, employers have a vested interest in the continuing commitment and welfare of employees, in order to maintain the viability of the business through the availability, quality and competitiveness of goods and services.

Sir Ken Jackson *(People Management*, September 2000) writes:

> It is clear that unions need to improve their ability to support their members. Our aim is to secure a better deal for them by adding value to their employers. We want to contribute to the success of the company by applying our representational talents with honesty, passion and industrial knowledge… It is only when managers are given intelligent, coherent criticism that they think through all the implications of their decisions. Equally, on many occasions, an informed union organisation will support managers' decisions and give them added credibility with the workforce.

3.4 Co-operation

According to the radical perspective, co-operation is merely collaboration in perpetuating oppression. According to the pluralist perspective, it is a negotiated process of mutual survival, taking into account the needs of the various stakeholders in the organisation. According to the unitary perspective, it is the natural mode of business relations and achieves greater productivity and satisfaction for all parties than conflict or competition. Whatever your opinion, it is worth bearing in mind the following points.

(a)   Co-operation has a rational appeal. It is demonstrable that a suitable number of people co-operating on a task will achieve a better result than one person doing the same task (synergy may enable 2+2 to equal 5) and that groups of co-operating individuals have higher productivity than groups of competing individuals. **However,** it has also been demonstrated that this is not always the case: collaboration can adversely affect individual and group performance, because of group norms, the distraction of group maintenance processes and the tendency of cohesive groups to become blinkered, self-protecting and risky in their decision-making.

(b)   Co-operation has an emotional appeal. It incorporates values about unity, teamwork, comradeship and belonging: as such, it is a useful cornerstone to the communication of corporate culture. **However,** Charles Handy (among others) has suggested that organisations are too quick to label and discourage differences, argument and competition as 'conflict': these are not only natural and inevitable (pluralist perspective) but potentially beneficial and fruitful.

(c)   Co-operation is a common cultural value-cluster: collectivist cultures such as Japan and Sweden emphasise inter-dependence. **However**, individualist cultures such as the UK and USA value independence more highly.

Activity 5   **(15 minutes)**

How might conflict in the form of differences, argument and competition be beneficial and fruitful for an organisation?

---

4   EMPLOYEE RELATIONS

4.1   HRM and industrial relations

Guest described four possible orientations to industrial relations strategy as follows.

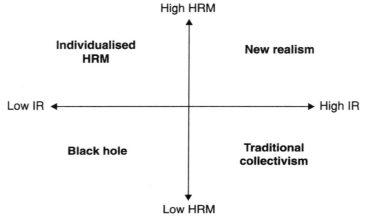

(a)   **The new realism: high emphasis on HRM and industrial relations.** Companies such as Rover, Nissan and Toshiba have initiated collaborative arrangements, extended consultation processes and moves towards single status, in order to facilitate greater flexibility, more multi-skilling, the removal of demarcations and improvements in quality.

(b)   **Traditional collectivism: emphasis on industrial relations without HRM.** Unions provide useful, well-established channels for communication and the handling of grievance/discipline/safety issues: it is easier to continue to operate a traditional pluralist industrial relations arrangement.

(c)   **Individualised HRM: emphasis on HRM without industrial relations.** This is an 'essentially piecemeal and opportunistic' approach which is only common among North-American firms.

(d)   **The black hole: no industrial relations.** HRM is not considered a policy priority for management, but neither is there seen to be a need for a traditional industrial relations system.

It has been argued that a thorough-going 'HRM' approach – with its unitary perspective and commitment-based strategies - renders the traditional 'industrial relations' approach irrelevant and marginalises the traditional roles of the trade union.

Activity 6   **(15 minutes)**

(a) What are the features of relations in the 'industrial relations' model and the 'HRM' model (Storey, Guest: see Chapter 11 if necessary)?

(b) What kinds of HRM policies, discussed in this Course Book, would reduce the perceived need for trade union representation?

At the TUC's 1994 conference, however, its HRM Taskforce reported that it found no direct relationship between HRM techniques and anti-unionism. In fact, HRM was most prevalent in unionised workplaces. Taskforce chair Bernadette Hillan said: 'If an employer is really trying to improve business performance, is committed to involving workers in the running of the organisation and is seeking to develop a real partnership with recognised trade unions, then HRM and collective bargaining can work in harmony.' She did, however, admit that some employers were using at least the language of HRM as an excuse to de-recognise unions.

The 2000 TUC conference was likewise told by its general secretary, John Monks, that: 'The most successful companies in the UK have the very best management practice, where unions are strong and working in partnership with management.'

4.2 From 'industrial relations' to 'employee relations'

The Industrial Relations Services (1994) identified four approaches to industrial relations (as cited by Armstrong).

(a) **Adversarial**: the organisation decides what it wants to do and employees are expected to fit in. Employees only exercise power by refusing to co-operate.

(b) **Traditional**: a good day-to-day working relationship, but management proposes and the workforce reacts through its elected representatives.

(c) **Partnership**: the organisation involves employees in the drawing up and execution of organisation policies, but retains the right to manage.

(d) **Power sharing**: employees are involved in both day-to-day and strategic decision-making.

Definition

Employee relations 'consist of all those areas of HRM that involve general relationships with employees, through collective agreements where trade unions are recognised [industrial relations] and/or through commonly applied policies for employee involvement and communications.' (Armstrong)

According to Armstrong (*Strategic HRM*), employee relations strategy will be concerned with how to:

(a) Build **stable and co-operative relationships** with employees that minimise conflict

NOTES

(b) Achieve **commitment** through employee involvement and communications processes

(c) Develop **mutuality** – a common interest in achieving the organisation's goals through the development of organisational cultures based on shared values between management and employees

He suggests that such strategies will result in the following kinds of policies.

(a) Changing forms of recognition, including single union recognition or de-recognition

(b) New bargaining structures, including decentralisation or single-table bargaining (discussed in chapter 19)

(c) The achievement of increased levels of commitment through involvement or participation – giving employees a voice

(d) Deliberately by-passing trade union representatives to communicate directly with employees

(e) Increasing the extent to which management controls operations in such areas as flexibility

(f) Generally improving the employee relations climate in order to produce more harmonious and co-operative relationships

(g) Developing a 'partnership' with trade unions (discussed in Chapter 19), recognising that employees are stakeholders and that it is to the advantage of both parties to work together

EXAMPLE 1

Strike Free: New Industrial Relations in Britain by Philip Bassett (1986) illustrated the height of the 'anti-union' phase of HRM in the UK. The following was the experience of the (then) leading-edge computer company, IBM. (Compare the attitudes and policies of McDonald's in the 1990s, as discussed in Chapter 15.)

Company management attribute the good employee relations to IBM's belief in respect for the individual. One aspect of this philosophy is that IBM does not recognise trade unions for collective bargaining purposes. To do so, they believe, would imply that without trade unions employees' interests would be neglected. Management are convinced that the company's record disproves such a belief.

IBM does not discourage its employees from becoming members of trade unions, but very few of them do so. Even of those who do, a significant minority are against collective bargaining. Pay in IBM is not a collective matter for employees; instead, the company conducts its own confidential survey of comparable companies and determines salary ranges centrally. There is scope for line managers to recommend increases for specific individuals based on merit.

The other traditional function of trade unions at plant level is to assist their members over the hurdles of the employer's grievance system. IBM believe that their own internal complaints procedures, which allow an individual to take a grievance to the very highest levels of management, remove the need for any union involvement.

Other companies, looking at IBM's industrially harmonious, strike-free, non-union record, have asked how they could emulate it. The answer given by a former personnel director of the company is simple: 'You start 30 years ago.'

EXAMPLE 2

Canadian-owned Sheerness Steel, Kent, is the first company in its industry to have de-recognised unions, led by the Iron and Steel Trades Confederation (ISTC), as part of a change to a single status company. According to the personnel director: "We have become a single status company with personal contracts, salaries, performance-related pay and no defined jobs – people do whatever they are trained to do. We realised that we no longer had anything to debate or discuss with the unions and that they were no longer necessary."

However, according to the ISTC, the workforce is not happy. Local conditions of high unemployment "had made it difficult for members to withstand company pressure to take personal contracts". The change to salaried work means that employees have lost overtime payments which, according to the ISTC, has severely affected their earnings. On the other hand, many of the old disciplinary problems, such as being late, are no longer a problem: just as well, perhaps, since the unions are no longer even allowed to represent individual members in disciplinary cases..."

(Personnel Management Plus, September 1992)

FOR DISCUSSION

Do the examples cited above reflect an HRM approach to employee relations?

We have already covered many employee involvement techniques in other contexts (such as reward, quality management, flexibility and development), and have discussed issues of involvement and empowerment of employees in our exploration of the HRM approach in Chapter 11. As you review such topics, bear in mind that they are part of the overall relationship of employees and management in the organisation. Specific mechanisms for employee consultation and participation (including Joint Consultation Committees and Works Councils) will be discussed in Chapter 19. We will merely summarise the types and examples of involvement techniques here.

4.3 Employee involvement techniques

Definition

> **Employee involvement** describes a wide range of policies and techniques for 'informing and consulting employees about, or associating them with, one or more aspects of running an organisation.' (Gennard & Judge)

Employee involvement concentrates mainly on individual employees and the degree to which they can be encouraged to identify with the goals of the organisation. It can be distinguished from employee participation (discussed in chapter 19), which concerns the extent to which employees are involved (via their representatives) in management decision-making.

The aims of involvement may be:

(a) To generate commitment to the organisation

(b) To help the organisation improve performance, especially in the face of change

(c) To enable the organisation to better meet changing customer requirements

(d) To improve the challenge and satisfaction of the work experience

(e) To aid the organisation in attracting and retaining skilled labour

(f)   To develop the business awareness of labour at all levels

    (g)   To increase employee incentives and accountabilities through tying reward to company performance and profitability, and/or

    (h)   To marginalise trade unions

Guest describes five ways to get employees involved.

- By improving the provision of information to employees

- By improving the provision of information from employees

- By changing the structure and arrangement of work

- By changing the incentives

- By changing relationships, through more participative leadership and informality

Activity 7   **(15 minutes)**

Suggest three techniques (already encountered in this *Course Book*) by which each of the above could be implemented.

Marchington *et al* similarly divide employee involvement schemes into four categories.

    (a)   **Downwards communications:** from managers to other employees and so on. This includes house journals, employee reports and briefings.

    (b)   **Upwards problem-solving forms:** designed to tap into individual and team knowledge and expertise. This includes suggestion schemes, attitude surveys, quality circles, customer care programmes and so on.

    (c)   **Financial participation:** linking rewards of individuals to the performance of the unit or business. This includes profit sharing, employee share ownership and factory-wide or value added bonus schemes.

    (d)   **Representative participation:** employees are involved in decision-making through their representatives on JCCs, advisory councils, works councils, or collective bargaining. (This may operate at different levels of involvement, from consultation and dialogue to co-determination and even to control, eg in worker-managed teams or co-operatives.)

In addition, involvement may be encouraged by:

    (a)   **Empowerment:** the devolving of control and responsibility to individuals or teams at the workplace or 'front line' customer-service level. Empowerment may be 'soft' (providing enhanced opportunities for involvement in decision-making, fewer status barriers, more open communication, greater flexibility) or 'hard' (devolution of responsibility and accountability: standards and targets, monitoring and control)

    (b)   **Inclusion in the cultural and strategic priorities of the business.** Employees are invited and encouraged to share in commitment to quality, customer care, continuous improvement, learning and so on. This is frequently linked to empowerment as a set of guiding values and objectives within which teams can be more or less self-managing.

NOTES

Chapter roundup

Industrial relations comprises all the rules, practices and conventions governing interactions between managements and their workforces, normally involving collective employee representation and bargaining.

Employee relations consist of all these areas of HRM that involve general relationships with employees, including industrial relations and employee involvement and communication.

The parties in industrial relations include: management and/or employers' associations, worker representatives (trade unions, staff associations or other forms of representation) and third parties, such as ACAS and Employment Tribunals.

Trade unions may be craft/occupational, general or industrial. After a period of declining membership (accelerated by HRM policies, the decline of manufacturing and Conservative government policy) the new recognition laws (Employment Relations Act 1999) may herald an upswing in unionism.

There are three basic perspectives on industrial relations: unitary, pluralist and radical.

Employee involvement is the process of informing and consulting employees about, or associating them with, one or more aspects of running an organisation. It may be accomplished by two-way communication, financial participation, representative participation, empowerment and inclusion in cultural programmes such as quality management and organisational learning

Quick quiz

1 What is an independent trade union?

2 What are the purposes of employers' associations?

3 Distinguish between craft, industrial and general unions.

4 What is a shop steward?

5 Give four reasons for the recent turnaround in the number of workers covered by union recognition agreements.

6 What was the closed shop and what happened to it?

7 Distinguish between the unitary and pluralist frames of reference.

8 In what ways might management and workers be said to have:

(a) Different interests, and

(b) Common interests

9 Outline Guest's four orientations to industrial relations strategy.

10 Give five examples of employee involvement techniques.

Answers to quick quiz

1 One which has been certified as being autonomous and financially self-supporting, not dominated by an employer. (see paragraph 1.2)

2 To give help and advice on employee relations issues; to represent members views to political influencers; to assist in dispute resolution; to negotiate sectoral agreements. (para 1.3)

3 Craft unions recruit employees who perform certain jobs. Industrial unions recruit all grades of employees in a particular industry. General unions organise workers from a variety of different jobs and industries. (para 2.1)

BPP PUBLISHING

4   A workplace union representative: the link between the work group, union officials and management.   (para 2.2)

5   Statutory recognition (Employment Relations Act 1999); Labour government support for partnership; recognition of unions as a useful and efficient mechanism for employee relations; increasing recruitment, supported by single union and partnership agreements.   (para 2.3)

6   An employee had to be a member of a particular union to secure or retain employment. The closed shop was stripped of legal support: dismissal for non-membership was made automatically unfair, selection on membership discriminatory and industrial action in support of a closed shop unlawful.   (para 2.5)

7   **Unitary:** all members of the organisation, despite their different roles, have common interests and objectives which unites their efforts. The management prerogative is recognised as being in everyone's best interests.

     Pluralist: organisations are political coalitions of individuals and groups which inevitably have their own interests. Management has to take into account the objectives of all the various stakeholders in the organisation, to develop a strategy of mutual compromise and survival.   (para 3.1)

8   Basically, differences arise from the labour market: trading off the objectives of buyers (management) and sellers (workers) of labour. Common interests arise from both sides' vested interest in the survival and prosperity of the organisation.
                    (See paragraphs 3.2, 3.3 for a full account.)

9   New realism: high emphasis on HRM and industrial relations eg through partnership agreements.

     Traditional collectivism: emphasis on industrial relations without HRM eg through collective bargaining.

     Individualised HRM: HRM without industrial relations eg through individual contracts.

     Black hole: no HRM or industrial relations eg authoritarian management.
                                                            (para 4.1)

10   Communication (eg briefings, journals)
     Up-down communication (eg suggestion schemes, quality circles)
     Financial participation (eg profit-sharing, share ownership)
     Representative participation (eg joint consultation, works councils)
     Empowerment (eg self-managed teamworking, delegation)
     Cultural programmes (eg TQM, customer care, learning organisation)
                                                            (para 4.3)

Answers to Activities

1   (a)   Lobbying politicians to obtain legislation to improve conditions of work (eg the minimum wage)

     (b)   Developing political affiliations with other trade unions, to create a power base for achieving political influence

     (c)   Providing financial support for a sympathetic political party (traditionally, the Labour Party)

     (d)   Establishing non-negotiatory processes for sharing management decision-making: eg by joint consultative committees or partnership agreements.

NOTES

(e)   Providing welfare help and support for members: funding during industrial action, say.

2   (a)   Conciliation (getting conflicting parties together for informal discussion to resolve a dispute)

        (b)   Mediation (providing a mediator or mediation board, which hears arguments and makes proposals and recommendations as a basis for settlement)

        (c)   Arbitration (assisting in the appointment of independent arbitrators who make a binding ruling)

3   Size is a variable insignificant in itself: size as a proportion of potential membership may be a more significant factor in determining the credibility of the union. The threat of industrial action even by a large union would be hollow if its membership represented a very small proportion of workers in the relevant organisation or sector. A union which is small in terms of membership numbers may have a very strong negotiating position if its members are of an occupational category which is significant to the organisation or national life (eg nurses, firemen).

4   The closed shop was encouraged by unions as a means of increasing their membership and bargaining power within a company. It was supported by some managements as a way of facilitating single-union agreements. Closed shops were criticised for interfering with individual rights of choice; constraining management decision-making on recruitment and retention; and strengthening the bargaining power of unions to the detriment of industrial relations.

5   (a)   Differences allow for diversity of talents, viewpoints, ideas: necessary for innovation, problem-solving, understanding human dynamics, flexibility. Differences reflect the diversity of the customer base: conformity may blinker the organisation to potential needs or problems. Suppression of diversity may cause stress and resentment.

        (b)   Argument is useful to clear the air, help divergent viewpoints to emerge, encourage empathy with different viewpoints: extremely helpful in conflict resolution, in change management (bringing resistance into the open), in encouraging emotional intelligence.

        (c)   Controlled competition between teams has been demonstrated to increase team cohesion/co-operation and motivation and improve performance. Competition tied to incentives is a powerful energiser of performance (particularly in individualistic cultures).

6   (a)   IR = low trust, collectivist, pluralist. HRM = high trust, individualist, unitarist.

        (b)   Examples include: direct voluntary communication and consultation on matters which will affect employees; worker involvement techniques; fair, consistent and transparent discipline and grievance handling; equitable and non-discriminatory recruitment, selection, appraisal and reward systems; health, safety and welfare policies clearly aimed at problem-solving and worker protection; programmes at improving the work environment; flexible remuneration packages (such as cafeteria benefits) encouraging individual aspirations and priorities.

7   (a)   Briefing groups and meetings, Joint Consultation Committees or works councils, open direct communication from managers,

encouraging informal networking, 360° feedback, consultation policy, noticeboards/memos etc.

(b)   Suggestion schemes, quality circles, upward appraisal, JCCs or works councils, attitude surveys

(c)   Increased delegation (empowerment), self-managed and/or multi-skilled teamworking, horizontal structures focused on the customer, job design based on whole meaningful tasks

(d)   Financial participation through profit-related pay, employee share ownership schemes; cafeteria benefits; learning/development opportunities

(e)   Participative management style; single status agreements; culture of informality (Management By Walking Around); role of supervisor as coach/facilitator.

Assignment 18   (1½ hours)

Semco is a Brazilian company which makes pumps, dishwashers and cooking units. The company attracted enormous media and business interest in the early to mid 1990s. Here's why.

(a)   All managers are rated by their subordinates every six months, on a scale of 1 to 100. Those managers who consistently under-perform are squeezed out.

(b)   Workers elect their own bosses: 'In a plant where everyone has a financial stake in its success, the idea of asking subordinates to choose bosses seems an eminently sensible way to stop accidents before they are promoted.'

(c)   Workers set their own salaries – but they know they might price themselves out of the department's budget if they aim too high.

(d)   The workers decide how much of the profits to share and how much to re-invest in the business.

(e)   Workers are encouraged to work from home.

(f)   Everyone 'from the cleaner upwards' has access to the company's books.

Semco's boss, Ricardo Semler, believes that democracy has been introduced to the work place: this is a radical departure from 'classical' organisation theory, but at a time when firms like IBM are being overtaken by smaller, more flexible competitors, his ideas are gaining currency. 'The trouble is that the corporate world is run by people not exactly busting keen to lose their parking lots, let alone to subject themselves to monthly scrutiny by people whom, currently, he can hire and fire. Even corporate turkeys don't vote for Christmas.' (Victor Keegan, *The Guardian*, 1993).

Compare Semco (as sketched in the above portrait) to a 'classical organisation' with a traditional 'industrial relations' approach.

Chapter 19 :

INDUSTRIAL RELATIONS PROCESSES

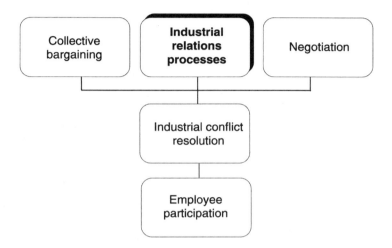

Introduction

In this chapter we explore some of the key processes in industrial relations: collective bargaining, and the related strategies and skills of negotiation; the management of industrial disputes; and employee consultation and participation.

In each of these areas, we will see signs of the shift towards a unitarist perspective discussed in Chapter 18, while at the same time recognising the differing interests of stakeholders in the organisation. Even industrial conflict must be managed in the context of an on-going relationship. This perspective is typified in the various measures taken to involve employees in decision-making, under the general banner of 'participation'. Voluntary 'partnership' between management and unions is currently in vogue, and we will examine partnership agreements as one form of employee participation, alongside European-led measures such as works councils and two-tier board structures.

Your objectives

In this chapter you will learn about the following:

(a)   The nature and scope of collective bargaining

(b)   The processes of negotiation

(c)   Negotiation strategy for a given situation

(d)   Different types of collective dispute

(e)   Dispute procedures and the resolution of conflict

(f)   The effectiveness of dispute procedures in resolving conflict in a given situation

(g) The effectiveness of arrangements made by organisations to involve their employees in decision-making

(h) The influence of the EU on democracy in the UK

(i) The implementation of (industrial relations) practice in the UK and that of other countries

1 COLLECTIVE BARGAINING

1.1 The nature and scope of collective bargaining

Definition

> **Collective bargaining** is the process whereby employee and employer representatives negotiate agreements by which terms and conditions of employment (and related matters) are determined for groups of represented employees, as an alternative to individually negotiated contract terms.

Collective bargaining is basically concerned with reaching two types of agreement.

(a) Substantive agreements, which determine the terms and conditions of employment. (For example, for Grade 1 staff, the pay scales will be such-and-such, or the annual holiday entitlement will be x days and so on.) Demarcation rules (what work is done by what grades and occupational groups of staff) are also substantive rules.

(b) Procedural agreements, which determine the methods and procedures for:

(i) Arriving at substantive agreements. (What negotiating machinery should be set up? Should a particular issue be discussed at national level, company level, local plant/branch level – or not at all?)

(ii) Settling any disagreements or disputes which cannot be resolved by normal negotiation. There might be arrangements to refer disputes at plant level to regional or national level, or to arbitration. Procedural rules would determine what the arbitration arrangements should be (eg involving ACAS).

1.2 Levels and parties in collective bargaining

Collective bargaining may take place at different levels.

(a) Some issues are discussed at national level, between representatives of employers for the industry or sector and national trade union officials. In France, Holland, Italy, Sweden, Finland, Belgium and Spain, for example, sectoral collective agreements are common. These may provide only a basic outline and floor of conditions (for example, minimum rates of pay, maximum weekly and overtime hours, paid holiday entitlements) which trade unions expect to elaborate and improve through company-level agreements.

(b) Other issues will be settled at company level, by representatives of management and the unions or staff associations recognised by the company. Ford, for example, have their own company-wide pay agreements, and do not join in national negotiations with an employers' federation.

(c) Other issues will be settled at more local level by 'domestic' bargaining, involving representatives of plant or factory management and local shop stewards. Phillips Electronics in the UK, for example, has abandoned its national bargaining structure in favour of plant by plant negotiations. This reflects the decentralisation of industrial relations (among other HRM functions) within organisations.

Decentralised bargaining has increased in recent years, because it provides greater flexibility than national agreements. This applies both to the employer (allowing for greater labour flexibility by tailoring work rules and pay agreements to the needs of specific plants) and to the employee (reflecting the desire for more direct influence in employment terms and conditions, which has created a further trend towards individualised contracts). It is also more easily changed, if necessary, because there is less (and more accessible) negotiating machinery. This relative flexibility may have drawbacks, however, if it results in fragmented and inequitable pay structures, inflationary 'leapfrogging' of settlements, and freedom to break or re-negotiate agreements at will.

1.3 Single-table bargaining

Definition

> **Single-table bargaining** describes a situation in which the terms and conditions of all represented workers employed by an establishment are determined in a single set of negotiations. This could involve a single union representing different types and grades of employees (manual and non-manual), or several unions which negotiate a bargaining position amongst themselves prior to negotiating with management as a single bargaining unit.

> **Activity 1** **(45 minutes)**
>
> What would you anticipate to be the advantages and disadvantages of single-table bargaining.

Beardwell and Holden argue that the significance of single-table bargaining is not primarily its advantages in simplifying and integrating bargaining processes, but the opportunity to extend consultation beyond the basic negotiation forum, to include matters which affect all employees: training and development, fringe benefits, the future direction of the business, change management and so on.

We will be covering employee consultation later in this chapter, but you should be aware that trade unions recognised for the purpose of collective bargaining are entitled to certain information.

1.4 Disclosure of information

An employer must provide information in response to a written request by a union representative, as long as:

(a) It relates to his (or an associated employer's) undertaking

(b) It is in his possession

NOTES

     (c)   It is in accordance with good practice (as laid down in an ACAS Code of Practice)

     (d)   Lack of the information would materially impede the representative in collective bargaining

The ACAS Code of Practice recommends that information should be disclosed on pay and benefits, conditions of service, human resources, performance (eg productivity, sales/order forecasts) and financial matters. It suggests that unions should define and request the information before negotiations begin, stating why they consider it relevant. A union may apply to the Central Arbitration Committee if it believes disclosable information has been withheld. If an employer refuses to comply with a Committee declaration that information should be disclosed, the CAC may make an enforceable award of terms and conditions, at the request of the trade union.

There is no obligation to give information relating to:

     (a)   Information given in confidence

     (b)   Information relating to particular individuals

     (c)   Information which – in any context other than collective bargaining – would cause injury to the undertaking

     (d)   Information protected by statute (say, in the interests of national security) or subject to legal proceedings

1.5 Attitudes to collective bargaining

Chamberlain and Kuhn (*Industrial Democracy*) traced a historical development in attitudes towards collective bargaining.

     (a)   At first, there was a **marketing theory**, in which collective bargaining was seen as pay bargaining for the supply of labour. Rates of pay would be settled on the basis of supply and demand.

     (b)   Later, a **governmental (or control) theory** developed. Collective bargaining was seen as a way of making rules of conduct and enforcing those rules in addition to pay bargaining.

     (c)   Finally, a **managerial theory** emerged, on the basis that decisions about matters in which both management and employees have a vital interest should be discussed and decided by collective negotiation.

A greater range of matters now come within the sphere of collective bargaining arrangements. Negotiations might cover not only pay, conditions of employment (holidays, hours of work etc) and demarcation lines, but also promotion and training opportunities, fringe benefits, health and safety, equal opportunities and so on.

As we saw in Chapter 18 on union recognition, a managerial approach to collective bargaining is arguably a systematic, efficient, relationship-building and equitable method of conducting industrial relations. It encourages a collectivist orientation which is suited to some cultures of employment and may encourage teamworking and identification with the organisation in others.

Activity 2	**(20 minutes)**

There has been a decline in collective bargaining in recent decades. From what you know of the development of trade unionism during this period, why might this be so?

BPP PUBLISHING

NOTES

2 NEGOTIATION

Definition

> **Negotiation** is a bargaining process through which commitments and compromises are reached, using the relative power of the parties involved.

2.1 Approaches to negotiation

There are two basic approaches to negotiation.

(a) **Distributive bargaining**, where negotiation is about the distribution of finite resources. One party's gain is another's loss: a 'win-lose' or 'zero sum' equation. If a pay increase of, say, 10% is gained, where the management budget was 5%, the extra has to be funded from elsewhere – profits, investments, other groups (such as shareholders), increased prices, increased productivity, cuts in training or whatever.

(b) **Integrative bargaining**, based on joint problem-solving, where negotiations aim to find a mutually satisfying solution to problems. This has emerged in recent years in a technique called the 'win-win' approach, a process of exploring and defining the needs and fears of all parties with a view not just to getting the best outcome for one's own party ('win-lose') or even compromise ('lose-lose') but to fulfilling the needs of all parties: a 'win-win' solution may not be available, but the process makes it possible. 'Win-win' negotiation is based on the desire to preserve a constructive relationship between the negotiating parties. 'Win-lose' outcomes can cause resentment or under-motivated performance by the 'losing' party, and perpetuates underlying conflict.

We will be outlining a negotiation process based on concessions and the attempt to find 'middle ground'. However, you should be aware of an alternative approach to collective bargaining, called 'pendulum arbitration'.

Definition

> **Pendulum arbitration is** a system whereby a third party will arbitrate on behalf of the two principals in collective bargaining, should they fail to reach agreement, by awarding the final position of one side or the other: either the employer's final offer or the employees' final claim.

Traditional arbitration draws from both sides of the negotiation in an attempt to find 'middle ground', and this may encourage principals to exaggerate their demands, knowing that they will eventually have to compromise or 'split the difference'. Pendulum arbitration encourages principals to moderate their final positions and to attempt to settle in good faith, knowing that an extreme position will rebound on them if the decision goes to the other side. It avoids the drawing out of the negotiation process by each side holding back from their final position during bargaining.

In practice, however, it is a difficult process, since disputes may involve complex multiple issues, and the final positions of each side on each issue may not be clear.

FOR DISCUSSION

What kind of industrial relations atmosphere is created by a concept such as 'pendulum arbitration'?

Do you think that a 'win-win' solution is possible in collective bargaining?

2.2 Preparing a negotiation

Formal negotiations, as opposed to informal 'arrangements', should follow broad guidelines.

(a) **Set objectives, parameters and priorities** which are achievable and consistent with industrial relations policy. These are likely to be couched in optimum, most likely and fall-back terms (see (e) below).

(b) **Research the background** of issues over which negotiations are to be conducted: trends in union responses, market pay rates, case studies from similar organisations/sectors, relevant legislation and court decisions and so on.

(c) **Recognise potential for conflict**. In an integrative framework, each side accepts that the objectives and perspectives of the other side are as genuine and legitimate as their own. Even in a distributive framework, it must be recognised that the outcome will have to be 'sold' to all parties, and the consequences of resistance, resentment and lost relationship managed. Recognition of the needs, wants and fears of the other party helps in managing expectations and in the process of devising a workable trade-off between divergent interests.

(d) **Establish relative bargaining power.** This may be approached by noting the costs and benefits to each negotiating party of a range of potential outcomes.

Chamberlain's model: Bargaining power of A

$$= \frac{\text{Costs to B of disagreement with A's terms}}{\text{Costs to A of disagreement with B's terms}}$$

And vice versa.

If the cost of disagreeing is greater than that of agreeing, the bargaining power of the other side is greater.

Activity 3   **(10 minutes)**

The Chamberlain model provides a quantitative measure of relative bargaining power. What other, more qualitative factors are there that might enhance or detract from the bargaining power of one side or the other?

(e) **Determine negotiating strategy.** Given a fair idea of what the other side's position and bargaining power are likely to be, the party in question should be able to predict any demands the other side will make, or what kind of offer is likely to be accepted. Each side should look for potential counter-arguments to its own case, without underestimating the potential gap between the parties.

NOTES

There are basically three possible outcomes for either side:

(a)   If we were to achieve all our objectives, what would be the ideal settlement?

(b)   If we were to make progress, but being realistic about the power of the other side, what is a realistic settlement?

(c)   If we were to concede, what is an acceptable fall-back position?

A position for each side should be estimated for each of the above situations, and areas of agreement concentrated on, as potential middle ground.

John Sawbridge (*People Management* 14 September 2000) suggests that:

The union will move only if it believes that:

- there is no other option
- its members will benefit
- it will be painful not to do so.

(f)   **Determine the agenda** ('terms of reference') of the meeting. The agenda for negotiation should be accepted (or acceptable) in advance by both sides. The order of items may have tactical significance: imposing time pressures for agreement on issues raised late in the day, say, or gaining momentum on related issues by placing them after a major point of agreement.

(g)   **Issue prior information.** This may be done:

(i)   As pre-conditioning: for example, advance announcement of poor trading results and intense competition as a prelude to negotiating pay awards, redundancies or productivity agreements.

(ii)   As a matter of legal obligation. Information relevant to collective bargaining must be disclosed to trade union representatives (see above).

(iii)   To allow all parties to do their homework, for better quality decision-making, (unless there is any assumed advantage in surprise disclosures).

(h)   **Select participants.** Representatives of management must be articulate, persuasive, acceptable to employee representatives and authoritative enough to implement agreed decisions. Face-to-face negotiations require particular skills in persuasion, personal rapport, reading of verbal and non-verbal signals and so on.

2.3   Conduct of negotiation

During the conduct of the negotiations themselves, participants should consider the following.

(a)   Opening statements: a broad statement of their position, leaving room for negotiation. This will be a clue to strategy – and may also be an opportunity for broad general agreement. It is recommended that the party seeking change be invited to state its case first.

(b)   Roles within the negotiating team. Negotiations can be highly ritualistic and appropriate roles will have to be adopted: the 'hard/soft' approach, for example, requires one conciliatory and one tough negotiator to disguise the team's true strategy and to expose any weaknesses in the other side. Sawbridge notes that negotiation 'is a group activity, involving speaking, persuading, listening, looking, recording and analysing. This is too much for one person to take on board. A successful negotiating team works together to support each member.'

BPP
PUBLISHING

(c) Argument and persuasive style. If an integrative outcome and goodwill are desired, participants should lead by example in maintaining a positive problem-solving approach. Sawbridge notes that negotiation has a dual purpose: to communicate your position clearly and concisely, providing evidence to support it; and to 'sell' your position, by convincing the other side of your commitment to it. The presentation should be aimed at the strategic pressure points suggested above.

(d) Use of the negotiating strategy and bargaining power. Items should be linked and packaged to achieve two-way momentum, so that no party gives away anything without getting something in return. Be firm on principles and flexible on details, so that there is room to move without compromising strategic priorities.

The meeting should be facilitated by an experienced chairperson, who will ensure that the meeting is conducted in a courteous and effective manner: sticking to the point of the agenda reached; giving alternating opportunities to speak (rather than a 'free for all'); and so on.

Activity 4   **(30 minutes)**

From your study or awareness of communication and persuasion techniques, suggest some techniques which you might use in negotiation.

Concessions, on one or both sides, are likely to be necessary in the process of negotiation. Tactical considerations again enter into the granting and acceptance of concessions. Early concessions may be taken for granted, or as a symptom of weakness. Tough concessions, attached to requirements for reciprocal concessions on the other side, and related to the main point of difference, may be more effective.

Adjournments may be used to give parties time to review progress, consider proposals, enter informal 'off-the-table' discussions which might help break an impasse, or just 'cool off' when negotiation reaches a heated stage.

All relevant details of the discussion should be recorded by a minute-taker, stenographer or sound recorder, in order to furnish minutes which can be used in formulating final agreements.

2.4 Settlement and follow-up

At the conclusion of negotiations, both parties must be satisfied that all issues have been discussed and that they understand exactly what has been agreed: the proceedings should be summarised and agreements 'played back' for confirmation by both sides. If there is any misunderstanding or ambiguity which raises objections, negotiations should recommence.

Once there is oral agreement, the points should be written up as a signed 'draft agreement', stating:

(a) Who made the agreement and on what date

(b) Who is to be covered by the agreement (groups and grades of employee, for example)

(c) When the agreement is to take effect, how long it is to run, and whether and how it may be amended or terminated prior to this date

(d) The contents (or 'clauses') of the agreement and any exceptions that may apply

NOTES

(e)   How disagreements and appeals will be dealt with once the negotiated settlement is implemented

The draft agreement should be circulated and checked by both sides, and clauses initialled once their wording is accepted. When all clauses have been approved by both sides, the agreement can be printed, formally signed and communicated to those affected by its provisions.

Having followed a negotiation through to a positive conclusion, let's consider what happens when negotiations break down or reach deadlock...

3   INDUSTRIAL CONFLICT RESOLUTION

3.1   Types of collective dispute

Individual disputes against employers are covered by disciplinary and grievance procedures (see Chapter 8): note that under the Employment Relations Act 1999, employees are entitled to be accompanied by a colleague or trade union representative in procedures concerning 'serious issues'. A trade union may get involved in an individual case where a principle of workers' rights is involved.

Collective disputes more typically involve pay, conditions of employment, job security or breach of contracts and negotiated agreements.

According to the Employment Act 1982, a 'lawful trade dispute' is one between workers and their own employers, wholly or mainly about work related matters, and *not:*

- Demarcation and other inter-union disputes
- Disputes between workers and employers other than their own
- Disputes other than those mainly connected with pay and conditions or
- Disputes overseas

3.2   Industrial action

Industrial action in pursuance of a dispute may take a number of forms (discussed below), but are classified on four basic dimensions.

(a)   **Official** action is supported by the trade union representatives of the employees in dispute, and conducted according to union procedure, including secret balloting of members.

(b)   **Unofficial** action is taken by a part of the workforce without recognition and support from union officials and without balloting and approval procedures.

(c)   **Primary** action is aimed at the employer with whom the participating union is in dispute.

(d)   **Secondary** action is aimed at employers who trade with firms in dispute, but who are not directly involved in the dispute themselves.

Activity 5   **(15 minutes)**

What do you think might be the purpose of threatening or implementing industrial action?

BPP
PUBLISHING

Definition

> **Strike action** is the withholding of labour in the course of a dispute with management

Various forms of primary industrial action by union members (in order of severity) include the following.

(a) Withdrawal of co-operation by the union (eg refusal to participate in disciplinary procedures).

(b) Insistence on formal rights by the union (eg raising trivial infringements as grievance issues, insistence on taking time off or limiting overtime, where there would normally be informal flexibility).

(c) A work-to-rule or go-slow: employees follow official work procedures and rules to the letter, thereby reducing productivity without doing anything to justify disciplinary action by management. This also highlights the extent to which management take for granted the commitment and voluntary contribution of employees.

(d) A ban on overtime and weekend working to restrict productivity, often highlighting issues of work organisation.

(e) A token withdrawal of labour: for example, a one-day strike by the union membership in the workforce, as a protest against management's unwillingness to make further concessions in negotiation. These may be repeated over a period of time, in order to provide a recurring disruption to the organisation's operations without a complete loss of pay: the 1996 London Underground dispute is one example.

(f) Indefinite strike action by the entire union membership in the workforce, either at national level, company level or plant level: the 1984 miners' strike is a historic example.

(g) Picketing: striking workers maintain a presence outside the employer's premises (a 'picket line'). The aim of the picket line is to highlight the protest and to inform and solicit the support of workers attempting to enter the workplace. In practice, this often takes the form of active discouragement and intimidation of strike-breakers, replacement workers and others. The Employment Act 1982 protects unions and their members against most civil and criminal actions 'in contemplation or furtherance of a trade dispute', including picketing at or near the place of work with a purpose that is 'peacefully to obtain or communicate information, or peacefully to persuade a person to work or not to work'. Secondary picketing (of organisations not involved in the dispute) is not protected, however.

FOR DISCUSSION

What are the corresponding sanctions which might be used by management in furtherance of an industrial dispute? Why might these be used as a 'last resort'?

3.3 Statistics on strikes

Official statistics on the use of industrial sanctions in the UK only cover strikes. They measure:

(a)   The frequency (number) of strikes

(b)   The size of strikes (that is, the number of workers involved)

(c)   The duration of strikes (that is, the number of working days lost) – since this figure on its own may give a distorted impression if there are a few very long strikes. For example, the 1984 miners' strike accounted for 83% of the total number of working days lost to strikes in that year!

All three measures peaked in 1979 (2,125 stoppages in progress, 4.6 million workers involved, and 29.4 million working days lost – of which 54% were accounted for by a strike of engineering workers). All three measures have since been steadily falling, and are currently at their lowest since records began in 1891. (The 1998 figures were 166 stoppages, 93,000 workers involved and 282,000 hours lost.) The Conservative opposition claims that the number of strike ballots has doubled following the new Employment Relations Act 1999, but trade union leaders respond that ballots are usually held to show employers the strength of disagreement over a particular issue and rarely result in industrial action. (As noted earlier, however, there has been a marked increase in the number of complaints made to Employment Tribunals in the wake of new employment legislation: managers cannot afford to get complacent!)

3.4   The law on strikes

Relevant provisions include the following.

(a)   Official industrial action requires the secret balloting of all affected members (Employment Act 1988). Seven days' notice must be given to an employer of a union's intention to ballot its members on industrial action (Trade Union Reform and Employment Rights Act 1993). The Employment Relations Act 1999 makes it harder for employers to challenge strike ballots, by giving the courts greater scope to disregard 'small accidental failures' in the organisation of ballots. It also clarifies the guidelines on balloting and allows the validity of a ballot to be extended by up to four weeks (if the union and employer agree) to give time for negotiations to continue.

(b)   In the course of a lawful and duly balloted trade dispute, the trade union, its officials and participants in the dispute are immune from legal action. However, members of the public have the right to apply for a court order restraining a union from taking **unlawful** industrial action (Trade Union Reform and Employment Rights Act 1993).

(c)   Picketing carries legal immunity only if the pickets consist of employees who normally work at the premises, former employees (if the dispute concerns their termination), and employees who have no fixed place of work or who cannot picket their own place of work (and who therefore picket the premises from which their work is administered). Picketing solely to obtain or communicate information is not unlawful, but may become so if it involves obstruction of the public highway or breach of the peace (Employment Act 1980). Secondary action of any kind is unlawful (Employment Act 1990).

(d)   An individual may not be unjustifiably disciplined by a union (eg by fines, expulsion, withdrawal of benefits or blacklisting) for refusing to strike, refusal to go slow if by so doing (s)he would be in breach of contract, or for crossing a picket line (Employment Act 1988).

(e)   It is unlawful to dismiss strikers for the first eight weeks of a strike (Employment Relations Act 1999): dismissal of workers during unofficial

BPP
PUBLISHING

NOTES

strike or other industrial action was previously excluded altogether from the statutory 'unfair dismissal' code.

3.5 No strike agreements

The 'right to strike' in enshrined in employment law. However, no-strike agreements may be made by voluntary agreement between employers and unions. The Trade Union and Labour Relations Act 1974 states that a no-strike clause in a collective agreement can only be made part of individual contracts of employment when the agreement provides expressly and in writing for its inclusion, and when the agreement is made reasonably accessible to employees at the workplace.

No-strike clauses effectively deprive union negotiators of the threat of strike action in the event of breakdown in bargaining, and arguably deprive workers of one of their only sources of power in the employment relationship. They therefore tend to be attached to collective agreements which support the managerial prerogative, such as single-union and partnership agreements. They also tend to be accompanied by pendulum arbitration facilities (see above), giving employees some scope for redress.

FOR DISCUSSION

Do you think certain categories of worker should be deprived of the right to strike, in the national interest? If so, which? (Think of times when your own life was disrupted by strike action.)

3.6 Dispute procedures and the role of ACAS

Detailed procedural agreements on disputes are generally made during collective bargaining or other (non-union) negotiated agreements. A typical dispute procedure would provide for the 'escalating' involvement of more senior representatives of both sides, with a guarantee of new industrial action until all stages have been followed through.

   (a)   Meeting of union representative and middle management

   (b)   Meeting of district union officer and senior management

   (c)   Meeting of regional and then national officials of the union and employers' association (in national disputes)

   (d)   Conciliation (if required)

   (e)   Mediation (if required)

   (f)   Agreement to abide by the decision of an independent arbitrator (as a last resort, since the decision then passes out of the hands of the parties involved)

If dispute procedures fail to re-open negotiation or resolve conflict, the parties may consider calling in ACAS to offer the services of conciliation, mediation and arbitration.

Conciliation is a voluntary process of discussion, facilitated by ACAS conciliators whose role is to make constructive suggestions, provide information and manage the process. At this stage, ACAS has no power to impose or recommend settlements.

If a voluntary settlement is not reached through conciliation, ACAS can arrange for mediation. This involves the appointment of an independent person or board of

BPP
PUBLISHING

mediation, who will hear both sides' evidence and arguments at a hearing. The mediator makes a formal proposal or recommendation as a basis for settlement of the dispute, but this is not legally binding on either party.

If both parties agree to arbitration:

(a) Terms of reference must be defined, setting limits to the arbitrator's powers and to the issues to be considered: traditional arbitration or pendulum arbitration (see above) may be used.

(b) Parties may select the independent arbitrator from the ACAS panel, or may let ACAS appoint an arbitrator.

(c) A date and venue are set for the arbitration hearing. Prior to the hearing, both sides exchange and submit to the arbitrator a written statement of their case and arguments, supporting documents, and a list of those attending (usually the negotiators). The arbitrator may also request a site visit, for example if the dispute concerns the conditions under which work is done or the level of skill required.

(d) An informal, private and confidential hearing is held, at which the arbitrator hears arguments from both sides. A typical procedure would allow each side an uninterrupted opportunity to state its case and critique the opposing case (as set out in the written submission), prior to questioning by the other side and by the arbitrator. The arbitrator then ensures that both parties have said or asked everything they wish to, and invites closing statements.

(e) The arbitrator considers the arguments after the hearing and delivers an award via ACAS, usually within two to three weeks.

Having discussed employee involvement in Chapter 18, we will now look at the related issue of employee participation, which more often involves collective representation.

4 EMPLOYEE PARTICIPATION

4.1 What is participation?

Definition

> **Employee participation** 'concerns the extent to which employees, often via their representatives, are involved with management in the decision-making machinery of the organisation. This includes joint consultation, collective bargaining and worker representation on the board.' (Gennard & Judge)

Activity 6 **(30 minutes)**

Outline four general reasons why an organisation may consider it desirable or necessary to work towards employee participation.

There are different degrees and methods of participation, reflecting the extent to which organisations wish to involve employees in decision-making.

BPP
PUBLISHING

NOTES

We discussed the social dimensions of the European Union in Chapter 10. Here, we will draw together the provisions on consultation and information, and industrial democracy.

4.2 Legal provisions for participation and consultation

The Companies Act 1989

An organisation employing more than 250 employees is required to include a statement in its Directors' Report describing the action taken in the previous financial year to introduce, maintain or develop arrangements for:

(a) Information/consultation of employees on matters affecting their employment

(b) Consultation with employee representatives to canvass their views on matters affecting them

(c) Financial participation of employees in the company's performance

(d) Extending employees' awareness of financial and economic factors affecting the company's performance

FOR DISCUSSION

Get hold of the Directors' Report (found as part of the Annual Report and Accounts) of any public limited company of your choice. Examine the statements made in regard to the above matters. Do they reflect genuine involvement or participation, from what you can gather?

The European Works Council Directive

The EWC Directive (extended to the UK in 1997: applicable from the end of 1999) provides for a European-level information and consultation system to be set up in all organisations with more than 1,000 employees in Member States and employing more than 150 people in each of two or more of these. A Pan-European Works Council (or alternative) has to be agreed between central management and a Special Negotiating Body of employee representatives from the countries involved. If no agreement is reached, a fallback system requires the establishment of a **European Works Council** of employee representatives with the right to meet central management at least once a year for information and consultation about the progress and prospects of the company. It may also request further consultation on transnational issues of concern, defined as 'measures significantly affecting employees' interests'.

EXAMPLE

Electrics giant Panasonic decided in 1994 to adopt a proactive view of the European Works Council Directive and to conclude a voluntary agreement with employee representatives, resulting in the establishment of:

(a) A 'Panasonic European Congress' (PEC), meeting yearly for consultation on transnational issues. The congress involves representatives from different nations; different types of operations (sales, manufacturing, R & D) and both unionised and non-unionised companies. In 1997, it was decided to give representatives training in their roles; different cultures, industrial law and climates; how to understand financial reports and figures; and Panasonic's structures and strategies in Europe.

BPP PUBLISHING

(b)   Two representative committees: an Employee Representative Committee and a Management Representative Committee, which meet three or four times a year to discuss the agenda for the annual meeting, agree the minutes and be informed and consulted on transnational issues. Each committee has three representatives from different nations.

(c)   A Panasonic UK Consultative Committee (PUCC), with 11 employee representatives from the different divisions of Panasonic UK Ltd. (The UK company was non-union and non-works-council, so there was no existing formal structure for information and consultation with elected employee representatives.) The PUCC meets with company directors every two months to discuss company performance, sales figures, health and safety, canteen and sports facilities, technological and structural changes and training and education. It is used 'as a means of communication between management and staff and acts as a sounding board for new ideas. It is also used to monitor opinions and debate the practicalities of staff suggestions or management ideas'.

The main contentious issues in creating a European forum proved to be the nature and timing of consultation, and the scope of negotiation. Delegates naturally want to compare and better their local terms and conditions – but the agreement clearly states that the purpose of European Works Councils is communication, information and consultation on transnational issues only. The personnel manager summed up (*People Management*, 1999):

> I believe it would be a mistake to underestimate the impact a European works council can have... Many multinational companies will undergo changes, restructuring and re-organisation that result in the need to inform and consult with their workforce and its representatives. The more informed employees are about pan-European activities and the better their understanding is, the more we can develop a feeling of partnership and trust. Building such a relationship takes time and effort... The costs of organising the annual meeting and the small committee meetings are high... However, if one takes a positive, proactive approach it is possible to view the EWC directive as an opportunity rather than a threat.

Draft directives: watch this space!

The **Draft Fifth Directive on Company Law** proposes that all EU-based limited companies with more than 1,000 workers adopt:

(a)   Collective bargaining on decisions or

(b)   A two-tier board structure, with elected worker representatives on the senior or 'supervisory' board to which the management or 'executive' board is responsible, or

(c)   A unitary board structure with worker representatives as non-executive directors, or

(d)   A sub-board level company council, solely comprised of worker representation

The **Draft Directive on National Information and Consultation** proposes that organisations with more than 50 employees will have to:

(a)   Provide information on recent and foreseeable development concerning the enterprise's activity and economic and financial situation

(b)   Inform and consult employees on the situation, structure and foreseeable developments relating to employment (particularly, threat to jobs)

(c)   Inform and consult employees on decisions that are likely to lead to substantial changes in work organisation and contractual relations.

The UK government (among others) is at the time of writing still opposing this directive, despite calls from the TUC. The general secretary of the GMB told the 2000 TUC conference: 'We need better rights to consultation and information. I look forward to the day when British workers hear about the changes in their employment from the lips of their managers and not from the pages of the *Financial Times* or the early morning news bulletins of the BBC' (referring to the recent incident in which 546 workers at Coats Viyella's textile factor near Leicester heard on local radio that they were to lose their jobs...).

Other UK law on consultation

UK law provides that employers are required to consult with recognised trade unions in areas such as health and safety, transfer of the undertaking, proposed redundancies and the contracting out of an occupational pension scheme from the state scheme. A 1994 decision in the European Court of Justice (*Commission of the European Communities v UK*) found that the UK had failed to comply with EU directives by restricting information and consultation to 'representatives of recognised trade unions' rather than 'representatives of the workforce'. The UK must now provide for consultation of representatives in non-unionised environments.

We will now look at some of the forms employee consultation and participation can take. Don't forget that the organisation may also use the full range of upward-downward communication and other employee involvement techniques mentioned in Chapter 18.

4.3 Joint consultation and works councils

Definition

> **Joint consultation** is a process by which management and employee representatives jointly examine and discuss issues of mutual concern.

Joint consultation is the main form of representative participation in the UK. Gennard and Judge distinguish between 'employee communication' (similarly concerned with the interchange of information and ideas within an organisation) and 'consultation', which involves managers actively seeking and taking account of the views of employees before making a decision. Consultation 'affects the process through which decisions are made in so far as it commits management first to the disclosure of information at an early stage in the decision-making process and second to take into account the collective views of the employees.'

Joint Consultative Committees (JCCs) – sometimes called 'Works Councils' – are composed of managers and employee representatives who come together on a regular basis to discuss matters of mutual interest. (Remember, these are non-negotiatory meetings.) Members should include senior managers (in order to demonstrate commitment and mobilise authority where required) and representatives of all significant employee groups (in order to be regarded as genuinely representative). Committees usually have a well defined constitution and terms of reference.

Like any committee or group meeting, a JCC meeting will need a skilled Chairperson to facilitate and control discussion, and a clear and manageable agenda, circulated in advance for member preparation. Minutes will need to be taken for feeding back to the parties represented (via briefing groups, noticeboards, intranet and so on). Management needs to demonstrate its commitment to genuine consultation by giving appropriate facilities, time off and training to committee members. In unionised organisations, issues such as pay bargaining are generally left to collective bargaining, so JCCs must also be given something of perceived importance to deal with if they are not to be marginalised as ineffectual 'talk shops'.

Activity 7   **(No time limit)**

What are the structures for joint consultation in your work organisation (or one you know well or can find out about). What issues are consultations designed to cover? What influence do they have on organisational policy? How are they regarded by employees in general?

EXAMPLE: INTERNATIONAL COMPARISONS

In **Germany**, the concept of consultation and participation is based on a system called **co-determination**, formally involving employees and their representatives in nearly all decisions relating to personnel and other aspects of company policy. Co-determination is supported by specific legislation. There are three methods by which workers can participate: by Works Councils, Supervisory Boards and Management Boards.

- In workplaces with more than five employees, the workforce elects a **works council** consisting solely of workers' representatives. This council has the right:

  (a) To receive information on health and safety, work organisation, jobs, work environment, the hiring of executives and planned changes which could adversely affect employees

  (b) To make suggestions during the formulation and implementation of HR plans, and specifically regarding vocational training (eg apprenticeships) and other training and development opportunities

  The views and suggestions of the council must be considered, although they are not binding on managerial decision-making.

- In companies employing more than 500 people, elected worker representatives sit on the **supervisory board** which meets four times a year. Worker representatives make up one-third to one-half of this policy-making body (depending on size), with other board members elected by the shareholders, under a 'neutral' chairperson. The supervisory board is responsible for deciding the overall direction of the enterprise; matters concerning corporate finance and structure (including mergers and takeovers); and the appointment, dismissal and remuneration of members of the executive or management board.

- The executive or **management board** is the full-time body responsible for the day-to-day running of operations.

Sweden also operates a co-determination system based on consultation with employees and the participation of representatives in decision making at both board and shop floor levels. Industrial democracy was developed early in Sweden, and techniques such as job enrichment, autonomous working groups and 'quality of working life' programmes were developed by companies such as Volvo back in the 1970s. The Swedish model is more highly unionised that the German model, with union membership over 80%.

Belgium, France, Italy, Spain and the Netherlands also have works councils supported by legislation, but the range of issues open to employee approval is smaller than in the German or Swedish co-determination models. Belgium and the Netherlands have an additional legal requirement for large companies to operate a two-tier (supervisory and executive) board of directors.

In **Japan**, employee involvement practices are deeply embedded in the collectivist and commitment-based culture of employment, in techniques such as quality circles, teamworking, concensus decision-making and long-term employee development. There is a unitarist assumption of the value of participation, supported by the training of group leaders and workers in the skills of participative working. However, observers note that employee involvement techniques are not primarily used as decision-making mechanisms or channels of communication (as in Europe) but as a cultural mechanism reinforcing identification with shared aims and goals.

4.4 Partnership agreements

Definition

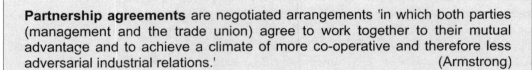

> **Partnership agreements** are negotiated arrangements 'in which both parties (management and the trade union) agree to work together to their mutual advantage and to achieve a climate of more co-operative and therefore less adversarial industrial relations.'   (Armstrong)

Partnership agreements generally include undertakings from both sides, linking job security, pay awards or participation (in the control of management) to productivity gains or greater flexibility in work organisation (in the control of unions).

EXAMPLE

Legal & General agreed a partnership deal with the MSF in 1997, an experience reported as follows in *People Management* (September 2000).

The objectives of the agreement are:

- To work together to further the success of the business by enabling a flexible approach in a time of rapid and continuous change

- To work together in a spirit of mutual confidence, partnership and co-operation, both formally and informally

- To work together to achieve fairness and equality in the treatment of staff, including transparent pay systems, contractual provisions that encourage equal treatment regardless of age, creed, disability, race or sex, and access to good vocational training and career development.

The parties set out to recognise both their differences and their shared interests. They committed themselves to avoiding conflict that would damage the business. MSF accepted management's right to manage. Legal & General acknowledged the union's right to represent its members both collectively and on individual matters of grievance or discipline.

Collective bargaining machinery was replaced by a Joint Employment Policy Forum (JEPF) meeting that would take place every six months. The JEPF was given wide scope to discuss business strategy, training and development, health and safety, reward and equal opportunities. Both sides preferred joint communication and informal methods of dispute resolution where possible, with the intention 'to talk at the earliest possible stage on all matters of mutual interest'. The agreement also committed management to give representatives training that would enable them to perform their union functions properly.

In April 2000, Legal and General and the MSF reviewed the agreement. Key concerns were that:

(a) Not all managers seemed to understand what partnership meant. This issued in failure to involve union representatives in employment matters, to give representatives time off for their duties or to encourage union membership.

(b) Union representatives were insufficiently trained and experienced to meet the demands of the partnership role, and the inequality in expertise between them and managers undermined the relationship.

(c) Employees were ambivalent about the deal. On the one hand, MSF didn't like the idea of 'freeloaders' (non-members who enjoyed the benefits of the agreement without paying union subscriptions). On the other, employees complained that the union had grown too close to management and lacked 'bite' in negotiations.

Further training, and greater promotion of the partnership concept, were two ways forward.

Activity 8	**(30 minutes)**
What advantages might parties in a partnership agreement be aiming for?	

> There are critics who see partnership as an illusory concept. Those on the left of the political spectrum… fear that unions, far from gaining influence, will be co-opted by management into their projects, effectively neutralising any chance of opposition. Critics from the right would argue that partnership hampers management's ability to manage, or, as the president of the CBI… believes, that it may even provide a "Trojan horse" through which unions could gain more influence.
>
> (*People Management*, 14 September 2000)

Chapter roundup

- Collective bargaining is the process whereby employee and employer representatives negotiate agreements on terms and conditions of employment (and related matters) for groups of represented employees. There has been a tendency to decentralise bargaining to plant level, in order to retain flexibility.

- Negotiating is a bargaining process through which commitments and compromises are reached, using the relative power of the parties involved.

- A lawful trade dispute is one between workers and their own employers, wholly or mainly about work-related matters. Various forms of sanctions are available to workers in pursuance of an industrial dispute, including strikes. Strike action has been strictly controlled by legislation and has correspondingly declined in severity and frequency.

- Employee participation concerns the extent to which employees, often via their representatives, are involved with management in the decision-making machinery of the organisation. It includes joint consultation, works councils, European Works Councils and worker representation on the board.

Quick quiz

1   What are procedural agreements in collective bargaining?

2   What is single-table bargaining?

3 · What does the ACAS Code of Practice recommend on the disclosure of information for collective bargaining?

4   What is pendulum arbitration?

5   What three outcomes of negotiation should negotiators plan in advance, as the basis of negotiating strategy?

6   Distinguish between primary and secondary industrial action.

7   List five areas of industrial action that are subject to UK legislation.

8   Outline the process of arbitration of a trade dispute and the role of ACAS.

9   What is a European Works Council? When is it compulsory to have one?

10   Outline the German model of co-determination.

Answers to quick quiz

1   Agreements which determine methods and procedures for arriving at substantive agreements (on pay, conditions and so on) and for settling disputes.   (see paragraph 1.1)

2   Terms and conditions of all workers (manual and non-manual) are determined in a single negotiation. This may be achieved by multiple unions pre-negotiating a bargaining proposal prior to collective bargaining with management.   (para 1.3)

3   Information should be disclosed on pay and benefits, conditions of service, human resources, performance (productivity, sales, orders) and financial matters. Unions should define and request specific information before negotiations begin.   (para 1.4)

4   Instead of the arbitrator finding 'middle ground' between the final offer/claim of each side, (s)he awards for one side's final position over the other: **either** the employer's final offer **or** the employees' final claim.
                                                                         (para 2.1)

5   Ideal settlement, realistic settlement, fall-back position.   (para 2.2)

6   Primary: aimed at the employer with whom the participating union is in dispute. Secondary (unlawful): aimed at employers who trade with firms in dispute.   (para 3.2)

7   Balloting of members; legal immunity for lawful dispute; outlawing of secondary action; individual member rights not to participate; unlawful dismissal of strikers in first eight weeks of dispute.   (para 3.4)

8   See paragraph 3.6 for a detailed account.

9   A Pan-European body of employee representatives with the right to meet central management at least once a year for information and consultation about the progress and prospects of the company. All organisations with more than 1,000 employees in the EU member states, with more than 150 people in each of two or more states, must establish some form of Europe-wide consultation on system: an EWC is the fallback system if unions and employee negotiators fail to agree on an alternative.
                                                                         (para 4.2)

10   See the International Comparison example in paragraph 4.3 for a detailed account.

Answers to Activities

1   **Advantages**

(a)   Less time and resources spent on negotiations than with multiple bargaining.

(b)   Takes account of more viewpoints, more representative: enhances likelihood of acceptance of decisions. (Particularly helpful for change management affecting multiple groups of employees.)

(c)   Encourages resolution of inter-union disputes as part of preparation for negotiation: saves wasted time and energy in harmonising separate agreements.

(d)   May help avoid demarcations and inflexible work rules, with overall bargaining perspective (needs for flexibility, quality etc).

Disadvantages

(a)   Agenda may be overcrowded by concerns of multiple groups.

(b)   Requires higher levels of negotiating and relationship management skills.

(c)   Inflexibility: management may be less able to differentiate and change agreements with different segments of the workforce.

(d)   Inter-union disputes may not be resolved prior to negotiation.

(e)   May hamper individual union attempts to recruit members.

2   Decline in collective bargaining, due to:

(a)   The decline in union membership, and therefore the number of workers covered by collective bargaining

(b)   The rise of individual- and team-based systems, with new emphasis on employees' responsibility for self-management and self-development: individual contracts, learning plans and career mobility; team-centred performance management, performance-related pay and so on

(c)   The rise of workforce flexibility, with the erosion of job descriptions, occupational demarcations and associated work rules

(d)   The decentralisation of employee relations (and other HRM) processes to line managers

(e)   The introduction of non-negotiatory consultation and involvement techniques

As we saw in Chapter 18, however, union recognition in the UK may be on the upturn: watch this space!

3   Quantitative elements of bargaining power include:

•   The intrinsic merit of each party's case or argument (the stronger your case, the better the prospect of achieving agreement on your terms)

•   The skill and ability of the negotiator

BPP PUBLISHING

- The potential for coercion (the power of underlying sanctions or 'threat' eg to close a plant, or initiate industrial action)

Note that bargaining power may be actual or 'real' and/or perceived, and that the one may be much higher or lower than the other...

4 (a) Gain agreements or commitments from the other side that can be used as a stepping stone for the logical progression of your argument.

   (b) Summarise periodically, especially to highlight common ground and consolidate progress.

   (c) Sell the benefits of your proposals to the other side: allow them to agree with you, without loss of face, whenever possible.

   (d) Preserve a tone of commitment, belief, even emotion: make your cause human.

   (e) Use questions. Positive, joint-problem-solving questions: 'What would it take to make this work?'. Probing, challenging questions: 'Where would the money for that proposal come from?' Push for answers where necessary.

   (f) Release information with a tactical awareness of its affects on negotiating position.

   (g) Use all interpersonal and communication skills: listening, empathy, accessible language, giving non-verbal cues (eg confident body-language) and interpreting non-verbal cues (eg signs of hesitation, tentative phrasing, suggestions of readiness to move).

5 Industrial action may be used as:

   (a) A demonstration of bargaining strength, by the threatened or actual withdrawal of labour and/or restriction of productivity, aimed at forcing management to enter negotiations or make concessions, or

   (b) A gesture of protest to highlight a grievance issue, aimed at management, government and other influential bodies, or at the general public. (For example, a literal 'go-slow' was staged by a transport union in Sydney, Australia in November 2000. Bus drivers drove at a crawl during the rush hour to highlight the failure of state government and policy to enforce city-centre bus lane rules, exposing drivers to stress, risk and commuter frustration: passengers and the media were handed leaflets explaining the purpose of the action and urged to support the protest.)

6 Participation may be desirable or necessary because of the following factors.

   (a) **Commitment**: the perceived need to obtain a higher level of identification with organisational goals and a higher degree of acceptance and support of strategies for change.

   (b) **Quality of decision-making**: the perceived need to involve employees with 'front-line' knowledge, experience and influence in areas such as quality management and customer care. Quality circles and empowered teams are developed on this basis.

   (c) **Trade union pressure.** Collective bargaining has been extended into areas traditionally considered as management concerns: human resource levels, training and so on. Joint consultation is another prevalent form of worker participation, where management discuss matters of concern regularly with union representatives, on Joint Consultative Committees (JCCs) or non-negotiatory staff forums. A more radical approach is the formation of partnership agreements with worker representatives.

(d) **Legal requirements**. Participation and consultation have occupied a high profile in employment protection and – most recently – in the social policy of the European Union, with provision for employee representation in decision-sharing structures such as Works Councils and Supervisory Boards.

7   Your own research and opinion.

8   Some advantages (identified by Legal & General and MSF in their partnership agreement) include:

(a) Increased flexibility, honesty and trust in relationships

(b) Better quality, faster decision-making, with decisions that were more likely to be readily accepted within the company

(c) Positive public relations for the company – and for the union ('rebranded' to attract new members)

(d) Having the right people focused on the right issues

(e) The development of an 'adult' relationship in which company and union could move in the same direction

---

Assignment 19   **(1 hour)**

You are the HR manager of a firm (in a sector of your choice). Your firm recognises the relevant union(s) for its sector for the purposes of collective bargaining, and at least one of these has shown itself to be militant in its approach to the use of sanction (industrial action) in the pursuit of claims for better pay and conditions. Management has made concessions over the years, but is unable to continue to do so without threatening the firm's viability. This argument is unlikely to impress the union. Line managers are saying that a major stoppage is on the cards again – although they do not know when, or on what issue, it will occur.

Devise a contingency plan for dealing with strike action if or when it occurs.

PUBLISHING

ANSWERS TO ASSIGNMENTS

Answer to Assignment 1

Class One Insurance Services

Matters for urgent attention might include:

- (a)   Recruitment of staff for replacement and growth
- (b)   Harmonisation of terms and conditions between sites and grades
- (c)   Develop grievance procedure to deal with perceived inequities
- (d)   Deal with miscellaneous but long-standing problems
- (e)   Set up regular visits to all sites
- (f)   Produce standardised procedures and policies for all divisions
- (g)   Collate salary information to get internal and external equity
- (h)   Examine pay strategy for sales staff
- (i)   Meet with trade union representatives on a regular, on-going basis
- (j)   Check health and safety procedures

Matters for longer term attention might include:

- (a)   Relocation of all staff to one site
- (b)   Reduction in numbers of administrative staff (especially at headquarters)
- (c)   Analysis of training needs
- (d)   Motivating long-serving staff
- (e)   Draw up age profiles to check future succession problems
- (f)   Conduct an attitude survey to test staff morale
- (g)   Establish a computerised records and pay system
- (h)   Check business plan and build personnel strategies around it
- (i)   Establish a system of performance appraisal
- (j)   Communicate business results to all staff

Answer to assignment 2

Flyblown and Fudgett

Research shows that mergers often fail because human considerations have not been taken into account. This case study suggests two very different organisational cultures meeting head-on. Fudgett appears to be a hierarchical, bureaucratic organisation with centralised decision making, whereas Flyblown appears flatter, with decentralisation and empowerment of line managers.

The benefits and drawbacks of centralised versus decentralised decision making have been discussed at length and you are advised to return to Chapter 2 to help you answer this question. In terms of organisational culture, we seem to have a head-on collision between the role culture of Fudgett (many levels, organisation by rules, slow decision making) and the network culture of Flyblown (few levels, project based team work, swift decision making). It would be unwise to allow these two cultures to co-exist: one must give way, and it is likely to be the role culture of the weaker partner in the merger.

You should also consider what might have happened before and during the merger itself. Here, communication would have been of key importance, and it is hoped that full consultation took place between the affected parties. The situation is not irretrievable but you should expect some casualties, primarily from the weaker party, ie Fudgett. You should also consider how best to manage those staff who remain (see notes on the 'survivor syndrome' in Chapter 10).

NOTES

Answer to assignment 3

Human Resource Planning at Quick-Send Ltd

1 (a) A bar chart would provide the best illustration of the age profile.

(b) The most striking point shown by the age profile is that 94 staff (43%) are over 50 years old. Quick-Send therefore have an ageing workforce. While such workers tend to have good attendance records and low absenteeism, the company will have to plan for replacements when they retire. The company should also have a clearly thought-out retirement policy.

A second factor is the number of young staff: 62 (28%) are under 30. The training requirements of such staff need to be considered.

2 (a)

Year	Total number of staff
X	217
X + 1	190
X + 2	160
X + 3	200
X + 4	231
X + 5	237

(b)

Year	Total number of staff needed	Shortage/surplus (before labour turnover) Shortage	Shortage/surplus (before labour turnover) Surplus	Labour turnover	Shortage/surplus taking into account labour turnover Shortage	Shortage/surplus taking into account labour turnover Surplus
X	217					
X + 1	190		27	9		18
X + 2	160		30	8		22
X + 3	200	40		10	50	
X + 4	231	31		12	43	
X + 5	237	6		12	18	

3 The figures show that for the next two years the warehouse and packing department will have a surplus of staff. After that there is a predicted shortage for each of the following three years.

Given that 20 of the current staff are currently over 60, it would not appear that the firm will have a problem for the first year faced with a predicted surplus of 18 staff.

Similarly, in the following year, the company could consider offering staff early retirement to overcome the predicted surplus of 22 staff. Voluntary redundancy could also be considered on a very limited basis.

The picture changes very much in the third year. If the predicted increase in orders and the stabilisation of the ratios is correct, the firm will be faced with a shortage of employees. Given the current ageing workforce, plans should be laid for recruitment and training of staff for these years, or the possibility of relocation from other areas of the organisation considered. Space and facilities for the increase in staff numbers is another consideration.

Answer to Assignment 4

Rottenborough District Hospital

The first point to note is that the three Rs are different (although they do overlap). There would be little point, for example, in developing a targeted recruitment policy if you made no efforts to keep your women returnees motivated and satisfied once working for you. You should also acknowledge the value of women workers and the problems you can expect as an organisation if they are under-represented.

Alternative ways in which you can attract, keep and encourage back your target group might include:

- (a)   Staff banks
- (b)   Term-time working
- (c)   Homeworking
- (d)   Jobshare and flexi-time
- (e)   Nursery and childcare vouchers

These are all relatively easy to implement. Longer term considerations might include:

- (a)   Reprofiling of jobs to create career pathways for non-professionals

- (b)   Analysing criteria for success at higher levels

- (c)   Improving the organisational image for recruitment

- (d)   Targeting women returnees more specifically in your recruitment campaigns

- (e)   Train all staff involved in recruitment and selection

- (f)   Review your job requirements to make essential skills specific

- (g)   Standardise and control questions asked of interview candidates

Once more, don't forget that the answer has to be in the form of a report to your Director of Human Resources.

Answer to Assignment 5

This was designed to be an active and inter-active learning exercise: there is no suggested answer.

For guidance, if needed, use some of the frameworks given in the text, as follows.

Task 1.   Paragraph 5.7, Chapter 4

Task 2.   Section 2, Chapter 5 (compare also with Application Form questions, paragraph 1.2)

Task 3.   Paragraphs 2.2-2.3, Chapter 5

Task 4.   Paragraph 2.3-2.4, Chapter 5. (Also see paragraph 1.3 on discrimination and privacy, and paragraph 1.3 to select options for further selection techniques.)

Answer to Assignment 6

Biotherm PLC

The overall purpose of the appraisal interview should be to encourage Alan Heath to become more a part of the personnel team (after all he has specialist knowledge which cannot be replaced). You cannot ignore his sickness record because it impacts on performance. However, you should attempt to understand the reasons behind his poor attendance rather than tackling it at this stage (this is best left for a separate occasion).

You should ensure at all costs that the appraisal interview does not become a disciplinary one.

Your plan should include the following:

(a) Discussion on achievement of past objectives

(b) Reasons behind failure to achieve objectives

(c) Problems and successes in current performance (you should have consulted in advance with the main people Alan interacts with, eg line managers, colleagues, external clients)

(d) Attempts to understand Alan's personal needs (he may be motivated by his 'expertise' for example, rather than any additional pay award)

(e) A discussion of Alan's job aspirations this will follow on from the previous point but you should have done your homework in advance on the requirements of the job immediately senior to his

(f) A commitment not to duck difficult issues but to explore you may find out some very good reasons behind his refusal to work beyond contracted hours, for example

(g) An attempt to agree a set of SMART objectives

Your approach to this interview should be 'problem-solving', rather than 'tell and sell' or 'tell and listen'.

Answer to Assignment 7

Ad Hoc Ltd

(a) See the table of paragraph 1.1 Chapter 7, to remind you of the advantages and disadvantages.

(b) **Overcoming weaknesses**

Some of the above weaknesses are such that they cannot be overcome in practice - they are inherent in the objectives of the technique. Their effects can be minimised, however, by choice of the particular method, the way in which the system is implemented and by building on the strengths of the technique. To a great extent the particular weaknesses of job evaluation, and ways in which they can be minimised, will vary according to the method used, the method of implementation, the training of the evaluator, and the attitudes of workers and management. In general terms, however, the value of the method can be enhanced as follows.

(i) Whichever method is used, evaluations must be kept up to date, with periodic reviews.

(ii) The process should (time, resources and expertise permitting) be as scientific as possible. A more qualitative approach, such as factor comparison or points rating, should be adopted, and the factors to be studied, the weightings and scores should be systematically determined. There must still be some element of subjectivity, but a visible attempt at objectivity is being made.

(iii) Job analysts and evaluators must be trained in the use of the appropriate techniques, must have access to job documentation and to job holders (for observation and interview), and their evaluations should be monitored or reviewed to ensure that they are keeping up with changes in the organisation and applying techniques correctly.

(iv)   It should be recognised by management, and by job holders, that job evaluation is only part of the pay/reward setting process. Job evaluation alone allows for no incentive level of reward: bonuses and increments for merit or performance will need to be added to the salary structure if there is not to be a demotivating effect. Moreover, job evaluation may be seen to be a threatening - or simply irrelevant - basis for salary structures, if it is not recognised that there are factors unrelated to job content which affect the value of jobs, such as equity ('felt fair' rewards), market rates of pay, negotiated pay scales, age and experience and so on.

(v)   Problems of acceptance by staff - since job evaluation is a highly political exercise - can be minimised by implementing the system in an open, sensitive way. The purpose, objectives and potential benefits will need to be 'sold' to staff in advance: it will in particular have to be made clear that it is the job, not the job-holder, which is being evaluated. The role of collective bargaining may have to be discussed with unions. Appeal and revision procedures will have to be built into the system, and employees must be allowed to voice any uncertainties, suspicions and objections they may have about the affect of job grading on earnings, confidentiality, promotion and so on.

Answer to Assignment 8

Your answer should cover most of the following points.

Lateness, absenteeism, and minor infractions of work rules will result in a first warning which will be oral but be recorded on the employee's record. If there are further occurrences of a similar nature, a second warning will be issued. This will be written and a copy will be retained on the employee's file. Any further breach will result in a final written warning. If there is yet another breach, it will result in dismissal.

At all stages the employee will be interviewed by the relevant manager and given the opportunity to state his/her case. The employee has the right to be accompanied by a fellow worker or trade union representative. The right of appeal is relevant at all stages and any appeal must be lodged with the relevant manager within 10 working days.

Answer to Assignment 9

Novalux PLC

The figures here have been designed not to provide a simple answer, and some statistical application is required. To test whether the differences between age groups in terms of staff turnover is significant or not, you would actually need to use a statistical test that is beyond the scope of this module.

However, the broader issue here is what else you can draw out from the figures provided, and what further information you might need in order to make other more meaningful conclusions. For example, you might consider finding out further information on the following:

(a)   The distribution of grades among leavers

(b)   What types of jobs they had

(c)   Which departments they come from

(d)   Whether any gender or ethnicity pattern emerges

(e)   Have reasons for leaving been given via an exit interview?

(f)   Do new employees go through an induction programme?

(g)   Are new employees trained properly?

(h)   What is the age profile of the organisation? For example, if it's a very young population the turnover figures by age might not be as alarming as they first appear.

Answer to Assignment 10

Q and R Ferries PLC

The dismissal of Roger Price is potentially fair, but the punishment is likely to be viewed by a tribunal as being too severe. They are therefore likely to rule unfair dismissal. Mary Gardner's case is likely to be viewed as fair dismissal, due to capability. However, Q and R Ferries are likely to be criticised by a tribunal for lack of consultation with the employee. Thus the areas of severity and consultation are likely to be the main points a tribunal will take into account.

You will shortly be interviewing the relevant department managers as part of your preparation for the tribunal cases. You should ask the following questions:

Roger Price's manager;

(a)   were all relevant procedures followed? (eg sick reporting)

(b)   did Roger Price know about the procedures?

(c)   did you follow the disciplinary procedures? If so, was dismissal the right level or should you have issued a warning?

Mary Gardner's manager;

(a)   were there any alternatives to dismissal? (eg career break)

(b)   were Mary Gardner's health problems known on appointment?

(c)   why didn't anyone talk to Mary Gardner?

Overall questions might challenge the wisdom of passing authority right down the line without overseeing it, and a possible recommendation of health screening on appointment.

Answer to Assignment 11

The basic points can be found in Chapter 11, sections 1 and 2. You may have chosen to use diagrams such as the Harvard map of HR territory to illustrate soft-hard approaches (perhaps drawing the employee life-cycle of the Michigan model); the 27-points-of-diffeence table is already well-suited to presentation.

In terms of format and style, you were given lots of leeway. Be as creative and professional as you can: the results may act as evidence of competence under Assessment Criteria 22.1. Remember to be concise (this is a summary): it will help you to sort out in your own mind what is important about the two 'theories' under discussion.

Answer to Assignment 12

Flex Consult

(a) The seaside holiday hotel will be able to anticipate peaks in demand on Bank Holiday weekends and during the summer holiday season. It will require a mix of unskilled and semi-skilled staff to cover extra demand. A typical solution would be to obtain skilled agency and/or seasonally contracted staff (perhaps annual regulars) with the addition of casual labour if required for general duties. There may also be a continual daily fluctuation of demand at the hotel, centred around housekeeping in the mornings, and around the bar/restaurant (if any) in the evenings: the employment of permanent part-time staff may be the solution here.

(b) The domestic appliance manufacturer might be able to anticipate peaks in demand in the fourth quarter of the year, with Christmas and January sales purchases. Such a regular seasonal fluctuation could be dealt with by securing extra hours of work through overtime or adding shifts, or by annual hours contracts stipulating a core period of labour before and during the peak period. These methods would have the advantage of utilising the existing skilled workforce, rather than obtaining outside labour who would require time and resources to 'get up to speed' with the product and production methods.

(c) The firm of management consultants needs to respond more flexibly to more or less random demands from new clients. It also requires access to highly-skilled professional people, without sufficient lead times to train them to meet immediate short-term demands. The firm will probably therefore rely on freelance consultants with whom it has a relationship of trust: possibly past employees who have set up on their own, or who have experienced training or collaboration with the firm and therefore know its 'house style' and methods. The firm should keep a group of 'associate consultants' on its books, and include them in consultant briefings and training programmes where possible.

Answer to Assignment 13

Glamour Products

You face a number of problems in this case study:

(a) Line manager and supervisor resentment

(b) Managing director's dismissive attitude to equal opportunities

(c) Adverse publicity for Glamour Products

(d) Impending IT case on unfair dismissal on grounds of race

(e) Uneasy relations with trade union

(f) Managing director's belief that training alone can deal with a complex problem

(g) Lack of any equal opportunities policy

You must attempt to deal with these, in particular the last two. Equal opportunities is a philosophy which should be embraced wholesale by an organisation if it is adopted. It is not something which can be packaged and delivered in a one-day training course. You should, therefore, undertake to do the following:

(a)   Investigate the grounds for unfair dismissal of Mr Patel

   (b)   Draw up an equal opportunities policy, having involved all interested parties (managers, staff, union representatives)

   (c)   Make it explicit that racist language will not be tolerated

   (d)   Attempt a long term education programme on equal opportunities: there is no point in simply ensuring compliance with the law: this will not make the problem go away and may serve to exacerbate existing negative attitudes

   (e)   Analyse other areas to ensure that equal opportunities are being observed for example, what is the representation of ethnic minority employees across different levels and functions in the organisation? Does your recruitment procedure support equal opportunities or work against it?

Don't forget to write your answer in the form of a faxed memo back to the Managing Director (as the question asks), pointing out the reasons why you feel a day conference isn't the right approach.

Answer to Assignment 14

Duntoiling Nursing Homes

To deal with this difficult situation effectively you need to do the following:

   (a)   Introduce a disciplinary procedure if none currently exists

   (b)   Consider the Health and Safety at Work legislation, particularly the employer's obligations of duty and care towards staff

   (c)   Define constructive dismissal (this means where an organisation has changed terms and conditions of employment to such an extent that the employees feel they have no other option but to resign)

   (d)   Consider the wisdom of unilateral changes in terms and conditions without notice (ie Cheeseman imposing these changes without any consultation)

   (e)   Consider reinstating the employee with possible concessions (eg counselling to give up smoking)

   (f)   Prepare your ideal and 'fall-back' positions when negotiating

   (g)   Question why the policy was introduced in the first place

   (h)   Ask why there was no involvement from the personnel function in implementing the smoking policy

   (i)   Develop a 'best practice' model showing how to introduce a smoking policy and do it again (remember the employer's duty to protect employees from the effects of passive smoking). The model should include:

        (i)   A consultation period (say 3 months)
        (ii)   Establishing a consultative committee
        (iii) Conducting a staff attitude survey
        (iv) Making provision for special cases
        (v)   Make formal changes to terms and conditions
        (vi) Retrain line managers in disciplinary matters
        (vii) Review and monitor the policy

Again remember that the question asks for your answer to be in the form of a brief to Mr Cheeseman.

Answer to Assignment 15

Kaizen Tomorrow Ltd

Limits to quality circles

The production director should be advised that the nature of the changes recommended by the quality circle will depend on the range of skills and experience of the circle members. The wider their skills are, and the broader their experience, the more significant and far-reaching will be the changes they might suggest. Groups of workers with similar skills are more likely to make suggestions for limited changes within the sphere of their own work experience. What range of skills should the circles have? How will unions demarcation lines (and the associated culture of inflexibility) be overcome?

The 'terms of reference' of the circles should be made clear. Are they to **recommend** changes to senior management, or will they have the authority to **decide** changes, and make them? Management does not currently enlist or invite worker input (unlike Japanese style): how will this be overcome?

Need for co-operation

Since the purpose of quality circles is to encourage innovation, the co-operation of employees will be crucial. The plans for setting up quality circles should therefore be discussed with the employees who will provide membership of the circles. How to create a culture of participation and consensus? Need for shared culture values/mechanisms to promote:

(a)   Identification with the organisation

(b)   Quality awareness/Japanese continuous improvement orientation)

Problems with quality circles

Possible problems with the introduction of quality circles might be:

(a)   Not enough support from top management

(b)   No co-operation from middle management

(c)   Discouragement because of unrealistic expectations of what the circles can do

(d)   Lack of support from trade unions

(e)   Poor choice of circle leaders – not experienced in facilitation of open discussion, seeking consensus

(f)   Insufficient training of circle members – not experienced in collective decision-making

(g)   Unwillingness to participate among employees – lack of identification with quality goals

(h)   Individual egos won't join in the circle 'team' spirit

Successful introduction of quality circles

The keys to a successful programme are:

(a)   Creating a proper atmosphere in which to launch them – a positive approach and good publicity

(b)   Giving circle members adequate training in quality circle techniques

(c)   Introducing circles slowly, one or two at a time, instead of setting up too many all at once; learning from experience; getting employees to accept the value of circles from their experience and observations over time

(d)   Full support from top management

    (e)   An enthusiastic 'facilitator' – a manager in charge of making the circles a success

    (f)   Setting up a good system for following up and evaluating proposals for change

    (g)   Giving recognition to circle members – for instance, rewards for successful changes

Answer to Assignment 16

No suggested answer: your Personal Development Plan is personal!

Answer to Assignment 17

Price-U-Like Stores

The first thing to note is that you should not draw up this training programme in isolation, but should seek the input of key managers and staff. The course should go through a 'pilot run' to iron out any problems which can then be changed. Importantly, the programme should be designed as a package which is capable of being transferred and delivered by other trainers (this is particularly important for multi-site organisations such as Price-U-Like Stores).

The style of the programme should be broad and mixed, allowing delegates to experience Customer Care first hand, then allowing them to reflect on what they have learnt and whether they can apply it to real situations they face. The programme should have clearly stated aims and objectives.

Indicative content of the programme might include:

    (a)   Icebreaker exercise
    (b)   Why have a Customer Care initiative?
    (c)   The importance of front-line staff to Customer Care
    (d)   Internal and external customers
    (e)   Listening skills, empathy, body language
    (f)   Why people complain

Delivery techniques might include discussion, role-play, brainstorming, videos, group problem solving, case studies, scenarios, lectures. You should also consider how to evaluate before, during and after the programme, taking into account different levels of evaluation (see Chapter 16).

Answer to Assignment 18

Some of the issues you may have raised are as follows.

Under a classical organisation/control/industrial relations system:

    (a)   Managers would be appraised by their managers (top-down): the idea of upward appraisal contravenes ideas of managerial status and authority. (Would not be possible in an elitist management culture, such as France or a high power-distance culture.)

    (b)   Managers would be appointed by the board or more senior managers. 'Leadership' by election (formal or informal) has always been acceptable – but 'management' traditionally implies authority delegated or conferred by position in the organisation. The idea of elected managers changes the whole culture of employee relations, blurring the lines between 'us' and 'them', while therefore increasing support for subsequent managerial decisions. It also affects the culture of the organisation, which traditionally reflects top-down managerial vision and values, as a form of control.

(c)(d) Salary levels would be set by top management, based on a rational structure of equity, differentials, market rates, cost-minimisation and so on, in line with the HR plan. Self-nominated salary places emphasis on the perceived value of a fair day's work for a fair day's pay – and the link between higher pay and more/harder/better work – to the employees themselves. This is effectively self-motivation. Financial participation in the form of work-nominated profit-sharing requires business/economic awareness and responsibility on the part of employees, including awareness of shared interest in the continuing competitiveness of the business, and the dynamics of the labour market.

(e) Working from home is a commitment rather than control-based system (HRM rather than IR), encouraging flexibility, reducing direct supervision and so on. This is perhaps the least radical of the measures for increasing employee discretion, but it reflects a culture of trust and assumed mutual interest that is typical of the new unitarist HR perspective.

(f) In the traditional IR framework, trade unions officials may be given access to this information prior to collective bargaining on wages. On-going, open access to financial information ('transparency') increases the accountability of management – but since workers share this responsibility, it is likely to increase both the sense of partnership and the quality of worker-manager decision-making (especially on financial matters).

Answer to Assignment 19

Your strike contingency plan should contain some of the following elements.

(a) Monitor employee and union attitudes, in the course of all formal and informal communications: ascertain likely duration, scope and severity of strike.

(b) Prepare strategies for negotiation, dispute handling, conciliation: lay out realistic and fall-back options. (Best scenario: union agreement to delay claims, relate claims to productivity guarantees/increases, engage in profit-sharing.) Prepare analysis of costs of various options.

(c) Communicate direct with workforce in attempt to avert strike. (Letters sent to employees homes, or with pay slips.) Emphasise need to work together, tighten belt in order to preserve firm/jobs in the face of external recession, competition. Lead by example on productivity, pay constraints.

(d) Public/financial relations exercise. Emphasise pressures on business, concern for jobs etc through editorial coverage in local (national?) press, broadcast, financial media. (Paid advertising as a last resort.)

(e) Take steps for protection of the firm's property and interests (security doors, check and secure keys, block access to confidential files, employ security guards if required).

(f) Take steps to ensure that materials and supplies can come in and orders go out freely (anticipate picket arrangements – notify police of potential for obstruction; arrange for transport/unloading/storage staff if affected by strike).

(g) Re-organise to minimise disruption by striking workers, maintain output or level of service sufficient to satisfy demand: schedule stock-take, equipment servicing during strike period to utilise down time; re-allocate tasks among workers not involved in strike action (supply cross-training if required); engage alternative sources of labour (temporary/casual); offer added incentives to non-striking workers to increase overtime and/or productivity.

(h) Stop pay of individuals on strike. Issue formal disciplinary warnings to strikers, with clear consequences for breach of contract. (NB If dismiss any strikers, must dismiss all.)

(i) Appoint Management Task Force to co-ordinate firm's response; provide on-going information to media; support non-striking workers.

(j) Brief legal advisers and take advice on actions available and consequences of options.

GLOSSARY

Accountability is the duty of an individual to report to his/her superior how he/she has fulfilled his/her responsibilities.

Assessment centres are an increasingly used approach, growing out of the War Office Selection Board methods during the Second World War. Although originally used for selection purposes, they have gained more and more value as assessment and development tools. The method assesses potential and identifies development needs, through various individual and group techniques. It is particularly useful in the identification of executive or supervisory potential, since it uses simulated but realistic management problems, to give participants opportunities to show potential in the kind of situations to which they would be promoted, but of which they currently have no experience.

Authority is the right to do something.

Centralisation and decentralisation refer to the degree to which authority is delegated in an organisation – and therefore the level at which decisions are taken in the management hierarchy.

Control   (1)   The process through which plans are implemented and objectives achieved, by setting targets and standards, measuring performance, comparing actual performance with standards and taking corrective action where necessary.

               (2)   A psychological and political process in which powerful individuals and groups dominate others and establish an order of behaviour.

Corporate planning involves devising a picture of how the organisation will look in three or five years time, and how it can reach that state during that time period.

Culture may be defined as 'that's the way we do things round here'. For Edgar Schein it is 'the pattern of basic assumptions that a given group has invented, discovered or developed, in learning to cope with its problems of external adaptation and internal integration, and that have worked well enough to be considered valid and, therefore, to be taught to new members as the correct way to perceive, think and feel in relation to these problems.'

Decentralisation Centralisation and decentralisation refer to the degree to which authority is delegated in an organisation – and therefore the level at which decisions are taken in the management hierarchy.

Decision support systems are a form of management information system. DSS are used by management to assist in making decisions on issues which are semi-structured or unstructured.

Delegation is the process whereby a superior gives a subordinate the authority and responsibility to carry out a given aspect of the superior's own task.

Development is job experience and learning from other managers, particularly one's immediate superior.

Devolution is the shift of responsibilities away from personnel specialists back towards ordinary management. (Stephen Connock).

Direct discrimination occurs when one interested group is treated less favourably than another (except for exempted cases).

Disabled person is 'A person who, on account of injury, disease, or congenital deformity is substantially handicapped in obtaining or keeping employment... of a kind which apart from the injury, disease or deformity would be suited to his age, qualifications and experience...' (Disabled Persons (Employment) Act 1944)

Education is that process which results in formal qualifications up to and including post-graduate degrees.

Employee records are those kept by an organisation about each of its employees. They are built up and added to as the employee's career with the organisation progresses.

Equal opportunities is an approach to the management of people at work (recruitment, selection, development, reward, relations and termination) based on equal access and fair treatment irrespective of gender, race, ethnicity, age, disability and sexual orientation.

Evaluation means comparing the actual costs of a training scheme with the assessed benefits which are obtained. If the costs exceed the benefits, the scheme will need to be redesigned or withdrawn.

Executive information systems provide the executive with the underlying performance facts and figures which have traditionally been under the control of middle managers.

Expert systems are computer programs which allow users to benefit from expert knowledge and information, and also advice.

Factory a place where manufacturing or processing work is done for the purposes of gain, and where the main purpose of the premises involves manual labour.

Human resource audit: corporate planning involves devising a picture of how the organisation will look in three or five years time, and how it can reach that state during that time period.

Human resource management is 'a strategic and coherent approach to the management of an organisation's most valued assets: the people working there, who individually and collectively contribute to the achievement of its objectives for sustainable competitive advantage'.

Human resource planning is a strategy for the acquisition, utilisation, improvement and retention of an enterprise's human resources.

Indirect discrimination occurs when requirements or conditions are imposed, with which a substantial proportion of the interested group could not comply, to their detriment.

Labour market consists of the group of potential employees, internal, local or otherwise, with the types of skill, knowledge and experience that the employer requires at a given time. It thus consists of people within the organisation, people who are out of work at that time, and also people in other organisations who may wish to change jobs or employers.

Management control is the process through which plans are implemented and objectives achieved, by setting targets and standards, measuring performance, comparing actual performance with standards and taking corrective action where necessary.

Managing diversity believes that the individual differences we currently focus on under equal opportunities (gender, race, age etc) are crude classifications of the most obvious differences between people, and should be replaced by a genuine understanding of the ways in which individuals differ.

Multinational company is a group with a head office and parent company in one country, and subsidiaries in other countries.

Objectives should be clear, specific and related to observable, measurable targets, ideally detailing:

   (a)   Behaviour – what the trainee should be able to do

(b)   Standard – to what level of performance, and

(c)   Environment – under what conditions

Performance appraisal is the process whereby an individual's performance is reviewed against previously agreed goals, and where new goals are agreed which will develop the individual and improve performance over the forthcoming review period.

Policy is a general statement or understanding which provides guidelines for management decision making.

Psychological contract is a set of values that determine what an organisation expects of its employees and what employees expect of the organisation.

Redundancy is defined by the Act as dismissal where:

(a)   The employer has ceased to carry on the business

(b)   The employer has ceased to carry on the business in the place where the employee was employed

(c)   The requirements of the business for employees to carry out work of a particular kind have ceased or diminished, or are expected to

Repetitive strain injury is discomfort – such as backache, eye strain and stiffness or muscular problems of the neck – which you may have experienced personally if you have ever worked for a long period at a VDU. This common term is actually somewhat inaccurate.

Responsibility is the liability of a person to be called to account for exercising his/her authority, actions and results.

Sexual harassment is any unwanted conduct with sexual connotations, physical or verbal.

Telecommuting describes the process of working from home, or from a satellite office close to home, with the aid of computers, facsimile machines, modems or other forms of telecommunication equipment.

Training   (a)   Is the formal learning activities which may not lead to qualifications, and which may be received at any time in a working career.

(b)   Is 'the systematic development of the attitude/knowledge/skill/ behaviour pattern required by an individual in order to perform adequately a given task or job.' (Department of Employment)

Training needs are represented by the gap between the requirements of the job and the actual current performance of the job-holders. In other words:

Required level of competence minus present level of competence = training need.

Transactions processing system is the lowest level in an organisation's use of information systems. It is used for routine tasks in which data items or transactions must be processed so that operations can continue. Handling payroll items for example.

Validation means observing the results of the course, and measuring whether the training objectives have been achieved.

Work study methods aim to set standards of staff-hours per unit of output, to achieve maximum productivity.

BPP PUBLISHING

INDEX

NOTES

BPP
PUBLISHING

NOTES

NOTES

BPP
PUBLISHING

NOTES

BPP
PUBLISHING

NOTES

ORDER FORM

Any books from our HNC/HND range can be ordered in one of the following ways:

- Telephone us on **020 8740 2211**
- Send this page to our **Freepost** address
- Fax this page on **020 8740 1184**
- Email us at **publishing@bpp.com**
- Go to our website: **www.bpp.com**

We aim to deliver to all UK addresses inside 5 working days. Orders to all EU addresses should be delivered within 6 working days. All other orders to overseas addresses should be delivered within 8 working days.

BPP Publishing Ltd
Aldine House
Aldine Place
London W12 8AW
Tel: 020 8740 2211
Fax: 020 8740 1184
Email: publishing@bpp.com

Full name: _____

Day-time delivery address: _____

_____

_____ Postcode _____

Day-time telephone (for queries only): _____

Please send me the following quantities of books:

		No. of copies	Price	Total
Core				
Unit 1	Marketing (8/00)		£7.95	
Unit 2	Managing Financial Resources (8/00)		£7.95	
Unit 3	Organisations and Behaviour (8/00)		£7.95	
Unit 4	Organisations, Competition and Environment (8/00)		£7.95	
Unit 5	Quantitative Techniques for Business (8/00)		£7.95	
Unit 6	Legal and Regulatory Framework (8/00)		£7.95	
Unit 7	Management Information Systems (8/00)		£7.95	
Unit 8	Business Strategy (8/00)		£7.95	

		No. of copies	Price	Total
Option				
Units 9-12	Business & Finance (1/2001)		£10.95	
Units 13-16	Business & Management (1/2001)		£10.95	
Units 17-20	Business & Marketing (1/2001)		£10.95	
Unit 21-24	Business & Personnel (1/2001)		£10.95	

		No. of copies	Price	Total
Other Material				
	Workbook (3/00)		£9.95	

Sub Total	£

Postage & Packaging

UK : Course book £3.00 for first plus £2.00 for each extra, Workbook £2.00 for first plus £1.00 for each	£
Europe : (inc. ROI) Course book £5.00 for first plus £4.00 for each extra, Workbook £2.50 for first plus £1.00 for each	£
Rest of the world : Course book £20.00 for first plus £10.00 for each extra, Workbook £2.50 for first plus £1.00 for each	£

Grand Total	£

I enclose a cheque for £_____ (cheque to BPP Publishing Ltd) or charge to Access/VISA/Switch

Card number: ☐☐☐☐☐☐☐☐☐☐☐☐☐☐☐☐☐☐☐☐☐☐

Issues number (Switch only): _____

Start date: _____ Expiry date: _____

Signature _____

REVIEW FORM & FREE PRIZE DRAW

We are constantly reviewing, updating and improving our Course Books. We would be grateful for any comments or thoughts you have on this Course Book. Cut out and send this page to our Freepost address and you will be automatically entered in a £50 prize draw.

Jed Cope
HNC/HND Range Manager
BPP Publishing Ltd, FREEPOST, London W12 8BR

Full name: _____

Address: _____

_____

_____ Postcode _____

Where are you studying?

Where did you find out about BPP range books?

Why did you decide to buy this Course Book?

Have you used our texts for the other units in your HNC/HND studies?

What thoughts do you have on our:

- Introductory pages

- Topic coverage

- Summary diagrams, icons, chapter roundups and quick quizzes

- Discussion topics, activities and assignments

The other side of this form is left blank for any further comments you wish to make.

Please give any further comments and suggestions (with page number if necessary) below.

FREE PRIZE DRAW RULES

1   Closing date for 31 July 2001 draw is 30 June 2001. Closing date for 31 January 2002 draw is 31 December 2001.

2   Restricted to entries with UK and Eire addresses only. BPP employees, their families and business associates are excluded.

3   No purchase necessary. Entry forms are available upon request from BPP Publishing. No more than one entry per title, per person. Draw restricted to persons aged 16 and over.

4   Winners will be notified by post and receive their cheques not later than 6 weeks after the relevant draw date.

5   The decision of the promoter in all matters is final and binding. No correspondence will be entered into.